Europe's Infrastructure Transition

Making Europe: Technology and Transformations, 1850–2000

Series editors: Johan Schot (SPRU – Science Policy Research Unit, University of Sussex, United Kingdom) and Phil Scranton (Rutgers University, USA)

Book series overview:

Consumers, Tinkerers, Rebels: The People Who Shaped Europe
by Ruth Oldenziel (Eindhoven University of Technology, the Netherlands) and Mikael Hård (Darmstadt University of Technology, Germany)

Building Europe on Expertise: Innovators, Organizers, Networkers
by Martin Kohlrausch (KU Leuven, Belgium) and Helmuth Trischler (Deutsches Museum, Germany)

Europe's Infrastructure Transition: Economy, War, Nature
by Per Högselius (KTH Royal Institute of Technology, Sweden), Arne Kaijser (KTH Royal Institute of Technology, Sweden) and Erik van der Vleuten (Eindhoven University of Technology, the Netherlands)

Writing the Rules for Europe: Experts, Cartels, and International Organizations
by Wolfram Kaiser (University of Portsmouth, United Kingdom) and Johan Schot (SPRU – Science Policy Research Unit, University of Sussex, United Kingdom)

Communicating Europe: Technologies, Information, Events
by Andreas Fickers (University of Luxembourg, Luxembourg) and Pascal Griset (Paris-Sorbonne University, France)

Europeans Globalizing: Mapping, Exploiting, Exchanging
by Maria Paula Diogo (New University of Lisbon, Portugal) and Dirk van Laak (University of Giessen, Germany)

Initiator: Foundation for the History of Technology (Eindhoven University of Technology, the Netherlands)

The Foundation for the History of Technology (SHT) seeks to develop and communicate knowledge that increases our understanding of the critical role that technology plays in the history of the modern world. Established in 1988 in the Netherlands, SHT initiates and supports scholarly research in the history of technology. This includes large-scale national and international research programs, as well as numerous individual projects, many of which are in collaboration with Eindhoven University of Technology. SHT also coordinates Tensions of Europe (TOE), an international research network of more than 250 scholars from across Europe and beyond who are studying the role of technology as an agent of change in European history. For more information visit www.histech.nl.

Europe's Infrastructure Transition

Economy, War, Nature

Per Högselius

Arne Kaijser

and

Erik van der Vleuten

© Per Högselius, Arne Kaijser, Erik van der Vleuten and Foundation for the History of Technology 2016, First softcover printing 2018

All rights reserved. No reproduction, copy or transmission of this publication may be made without written permission.

No portion of this publication may be reproduced, copied or transmitted save with written permission or in accordance with the provisions of the Copyright, Designs and Patents Act 1988, or under the terms of any licence permitting limited copying issued by the Copyright Licensing Agency, Saffron House, 6–10 Kirby Street, London EC1N 8TS.

Any person who does any unauthorized act in relation to this publication may be liable to criminal prosecution and civil claims for damages.

The authors have asserted their rights to be identified as the authors of this work in accordance with the Copyright, Designs and Patents Act 1988.

First published 2016 by
PALGRAVE MACMILLAN

Palgrave Macmillan in the UK is an imprint of Macmillan Publishers Limited, registered in England, company number 785998, of Houndmills, Basingstoke, Hampshire RG21 6XS.

Palgrave Macmillan in the US is a division of St Martin's Press LLC, 175 Fifth Avenue, New York, NY 10010.

Palgrave Macmillan is the global academic imprint of the above companies and has companies and representatives throughout the world.

Palgrave® and Macmillan® are registered trademarks in the United States, the United Kingdom, Europe and other countries.

ISBN: 978–0–230–30799–5 (HB)
ISBN: 978–0–230–30800–8 (PB)

This book is printed on paper suitable for recycling and made from fully managed and sustained forest sources. Logging, pulping and manufacturing processes are expected to conform to the environmental regulations of the country of origin.

A catalogue record for this book is available from the British Library.

Library of Congress Cataloging-in-Publication Data

Högselius, Per.
    Europe's infrastructure transition : economy, war, nature / Per Högselius, Arne Kaijser and Erik van der Vleuten.
       pages cm.—(Making Europe)
    Includes bibliographical references and index.
    ISBN 978–0–230–30799–5
     1. Infrastructure (Economics)—Europe—History. 2. Europe—Economic integration—History. 3. Europe—History. I. Vleuten, Erik van der. II. Högselius, Per, 1973– III. Title.

HC240.9.C3K35 2015
363.6094—dc23   2015001279

Dedicated to the memory of Thomas P. Hughes (1923–2014)

Contents

Making Europe: An Introduction to the Series — xi

Acknowledgements — xix

Introduction: Chevalier's Dream — 1
    Manifesto for a New Europe — 1
    Europe's Infrastructure Transition — 5
    Building Systems, Making Europe — 9
    The Grid of History — 16

Part I   Connecting Europe

1   Manipulating Space & Time — 21
    To the Finland Station — 21
    Europe's Transport Revolution — 24
    The Rise of Telegraphy — 32
    Building Borders — 36
    Competing European Visions — 40
    Cold War Networks & Borders — 47
    Infrastructure & Communism's Collapse — 53
    Toward a New Europe? — 56
    Space & Time Annihilated? — 59

2 Fueling Europe — 65
- Europe Unplugged — 65
- From Renewable to Fossil Fuels — 67
- The Rise of Europe's Dedicated Energy Infrastructure — 70
- Electrifying Europe: Integrations & Divisions — 72
- The European Oil Geography — 82
- Natural Gas: Deconstructing the Iron Curtain — 85
- Nuclear Europe — 91
- A Changing Political & Economic Environment — 94
- Europe through the Lens of its Energy Infrastructure — 101

Part II Economy & War

3 Networked Food Economy — 107
- Networked Harbor — 107
- A Cavalcade of Economic System-Builders — 111
- The Far Reaches of Europe's Food Economy — 115
- Food Borders & National Food Systems — 124
- The Pros & Cons of Regional Food Integration — 131

4 Factory & Finance — 141
- Entrepreneurial Energies — 141
- Coal & Chemicals — 144
- Fragmented Fabrication — 147
- Cold War Chemicals — 151
- Capital & Communications — 159
- Capital & Crisis — 165
- Capital in Cyberspace — 168
- Flash Crash — 177

5 Logistics of War — 183
- August 1914 — 183
- Railroads & Telegraphs in Military Planning — 185
- Infrastructure & Colonial Control — 188
- The First World War — 189
- Blitzkrieg in Snow & Mud — 193
- Bombing the Enemy — 198
- The Tonnage War — 203
- Racial War — 207
- Military System-Building in the Cold War — 210
- Losing Control of Colonies — 218
- The Infrastructure of a Dark Continent — 222

Part III Networking Nature

6 Linking Land — **229**
- Networked Mountain — 229
- Knowing Land — 233
- Using Land — 242
- Urban Systems — 245
- Connection & Rupture in Agriculture — 248
- Preserving Land — 254
- Europe's Ecological Networks — 258
- *Parnassius Mnemosyne* or *Lepus Europeus* — 265

7 Troubled Waters — **269**
- The "Molotov–Ribbentrop Pipeline" — 269
- Charting Inland Waters — 272
- Mapping the Sea — 275
- Improving Europe's Rivers — 278
- The Coming of Hydropower — 282
- Transferring Water — 286
- Improving Europe's Seas — 288
- Energizing the Sea — 294
- The Rise of Transnational Pollution — 297
- Toward Ecological System-Building — 302
- Europe through the Lens of Wet Systems — 305

8 Common Skies — **309**
- "A Cupola of Polluted Air over Europe" — 309
- Mapping the Sky — 311
- Weather & War — 317
- Computers & Satellites — 318
- Sharing & Allocating Radio Waves — 320
- Creating an Aviation Infrastructure — 328
- Handling Congestion in the Air — 333
- Using the Sky as a Sink — 336
- Ecological Networks for Birds — 344
- Intermeshed Appropriations of the Sky — 346

Conclusion — **349**
- How Did Europe's Infrastructure Space Emerge? — 351
- How Did Infrastructure Alter Europe's Economic Relations & Warfare? — 357
- How Did Infrastructure Interact with Europe's Natural Environments? — 361

Endnotes	367
Bibliography	395
Illustration Credits	433
Making Europe: Series Acknowledgements	439
Index	441

Making Europe:
An Introduction to the Series

In a typical conversation about twentieth-century European history, the subject of war will almost certainly arise—whether it is the Great War, the Second World War, or the Cold War. Similarly, historians who write about contemporary European history often view war as the twentieth century's iconic event. In fact, many scholars rely on Europe's political history, rife as it is with military conflict, to set the timeframe for their work. The influential historian Eric Hobsbawm, for example, defined the twentieth century as beginning with the First World War and ending with the collapse of the Soviet Union; Hobsbawm named this period—1914 to 1991—The Short Twentieth Century. Indeed, the topic of war and rupture has dominated the discourse on Europe in the twentieth century—and understandably so.

We, the editors and authors of the *Making Europe* series, however, have taken an alternative approach to our subject. We offer a European history viewed through the lens of technology rather than war. We believe that a European history with technology at its core can help to understand the continuities that have endured despite the rupture of wars. *Making Europe* places continuities—from the rise of institutions like CERN to the evolution of hacker networks—in a longer-term perspective. The *Making Europe* narrative suggests that recent European history is as much about building connections across national borders as it is about playing out conflicts between nation-states. This view of technology from a transnational perspective has proven to be felicitous. As a phenomenon, technology has always been particularly mobile; this mobility has allowed new technologies to help shape international relations between countries, companies, organizations, and people.

To understand the role of technology in this history, we required ourselves to rethink the very meaning of technology: referencing far more than machines alone, technology also embraces people and values; ideas, skills, and knowledge. Technological change, in our view, is a deeply human process. Technology was—and still is—central to the creation of Europe. And given its centrality, technology has been hotly contested—politically, economically, and culturally—in the making of Europe.

Technology's role in shaping Europe coalesced around 1850, when a new era began, an era from 1850 to 2000 that we refer to as The Long Twentieth Century. It was during the mid-nineteenth century that a newly globalizing world began to emerge. This was a world in which the many new transportation and communication technologies played a decisive part. At this time, technology became a reference point for European superiority—both within and beyond Europe. Cross-border connections and institutions thrived; the knowledge-sharing practices that fostered these connections were widely circulated and adopted. This circulation of knowledge led to a worldwide imagining, negotiating, and experiencing of Europe that still exists today. This was also the foundation for the formal process of European integration that gained traction in the 1950s. Our perspective simultaneously decenters the European Union and its direct predecessors—which, after all, comprised only one force of Europeanization among many—and places the process of European integration in long-term historical context. Acknowledging that this dynamic of integration continues today, *Making Europe* presents and interprets a history that is still in the making.

That said, it is clear to us as historians that the decade 1990–2000 marks another watershed: it was in this period that the digital revolution gained new momentum, as did shifting power relationships at the global level. This spurred the European Union to become a hegemonic force of Europeanization, and it helped globalization to enter a new phase. Simultaneously, however, the processes of integration and globalization in this apparent new phase have proven to be fragile: in light of the global economic crisis, Europe's future, called into doubt, has become a pressing issue, and one with a sharp political edge. Accordingly, Europe's past has also come under fresh scrutiny. We contend that technology will continue to play a central role in defining Europe; that the politics of Europe is the politics of technology as much as anything else; and that now is the opportune time to explore technology's historical role in the creation of Europe.

Making Europe provides a perspective on European history that transcends borders. The volumes in the series examine the linking—and, in some cases, the disruption—of infrastructures and knowledge networks that operate beyond nations and states. Also mapped here is the transnational circulation—and appropriation—of people, products, and ideas. The people and organizations featured in this series employed particular notions of Europe in building their cross-border connections. Indeed, they imagined and invented new Europes, often making clear distinctions between which people and places belonged and which were alien to the concept and the reality of Europe. *Making Europe* asks: Who projected their ideas of Europe? When did these projections take place—how, and why? The series looks at the people and the organizations that perceived themselves as central—and peripheral—to Europe, its colonies, and the transatlantic crossings that were part of the European imagination. Examined here are migrants and experts, foods and inventions, markets and regulations—virtually everything that was identified, experienced, and communicated as "European." This Europeanization, we find, had significant—and sometimes unintended—consequences: some connections between people and institutions were lasting, others broken, these continuities and ruptures shaping Europe as both an imagined place and a living community. *Making Europe* explores the stability and fragility of these European connections, communities, and institutions.

The majority of existing studies of Europe have been based on one of two approaches. First is the, often massive, single-author narrative. Second is the essay collection, which presents many voices, in some cases edited to align the authors' themes. In the field of European history, single-author volumes have tended to be broad-ranging and to address different timeframes and regions. Often, single-author volumes are a compilation of national stories; at their best, compilations transcend their individual stories to posit a complete European picture. Essay collections, for their part, have generally assumed a sharper focus—on particular communities, ethnicities, and empires, for example. These usual approaches point to a distinctive feature of *Making Europe*: in this series, five of the six volumes have two authors; one book has three writers. These voices, thirteen in all, create multiple narratives. The six sets of *Making Europe*'s co-authors have worked as a team to draft a series of volumes with coordinated yet individual themes (see www.makingeurope.eu). These six volumes contain six distinct points of view; as editors, we have imposed neither uniformity nor the pressure to harmonize narratives. In our opinion, the most informative new contributions to European history embrace diverse actors and diverse meanings, a range of purposes and understandings. *Making Europe* captures this diversity, reflecting a dynamic European history that continues to unfold.

All of the authors in the series have drawn on the European Science Foundation's "Inventing Europe" collaborative research initiatives as well as the Foundation for the History of Technology's "Tensions of Europe" project, begun in 1998 (see www.tensionsofeurope.eu). They have profited from an intensive period of discussion and joint research and writing at the Netherlands Institute for Advanced Study in the Wassenaar dunes in 2010–11. The fruits of these initiatives include the *Making Europe* book series as well as a web-based exhibit "Inventing Europe, European Digital Museum for Science and Technology" that encompasses a dozen of Europe's technology and science museums (see www.inventingeurope.eu) and scores of scholarly publications. All aim to promote creativity in fostering a more inclusive understanding of technology's role in refashioning Europe—an ongoing process that is as fascinating as it is contentious. The authors of *Making Europe* have asked themselves what shape an open-ended European history of technology would take. They provide their answers in the form of this book series.

The first volume in the *Making Europe* series, entitled *Consumers, Tinkerers, Rebels: The People who Shaped Europe*, is written by Ruth

Oldenziel and Mikael Hård. This volume spotlights the people who "made" Europe by appropriating and consuming a wide range of technologies—from the sewing machine to the bicycle, the Barbie doll to the personal computer. What emerges is a fascinating portrait of how Europeans lived during The Long Twentieth Century. Explored here are the questions of who, exactly, decided how Europeans dressed and dwelled? Traveled and dined? Worked and played? Who, in fact, can be credited with shaping the daily lives of Europeans? The authors argue that, while inventors, engineers, and politicians played their parts, it was consumers, tinkerers, and rebels who have been the unrecognized force in the making of Europe.

The second volume in the series, entitled *Building Europe on Expertise: Innovators, Organizers, Networkers*, is written by Martin Kohlrausch and Helmuth Trischler. Here the focus shifts from consumers of technology to a new breed of professionals: the technical and scientific experts whose influence soared from around 1850 onward. The authors show how these experts created, organized, and spread knowledge—enabling them to shape societies, create cross-border connections, and set political agendas. During Europe's Long Twentieth Century, technoscientific experts became a strategic resource for serving national, international, and transnational interests, the authors argue. They revisit experts' visions of Europe, showing how these visions manifested in the dictatorships of Nazi Germany and Stalinist Russia—as well as helping to build Europe's vast research networks during the Cold War. *Building Europe on Expertise* ends with today's efforts to reinvent the European Union—as a knowledge-based society defined by experts.

The third volume in the series, *Europe's Infrastructure Transition: Economy, War, Nature*, is written by Per Högselius, Arne Kaijser, and Erik van der Vleuten. This book elaborates on the first two volumes by introducing a new cast of historical actors: system-builders. These individuals and organizations helped to transform Europe by envisioning, constructing, and manipulating large-scale transport, communications, and energy systems. Their efforts reshaped Europe as a geographical entity by forming massive new material interconnections—and divisions—between places. This had far-reaching implications for European integration; for peaceful economic exchange; for military planning and logistics. System-builders challenged Europe's natural barriers, from the Alps to northern Europe's forests and the vast marshlands to the east. But Europe's water, air, and land were not only connected, they were transformed radically, sometimes destroyed. In response, system-builders eventually turned much of Europe's environment itself into infrastructure, interlinking isolated ecosystems via human-made corridors and networks.

The fourth volume, *Making the Rules for Europe: Experts, Cartels, International Organizations* is written by Wolfram Kaiser and Johan Schot. Here, the focus becomes the norms and standards of technological innovation—discussed in depth for transport and heavy industry. Featured are the people and organizations that debated, negotiated, and regulated the cross-border issues raised by innovation. Presented here are individuals with special—and often interdisciplinary—expertise in technology, business, and law. Often, these experts sought to de-politicize issues by deeming them technical; this yielded workable solutions to shared problems. It also paved experts' way in rule-making for multiple, distinct yet overlapping, and frequently competing "Europes." In the pursuit of finding technological solutions, many institutions' transnational practices survived ruptures, including the two World Wars. After the Second World War, the European Union was obliged to accommodate—and to compete with—other institutions' established practices in order for the EU to gain greater influence in shaping Europe.

The fifth volume, *Communicating Europe: Technologies, Information, Events,* analyzes Europe's information and communication systems from roughly 1850 onward. Authors Andreas Fickers and Pascal Griset place these technologies at the very heart of European society. Presented here is a global vision of media, telecommunications, and computers that reveals the tensions inherent in designing and appropriating electrical and electronic devices. The authors argue that the control in the material realm by research and entrepreneurship and the emergence of new forms of creativity and new ways of life are two sides of the same coin, mostly driven by political and cultural forces. Examined in this volume are the political, economic, and cultural realities and meanings of information and communication technologies on a European level. This perspective, which extends over the long term, provides the tools for a new critical understanding of the digital revolution.

Making Europe: An Introduction to the Series   xvii

How did today's globalized, thoroughly mapped-out world emerge? What part did technology play in Europe's international encounters, colonial and otherwise? *Europeans Globalizing*, written by Maria Paula Diogo and Dirk van Laak, concludes the *Making Europe* series with a study of how Europe interacted with the rest of the world from 1850 until the close of the twentieth century. The volume details how technologies were applied and creatively adopted–from India to Argentina, South Africa to the Arctic. From the turn of the twentieth century onwards, we witness assumptions about Europe's technologically-based superiority being continuously challenged. And we discover that globalized Europe in its present form looks quite different from what Europeans once imagined.

Consumers and tinkerers; engineers and scientists; system-builders and inventors. Experts in technology, law, and business; communicators and entrepreneurs; politicians and ambassadors. This is a cross-section of the actors represented on *Making Europe*'s pages. These actors, through the institutions and organizations they cultivated, the connections they created, the rules and practices they fostered, co-created Europe. Narrated from contrasting as well as complementary viewpoints, the six volumes in the series create a collage of co-existent portraits that depict Europe's Long Twentieth Century; its technologies; and its meanings. Together, these histories form the view of modern Europe that we and the authors wish to contribute to the historical record at this time.

Johan Schot & Philip Scranton
Making Europe Series Editors
Amsterdam, the Netherlands & Camden, New Jersey, USA
July 2013

Acknowledgements

This book tells the story of how Europe, in the nineteenth and twentieth centuries, went through what we call an infrastructure transition. It shows how the creation of physical connections and ruptures was deeply intertwined with the shaping of Europe's modern economy, its wars, and its natural environment. Europe's transport, communications, and energy infrastructure reached out across and beyond the continent, even across the globe. So did its economic, military, and environmental relations. This makes the infrastructure transition one of the most profound and wide-ranging transformations in modern European history. It also made writing this book a daunting endeavor. We had to address a wide range of topics in a vast geographical and temporal scope. This could not have been done without the generous support from numerous individuals and organizations.

In the context of the "Tensions of Europe: Technology and the Making of Europe" research network (www.tensionsofeurope.eu), we were extremely privileged to be able to work together with historians from all over Europe and North America for nearly fifteen years. Many of the ideas presented in this book stem from discussions with colleagues at Tensions seminars, workshops, and conferences. We may distinguish three overlapping phases in this research journey.

Our common journey began in 1999 with the Tensions of Europe research program. In its thematic subprogram Networking Europe we worked with Irene Anastasiadou, Pär Blomkvist, Angel Calvo, Maria Paula Diogo, Alexander Gall, Léonard Laborie, Helmut Maier, Robert McWilliam, Judith Schueler, Ana Paula Silva, Lars Thue, Aristotle Tympas, and Geert Verbong to open up a novel research field, develop a research agenda, and make case studies of transnational railroad, telegraph, highway, and electric power networks. Our collaboration resulted in an edited volume, *Networking Europe: Transnational Infrastructures and the Shaping of Europe, 1850–2000* (2006). We realized that this form of collaboration with scholars from different parts of Europe was a very fruitful and rewarding way of carrying out transnational research, and in 2006 we were able to continue the journey in a new phase.

In this second phase we welcomed the opportunity to do more in-depth research within a European Science Foundation EUROCORES Programme called "Inventing Europe." Together with a partly new group of European colleagues we received funding for a large project—EUROCRIT, as we called it—focusing on Europe's "critical" infrastructure and more specifically on the historical roots of present day infrastructure vulnerabilities. Apart from fruitful complementarities in language skills and access to diverse archives and literatures, we found it particularly rewarding to learn about the profound differences between different parts of Europe when it comes to infrastructure developments and infrastructure vulnerabilities. This project also resulted in an edited volume, *The Making of Europe's Critical Infrastructure: Common Connections and Shared Vulnerabilities* (2013). We would like to thank our dear EUROCRIT colleagues: Anna Åberg, Stathis Arapostathis, Eefje Cleophas, Lars Heide, Ivaylo Hristov, Yiannis Garyfallos, Anique Hommels, Vincent Lagendijk, Karl-Erik Michelsen, Tihomir Mitev, Ivan Tchalakov, Lars Thue, Aristotle Tympas, and Katerina Vlantoni. Our lively and enjoyable workshops in Utrecht, Sigtuna, Helsinki, Lisbon, Athens, and Sofia demonstrated that exciting research and fun go hand-in-hand!

One other parallel project deserves particular mention. The Eindhoven-based TIE (Transnational Infrastructures and the Rise of Contemporary Europe) project, led by Johan Schot, gave extremely important input to us in the form of several PhD theses—much cited in this book—on transnational infrastructure, authored by Judith Schueler, Vincent Lagendijk, Frank Schipper, Irene Anastasiadou, and Suzanne Lommers. Also Johan Schot, Alec Badenoch, Barbara Bonhage, Cornelis Disco, Andreas Fickers, Christian Henrich-Franke, Patrick Kammerer, Eda Kranakis, Dirk van Laak, and Waqar Zaidi made important contributions. From 2006, a follow-up program called "Hidden Integration in Central, Eastern and Southeastern Europe" added the transnational infrastructure theses by Ivaylo Hristov and Jiří Janáč.

A third, synthetic phase arrived with the six-volume Making Europe book series project, which provided the immediate context for this book. In this phase we widened our transnational analysis by setting out to write a modern history of Europe—focusing, in particular, on its economy, its wars, and its natural environment—through the lens of infrastructure. This book is a product of intense collaboration across geographic and disciplinary boundaries. We are most grateful to colleagues who gave valuable comments about the book as a whole and about the individual chapters, for which we divided the storyline and final responsibility among ourselves (Högselius: chapters 1, 2, 7; Kaijser: chapters 5, 9, Conclusion; van der Vleuten: Introduction, chapters 3, 4, 6). We benefitted enormously from the inspiring intellectual atmosphere of the Netherlands Institute of Advanced Studies (NIAS), located in a lovely mansion close to the sea, for five months in 2010–11. This gave us a unique chance to engage in frequent and inspiring discussions with other Making Europe project members, including Alec Badenoch, Maria Paula Diogo, Andreas Fickers, Pascal Griset, Mikael Hård, Dagmara Jajeśniak-Quast, Wolfram Kaiser, Martin Kohlrausch, Dirk van Laak, Suzanne Lommers, Sławomir Łotysz, Matthias Middell, Ruth Oldenziel, Emanuela Scarpelini, Johan Schot, Phil Scranton, and Helmuth Trischler. They read and commented on early versions of the book design and our chapters, and we also jointly developed ideas that have guided the character of the book series as a whole. The Making Europe project involved many more than the authors and editors. Serkan Karas and Fotini Tsaglioti worked as research assistants for our volume, Pál Germuska generously contributed a valuable report, and many other colleagues offered constructive criticism at a number of conferences and workshops.

The parallel production of the virtual exhibition Inventing Europe (http://www.inventingeurope.eu) also gave us new ideas and insights.

Two anonymous reviewers and two non-anonymous, Maarten van der Vlist and Bert Toussaint, commented on the entire manuscript and we are extremely grateful for their critical and constructive reports. Further, we received advice, reading tips, and insights on many topics of relevance for our book from Nils Bruzelius, Johan Gribbe, Ernst Homburg, Sabine Höhler, Vincent Lagendijk, Thomas J. Misa, Kiran K. Patel, Pierre-Yves Saunier, Frank Schipper, and Nina Wormbs. In addition, we have presented draft chapters and book outlines at a number of seminars and workshops outside the Tensions of Europe network and received valuable feedback. Needless to say, the historical interpretations and errors in this book remain our sole responsibility.

The images form an important part of this book, illustrating and explaining its arguments. Katherine Kay-Mouat and Jan Korsten gave us invaluable support in the picture selection process. Camiel Lintsen, as usual, did a fine job drawing maps. Phil Scranton and Lisa Friedman provided the necessary editing expertise to create a smooth text, and Jenny McCall, Holly Tyler, and Philip Hillyer at Palgrave helped produce the book.

We also wish to express our gratitude to the organizations that contributed financially to making this book possible: the European Science Foundation (ESF), the Foundation for the History of Technology (SHT), the Netherlands Institute of Advanced Studies (NIAS), and the Swedish Foundation for Humanities and Social Sciences (Riksbankens Jubileumsfond).

Our editors, Johan Schot and Phil Scranton, deserve special mention. With his extraordinary enthusiasm, energy and managerial skills, Johan has been the driving force in the Tensions of Europe network since its establishment, and without him the Making Europe series would not have come about. Throughout the writing process Johan and Phil have been an enormous support, helping us strengthen our arguments. They have kept us on track and encouraged us when we most needed it. In the final stage, Phil with his editing skills played a crucial role in producing a readable manuscript. We feel very lucky to have had such inspiring and helpful editors—thank you Johan and Phil!

Finally, one person stands above all in inspiring this volume and, indeed, the field from which it sprang. While finalizing this book, we received the sad news that Thomas P. Hughes had passed away. It was Tom's scholarship that encouraged the three of us—as well as many others—to begin studying large technical systems and their interactions with society. He was an enthusiastic supporter of our collaborative European research projects that laid the foundation for this book. With his deep knowledge and his gentle and generous manners, he was a strong source of inspiration for us, and will continue to be so. We dedicate this book to his memory.

Per Högselius, Arne Kaijser, and Erik van der Vleuten
Stockholm and Eindhoven, June 2015

Introduction: Chevalier's Dream

Manifesto for a New Europe

Eradicating poverty. Achieving independence from nature. Creating lasting peace.

These were key aspirations embraced by Michel Chevalier and other engineers of his time. It was July 1830, the start of the Second French Revolution, and the future of Europe worried the 24-year-old Chevalier. As a graduate of the engineering schools *École Polytechnique* and *École des Mines* in Paris, he had been steeped in ideology: modernization was paramount—but not at the cost of peace. And so Chevalier felt deeply conflicted about the revolution. Like many in his circle, he fervently supported the revolutionaries' "modern" liberal, democratic agenda. But, as an emerging pacifist, he abhorred the violence and suffering of war.

To resolve his inner conflict, Chevalier joined the pacifist reform movement, becoming a so-called Saint Simonian. The movement's leader, Barthélemy Enfantin, enlisted the spirited Chevalier as editor-in-chief of the new Saint Simonian newspaper *Le Globe*. During the next two years, Chevalier elaborated his vision on the pages of *Le Globe*. Europe, he contended, was mired in violence—and had been for millennia. Neither the military efforts to settle conflict nor the peace conferences of the time (such as the Congress of Vienna, after the Napoleonic Wars) could establish lasting peace. Peace, all agreed, depended on harmony between nations and accord between social classes. But, to Chevalier's dismay, the revolutionaries of 1830 proclaimed that peace could only be won through war. Woefully, Chevalier observed that the progress of humanity had "its passport written on a cannonball."[1] From Paris to Brussels to St. Petersburg, Europe's revolutionaries embraced violent means—and aristocratic rulers responded in kind; the cycle of violence continued.

Chevalier proposed an alternative. His idols, Enfantin and the late Count Claude Henri de Saint Simon, saw "bathing Europe in fire and blood" as no solution.[2] Chevalier and his mentors advocated instead a process of joining people in a "universal association," building businesses and industries together, as equals. Chevalier argued that warmongering royalists and republicans failed to acknowledge the signs of this emerging association. Increasingly, "the continuous exchange of sentiments, ideas, and material goods" connected Europeans across class lines as well as local, national, and continental borders.[3] At the same time, powerful new networks promised to inspire cooperation and enable economic progress for all countries, all social classes, and all individuals like never before. These new "material networks"—primarily railroads and steam-ship lines—and "intangible networks" like credit would promote peace, progress, and liberty more efficiently than peace treaties and political constitutions. For Chevalier, it was these tangible networks—now known as infrastructure—and intangible networks that would forever change the human condition. One of his translators even published a book of Chevalier's collected newspaper articles entitled *The Railroads, Constituting the Primary Material Means of Creating Peace in Europe and Happiness for Humanity*.[4] In a later piece, Chevalier stated that "railways have more in common with the religious spirit than we think; never before has an instrument so powerful existed to connect scattered peoples."[5] Chevalier called his vision the circulation society; today we speak of the network society.

An impressive plan for a transcontinental railroad and steamship system underpinned Chevalier's vision. Railroads would help connect the Mediterranean, the Black Sea, and the Caspian Sea from Cadiz and Tangiers to Constantinople (Istanbul) and Teheran. Northbound lines would link these eastbound axes to the North and Baltic Seas, while another ambitious eastbound railroad would connect Flanders at the North Sea via Warsaw, Vilnius, Riga, and St. Petersburg to the Russian Pacific. In all, Chevalier envisioned 60,000 kilometers of interconnected, double-track railroad as the basis for Europe's "universal association." Simultaneously, thousands of steamships would traverse the seas. In true pacifist style, he argued that the necessary funding of 4.5 billion francs was feasible; after all, the sum did not exceed the total French military loans of the previous forty years.

During his lifetime Chevalier worked diligently toward this dream. A two-year stay in the United States confirmed his belief in the power of infrastructure to build nations. Once back in France, Chevalier successfully promoted domestic railroads, the transalpine Simplon tunnel, and the Suez and Panama canals. He was well positioned as a professor of political economy and later as a member of Napoleon III's Council of State and Imperial Senate. Contemporaries knew him as the French signatory of the Cobden–Chevalier Treaty, the Anglo-French free-trade agreement of 1860 that prompted many others, boosting world trade.[6]

After his death, Chevalier's name faded from public memory, but his dream—of European prosperity and peace though infrastructure—endured. In the spirit of Chevalier, many since have dreamed of and built ambitious infrastructure projects. Everything from Europe's system of waterways to its energy and digital networks has promised prosperity and peace. Just as Chevalier campaigned for railroads in the nineteenth century, today's social-media marketeers promise to "give people the power to share and make the world more open and connected," as Facebook's mission statement reads. The dream lives on; historians now see Chevalier's 1830s vision as a manifesto for our current Network Age.[7]

We see that Chevalier's dream was shared by many others. But did that dream deliver on the promise of prosperity and peace for all? This question drives the three main parts of this book.

In Part I, we explore this claim of equality and ask what came of Chevalier's vision for integrating Europe via infrastructure rather than through political treaties. We examine different kinds of infrastructure, from transport, to communications, to energy. In Part I and throughout the book, our analysis of building Europe through infrastructure transcends the European Union—because infrastructure itself transcends physical and political boundaries. We contrast the dream of a uniformly connected, harmonious Europe with the reality of a Europe with an uneven infrastructure in which some inhabitants are hyper-connected, others marginalized. In short, Part I of this book investigates how Europe's infrastructure space developed and what it came to look like. Who was connected to whom; who was left out, and why?

In Part II, we ask what came of Chevalier's hopes for economic progress and peace for humankind. For Chevalier, it was not about building infrastructure for its own sake. Infrastructure was to foster prosperity for all nations and individuals on a poverty-ridden continent; economic cooperation would create peace between rival nations and between competing social classes. After all, why attack one's own collaborators? In this section, we outline the ways in which Europe's economy has indeed been built on infrastructure. It is this infrastructure-based economy that achieved spectacular gains in living standards, although inequalities persisted, as did war. Contrary to Chevalier's expectations, the twentieth century became Europe's bloodiest and most destructive ever. We show that the same railroads used to distribute food and improve health also helped Europe's military forces to wage war on an ever-larger scale. Ironically, infrastructure connected people and places for the purposes of peace as well as war, producing prosperity as well as previously-unimagined violence.[8]

In Part III, we consider Chevalier's belief that infrastructure would liberate Europeans from their restrictive dependence on nature. Steamships would turn seas that divide into arteries that connect. Railroads would traverse mountains and "liberate" isolated territories such as Russia, whose inhabitants Chevalier referred to as "a paralyzed people locked in by snow."[9] In Part III we demonstrate how infrastructure of all kinds helped tame the natural environment and use it for human purposes. Many today note that our hard-won freedom from nature comes at a price: they *blame* transport and energy infrastructure for a host of environmental problems, from pollution and resource depletion to climate change and loss of biodiversity. To activists, infrastructure connected Europeans—and indeed the world—to create a shared catastrophe: the ecological crisis. Part III asks how infrastructure affected Europe's natural environment, particularly its land, water, and air, for better or for worse.

Infrastructure played a far more complex role in the making of modern Europe than Chevalier had ever imagined. This is the essence of Europe's modern infrastructure transition: Europe's infrastructure, its overlapping economies, its wars, and its natural environments interacted in an unpredictable, exceptionally dynamic process of historical change.[10] This book traces the making of this complex web of connections, and the ruptures within, that transformed Europe beyond recognition.

Europe's Infrastructure Transition

How do we locate Europe's infrastructure transition in time and space? By the 1830s, when Chevalier developed his vision, significant threads in Europe's infrastructure fabric had already been woven. For example, in the previous centuries, long-distance trade routes by land and sea had already come to cover vast territories; shipping networks spanned the globe. In fact, seventeenth- and eighteenth-century observers praised England and the Low Countries, in particular, for their advanced maritime and inland canal infrastructure. Historians have also shown that seventeenth- and eighteenth-century Europeans were much more mobile than previously believed. These centuries saw occasional mass migrations and the expansion of mega-cities such as London, Paris, and Amsterdam, which drew primarily on imported labor, food, and energy.[11]

These developments, in the context of their times, were indeed impressive; yet the present-day traveller would have found Europe's pre-nineteenth-century infrastructure to be terribly slow, dangerous, and cumbersome, not to mention sparse. For example, the prevailing forms of transportation and communication were pedestrian, animal (horses and oxen, for example), and wind (sailing ships). The great Roman roads had long fallen into decay; roads were local and unpaved. Natural formations, from mountain ranges to lakes, and even heaths and moors, constituted huge barriers to mobility. Often, states chose these natural formations as political boundaries and military defense lines; conveniently, these physical barriers necessitated only a limited number of man-made fortified passage points. Weather conditions, from drought to rain, storms to icy waters, transformed travel from a slow process into an ordeal. For this reason, travel was mostly the province of aristocrats, sailors, soldiers, merchants, wandering artisans, rural emigrants, and seasonal workers. At this time—the first half of the nineteenth century—the average number of migrations undertaken by these groups languished at roughly one million per year—in a European population of roughly 180 million![12] For the great majority of people, peacetime contacts with other communities were limited to neighboring villages. For the average European, local energy, food, information, and security shaped daily life. Present-day travellers would be shocked by their early-nineteenth-century counterparts' poor diets, harsh living standards, and average life expectancy of well below 40 years of age.

It was only at the time of Chevalier's coming-of-age—around 1830—that changes in Europe's infrastructure began to accelerate in earnest. Over the following two centuries, Europe has become interconnected by colossal networks from steel rails to asphalt roads, from copper wire to electromagnetic waves to fiber optic cable.[13] These physical networks and systems enabled the far-reaching circulation of people, of food and water, of goods and credit, of news and entertainment, as well as the circulation of energy and pollution. Today, virtually all Europeans commute or travel on a daily, weekly, monthly, or at least yearly basis; Europeans rely on resources—from food to information—that are produced outside their local communities. Europe's physical infrastructure, and the economies it fostered, has transformed life radically. Indeed, food and energy have become abundant and cheap, while life expectancies have doubled.

At the same time as it has improved standards of living, Europe's elaborate physical infrastructure has increased the risk of harm. As we discuss in Parts II and III, this vast web contributed to escalating the scale of war as well as the scale of environmental damage. Thus, *Europe's Infrastructure Transition* focuses on the period from the mid-nineteenth century or so to the present, the time in which an intricate web of connections was formed. These were the connections that changed Europe—for better and for worse.

When it comes to locating Europe's infrastructure transition in physical space, our inquiry transcends the boundaries defined by either states or by continents, by natural boundaries like

Introduction: Chevalier's Dream | 7

Fig. 0.1 Piercing the Alps: *During Europe's infrastructure transition new transport, communication, and energy connections pierced major natural obstacles. In May 1882, some six hundred guests from all over Europe celebrated the opening of the railroad tunnel through the St. Gotthard massif in Switzerland. Financed by the Swiss federal and canton governments, the Kingdom of Italy, and Imperial Germany, the line symbolized the connection between Europe's North and South. In the course of the next few decades, telegraph, telephone, and electric power lines also penetrated the Gotthard massive. The first road tunnel came in 1980.*

mountains, or by the politics of the European Union. Instead, we use infrastructure itself—with its associated economic, military, and environmental systems—as the framework for defining boundaries. After all, infrastructure crossed conventional political and natural boundaries, time and time again. In the 1830s, Chevalier chose railroads and steamships precisely because of their ability to reach beyond borders. Less than a century later, new connections indeed challenged traditional definitions of Europe. "The railway ... is a lesson in the futility of artificial restrictions on progress," noted an anonymous reporter at the International Railway Congress in 1910: "The passenger boards his train at Calais and frontiers are wiped out between the English Channel and Brindisi; or he sets out on his journey from St. Petersburg and his destination is the distant port of Vladivostok in the Far East. For him the artificial distinction that calls this 'Europe' and that 'Asia' is wiped out."[14]

Accordingly, the authors of this book do not set out to study Europe's infrastructure transition within a predefined spatial container called "Europe"; instead, we examine how the infrastructure transition changed the very shape of that container.[15] We trace the making of modern Europe as a web of global connections, from Siberian gas fields to Colombian coal mines; Senegalese groundnut plantations to Australian cattle farms; the New York Stock Exchange to the battlefields of Vietnam, the cables of the ocean floor to the pollutants in Earth's stratosphere.

Infrastructure has proven both its power to connect and its power to divide. For this reason, we analyze Europe's global connections as well as its hierarchies and ruptures. One example is Britain's famously-extensive telegraph network that runs beneath the ocean floor. This network, which was in place by 1900, was designed specifically to bypass land-based telegraph systems in territories beyond British control. Infrastructure could create new borders or reify existing ones: new canals, railroads, and highways actually cut local neighborhoods in two. When the Soviet Union incorporated the Baltic States after the Second World War, Baltic telephone connections to the West were cut, and all telephone calls were rerouted through Moscow. The Iron Curtain was a massive attempt at de-linking infrastructure and building borders. Twin electric power lines on either side of the French–German border duplicated that boundary rather than eliminating it. This also held true for national road networks in Bulgaria and Romania: even in 2011, only one structure, formerly known as the Friendship Bridge, crossed their 470-kilometer border along the Danube River. In Hungary, by contrast, nine bridges crossed the Danube in the capital city of Budapest alone.

Infrastructure connections alone did not guarantee mobility: checkpoints and tariffs restricted the circulation of everything from people to money to products. Consider Europe's Channel Tunnel that connects France and Britain. Since 1994, this iconic cross-border link has enabled the free circulation of businesspeople, tourists, and cargo. At the same time, high-security fencing; extensive monitoring equipment; and more than one hundred armed guards have prevented access by tens of thousands of migrants and asylum seekers who also tried to enter Britain via the tunnel. In practice, universal connectivity has proven to be elusive, despite the promises offered by everyone from Chevalier to the founders of Facebook. In the landscape of infrastructure linkages, some have become "more equal" than others.[16] Accordingly, this history of Europe's infrastructure transition traces far-reaching connections as well as connectivity hierarchies, boundaries, and asymmetries.

Building Systems, Making Europe

In the making of modern Europe, the infrastructure transition was fundamental because it transformed—unpredictably yet powerfully—Europe's physical connections, its economies, it wars, as well as its natural environments. How can we understand the dynamics of this transition? How do we trace its tightly-woven fabric of connections?

We emphasize that this fabric did not emerge as a result of impersonal forces such as technological advance, globalization, and Europeanization. To the contrary, the web resulted from the concrete preferences and choices of its makers. Many contributed to building Europe's modern infrastructure, its economic and military systems. Among them were individuals, companies, and governments; engineering communities, international organizations, and others. These were Europe's system-builders; it is they who spun its web of connections and decided, implicitly and explicitly, whom to connect and whom to bypass; how to use infrastructure for economic and military purposes; and how to treat the natural environment. This book documents the visions, priorities, and choices of Europe's system-builders as they constructed or blocked connections in infrastructure, the economy, the military, and the environment.[17]

Who, exactly, built which parts of modern Europe? Europe's infrastructure transition involved many kinds of system-builders who constructed connections and borders within and between infrastructure, economic, military, and environmental systems. Part I (chapters 1 and 2), titled Connecting Europe, focuses on system-builders who connected Europe through transport, communications, and energy infrastructure. Some worked toward what they perceived as the betterment of Europe. For example, around 1930, walking in the footsteps of Chevalier, visionary engineers Oskar Oliven, Georges Valensi, Piero Puricelli, and Hugo Junkers proposed unity via pan-European electrical networks, telephony, highways, and airline networks, respectively. Historically, many different organizations strove to integrate European infrastructure. These groups included: the International Railway Union (1922), the International Broadcasting Union (1925), the United Nations (The Economic Commission for Europe, 1948), and the European

Conference of Post and Telecommunication Administrations (1959). And, since the 1990s, it has been the European Union that champions the construction of so-called Trans-European Networks (TENs) in an effort to create a coherent European economy and society.

All these system-builders, from Chevalier to the current EU commissioners, shared the goal of integrating Europe's infrastructure. But each expressed distinctly divergent views on *how* to integrate Europe's infrastructure, embracing, as they did, different visions of Europe—some inclusive, others exclusive. For example, Gunnar Myrdal—Secretary General of the United Nations Economic Commission for Europe (1948) and a Nobel Prize winner in economics—advocated an inclusive agenda. Myrdal promoted the so-called E-road plan and other infrastructure as "all-European" connections that should integrate the socialist East and capitalist West. His aim was to prevent a third world war, no less. He heavily criticized infrastructure projects limited to a few countries, such as efforts by the European Economic Community (a forerunner to the European Union) at infrastructure integration for its six member states only. Myrdal condemned use of the term "Europe" in such "sub-regional" initiatives as "intensely inimical" to his own organization's work.[18]

Most infrastructure system-builders, however, did not aim primarily at European integration. Private companies, imperial governments, and bilateral projects dominated the international scene with infrastructure visions and objectives of their own. In this arena, even such apparently powerful international organizations as the European Union find their influence on Europe's infrastructure development to be severely restricted.[19] Moreover, domestic infrastructure building was much larger than any international initiatives—whether or not they were aimed at building an integrated Europe. Over the last two centuries, national and municipal governments have accumulated unprecedented power, budgets, and manpower. National and local infrastructure projects have followed suit, while national and urban spaces have emerged as magnets in Europe's infrastructure geography. Any transnational history of Europe's infrastructure transition must acknowledge that the age of European integration and globalization was also the age of the nation state and the municipality.[20]

Finally, we note that infrastructure builders, at times, deployed the 'European integration' mission strategically. For example, hydraulic engineers Antonin Smrček, Jaroslav Kubec, and others promoted the Danube–Oder–Elbe canal as the missing link in Europe's inland navigation system. For more than a century, engineers worked to construct this canal that would connect the North Sea, the Baltic Sea, and the Black Sea. What kept their partly-built project alive was the ability to adapt their designs and visions to competing and successive political agendas, including Czech nationalism, Moravian regionalism, Central European integration efforts, Nazi *Neuropa*-building, postwar Pan-Europeanism, and socialist integration. When the European Union gained importance, engineers lobbied to make the canal a priority project of the Trans European Network program.[21]

As for system-builders creating ruptures in Europe, examples also abound. Consider the disintegration wrought by Cold War infrastructure: everything from border crossings to barbed-wire fences to the entire constellation of technologies that constituted the Iron Curtain. Contemporary versions of these ruptures also abound: the European Union agency for external frontiers management, Frontex, is a controversial and telling example of a border builder today. In the name of European solidarity and migrant safety, EU member states supply Frontex with aircraft, ground-patrol units, and equipment to intercept migrants who try to cross the EU's Greek-Turkish, Mediterranean, and Atlantic borders. Individuals and families are imprisoned in detention centers which, by Council of Europe standards, qualify as "inhumane." Whenever possible, would-be migrants are returned to their countries of origin. And, while EU ministers praised the democratic revolutions of the 2011 Arab Spring in Northern Africa and the Middle East, they also accelerated development of Frontex's European External Border Surveillance System (EUROSUR) to guard against the anticipated surge in illegal immigration from these territories. An unprecedentedly-advanced infrastructure, EUROSUR consists of coastal radar, satellite tracking systems, drones, and autonomous targeting systems. The goal is to detect small vessels as they approach EU territory and to transform the edges of the EU into so-called "smart borders."[22] Today's European Union functions like the infrastructure system-builders have historically: the EU envisions and builds connections as well as borders.

Part II of this book (chapters 3, 4, and 5), Economy and War, addresses the role of infrastructure in the making of peace and war.

In Chevalier's pacifist vision, "material" railroad and shipping networks and "immaterial" credit networks would unite Europe in a common economy and reduce the risk of war. He wrote: "Industry is eminently peaceful. Instinctively it rejects war; that which creates does not combine with that which kills."[23] Many since Chevalier have reiterated this argument. In order to unravel how peoples and places became connected (and divided) through wars and economics, we study the historical makers of these connections.

In chapters 3 and 4, we investigate how various actors—individuals and companies, governments and international organizations—mobilized infrastructure to build Chevalier's so-called networks of peace, now known as Europe's network economy. These actors served as veritable "economic system-builders": using infrastructure links, they connected farms, factories, stores, and consumers into economic systems for the production and allocation of scarce goods and services.[24] For example, starting in the late nineteenth century, William and Edmund Vestey expanded their Liverpool-based family butchery to cattle farms, meat processing plants, and cold stores in Argentina, Uruguay, Venezuela, and Australia. The Vesteys built—or corralled others into building—railroads that connected their inland cattle farms to harborside meat processing plants, stores, and docks. They set up their own Blue Star Line shipping company to connect these overseas facilities to their new cold stores at the London docks. From here, existing inland transport networks facilitated further distribution to shops in London. The Vesteys had built an intercontinental food chain, and British meat consumption rose steeply as retail prices dropped.

Many other economic system-builders, both local and international, built and deployed infrastructure to forge Europe's food connections. Together, they created one of Europe's most fundamental economic transitions ever, a transition from widespread hunger and monotonous diets to abundant food and varied diets. Similarly, industrial entrepreneurs used transport, communications, and energy links—from trains transporting coal to gas pipelines—to set up Europe's heavy industry; financial traders used telecommunications to build Europe's financial market connections, which fueled economic expansion as well as financial crises.

Unfortunately, Europe's transnational economic systems did not eradicate the possibility of war, as Chevalier discovered in 1870.

Introduction: Chevalier's Dream | 13

Fig. 0.2 **Rails of War:** *The development of war trains illustrates the entanglement of infrastructure systems and military systems. The Polish army captured the Śmiały (Polish for "bold") war train from Austria-Hungary in 1918. In 1918–21 it successfully used the Śmiały and other armored trains in the Greater Poland Uprising, the Polish–Ukrainian war, and the Polish–Soviet war. In 1939 the Śmiały both destroyed German tanks and fought the Soviet invaders, before it surrendered to the Red Army. In 1941 the Germans captured it from the Soviets, then used it on the Eastern front.*

He was the only member of Napoleons III's Imperial Senate to vote against war with Prussia. The Franco-Prussian War came as a shock to the French military, though it eventually opened their eyes to the destructive power of infrastructure. Pre-1870, in processes akin to economic system-building, the Prussian army had learned to mobilize railroads and communications systems for military purposes. Military system-builders such as Helmut von Moltke the Elder, Chief of the Prussian General Staff as of 1857, had developed elaborate mobilization plans. In the Austro-Prussian War of 1866, for example, the Prussian army had used railroads to transport nearly 200,000 men and 55,000 horses. Given their ability to rapidly concentrate troops and ammunition in decisive battles, the Prussians were able to outmaneuver the Austrian armies. This marked Prussia's military intervention with railroad construction. New lines were designed for military peak demand, which greatly exceeded day-to-day civilian demand. In 1870, within eighteen days of the declaration of war, von Moltke's staff directed approximately 400,000 troops to predetermined border positions. Outmaneuvering the French, they captured Emperor Napoleon and his army a month later. Chapter 5 investigates how, in response to these Prussian victories, other European military powers used infrastructure to build powerful logistics systems for warfare by land, air, and sea. The chapter also looks at the ways in which military infrastructure—NATO, for example—has aimed to integrate Europe.

In Part III of this volume (chapters 6, 7, and 8), Networking Nature, we examine how Europe's infrastructure transition created entanglements with the natural environment—water, air, and land. In order to trace the role of infrastructure in the construction and fragmentation of environmental connections, we again follow the makers of such connections. For example, system-builders manipulated nature to make their systems work. They modified natural waterways in order to "fit" them into networks of many different descriptions: drainage, navigation, water-supply, and hydroelectric power, to name just a few. Other system-builders claimed and redefined airspace for aviation, transmission of radio waves, and the disposal of emission gasses from power plants, factories, and vehicles. Still others manipulated mountains, forests, and moors for infrastructure purposes serving human needs. Knowingly or unwittingly, these professionals generated new environmental connections and ruptures, for better or worse.

To spotlight infrastructure's role in changing Europe's ecological systems, we also track the intermediaries who spoke on behalf of nature. As we will see, scientific organizations such as the International Meteorological Organization and the European Geodetic Association built systems to understand nature: they

Fig. 0.3 Gray-Green Junctions: *Europe's infrastructure transition fundamentally changed landscapes. First, railroads, canals, pipelines, and especially motorways caused habitat fragmentation for Europe's wild plants and animals, threatening biodiversity. Then, nature conservationists started building their own infrastructure: ecological networks reconnecting isolated patches of nature on regional, national, and pancontinental scales. "Wildlife crossings" or "ecoducts," first built in France in the 1950s, are key nodes in such networks. The photo shows the ecoduct "het groene woud" (2003), allowing red deer, foxes, badgers and other species to cross the A2 motorway in the Netherlands. Local youth, to the dismay of conservationists, use it as a motocross passage.*

used telecommunications to connect observation posts that dotted the Continent and the skies, creating pan-European knowledge systems. These systems have yielded a more integrated understanding of Europe's lands, its bodies of water, and its air. For example, geographers, map-makers, and the like "integrated" Europe on paper via finely-detailed coordinate grids and models that defined Europe's landscapes and its skies.[25]

In addition, from the late nineteenth century to the present, nature conservationists have asserted the detrimental effects of the relationship between infrastructure and ecological habitats. "One of the most important issues is fragmentation of landscapes by human activities and infrastructure—a major cause of the alarming decrease in many European wildlife populations," noted European Environment Agency director Jacqueline McGlade and her Swiss colleague Bruno Oberle in a 2011 report.[26] Historically, conservationists have responded to these assertions by protecting and restoring nature in the form of nature reserves and ecological connections. For example, they built fish ladders to bypass hydropower dams; ecological corridors to traverse cultivated fields; and ecoducts (animal viaducts) to enable wildlife to cross highways. Indeed, the construction of national ecological networks began in the 1970s. And, in the 1990s, work commenced on a pan-European ecological network for the transcontinental circulation of plants and animals. Increasingly, ecological system-builders talked about these networks in terms of constructing "green infrastructure."[27] In Part III, we investigate how system-builders tried to valorize, understand, and build their natural environments—and how this changed Europe's land, water, and air.

The Grid of History

On the surface, our modern world of technology appears smooth and ever accelerating, propelled as it is by promises of connectivity and universal access. Our purpose in this book is to delve beneath this surface of technology—technology that is almost mythically complete, modern, and irreproachable. After all, the infrastructure of the modern world—indeed, infrastructure throughout history—usually remains invisible. Often, only a critical event—an electricity blackout or gas crisis, a food emergency or an ecological upset—reveals the infrastructure that makes it all work. These events expose asymmetries and dependencies, ruptures within our otherwise "connected" lives. In this book, we aim to make visible the hidden infrastructure dynamics of our modern world, to examine how these dynamics came into being.[28]

Indeed, our book portrays Europe's infrastructure transition as embracing several interrelated processes: the building of infrastructure, the construction of economic and military systems, and the manipulation of Europe's natural environment. In charting the making of modern Europe, most historical studies focus on one of these processes only: either physical infrastructure or economic systems, military systems or the environment. Juxtaposing these processes allows us to examine the interactions between them, in all their complexity and unpredictability. These interactions, we claim, also produced the vigorous infrastructure dynamic of Europe's remarkable evolution and, at times, its devolution.

Interweaving these four processes takes us into many different fields. For example, our history traces railroad projects all the way from Chevalier's early-nineteenth-century visions to Operation Barbarossa, the Nazis' failed invasion of Russia. We chart telecommunications from Napoleon's optical telegraphs to the dotcom crash of 2001. We look at developments in energy from early logging networks in Scandinavia to the construction of Europe's organic-chemical industries along its transcontinental and overseas oil networks. We analyze food chains from ice-cooled butter transports on the Trans-Siberian Railway to the Aboriginals' walk-out at a Vestey company meat farm in Northern Australia. We look at changes in Europe's natural environments, from satellite imaging of land uses to acid rain in Scandinavia.

It is by presenting these diverse yet interrelated processes, system-builders, and events that our history of Europe takes shape. To paraphrase historian Norman Davies: we use the history of the grid to reinterpret the grid of European history.[29]

I
CONNECTING EUROPE

1
Manipulating Space & Time

To the Finland Station

In central St. Petersburg, on the northern bank of the Neva, there is a railroad station. It is a fairly small one, with only a few tracks, but it has a particular place in Russian history: Vladimir Ilyich Lenin arrived here in spring 1917 to initiate the Great Socialist October Revolution. The Finland station can be regarded as the physical place of a new era's arrival in Russia. *To the Finland Station* was the title of American historian Edmund Wilson's classic study of the evolution of socialist and revolutionary thinking in Europe, indicating that it was a long and troublesome journey, metaphorically speaking, that eventually led Lenin to get off the train here.[1]

But the journey to the Finland station was long and troublesome not only in a metaphorical sense, but also in a more mundane way. Lenin arrived in St. Petersburg (or Petrograd, as the city was called at the time) after a lengthy period of exile in Switzerland. As its name indicates, however, the station where he got off welcomes the arrival of trains from Finland rather than from Central Europe. Lenin's trip was unusually complicated. He first rode a train to Sassnitz on Germany's Baltic coast, where a steamer waited to take him on board. He debarked in southern Sweden, continued to Stockholm and, after a break, traveled north to Haparanda near the Polar Circle. There, at the border between Sweden and the Russian Grand Duchy of Finland, Lenin had to step out and change to a horsedrawn sledge, which carried him across the border to the Finnish railroad station at Tornio. From there, the final leg of the trip awaited, taking him in a southeastern direction across most of Finland and eventually into Russia proper. He arrived in the Imperial capital just before midnight on April 16, 1917.[2]

All in all, Lenin's journey took more than a week. This was absurd, at least if seen in relation to the existence of efficient transport networks through which Western and East-Central Europe, ever since the mid-nineteenth century, had been connected with Russia. But traveling across Europe in spring 1917, when the Great War was raging, was not an easy thing; and it was even more cumbersome for someone widely known as a communist revolutionary. The war had disrupted much of Europe's regular international rail traffic, and crossing state borders was extremely complicated. The fact that Lenin's journey was possible at all was the result of

Fig. 1.1 Arrival of an Era: *Vladimir Ilych Lenin's 1917 arrival at Petrograd's Finland Station has often been interpreted as the starting point for the October Revolution and the Soviet era in Russian history. Lenin's journey from Switzerland to Russia, in the midst of the First World War, was extraordinarily complicated. In the end it took more than a week, since the most direct railroads could not be used. In this Soviet-era painting Joseph Stalin, who was not actually present at the event, is fictitiously depicted as standing behind Lenin.*

difficult diplomatic negotiations involving several countries. In the end Lenin was permitted to travel from Switzerland to Russia. However, he was prevented from arriving quickly and comfortably by way of Warsaw, as Count Myshkin had done a few decades earlier in the opening pages of Fyodor Dostoyevsky's famous novel *The Idiot*, or from Lübeck by ship, as Dostoeyvsky's idol Nikolai Gogol had done in the early nineteenth century, on his one and only trip outside Russia.

The Warsaw–St. Petersburg railroad, at the time of its inauguration in 1862, had seemed to revolutionize travel between continental Europe and the Russian capital city. The railroad was built as an almost straight line between the two cities, passing through Vilnius, Daugavpils, and Pskov, cities that experienced a marked upswing following its completion. Russia seemed to be coming much nearer to the rest of Europe. During the following century, however, European conflicts and border changes altered the railroad's prospects. In the 1920s a whole array of new, independent states (in what had earlier been western Russia) first made movement along the railroad more complicated. The expansion of Soviet power after 1944 annulled the interwar borders and made traveling easier again. But the hardest blow to the route was still to come, in 1991, when the Soviet Union collapsed and, in 2004, the Baltic States and Poland accessed the European Union. From then on, a train passing along the straight path from Warsaw to St. Petersburg had to cross no less than five national borders, entering and exiting the European Union (EU) twice. Moreover, part of the route was on the West European 1.435 m standard gauge, and part on Russian 1.520 m tracks. Not surprisingly, then, the old railroad built in the 1860s hardly operates anymore. While the tracks still exist, traffic is redirected along less complicated routes. Much cargo en route to present-day St. Petersburg even travels the way Lenin did in 1917: through Sweden and Finland.[3]

How then, can we understand Europe's infrastructure transition in the field of transport and communications? The above examples illustrate that it would be an error to view it as a linear process of steady growth, expansion, and ever more efficient connectivity among countries and regions. Rather, the making of Europe must be viewed as a highly volatile, ambiguous, and contested development. This chapter analyzes the construction of modern transport and communications infrastructure in Europe from the perspective of system-builders, but also from the perspective of border-builders seeking to control and delimit long-distance flows of people, goods, and information. It is precisely in the dynamic interaction between system-building and border-building that we must look for infrastructural Europe taking shape.

Europe's Transport Revolution

A century before Lenin's legendary return to Russia, Europe was in the process of recovering from decades of revolutionary turmoil and bloody wars. In 1814, hoping to create a more stable international order and avoid future chaos, government representatives had come together at the Congress of Vienna. Its most important outcome was, arguably, that many micro-states, a typical feature on older European political maps, disappeared. Napoleon had already implemented a large number of radical border changes and inter-state mergers. Many of these were now made permanent. The reforms allowed for strong and centralized state bureaucracies to be formed in parts of Europe—notably Germany—where local and micro-regional forms of government had earlier dominated. Taking inspiration from France and other countries, government agencies in charge of "public works" formed virtually everywhere. As the nineteenth century progressed, these organizations undertook infrastructure system-building on unprecedented scales. State-wide transport and communications networks, whether aimed for military or civilian use, were increasingly eyed as a panacea for modernization and nation-building.

Indirectly, the disappearance of the micro-states also encouraged infrastructural projects at the *international* level. In the eighteenth century, such projects had often been virtually impossible to carry out, given the myriad of incompatible state forms and the chronic lack of competence and capital in many small polities. On the very occasion of the Congress of Vienna, Michel Chevalier's idol, the French philosopher Claude Henri de Saint-Simon, took the opportunity to point at roads and artificial waterways as important means for integrating Europe, envisioning a European Parliament that would be responsible for large-scale public works—including, in particular, a giant pan-European canal and river system.[4]

Saint Simon's vision did not materialize, but his ideas would inspire later generations of infrastructure enthusiasts. Moreover, the diplomats in Vienna eventually did agree that the "powers whose states are separated or crossed by the same navigable river engage to regulate, by common consent, all that regards its navigation." Navigation on these "international" rivers, the delegates decided, "shall be entirely free, and shall not, in respect to commerce, be prohibited to anyone." For this purpose the Congress stipulated that a number of international "river commissions" be formed, to ensure that physical and institutional obstacles to this new navigational freedom were removed.[5]

Overall, however, the national emphasis in post-Vienna system-building was unmistakable. Numerous ambitious projects, many of which were perceived as being of great national significance, were launched throughout Europe, ranging from the construction of carefully planned and regularized networks of roads, radiating from capital cities such as Paris, Berlin, and Munich, to new, expensive waterways both in already industrializing regions and in other, less-developed countries such as Sweden and Spain.[6] Even river improvement projects, while often being of international significance, were organized—and funded—by government agencies rather than by the new river commissions, and they were typically framed as projects of national rather than European importance.[7]

The efforts to improve Europe's roads and waterways built on the experiences from centuries of pre- and early-modern system-building. They did not constitute any radical break with the past. As the nineteenth century progressed, however, these traditional infrastructural projects were overshadowed by activities of a totally different kind. Steam propulsion was the decisive factor in this context, being introduced first on water and then on land.

Already in the 1810s, steam-propelled vessels had started traversing busy European rivers such as the Clyde, the Rhine, and the Po. Soon shipping companies started experimenting with steamships in coastal shipping and, ultimately, trans-oceanic navigation as well. The new mode of transport had a tremendous impact as steamers were able to operate more or less independently of weather and winds. In a way unimaginable for eighteenth-century

Europeans, voyages could be planned far in advance and detailed time-tables for connections between distant ports created.[8]

Mail services and first-class passenger transport on Europe's Atlantic seaboard were among the first to be reshaped by steam. In 1839, then, two steamship companies, the Great Western and the British American, inaugurated regular trans-Atlantic passenger services. Another company, created by Nova Scotian Samuel Cunard, was awarded a monopoly on Britain's trans-Atlantic mail services. Liverpool became its base. In continental Western Europe, Bremerhaven in northern Germany attained a similar hub position, turning into "America's continental post office."[9]

In the 1860s and 1870s more powerful steamships started carrying masses of migrants, too, across the Atlantic. Significant migration to North America had started earlier, using sailing vessels, but from around 1850 entrepreneurs identified the new screw-propelled, iron-hulled steamships that began to appear around this time as an opportunity in the increasingly competitive migration business. On this basis, the Inman Line, the White Star Line, Bremen's Norddeutscher Lloyd, Cunard, and a few other companies became highly successful builders of steam-powered trans-Atlantic passenger connections.[10]

In the meantime steam propulsion transformed overland transport, too. Most actors originally viewed steam-powered railroads as an auxiliary form of transport, supplementing already existing waterways and road networks. Very soon, however, leading visionaries enthusiastically embraced the idea of railroads forming a large-scale system in their own right. Thomas Gray, Britain's most important early railroad promoter, in the early 1820s argued forcefully in favor of a nationwide system. In actual practice, the myriad of entrepreneurs who gradually organized the construction of Britain's railroads did not follow any such national vision, but rather focused on improving connectivity between certain specific localities. Even so, the sum of individual projects, carried out without much coordination, had by the late 1830s generated a system that enabled passengers and light cargo to move from one corner of England to the other.[11]

It did not take long before railroad fever seized large parts of continental Europe as well. Belgium became the first continental country to build a primary network of railroad lines. In marked contrast to the British case, leading representatives of the young

Belgian state identified railroad-building as a task that under no circumstances could be left to uncoordinated private initiatives. Belgian Prime Minister Charles Rogier, inspired by the Saint-Simonian movement, forcefully argued that the country's liberal constitution had "to be completed with a material act of the same scope," and that this act would have to be "the construction of a railway."[12] Initially, the Belgian focus was on creating a link with Germany. Gradually, however, the engineers charged with the planning, Pierre Simons and Gustave de Ridder, widened their ambitions. By 1833, the initial project had been transformed into a grand plan for a nationwide—but internationally connected—network of trunk lines. Such a network represented an economically crucial and symbolically important project for the vulnerable Belgian nation, whose declaration of independence had not yet been recognized by its former Dutch rulers.[13]

France was not far behind Belgium in terms of governmental ambitions for a nationwide network. However, implementation of the government's 1833 vision for a national system largely failed. Instead, the early phase of French railroad system-building became a highly-decentralized process in which multiple private actors, not unlike their British counterparts, played the main roles. By 1850 the French railroad system was little more than a regional network covering the northernmost departments of France and the area around Paris. In Germany, by contrast, it was already possible to travel by train among most major cities and industrial centers. The rapid German development was remarkable in view of the far-reaching political fragmentation of the territories through which the newly-built lines passed. The Prussian government was very active in forging railroad links between its geographically-distributed territorial constituents, but since this involved transit through other German states, its ambitions inspired the construction of a larger German network.[14] Such a national system was convincingly argued for by Germany's main railroad visionary, Friedrich List, who pointed to a wide range of advantages, ranging from military aspects and economic gains to its expected impact on the spirit of the nation. Together with waterways, roads, and steam navigation, railroads would also enable an eastward expansion of German political and economic influence. Although List's vision of a "German-Hungarian economic space," bounded by the North, Baltic, and Black Seas, remained a distant

Fig. 1.2 **Early Adopter:** *Postal services have always been among the very first to make use of new infrastructure—from railroads and steamships in the nineteenth century to aviation and the Internet in the twentieth. Here a steamship has just unloaded a batch of continental mail in the port of Dover, for further rail-bound distribution to London and other British destinations.*

dream, railroad-building in the period that followed stimulated Germany's political unification.[15]

During the next few decades, railroad companies—state-owned and private—projected and built state-wide networks in many European countries. Almost everywhere railroad-building was perceived as being of vital importance for nation-building. This did not mean, however, that national networks would form closed systems. Their development in Belgium, the Netherlands, Switzerland, and Greece, where international interconnectivity figured prominently in national system-building visions, made clear that national projects were deeply embedded in a wider European context. In 1843 Europe's first cross-border railroad was inaugurated, connecting Belgium with Prussia. It was soon followed by other links. By 1850, it was already possible to travel by train from Paris to Warsaw and from Hamburg to Zagreb—although lack of coordination typically forced travelers to spend long hours waiting for connecting trains, which, moreover, might be departing from a different station.[16]

Importantly, the overall increase in international connectivity was not the result of any grand Chevalierian dream in which

Europe as a whole was at focus, but of bilateral and mostly uncoordinated efforts. These were complemented by the initiatives taken by trade organizations such as the Association of German Railway Administrations (*Verein Deutscher Eisenbahnverwaltungen*, set up in 1847), private companies such as Georges Nackelmackers's International Sleeping Car Company (formed in 1872), and state governments.[17]

Apart from state borders, system-builders early on set out to subjugate giant natural obstacles in the European transport geography. This concerned, in particular, the Alps. The first trans-Alpine railroad connections—the Semmering and Brenner railroads, completed in 1854 and 1867—took the form of domestic lines designed to strengthen Vienna's control of the Habsburg provinces south of the Alps. Other projects were much more international in style. The determination of Italy's government to connect its emerging railroad network with those of France and Germany was decisive in this context. Northern Italy was emerging as a rapidly-industrializing region, but the fear of becoming isolated from northwestern Europe's industrial heartlands was omnipresent in Turin, Milan, and the other Italian manufacturing hotspots.

A first connection, initiated by the Italian government shortly after the country's unification, took the form of a tunnel under Mont Cenis into France. More ambitious, however, was Switzerland's Gotthard Tunnel, through which Italy's connections with Germany were radically improved. Initiated in the late 1860s, it was able to profit from the availability of dynamite, which opened up completely new possibilities in tunnel construction. Albert Escher, a former president of the Swiss Federal Council, proved crucial in merging Swiss national interests with German and Italian ones. Two decades earlier, Escher had played a leading role in turning railroad construction into a Swiss national interest. Shifting his attention to the international context, he persuaded the Italian and German governments to pay a total of 65 million Swiss Francs—corresponding to more than a third of total project costs—for a railroad link built solely on Swiss territory. This, if anything, signified the enormous perceived importance, far beyond the Alpine countries themselves, of creating efficient trans-Alpine transport connections. Yet the Gotthard Tunnel was also highly significant in the domestic Swiss context, both symbolically and physically interconnecting northern Switzerland and Ticino, the country's Italian-speaking canton in the south.[18]

Europe's seas posed additional natural divides that system-builders eagerly set out to challenge. This was so, for example, in forging Denmark's national railroad system, but also in enabling a number of international railroad connections. Sweden, for example, was integrated with the rest of Europe through specially-designed railroad ferries to Denmark and northern Germany.[19] In southern Europe, the French-Italian engineer Philippe Vitali succeeded in bringing about a connection from Calabria to Sicily. He then proceeded, in 1869, to lobby the Greek government to support a more ambitious project aimed at linking Athens by a "direct and fast 26-hour connection to Brindisi, Italy, and from there, to the whole of Western Europe."[20] At the time, the Greek government was much concerned with Greece "lying at the end of Europe," and accordingly was susceptible to such grand schemes.[21] In the end, however, it found Vitali's proposal too costly. Instead, Greek railroad builders ultimately linked up with the rest of Europe through Balkan lines.[22]

Other system-builders expanded Europe's railroad network into previously more or less inaccessible territories. Tracks were laid through the vast forests, tundra, and swamps of northern and eastern Europe, and across the Urals into Siberia and Central Asia. After a period of uncoordinated Russian railroad construction led by private actors in the 1860s and 1870s, the Imperial government seized control over system-building. Under the leadership of Sergei Witte, Russia's capable finance minister, the Empire embarked on several unprecedented projects serving political and military rather than economic purposes, notably the Trans-Siberian Railway and two geographically-daunting lines into Central Asia. Additional tracks created links to Russia's newly-conquered Caucasian provinces. These projects challenged the very perception of the Urals, the Caucasus, and the Caspian as "natural" borders between Europe and Asia.[23]

Ferdinand de Lesseps, the Suez Canal's famed engineer, initiated a vivid debate in Europe by proposing that Russia's Central Asian railroads be extended into Afghanistan and British India. Some observers regarded such a connection, especially if combined with a railroad tunnel under the English Channel, as the most promising way of establishing overland transport links between

Fig. 1.3 **Integrating Eurasia:** *The Trans-Siberian Railway revolutionized overland transport between Europe and Asia. In Manchuria, it linked up with the emerging Chinese railroad network, much of which likewise resulted from European system-builders' efforts. This early-twentieth-century photo shows a train approaching the town of Khilok in eastern Siberia, en route from St. Petersburg to the Pacific. The Transsib remained a popular—and by far the fastest—route for European travelers on their way to the Far East even after the Bolshevik takeover of Russia in 1917.*

the British Isles and the Empire's jewel in the East. In the end, however, nothing came of de Lesseps's proposal. More successful were the efforts of European railroad builders further east. Witte's engineers, for example, while building the Trans-Siberian, became deeply involved in railroad construction in Chinese Manchuria. The British were also highly active in Chinese railroads, and in the end it was in China rather than in Central Asia that Russian and British system-building became interlinked. In 1899 the two European powers signed an agreement defining their respective spheres of Chinese railroad concessions.[24]

In a similar vein, prospective system-builders envisioned radical infrastructural expansions into the Ottoman Empire, the young nation states of Latin America, and resource-rich colonial territories in Africa. The famous Orient Express started running from Paris to Constantinople in 1883, but Constantinople, in the imperial visions of Britain, France, and Germany, was never thought of as the final destination. Instead, it was regarded as a future hub and point of departure for further railroad construction in both eastern and southern directions. While German engineers, following the conclusion of an alliance between Kaiser Wilhelm II and the Ottomans, set about building the Berlin–Baghdad railroad, the Prime Minister of the British Cape colony, Cecil Rhodes, sought support for a "Cape to Cairo railway" through the whole of Africa. The latter proposal clashed with the interests of France and Portugal, both of which aimed to construct trans-African railroads from West to East. In the same way as the Baghdad project aroused controversy far beyond the Middle East transport realm, the quest for imperial rail and communications corridors through Africa became an important factor in the geopolitical scramble for Africa.[25]

The far reaches of European system-building also influenced the perception of the railroads built in Europe itself. What at first sight appeared to be intra-European railroads were, in the eyes of their promoters, more often components in colonial, imperial, and global network visions. The Gotthard Tunnel, for example, served not merely to unite Switzerland's cantons or improve the connectivity between southern and northern Europe, but was widely interpreted as an extension of the Suez Canal and as a link between the Rhine countries and the Orient. In a similar way, the railroad lines to Europe's Atlantic ports in effect did not end there, but continued through shipments of goods, mail, and passengers to the Americas.[26]

The Rise of Telegraphy

Traditionally, transport and communications had been one and the same thing, as people, goods, and information moved together. This changed with the rise of a radically-new mode of communications: telegraphy. Optical and, in particular, electrical telegraphy proved a remarkable addition to Europe's infrastructural landscape, for the first time enabling regular long-distance communications at a speed much greater than what any transport system, even the railroad, was able to offer. As a result, it started to make sense to think of transport and communications as separate realms.

In optical telegraphy, the French inventor and engineer Claude Chappe led the way. A political and military interest in fast long-distance communications during the Revolutionary and Napoleonic

Wars generated state support for Chappe's and similar undertakings. The French built a vast network of optical telegraphy lines, which was subsequently expanded throughout most of French-occupied Europe. Somewhat less ambitious optical networks arose in Sweden, England, and Prussia.[27] Then, starting in the 1830s, inventors launched serious experiments with low-voltage electricity signals. The breakthrough for electrical telegraphy came in the late 1840s, coinciding with the European railroad boom.

In Britain, private actors played an important part in constructing the first electrical telegraph lines. In most other countries, however, national governments identified telegraphy as a domain for state control. This was so especially after the European turmoil in 1848 and the Crimean War (1853–6), events that demonstrated the military and political potential of the new technology. Unsurprisingly, then, state-run telegraph administrations became the main system-builders.

International connections played an important role from the outset. In 1849–50 Prussia, Bavaria, Saxony, and Austria signed a series of interconnection treaties. In 1850, these four states set up the Austro-German Telegraph Union to regulate tariffs and the construction of new interconnections. In 1851, the Union organized a conference in Vienna, whereby the Morse system was defined as a common standard in telegraphic communications. This spurred further bilateral and multilateral interconnection agreements between state telegraph agencies. In 1855 France and most of its neighbors (Belgium, Switzerland, Sardinia, and Spain) formed the West European Telegraph Union, soon joined by several other countries. A decade later, following another initiative by Napoleon III's government, nearly all European state telegraph agencies came together in forming the International Telegraph Union (ITU). By then, the European telegraph network had already become an impressively-integrated structure, covering most of the Continent and interconnecting 2,800 cities and towns.[28]

As in the transport case, nature imposed significant barriers to telegraph system-building. This concerned in particular the construction of underwater connections. Absent these, the Scandinavian countries, the British Isles, and the large Mediterranean islands could not achieve connectivity with the rest of Europe. The dilemma was that the electrical signal was distorted through its contact with seawater. This practical problem was solved through the discovery that gutta percha, harvested from the jungles of Southeast Asia, was an effective insulator. After a failed attempt in 1850, three British entrepreneurs—the Brett brothers and the well-known railroad engineer Thomas Crampton—were able to install a cable beneath the English Channel. Having founded the Submarine Telegraph Company, they opened a direct telegraph connection between London and Paris in 1852. Their success stimulated other actors to lay submarine cables in the North Sea, the Baltic, and the Mediterranean. In 1853 England connected with Ireland and in 1854 Denmark was linked with Germany. In 1855 the state telegraph administrations of Sweden and Denmark completed a cable across the Sound, which together with the German–Danish connection, enabled Sweden to communicate with the Continent. Before long, all North and Baltic Sea coastal states had become interlinked.[29]

The difficulties were much greater when bridging the Mediterranean and the great oceans. In the Mediterranean, John Brett's company succeeded in connecting Corsica and Sardinia with Genoa on the Italian mainland. When setting out to bridge the much deeper waters that separated southern Europe from North Africa, however, Brett's ambitions met with troubles of the same magnitude as the Alps imposed on railroad engineers at about the same time. His efforts proved unsuccessful. Attempts to lay cables on the bottom of the Red Sea and across the Atlantic in the late 1850s also failed, although one of the first Atlantic cables, championed by the American entrepreneur Cyrus Field, did enable trans-Atlantic telegraphy for a few weeks.[30]

For some time, system-builders retreated to land-based routes for linking Europe with the rest of the world. In this situation, Western Europe's colonial powers, eager for contact with their geographically-dispersed possessions, found themselves dependent on transit through countries such as Prussia, Russia, Persia, the Ottoman Empire, and Egypt. Britain, for example, signed agreements with the Persian, Russian, and Ottoman governments in a first attempt to establish electrical communications with India. This British–Indian connection went online in 1865, but it worked poorly. Through cooperation with Siemens & Halske's skilled engineers and the Prussian government, the Britons improved the connection decisively during the next few years. In addition, they cooperated with a Danish telegraph company, the Great Northern.

Fig. 1.4 Networking the Ocean: *Up to 1866 no one knew whether it would ever be technically possible to lay durable telegraph connections across the Atlantic. In 1858 the American entrepreneur Cyrus Field championed a first attempt, pictured here, using the combined steam and sailing ship HMS Agamemnon. The project was initially hailed as a success, but the cable stopped working after only a few weeks. It would take another eight years before the Atlantic could be telegraphically bridged on a more permanent basis.*

The Danes managed to attain an unexpected key role in linking up England with Russia and the Far East by way of the Baltic Sea rather than continental Western Europe. At one point it seemed that Russian cables, extended across the Bering Strait, would also become the preferred telegraph route to the Americas.[31]

When improved technology and cable-laying methods yielded a breakthrough in deep-sea submarine telegraphy, the political geography of the growing system changed. Britain was able to reduce its dependence on foreign partners. In 1866 the private Anglo-American Telegraph Company, formed on the initiative of the Manchester industrialist John Pender, managed to lay a much-improved trans-Atlantic cable. Its instant success soon spread to other seas. Forging a symbiotic relationship with the British government and its Colonial Office, Pender's Eastern Telegraph Company quickly expanded submarine telegraphy to nearly all corners of the maritime world. Eastern's London headquarters rose to become the hub of the world's telegraph network. As a result, by the 1870s continental Europe was more dependent on Britain for its worldwide communications than the other way round. Only toward the end of the century did the other colonial powers, which by then had come to include Germany, attempt to challenge Britain's global dominance.[32]

From the late 1870s, telegraphy was complemented—and challenged—by another wired communications infrastructure: telephony. Here, the American Bell company became the most important system-builder, constructing telephone systems in many European cities. Long-distance telephony, once it proved technically feasible, started spreading from the 1880s, including a few early cross-border connections. Yet serious plans for interconnecting Europe were not developed before the First World War.[33]

Of greater importance for international communications was the new technology of radio transmissions—or wireless telegraphy—which saw its breakthrough in the years around 1900 and developed rapidly during the decade before the First World War. It was early on identified as an invention of great significance not least for communications at sea. Later it would find a range of other uses as well. The British Marconi company played the most important role in initial technology development, but the German government took the lead in organizing international cooperation. Problems to be dealt with in this context included the establishment of rules for retransmitting international messages in transit and of schemes for countries' sharing of the electromagnetic spectrum. Some of the technological, institutional, and political challenges were successfully dealt with before the outbreak of the war in 1914. Similar to telephony, however, the European radio transmission infrastructure would enter a period of even more dynamic development during the interwar years.[34]

Building Borders

European connectivity depended not only on the physical availability of efficient transport and communication networks. Equally decisive were the institutional possibilities for moving goods, people, and information over long distances. Traditionally, long-haul transports were severely hindered by a myriad of tolls, customs, and other obligations on the way from one location to another. The eighteenth century, however, generated an emerging trend toward liberalization, and the Vienna Congress further pushed this development. By 1850 key European rivers such the Rhine and the Po had been almost totally freed of their once complex webs of tolls. Inland tolls on the Elbe ceased in 1866 and on the Weser gradually disappeared during the 1850s and 1860s. Access to the Lower Danube improved after the Crimean War, although the European Danube Commission collected a toll for the purpose of funding and maintaining river improvement schemes. In northern Europe, the Danish Sound toll, collected from ships passing into and out of the Baltic Sea, ended in 1857. Meanwhile coastal shipping in most parts of Europe, from Finland to Spain, was also liberalized. This trend was further strengthened through numerous bilateral free trade treaties, starting with the 1860 Cobden–Chevalier agreement.[35]

From the 1890s a growing wave of resistance toward the freedom of flows challenged this period of liberalization. This trend culminated in the outbreak of the First World War. Wartime civilian transport across Europe became exceedingly difficult or even impossible as states strengthened border controls everywhere. The original idea was that this regime would be provisional. In reality, it largely persisted throughout the interwar years.[36]

In order to prevent illegal flows of people, goods, and information, some roads, waterways, railroad tracks, and telegraph lines were decommissioned or even destroyed. A new category of actors appeared, for whom the main goal was not to build new systems, but to control and restrict flows and channel them physically toward a smaller number of border-crossing points. These border-builders included not only political actors, but also a range of customs officials, traffic managers, and engineers. Their activities focused on the formulation and implementation of new laws and rules, but also on the concrete design of frontier stations, including the construction of suitable material obstacles to cross-border passages and new communication systems employed for keeping detailed track of flows.

The actual making of a border was often a lengthy process. The postwar Polish–German border, for example, was traversed by a myriad of old railroad lines, waterways, roads, and telegraph lines. Many of these were physically dismantled or adapted for border-control purposes, but not immediately. In the case of railroads, the Polish and German governments reached an agreement on principles and procedures for handling cross-border transport only in 1926. On its basis the Polish and German railroad administrations set out to dismantle several railroad lines, the overall purpose being to concentrate all cross-border traffic into a limited set of passageways. The railroad junction of Bentschen (Zbąszyń), for example, located between Berlin and Poznań, was radically re-engineered for the sake of border controls. Several East–West waterways in the same area, having seen a remarkable upswing in the decades before the war, were likewise taken out of use.[37]

The Polish–German border was only one of many in interwar Europe along which governments ordered frontier stations to be built. Border-builders in the new nation states of the Russian, Habsburg, and Ottoman Empires took to their task with enthusiasm. They joined forces with national infrastructure visionaries who were eager to reconfigure old Imperial system segments into national networks. Poland, for example, invested heavily in a railroad line from Upper Silesia to its new Baltic port at Gdynia in order to avoid dependence on expensive and time-consuming transit through East Prussia or the Free City of Danzig. In western Romania, where the towns of Arad and Oradea had been interlinked by way of what was now eastern Hungary, the railroad administration likewise set out to build new links that eliminated tedious border-crossings. Following the same logic, the German *Reichsbahn* built the Hindenburgdamm, which connected the mainland with the North Sea island of Sylt. Before its completion, the

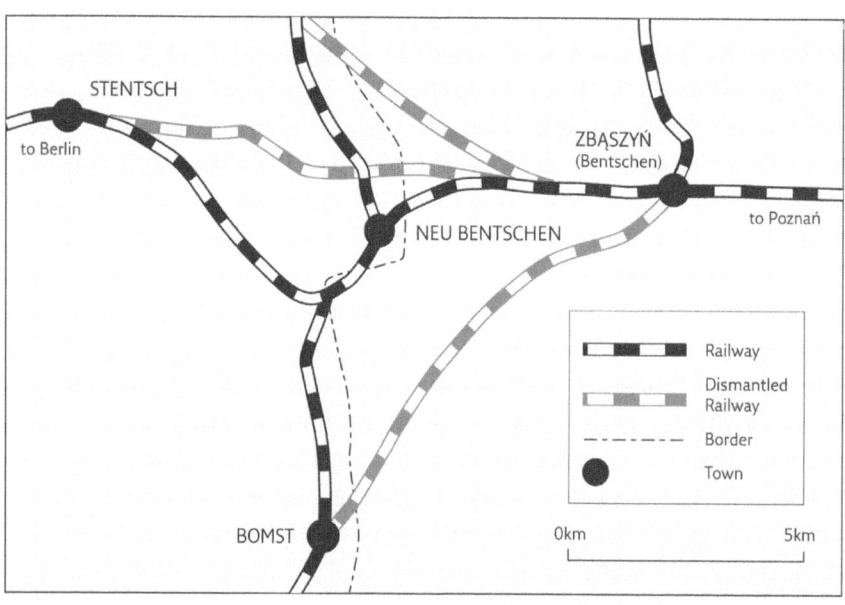

Fig. 1.5 **Borders in the Making:** *During the interwar years border-builders played a salient role in reconfiguring Europe's transport and communications infrastructure. This map visualizes the re-engineering of railroad lines at the most important border-crossing along the new German-Polish frontier. On their side of the border, the Germans created the new town of Neu Bentschen, which was almost exclusively inhabited by railway workers, customs officials, border guards, and postal employees.*

only way to reach Sylt had been through territory that, as a result of the war, had been ceded to Denmark. All in all, border-building and national system-building went hand in hand.[38]

In this new age, queuing and waiting at borders became an important feature of international travel. Those who had grown up in the much more liberal prewar era were upset by the "many formalities in connections with passports, customs, and the filling up of many forms—in a word, the political barriers to the freedom of travel, which sometimes seem unnecessarily complicated and vexatious."[39] A pan-European journal compared this situation with the much smoother one in the United States, complaining loudly about "these artificial and unnecessary quibbles! These visas, these revisions and controls, these getting up and changing! How comfortable is, in contrast, the much longer journey from New York to San Francisco!"[40] In the end, traffic along important prewar railroad lines such as those from Budapest to Czernowitz and from Berlin to St. Petersburg sharply declined in view of the six and seven frontiers, respectively, that now lay in between. The Hungarian railroad expert and former foreign trade minister Elemer Hantos described the big stations of international traffic of the prewar era as resembling "cemeteries."[41]

The situation was much the same in Europe's newest transport system, aviation. Almost immediately after the ceasefire in 1918, several European countries established state-sponsored airline companies, which started offering both national and international services.[42] As it turned out, however, border-builders were able to restrict international air travel in a number of ways. Customs officials could not physically control airplanes as they crossed an international border, but they were very eager to check them as soon as they landed. The customs usually insisted on examining an airplane at the first frontier station rather than at the city of destination, which led to considerable delays. Moreover, if an airplane was blown off course and had to make a landing at a small airport without customs, the pilots were required to stay there until customs and immigration officers arrived. Airplanes in transit, which only landed to refuel, were also carefully checked and some countries even levied duty on goods and baggage in transit.[43]

Italy refused to grant landing rights to Britain's Imperial Airways on flights to the latter's colonial possessions in the East—unless it shared its receipts equally with an Italian airline. The airline refused to do so. As a result, when Imperial Airways opened its first service to the Near East (Baghdad and Basra) in 1926, the passengers had to make their way to Marseilles, take a boat to Port Said in Egypt and then fly from there. Turkey, meanwhile, prohibited transit flight over its territory altogether, primarily for military reasons, while Greece required all foreign airlines passing over its territory to land in Athens and coordinate their schedules with domestic air services. In a similar vein, when first attempts to bridge the Atlantic were made in the late 1930s, the Portuguese government used its privileged position, in holding the Azores, to demand that all planes wanting to land there also had to land in Lisbon. After 1939, Spain, for its part, reserved landing and transit rights to companies from countries that had supported Franco in the Civil War.[44]

Competing European Visions

Unsurprisingly, the activities of Europe's border-builders were criticized and challenged by international system-builders. Just as Chevalier and others had done after the Revolutionary and Napoleonic Wars, many post-First World War advocates judged that only a greater degree of European integration might prevent new wars and aggression and stimulate economic development—and once again, industry and infrastructure were viewed as crucial components in such integrative efforts. By the late 1920s, arguments of this kind had gathered unprecedented momentum.

One of the most influential critics was Albert Thomas, the French director of the International Labour Organisation (ILO), who suggested that political unification initiatives, such as those of French Prime Minister Aristide Briand or Pan-Europa movement leader Count Richard Coudenhove-Kalergi, must be complemented by a comprehensive plan for "European public works."[45] Railroads and waterways were in focus, along with new infrastructure such as motorways and—in the energy field—electricity networks.[46]

Among other things, Thomas directly contributed to convening two European motorway congresses, held in 1931 and 1932. Like aviation, motorways constituted a new transport infrastructure

Fig. 1.6 Envisioning the Automotive Age: *In interwar Europe, motorways emerged as a radically new transport infrastructure. Italian engineer Piero Puricelli was their most prominent visionary, first in Italy, then at the international level. This image shows a proposed European network map Puricelli developed in cooperation with the International Labour Organisation's director Albert Thomas. Adopted at the 1931 Congrès International des Autoroutes as a point of departure for pan-European system-building, it had a clear West European bias. East-Central Europe was only partly included.*

that experienced a breakthrough in the interwar years. Italian engineer Piero Puricelli, in a private initiative, had succeeded in constructing Europe's first motorway—an *autostrada* near Milan—in 1924. During the following years he not only extended the Italian motorway network, but also started sketching a pan-European system. Already a sought-after person by motorway promoters in Germany and elsewhere, Puricelli became Thomas's obvious choice as a partner. At the 1931 congress, the point of departure for discussion was a preliminary plan, prepared in advance, for a European motorway network. Thomas was its nominal, Puricelli its actual author.[47]

Thomas further urged the League of Nations to take a leading role in the "execution of extensive public works of an international character."[48] The League had created an Advisory and Technical Committee on Communications and Transit, consisting of high-level governmental officials from national public works departments. In the early 1930s the committee's efforts gained new momentum and Europe appeared as an emergent category in its infrastructural visions. This was precisely what Thomas had wanted. Yet the idea of European networks was not embraced by everyone. It clashed both with strong national interests and with regional initiatives in which concepts such as "Central Europe" or "Latin Europe" formed geographical points of departure for cooperation.[49]

The Association of German Railway Administrations (*Verein Deutscher Eisenbahnverwaltungen*), which in late 1929 changed its prefix from "German" to "Central European" and moved on to establish cooperation with Scandinavian railroads, and the Central European Economic Conference (*Mitteleuropäische Wirtschaftstagung*, MWT) were two of the most prominent actors with regional visions.[50] League of Nations delegates from outside Central Europe were deeply upset by MWT's desire "to regulate the problem of communications and transit in central Europe within a regional framework to the exclusion of the states in western Europe."[51] Governmental agencies in the former Austro-Hungarian realm, for their parts, interpreted MWT as an Austrian political instrument to re-establish the Habsburg Empire, or as a tool for strengthening German interests in the region.[52]

The debate about Central European waterways exemplifies this competition. In the decades around 1900, public works agencies in Imperial Germany and Austria-Hungary had started serious discussions aimed at the construction of canals interconnecting the Danube with the Oder, the Elbe, and the Vistula. This vision lived on in the interwar period, much thanks to continuity among the key hydraulic experts involved, notably Leo Sympher in Germany and Antonin Smrcek in Czechoslovakia. The project was debated in a multitude of national and international locales. It had a Central European flair, but depending on the context of discussion, it was also framed as a project of pan-European importance or as a national project of great significance for newly-independent Czechoslovakia. In Prague it became controversial as political leaders feared the consequences of stronger physical integration with Germany, while Smrcek and his colleagues pointed to the unique hub position that the proposed canal would lend the Czechs in Europe as a whole. Politicians also sought to appropriate the project by transforming it into a national system designed for domestic transport, or chose to neglect it in favor of railroads as the main integrative force.[53]

As for railroads, Europe had become an impressively integrated entity already in the nineteenth century. During and after the First World War, however, vigorous attempts were made to radically reconfigure the network. As Allied border-builders set out to isolate Germany to the greatest possible extent, system-builders in countries such as France and Italy saw a chance to attain central positions in international railroad traffic. A key project was the "Line of the 45th Parallel," proposed in 1916 by the French poet, economist, and diplomat Paul Claudel.[54] Running from Bordeaux to Odessa, while avoiding Germany, this line was interpreted as a way of stimulating friendship among the Latin peoples and spreading "Latin civilization" eastwards.[55] The line was referred to as a grand "Trans-European artery," but also as an "anti-Germanic barrier" deliberately designed to exclude some parts of Europe.[56]

Other French activists proposed that the new East–West artery be combined with a North–South line running from England and the Benelux region through France, onwards across the Pyrenees into Spain, and continuing to Africa through a tunnel under the Strait of Gibraltar. From North Africa, it would be extended across the Sahara and eventually reach Dakar in the French colony of Senegal. The French eyed Dakar as an ideal port for transshipments to South America and thus as a promising future hub in overall trade between Europe and South America. The latter continent was regarded as a natural extension of Latin Europe. The vision also included new railroad projects in South America itself.[57]

In actual practice, however, hardly any of these grand interwar visions—whether limited to the European peninsula or extended to overseas regions and colonies—gained sufficient support, and most completely failed to take off. In the interplay between European, regional, and national schemes, the national dimension clearly triumphed, at least for the time being. To the extent that new "European" transport and communications networks came into being, they were patchworks of national grids linked to each other on the margin. This was evident not only in old transport systems such as water and rail, but also in new motorways, airways, and telecommunications infrastructure.

In aviation, the newly-created national carriers led the way. Organizing themselves into an international pool, they were able to create a dense network of services covering large parts of Europe. In Western and Central Europe, Germany's Lufthansa led the

Fig. 1.7 Colonial Connections: *The rise of aviation was of significance not only for Europe's internal integration, but also for its links with the rest of the world. Western Europe's colonial powers early on set up regular flights to their possessions in Africa, Asia, and Australia. This commercial poster from Belgium's Sabena, which established a connection between Europe and the Congo, contrasts the romance of camel travel through the Sahara with the modern technological miracle of flying.*

development, with Berlin emerging as the most important aviation hub. Further East the Soviet Union's Aeroflot, set up in 1932, developed air services spanning nearly all corners of the communist empire, from Leningrad to Vladivostok.[58] The airlines of the West European colonial powers prioritized the creation of links to their colonies. Britain's Imperial Airways and the Netherlands' KLM competed fiercely in establishing air services to the Far East. By the 1930s both were able to offer regular flights from Europe all the way to Sydney. Cairo emerged as the British hub for flights to its colonial possessions in both Asia and Africa. Air France opened routes to West Africa and to French Indochina, and together with associate companies, connections from West Africa to Madagascar. Belgian Sabena created services to and within Belgian Congo, and Italian Ala Littoria a route via Libya to Addis Ababa. Only high-ranking government officials or very wealthy businessmen could afford to fly on these planes. Yet the establishment of fast mail services to the colonies was of great significance for a much larger number of people, both in the colonies and their mother countries.[59]

Telecommunications also developed rapidly during the interwar years. Pan-European planners early on identified both broadcasting and international telephony as great opportunities in the face of political, economic, and cultural integration. In 1924, Europe's national public telegraph and telephone administrations (PTTs) formed the Consultative Committee for International Telephony (CCIF). It assumed a leading role in coordinating the expanding transnational telephony network. Earlier telephone system-building had produced differences in technical design. CCIF set out to counter this state of affairs through international standardization. A coordinating body, it could only make recommendations, and member organizations could choose to follow these or not. Yet it turned out that CCIF was able to create consensus about many of its recommendations; and by the late 1930s, it was possible to make international phone calls throughout most of Europe. However, the cost was very high, especially in comparison with long-distance telephony in North America. From an economic point of view, CCIF's members used their total control over the European telephony market to maintain a very profitable oligopoly.[60]

After 1938, international system-building was undermined by Hitler's quest for *Grossraumwirtschaft*. Not unlike Napoleon, another "infrastructure-friendly dictator," the Fuhrer pushed infrastructural

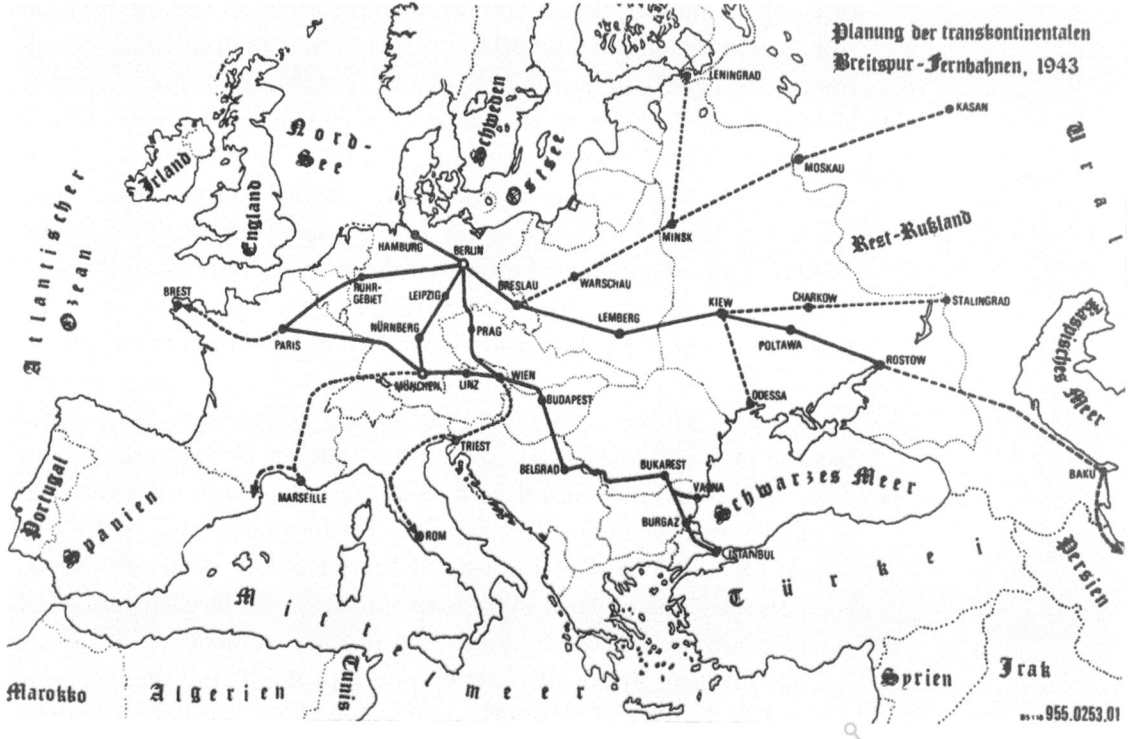

Fig. 1.8 **Hitler's Hubris:** *The Nazi German attempt to establish a transcontinental European empire went hand in hand with ambitious infrastructure visions. The idea of a super-broad-gauge railroad network, to be superimposed on the existing European railroad system, was enthusiastically championed by Hitler personally. Albert Speer's Ministry of Transport and the German Reichsbahn both opposed the project, arguing that all transport requirements could be better satisfied using standard-gauge railroads. Like many other Nazi visions, it never materialized.*

integration throughout the domains successively brought under Nazi control, a symbolically, politically, and economically important development.[61] Initially Hitler's infrastructure focus was on East-Central Europe, but once the war broke out and new territories were occupied, the visions extended to include continental Europe as a whole. Leading Nazi infrastructure promoters such as Fritz Markmann elaborated a number of impressive projects, for example, an all-European waterway system stretching from the Atlantic to the Caspian, an extended *Mittellandkanal* forming its main East–West axis. Similarly, the Nazi-controlled road network was to be extended "to the southernmost point of Crimea and to the Caucasus."[62] This was paralleled by the vision of a super-wide-gauge railroad network with lines to Istanbul, Baku, and northern Russia. A Nazi "European Union of Posts and Telecommunications" was meanwhile installed in Vienna. But as the tide turned and the war was lost, Hitler's grand European fantasy failed to materialize.[63]

Cold War Networks & Borders

The end of the Second World War and the onset of a Cold War placed infrastructure promoters and system-builders in a completely new political and geographical setting. The realm of transport and communications became both a political tool and a battleground in the intense post-war struggle to shape Europe. Although the idea of a *politically*-unified continent quickly dwindled in the surging antagonism between the superpowers, an *infrastructurally*-unified Europe continued to hold promise, for better or for worse, as a real possibility. It was interpreted by some as an opportunity that, in the Chevalierian spirit, must be exploited for the sake of all-European prosperity and peace, and by others as a danger and a threat that under all circumstances must be obstructed. To be sure, the latter were not opposed to international cooperation as such. They only argued that it must be contained in appropriate ways and centered on regional (for example, exclusively West European) initiatives.

Immediately after Germany's surrender in May 1945, the Allies formed the European Central Inland Transport Organization to deal with restoration of mobility on the Continent. This body was transformed into an Inland Transport Committee within the UN's Economic Commission for Europe (UNECE), once that organization was created in 1947. Initially a consensus seemed to emerge that UNECE was the ideal organization for coping with infrastructural integration and cooperation on the war-torn Continent. As the Cold War intensified, however, suspicion grew from the United States and other Western countries. Upset by the harsh, undemocratic political developments in the East, they increasingly encouraged the formation of exclusively West European organizations to deal with international infrastructure issues.[64] The Marshall planners, for example, opted to divert their efforts into the "European Recovery Program." The West Europeans also formed the European Conference of Ministers of Transport (ECMT). It had grand ambitions, hoping to turn itself into "a sort of super-system-builder coordinating and amplifying the work of other players in the field."[65] In Eastern Europe similar organizations for infrastructure formed, notably as subcommittees within the Council of Mutual Economic Assistance (CMEA or Comecon).[66]

Formation of these exclusively Western and Eastern bodies went hand in hand with border-building and in particular with the making of the Iron Curtain. At the outset the Iron Curtain was only a metaphor and did not exist in material terms. It had to be created by a new generation of border-builders, and once in place it had to be maintained and defended against those who wanted to "tear this wall down."[67] The Iron Curtain erectors could draw on ample experience from the interwar era's border-building efforts, but the political and military stakes were now higher. As before, constructing the Iron Curtain was not merely a matter of cutting existing East–West links and preventing new ones from emerging. Total isolation was never an ambition; the challenge was rather to establish efficient ways of regulating, controlling, and restricting East–West flows to the desired extent.

Iron Curtain builders faced their greatest challenge in the defeated Third Reich, where no border at all had existed before 1945. Before the war, no less than 47 railroad lines, 3 motorways, 31 long-distance roads, 80 country roads, thousands of smaller public and private roads, and numerous waterways and telecommunications lines had crossed this internal non-border.[68] The focus of the immediate postwar period was on restoring numerous transport links that had been destroyed during the war. In May 1952, however, the East German Council of Ministers issued a decree on "measures at the demarcation line between the German Democratic Republic and the west German zones of occupation."[69] The Ministry for State Security (Stasi) ordered the creation of a 5 km wide closed zone next to the border. Identifying local transport in this area as a security threat, Stasi gained the Party's support for shutting down all traffic on 9 cross-border railroad lines, and many tracks were taken out of use. The government ordered the East German *Reichsbahn* to concentrate all cross-border traffic at a handful of frontier stations. Roads and waterways faced similar constraints.[70]

But this was not the end of the story. While East Germans faced increasing difficulties obtaining travel permissions, the Western Allies in 1953 decided to liberalize inter-zonal travel. In the case of rail, the result was a vastly-increased demand for passenger services from West to East Germany. The West and East German railroad administrations responded by agreeing to double services, from 12 daily trains across the border to 24 daily trains, supplemented by an additional 24 trains on holidays. The number of possible destinations in East Germany also increased. Gradually

Fig. 1.9 Controlling the Iron Curtain: *Cold War border-builders did not aim to eliminate East–West transport and communication flows altogether. Their challenge was, rather, to facilitate desirable flows while preventing undesirable ones. This stimulated the development of innovative border-control technologies. East Germany's railroads deployed so-called derailing points (Entgleisungsweichen), which, in combination with advanced signaling techniques, prevented unauthorized trains from escaping into the West. This photo shows the derailing point along the East–West transit track at Staaken.*

the two railroad administrations developed a fruitful cooperation, including annually held bilateral timetable conferences.[71]

The construction of the Berlin Wall in 1961 did not immediately influence East–West rail travel. However, a few months after the wall had been built, an East German railroad engineer, Harry Deterling, managed to flee to the West by driving a whole train illegally across the border from East Germany into West Berlin. Shocked by this spectacular event (which later on became a movie), Stasi and the East German Border Police developed a new set of "principles concerning special measures at frontier railway stations."[72] In cooperation with the *Reichsbahn*, they meticulously re-engineered the country's frontier stations, deploying innovative border-control technologies. For example, carefully-constructed derailing points (*Entgleisungsweichen*) were built at the border stations, inevitably causing any unauthorized train attempting to pass the border to derail. The Border Police was especially concerned about the risk that a fleeing train might follow a regular cross-border train close behind. This made it imperative to complement the derailing points with fast and reliable signaling systems through which the points could be activated automatically as soon as the regular train had passed.[73]

The legal cross-border traffic continued to increase. As of the late 1960s no fewer than 20,000 West German citizens traveled every day across the East–West border, and about 3,500 East German citizens moved in the opposite direction. The difference gives an idea of the difficulties East German citizens had obtaining travel visas. The flows grew further after West German Chancellor Willy Brandt negotiated a new transport agreement with East Berlin in the early 1970s. All in all, the intra-German border was probably the most intensely guarded and at the same time the most trafficked along the Iron Curtain as a whole.[74]

UNECE and other pan-European actors sought to prevent the Iron Curtain builders from realizing their expectations. Their degree of success in doing so varied. In road transport UNECE early on seemed to emerge as a leader, successfully keeping the Iron Curtain builders out. Its flagship project was the E-Road initiative, in which the interwar programs for a transcontinental motorway network were brought up again in somewhat new forms.

UNECE's experts imagined a pan-European network that would transcend the Iron Curtain while also extending into North Africa and the Middle East. In 1950 the seminal "Declaration on the Construction of Main International Traffic Arteries" was signed, initially by Belgium, France, Luxembourg, the Netherlands, and the United Kingdom, and subsequently by Austria, Greece, Sweden, Norway, Portugal, Turkey, West Germany, Italy, Poland, Spain, Yugoslavia, Bulgaria, Hungary, Finland, Romania, Denmark, Ireland, and Czechoslovakia (in that order, with Czechoslovakia's assent taking place in 1973). The Soviet Union, however, did not sign. Some 22 main traffic arteries—numbered E1–E22—formed the backbone of the proposed system, complemented by a set of secondary routes—numbered E31–92—forming branches and feeders. The signatories promised to build (or rebuild) these roads adhering to European, expert-negotiated standards.[75]

The E-road map as a whole derived from proposals submitted by individual countries. UNECE played a key role in ensuring efficient coordination of national plans, information exchanges, functional border-crossings, and harmonization. Other organizations, such as the International Bank for Reconstruction and Development and the International Road Federation also played active and supportive roles. The former contributed loans, especially for cross-border connections, and the latter, whose interest lay in increased motorization more generally, provided hundreds of European road planners with scholarships for studies in traffic engineering at Yale University in the United States. In addition, ECMT and the EEC contributed to the E-Road project in constructive ways.[76]

Waterways was another domain where UNECE initially held high hopes for East–West cooperation. Here, however, it was not at all as successful. There was no lack of wet system-building visions in Cold War Europe, and some were exceptionally ambitious. Czechoslovakia's hydraulic engineers, for example, fancied a pan-European network extending from the Rhine to Moscow and, as imagined by Jan Smetana, the director of Prague's Water Research Management Institute, onward across the Urals all the way to the Pacific. The Czechs sought to mobilize the Soviet Union as an ally in advocating this and other interconnection ideas within Comecon and UNECE. In particular they sought to revive the dream of a Danube–Oder–Elbe Canal.[77]

Hydraulic engineers in different countries showed some enthusiasm for these projects, but on a higher political level most West European countries opposed them, interpreting the very idea of a unified waterway network as an "East European interest" only.[78] After 1967, the group of experts that had been charged with investigating the East–West unification issue stopped meeting. Integration between the Danube and the West European river systems continued to be promoted, but the emphasis was increasingly on the more western-centric Rhine–Main–Danube Canal, which started to be built in Bavaria in the 1970s. The Danube–Oder–Elbe project was revived again in the mid-1970s, but it now centered on bilateral cooperation between Czechoslovakia and Poland. Its previous pan-European image was lost.[79]

East–West cooperation in telephony, mainly within CCIF, largely ceased after 1945. To the East of the Iron Curtain, Europeans found it difficult or impossible to make international phone calls, disappointing residents in countries such as the formerly independent Baltic states. In the interwar years, the Baltic PTTs had developed their own international telephone connections and the Latvians had been especially active in CCIF. Following Stalin's annexation of the three countries in 1944, the Soviet Ministry of Communications decided to cut the Baltics' international lines, forging a new regime in which all international calls were routed through Moscow. There, only a few international lines were made available for the general public. The Moscow connection was troublesome in a double way, since long-distance connections between the Baltic region and the Soviet capital city were rudimentary at best.[80]

Western system-builders were not necessarily more interested in East–West communications than were their Eastern peers. In 1954–5, for example, Bulgaria repeatedly pushed for re-establishing telephone connections with Greece, whose government, however, did not show any corresponding enthusiasm. Only in 1964 was a direct connection between the two Balkan nations brought into operation. As in railroads, the most permeable section of the telephonic Iron Curtain was probably the intra-German border. There, many prewar lines continued to function, the notable difference being that both Stasi and its counterpart in West Germany, the *Bundesnachrichtendienst* (BND), monitored virtually every East–West phone call.[81]

Within the West, meanwhile, connectivity improved markedly. PTTs expanded their existing intra-West European connections while also linking up with North American telephone companies. The connections improved further through the introduction of Subscriber Trunk Dialing technology, through which users could make long-distance—including international—phone calls on their own, that is, without the help of an operator. In 1956 the French and Belgian PTTs pioneered this technique.[82]

Starting in the 1970s, the greatest challenge for the West European PTTs was to digitalize telephone switching and build data communications networks. In 1976 the PTTs of Canada, France, and Britain proposed an international standard for data communications: X.25. Before 1980, several national data networks in Europe, North America, and Japan, plus a multinational data network developed under the auspices of the EC Commission (EURONET), had adopted it.[83] To their surprise, however, the PTTs early on found that they were not the only actors with ambitions in data system-building. Apart from many large multinational corporations that started constructing worldwide, company-internal networks based on leased lines, a sprawling community of entrepreneurs with roots in computer science appeared on the scene. Their focus was on improving long-distance scientific data exchange and academic communications.

To the PTTs' dismay, the newcomers did not view the existing telephone networks as the centerpieces of future data communications systems. Their emphasis was on interconnecting a variety of—mainly local—heterogeneous computer networks with each other. Such networks could not always be incorporated into X.25 systems, fueling hostilities between computer scientists and PTTs. To accommodate as wide a network of networks as possible, the former proposed to use—and contributed to developing—rival solutions, notably the Internet Protocol (TCP/IP).[84]

The conflict over standards and protocols peaked around 1980, at which time it seemed that the PTTs would triumph. The French PTT, for example, succeeded in persuading the government to cut funding to leading IP-oriented projects and, instead, channel investments to its own X.25 Transpac network. This subsequently became a much-publicized success, with millions of users accessing it from special Minitel terminals, enabling the use of various Videotex services. Yet the struggle had only begun. The enormous growth of and rising expectations for computerization and data communications increased the stakes. By the mid-1980s a new, unprecedented dynamism had come to characterize the whole communications field, both nationally and at the European level, with seemingly unpredictable consequences for the future.

Infrastructure & Communism's Collapse

In November 1989 the Berlin wall fell. Two years later the Soviet Union dissolved, giving way to 15 independent nations. Czechoslovakia, meanwhile, split into a Czech and a Slovak Republic in January 1993. The division of Yugoslavia, which became a much more painful and bloody experience, would find its end-point only with Kosovo's declaration of independence in 2008. The extreme process of fragmentation mirrored the break-up of the Russian, Habsburg, and Ottoman Empires after the First World War, and system-builders now faced similar challenges as had their predecessors.

The fate of the giant Soviet railroad system illustrates how actors, in the face of a near-total breakdown of political structures, sought to rescue transport and communications in the former communist bloc. The prime mover in the early phase of system transformation was the Soviet Railway Ministry and, in particular, a group of technocrats known as the ministry's Collegium. Comprising leading transport officials from various republican and regional railroad administrations, the Collegium agreed that "whatever might happen politically, everything should be done to maintain the Soviet railroad system as a single network."[85]

When in December 1991 the Soviet Union was formally dissolved and all republican railroad administrations gained independence from Moscow, cooperation was not disrupted. The Collegium transformed itself into a multinational Railway Transport Council, tasked to coordinate interaction among the independent systems of the former Soviet Union. The Council distanced itself from the chaotic political developments, in January 1992 self-confidently declaring that "while politicians argue, transport people are uniting."[86] The Finnish and Mongolian railroad administrations started participating in the Council's meetings, and in effect the new body thus came to include all broad-gauge railroads across the Eurasian continent. Through this cooperation, the Soviet Union, although with somewhat different borders, lived on in the railroad realm. After some controversy, Russian was accepted as the council's official language.[87]

The Council emerged as a system-rescuer as well as a system-builder. While it dealt with acute problems such as "certain railroads that were failing to promptly return freight-cars that did not belong to them" and "elimination of unjustified frontier stoppages," it also took charge of timetable coordination and completion of an interstate railroad computer network.[88] However, a plethora of new border-builders in the 15 independent ex-Soviet republics contested these activities. For freight trains, customs inspections and documentation often took several days, as duties and other charges had to be paid.[89]

The Council initially decided to adhere to the old Soviet practice of sending trains by the shortest route, but in the face of excessively complicated frontier procedures it soon abandoned this approach. Instead, fully loaded trains, typically Russian freight trains bound for Baltic ports, were allowed to travel a longer route to minimize the number of border-crossings. One effect was that some key railroad hubs, such as Daugavpils in southeastern Latvia, became virtually deserted. The Kremlin complained loudly about what its officials regarded as excessive border-building by the Baltic governments and customs agencies. Moscow's response was to invest heavily in a new port infrastructure near St. Petersburg, the purpose of which was to reduce Russian dependence on rail transit through the Baltics.[90]

Meanwhile the Baltic railroad administrations sought to improve their connectivity with Western Europe. The only existing railroad line from the Baltic region that did not pass through Russian or Belarusian territory was a single-track line reaching the southern

Lithuanian town of Šeštokai, near the Polish border. At that point, the railroad connected to the narrower West European gauge. Initiatives were launched to strengthen the link and manage the break of gauge. Following years of discussions and delays, a system for automatic changing of bogies (undercarriages) eventually became operative in 1999.

In the meantime, however, a gradual shift to road transport, shipping, and aviation as the main modes of East–West interaction had already taken place in the Baltic region. For passenger transport, it proved exceedingly difficult to maintain an economically-viable regular railroad service. An agreement signed in the 1990s had stipulated that one Lithuanian and one Polish passenger train would travel the route between Vilnius and Warsaw on a daily basis. In reality, the national Lithuanian railroad company never managed to launch its service, while its Polish counterpart, having operated for a few years, closed the link in 2005. The Baltic railroads, even long after their accession to the EU, thus largely continued to operate in isolation from Central and Western Europe.[91]

In other, more flexible kinds of infrastructure, it proved easier to unite East and West. Most former communist countries invested heavily, often with help from the EU, the European Bank for Reconstruction and Development, the World Bank, and other international institutions, in refurbishing their seaports and airports, while setting up shipping companies and national air carriers. In the Baltics, whose airports had earlier been used for flights in eastern directions only, the new carriers immediately established regular services to Frankfurt, London, and the Nordic capitals. East–West ferry connections also proliferated, only temporarily halted by the September 1994 *Estonia* ferry tragedy, in which 852 people lost their lives en route from Tallinn to Stockholm.[92]

Mobile telecommunications further helped East-Central Europe reconnect with the West. In the immediate post-Cold War era, virtually all former communist countries set up analogue mobile phone networks. One of the fifteen Soviet republics, Estonia, even managed to become part of the sprawling Nordic Mobile Telephony (NMT) system prior to achieving political independence. In 1990, informal discussions between Soviet Estonia's Minister of Communications, Toomas Sõmera, and the Swedish and Finnish PTTs paved the way for an unusual arrangement in which Estonia became technically part of the Finnish PTT's NMT network. Estonian, Finnish, and

Swedish engineers and technicians cooperated in installing a few Swedish-made radio base stations on Soviet Estonian territory and a radio link across the Gulf of Finland, while refraining from creating an Estonian NMT exchange. In this way Sõmera's Ministry was able to offer Soviet Estonian subscribers high-quality mobile services—with Finnish telephone numbers.[93]

The first subscriber joined the system in early July 1991. The network came to play an important role sooner than anybody had imagined. When Soviet troops attempted to put an end to Estonia's struggle for political independence in late August 1991, all long-distance fixed lines were cut, isolating the tiny republic from the rest of the world—but the Estonian–Nordic NMT system kept working. The separatist Estonian government was at this time spread out, with the Prime Minister temporarily residing in Stockholm and other ministers in Helsinki and Tallinn. Through the NMT network, designed as it was for international interoperability, the government's activities could nonetheless be coordinated. This helped the Estonians in their aspirations to become part of Western Europe not only in telecommunications, but politically and economically as well.[94]

Toward a New Europe?

At the time when East European communism started to crumble, Western Europe's infrastructure was already entering a new intense period of change. The Commission of the European Communities, under the strong leadership of Jacques Delors, sought an active role in forming Europe's future infrastructure. Under the influence of neoliberalism, and linking up with powerful groupings in the private sector, notably the European Round Table of Industrialists (ERT, formed in 1983), the Commission forcefully argued that more competition was necessary in infrastructural fields and that "more Europe" could be achieved by community-wide liberalization of transport, communications, and energy. Moreover, the Commission argued that there was an urgent need to view European infrastructure in its totality, rather than, as the sector-specific international organizations typically did, as a collection of single systems. A key challenge was to make connections between different kinds of systems more efficient. Intermodality became the new buzzword. Another urgent task lay in reducing infrastructure's destructive impact on the environment. In the transport field, the Commission argued, environmental performance could be improved, for example, by transferring traffic flows from road to rail and water. The environmental dimension thus offered another argument for a comprehensive approach.[95]

By the early 1990s, Western Europe found itself plagued by economic recession. In this situation the Commission put infrastructure system-building center stage in its competitiveness strategy. The symbolically most important initiative in this context was the Trans-European Networks (TENs) program, formally launched in connection with the 1992 Maastricht Treaty. It became the new EU's "big idea for dealing with many of its economic problems."[96] Starting in 1994, member states jointly started to work out concrete lists of projects that, supposedly, would strengthen the EU as a whole.[97]

In actual practice, the EU seriously underfunded the TENs program, and it mainly played an auxiliary role in projects launched by other system-builders. While prestigious international efforts such as the Danish–Swedish Øresund connection and the British–French Channel Tunnel were listed as priority TENs projects, most analysts judged that these would have come about even without any EU involvement. In the end national and regional system-builders mainly used the TENs program to boost their favorite projects at home.[98]

The US government proposed to strengthen the supranational dimension of European system-building by forging a European Infrastructure Agency.[99] This, however, went far beyond what national actors in Europe could possibly accept. Of much greater significance was the Commission's relentless struggle for EU-wide liberalization of transport and communications markets. Liberalization, while greatly contested, made it possible for a variety of new—mainly private—system-builders to participate in Europe's infrastructure transition. This was so particularly in the communications field.

In mobile telephony, for example, it became common, starting in the 1990s, that two or three companies, independently of each other, built overlapping national networks—a previously unthinkable phenomenon in most infrastructural domains. In data communications this went even further. Anticipating enormous growth in data traffic, both public and private actors rushed to build expensive networks based on optical fibers, yielding hundreds of overlapping data communications systems. These were not necessarily national in scope, and countries were not connected to each other merely on the margin. On the contrary, international data traffic was at their core. Many private system-builders, aiming for the most lucrative markets, prioritized connections between Amsterdam, London, Paris, and Frankfurt, since these, in their roles as financial centers, generated no less than 60 percent of the EU's total data traffic.[100]

By the mid-1990s, the volume of data traffic had overtaken that of voice telephony in Europe. In this situation, the PTTs' earlier perception of data communications merely as an extension of the existing telephone system became impossible to sustain. The result was a weakening of the PTTs' role in the data communications field and a transition to the Internet Protocol as the de facto standard for long-distance data transmission. In the 1990s, Europe's Internet system-builders—many of which were offshoots from the academic sector—started cooperating by setting up joint system nodes called Internet Exchange Points (IXPs). Through these years, tens and even hundreds of network operators joined each IXP, incorporating them into their respective Europe- or near-Europe-wide systems. By 2001, no fewer than 27 carriers operated data networks with a more or less pan-European reach, although only five of them actually built fiber networks in a physical sense; the rest relied on leased capacity or joined forces with others. Incumbent telecoms administrations did not necessarily play any leading role in this process. Through their ownership of most local telephone lines, however, they remained immensely important to residential and other small users' ability to access the Internet.[101]

In the transport field, the Commission's liberalization policies most fundamentally transformed aviation. Here, new system-builders in the form of low-fare airlines appeared. The most successful was Ryanair, founded in 1985 by three Irish entrepreneurs. Apart from operating a dense network of routes, Ryanair skillfully aligned itself with municipalities to redevelop small regional airfields, many of which had been used for military purposes during the Cold War. By the 2010s, the company had become a nearly pan-European system-builder, with a network that extended to all corners of

Fig. 1.10 **Internet Geographies:** *In contrast to telegraphy and telephony, early data communications system-building featured a multiplicity of private actors, many of which built systems with a pan-European or even near-global reach. This network map from Interoute, a private company headquartered in London, exemplifies how Internet system-builders generated new European geographies, with the various sub-networks not necessarily coinciding with state borders. Note the inspiration taken from urban subway maps.*

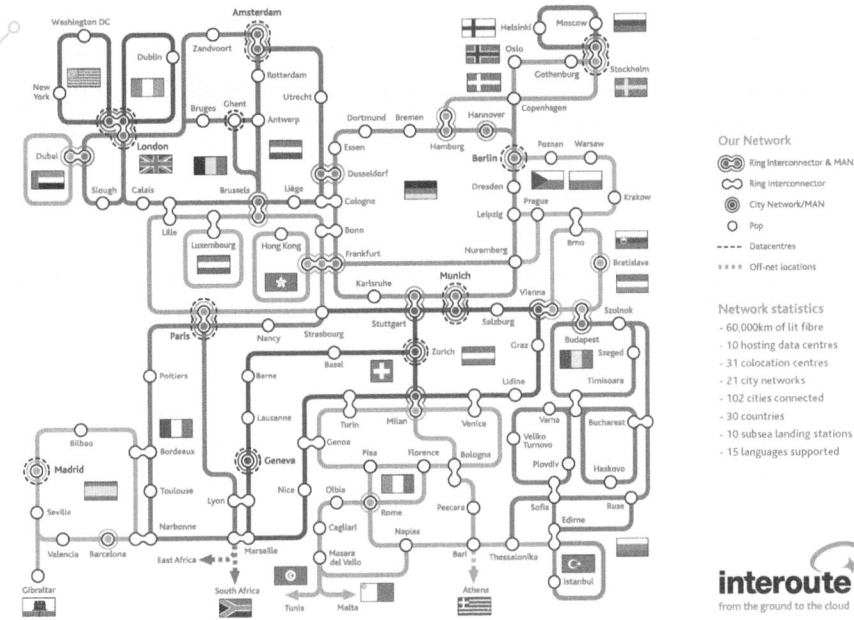

the EU's liberalized aviation market, as well as to Norway and Morocco. Not unlike its counterparts in Internet system-building, it relied on a number of particularly important hubs, into which traffic from more peripheral regions was funneled. Like the main IXPs, other low-fare airlines subsequently joined these hubs.[102]

Space & Time Annihilated?

This chapter has outlined Europe's infrastructure transition in the transport and communications field. But how can we understand the outcome? In particular, to what extent have new modes of transport and communications actually brought different European localities and their populations closer to each other?

Contemporaries perceived the coming of steamships, railroads, and telegraphy as revolutionary. Travel times between Europe's major cities and industrial regions shrank drastically. In Sweden, for example, a journey between Stockholm and Gothenburg, which would normally have involved rounding the Scandinavian peninsula by ship, had traditionally taken several days. From 1862, when the first rail connection between the two cities was inaugurated, the travel time suddenly dropped to 12 hours.[103] Belgian engineers, designing the first international rail link in Europe, similarly noted that "a train could travel from Antwerp to Cologne in less than 24 hours, whereas by boat it could take up to eleven days."[104] In the case of trans-Alpine travel, a journey from Lucerne in Switzerland to Milan in Italy, using the available steamship service across the Lake of Lucerne and then the mail coach over the Gotthard Pass, took 32 hours before 1882 (already an impressively short journey), but only 9 hours and 21 minutes once the Gotthard Tunnel opened.[105]

Chevalier and other Saint-Simonians early on pointed with enthusiasm to the condensed transport space. The very concepts of space and time seemed to be in flux. In 1839, the French economist Constantin Pecqueur already predicted an emergent "new geography of France."[106] The German poet Heinrich Heine, living in Paris, noted at about the same time that "space is killed" not only nationally, but internationally as well. "I feel as if the mountains and forests of all countries were advancing on Paris," he exclaimed. "I can smell the German linden trees; the North Sea's breakers are rolling against my door."[107]

The trans-Alpine railroad projects were seen to bring northern and southern Europe closer together, whereas steamships had a most remarkable impact on distances in the maritime domain.[108] The Mediterranean supposedly had "shrunk into a lake," whereas the Atlantic had "dried up to less than half its breadth."[109] Through the subsequent advent of telegraphy, space and time no longer seemed relevant at all: "The Atlantic, with all its waves, is as nothing," as one observer put it at the inauguration ceremony for the first telegraph connection between Europe and North America.[110] This perception would be further accentuated through the rise of trans-Atlantic aviation and telephony in the 1950s.

But Europe's infrastructure transition was highly ambiguous. It meant different things to different localities. For population centers located on major trunk lines or with easy access to the emerging systems, space-time was completely transformed. Places located further away from train stations, airports, motorway entrances, telegraph offices, or Europe's great ports were not affected in the same way. For them, the rise of the new systems often established a new level of inequality. This was also the case when traditional transport and communication routes such as the mail coach routes across the Alps, which for centuries had contributed to regional prosperity, were replaced by trans-Alpine tunnel traffic.

Of course, access to the new networks also depended on users' ability to pay for the available services. This concerned not only the poor, but also seemingly-influential companies and organizations. Newspapers and news agencies in Europe represented the most important civil society users of the telegraph network, but since many newspapers were not published daily, some opted not to invest in expensive telegram subscriptions. As far as private telegrams were concerned, sending them in the nineteenth century was for most people so expensive that it was rarely considered practical other than at extreme moments. As of 1857, for example, a single telegram from the north Swedish town of Sundsvall to Stockholm cost as much as a one-year subscription to the local newspaper. A telegram to Paris cost ten times as much. The rise of long-distance telephony did not change this situation much. In other words, the paradoxical pre-modern world, in which global interconnectedness for the few had coexisted with local isolation for the rest, lived on in a new form.[111]

In the age of border-builders that set in after 1914, it became clear that the perceived compression of space and time could be reversed. Lenin, referred to earlier, was among the first to experience this reversal. It was not merely a wartime phenomenon. As of 1935, it still took half an hour longer to travel by train from Vienna to Berlin than in 1914, notwithstanding two decades of far-reaching technological progress. To Istanbul, the journey had become seven hours longer. Moreover, whereas before the Great War there had been no less than 161 trains per week from Vienna to Berlin and 28 to Istanbul, there were now only 70 and 14, respectively. The growth of road and air transport during the interwar years was not able to compensate for this regress.[112]

After the Second World War some regions in Europe came closer to each other, whereas others moved farther away. Traveling by train in Germany had always seemed efficient and simple. During the Cold War, however, trains from the West to the East typically had to stop for 40 minutes on the Eastern side of the intra-German border. Trains en route to West Berlin were halted for up to one hour at the new frontier stations, before the new transit agreement negotiated by Willy Brandt shortened the delay to 5–20 minutes.

In the communications field, by the outbreak of the Second World War it was possible to make international phone calls throughout most of Europe, and international radio transmissions were commonplace. The average waiting time for international phone calls had decreased from one hour to eight minutes, thus deepening the process of space-time compression. But after the war it was often not possible to make any phone calls at all across the Iron Curtain, and to the extent that it was possible, waiting times were typically longer than they had been in the 1920s and 1930s.

The Iron Curtain was certainly visible in much of Europe's network geography. Yet Europe, seen through the lens of transport and communications, also featured its own internal and external boundaries, which did not necessarily coincide with well-known political, economic, or cultural divides. During the Cold War, for example, technical incompatibilities in railroad gauge generated longer waiting times at Brest, on the intra-Comecon Polish–Soviet border, than at the intra-German frontier stations along the Iron Curtain. On the Swedish–Finnish border, which similarly marked the East–West break of gauge, there was no traffic at all. Like Lenin on his journey in 1917, travelers had to use other means of transport. An analogous gauge divide, invisible on political maps, separated France from the Iberian Peninsula. These boundaries, whose existence stemmed from nineteenth-century system-building activities, were not eliminated after the Cold War.

In the realm of road transport, Europe was for a long time divided into territories with right- and left-hand traffic. During the nineteenth century few nation states followed uniform rules. Micro-regional habits dominated. With the rise of the automotive age, however, long-distance traffic grew and a continental trend toward harmonization set in—notably toward right-hand traffic— further encouraged through the work of organizations such as UNECE and its E-Roads project. Islands or peninsulas such as Britain, Malta, Cyprus, Iceland, and Sweden were the ones most stubbornly opposing the trend. The latter two eventually changed to right-hand traffic in the 1960s. From then on, drivers kept to the right from Bergen and Lisbon to Vladivostok and Shanghai.

The main divide in Waterway Europe was a hydrological-geographical feature known as the Main European Watershed. Invisible on political maps, it extended across Europe from the northeast to the southwest, traversing the Valdai Hills in Russia, much of Czechoslovakia, and the Alps. On either side, and particularly so to the West, impressive canal-building and river rectification projects generated tightly-integrated meso-regions, though with very limited connectivity across the main divide. Efforts to overcome the Main Watershed had been undertaken already in the seventeenth century, but in actual practice only a few, fairly unimportant canals were completed. Only in 1992, when the important Rhine–Main–Danube canal opened, did the situation change in a significant way.

Transport and communications Europe featured few external borders. By following system-builders in their vigorous efforts to expand and extend their networks, we may even argue that Europe became a global geographical entity. This was most obvious at sea, where the only real barriers to expansion were the frozen Arctic seaways. By the early twenty-first century, technology and melting sea ice were about to open both the Northwest and the Northeast passages, thus completing the process of globalization in maritime transport. The struggle for control over the new Arctic routes was already becoming intense.

From the late nineteenth century, system-builders used the near-global seaways to extend Railway Europe into Asia, Australia, Africa, and the Americas. Roads in the same regions added to the sprawling system. Still, Transport Europe did not extend everywhere, and some expansion attempts failed. For example, while Railway Europe expanded across the Urals into Siberia, Central Asia, and China, visions of alternative, more southerly "Iron Silk Roads" failed to materialize.[113] European system-builders also failed to build railroads across the Sahara, which thus—more so than the Mediterranean—remained a major southern barrier.

All in all, Europe's infrastructure transition in transport and communications was in no way a simple, linear process with a predetermined outcome. The efforts of system-builders and border-builders ultimately produced a geography of networks that featured many surprising and contradictory patterns. Michel Chevalier and his contemporaries would have found it hard to anticipate the European regions that took form in different transport and communication fields, and the barriers and divisions that separated these from each other—sometimes on a temporary, sometimes on a seemingly permanent basis. Today, Chevalier's followers still face immense challenges in their attempts to build Europe on infrastructure.

2
Fueling Europe

Europe Unplugged

On January 1, 2006, Russian energy company Gazprom interrupted its delivery of natural gas to neighboring Ukraine. During a few dramatic days the decision gave rise to worries in large parts of Europe, particularly in the countries situated further downstream along the same pipeline. On January 2, gas companies in Hungary, Slovakia, and Austria reported a drastic drop in pressure—at a time of peak winter heat demand. Operators farther west did their best to counteract the emergency situation by rescheduling and redirecting gas flows, seeking to compensate for the absent Russian supply with gas from Norwegian, Dutch, and Algerian sources. Still, a crisis threatened a vast number of households, municipal institutions, industrial enterprises, and power plants. At stake was millions of Europeans' access to electricity, space heating, hot water, and gas for cooking, along with a variety of industrial gas needs.

The immediate reason for the crisis was Russia's and Ukraine's failure to agree on the renewal of gas export and transit contracts. This problem was in turn related to the strained relations following the recent Orange Revolution, which had marked the onset of a more Western- and less Russian-oriented political stance in Ukraine. The acute delivery problems were soon solved through negotiations and the signing of a new Russian–Ukrainian gas contract. Yet the crisis gave rise to dismay and perplexity. Within the EU, demands for sanctions against Russia were raised. From a German perspective, the incident seemed to confirm the need for a new natural gas connection between Germany and Russia through the Baltic Sea—the Nord Stream pipeline—as an alternative to the apparently unreliable transit through Ukraine, Slovakia, the Czech Republic, and Poland.[1]

Later the same year, Europeans found further reason to worry about their energy supplies. This time, on the evening of November 4, 2006, electricity rather than natural gas was at stake, and everything happened very quickly. The troubles started when a German transmission system operator, E.ON Netz, disconnected a high-voltage power line over the Ems River on a shipyard's request. This would allow a large cruise ship, the *Norwegian Pearl*, to safely pass from the yard to the North Sea. During the disconnection, other power lines were scheduled to take over the duties of the disconnected line, in accordance with established practice.

This evening, however, was different. When E.ON Netz switched off line, the burden on other connections in the network increased, as expected. Several of these then were operating near their maximum capacity. Further fluctuations of electric currents caused one line to overload and automatically shut down. The following sequence of events was astounding. Within a mere fourteen seconds, a cascade of overloads and power line shutdowns spread throughout Germany from northwest to southeast, each tripped line increasing the burden on the rest of the system. In the next five seconds the failure cascaded as far as Romania to the East, Italy to the South, and Portugal to the Southwest. The incident affected electricity supply in nearly 20 countries, and supply was cut selectively to some 15 million households. Via a submarine cable across the Strait of Gibraltar, the disturbance even reached Morocco, Algeria, and Tunisia, where breakers cut electricity powers and citizens were left in the dark or trapped in elevators.[2]

Similar to the natural gas crisis, the electricity crisis was soon overcome, allowing regular flows of energy to resume. In media and political circles, however, the event continued to be discussed. The European Commission, in particular, took the blackout as evidence of the need for better coordination and integration at the EU level in the field of electricity. Yet to most Europeans, if the 2006 gas and electricity crises demonstrated anything, it was the remarkable extent to which different parts of Europe—and not only EU member states—were already tightly interlinked. The 2006 events exposed a hidden European integration on which millions of Europeans depended, but of whose extent few had been aware.[3]

How had it been possible for this integration to come about? Why had governments and energy companies in countries and regions agreed to link their networks to those of their neighbors and thus accepted a troublesome dependence on one another? Who had been in charge of envisaging, planning, and constructing this daunting infrastructure? And why were some parts of Energy Europe more strongly interlinked—and thus more affected in times of crises—than others? These questions form the point of departure for this chapter.

From Renewable to Fossil Fuels

Like information, energy in pre-modern Europe did not have an infrastructure of its own. The only way to transfer fuel over long distances was by general transport. Firewood was sometimes moved through log-driving on rivers and streams and in some cases by ship along coasts or across the sea. As a rule, however, the technical difficulties and high costs of such transport meant that Europe's energy supply, to an overwhelming extent, was local.

In the early modern period artificial waterways were increasingly enlisted. The Dutch Golden Age, for example, is difficult to imagine without abundant and cheap access to peat and the unique canal network built for transporting this fuel. Later on canals started to be used for coal transports, too, whereby coal companies often took active part in new canal construction. In England, for example, coal mine owner Francis Egerton built the famous Bridgewater Canal (1761), designed for shipments to Manchester's important coal market. Many canals in France, both before and after the French Revolution, were likewise heavily used for coal deliveries. The coming of rail further widened the

Fig. 2.1 **Coal and Canals:** *Artificial waterways quickly attained a key role in long-haul fuel transports. Britain's famous Bridgewater Canal, depicted here at its intersection with the Barton Swing Aqueduct, was not the only canal built for this purpose. Horse-towed coal barges like this one became a frequent sight as Europe industrialized and energy consumption grew.*

opportunities. Many railroads, ranging from England's pioneering Stockton–Darlington line to colonial projects like Germany's Shantung Railway in China, operated primarily for coal shipments. Since railroad companies were themselves major coal users, railroad construction and the expansion of coal movements mutually supported each other.[4]

By the late nineteenth century, a major European coal trade had emerged, enabling industrial enterprises to acquire coal for smelters, industrial steam engines, locomotives, and ships as well as for space heating. Coal gradually emerged as a universal fuel, amenable to nearly any purpose. Through the intense efforts of mainly private coal dealers, much of the fuel produced in the leading mining regions—Britain, Belgium, northern France, and increasingly the Ruhr and Silesia in Germany—was exported. Regions such as Scandinavia, northwestern Russia, Italy, and Portugal became highly dependent on coal from these sources. Imports to Europe from faraway suppliers such as Australia or the Americas, however, were still "prohibitively expensive" by the First World War.[5]

The late nineteenth century featured rapid growth of another fossil fuel: petroleum, or mineral oil. It was mainly used in refined form for lubrication and lighting purposes. Europe's oil geography differed markedly from that of coal. Galicia on the outskirts of the Austro-Hungarian Empire, Romania in Europe's southeast, and Baku in Tsarist Russia's recently-conquered Caucasian lands emerged as the leading production sites. The availability of railroads and steamships made it economically feasible for producers to extract much more oil than the regions themselves could possibly absorb. This led export-oriented entrepreneurs to invest in further prospecting and exploration. A lucrative international trade emerged. In contrast to coal, oil was also imported into Europe from overseas, notably from the United States and the Dutch East Indies.[6]

Where existing transport links were weak, Europe's oil producers became active in improving basic infrastructure. Throughout the 1870s, oil from Baku, shipped in wooden barrels across the Caspian to Astrakhan, was reloaded onto river barges and sent up the Volga. At Tsaritsyn (later renamed Stalingrad and Volgograd) it was transferred into railroad cars for further transport to customers within the Russian Empire. The process was tedious and expensive, making it almost impossible for Russian oil to compete, outside

Fig. 2.2 Oil and Agitation: *From the late 1870s Baku in the southernmost corner of Tsarist Russia spectacularly emerged as one of the world's most important oil production sites. With a steadily growing population of oil industry workers, it also became a hotspot for socialist revolutionary activity. Some of the twentieth century's most influential communist leaders started their political careers in this environment. This drawing depicts a young Joseph Stalin addressing a meeting of Baku oil workers in 1908.*

Russia itself, with American imports. The Swedish-owned Branobel company, which dominated Russia's oil industry, responded by constructing a new railroad link, connecting Baku with the nearby Trans-Caucasus Railway and thus with the Black Sea. The link's opening in 1883 paved the way for intensified competition between American and Russian oil in Western Europe.[7]

In both coal and oil, international trade thus grew rapidly. Developments in one part of Europe were increasingly linked to developments elsewhere. The price of coking coal or household kerosene in Helsinki or Athens became linked to the corresponding market prices in Dublin or Moscow, and a strike, blockade, or accident in a major coal mine or oil field sometimes had repercussions on energy supply throughout the Continent. Such interdependencies were the result of importers' and exporters' intense use of railroad, canal, and shipping networks that covered ever larger parts of Europe and the world. Without these transport systems, Europe's transition from renewable to fossil fuels would have been impossible.

The Rise of Europe's Dedicated Energy Infrastructure

As energy use grew, inventors and entrepreneurs started experimenting with improved production, refinement, and distribution systems. This ultimately resulted in the creation of networks that did not rely on general transport, but constituted a separate, or dedicated energy infrastructure.

An early example was the construction of networks for distributing gas through pipes. The gas in question, which was used for lighting purposes, was derived from coal; and the main producers were municipal and industrial gasworks. London's Gas Light and Coke Company built Europe's first urban gas system, inaugurated in 1814. During the following decades, similar systems were built in both large and small cities throughout Europe.[8]

Toward the end of the nineteenth century, electricity saw the light of day. A refined form of energy, like coal gas, it had to be generated either through the combustion of fossil or renewable fuel, or electromechanically in hydropower plants. Electricity initially

Fig. 2.3 **Diverging Distribution Modes:** *Dedicated energy infrastructure such as gas and electricity networks required huge investments, but once built they saved much manual labor. This photo shows a laborer carrying in a large sack of coal for a terraced house in Salford, Manchester. He walks by an elegant Victorian gas lamp, which receives its fuel through a hidden network of pipelines buried under the street.*

competed with gas on the lighting market; its system-builders took inspiration from their counterparts in the gas industry, constructing local distribution networks in major cities. Increasing dynamo scale, however, soon enabled visionary actors to experiment with it as a source of motive power as well. In this way electricity was able to replace—or complement—steam engines and traditional watermills, making industrial operations easier, cleaner, and more power-intensive.[9]

At the turn of the century, both gas and electricity networks were mainly local constructs. Yet since both depended on access to primary energy sources (mainly coal), they were in actual practice integrated into much wider systems. Many local networks depended on primary fuel supplies from abroad. Cities such as Milan, Lisbon, and Stockholm imported coal for their municipal gas systems from Britain. Some cities relied on imports despite the availability of abundant domestic coal resources. In Russia, for example, the lack of railroad connections from the coal mines of the Donets Basin (Donbass) made domestic coal much more expensive than foreign supplies. This prompted St. Petersburg's gasworks and industrial enterprises to import large volumes of both British and German coal, which could be transported cheaply by ship across the Baltic Sea.[10]

The First World War highlighted the vulnerability of these intricate connections. Cities went dark as gas and electricity supplies were disrupted, and a range of traditional energy sources, such as firewood, vegetable oil, and peat, made unexpected come-backs.[11] These traumatic experiences generated an interwar wave of prospecting and exploration for domestic energy resources. From then on, governments increasingly identified energy supply as a national security concern—and thus as a field in which the state must assume a leading role.

Electrifying Europe: Integrations & Divisions

The interwar era coincided with a technical debate in which experts argued that electricity systems must scale up. In Britain, for example, wartime efforts had demonstrated the fuel-saving advantages of power pools, in which many power plants jointly supplied a large area. This was technically possible and economically feasible if all generators and electrotechnical machines operated synchronously, that is, in tune at one frequency. The key technology in this context, alternating current (AC) transmission, had seen its breakthrough before the war. In the course of the 1920s, almost all European governments, who were now very eager to take control over system-building, identified the striking economic benefits of power pools as a legitimate way to strengthen their influence, envisioning state-wide electricity systems.

Fig. 2.4 **Electrical Integration and Fragmentation:** *In 1930 Europe's electric power system was still in the making. Most power stations functioned as isolated electricity supply systems: they used local or regional hydropower or fossil fuel (and, if local energy sources were not available, coal supplied by ship and train) to produce electricity for consumers. Central Europe and Sweden pioneered the construction of long-distance, high-voltage interconnections between power stations. Britain and the USSR sought to reverse their "electrical backwardness" by constructing national grids (projected, but not yet built in 1930). National grids would become key building blocks in trans-European electric power collaborations.*

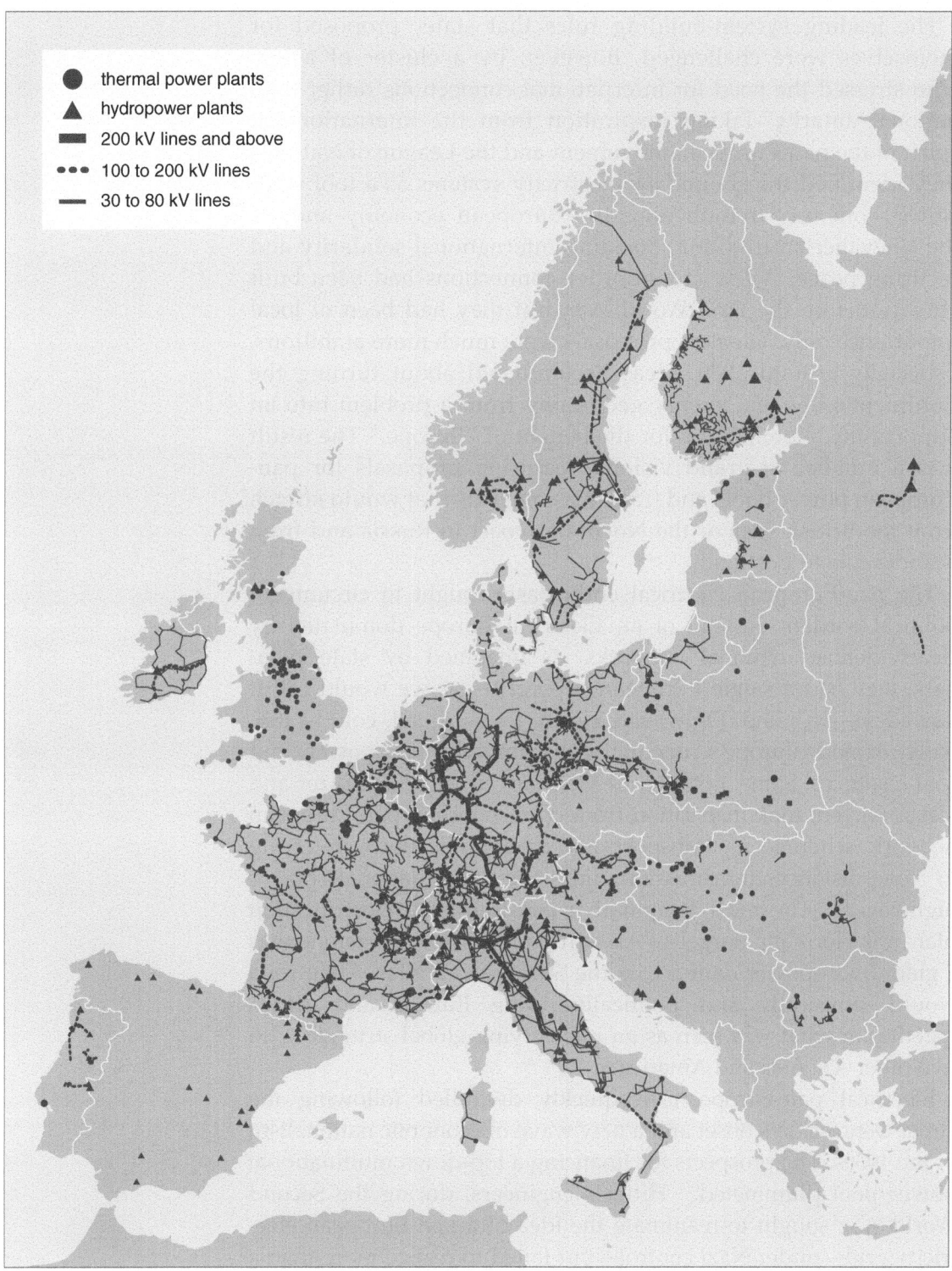

The leading system-building roles that states proposed for themselves were challenged, however, by a cluster of actors who stressed the need for international connections rather than national autarky. Taking inspiration from the internationalist spirit of the pan-European movement and the League of Nations, they identified transboundary electricity systems as a tool well-suited both for strengthening the European economy and, in the Chevalierian tradition, boosting international solidarity and securing peace. A few cross-border connections had been built already before the First World War, but they had been of local importance only. The new proposals were much more ambitious. Especially around 1930, ideas accumulated about turning the Continent's unequal energy geography from a problem into an opportunity, mobilizing it for the benefit of "Europe." The result was a number of grand visions, featuring proposals for pan-European power pools and transmission grids that would stretch from the British Isles or the North Sea coast to Russia and from Scandinavia to Portugal.

The pan-European electrical enthusiasts sought to circumvent political borders. Instead of an Electrical Europe dominated by clearly-defined national networks, as imagined by state planners, they had a single European supergrid—as we would call it nowadays—in mind. Only such a grid, they argued, could rationally exploit Europe's unequally-distributed hydropower and coal resources. Some, notably the Germans Ernst Schönholzer and Oskar Oliven, took inspiration from corresponding pan-European network schemes in transport and communications, referring to long-distance transmission lines as "international power highways."[12] The most imaginative pan-European electrification plan was Hermann Sörgel's "Atlantropa," whose cornerstone was a giant hydropower dam across the Strait of Gibraltar. Atlantropa would—physically and politically—bring Europe and Africa together in what was seen as an intensifying global struggle with two other A's: Asia and America.[13]

Electrical pan-Europeanism quickly dwindled following the Great Depression's onset and a new wave of economic nationalism in the 1930s. The prospects for financing a top-down multinational power pool plummeted.[14] Hitler's engineers, during the Second World War, sought to reanimate the idea of a pan-European electricity grid—under Nazi control—but failed to realize more than a handful of relatively-minor projects.[15]

Fig. 2.5 High-Voltage Visions: *Pan-European visionaries identified electricity systems as tools for strengthening European competitiveness, boosting transboundary solidarity, and securing peace. This pair of maps shows Hermann Sörgel's radical Atlantropa vision. The perceived connection between infrastructure and Europe's political future is here made explicit through the argument that "only a joint, simultaneous chaining through a high-voltage grid creates a European Union."*

Abb. 40. Das Raubtier „Mensch". Europa ist ein großer Käfig mit Einzelzellen.

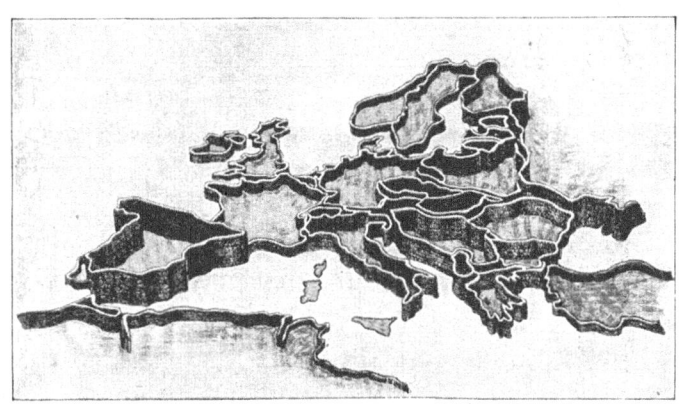

Wer es einer bloßen schönen Idee zuliebe wagen würde, seinen Käfig zu öffnen, wäre die Beute der anderen.

Abb. 41. Statt trennender Mauern: bindende Leitungen!

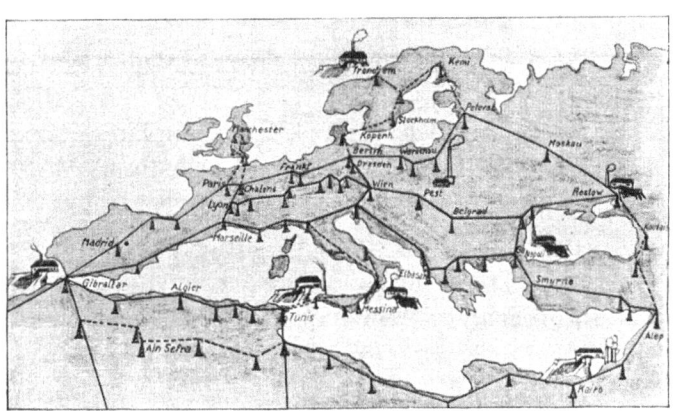

Nur eine gemeinsame, gleichzeitige Verkettung durch ein Groß-Kraftnetz schafft eine Europa-Union.

The radically-new political geography of the postwar era forced system-builders to rethink Europe's electrical future. Should national borders, along with ideological and military divides like the Iron Curtain, be allowed to determine the geographical patterns of electricity flows? Or should Europe's natural geography, in terms of the distribution of fossil fuels and waterfalls, form the point of departure for further system-building?

The Director General of the United Nations Economic Commission for Europe (UNECE), Gunnar Myrdal, wished to "draw up a program which would take account of geological factors irrespective of political frontiers."[16] The Iron Curtain should not be allowed to play any role in designing Energy Europe. While regarding the interwar pan-European supergrid proposal as "a somewhat utopian scheme which is not economically justified," the Chairman of UNECE's Committee for Electric Power, Pierre Smits, thought that policymakers would have to learn to "think in European terms."[17] Among other things, this translated into large-scale transfers to Western Europe of hydropower from Norway, Austria, and Yugoslavia and of thermal power from Poland and Czechoslovakia.[18]

The two superpowers opposed such views. While recognizing the benefits of international cooperation, they anticipated the formation of at least two distinct European electricity grids—one in the West and one in the East. Each of them might involve strong international connections, but under no circumstances should the two be allowed to become interdependent. Nature-based synergies across the Iron Curtain were thus not to be exploited; economics and efficiency were to be sacrificed for the sake of political, military, and ideological considerations.

Within the West, U.S. Marshall planners and in particular the European Recovery Program's leading electricity advisor, Walker Cisler, pushed for a tightly integrated West European system. The degree of integration within capitalist Europe should be as high as possible, and national interests should play a subordinate role in this context. In order to maximize overall West European benefits, projects should be "selected without regard to national frontiers."[19] The difference, compared to UNECE's competing vision, was that East-Central Europe must be excluded.[20]

Cisler's proposal, however, clearly undercut not only the UNECE's interests, but also those of Europe's regional and national power companies. During and after the war, governments throughout the Continent had seized or strengthened control of the electricity systems in their respective countries, and they were in no way willing to give away that power to the prospective operator of a West European supergrid. In the end, governments and utilities succeeded in diverting most Marshall Aid for electricity (re)construction to distinctly national projects, with cross-border links playing a subordinate role, subject to bilateral negotiations between power companies in different countries.

As a result, the triumphant model for integrating Western Europe electrically centered on distinct national or subnational systems that were interlinked with each other only on the margin. But power companies were still eager to cooperate with each other. While all countries wished to retain self-sufficiency in electricity supply, engineers identified cross-border connections as a vehicle for improving grid stability and economizing on reserve capacity. In 1951, company representatives from six NATO countries—Belgium, France, Italy, Luxembourg, the Netherlands, and West Germany—plus Austria and Switzerland established a joint non-governmental organization to coordinate building and operating cross-border power links. It was dubbed the Union for the Coordination of Production and Transmission of Electricity (UCPTE). In 1958, the power companies started synchronous operation of the entire UCPTE supply area. Although this area covered only a very small portion of the territory previously imagined as a pan-European electricity space, UCPTE presented itself as the main European grid.[21]

Northern Europe's electricity companies were invited to join UCPTE's power pool. Although their region consisted of capitalist nations that were also recipients of Marshall Aid, however, they opted not to accept. Instead, inspired by the postwar surge in Nordic cooperation, they opted to create a Nordic counterpart to UCPTE in 1963. The resulting divide between Northern and Western Europe originated in the technical difficulties and high costs of laying undersea synchronous links. Since the main barrier was between Western and Eastern Denmark, Western Denmark did not join the Nordic electricity pool. Instead, it linked up with UCPTE. A number of asynchronous connections in the form of High-Voltage Direct Current (HVDC) links, laid on the bottom of the sea, eventually enabled a certain degree of interaction between the Nordic and the West European blocs.[22]

In southern Europe, Spain and Portugal, because of their non-democratic regimes, were not invited to join UCPTE. Instead, the main Iberian electricity companies developed their own partnership, building connections with each other. Moreover, in 1962 Spanish, Portuguese, and French power sector representatives introduced a Franco–Iberian electricity union, modelled on UCPTE. Two years later a similar organization was established to enable cooperation between Austria, Italy, and communist Yugoslavia.

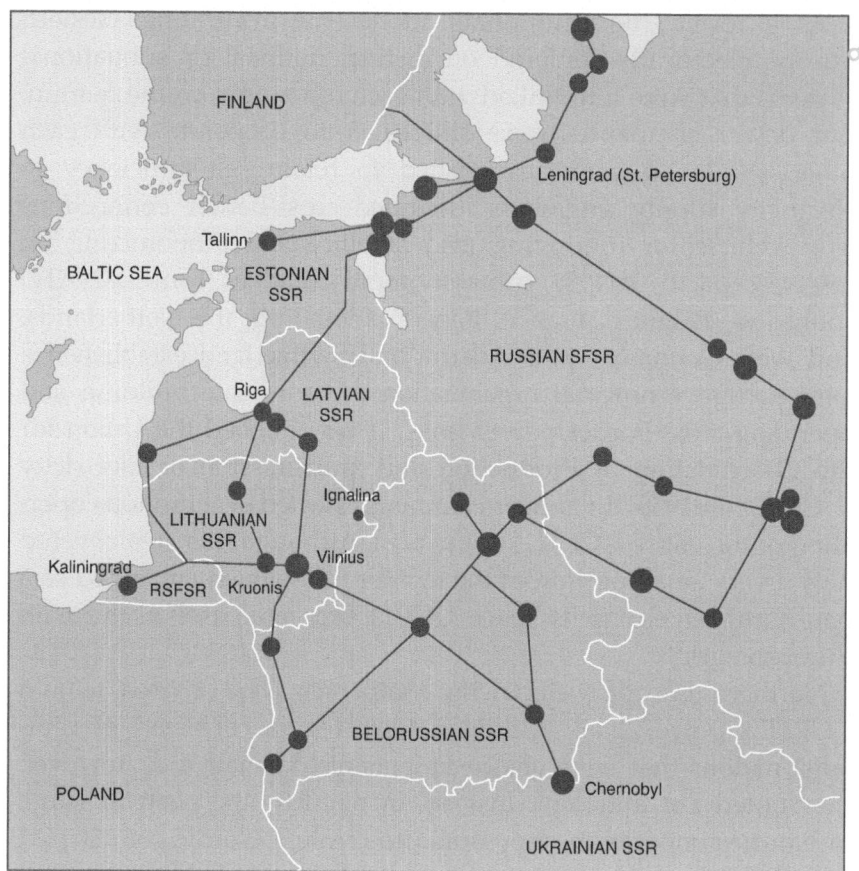

Fig. 2.6 **Electricity and Empire:** *As a result of the Second World War, the Soviet Union's territory grew radically in the west. During the postwar period, electricity system-building played an important role in physically integrating the newly-conquered areas with the communist empire's heartlands. This map shows the resulting "North Western Ring," as the most important part of this supergrid was called, during the early 1980s. The system was later strengthened through construction of the Ignalina Nuclear Power Plant and its connection to the Ring.*

Both Austria and France thus participated in two regional electricity organizations.[23]

In communist East-Central Europe, the Soviet ambition to create a supergrid was more successful than the U.S.-led attempt in Western Europe. The vast oil-shale reserves of the new Estonian Soviet Socialist Republic, which in the interwar years had catered to Nazi needs for oil, acquired a new function as a set of large shale-fueled power plants came online in the 1950s. Transmission lines linked these thermal plants with Latvian and Karelian hydropower as well as with thermal capacities in Lithuania, Belarus, and Kaliningrad (the former German city of Königsberg). By the mid-1960s, a "North Western Ring" had been created, the topography of which no longer provided any clues about prewar political borders. The supergrid's control center was in Latvia, which hosted the main balancing hydropower capacities, whereas the Estonian thermal plants, whose output far exceeded Estonia's own needs, provided the base load. Leningrad was the system's most important consumption center.[24]

Several analogous power pools materialized further east and south throughout the Soviet Union. In 1967, Brezhnev's engineers, under the command of the powerful Soviet Minister of Electrification, Piotr Neporozhny, created a Central Dispatch Center in Moscow, through which the different pools were synchronously linked to each other. They also built a set of new high-voltage transmission lines, most of which disregarded the boundaries between power pools in a way that would have been unthinkable in Western Europe. This allowed for massive "exports" of electricity from one pool to another, with deliveries toward Moscow playing a particularly important role.[25]

At the same time, the Soviet satellite states in East-Central Europe struggled to expand electricity supply, identifying it as a crucial factor in developing heavy industry. Taking inspiration from UCPTE, national system-builders proposed forming a Central and East European power pool. Party leaders enthusiastically supported the idea of this electrical communist brotherhood, while central planners viewed it as part of broader efforts to unify the economic plans of individual states. Cooperation started in 1956, when Comecon set up a commission for electric power exchange and utilization of the Danube's hydropower potential. Three years later, this body became the Standing Commission on Electric Power, expected to unite the grids of Bulgaria, Romania, Hungary, Czechoslovakia, Poland, East Germany, and parts of the Soviet Union.

A previously-constructed transmission line between Hungary and Czechoslovakia functioned as the basis for this effort. In 1960, Poland and East Germany linked their grids with Czechoslovakia, and indirectly with Hungary's network. In 1962, then, the Hungarian system merged with the network of what on the interwar European map had been eastern Poland. Given Soviet annexation in 1944, this region had become part of Soviet Ukraine, but its electricity system had not yet been integrated with the rest of the USSR. In electrical terms, the former east Polish territories were thus hardly a Soviet region; its interwar political legacy remained electrically visible. Romania and Bulgaria joined the Comecon system in 1963 and 1966, respectively. Prague was the heart of the

Comecon integrated system, as it hosted the central dispatch center, whence orders could be sent to power plants and grid operators in the other communist countries.[26]

As for connections across the Iron Curtain, both Washington and Moscow spotted more risks than opportunities. Among European power company representatives, by contrast, the division was not necessarily that popular. Joining forces with the UNECE's pan-European interests, numerous electrical engineers and company managers became active in seeking to overcome the irrational division and exploit Europe's nature-given energy resource geography in a more efficient way. Soviet, Polish, Czechoslovak, Bulgarian, and Yugoslavian government representatives, for their parts, identified electricity exports as a way to obtain hard currency and Western technology.[27]

Both Western and Eastern electricity companies thus sought interconnection opportunities, and a number of East–West connections did materialize. Austrian state power company Verbund led by linking up to Yugoslavia in 1959. The Greek state-owned power company, PPC, followed the Austrian example. In 1961, it built a first cross-border connection to Yugoslavia, significantly improving the Greek national network's stability and providing greater access to the Balkan Peninsula's vast hydropower resources. This positive experience provided a stimulus for PPC to negotiate for further connections not only to Yugoslavia, but also to Albania and Bulgaria. Remarkably, these relations to several communist countries and military enemies evolved most dynamically during the rightwing authoritarian regime in Greece (1967–1974). Bulgaria, in addition to its Greek link, in 1975 built a 400-kV line to western Turkey, which soon became highly dependent on Bulgarian electricity imports.[28]

The German power companies were the largest potential importers of electricity from beyond the Iron Curtain, but realizing this potential proved difficult. In southern Germany, early discussions within UNECE seemed to pave the way for an elegant technical solution by which Bayernwerk, Bavaria's main electricity provider, would import thermal power from Czechoslovakia or Poland. Yet these efforts eventually failed due to resistance from the United States. Instead, Bayernwerk's system-building efforts shifted toward constructing links to the powerful transmission grids in northern Germany and expansion of local power plants fueled by imported oil.[29]

Fig. 2.7 Europe's Hidden Disintegration: *The Cold War strongly influenced European electricity system-building. The United Nations Economic Commission for Europe (UNECE) sought to encourage the construction of links across the Iron Curtain, though mostly in vain. This UNECE-produced map from the late 1960s shows the resulting East–West divide, most clearly visible in the borderlands between West Germany, Czechoslovakia, Austria, and Hungary. But the mapmakers did their best to ignore the divide, opting not to highlight it graphically and even refraining from inserting country names. The mapmakers also chose to include several transmission lines between East and West Germany, which in reality had been taken out of use.*

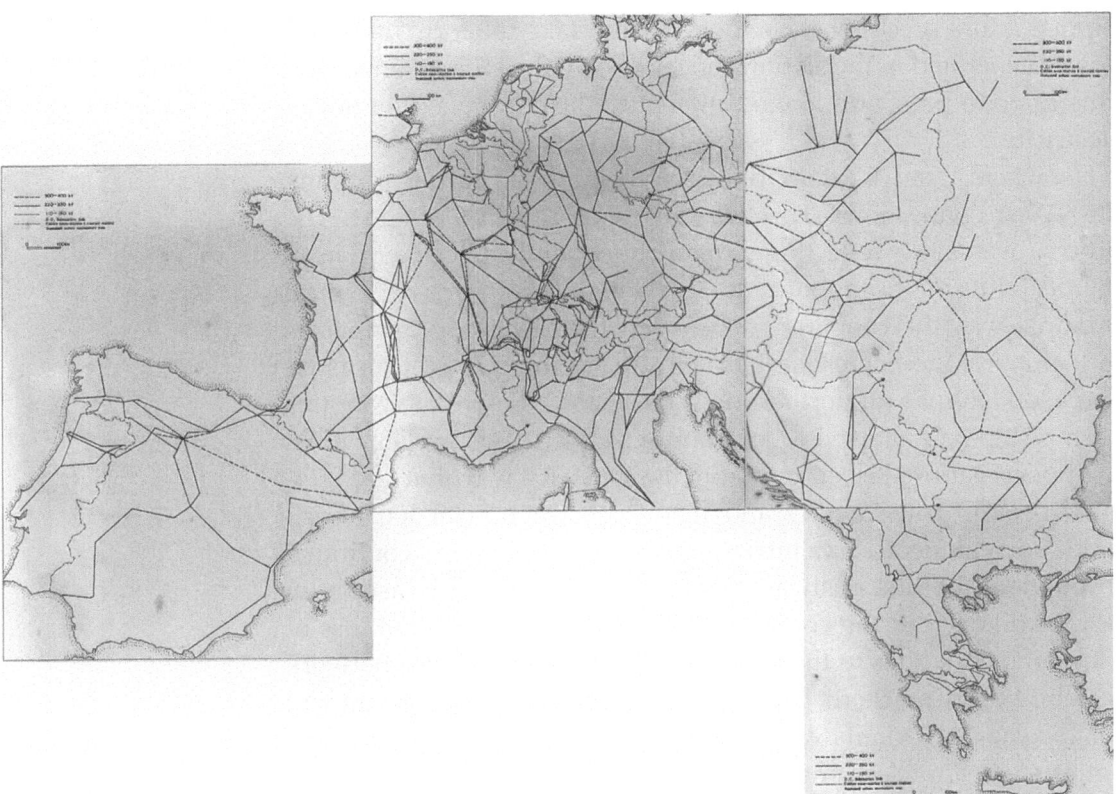

Another issue was whether or not already existing links across the postwar East–West divide should be dismantled. Finland, for example, while participating actively in the Nordic power pool, faced the challenge of managing its electrical relations with the Soviet Union. In the interwar years, Finnish engineers had harnessed the hydropower potential of the mighty Vuoksi River, which flowed from Lake Saimaa to Lake Ladoga. With four major hydropower plants, it formed the heart of the Finnish electricity system. Through the border changes in 1940 and 1944 most of the river, including the most important hydropower plants, came under Soviet control.

The new political situation, however, did not necessarily imply that Finland lost access to the Vuoksi's hydroelectricity. When the Soviet Union grew to become the most important export market for Finnish industrial goods in the postwar period, the idea emerged that the Soviets might pay for these goods through electricity exports. More precisely, the exports would take the form of hydropower generated in the stations once built by the Finns themselves. This came to pass, and Finland thereafter heavily relied on Soviet electricity.[30]

Elsewhere, Iron Curtain builders triumphed, cutting existing East–West connections. This was so especially in Germany. The process was slow, reflecting general uncertainty over Germany's political future throughout the early Cold War era. A typical example was the cooperation between the electricity companies in Hamburg and Schleswig-Holstein (in northern West Germany) and Mecklenburg (in northern East Germany). Before the war, this partnership had allowed Mecklenburg's electricity supplier, MEW, to import coal-fired electricity from the West in a way that strengthened overall grid stability and made construction of local coal-fired units unnecessary. Intriguingly, the cooperation continued throughout the first postwar decade. Only in 1954 did East Berlin order MEW to cut the connection. Over the long term the loss of Mecklenburg's links to the West, which generated serious network instabilities in northern East Germany, became a main argument for the choice of Greifswald in the far north as the location of the country's first nuclear power plant.[31]

The European Oil Geography

In 1950 Europe was still 90 percent fueled by coal. Wartime experiences, however, in which access to oil had proven key to victory, and the rise of mass motorism identified oil as a fuel of the future.[32] As oil consumption grew, so did oil transport needs. Pipelines here emerged as a new dedicated energy infrastructure, being regarded as a powerful means to make oil shipments both cheaper and safer.

Oil pipelines had played a role already in the nineteenth century in several oil-producing regions. In the Caucasus, for example, the Nobel brothers complemented and partly replaced the 1883 railroad connection from the Caspian to the Black Sea by a 70-kilometer pipe. Later on they sought to build a similar connection to the Persian Gulf, a venture that eventually failed due to British resistance. More successful was the military pipeline grid that was built in Britain itself during the Second World War, designed for supplying the country's air bases with American aviation fuel.[33]

After the war actors took inspiration from these earlier experiences and initiated the construction of commercial long-distance oil pipelines in Europe. In the West, American- and European-owned oil companies joined forces with the chemical industry and state interests. The aim was to bring oil from America, North Africa, and the Middle East to landlocked continental regions in Western Europe and possibly into communist East-Central Europe as well. Major nodes in this system were the ports of Wilhelmshaven, Rotterdam, Bordeaux, Marseilles, Genoa, Trieste, Rijeka, and Thessaloniki, whence pipelines started threading toward inland regions in Germany, the Netherlands, Belgium, France, Austria, Switzerland, Yugoslavia, Hungary, and Czechoslovakia. There was no joint planning for this network, although cooperation and cross-consultations did occur.[34]

One of the most notable West European oil pipeline builders was Bavaria's Minister of Economy Otto Schedl. Schedl identified North African and Middle Eastern oil as a weapon in the intra-German economic struggle against the coal-rich north German lands. For this purpose he initiated several cooperative projects with Italian, French, Austrian, and Swiss actors, aiming to establish major south–north pipeline routes. The most prestigious was the Trans-Alpine Pipeline, which reached Bavaria from Trieste by way of western Austria. In other cases the main initiative came from private actors. The envisioned pipeline from Thessaloniki to Skopje in Yugoslavia, for example, was most eagerly promoted by Tom Pappas, a Greek-American businessman having excellent personal relations with both the American oil company Esso and the Greek junta.[35]

The emerging West European pipeline system was, to an overwhelming extent, fed by oil from faraway regions. Before the Second World War the United States had been the world's biggest oil producer, and large volumes of American oil had been exported to the Old World. In the postwar period, the global oil geography changed dramatically as the Middle East rose to become the most important producing region. During the interwar years, American and European oil companies had led the deployment of a Middle Eastern oil industry. In the the 1940s they concluded a series of new agreements with governments in the main producing countries, paving the way for continued Western involvement during a period of rapid growth in oil consumption. This included not only developments in the oil fields themselves, but also various projects to accommodate scaled-up oil transport. The Suez Canal was successively deepened to allow for ever larger oil tankers to pass through, and new pipelines were built across the desert from Arab oil fields to Mediterranean ports.

During the 1956–7 Suez Crisis, however, both the canal and the pipelines were subject to sabotage, severely affecting Western Europe's oil supply and demonstrating its vulnerability. American oil temporarily came to the rescue. In what followed, traumatized European governments stepped up their support of geographical diversification through prospecting and exploration in Europe and other parts of the world. Africa, in particular, emerged as a new frontier. Shell, British Petroleum, Italy's ENI, and several French oil companies became very active system-builders there. In both Africa and the Middle East, however, the companies faced enormous difficulties in their attempts to maintain and scale up oil production and shipments, as their activities became deeply intermeshed with difficult decolonization processes, local conflicts, and general opposition to Western involvement.[36]

East-Central Europe's oil supply was much less integrated with the Middle East, Africa, and the Americas. Many Central European countries did import sizeable volumes of oil from the Arab world and elsewhere, and communist oil experts were very active in many friendly Third World countries, notably Egypt, Syria, and Iran. Yet their impact on and control over global oil flows was insignificant in comparison with the West's aggressively expanding oil majors'.

The main source of supply for communist East-Central Europe was the Soviet Union. To manage rapidly-growing flows of Soviet oil, Comecon initiated construction of an ambitious pipeline system. Its 1958 plan called for the creation of an immense infrastructure designed to bring massive flows of oil from the provinces around the Volga to the Soviet Union's westernmost regions, Poland, East Germany, Czechoslovakia, and Hungary. The system, constructed in the 1960s, consisted of two major lines, one going through Poland and continuing into East Germany and the other taking a more southerly route, heading for Czechoslovakia and Hungary.[37]

Although none of its branches crossed the Iron Curtain, the Eastern system, referred to as the Druzhba (the Russian word for friendship), had a considerable impact not only on East-Central Europe's oil supply, but also on West European markets. This was because Soviet oil piped to Czechoslovakia or East Germany could easily be reloaded into rail- or barge-bound tanks and shipped west. The Druzhba thus made it easier and less costly for the Soviet Union to export oil to Western Europe. It was almost as if the giant oil fields in the Volga-Urals region, located several thousand kilometers to the east, had moved to Bratislava and Schwedt.

Western oil companies feared that the Soviets might deliberately use the new system to disturb West European oil markets through dumping and other means of unfair competition and manipulation. Lobbying their own governments to prevent or at least delay the project's completion, the international companies also argued that the system might turn out to be of great military-logistic importance in case of a Soviet attack on Western Europe.[38] Oil customers, in contrast, were happy to see competition between Eastern and Western suppliers toughen. The first sections of the Druzhba system eventually went on stream in 1962, and it was completed in 1964. By that time several pipeline projects involving France, Switzerland, West Germany, and the Benelux region had also been taken into operation. Schedl's Bavarian plans were realized shortly afterwards, the Trans-Alpine Pipeline being inaugurated in 1967. The Greek–Yugoslavian project, in contrast, failed to materialize during the Cold War period, and the Yugoslavian pipeline from the Croatian coast became operational only in 1989.

Natural Gas: Deconstructing the Iron Curtain

Another large-scale energy infrastructure that recorded its breakthrough in the postwar era was pipelines for natural gas. Eventually evolving into a near pan-European network, the gas system drew on local and regional experiences from the early twentieth century, at which time the focus was on manufactured rather than natural gas. The already existing urban systems aside, the first gas networks arose in Europe's main coal-mining regions, where coke plants produced large volumes of gas as a by-product. Much of this gas was used in industrial processes, but increasingly coke plant owners sought partnerships and interconnections with urban networks. In this context a new category of system-builders, the regional gas companies, entered the scene. The most powerful in Europe was Ruhrgas, set up in 1926 by the German coal industry and regional interests. Like the early electricity systems, regional gas grids were sometimes built across national borders. Ruhrgas, for example, linked up with the coke gas networks of the southeastern Netherlands, eastern Belgium, and northeastern France. Following Hitler's occupation of Czechoslovakia, the German gas industry also undertook to bring Czechoslovak coke gas to nearby Saxony and Bavaria.[39]

In the interwar years coke and town gas started to be complemented by supplies of natural gas. Before the Second World War, the largest known gas fields in Western Europe were those in southern France, Italy's Po Valley, and Lower Austria. In the 1930s, gas companies started distributing the gas from these fields to nearby users. In East-Central Europe, the leading natural gas regions coincided with major oil-producing areas like Galicia in eastern Poland and Azerbaijan in the Soviet Union. The Nazis, occupying Galicia in 1941, became very active in seeking to bring the region's gas riches westwards, and had a pipeline built to the industrial town of Stalowa Wola. After the war, the Soviet Union annexed Galicia but not Stalowa Wola. The pipeline continued to operate, thereby for the first time making natural gas an internationally-traded energy source.[40]

Apart from the Galician line, European natural gas for the next two decades remained a fuel of domestic importance only. Among Western Europe's gas fields, only the French Lacq deposit was large enough for international trade to be considered, but France was itself a large market and the responsible agencies eventually opted to reserve Lacq for domestic use.[41] Instead, the first serious considerations of large-scale gas exports emerged in French Algeria. There, a supergiant gas field, Hassi R'Mel, was discovered in 1956. Its relative proximity to West, or at least South European, markets inspired a vivid discussion of possible arrangements through which its gas could be brought to users in Europe. Both private actors and international organizations such as the UNECE took great interest in the field's potential.[42]

The French gas industry was particularly enthusiastic about Algerian gas, even though it was perceived as risky, both from a technological and a political perspective. Technologically, the main challenge was seen to lie in the development of gas liquefaction methods, the goal being to enable sea transport of liquefied natural gas (LNG) in tankers across the Mediterranean. Subsurface pipeline-laying, by contrast, was seen exceedingly difficult or even impossible because of the Mediterranean's great depth. Proponents of Algerian gas imports further had to cope with the fact that an armed conflict raged between rebel forces and the French colonial power, with the former demanding Algerian independence.[43]

The outlook for Western Europe changed radically in 1959, when Shell and Esso, which together owned the Dutch Oil Company (NAM), struck gas at Slochteren in the northern Netherlands. The field was so immense that it threatened to upset the whole European energy system. Its size seemed to open up totally new opportunities for natural gas as a fuel, enabling it to compete aggressively with other energy options. For potential importers, this made the Dutch discovery a mixed blessing. On one hand, it gave countries and regions located in reasonable proximity to the Netherlands potential access to a high-quality fuel. On the other, incumbent energy suppliers—particularly the coal industry—felt threatened. This conflict between interests was evident within the Netherlands, too.[44]

Germany's Ruhrgas and Thyssengas, Belgium's Distrigaz, and Gaz de France became the first importers of Dutch gas. Slochteren's riches started flowing into Belgium and Germany in 1966 and into France in 1967. Esso's and Shell's experienced gas experts—many of whom had taken an active part in similar system-building activities in North America—led the negotiations paving the way for this trade. In the end the two companies also managed to become shareholders in some of the importing companies. This gave them unprecedented influence over the West European gas industry and its further evolution.[45]

While the Netherlands-centered pipelines were still under negotiation, a further potentially large-scale exporter of natural gas appeared: the Soviet Union. Its entry onto the West European gas scene was related to the discovery of several supergiant natural gas deposits in northwestern Siberia during the first half of the 1960s. Up to then, Galician (western Ukrainian) gas had been the focal point of Soviet gas system-building. Apart from Ukraine itself, five adjacent Soviet republics—Belarus, Lithuania, Latvia, Moldova, and Russia—"imported" Galician gas. The new Soviet

Fig. 2.8 **The Future is Open:** *As of the early 1960s the "European long-distance gas grid," as visualized in this German map, consisted mainly of local and regional grids that lacked connections with each other. It was still uncertain whether the Soviet Union and North Africa would be connected with Western Europe. The darker lines in northwestern continental Europe show older pipelines built for the transmission of manufactured gas.*

strategy, which was linked to a massive scale-up of the country's gas supply, expected the newly discovered gas to flow in the opposite direction: from Siberia to the westernmost Soviet regions, and onward to Central and Western Europe.[46]

Czechoslovakia became the first country, save Poland, to import Soviet natural gas. For this purpose the Soviet Gas Ministry and its Czechoslovak counterpart built an interconnecting pipeline from Ukraine to Slovakia, named Bratstvo (the Russian word for brotherhood). By the time deliveries started in summer 1967, Soviet agencies had also initiated negotiations with the Austrian state-owned oil and gas company ÖMV and its Italian counterpart ENI. Both had well-developed relations with the Soviet oil industry and regarded it as natural to expand these relations to include gas. ÖMV, ENI, and the Soviets collaborated on a pipeline that both Western and Eastern media referred to as the "Trans-European Pipeline."[47]

Bavarian Minister of Economy Otto Schedl, following up on his experience of negotiating several oil import deals, thought that southern Germany, too, might profit from Soviet gas imports. The West German government, however, feared negative consequences. The Federal Ministry of Economy's energy experts thought that the Soviet Union, on the one hand, might use the threat of gas supply disruptions for political blackmail, while, on the other hand, could seek to flood the German market with cheap natural gas, deliberately disturbing the Ruhr's coal industry. Moreover, the main German gas company, Ruhrgas, which was now controlled by Shell, Esso, and coal interests, argued that southern Germany could be supplied more efficiently through domestic German gas and imports from the Netherlands. Otto Schedl's attempts to get hold of Soviet gas thus failed—for the time being.[48]

Austria was luckier. Not only was its center-right government highly supportive of the Trans-European project, but the Kremlin was at the time also looking for ways to counteract Austria's attempts to associate itself more closely with the European Economic Community (EEC). Natural gas thus became a pawn in a wider European power struggle. ÖMV concluded a deal with the Soviet Ministry of Foreign Trade in June 1968, and the gas started flowing in September—only ten days after Warsaw Pact forces invaded Czechoslovakia, brutally crushing the Prague Spring. Voices were raised urging the Austrians to publicly criticize the shocking Czechoslovak events by refusing to start up Soviet gas imports. Facing the possibility of a major conflict with the Soviets, however, and by extension a national energy crisis, the Austrian government found itself unable to support such a radical proposition.[49]

ENI initially failed to reach an agreement with the Soviets. The talks broke down in late 1967, only to be revived again in 1969. By then new trends in West Germany's foreign policy allowed for a reassessment of a possible Soviet–German gas trade, too. Soviet gas was framed by new foreign minister Willy Brandt's advisor Egon Bahr as a catalyst for the Social Democrats' "Neue Ostpolitik." Agreements on Soviet gas exports were reached with both Italy and West Germany by early 1970.[50]

The first cubic meters of Soviet gas flowed into West Germany in late 1973 and into Italy by spring 1974. Finland also started

Fig. 2.9 Pipelines versus Tankers: *Originally natural gas could only be transported by pipeline. Experiments with liquefied natural gas (LNG) started in earnest in the 1950s. Today piped deliveries continue to account for the vast majority of European gas supply, but LNG's share is growing. A few countries, especially Spain, rely heavily on LNG shipments from North Africa and elsewhere. This photo shows the impressive* Adamawa *LNG tanker passing through the Strait of Gibraltar.*

importing Soviet gas in 1974 and France followed in 1976. Except for Finland, all importing countries received their gas from the same pipeline route, going through Ukraine and Czechoslovakia. For West Germany, this was not necessarily optimal; a route through Poland and East Germany would have been much shorter. Politically, however, the Polish–East German route was regarded as more problematic than the Czechoslovakian alternative. When East Germany itself started purchasing Soviet gas in 1973, it used the same route as the Western importers. Bulgaria also started importing Soviet gas, through a more southerly pipeline that traversed Romania.[51]

Meanwhile the Netherlands, which already exported gas to West Germany, Belgium, and France, concluded further agreement with Italy and Switzerland, paving the way for these countries to link up with the Slochteren-based system. The Dutch gas company, renamed Gasunie, further hoped to construct a pipeline under the English Channel. Discoveries of vast gas resources in the British sector of the North Sea, however, killed this idea. Britain did embark on minor imports of Alge rian natural gas, which arrived by way of LNG tankers. The main recipient of Algerian LNG, however, was France. Overall, the North African gas trade, which apart from Algeria also included Libya as an exporter, developed much more slowly than initially anticipated.[52]

From the late 1960s, world fuel markets entered a period of turmoil and instability, culminating in the two oil crises of 1973–4 and 1979. Facing massive price increases and fearing the OPEC's "oil weapon," European governments favored diversification to non-oil energy sources. This made natural gas appear even more attractive as a fuel. Governments and companies that had embarked on controversial East–West gas pipeline projects found the soundness of their visions confirmed, and by the mid-1980s gas companies had built additional East–West gas capacities. Soviet gas exports to capitalist Europe more than doubled during the second half of the decade.[53]

In Northern Europe, Denmark and Norway emerged as further fuel exporters. Massive Norwegian gas exports, enabled through a new pipeline network on the North Sea floor, quickly came to be regarded as a guarantor of West European gas security. Moreover, in 1983 Italy's ENI and its Algerian counterpart SONATRACH, which for nearly a quarter of a century had been discussing a possible Trans-Mediterranean Pipeline, eventually managed to bring this project on stream. Stretching from the Sahara through Tunisia and Sicily to the Italian mainland, the Trans-Mediterranean vastly increased the scale of Algerian gas sales to Europe. The Netherlands, in contrast, gradually reinterpreted its role as a gas exporter and did not sign any new international contracts. The government concluded that Dutch gas would have to be saved for future domestic use.[54]

Nuclear Europe

Like the gas industry, electricity companies also hoped to take advantage of the two oil crises. This concerned, in particular, the prospects for nuclear power to replace oil. Since the mid-1950s, many governments had regarded nuclear power as an extremely promising energy source. Resource-poor nations interpreted it as a way to reduce energy import dependence. The nuclear power plants that were actually built, however, relied almost exclusively on uranium from faraway regions of the world and frequently also on foreign conversion and enrichment services.

Europe's colonial powers initially regarded their resource-rich possessions in Africa and Asia as guarantors of independent

Fig. 2.10 **Radioactive Railroads:** *Many European countries tend to regard their nuclear power as a domestic energy source, even though virtually all their nuclear fuel is imported from non-European sources. Nuclear operators face enormous challenges in arranging the international logistics of both fresh and spent nuclear fuel. In addition, they have to deal with massive opposition from the anti-nuclear movement against radioactive transports. This photo shows a group of German activists trying to block, in a 1997 campaign, transport of highly radioactive nuclear waste by physically destroying a railroad track.*

nuclear fuel supply. The French Commissariat for Atomic Energy (*Commissariat à l'Énergie Atomique*, CEA), for example, early on sent out its geologists to map the uranium resources in Madagascar, Gabon, and Niger. Like Europe's oil companies, however, they soon faced the daunting challenge of sustaining their operations in a turbulent era of decolonization. In accordance with a treaty signed in connection with Niger's independence in 1960, Niger gave France priority access to its uranium. After years of debate and repeated interventions by Presidents Charles de Gaulle and Georges Pompidou, two French-controlled mining companies were tasked to direct the build-up of a Nigerien uranium industry.[55] By the early 1970s Niger's Saharan uranium resources were considered "indispensable to the French energy boom."[56] Following a 1974 military coup in Niger, however, France's control over Nigerien fuel flows decreased. Among other things, the CEA-created mines started delivering uranium not only to France, but also to Libya, Iraq, and Pakistan. Rather than strengthening French energy independence, France's (post)colonial uranium hunt thus had the effect of helping a number of authoritarian regimes in their—mainly military—nuclear ambitions.[57]

In parallel with these external nuclear developments, intra-European ties also formed and strengthened. Nuclear operators in countries such as Sweden, Finland, East Germany, Czechoslovakia,

Hungary, Romania, Bulgaria, Yugoslavia, Italy, and Spain became major importers of conversion, enrichment, and reprocessing services from France, Britain, Germany, and the Soviet Union. As more and more nuclear power plants came online, nuclear fuel increasingly crisscrossed Europe in specially designed trucks, trains, and seagoing vessels.

Managing this nuclear fuel infrastructure was often exceedingly complicated. For example, the Finnish nuclear operator TVO in the late 1970s purchased uranium from Canada, which was then shipped across the Atlantic to Le Havre on the French coast for conversion—in the same facilities that processed France's African uranium—into uranium hexafluoride. After that, the fuel embarked on another lengthy voyage, heading for the port of Riga in Soviet Latvia, where it was reloaded onto railroad cars for transport to the Mayak nuclear complex in the eastern Urals. Enriched in the Soviet Union, the fuel reappeared a few weeks later in Leningrad. Next, it floated across the Baltic to the fuel element factory at Västerås, Sweden, after which it could eventually be transported, in its final form, to TVO's nuclear power plant at Olkiluoto on the Finnish coast. For each step in the supply chain, TVO concluded a detailed contract with the respective supplier.[58]

The Soviet Union identified nuclear power as a political tool in its efforts to increase the interdependence between different Soviet republics. Nuclear power plants such as Chernobyl (in Ukraine) and Ignalina (in Lithuania) were deliberately placed in the immediate vicinity of republican borders, so that two or more union republics became dependent on the same plant. Directly linked to nuclear expansion in the East was also the grand vision of a new East Bloc electricity supergrid, in which a set of 750-kV transmission lines would tie the different communist countries to each other much more strongly than before.[59]

In 1978, the Siberian Unified Power System and the Mongolian national network were synchronized with the European part of the Soviet Union. In a next step the Soviet Ministry of Electrification aimed to build links to the other communist countries and to synchronize the Soviet grid with the unified Central European grid. In the mid-1980s, two major 750-kV transmission lines went operational, built to deliver electricity from Ukrainian nuclear power plants to the national grids of Poland, Romania, and Bulgaria. From then on, electrical generators and machines operated in parallel over a vast area stretching from Berlin to Ulan Bator. At the same time, Soviet planners looked forward to an even more powerful, 1500-kV network.[60]

After the Chernobyl disaster in 1986, nuclear ambitions throughout Europe stagnated. In the Soviet Union itself, the tragedy's aftermath swallowed the entire nuclear budget and forced a moratorium on all new projects. Poland abandoned its Żarnowiec nuclear power plant, then under construction on the shores of the Baltic. In the West, Italy decided to immediately phase out all its nuclear power reactors, and instead turn to nuclear electricity imports from France. Sweden renewed an earlier decision to terminate its nuclear program by 2010. The reaction was not as radical in other countries, but overall the prospects for future nuclear expansion seemed to evaporate.[61]

A Changing Political & Economic Environment

The Chernobyl disaster was one of several events that, by the mid-1980s, pulled Energy Europe into a new era. Other crucial developments included an accelerated environmental debate, a pervasive political shift toward neoliberalism, a radical internationalization of European business, a sense of toughening economic competition, and the breakthrough to the information age. As in transport and communications, these trends crucially affected European energy system-building activities. After 1989, communism's collapse in East-Central Europe, Germany's reunification, and the dissolution of the Soviet Union, Czechoslovakia, and Yugoslavia generated additional challenges.

System-builders were quick to respond to these new political, economic, and technological trends. One of the most ambitious attempts to exploit the new times stemmed from the Commission of the European Communities. The Commission had so far failed to play any decisive role in shaping the European energy system. The initial promises linked to the European Coal and Steel Community (founded 1951) had been watered down by coal's rapidly declining importance, whereas Euratom (founded 1958) had failed to have any decisive influence on European developments in the nuclear field. Repeated attempts to formulate a common EC energy policy had led to nothing. International cooperation had to an overwhelming extent been handled through non-EC agencies.

Starting in the mid-1980s, however, the Commission renewed its efforts. In particular, it pushed with great enthusiasm for EC-wide liberalization of energy markets. This was controversial. Leaving immensely complex technical systems such as electricity and natural gas grids to market forces had traditionally been regarded as dangerous or even impossible without adverse impact on supply security. The revolution in information and communications technologies, however, seemed to open up new prospects. The new neoliberal political climate made such opportunities extremely interesting both for the Commission and for some national governments—not only in Margret Thatcher's Britain but also in traditional social-democratic strongholds like Norway and Sweden. Economists began to think of gas and electricity as "normal" commodities that, potentially, could be traded just like any other goods or services, through commercial transactions between a myriad of buyers and sellers.[62]

The Commission argued that liberalization must take place not only in individual member states, but also at the level of the EC as a whole. In other words, customers in one member state must be allowed to buy their gas and electricity from producers in other member states. This, the Commission believed, would stimulate competition, lower gas and electricity prices, and strengthen the European economy's competitiveness. The Single European Act, signed in 1986, stated that a common energy market would be realized within the EC by 1992. Many of the large gas and power companies criticized these goals, making implementation difficult. As a result, the target date was subsequently postponed. Yet from the late 1980s there was an unmistakable feeling that it was only a matter of time before energy markets would become subject to competition.

The EC Commission and its Chairman Jacques Delors complemented market reform initiatives by supporting infrastructural projects. Only the existence of efficient transmission systems—nationally and internationally—would, they argued, make EU-wide gas and electricity liberalization meaningful. As in transport and communications, the most publicized tool in this context was the Trans-European Networks program. By 1990 the Commission had compiled a first list of gas and electricity interconnection priorities, comprising new links to be built both between and within member states. Notably, they also included connections to non-member states, such as transmission lines to Austria and Switzerland and gas pipelines from North Africa and Norway. The latter were considered important for increasing the gas volumes that could contribute to intra-EC trade.[63]

A side-effect of denser gas and electricity links was that they strengthened supply security. Throughout the 1990s, this aspect remained in the shadow of the liberalization debate. In the early 2000s, however, several large blackouts and gas crises—of the type referred to earlier in this chapter—brought the security issue firmly onto the EU's agenda. By that time a more general security debate was raging in Europe, following events such as the terrorist attacks in the United States and several European countries, concerns over IT security in connection with the Internet's breakthrough, and the Year 2000 Problem.[64]

The EU Commission seized the opportunity, asserting that blackouts and gas crises were "unacceptable" and that the solution was more EU-wide coordination and cooperation—both in intra-EU energy affairs and in the EU's external relations with key gas suppliers such as Norway and Russia. The new EU member states in East-Central Europe were instrumental in mobilizing support for a strong EU role in these matters.[65]

Large energy companies and transmission system operators initially remained skeptical of the EU's growing ambitions. In electricity, UCPTE and the other meso-regional organizations that existed for half a century argued that a stronger EU role would not strengthen but, on the contrary, would weaken security of supply. Gradually, however, the organizations changed their strategy, initiating a dialogue with the Commission in which they sought to influence rather than stop the latter's plans and reforms. Eventually the sector organizations also followed the European Commission's suggestion that they merge into an EU-wide European Network of Transmission System Operators for Electricity (ENTSO-E). Accordingly, the old meso-regional electricity organizations were terminated in 2009. A similar body, the European Network of Transmission System Operators for Gas (ENTSOG), was formed in natural gas.

The EC Commission further identified Europe's pressing challenges in the environmental field as an opportunity. Brussels bureaucrats skillfully exploited global warming's breakthrough as a political issue in the early 2000s. Stressing the intrinsically transboundary nature of climate change, they convincingly argued that the EU must be allowed to take an active part in guiding Energy Europe

Fig. 2.11 New Atlantropa: *Twenty-first century electricity visionaries seem to be taking inspiration from their interwar predecessors. While the focus is now on "smart grids" and on sun and wind as the main future sources of energy, the similarities with older visions are often striking. This map shows the Desertec plan, in which a new supergrid forms the basis for Europe's electrical integration with Africa and the Middle East. It remains to be seen whether this idea will find it easier to materialize than Hermann Sörgel's interwar Atlantropa vision.*

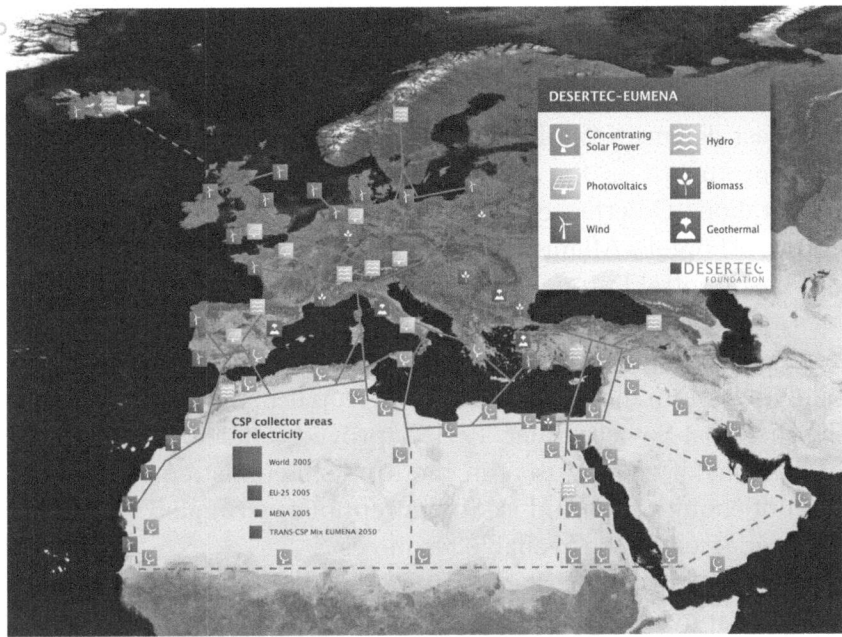

away from fossil to renewable energy sources. The cornerstone of EU activity in this field was its emissions trading system, the vision being to create yet another free market and use it as an instrument to shift energy-related investments in a more sustainable direction.

Apart from its Trans-European Networks Program, however, the EU did not aspire to become a physical system-builder in renewable energy. Instead, several organizations and ad hoc actor networks took the lead. These identified the adaptation and redesign of electricity grids as a key technical challenge, necessary for integrating vast amounts of future wind, solar, and other intermittent power without adverse effects on supply security. In December 2009, nine European states signed a declaration referred to as the North Sea Countries Offshore Grid Initiative. Its idea was to build a new European electricity grid based on massive North Sea wind farms. Scandinavian and Alpine hydropower, and to a smaller extent, gas-fired facilities on the Continent and in Britain, would fulfil a regulating function. ICT would play a crucial role in controlling and stabilizing the system. The European Commission supported the initiative.[66]

Another much publicized move was the German-centered Desertec Foundation's study of potential interconnections between future solar power production in North Africa and the Middle

East and the electricity-devouring European lands. Like the North Sea vision, Desertec's Eurafrican vision relied heavily on elaborating a new supergrid for efficient electricity transmission over vast distances. While building on earlier discussions within a forum known as the Trans-Mediterranean Renewable Energy Cooperation, Desertec exhibited some intriguing parallels with Hermann Sörgel's Atlantropa vision of the 1930s.

In East-Central Europe, the main focus was less on radical initiatives and more on mundane tasks arising from the Cold War's end. A first challenge was to prevent the political and economic chaos following communism's collapse from jeopardizing energy supply. The first post-Soviet winter, 1991–2, proved a horrible experience for millions of energy users in the former Leninist empire. There was not enough fuel, and ex-Soviet republics struggled with each other for access to the available resources.[67]

But new opportunities were also spotted. In the European natural gas geography, for example, transmission companies made use of new routes, such as from Russia to the West through Poland and the former East Germany. The Russian and Polish governments, with Presidents Boris Yeltsin and Lech Walesa personally attending, signed a corresponding agreement in 1993. The EU subsequently included it as a priority project in its Trans-European Networks program. Later on the ex-Soviet Gas Ministry, renamed Gazprom and partly privatized, joined forces with several old and new West European partners to build additional East–West links across the Baltic and Black Seas. In addition to Russia's traditional partners in Western and Central Europe, Turkey became an important consumer of Russian gas.[68]

Ironically, however, as testified by the recurrent gas crises of the early 2000s, in the supposedly relaxed post-Cold War era, gas exports from the East were increasingly viewed as a problem throughout Western Europe and particularly in Central Europe. Against this background gas companies, supported by the EU, worked hard to diversify supplies by planning new pipelines, beyond Russia's reach, to Central Asia and the Middle East. They also initiated several new LNG supply lines, enabling gas from countries such as Nigeria and Qatar to reach European markets.

Power companies followed the gas industry's example by building several new East–West connections, especially across the former intra-German divide. The Berlin Wall in electricity did not

Fig. 2.12 Controlling Europe: *Europe's dependence on Russian natural gas is sometimes argued to constitute an "energy weapon." This suggestive photo, showing Russian Gazprom's computerized control room in Moscow, conveys the impression that a mouse-click is all that's needed to disrupt the massive gas flows from Russia to the West. As of 2014, following civil war in eastern Ukraine and Russia's annexation of Crimea, political uncertainty over European gas relations increased sharply.*

fall in 1989, but only in 1994. That year West Berlin's electricity supplier Bewag ended its insular existence on the European map by linking up with the rest of Germany. At about the same time, most former Comecon countries started synchronous operation with the UCPTE system, which thus enlarged their power pools.[69]

However, the electrical Iron Curtain that during the Cold War had divided Europe did not collapse, but merely moved east: the boundary between the Eastern and Western synchronized grids now followed a line from northeast Poland to the Turkish Black Sea coast. Intriguingly, the three Baltic States, which by 2004 had become members both of the European Union and of NATO, remained on the Eastern side of the new divide, retaining synchronized operation with Russia and Belarus. This continued to be the case even after a new, asynchronous transmission line across the Gulf of Finland, laid in 2006, linked the Baltic networks to the Nordic grid. Power companies reasoned that cooperation within the Soviet-era Northwestern Ring strengthened grid stability, while foreign trade agencies in Estonia and Lithuania were reluctant to relinquish profitable electricity exports from their oversized, Soviet-era power plants to Russia and Belarus.[70]

In parallel with the construction of new East–West connections, the 1990s saw a strengthening of links between the Iberian Peninsula and North Africa. In 1996, the complete Gaz Maghreb Europe pipeline brought Algerian gas across the Strait of Gibraltar to Spain and Portugal; and in 2004 a new link connecting Libya with Italy was inaugurated. In electricity, UCPTE in 1997 started synchronous operation with power companies in Morocco, Algeria, and Tunisia, making use of a new submarine connection across the Strait of Gibraltar.[71]

Less visible was the growing interconnectedness between Europe's electricity system and a variety of faraway coal-mining regions. Coal, on which power companies depended for a sizeable share of their electricity production, had traditionally been traded mainly on an intra-European basis, and several countries had enjoyed self-sufficiency in supply. By the early twenty-first century, however, Britain and Germany, which once had been the world's largest coal exporters, had become Europe's largest coal importers. Given lower transportation costs, removal of trade barriers, liberalization of electricity markets, and competition from other energy sources, leading coal producers such as British Coal and Germany's Ruhrkohle increasingly found themselves uncompetitive in the face of alternative, overseas supplies.

West European electricity demand made it economically feasible to launch breathtaking new mining projects such as Colombia's huge open-pit mine at El Cerrejón and Australia's Drayton Mine. Europe's electricity system-builders and traditional coal miners as a rule did not take any direct part in these ventures. More active in orchestrating and organizing mining projects in and coal flows from overseas were, paradoxically, Europe's oil and gas companies. Shell, Total, and ENI all found their experiences from the oil industry valuable when the coal market, starting in the 1980s, entered a phase of intense globalization. An important motivating factor in that context was the decreasing profitability of oil production following the so-called reverse oil price shock in 1986. Overall, however, active European involvement in the global coal industry remained quite limited, and by the early twenty-first century most electricity companies increasingly relied on the spot market for securing their coal supplies.[72]

The perceived need for a shift toward renewable electricity production generated further European supply lines. Wind and solar power (in addition to hydropower, which had a longer history) were the main foci in Europe's renewable electricity initiatives, but biomass was not far behind, particularly when electricity was generated as a by-product in heating plants. Here, just as in the coal case, inexpensive transportation made it attractive for European heat and power companies to rely on cheap imported biofuels—even in cases when domestic sources were physically available. After the Soviet Union's collapse, for example, many Swedish and Danish district heating companies shifted to biomass imports from the former Soviet Union. They also started sourcing tall oil and pellets, paper, and lumber mill by-products from North America. In the Swedish case, this development was remarkable given this country's extremely rich domestic forest resources.[73]

Dutch and British actors, for their parts, identified palm oil from South East Asia as a promising basis for meeting the EU's demand for 20 percent renewable energy by 2020. As in coal, many oil companies took an active interest in the palm oil sector, though not so much in production as in refinement and transportation. Neste Oil, for example, invested heavily in facilities for handling palm oil imports at Rotterdam, anticipating its rise as a European "biomainport." The Rotterdam Port Authority also became very active, forming a joint venture with Borneo's Lahad Datu, which was eager to become the main port at the export end of the supply line. These and other biofuel projects, however, were fiercely criticized by NGOs, who argued that European biomass imports, while stimulating sustainability in Europe, contributed to environmental degradation and social problems elsewhere in the world.[74]

Europe through the Lens of its Energy Infrastructure

This chapter has traced a remarkable growth and reconfiguration of Europe's energy system during the past two hundred years. The infrastructure transition in energy started on a modest scale during the early modern period, as Europeans started to use waterways on a significant scale for transporting firewood, peat, and coal. It accelerated in the mid-nineteenth century through the construction of railroads and their use for fuel movements. The defining moment, however, came with electricity system-building and the construction of oil and gas pipelines. In contrast to railroads, canals, and maritime transport links, these formed a new, dedicated category of energy systems. They were designed specifically for moving energy and could not be used for any other purpose. Their rise enabled a massive scale-up of European energy supply.

In the course of this transition, seas, mountains, forests, tundra, and swamps ceased to be obstacles in energy transmission and distribution. Oil and gas now moved swiftly across the Alps, the Carpathians, and the great Caucasian ridges, across the North, Black, Baltic, and Mediterranean Seas, across the vast Central Asian deserts and much of the Sahara, as well as across the permafrost, taiga, and wild wetlands of Russia. By the early twenty-first century, most Europeans could access a variety of energy sources regardless of whether they happened to live in a resource-rich or a resource-poor region.

Through the construction of large-scale energy infrastructure, Europe also went through a pervasive integration. However, the inner structure and external and internal borders of Energy Europe differed considerably from the definition of Europe as a political, economic, and cultural space. Energy Europe was a wider geographical realm that did not necessarily halt at the Urals or the Mediterranean, at the EU's external borders, or on the shores of the ocean. But its reach was not unlimited: Gas Europe, for example, included northwestern Siberia, much of Central Asia, and North Africa, but not to any notable extent the Americas, India, sub-Saharan Africa, or the Far East. Oil Europe, by contrast, was almost born global, early on encompassing oil fields in the Dutch East Indies, Caucasia, and the United States. But in the course of the twentieth century, it shrank. The Middle East, North Africa, the Soviet Union, and the North Sea emerged as integral components of the European oil geography, while Trans-Atlantic and Far-East links became virtually irrelevant in terms of material flows of fuel. Electrical Europe, meanwhile, made halt at the Urals until 1978, after which it transcended this traditional geographical boundary.

Parts of North Africa were incorporated two decades later. Indirectly, through its high dependence on primary energy sources such as coal, uranium, and biofuels, Europe's electrical domain also expanded into Canada, Australia, sub-Saharan Africa, Southeast Asia, and parts of South America.

In Energy Europe as a whole, the traditional imagined boundaries between Europe, Asia, and Africa lost much of their significance and meaning. Yet there were also some clear divides, the most significant separating Europe from the world's three most populous nations: China, India, and the United States. To the extent that Europe and the United States were interlinked at all, the relation had diminishing importance. Trans-Atlantic infrastructure connections in energy thus shifted in a direction opposite to Trans-Atlantic military and political relations, which strengthened.

At the same time Energy Europe developed its *internal* borders, structures, and configurations. These differed strongly from one infrastructure to the other. Electricity networks, breathtaking interwar visions notwithstanding, remained largely national in character, with cross-border exchanges being marginal add-ons. As a rule, electricity companies rarely built cross-border transmission lines for the purpose of electricity trading, but rather for grid stability and reserve capacity purposes. Oil and gas networks, in contrast, had from the outset relied on international relations, and in the absence of large-scale flows across borders they would have been meaningless. A notable difference between oil and gas, however, was that Cold War Europe's oil pipeline network did not transgress the Iron Curtain, whereas in natural gas that political barrier was hardly visible. In the electricity case, there seemed to be several Iron Curtains, defined by the borders that separated synchronously-operating blocs of national and sub-national grids.

Political borders were often visible in the topography of networks, and some were more visible than others. During the Cold War, the most prominent political barriers were East Germany's. With the exception of the Druzhba oil pipeline, the northern branch of which stretched from the Soviet Union through Poland and across the border to Schwedt, East Germany's only direct energy connections to the outside world went through Czechoslovakia. The country's far-reaching political isolation was thus reflected in Europe's energy geography. Its fate can be contrasted to countries and regions that managed to turn themselves into hubs in the growing flows of energy. To these belonged, in particular, Czechoslovakia and Austria, both of which managed to link up with nearly all their neighbors in terms of oil and gas pipelines and electricity links. Bulgaria was not far behind, emerging, toward the end of the twentieth century, as a "power hub of the Balkans" and a major transit route for Russian gas en route to Turkey and Greece. Switzerland became another important hub. With its vast hydropower resources, it played a major role in the UCPTE's synchronized electricity network, and from the mid-1970s it provided an important transit corridor for Dutch natural gas en route to Italy. Oil from the Middle East and North Africa moved in the opposite direction through Swiss territory, from Mediterranean harbors to landlocked German regions.

Competition among companies, regions, and nation states for the status of hubs in the European energy geography reflected their perception of opportunities as well as of threats and risks. A hub position meant power in relation to neighboring energy networks. Similarly, being connected to gas pipelines or transmission lines from several different directions was seen advantageous from a security point of view—a logic that contributed strongly to the deepening of energy links in Europe.

International organizations such as NATO, the EEC, Comecon, and the International Energy Agency consistently pushed for greater energy integration among their member states, a main goal being to reduce vulnerability in the face of oil embargoes, gas crises, nuclear disasters, and other unexpected events. Other actors, such as the interwar era's electricity visionaries or Cold War détente proponents like Willy Brandt, pushed for European energy integration with a view to its political implications. Today, Europe's energy infrastructure is omnipresent both in the broader quest for "security," in the various meanings of this concept, and in the debate about Europe's political and economic future. Europe's infrastructure transition, clearly, is not yet finished.

II
ECONOMY & WAR

3
Networked Food Economy

Networked Harbor

Sunday, July 7, 1907. In response to an escalating labor conflict, Dutch army and naval forces entered the Rotterdam harbor in the estuaries of the Rhine and Meuse Rivers. At stake was the pneumatic pumping of bulk grain from sea vessels to river barges. Compared to the traditional manual unloading of grain sacks, the new harbor infrastructure promised to save 94 percent of the labor previously needed and boost Rotterdam's grain trade. The German milling trade association (*Verein deutscher Handelsmüller*), for which Rotterdam was a major transit node, and the Rotterdam Chamber of Commerce promoted the new infrastructure. A few grain companies started to use it, but most preferred the old system—until the labor conflict got out of hand. Port workers called the new machines "bread robbers": They sucked the lifeblood out of workers as they sucked grain out of ships. A first strike in 1905 seemed successful. When a few grain companies again started to use pneumatic unloaders in 1907, another boycott followed. Now violence escalated. Workers attacked the grain ship SS *Hillhouse* to assault strike breakers brought in by the companies. Port worker

Hein Mol remembered how "in blind anger the workers hit on the strike breakers, there was no pardon. Some of them jumped overboard in mortal fear... many paid with broken limbs. The ones that did not jump were simply thrown over. The screaming was terrible. One policeman was knifed, others surrendered their sabers and begged for mercy."[1] The Mayor declared a state of siege and sent for the nation's navy and cavalry. Grain trade companies closed ranks and rapidly introduced grain elevators to break the revolt. Further worker resistance proved futile. By 1913 virtually all grain that entered Rotterdam was unloaded pneumatically.

Whether by conflict or cooperation, by local initiative or foreign demand, stakeholders in other Rotterdam bulk trades also introduced mechanical cargo handling. From the 1880s German and American oil companies used steam-powered pumping to deliver oil from vessels to storage depots, Rhine barges, and rail tankers. In the 1890s the Rotterdam municipality bought electric cranes for vessel-to-railroad transshipment of iron ore destined for the German steel industries. German coal exporters convinced the municipality to purchase coal tips, which inverted incoming German coal wagons for discharge into vessels. Later, especially in the 1950s and 1960s, new pallet and container handling infrastructure also mechanized break-bulk cargo handling.[2]

Rotterdam harbor entrepreneurs and politicians pushed equally hard for external network connectivity. After all, their business model was to create locally-added value by cargo transfer from one external infrastructure to another (later business models added on-site industrial processing of incoming products to higher-value outgoing products). For instance, when Rotterdam industrialist and former municipal council member Gerardus Henry Betz became Minister of Finance, he persuaded his government to finance and build a very expensive artificial river mouth. The so-called New Waterway (1864–1872) would greatly improve Rotterdam's connection to maritime navigation networks. Betz convinced Parliament with the argument that Rotterdam's economic interest was also a national one: The Netherlands are "a funnel through which world trade connects to half of Europe ... the larger the funnel, the larger the trade flows." Besides, Prime Minister Johan Rudolph Thorbecke added, "A country's trade has its natural gravity centers where traffic runs as blood in a human body ....The stasis of such a traffic heart would hurt the entire country."[3]

Fig. 3.1 Rotterdam Trade Junction:
Economic system-builders built massive coal, ore, grain, and later oil flows through Rotterdam. This required mechanized, on-site transshipment of goods between ships, barges, railways wagons, and trucks. The heavily-contested introduction of pneumatic grain elevators, which triggered a major strike in 1907, illustrates this development. The photo shows five very large grain elevators at work in Rotterdam harbor in 1961. From 1962 Rotterdam harbor officially ranked as the world's largest, thanks to its vast new oil harbors connected to local, regional, and international oil pipelines.

Rotterdam firms and their municipality also teamed up with a major railroad to secure rail connections to Germany's industrial heartland. The *Staatsspoorwegen* company, privately owned despite its name, then used pricing incentives to attract traffic through Rotterdam. In the 1880s its director acknowledged a "most friendly relationship with several steamer companies," and the Rotterdam mayor took a seat on the company's board.[4] Harbor stakeholders also strove for early telegraphy, telephone, and energy network connections. Rotterdam's telephone network explicitly serviced trade, finance, and insurance activities. Its municipal electric power station, the first in the Netherlands, prioritized powering the harbor cranes before supplying other city consumers. Half a century later, the Municipal Port Authority built the vast *Europoort* harbor complex (1958–64), including a new canal on the harbor's sea side, to attract ever larger oil tankers. On the land side another new canal improved inland waterway access, new roadways provided trucking access, and Royal Dutch/Shell (now operating a huge plant in the area) and its partners built the Rotterdam–Rhine oil pipeline to refineries in Germany. These combined efforts paid off. "Congratulations Rotterdam" read a telegram from the New York Port Authority to their Netherlands colleagues in 1962: "you overtook New York as the world's number one port."[5]

In order to preserve that position, Rotterdam harbor stakeholders continued to seek premium connectivity. Most notorious today is their well-organized lobby for a high-capacity, cargo-only railroad to the German border. For the European Commission's

Trans European Network executive agency, this priority project (part of the Rotterdam–Genoa freight corridor) now "undeniably counts among the success stories of TEN-T policy."[6] Within the Netherlands, however, this so-called Betuwe route project generated nationwide controversy. During the conflict, opponents revealed how harbor companies, the Municipal Port Authority, and other interested parties had manipulated national government decision-making from the mid-1980s. A Parliamentary Inquiry confirmed that lobby group members sat on all relevant government commissions, made the railroad a national and EU priority project, and got taxpayers to foot the bill. As in the case of Rotterdam's artificial river mouth over a century earlier, a prominent local politician shepherded the project as a Transport Minister. After her term, Nelie Kroes continued to support the railroad as chair of the distribution sector's national lobby organization and as a high-level expert on several EU transport commissions. The line was officially inaugurated in 2007, despite the lack of a high-capacity connection on the German side of the border.[7]

The Rotterdam story illustrates how the making of Europe's modern economy relied on infrastructure projects. To turn their harbor into a trade hub for European and global economies, Rotterdam harbor stakeholders linked up their terminals, stores and plants with local transshipment technologies and long-distance connections. They were economic system-builders: unlike the specialized infrastructure system-builders in previous chapters, they mobilized a broad range of infrastructure and logistic services to create and sustain economic flows through Rotterdam. If such infrastructure was beyond their branch's direct reach (say national and international rail planning), they tried to influence it nevertheless. Conversely, railroad and steamer infrastructure companies supported the development of the Rotterdam harbor. In Europe's infrastructure transition, infrastructure and economy building intertwined in many ways.[8]

This chapter and the next focus on the making of Europe's economic connections and borders, and the role of infrastructure therein. After a brief discussion of important economic system-builders, these chapters show how they used infrastructure to build key branches in the primary, secondary, and tertiary sectors of Europe's network economy.

A Cavalcade of Economic System-Builders

Across the nineteenth and twentieth centuries, all over the subcontinent and beyond, firms, sector associations, urban and state governments, international organizations, and many others beyond infrastructure sectors manipulated and used infrastructure to build production, trade, and distribution systems and to create competitive advantages. Constructing a harbor, a factory, a farm, a bourse, a mine, a market, or a local, regional, national, international, or corporate economy always involved internal and external transport, communication, and energy connections.

Compared to the infrastructure building discussed already and military system-building addressed later, the playing field of economic system-building was extremely fragmented. A tremendous variety of historical agents built Europe's systems for the production and allocation of scarce goods and services. They did so in complex processes of infrastructure collaboration and competition. For instance, the Rotterdam harbor competed fiercely with the Antwerp and Amsterdam harbors on infrastructure connectivity to attract Rhine Valley trade; the latter two even convinced their governments to build canal and 'Iron Rhine' rail connections for this purpose. Jointly, they boosted cargo flows through the valley. So did upstream Rhine cities such as Cologne, Mainz, Koblenz, Mannheim, Strasbourg, and Basel, which competed on shipping, rail, and road access to attract river head storage and transshipment business. Small and large companies—including global players such as BASF, Bayer, Hoechst, Krupp, Mannesmann, Royal Dutch/Shell, RWE, Sandoz, Thyssen, and Unilever—connected mines and factory sites to the Rhine valley artery, which also became a coal, oil, and electric power backbone. By the late nineteenth century these joint downstream and upstream connectivity projects underpinned what economic historians call the *transnational Rhine economy*. Individually, of course, many Rhine valley firms did not aim to create a Rhine economy in itself. Rather, they mobilized infrastructure links to expand their particular production and distribution systems across Europe and the globe, and create their own corporate transnational economies. Such fragmented, bottom-up economic system-building by firms and municipalities proliferated throughout Europe and beyond.[9]

In addition, state governments played a key role in economic system-building. Governments promoted, financed, and built cross-border infrastructure to facilitate economic exchanges; these include the nineteenth-century Alpine tunnels that extended the Rhine economy into the so-called *Blue Banana*, Europe's primary economic corridor curving from prominent North Sea harbors to Italy's Mediterranean ports.[10] Moreover, state governments invested massively in domestic infrastructure to expand national economies. Domestic economic system-building usually involved protectionist tariff borders, domestic infrastructure investments, nationwide distribution systems and markets, and convincing users to buy domestic products. When the Soviet Council of People's Commissars, *Sovnarkom*, secretly allocated no less than 40 percent of its gold reserves to improve the internal railroad system in 1920, it aimed at economic system-building: "the reconstruction of transport is the surest way to the reconstruction of the country's whole economic life."[11] A year later Lenin's New Economic Policy enforced the leap from a peasant to an industrial economy through an ambitious state electrification program, as well as by transport and communication reforms. Subsequent five-year plans continued to employ infrastructure to move the Soviet economy forward. The British government's economic priorities were little different, though its means of implementation were. To repair economic and industrial stagnation and decline in the 1920s, the British state built a national power grid and reorganized the fragmented transport sector. After the Second World War the full nationalization of electric power, gas, coal, railroad, canal, dock, aviation, long-distance road haulage, and telecommunications networks underpinned reconstructing the national economy. In between Europe's East and West, many governments followed the infrastructure road to economic nationalism. Jointly they made national economies the key building blocks of Europe's economic geography.[12]

The playing field of economic system-building was even more crowded. In addition to the great variety of corporate, sector, municipal, and national actors, a number of international organizations explicitly set out to construct a "European" economy. They, too, targeted infrastructure as a means to this end. "Geographically, many countries of the continent have complementary resources; and they have for centuries been tied together by movements of trade, capital, and labor," noted the most comprehensive of these organizations, the United Nations Economic Commission for Europe (UNECE, founded 1947).[13] This perception led the young United Nations to break with its ideal of universal organization and establish a *European* commission to build a *European* economic system. Of course, as in the history of many international organizations, other agendas thrived behind the scene. Polish labor minister Jan Stanczyk worked for coal exports to Western Europe; French negotiators desired access to German coal and ores; the U.S. and U.K. governments sought to contain Soviet influence and—originally—prevent an East–West split of Europe; and Moscow strove for influence on expected American aid to East-Central Europe. Yet once the organization was established, Secretary General Gunnar Myrdal, the former Swedish Trade Minister and future Nobel Prize winner in economics, and his staff developed a strong sense of mission. Their task was to bind all of Europe's nations, both East and West, together into one international economic system, thus creating a division of labor, larger markets, and common prosperity. In addition all-European economic interdependency would mitigate national rivalry, mend the escalating East–West cleavage, and ultimately prevent the outbreak of a Third World War. The United Nations General Assembly accepted these claims when it made its first regional commission permanent in 1951.[14]

How to go about building a pan-European economy? As in the case of the Rotterdam harbor, UNECE planners did not focus on the abstract generalities of economic theory. Instead they engaged with "such tangibles as coal, steel, railroads and highways" on a "down-to-earth level," as an enthusiastic American observer put it.[15] Myrdal and his secretariat organized secret trade negotiations between Eastern and Western governments to get economic exchanges going, and set up committees for specific trade domains such as industry and materials, timber, agriculture, housing, and steel. Yet an international division of labor did not make sense without an international infrastructure to sustain economic exchanges. Accordingly, the secretariat found the UNECE committees for coal, electricity, gas, and inland transport pivotal to any attempt at all-European economic system-building.

Since the organization aimed at a pan-European international economy, superseding national and Cold War rivalries, its infrastructure projects explicitly aimed to erase national boundaries and cross the Iron Curtain. The Inland Transport Committee, the most active of all UNECE committees, worked on E-roads, the TIR carnet (Europe's international customs transit system for sealed vehicles), and international traffic signs conventions. In energy, Myrdal noted that "in a united Europe we should be able to think ... in terms of the construction of oil and gas pipelines from the Middle East serving the great consuming centers as these fuels move from East to West, from South to North, through the continent ... We should look upon the coal resources in all parts of Europe as a whole and draw up a program which would take account of geological factors irrespective of political frontiers."[16] The Electricity Committee and Gas Committee also focused upon connection projects that bridged major borders, such as the (failed) electric power connection of Polish coal fields to Southern Germany's energy-thirsty industries, and the (successful) connection of Eastern and Western power grids through Yugoslavia.

The UNECE was Europe's most comprehensive, but not its only, international economic system-builder. Others preceded, joined, rivaled, and eventually displaced it. Tellingly, these organizations too translated their preferred versions of a European economy into clear infrastructure priorities. In the 1920s and 1930s the global (yet Eurocentric) League of Nations' Organisation for Communications and Transit pushed equally international (yet Eurocentric) rail, road, water, and electricity infrastructure schemes. The Nazi vision of a German-led, Pan-European economy (*Grossraumwirtschaft*) aimed to overcome liberal democracy's crises of unemployment, inflation, deflation, and labor unrest; plans followed for German-centric railroad, highway, waterway, and electric power networks (*Grossraumtechnik*) for the Third Reich.[17] In the post-war era, much of the Marshall Aid for European economic recovery went to infrastructure projects; to Myrdal's bitter disappointment, the UNECE lost its bid for administering these funds to the Organisation for European Economic Co-operation (OEEC, founded 1948). Contrary to the international, border-erasing priorities of its American financiers and the UNECE, the OEEC only served "Western Europe ... to retain its position in this competitive world and to continue to raise its standards of living."[18] Accordingly, it spent most effort and funds on national rather than cross-border infrastructure projects. Likewise, its Eastern counterpart, the Council of Mutual Economic Assistance (Comecon, founded 1949), prioritized transport, communications, and energy infrastructure as "a material instrument of socialist economic integration" to serve "more effective economic activity and raising the living standards in the fraternal countries."[19] Here as well international economic connections came second after domestic economic system-building.

Finally, within the Western bloc, the six governments of Belgium, France, Germany, Italy, Luxembourg, and the Netherlands judged all-European and Western European economy building too slow. Their European Economic Community (founded 1957) experimented with supranational decision making to speed things up. Accordingly, the Community aimed at 'supranational' rather than intergovernmental infrastructure construction, use, and governance, though with little success until the 1980s. Illustrating the discord among self-declared European economy builders, UNECE's Gunnar Myrdal loathed such Western claims to "Europe" for the happy few: "I always reacted... to the increasingly common application of the term 'Europe' to that narrow strip of our Continent and the term 'European' to its subregional organizations. This... indicates a deeper inclination which is *intensely inimical* to our [pan-European] work."[20]

The fragmentation of European economic system-building was a fact of life. Corporate, municipal, national, international, and other initiatives proliferated side by side in complex patterns of infrastructure cooperation and competition. To inquire how these processes worked in practice and what economic geographies of connection and rupture they ultimately produced, we now take a closer look at selected cases. The remainder of this chapter will study the networking of Europe's food economy, which evolved principally along transport arteries and used communication and energy as auxiliary infrastructure. The next chapter will zoom in on the pivotal roles of energy infrastructure in the shaping of Europe's chemical industry and of ICT infrastructure in developing Europe's financial services.

The Far Reaches of Europe's Food Economy

In the making of Europe's economy, food supply holds a most prominent place. Food was and is among the foremost necessities of life, and food supply counted as one of the most durable economic challenges of the last one-and-a-half centuries. In this period Europe's population grew rapidly, but its food economy did more than just keep up: In two overlapping food transitions, it radically shifted from structural hunger to abundance, and from monotonous to varied diets. Port worker Hein Mol, our eyewitness to the 1907 Rotterdam harbor grain conflict, grew up in one of the richest countries in the world. Yet he remembers being in a state of permanent hunger as a kid still in the 1890s. If the season was right, he and his brothers feasted on the nearby cabbage fields to supplement their breakfasts before going to school in the morning. Over a century later, after Europe's food transitions to abundance and variety, children today rarely share his enthusiasm for cabbage. Instead of calorific deficits, nutritionists throughout the developed world now worry about epidemic over-eating and associated health hazards such as obesity and diabetes. Current over-nutrition talk, however, should not blind us to the remarkable increases in height and health of individuals facilitated by Europe's nineteenth- and twentieth-century food transitions. Improved diets resulted in increased resistance to infectious diseases and triggered the dramatic rise of average life expectancy from below 40 in the mid-nineteenth century to well over 70 by the 1970s.[21]

Underpinning Europe's food transitions from want to plenty and from monotony to variety, food system-builders used infrastructure to tie fields, farms, factories, stores, shops, and kitchens together in ever expanding food chains. Energy, water, and telecommunications infrastructure provided auxiliary linkages facilitating these food chains; think of energy inputs into greenhouse agriculture, drainage networks undergirding fields, or ICT networks connecting barcode scanners at supermarket counters to central warehouses, ready to wheel in new supplies as stocks run low. As in the Rotterdam harbor case, however, transport was and is at the heart of this kind of economic system-building.

Long before the age of infrastructure, overseas trade co-existed with village-scale food chains connecting fields, market, and kitchens by local roads. During Europe's infrastructure transition, local food circulation continued to develop, supported by home-canning, allotment gardens, and other local food technologies. Such food chains got many households through the World Wars and economic crises. They made another comeback in the 1970s, and inform today's slow food movement.[22]

Since the second half of the nineteenth century, however, the intercontinental expansion of Europe's food economy accelerated, increasingly outgrew local supply, and heavily influenced European food patterns. Overseas food system-building involved the production or acquisition of cheap foods overseas, the emergence of free trade policies to construct an international food market, and the rapid development of cheap and fast transport connections. Derk Mansholt—grandfather to the European Community's first and long-term Agricultural Commissioner, Sicco Mansholt—observed in 1873 that wheat prices in London still exceeded those in the American interiors by a factor of ten. Yet by 1880 railroad and steamboat transport costs had collapsed, imported grain prices undercut domestic grain, and foreign wheat flooded Europe. In the following decades meat, sugar, oilseeds, fruits, and vegetables became the next largest flows, though for the time being mostly directed toward Britain. While European consumers filled their bellies with ever cheaper foods, domestic agriculture succumbed to crisis. Again the British case is most telling: starting with the Cobden–Chevalier treaty between Britain and France in 1860, the British government led Europe into the free trade era through a set of bilateral treaties that greatly reduced import restrictions. Thereafter its financial sector boomed and its citizens ate cheap bread and meat, but much domestic arable land went out of cultivation. Agriculture's share of the British national income fell from one-fifth in 1850 to one-sixteenth in 1900.[23]

Maritime steam shipping, inland railroads, and telegraphy provided the long-distance infrastructure hardware for this food trade globalization.[24] Mobilizing shipping connections for grain, oil seed, or sugar was not too complicated. These trades could largely use existing navigation infrastructure and were soon institutionalized. For instance, the London Corn Trade Association developed standard contracts to govern grain deals between overseas sellers and European buyers. By the interwar years it had over seventy-five such standard contracts. E. Friis, a grain trader in Copenhagen, Denmark, explained how he most often used contract no. 30 for trade in United States and Canadian wheat, rye, barley, and maize. The contract was subtitled "by steamer or motor vessel to the continent." Next to pricing, insurance, and disclaimers, it specified the ports of origin and destination, name and class of the ship, packaging methods for withstanding long journeys, how the skipper should act in case of harbor strikes, and many other shipping issues. In most such grain deals, the seller would then hire a shipping company; these were "cif" (cost, insurance, freight included) deals. In less frequent "fob" (free on board) deals, the seller would simply deliver the grain in the export port to a ship arranged by the buyer. Incidentally, grain from the Americas or Southern Soviet Republics usually arrived in Copenhagen after transshipment by pneumatic grain unloader in Rotterdam or Antwerp.[25]

Long distance transport of perishable foodstuffs was more difficult to organize. The trade in high value, but highly perishable, meat increasingly required infrastructure adaptations. When the American meat exporter T.C. Eastman delivered his first shipment of frozen meat to London in 1873, he used a standard dry cargo vessel carrying meat on natural ice. He sent part of the overseas beef to Windsor Castle, where Queen Victoria found the meat "very good"; Eastman Ltd. acquired a Royal Seal, and by 1885 twenty-five steamships ran regularly between the two countries.[26] Eastman's cold chain needed an auxiliary natural ice infrastructure to supply meat factories, export ports, and import ports; the London docks got their first natural ice cold store in 1874.

By then, several meat traders and refrigeration engineers experimented with mechanical refrigeration equipment to create overseas cold chains. Among them the Uruguayans Federico Nin Reyes and Francisco Lecocq contemplated meat exports to Europe and financed the experiments of the French refrigeration engineer Charles Tellier. Tellier's first frozen meat shipment from Montevideo to London in 1868 broke down; the meat had to be eaten on board before it rotted. Yet his Rouen–Buenos Aires–Rouen journey in 1876–7 counted as a major success, even though the deputy president of the Argentine Rural Society found the "flavor of the greater part [of the outward cargo] rather unpleasant."[27] In 1879–80 the British firm McIlwraith, McEacharn & Co. carried 40 tons of frozen beef and mutton from Australia to Plymouth on the SS *Strathleven*, a dry cargo vessel fitted with a freezing plant supplying "cold dry air through pipes to the room in which the meat is stored."[28] Two years later the New Zealand and Australian Land Company delivered a frozen cargo of 3,521 sheep, 449 lambs, and 22 pigs in a condition "as perfect as meat could be."[29]

In the last decades of the nineteenth century, the overseas meat trade rapidly took off. Mechanically-refrigerated transport ousted

Fig. 3.2 Empire Food Ships: *The so-called Empire food ships were the eye-catchers of Britain's transcontinental food chains. They connected the meat export harbors of Northern Australia, New Zealand, Uruguay, and Argentina—among others—to cold storage facilities on the London docks. The illustration shows the construction of the* Waipawa *at Harland and Wolff shipyard in Belfast, June 1934. The ventilator shafts are the most visible elements of its refrigerated capacity of over 14,000 cubic meters. The* Waipawa *and its four sister ships became crucial in maintaining Britain's food supply during the Second World War. Only the* Waipawa *survived.*

natural ice cooling, and specially-designed refrigerated meat ships replaced modified dry cargo vessels. Britain, which dominated the meat trade, built the majestic Empire food ships: these huge cooling vessels could carry up to 18,000 cubic meters of frozen meat. The British empire of the 1930s, notes one historian, was bound together by Imperial Airways, the BBC Empire service, and such Empire food ships.[30]

In addition to mobilizing overseas shipping links, food companies built mechanically-refrigerated abattoirs in exporting countries and cold stores in reception countries as key elements of their transnational food chains. For instance, from the 1890s William and Edmund Vestey expanded their Liverpool-based family butchery with cattle farms and meat processing plants in Argentina, Uruguay, Venezuela, and Australia, mechanically-refrigerated cold stores in London, and ultimately their own Blue Star Line shipping company to integrate the Vestey intercontinental food system. While Vestey became a major player in the Britain-centered global food system, British consumers benefited: at the eve of the Great War, they on average ate 60 kg of meat per head per year. This level would be reached in parts of mainland Europe only in the 1930s, and in much of Southern and East-Central Europe in the 1960s.

These overseas cold chains increasingly carried other foods than meat. The Vesteys moved into Chinese eggs, and the Elders & Fyffes company's first refrigerated banana ship arrived from Jamaica in 1901, supported by a £40,000 subsidy from a government keen on developing the Jamaican colonial economy. Other British, French, German, Italian, Canadian, and Norwegian banana skippers soon joined the action, and helped turn the banana into a mass market commodity.[31]

Some transatlantic food flows moved in the opposite direction. In the 1920s and 1930s the Norwegian Trade Ministry subsidized the construction of cold stores along the Norwegian coast, so distant fishing grounds all the way up to Finnmark at the Barents Sea could be drawn into the export economy. Johannes Jacobsen and his Norwegian Fish Fillet Company (*Norske Fiskefilet Kompani*), carrying half of all Norwegian fish exports by the late 1930s, first targeted the United States because American producers had already convinced their consumers to accept frozen fish as "fresh." Norway's "finest cod in the world" reached Chicago in 1931. Exports "to Europe" followed later, together with a massive advertising campaign marketing frozen fish as fresh.[32]

Next to mobilizing overseas infrastructure, the far reaches of Europe's food economy stretched inland by river, railroad, or road. In Argentina, opening up the plains to European cattle and grain farmers in the 1880s and 1890s generated South America's largest railroad system. By 1900 twenty-four railroad companies, overwhelmingly financed by British traders and investors, had built some 16,000 km of track to the Buenos Aires harbors. To ease construction of this combined infrastructure–settlement–food system, the Argentine military had ruthlessly cleared the Pampas of indigenous peoples: "Our self-respect as a virile people obliges us to put down as soon as possible...this handful of savages who destroy our wealth and prevent us from definitely occupying...the richest and most fertile lands of the Republic," noted Minister of War and later President Julio A. Roca, who led the most violent campaigns.[33] Food system-building was not necessarily nice and peaceful.

In the United States, too, the inland expansion of settler agriculture and its subsequent linkages to Europe's food economy came with railroad expansion and Indian Removal policies. In Australia, the Commonwealth provided the railroad connections to Vestey Brothers' inland cattle stations to support the export economy. These cattle stations claimed large grasslands for their herds that now competed with the indigenous population for waterholes and edible plants. Vestey's and other firms found that landless Aborigines were good cattle herders and offered board and lodging in return for labor, in what activists later called a "feudal system." It is no coincidence that the movement for Aboriginal rights started with a collective strike and walk-off from the huge Vestey cattle ranch at Wave Hill, Northern Territory, in 1966.[34]

Meanwhile the Trans-Aral, Trans-Caspian, and Trans-Siberian railroads, combined with Tsarist peasant relocation policies, expanded the Russian food economy into Asia. From the mid-1890s, Siberian wheat transports filled the Trans-Siberian Railway's haulage capacity to the top; by the 1900s it carried an annual 500,000 tons of wheat westward to domestic consumption centers and export ports. After 1898, when the Railway reached Irkutsk and Lake Baikal, iced wagons also carried Siberian butter. For this purpose the Railway was flanked by re-icing stations. Soon mechanically-refrigerated wagons followed, and the two refrigeration methods would co-exist until the mid-1960s. By 1908 Russia easily had Europe's largest fleet of some 1,900 refrigerated freight cars; there were about a thousand in the rest of Europe.[35]

The extension of Europe's food economy into colonial Africa was a major logistical challenge that met with varying success. Consider the groundnut, West Africa's chief cash crop that came to supply the fat intakes of European consumers via direct consumption, cooking oil, and margarine production—alongside non-food applications. To set up this major overseas business, colonial trading firms established inland trade stations or plantations, inland infrastructure carrying the groundnuts to entrepôt ports, and maritime shipping links to European harbors. The British United Africa Company and the River Gambia Trading Company, or the French equatorial Africa shipping company (*Compagnie française de l'Afrique équatoriale*) and Senegal merchant shipping company (*Société des messageries du Sénégal*) tellingly named their inland stations after the infrastructure used to evacuate agricultural produce. "River stations" proliferated rapidly from the 1880s, and railroad "line stations" from the early 1900s. "Road stations" emerged by the 1920s and would displace the others in the 1950s and 1960s. To mobilize the Gambia, Senegal, Niger, and other rivers for business, these trade companies set up inland vessel fleets, fuel storage sites, and repair yards. To enable railroad trade, they usually lobbied their colonial governments; the French administration built the 1,200 km railroad from the deep sea port of Dakar, Senegal to the upper Niger in landlocked French Soudan (now Mali) because the financial risks were too high for any commercial company.[36]

When at midnight on October 10, 1947 some twenty thousand African workers on the Dakar–Niger, Abidjan–Niger, Benin–Niger, and Conakry–Niger railroad lines went on strike and blocked exports from French West Africa until March 1948, inland infrastructure suddenly became a key site and symbol of anticolonial resistance. Angry colonial authorities reacted with a starvation policy and cut food and water supplies to striking railroad employees. The measures proved counter-productive, for they mobilized wider populations to feed the workers and join the anticolonial cause.[37] Independence came in 1960, but did not change overseas food flows. The new governments joined forces to exploit the same transport arteries for the same groundnut exports to the same European markets—at least until European Economic Community protectionism shut the door.

Sometimes the inland expansion of Europe's overseas food chains failed dramatically. To imitate the West African groundnut export economy, the United Africa Company (now controlled by Unilever), the British colonial government, and the Labour government cooked up the infamous East African Groundnut Scheme in 1946–8. The plan aimed to enhance British fat intakes and pacify

Fig. 3.3 Groundnut Economy: *Colonial trade companies expanded Europe's food chains into Africa. In French West Africa, they built a monoculture economy based on groundnut plantations and river or rail transport. River and ocean steamers then carried the groundnuts to Europe, where fat was in high demand for cooking, food, and nonfood purposes. In Europe, groundnuts are called peanuts.*

social unrest in Britain about food shortages. The Ministry of Food established the Overseas Food Corporation to develop over 3 million acres (13,000 km²) of large-scale groundnut plantations in Tanganyika (Tanzania), Kenya, and Northern Rhodesia (Zambia). As one of the largest and most expensive development projects in colonial history, it involved some forty thousand workers. The corporation shipped in "the largest force of heavy tractors ever assembled."[38] The existing Dar-es-Salaam deep sea port and its inland railroad connection determined the location of the first plantations. This turned out disastrously, for soil and climate conditions proved suboptimal and output levels were poor. The master plan also called for expanded harbor, rail, and road capacity, but delays made infrastructure a bottleneck. The single-track 1 meter gauge railroad already became congested in the construction phase. It proved unable to supply more than half of the fuel required by the tractors—let alone spare parts when they regularly broke down on the sturdy soils. Scheduling failures also hit the construction of a new deep sea port and railroad further south at Mtwara, which never reached completion. In 1951 the combination of infrastructure delays, budget overruns, and poor yields led the British government to cancel the project. The groundnut scandal had cost

£49 million of taxpayer money, undermined Labour government credibility, and left the lands dusty and ruined.

Food Borders & National Food Systems

Europe's overseas food commerce had relied on free trade policies and international food chains. Its subsequent national fragmentation likewise involved national food chain building as well as protectionist policies. In the 1860s many European countries had followed Britain into the free trade era; by the 1870s their farmers had felt the backlash, and started campaigns for protectionism. From the 1880s governments in the German and Austria-Hungarian empires, Italy, Sweden, Spain, and Portugal supported domestic food suppliers with import barriers and export subsidies. Others soon followed. A few export-dependent countries such as Denmark and the Netherlands resisted the trend. Other exports collapsed: French tariffs on Greece's primary export product, currants, and a ban on their use in winemaking evolved into a major crisis. Combined with excessive foreign debts, it triggered the Greek bankruptcy of 1893 and massive Greek emigration.[39] Meanwhile national agricultural associations such as the German *Bund der Landwirte*, the French *Société des Agriculteurs de France*, the Italian *Liga di Difesa Agraria*, and the Spanish *Asociación de agricultores de Espana* welded domestic agricultural interests into national lobbies for further protectionism. Their joint International Agricultural Congresses did not counter this trend; instead, delegates agreed that "we want to negotiate internationally in order to enable a national economic policy for each of us."[40] International collaboration should—they thought—also weaken American competition by stimulating European technological innovation, schooling, and credit institutions.

Two World Wars and a Great Depression further promoted the assault on international food chains. Soon even former free trade champions gave in. In response to the Depression, Britain and its Commonwealth partners negotiated the Ottawa agreements of 1932: twelve bilateral treaties introduced dominion-preference of British food imports, common Commonwealth tax barriers, and increased external tariffs. The British free-trade era gave way to an "insular capitalism" that protected the Empire. This in turn led Denmark and the Netherlands, whose agriculture specialized in exports to the British market, to join the protectionist dance. Food barrier building also entered socialist and fascist alternatives to liberal democracy. In several books Richard Walther Darré connected the fate of the Aryan race to a return to the soil, and convinced many German farmers to support the Nazi Party in the 1933 election. As Hitler's Minister for Food and Agriculture from 1933 to 1942, Darré shielded domestic agriculture from the international market, introduced price supports for domestic agriculture, and abolished farm bankruptcies. Across the border, Dutch farmers looked on with envious eyes—at least initially.[41]

A few years later, the Second World War killed as many people by food chain disruption as by direct military action.[42] After the war, national governments combined their concern for national food security with the traditional protection of domestic farming interests. By the early 1960s UNECE reports called agriculture "the problem child of international trade."[43] National governments in market and socialist economies alike defended farming by means of financial, technical, and educational support and the protection of domestic food markets. In between East and West, non-aligned and social democratic Sweden likewise made food self-sufficiency a cornerstone of its neutrality policy, together with vast military spending: "it is important for every nation, and for the feeling of safety and independence, that food could be produced with our own means."[44]

While tariff barriers constrained international food chains, domestic players actively engaged in national food chain and market development. Sometimes the state took charge as a national food system-builder. Food was as key to the shaping of the Soviet economy in the late 1910s and 1920s, as it was to its demise in the 1980s. The Soviet authorities radically altered the Tsarist food economy, employing a railroad system that carried Russian grain to major cities and export ports. The 1891–2 famine had already shown the vulnerability of the old system. When repeated crop failures hit Russia's inland agricultural regions hard, the Imperial Government in St. Petersburg temporarily banned exports and set up an enormous food relief program. Yet the export-orientation of the railroad network complicated its use for internal emergency food reallocation. Due to a lack of rail capacity, thousands of boxcars with Caucasian grain heading north to the starving regions got stuck midway at railroad yards in Rostov and elsewhere. The relief authorities then redirected Caucasian grain to the nearest export harbor of Novorossiysk at the Black Sea. From there seagoing vessels carried the supplies to export harbors further West, such as Sevastopol and Odessa, from where other railroads moved the grain inland to the affected regions. Simultaneously American relief organizations shipped grain across the Atlantic to Russia's Baltic Sea harbors, also using the export-oriented railroad system to travel inland. But hunger had already been compounded by cholera, and hundreds of thousands had died. Despite unprecedented Russian and international relief efforts, the catastrophe triggered fundamental criticism of Tsarist rule—famously articulated by Leo Tolstoy—and several revolutionary movements.[45]

When the Bolsheviks took power in 1917, their initial economic policy of "war communism" (1917–21) expropriated the complete food chain from farmland and factories to railroads, stores, and shops. This shock therapy backfired when impoverished peasants decreased their crop production even further, which together with the 1921 drought, triggered an even more devastating famine. Despite a strengthening of the railroad system in the meantime and another round of massive foreign emergency aid, the new famine caused millions of casualties. Mass deaths and peasant uprisings inspired Lenin's New Economic Policy (1921–8), which abandoned the mandatory procurement of agricultural produce from farmers. Later, Stalin's five-year plan (1928–33) reintroduced it. Though their differences were important, these economic policies converged in building internal food chains to establish national food self-sufficiency, combined with food exports to acquire hard currency. This approach translated into vast spending on railroad infrastructure: The 1920 deal to allocate 300 million gold rubles, or 40 percent of the national gold reserves, for railroads addressed the food problem. As Trotsky told the Seventh Congress of Soviets in December 1919, "the food supply system has a large quantity of food stored in elevators and warehouses. So where is the problem? Transport!"[46]

To mobilize the rail system further to move refrigerated goods, state institutions boosted the manufacture of refrigeration equipment, built new ice factories and cold stores, fitted mobile ice

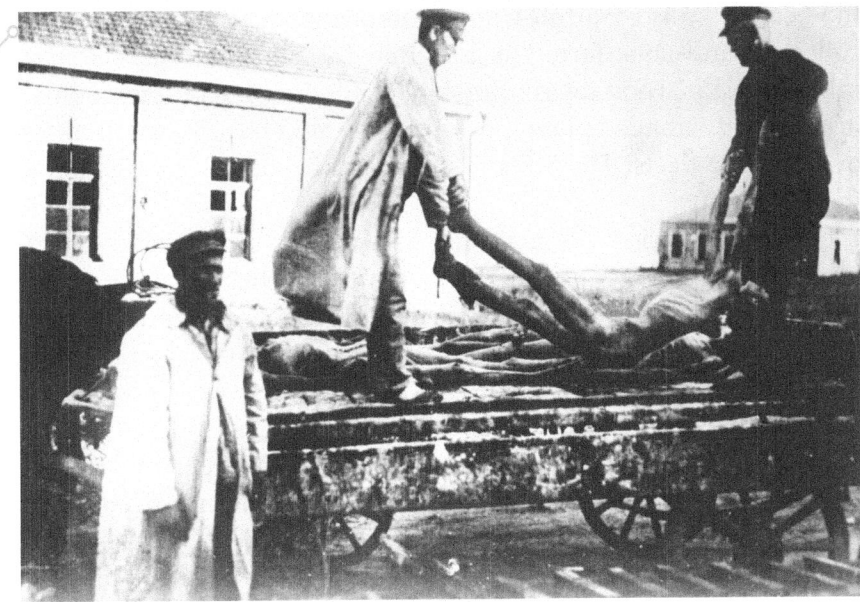

Fig. 3.4 Famine in Ukraine: *The construction of transport-based, long-distance food chains made many Europeans independent of local harvests. On the other hand, local communities became vulnerable to the mismanagement, misuse, breakdown, or other failures of the large-scale food system. Repeated mass famines in the Soviet Union were among the harshest examples. The photo illustrates starvation in the famine of 1932–3, currently known in the Ukraine as the* Holodomor, *that killed millions.*

factories onto railroad wagons, and expanded the refrigerated wagon fleet to 6,500 by 1925. To boost grain flows, a state grain monopoly set up collecting agencies to procure wheat from farmers; these in turn organized storage, distribution to consumers, and rail transport to central consumption centers and export harbors. When Stalin's government aggressively stepped up mandatory procurement quotas, harvests failed two years in a row, and secret police kept desperate farmers from leaving the lands. As a result, farmers once more suffered starvation in absurd numbers. Millions died in the Ukraine and Russia's Caucasus and Volga regions in 1932 and 1933. In 2006 an anti-Russian Ukrainian Parliament would proclaim this so-called *Holodomor* a deliberate and centrally-planned Stalinist genocide. Historians disagree about the planned character of the catastrophe.[47] The inflexible and suspicious state apparatus may have mistaken hunger for the political resistance that it sought to combat; thus it acknowledged the catastrophe too late, classified it as top secret, and temporarily diverted wheat exports to emergency relief. Either way political coercion and large-scale famine and starvation, again, were part and parcel of Soviet national food system-building. Nevertheless Soviet planners continued to refine their centralized food production and distribution system; after the Second World War all-Union authorities distributed trucks to collective and state farms to get grain to factories, markets, and railroad heads. Food distributors on an all-Union, republic, county, or city level arranged planning, wholesale, and transport with their own vehicle fleets. The Soviet Union had become a vast national food economy.

In small countries with marginal state intervention, national food systems also emerged. In the Netherlands, horticultural organizations founded a common Central Bureau to reorganize the sector in a nationwide collaboration in 1918. Participating farmers traded their produce through the Bureau's national network of auctions, and the Bureau created national quality control and packaging standards, set up cold stores, and organized large advertising campaigns to promote domestic consumption. Industrial food producers developed increasingly affluent home markets by product branding, marketing campaigns, and building alliances with large retailers. These retailers set up company fleets of trucks and barges to connect central warehouses to increasingly dense national networks of local shops. In response to these large retail companies, small retailers joined forces to build similar networks: Adriaan van Well founded the DE SPAR cooperative in 1932 to set up a national retail system, which by 1939 involved 2,200 shops and fourteen wholesalers. The latter carved up the country into fourteen regions and operated the DE SPAR truck fleet. Local distribution added DE SPAR freight bicycles. In the late 1940s the initiative went international, ultimately drawing over 12,000 stores in thirty-four countries into voluntary cooperation. Domestically, these food system-builders— together with national food research and home economics institutes promoting national dietary recommendations—produced a veritable national meal pattern by the early 1960s: never before, or after, did Dutch households of all social classes and in the most remote corners of the country eat such similar meals at the same times of the day in the same way. At the time, they almost invariably favored wheat bread for breakfast and lunch, and a standard dinner of soup, a main dish featuring potatoes, salad, and a modest piece of meat or fish, then a milk-based dessert.[48]

Other countries, too, built national food chains with varying degrees of state intervention. Since the mid-1880s, the German dairy sector had developed a so-called "railmilk" system; by the 1920s enterprises might collect raw milk from farms in one or several states by rail for central processing. After 1933 Nazi food minister Darré set up the Reich Food Cooperation (*Reichsnährstand*) to weld individual farmers, their national associations, food factories, distribution systems, and shops into one autarchic all-German food system. Less intrusive, in Belgium a State Refrigeration Service helped rebuild the meat chain and later transformed itself into the state company REFRIBEL. In the mid-1930s the Bulgarian Ministry of Agriculture and State Property ordered the central collection of raw milk in each of the country's dairy regions; urban dairy stations then gathered milk from these collection stations by truck or cart.[49]

In a few important instances, national food system-builders sought to cross national boundaries. The Italian and German governments translated national food autarky into the annexation of bread baskets such as Ethiopia and Soviet Ukraine to feed domestic populations. Both schemes backfired, with devastating implications for indigenous populations. Mussolini's settlers in newly-conquered Ethiopia did not manage to get Italian-style agriculture off the ground; rather than sending food to Italy, the colonists themselves needed food supplies from Italy.

As for Nazi Germany, Hitler noted that "I need the Ukraine, so that no one is able to starve us."[50] Herbert Backe, about to succeed Darré as food minister, developed the 1941 Hunger Plan as part of the invasion of the Soviet Union. The scheme diverted Russian and Ukrainian wheat flows from Soviet to German mouths, feeding the invading *Wehrmacht* and citizens back home, while simultaneously starving indigenous populations to death or forcing emigration. Ironically, again, the invaders could not cope with the logistic challenges—the lack of truck fuel and railroad wagons—and when the tide of the Soviet invasion turned, many Nazi troops themselves fell victim to exhaustion from food shortages and winter cold. The Nazi leadership then used the food diversion policy in occupied Poland with equally deadly consequences for local populations.

Meanwhile the war and its food struggles destroyed international food chains that had survived the 1920s and 1930s, for international food dependency presented a tremendous vulnerability.

Throughout Europe, national war cabinets took control of the domestic food system. Even in Britain, farming made a comeback, as the wheels of the Commonwealth clogged. When the Japanese occupation of Burma cut rice supplies to British India's Eastern provinces, neither the British and Indian governments, nor the Commonwealth managed to redirect food flows. To the contrary, Churchill's War Cabinet anticipated further Japanese invasions and wheeled stocks out of Calcutta (Kolkota) in a kind of scorched earth policy. The Cabinet's priority-use of remaining food stocks for soldiers and British citizens, and its blocking of emergency food aid from either Canada—ships were needed elsewhere—or the United Nations Relief and Rehabilitation Administration (UNRRA), aggravated the situation. The Bengal famine of 1943–4 and associated diseases killed an estimated three million, and further mobilized Indians against British rule. Upon noting the Allied food airlift from Britain to the Northern Netherlands in spring 1945, in which eight hundred planes dropped some 7,558 tons of food, Viceroy of India Archibald Wavell expressed disgust at the British government for its "very different attitude toward feeding a starving population when the starvation is in Europe."[51] In the 1830s Chevalier had dreamt of infrastructure connectivity, economic growth for all, and equality. Over a century later, inequality ruled Europe's food chains both in war and peace.

After the war's disruption of international food chains, national food border and domestic system-building peaked. Governments in Europe and beyond intensified national tariff borders and stepped up the domestic production and distribution of starchy staples to provide basic calories. As for perishable foods, the French Ministry of Agriculture developed a postwar refrigeration policy and directed public and private ventures toward a common national cold chain. From 1948 the Spanish government pushed a national refrigeration network, and invested massively in cold stores and refrigerated wagons and trucks. In Norway the state had subsidized a coastal cold store infrastructure for fish exports in the 1930s; now, stagnating exports and domestic shortages led the Trade Ministry to focus on inland fish distribution and build a nationwide cold store system. The new command economies of East-Central Europe followed the Soviet example: collective and state farms met with varying success, yet all socialist governments built national food systems, aimed at self-sufficiency to feed their peoples and minimize expensive imports. They nationalized food enterprises and set up institutions to collect and distribute foods on state, regional, and municipal levels. State trading firms provided logistical services. In Bulgaria, for instance, the State Economic Union set up several nationwide transport companies, which divided the country into sections to be served by their trucks.[52]

By 1960 Western European countries produced within national boundaries an estimated 86 percent of their wheat consumption, 95 percent of their meat, 96 percent of their eggs, 88 percent of their butter and 99 percent of their cheese.[53] National food circulation characterized East-Central Europe's food economy even more. Some countries deviated significantly from the aggregate pattern: Import-dependent Britain produced merely 40 percent of its wheat, 60 percent of its meat, and less than 10 percent of its butter. Finland, Denmark, the Netherlands, Norway, Poland, and Portugal needed substantial wheat imports, but largely produced their own perishable foods. Bulgaria, France, Greece, Romania, the Soviet Union, Spain, Sweden, Turkey, and Yugoslavia achieved self-sufficiency in all basic foods. National food chains, not international ones, dominated Europe's food economy. As for the remaining cross-border food trade, intercontinental food chains prevailed; an all-European food economy was nowhere in sight. By 1960 Western European countries acquired only 3 percent of their food imports from East-Central Europe, 29 percent from other Western European countries, and no less than 68 percent from other continents. Soviet bloc countries traded mostly with each other, followed by trade with other continents and—finally—Western Europe.

The Pros & Cons of Regional Food Integration

The nationally-fragmented, intercontinentally-connected character of Europe's food economy made it a target for postwar regional integration initiatives. As noted above, several European food system integration programs co-existed and competed, although these had very different implications for Europe's food chains.

The United Nations Economic Commission for Europe made a first call for an integrated European food economy. In line with the organization's aims this would be an all-European economy erasing the Cold War cleavage and national boundaries alike. The UNECE particularly focused on perishable foodstuffs. Experts agreed that by the late 1940s, hunger and starvation had by and large been eradicated in Europe. But they still found malnutrition, the lack of vital nutrients, a tremendous problem: "What is most harmful is not occasional fasting but prolonged and unremedied malnutrition, which eventually slows down the activity of a whole nation. Endemic malnutrition, therefore, is the enemy," warned Myrdal's UNECE secretariat in 1949.[54] Malnutrition stemmed from monotonous diets based on grains and potatoes. In terms of contemporary food science insights, increased consumption of fresh milk, cheese, meat, offal, fish, and eggs should boost protein intakes. Improved cream and butter supply should provide fats and fat-soluble vitamins. Vegetables and fresh fruits could provide mineral salts, water-soluble vitamins (A, B, and C), and cellulose. As ever, transport infrastructure was key to Europe's upcoming food transition: "Victory lies not only in increasing production, though this is of course necessary, but also, and perhaps to a greater extent, in a more even distribution of the foodstuffs produced, a sphere in which transport plays a technical role of the first importance."[55] The health of Europe's individuals and nations hinged in particular on the infrastructure known as the "refrigerated chain" or "cooling chain." The foods providing missing nutrients were highly perishable and required cooled transport facilities. A new UNECE Working Party was to "take any immediate action" to improve the circulation of such foodstuffs.[56] In short, it should build the transport links of an all-European food economy.

The Working Party teamed up with a wide range of food sector players, including the UN Food and Agriculture Organization, as well as infrastructure organizations such as the International Railway Union, the International Road Transport Union, the European Union of Coachbuilders, and the International Freight Train Time Table Conference. Jointly these organizations embarked on an ambitious all-European food system-building program.[57] They focused on mobilizing existing infrastructure for food purposes rather than constructing new roads or rails, although a

Fig. 3.5 **Continental Cold Chain:** *After the Second World War, the United Nations Economic Commission for Europe identified monotonous diets and malnutrition as Europe's postwar enemies. In order to boost the intakes of crucial vitamins and minerals, it set out to build a pan-European cold chain for the distribution of fish, vegetables, fruits, and other perishable foods. The Commission identified the International Railway Company for Refrigerated Transport (Interfrigo) as a key element of this system. The photo shows the loading of fish in refrigerated Interfrigo wagons in 1959.*

tunnel under the English Channel was on their wish list. However, even the mobilization of existing transport links for food purposes required extensive technical, organizational, and legal work. Much effort went toward the design of mechanically-refrigerated railroad wagons, lorries, and containers. Think not just of complete wagon designs, but also of specific elements such as wagon walls of stainless steel or aluminum alloys to withstand frequent chemical cleaning after fish or fruit transport; shock-absorbing devices; or standards for the airtightness of vehicles. In addition speed was of the essence, so the Working Party and its partner organizations aligned railroad timetables, designed international transport documents, and negotiated priority for perishable transport at border checkpoints. Next came international standards for perishable foods, their packaging, and their transportation. By the mid-1960s so-called "European standards" existed for the size, color, and classification of twenty individual foodstuffs. Soon followed standards for refrigeration equipment, testing procedures, and maximum transport temperatures for a range of foods. For instance, frozen fish was to be transported at max. −18 °C, frozen butter at −10 °C, non-frozen poultry at +4 °C, and non-frozen fish "must always be carried in melting ice."[58] Finally the International Railway Company for Refrigerated Transport (Interfrigo), owned by Western European railroad administrations, would operate the rail-based cold chains. The Working Party asked the International Road Transport Union to found a similar organization for roads. Transfrigoroute Europe came into being as an association of cold transport firms in 1956, and already in 1960 it claimed that its "rolling refrigerators" had created an "unbroken cooling chain on roads."[59] By 1976 it had 1,175 members; in 2005 it claimed to serve some 80 percent of Europe's temperature-controlled road transport. Intercontainer, finally, offered combined rail–road refrigerated services.

By 1970 the key elements of a pan-European cold chain for perishable foods seemed to be in place. In the meantime, however, UNECE all-European food system-building efforts had been superseded by the proliferation of national cold chains, witness the absolute dominance of domestically-produced foods in national food consumption statistics. The national cold chains described above, not international ones, deserve the credit for Europe's second food victory. Domestic cold chains beat the malnutrition enemy, a few decades after the eradication of structural hunger, and did so throughout Europe. UNECE analysts observed that consumers from Belgium to Bulgaria and from Sweden to Spain now craved and ate varied diets. Even the traditional Mediterranean food culture had split into a diverse diet on its Northern shores and a monotonous one on its Southern and Eastern edges.[60] So Europe's food system remained fundamentally splintered. Even within the remaining cross-border food trade, an all-European food economy faltered: by the mid-1980s Western European imports from East-Central Europe still lingered at 3 percent, as they had in 1960. Despite Polish meat and Bulgarian and Hungarian egg exports to Western Europe, despite Greek citrus fruit, grape, and olive exports to Comecon members, food trade across the Iron Curtain remained marginal.[61]

About 1960 UNECE analysts wondered whether recent intra-regional integration initiatives by Comecon and the European Communities would change Europe's food economy more fundamentally. Comecon members accepted the "Fundamental principles of the international socialist division of labour" at their fifteenth session in Moscow in 1962, promising increased agricultural specialization among countries. For the time being, however, that pledge did not fundamentally challenge the paradigm of national food self sufficiency: The same document recommended that each member state develop "an agriculture capable of meeting to the maximum extent possible the country's requirements as regards foodstuffs."[62] Grains and animal production should be optimized in each country individually. Bulgaria deviated from the pattern by developing fruit and vegetable chains to become the main exporter in the region; its export system stretched beyond the Comecon bloc. Bulgarian state trading companies merged, and by 1980 their 4,000 trucks served a motoroute-based trade network from Spain and France in the west to Iraq, Iran, and Pakistan in the east.[63]

Within the Western bloc, the European Economic Community implemented a more radical food integration initiative. In the mid-1980s UNECE analysts could observe that Western Europe's imports from East-Central Europe remained stagnant, but the share of imports from other Western European countries had increased from 29 percent to 55 percent. At the same time the percentage of imports from overseas had declined from 69 percent to 42 percent. These changes almost exclusively reflected developments within the European Economic Community.[64]

Ironically, Community food market integration stemmed from the very same protectionist concerns that had produced the national compartmentalization of Europe's food economy. Sicco Mansholt had been a life-long proponent of protectionism.[65] He came from a socialist farming family in one of the most radical pro-Soviet villages in the Netherlands, and he had literally read and reread his grandfather's 1896 critique of the free grain trade to tatters. During the Nazi Occupation Mansholt organized clandestine food supplies for the resistance movement, which earned him an invitation to become the postwar Dutch Minister of Agriculture at the age of 37. In this position of power, Mansholt joined his French colleague Pierre Pflimin in the early 1950s, calling for joint European protectionism against overseas competitors. The first round of negotiations for a so-called Green Pool in 1953 failed, but agriculture was included in the 1958 European Economic

Fig. 3.6 **Butter Mountain:** *The European Economic Community established its Common Agricultural Policy to strengthen food exchanges within the EEC, and reduce its dependence on transcontinental food imports. In order to guarantee minimum prices to Community farmers despite overproduction, the EEC occasionally bought large amounts of butter, milk, wine, and other products. This effort consumed most of the EEC budget, and eventually produced huge food stocks known as the "butter mountain," the "milk lake," and the "wine lake." The photo shows what a butter mountain really looked like: butter packages neatly stacked in cold storage at Gross-Gerau, West Germany, in 1979.*

Community, and Mansholt became the Community's Agriculture Commissioner from 1958 to 1972. European farmers came to benefit tremendously from the Common Agricultural Policy that Mansholt, with French support, managed to place center stage in Community politics.

Mansholt and his colleagues expected that the Community's Common Agricultural Policy would increase agricultural productivity, ensure a fair standard of living for the agricultural sector, and guarantee security of food supply and reasonable consumer prices. The policy's key tools were market unity, community preference, and financial solidarity. Market unity meant removing national food borders (levies, monopolies, quotas) and establishing similar prices throughout the Community's member states, the number of which increased from six in 1958 to twelve in 1986. Community preference meant privileging members' products over imports from third countries by means of joint external tariff walls and quotas. Financial solidarity, finally, meant that member states jointly paid for Community market interventions, such as buying community products to avoid price drops beneath a set minimum. In 1992 agriculture price support accounted for about half the EU budget; it kept many farmers in business in adverse times, but also produced the huge food stocks known as the butter and meat mountains and the milk and wine lakes. The Community repeatedly used export subsidies to dump these goods on foreign markets, where they disrupted indigenous food production. The common market benefited European Economic Community members at the expense of non-members in more than one way.

Community policies primarily focused on political and financial mechanisms rather than down-to-earth food system-building. The latter was not needed. After all, Community members and their associated partners could piggyback on a transnational food infrastructure established by the UNECE and other organizations. In the case of cold chains, Community directives simply appropriated UNECE frozen foods definitions, specified (voluntary) temperature control instructions for member states, and authorized broader road vehicles with thicker insulated walls. Moreover, Community members and their closest trade partners were the frontrunners in UNECE food working party work. Dutch, French, and Italian national representatives with a stake in agricultural exports pushed new initiatives, and their community and associated trade partners signed, ratified, and implemented cross-border cold chain measures well ahead of other states. Food companies did the rest by focusing their cross-border system-building activity on the Community and its associated trade partners. Food retail companies such as DE SPAR proliferated, particularly on Community and partner territory. So did cold transport associations such as Interfrigo and Transfrigoroute. The leading deep freezing carrier, Frigoscandia, built a Swedish cold chain in the 1950s and by the mid-1970s circulated its 350 trucks and 50 rail wagons among ten Western European countries. When Sweden entered the European Union in the mid-1990s, a thousand trucks served an area roughly corresponding to Union territory plus Norway and Switzerland. Only in the 1990s did food companies massively enter former communist territories.[66]

Looking back as an 86 year old, Sicco Mansholt credited his Community policies for making 'Europe' much less dependent on overseas imports—Europe's third food victory perhaps, after its earlier victories over the enemies of structural hunger and monotonous diets. Tellingly, when Greece joined in 1981, the 31 percent share of Community countries in its agricultural imports of the late 1970s rose to 68 percent by 1983.[67]

There are, however, several caveats. First, within Europe national boundaries continued to matter, as they did for other commodities.[68] More important, perhaps, is that "third countries" footed the bill of European food integration efforts. "What did we do in Europe?", asked a regretful Mansholt; "we drove third world farmers into despair and urban slums...we got stuck with intensive pig farming and manure mountains...a sticky mess of ridiculous legislation. Dramatic."[69]

Some developing countries lost domestic farmers due to Community dumping policies. Others lost important export markets. Consider one last time our West African groundnut story. Senegal's groundnut production peaked in the mid-1960s at almost 1.2 million tons, accounted for 75 percent of its agricultural earnings, and directly or indirectly employed 90 percent of the active population. In the French Union, it enjoyed full access to the French market and protection in the form of quotas and minimum prices. After independence, the Senegalese government expected association with the European Economic Community's common agricultural market on a par with the remaining French colonies. It anticipated a continuation of its exports to France, privileged access to other Community markets, and even winning German, Dutch, and Italian tastes for groundnut oil products.

Mansholt and the French negotiators supported this effort, but not fiercely enough to convince the other Community partners. Italian negotiators sought to promote Italian olive oil exports. German and the Benelux partner representatives prioritized cheaper fat imports to their domestic industries at world market prices. After a decade of strained negotiations, Senegal received funds to prepare for world market conditions, but not the expected participation in the European Economic Community's common market. Henceforward it qualified for marginal "development aid" rather than profitable economic association. By the early 1970s its European exports had collapsed, annual production almost halved, and many indebted peasants had sold their equipment and returned to a subsistence economy.[70]

Economic system-building again had created connections as well as disconnections, winners as well as losers. And European history is full of ironies. For in time, Senegal's food disconnection would inspire a very different type of connection to European Union territory; small and quite dangerous fishing boats would carry impoverished illegal migrants across the Atlantic from Senegal and its neighbor countries to Spain's Canary Islands. Many, as we know, did not make it alive.

4
Factory & Finance

Entrepreneurial Energies

Friedrich Engelhorn had earned his citizenship and guild rights in Mannheim, in the German Grand Duchy of Baden, as a gold and silver smith. His 1847 marriage to Maria Magdalena Brustling, the daughter of an affluent local brewer, made him professionally independent and enabled a change of career. A tenant in the young couple's new house provided direction. The visitor, the Belgian inventor Guillaume Smyers, was thrilled by the booming coal gas business. He inspired Engelhorn to become an energy entrepreneur: In 1848 Engelhorn, Smyers, and a local financier founded the limited liability company *Engelhorn & Cie* to produce and sell bottled coal gas. In 1851 Engelhorn took another step and co-founded the Baden Gas Company (*Badische Gesellschaft für Gasbeleuchtung*) that operated gas works in about nineteen towns at its peak. Engelhorn himself became the director of its Mannheim gas works.[1]

In this capacity, Engelhorn soon spotted yet another business opportunity that built directly on his energy infrastructure. Like other gas and coke works, the Mannheim gas works produced large amounts of tarry residues as a by-product of coal gasification.

Thus Engelhorn became fascinated by a series of scientific breakthroughs in the organic chemistry of coal-tar hydrocarbons and their derivatives. By the mid-1850s researchers at the Royal College of Chemistry in London had managed to isolate the principal coal-tar component benzene (C_6H_6), and transform benzene into aniline ($C_6H_5NH_2$). In 1856 William Henry Perkin sensationally transformed aniline into an intensely purple dyestuff later called mauveine. Great commercial possibilities came into view: synthetic dyes from worthless coal-tar could replace expensive natural and semi-natural dyes in the textile industries. The mauve mania—the British humorist magazine *Punch* wrote of 'mauve measles'—immediately spread to France and Germany. In Lyon chemists synthesized aniline red (fuchsine) in 1859. In Mannheim, Engelhorn and his business partners built a factory next to their gas works for the "preparation of aniline and coal-tar dyes ... later to extend to other chemical products."[2] They bought the inorganic chemicals (lime, soda, sulphuric acid, nitric acid) needed to manipulate coal tar hydrocarbons from an external manufacturer. To combine dye production with in-house control of such auxiliary chemicals, Engelhorn established the *Badische Anilin- & Soda-Fabrik* (BASF) in 1865. Engelhorn left the gas works to lead the new company. So began the construction of a giant industrial system that acquired fossil fuels—first coal, later oil and natural gas—and transformed these into chemical products for domestic and export markets. By 1900, the Paris World Fair's catalogue exclaimed that BASF possessed "without question the largest chemical factory in the world."[3]

Engelhorn's contemporary François Blanc had different passions. As children, François and his twin brother Louis were fascinated by the card tricks of a traveling circus magician who visited their hometown in Southern France. They decided to join the circus as the magician's assistants, learned the trade, and came to work at the Marseille casino and other gambling houses. By 1834 they had earned enough money to move to Bordeaux, where they, among others, speculated in bonds at the local stock exchange. They set up an ingenious scheme. The rates of French government bonds on the Paris Bourse came to Bordeaux by mail coach. Fellow speculators such as the Rothschilds, François would later remind the jury at his trial, used messengers, carrier pigeons, and windmill signals to beat the official information channels.[4] The brothers, for their part, bribed an operator at a state optical telegraph office in Tours on the Paris–Bordeaux line. An accomplice in Paris sent the operator in Tours a white or grey glove by coach, signifying whether the bond rates went up or down. The operator then secretly added signals to official government telegraph messages. Accomplices in the Bordeaux telegraph office decoded this hidden information, and the Blancs cashed in their information advantage on the Bordeaux stock exchange.

The police discovered the hacking of state telegraph services in 1836 and arrested the Blancs. Their trial boosted existing anti-speculation sentiments; summarizing the mood of the day, one Member of Parliament exclaimed that private use of telegraphy would only serve "to rob those who do not have news of the Paris Bourse."[5] François and Louis countered that "no one was robbed. We fought our opponents with lawful weapons only," for no law explicitly prohibited their use of the state telegraph network.[6] They got away, only paying the trial costs. While legislators repaired the legislative loophole, the Blancs used their earnings to set up casinos in Paris, Luxembourg, and Bad Homburg, before they were headhunted by Princess Maria Caroline of Monaco. When Engelhorn founded BASF, the Blancs inaugurated their Monte Carlo casino and ignited Monaco's gambling boom; François became widely celebrated as "the Magician of Monte Carlo."

For all their differences, Friedrich Engelhorn and François Blanc were both economic system-builders. The previous chapter explored how food system-builders constructed Europe's food economy through transport infrastructure (using energy and telecommunications as auxiliary networks only). In a similar fashion, Engelhorn and other chemical system-builders built a vast industry "on top of" Europe's energy infrastructure, which they also altered in the process. Their production and distribution systems accessed foreign and domestic sources of fossil fuel hydrocarbons (coal, later oil and gas), fed these to factories for transformation into an ever increasing range of products, and distributed these to domestic and export markets.[7] Latching on to Europe's energy geography, they fashioned new layers of processed hydrocarbon flows that would ultimately pervade the human habitat with fossil fuel-based chemicals such as dyes, explosives, fertilizers, detergents, pesticides, cosmetics, plastics, anti-freeze, pharmaceuticals, vitamins, and foods.

The Blanc brothers' telegraph scam hints at a similar entanglement of communication infrastructure and the making of Europe's financial systems. Financial system-builders from the Rothschilds to present-day banks and High Frequency Traders used information and communication technology (ICT) links to hook up financial sector nodes such as bourses, banks, brokers, and investors. Later followed automatic salary payment systems connecting employers and employees, PIN machines in shops, automated teller machines in streets, home banking, and more. Through information and communication infrastructure they built the financial transaction systems that came to carry Europe's value flows.

The fossil fuel-based organic chemical industry became a cornerstone of Europe's so-called industrial "real economy." The ICT-based "financial economy" facilitated, reflected, and occasionally undermined that real economy. This chapter traces the making of infrastructure-based geographies of connection and rupture in both types of economy.

Coal & Chemicals

Most histories of the organic chemical industry focus on scientific discoveries and business strategies. It is in its energy-based economic system-building, however, that we find the spatial configuring of Europe's chemical economy. Up to the First World War, BASF and other Rhine valley firms such as Bayer (then *Farbenfabriken vormals Friedr. Bayer & Co*) and Hoechst dominated Europe's coal-based dyestuff economy. To understand the shaping of their prewar production and distribution systems, let us take a closer look at the biggest player.

Food system-builders had connected fields, factories, stores, shops, and kitchens by means of transport links. So, too, Engelhorn and his technical directors built the BASF production system by connecting plants through hydrocarbon fuel flows. In the history of chemical technology, the concept of a chemical "complex" denotes dense local flows of chemicals where products and by-products from one factory serve as raw materials for the next. In the dawning age of organic chemistry, Engelhorn and his collaborators set up such a large dyestuff production complex in Ludwigshafen, right

Fig. 4.1 Chemical System-Building: *The BASF factory complex at Ludwigshafen, Germany, in 1881, as painted by Robert Friedrich Stieler. Rhine barges and rail wagons bought in German, Belgian, French, and even British coal and coal tar as energy sources and raw materials. By 1900 a multitude of on-site animal and hand carts, conveyor belts, and 46 km of local railroad moved coal, tar, intermediate, and final products among over 400 buildings on 32 hectares of factory premises. Finally, processed hydrocarbons— intermediate or finished products—left the factory for consumers worldwide.*

across the Rhine River from Mannheim. They first built plants for producing auxiliary inorganic chemicals such as sulphuric acid, nitric acid, soda, caustic soda, sulphate, hydrochloric acid, and calcium chloride. These fed into core production lines constructed next. Ten buildings housed the extraction of benzene from coal tar, originally supplied by the Mannheim gas works, and its subsequent transformation into aniline and aniline dyes. By 1870 a second product line extracted anthracene from coal-tar to produce alizarin dyes, starting with the synthetic duplication of natural red madder (a favorite Victorian color). In the following decades tar-aniline-azo dye and tar-naphthalene-indigo sections followed. By 1900 over 6,000 employees worked in well over 400 buildings on 32 hectares (over 100 acres) of factory premises, excluding the neighboring worker housing. Interconnecting these buildings, animal and hand carts, conveyor belts, and 46 kilometres of local railroad moved coal, tar, inorganic inputs, and intermediate and final products around the premises. Other local infrastructure included new on-site gas, electricity, water, and heat works and their distribution systems; all were fired with coal, which simultaneously served as feedstock and fuel. Half a century later, in the era of petrochemicals, a multitude of local oil and oil product pipelines would follow.[8] Meanwhile BASF expanded from dyestuffs into other product lines and complexes. Fertilizer demand inspired the establishment of the Oppau works next to Ludwigshafen in 1913, and from 1916 a huge complex at Leuna in Eastern Germany turned local brown coal into explosives.

In addition to dense flows of (processed) hydrocarbons in local chemical complexes, BASF system-builders reached outward. Mannheim had become the Rhine river head and a well-connected railroad junction; BASF Ludwigshafen eventually drew most of its hydrocarbon inputs from the Ruhr coal region by waterway, from the Saarland coal region by rail, and from British, Belgian, and French coal tar exporters by combined transport. Underscoring the fossil fuel basis of its production system, BASF purchased the *Auguste Victoria* hardcoal mine in the Ruhr region in 1907, and the *A. Riebeck'sche Montanwerke AG* lignite quarries and tar production facilities near Leuna in 1925. Later in the twentieth century, BASF's transport-based hydrocarbon flows would be supplemented by dedicated long-distance oil, naphtha, and ethylene pipelines from North Sea and Mediterranean harbors and natural gas pipelines from Dutch, German, and Siberian gas fields.[9] Next to mobilizing long-distance hydrocarbon feedstock networks for inputs, BASF used transport networks to export processed hydrocarbons—both intermediate and final products. By the 1880s the textile industries in the United Kingdom, United States, Russia, France, and the Austria-Hungarian Empire were BASF's main export markets. These product flows constituted yet another layer in Europe's hydrocarbon geography. Incoming and outgoing flows of raw and processed hydrocarbons were its core business, but the company also mobilized transport infrastructure for a vast trade in auxiliary inorganic chemicals. Lime came in from the Rhine valley, pyrites from Spain, and China-gallen from China. Nitrated salts (saltpetre) arrived from Chile, until BASF started on-site extraction of nitrogen from the air, using the so-called Haber-Bosch process at the Ludwigshafen-Oppau works in 1913.

Combining dense local production complexes with European and global outreach, BASF had prefigured the "glocal" production system that sociologists today associate with the network society. Together with similar production systems of competitors such as Bayer and Hoechst, it carried over 80 percent of world production and 90 percent of world trade in synthetic dyes by 1913. Europe's prewar dyestuffs economy was highly international: no less than three-quarters of all artificial dyestuffs moved across national borders to export markets.[10] This, however, was about to change.

Fragmented Fabrication

The First World War greatly challenged this German-centric, export-oriented economic geography. Industries and governments from Britain to the Soviet Union and from Denmark to Italy sought to cut their dependence on Germany and build national chemical economies. The largest dye user, Britain's huge textile industries, had become largely dependent on German imports after Perkin and other pioneers had retired in the 1870s. British coal-tar producers exported their raw material to Germany instead. By 1913 Britain imported no less than 80 percent of its synthetic dyes. Yet the war turned dye production into a strategic asset, for intermediates could easily be diverted to explosives manufacturing. Trinitrotoluene (TNT) is a nitrified cyclical hydrocarbon just like aniline; dynamite is a simpler nitrified hydrocarbon. In Germany the Ludwigshafen-Oppau complex had already converted to explosives production. For this reason it became one of the first air raid targets ever when French aircraft bombed the factory premises on May 27, 1915. In Britain the national government now merged a number of chemical firms into British Dyes Ltd, injected £1.7 million, and converted plants to explosives production. After the war the industry further consolidated into the British Dyestuffs Corporation in 1919 and the Imperial Chemical Industries (ICI) in 1926, which soon dominated the domestic market. The British government further supported national chemical system-building with the 1920 Dyestuffs Act, prohibiting all synthetic dyestuffs or intermediates imports for ten years, except under Board of Trade licence. Its interpretation as a military measure overruled free trade sentiments in Parliament. Throughout the 1920s the government ignored the furious textile dyers lobby for cheaper German products, and repeatedly extended the import prohibition. Practically all British colonies banned German dyestuffs too and helped ICI to build an imperial monopoly. Britain had secured its organic chemical industry fed by British coal. The share of domestic production in British dyestuffs consumption increased from a mere 20 percent in 1914 to over 90 percent by 1928.[11]

In mainland Europe, chemical border-building and domestic chemical system-building also proliferated. French Armaments Minister Albert Thomas and Trade Minister Etienne Clémentel banned German dyes, and pushed cooperation of the domestic dye industries in the syndicate that later became the *Centrale des Matières Colorantes* (CMC). After the war, French chemical engineers believed that the annexed Saarland coal mines would underwrite national hydrocarbon self-sufficiency. The Italian government banned German dyestuffs and stimulated the *Industria Nazionale Colori di Anilina* in Milan (later absorbed by *Montecatini*). Spain got its *Sociedad Espanola de Productos Quimicos* in Barcelona. In Czechoslovakia the *Aussiger Verein* expanded from inorganic chemicals into carbochemistry, and the new Soviet leaders established a Bureau for Aniline Manufacture in 1918 that soon controlled seven factories. Danish university professors Peter Esch Raaschou and Einar Biilmann aimed at a national dyestuffs industry based on tar from urban gas works, and set up their first factory near Copenhagen; similarly, Dutch university professor and factory director Gerrit Hondius Boldingh organized the Netherlandish Dyestuffs Factory (*Nederlandsche Kleurstoffen Fabriek*), processing coal-tar from domestic gas works as well as oil derivates from the oil company Royal Dutch/Shell. In Switzerland and Germany, finally, dyestuffs manufacturers started to collaborate in national syndicates (so-called *Interessen Gemeinschaften*). In Germany, for instance, the lead firms joined forces in a syndicate and in 1925 amalgamated into the *IG Farben* group. Whether by national cooperation or merger, nation-centered system-builders pushed Europe's chemical economy toward national flows based—if possible—on domestic fossil fuels (Switzerland, Denmark, and Italy at the time did not mine coal). As for the final products, national border-building and domestic system-building reduced the share of all dyestuffs exported from three-quarters in 1913 to one-third in the interwar years.[12]

And yet, interwar chemical system-builders produced a different space of flows than Europe's food system-builders did. Whereas a multitude of fields, farms, and factories fed Europe's food economy, just a few giant local complexes located near major coal deposits remained the undisputed centers of gravity for Europe's chemical geography. Moreover, Europe's major chemical companies managed to prevent the almost complete splintering along national lines that happened in Europe's food economy. They were particularly concerned by the buzz of activity causing overproduction, competition, and price drops: "Today the dye making capacity of the world is nearly four times in excess of the world's present requirements," noted the chairman of the British Dyestuffs Corporation in 1925.[13] The German, Swiss, British, and French initiatives fared fairly well, but other national projects disappointed or collapsed. In Denmark, Raaschou and Biilmann's company could not compete on the overcrowded world market. By the late 1920s they sold their tar to road and roof builders instead. Soviet planners chose vast additional imports from Germany to supply their domestic market; only in the 1930s did Stalin's five year plans aim at chemical self-sufficiency. In Czechoslovakia the *Aussiger Verein* produced merely 5 percent of domestic dyestuffs consumption by the mid-1920s; the rest was imported, mostly from Germany. In the Netherlands, Boldingh also found it difficult to compete on the flooded world market. Besides, German dye manufacturers sabotaged his initiative by secret deals with Dutch textile producers and stock purchases, which gave them influence on the boards of directors. Boldingh gave up in the early 1930s and sold his factory equipment to his German competitors.

It is telling that Royal Dutch/Shell, a few decades later the largest petrochemical corporation worldwide, could have saved this last national project but chose not to do so. By 1906 its researchers had discovered that unsalable heavy Borneo oil contained hydrocarbons similar to coal tar. By 1909 the company shipped Borneo oil to a new refinery in Rotterdam, moved toluene-rich distillates by Rhine tanker to its new factory near Düsseldorf within the German tax barriers, and there synthesized nitrified toluene for German dye producers. During the war Royal Dutch/Shell produced explosives in England and France, while its researchers mapped potential chemical product lines derived from petroleum instead of coal. After 1918 Royal Dutch/Shell directors felt quite sympathetic to national projects that aimed to become "independent from the German dye monopoly, the more so as...petroleum derivates can be used as starting material."[14] However, company president Henry Deterding anticipated postwar overproduction and protectionism, and judged the Dutch home market too small to proceed at full speed. Royal Dutch/Shell chose to participate only marginally in Boldingh's national dyestuffs project.

Moreover, when the Royal Dutch/Shell board finally did make a full chemical turn in 1927, it largely bypassed the home market. Its chemical enthusiasm targeted the booming demand for artificial fertilizer, which Royal Dutch/Shell engineers could produce by binding hydrogen from oil to nitrogen from the air. Negotiations on cooperation with BASF failed, especially after BASF President Carl Bosch threatened to "kill the world's oil industries" as his company had previously killed the natural dyestuffs industries. The Dutch–British company was not deterred: "I expect we shall be just as important in the chemical industry as we are in the oil industry," wrote technical director Guus Kessler, "We have got the money, the best raw material, and the best geographical position."[15] This "best geographical position" referred to Royal Dutch/Shell's global oil system instead of a protected national market in a small European country. Apart from a few pilot plants, its first chemical complex emerged near the Shell refinery in Martinez, California, transforming natural and refinery gas into fertilizers, solvents, and pesticides.

As a result of these chemical system-builder choices, quarrels, and fortunes, Europe's interwar organic chemicals economy came to center on production and distribution by a handful of very large companies. Their large home markets explain the statistical dominance of domestic flows in organic chemicals movements. From the late 1920s these players further consolidated their position through cartel agreements. For the most profitable product group, dyestuffs, German IG Farben and French CMC agreed to pool research, profits, and production in 1927. The Swiss joined in 1929, British ICI in 1932. Each partner in this so-called Four Party Cartel held priority in its home market. Cartel partners had preferential access to any remaining domestic demand. The group also coordinated exports, used its joint power to wage price battles with competitors, and set up subsidiaries abroad. For instance, cartel partners controlled half of Poland's dye production, and bound the remaining companies to fixed production volumes and market shares. Competitors succumbed, such as Boldingh's Dutch initiative, or accepted binding contracts, such as the Polish companies. The Czechoslovakian *Aussiger Verein* was the last competitor in Central Europe to negotiate a production and sales agreement with the cartel. In the 1930s, cartel-members came to control 65 percent of world dye production directly and almost 70 percent including third party contracts, and 90 percent of world exports. Internally, the cartel distributed 66 percent of its sales to IG Farben, 17 percent to the Swiss IG, 8.5 percent to the French CMC, and 8.5 percent to British ICI; the German manufacturers were its undisputed leaders.[16] In terms of systems and flows, the cartel's production and distribution machinery fed German, French, and British coal into local factory complexes creating products exported to European and global dyestuffs markets, supplemented by (sub)national flows based on indigenous coal in several countries. Similar system-building processes governed other product groups.

Cold War Chemicals

The Second World War and its immediate aftermath overrode cartel agreements and initially stimulated self-sufficient national chemical economies. It was to secure chemical autarky that IG Farben and the Reich Ministry of Economics set up the infamous chemical complex *Buna Werke* in Auschwitz in occupied Poland, using local coal and slave labor to produce synthetic oil, rubber, and explosives for the war economy at a seemingly safe distance from British airstrikes. After the war, the new Allied rulers dissolved IG Farben into its original (West German) founder companies, which were separated from their Eastern complexes and lignite fields. The Russian occupation authorities transferred BASF's Leuna complex to the new East German state as the publicly owned enterprise *VEB Leuna-Werke "Walter Ulbricht,"* named after the new country's leader. The Polish state turned the Auschwitz complex into the state company *Chemiewerke Oświęcim*. The Czechoslovak state took over the *Aussiger Verein* complexes. In line with the autarky policies of their governments, these state companies aimed at national, self-sufficient production and distribution systems. In the Soviet Union, finally, the Autonomous Soviet Socialist Republics of Bashkiria and Tataristan held the Soviet Union's largest oil reserves known at the time. When the invading Nazi army in 1942 targeted Soviet oil production at Baku in the Azerbaijan SSR, the Soviet State Defence Committee transferred eleven thousand oil workers and trainloads of equipment from Baku to this inland region, henceforward known as the Union's "Second Baku." Here, large petrochemical complexes emerged at Ufa and Salavat in Bashkiria and at Kazan and Nizhnekamsk in Tatarstan, which expanded rapidly in the 1950s.[17]

From the mid-1950s, however, Comecon challenged this national fragmentation of the chemical industry. The organization set up a permanent commission for the chemical industry in 1956. Moreover, at its tenth congress in Prague on December 18, 1958, the vice-chairmen of the GDR, Hungarian, and Polish State Planning Commissions, the Soviet State Committee for Foreign Economic Relations, and the Czechoslovak Foreign Trade Ministry agreed on the 3,840 km Druzhba oil pipeline, mentioned in chapter 2. The 'friendship' pipeline was to do more than energy transport. It also would facilitate Khrushchev's plan "to create an integrated chemical industry throughout the Communist world."[18] East-Central Europe's chemical industries would be recast along this shared fossil fuel infrastructure, which would feed Second Baku oil into an array of petrochemical complexes that would supply products to domestic markets.

Back home, the relevant state committees embedded their shares of the pipeline and chemical production complexes in their national three, five, or seven year plans. In the Soviet Union, for instance, the Central Committee of the Communist Party developed, in the words of a *Pravda* journalist, a "grandiose plan for the chemicalization of the U.S.S.R. national economy as new proof of the might of the Land of Soviets and its enormous successes in the development of the socialist economy."[19] The Druzhba combined international hydrocarbon flows with such national "chemicalization" programs. It is an excellent example of the two-way interplay between energy and chemical system-building.

On its way from Second Baku to Central Europe, the Druzhba pipeline first fed new complexes within the Soviet Union. For instance, a 960 km Northern branch line to the Baltic Sea would supply a new petrochemical complex in Polotsk, Belarus. On its way west, the Druzhba hydrocarbon backbone split into a Northern and a Southern branch. The Polish Council of Ministers erected a new petrochemical complex at Plock, where the Northern branch crossed the Vistula River. The complex had refineries and plants for plastics, artificial fibres (viscose, rayon, acrylic), and synthetic rubber. From Plock the northern pipeline further extended across the border to Schwedt in the German Democratic Republic. In addition, the state built an oil harbor at Rostock for seaborne oil imports. Initially rail tankers carried oil from the harbor and the Druzhba end station to the Leuna chemical complex, but soon the domestic Rostock–Schwedt (1969) and Schwedt–Leuna (1974) pipelines replaced them. Along the Southern Druzhba branch, similarly, the Hungarian state built huge petrochemical complexes at Leninvaros

**Fig. 4.2
Chemicalization of the Comecon:** *In the postwar decades, oil replaced coal as Europe's lead energy source. Chemical system-builders now recast the organic chemical industry along oil infrastructure lines. Western chemical companies built complexes near major sea ports to tap into Europe's maritime oil infrastructure. Eastern European system-builders, by contrast, made the new* Druzhba *(friendship) oil pipeline the backbone of their chemical system. The world's longest pipeline fed oil from the Tartarstan and Samara oil fields to refineries and chemical complexes in most Comecon member states. The photo shows the control panel of the Druzhba pipeline near Almetyevsk in 1971.*

in the east and at Százhalombatta outside Budapest. The southern Druzhba then extended westward into Czechoslovakia to feed the Bratislava refinery that had hitherto run on local oil, as well as the Prague and northwestern chemical complexes, replacing local lignite as feedstock. Outside the Druzhba reach, Romanian planners expected to be self-sufficient in oil for another fifteen years or so to supply their petrochemical complexes. The Bulgarian government opted to feed its petrochemical industry with oil delivered to the country's Black Sea ports.[20]

In the following decades this East-Central European geography of a common long-distance raw materials and energy backbone, local petrochemical complexes, and national markets developed further. The emerging natural gas infrastructure provided an additional long-distance supply line. From the early 1970s the Bratstvo (brotherhood) gas pipeline provided Siberian gas to Central European complexes. When oil and gas yields fell in Second Baku, managers transferred Siberian gas by rail and pipe to the Tartarstan and Bashkiria complexes.[21] Moreover, Comecon partners added a regional dimension to this chemical geography. Ethylene (C_2H_4) is a light gaseous refinery product and base chemical for polyethylene and PVC. Comecon engineers believed it an "economical necessity" to pool this important resource between petrochemical complexes up to a few hundred kilometers apart. In 1971 the East German and Czechoslovak governments agreed to connect Leuna to Czechoslovakian petrochemical complexes by a 150 km ethylene pipeline. The Hungarian and Soviet governments also invested in a 350 km ethylene pipeline to supply the Kalush plant in western Ukraine from the Hungarian Leninvaros complex. When Kalush received an ethylene plant of its own in 1987, ethylene flows reversed from Ukraine to Hungary. In the Soviet Union, such micro-regional infrastructure crossed internal state borders between the Tartaristan and Bashkiria complexes. Thus, concluded Czechoslovakian engineer Jan Pantoflicek, "it has been clearly demonstrated that the development of petrochemistry... cannot be achieved individually ... The current ethylene-based petrochemical developments in Eastern Europe serve as an example of... a broader economic integrative program among Comecon members."[22]

In Western Europe, a similar shift from coal to oil stirred up the chemical industry's economic geography. To keep foreign currency expenses down while oil imports rapidly went up, governments and Marshall planners promoted crude oil refining near European harbors rather than in countries of origin. Oil and chemical companies responded to this trend by establishing petrochemical complexes near a number of new or upgraded waterside refineries—in Marseille, Barcelona, Sicily, and Sardinia in the Mediterranean and Le Havre, Antwerp, Rotterdam, and Teesside at the Channel and North Sea. In 1960 alone, petrochemical plant construction in Europe as a whole grew by a staggering 41 percent.[23] While East-Central Europe's organic chemical industry reoriented to Second Baku oil, Western Europe's industry latched itself onto its overseas oil supply network.

Of these new complexes, Rotterdam–Antwerp became the largest by far. It was to petrochemistry what BASF Ludwigshafen had been to carbochemistry. Unlike Ludwigshafen, however, many system-builders joined forces to build this huge complex. Immediately after the war, which had left Rotterdam in ruins, the Rotterdam municipality teamed up with Royal Dutch/Shell and the Dutch national government. The municipality endorsed industrialization to reduce the vulnerability of harbor incomes to trade flow changes. It expanded Rotterdam's facilities with large oil terminals in the new *Europoort* in the late 1950s. The national government

Fig. 4.3 The Rotterdam–Antwerp Chemical Complex: *In the age of oil, Europe's petrochemical system builders used pipelines to connect oil terminals, refineries, and a multitude of chemical plants and complexes into vast transnational chemical industry systems. The cross-border industrial zone between the Rotterdam and Antwerp harbors became one of the world's largest chemical complexes. By 1970 its crude oil, naphtha, ethylene, chlorine, and oxygen pipelines interconnected harbor terminals and over seventy plants and complexes (which in turn consisted of many plants) from over thirty chemical companies. High-capacity pipelines linked this complex to other Western European chemical complexes.*

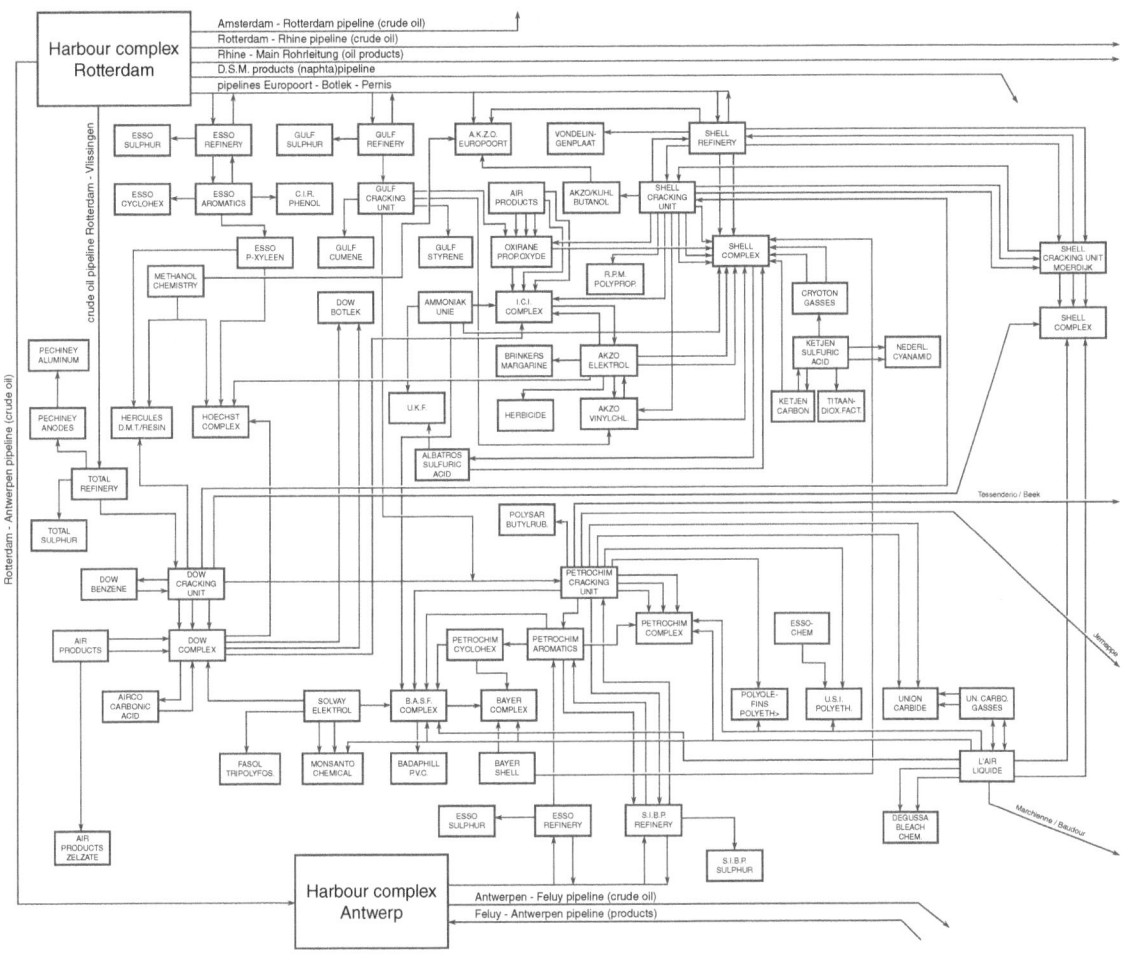

saw a high-value chemical export sector as a boost to the national economy, and subsidized chemical plant construction. Royal Dutch/Shell directors applied their California experiences to petrochemical complexes elsewhere in the U.S. and in the Netherlands, U.K., France, Germany, Canada, and Australia. In Rotterdam the company built a vast refinery and plants for synthetic detergents and vinyl chloride, a basic ingredient for PVC plastics. By the late 1950s Shell's Rotterdam output had expanded to over a thousand products for the Western European market.

Meanwhile Frans Posthuma, a future Municipal Port Authority director, had visited the United States and concluded that Rotterdam should attract American oil and chemical companies as well. The municipality and national government then lured foreign companies to Rotterdam with promises of cheap building sites, modern harbor facilities, tax advantages, and premium access to the projected European Economic Community market. From the mid-1950s American corporations such as Dow Chemical, DuPont, ESSO Chemical, Hercules, and Gulf constructed refineries and chemical plants near Rotterdam. Soon followed British ICI and industries from EEC partner countries, for whom the presence of other chemical companies and their (waste) products was a key location factor. By the early 1970s railroads and crude oil, naphtha, ethylene, chlorine, and oxygen pipelines interconnected harbors and over seventy plants and complexes (which in turn consisted of multiple production facilities) of over thirty chemical companies in the cross-border region between the Rotterdam and Antwerp harbors. The Dutch government financed a 72 km long, 100 m wide 'pipeline street' from Rotterdam to Antwerp as a chemical infrastructure backbone. The Rotterdam–Antwerp micro-regional, cross-border, multi-company production system turned overseas oil into thousands of products for the EEC market. From the late 1960s Dutch natural gas from the Slochteren fields became an important feedstock as well.[24]

By then, incumbent industries in the German and Swiss Rhine valley had also switched their inland complexes to oil. Coal had stagnated in Europe's fuel economy, and the coal industry could no longer supply sufficient quantities of tar. Thus, BASF general manager Bernhard Timm concluded in the early 1960s that "oil is our chemical raw material; coal and oil are the two raw materials for our energy supply."[25] His and other companies had already teamed up with oil giants to tap into Europe's overseas oil flows. In early 1959 Esso, British Petroleum, and several chemical companies opened the 391 km North-West oil pipeline (*Nord-West Ölleitung*) connecting the Wilhelmshaven North Sea harbor to refineries in the Rhine-Ruhr area—with massive financial support from the German federal government. Royal Dutch/Shell and its collaborators opened their own high capacity, 263 km Rotterdam–Ruhr pipeline in 1960 to deliver cheap supplies to Shell's German plants and other clients. BASF and the Swiss chemical firms teamed up with Esso, Shell and others in the Southern European Pipeline (*Pipeline Sud-Européen*), connecting the oil harbors of Marseille to French, Swiss, and German plants by 1963. Later followed the Central European Pipeline from

Fig. 4.4 BASF in the Age of Oil: *The BASF Ludwigshafen complex today is structured around "pipeline streets," which connect some 250 production plants (next to hundreds of research labs, technical centers, and offices).*

Genoa and the Trans-Alpine Pipeline from Trieste, as well as a number of gas pipelines. Illustratively, in 1968 BASF acquired the gas company *Wintershall* to access German natural gas. By way of cooperation, oil companies and chemical manufacturers also constructed an ethylene pipeline network connecting Rotterdam, Antwerp, and the main German chemical companies a few years before its East-Central European counterparts.[26]

From the late 1960s oil, gas, and ethylene pipelines criss-crossed the area between Rotterdam, Le Havre, Ludwigshafen, and the Ruhr that became known as the "chemical square of Europe," providing roughly 50 percent of Western Europe's petrochemical production in 1980.[27] Contrary to the East-Central European production system that refined Russian oil into products for national users, the chemical square transformed overseas oil and Dutch and German natural gas into products for the European Economic Community market.

Compared to these integration efforts within both the Eastern and Western block, connections between the two remained scarce.

Even the nearby petrochemical sites in Vienna and Bratislava did not cooperate. They drew oil from the Transalpine and the Druzhba pipelines respectively, and did not exchange ethylene.

There were a few notable breaches in the Iron Curtain though. In the North, the Finnish state oil company *Neste* built a large ethylene plant next to its Porvoo refinery on the Gulf of Finland to process Soviet crude oil in the early 1970s. In Central Europe, BASF connected its Ludwigshafen operations to the Comecon gas pipeline system in the mid-1970s. In the Balkans, Yugoslavia pragmatically built connections to Comecon and OECD partners. In the early 1970s the Yugoslavian, Hungarian, Czechoslovakian, Polish, and Austrian governments negotiated an oil pipeline from the Adriatic coast to their refineries and chemical complexes; in the end the Adria Pipeline only supplied Yugoslavia's new Pančevo complex (known for the NATO bombing in 1999 that released toxic chemicals on civilian populations) and its counterparts in Százhalombatta, Hungary and Timișoara, Romania. Simultaneously the Greek-American Thomas A. Pappas lobbied the Greek dictatorship for a pipeline connecting his Thessaloniki refineries to a refinery and petrochemical facilities in Skopje in Yugoslavian Macedonia. Greek officials declined, fearing, then as now, Macedonian claims on Thessaloniki. Pappas railwayed oil into Yugoslavia nevertheless. After the Cold War and Yugoslavian wars, the Greek state company Hellenic Oil bought the Skopje refinery and completed the pipeline.[28] Thanks to these and other breaches in the Iron Curtain, chemicals made up about 7 percent of total East European exports to the West and 17 percent of total West European exports to the East during the period 1965 to 1980. In stark contrast with the next case, financial systems, this East–West trade in chemicals was much larger than the transatlantic trade.[29]

Nonetheless, the chemical East–West cleavage persists today. After the Cold War, chemical system-builders established a few East–West connections, including Dow's ethylene pipeline from the German North Sea to Leuna in 2003. In the same year the Association of European Petrochemicals Producers, after years of lobbying, managed to get an ethylene and propylene pipeline program into the European Union's Trans-European Energy Networks plan. This feat once more underscores the entanglement of energy and chemical system-building. Yet the EU Parliament felt that public money should benefit electricity and gas rather than industrial hydrocarbon infrastructure. Ten years later, the feedstock part of the TEN energy program was still on hold.[30]

Capital & Communications

The making of Europe's "real economy," of which the chemical industry became a cornerstone, intimately intertwined with the construction of a transnational "financial economy." For one, the booming financial system increasingly counted as an indicator of the state of the real economy. "Stocks and bonds have come to represent the wealth of the world," noted University of Pennsylvania Professor of Insurance and Commerce Solomon S. Huebner by 1910; "our stock exchange markets may be said to represent the pulse of our economic life."[31] Moreover, financial services increasingly facilitated and occasionally undermined the expanding real economy. Nineteenth-century financial markets provided funds and investors to much of the world's railroad, water works, gas, electricity, telegraphy, and telephony infrastructure. The same goes for food supply, the chemical industry, and other economic systems. The Mannheim bank *W.H. Ladenburg and Söhne* helped Engelhorn to incorporate BASF as a limited liability company in 1865, raising 1.4 million guilders from shareholders to create the Ludwigshafen-based production and distribution system. Later, BASF and Europe's other chemical companies repeatedly issued shares to finance expansion. Even in the Soviet Union, where a free capital market was first restricted and later abolished, economists vigorously debated how their state-regulated financial system could channel funds into the chemicalization of the Soviet Union, for "under the conditions of socialism, finance [serves] material production."[32] Throughout Europe and beyond, financial services intertwined with the development of infrastructure and industry. They were a core constituent of Europe's infrastructure transition. And, from the Blanc brothers' scam to present-day High Frequency Trading, information and communication infrastructure was at the heart of financial system-building.

Of all financial services, speedy communication was most critical to the capital market, where governments and firms raise long-term funds by issuing securities such as bonds and stock. Transferable securities date back to the medieval Italian city states; and since the sixteenth century national governments have introduced permanent national debts to fund expensive projects, especially wars. Investors could henceforward trade transferable government bonds among themselves, while government loans and interest payments shifted the burden of warfare to future generations. In the early seventeenth century the Dutch and English East India Companies pioneered a similar financing scheme for joint stock companies.

By the 1820s, national debt and private equity had inspired a flourishing business of professional mediation between buyers and sellers. Stock exchanges proliferated, and securities traders from the Rothschilds to the Blanc brothers connected these exchanges by mail coaches, messengers, carrier pigeons, and optic telegraphy. Legally or illegally, knowingly or unknowingly, they aligned prices between different markets. Prior to the electric telecommunications revolution, the Amsterdam and London stock exchanges followed each other's price movements with a three-day delay; news of French government *rentes* took twelve hours to get to London.

At that time, however, international capital flows were still minor. National stock exchanges traded overwhelmingly in domestic government debt. Even at the London Stock Exchange, the future center of international finance, 70 percent of the trades involved British government bonds still in 1853; domestic railroads made up another 16 percent. Furthermore, a large and growing number of local exchanges brought local investors together with local canal, gas, water, mining, and railroad companies. These functioned largely independently of each other, their national exchange, and the wider world.[33]

From the 1840s, however, financial system-builders increasingly mobilized electric communications to tightly integrate and expand capital markets. London traders were particularly successful at accessing trade in any local, national, or foreign asset of sufficient size and profitability. Indeed, London soon became the undisputed center of global telecommunications as well as the global capital market. This powerful entanglement survived the demise of Great Britain as a superpower; still today financial experts perceive London as the financial "navel of the world."[34]

Following expansion of the telecommunications network, London traders first reached out to British provincial town exchanges.[35]

By the late 1840s telegraph lines connected all major British cities; stock exchanges now hosted telegraph offices in or next to their buildings, and exchange owners and traders lobbied for direct connections between exchange buildings that bypassed public telegraph offices. By 1870 the London Stock Exchange had eleven such dedicated lines to provincial exchanges. By 1899 sixty dedicated lines carried a staggering 28,142 telegrams per working day. Inside the exchange building, pneumatic tubes linked the trading floor to the telegraph office.

Starting with the 1851 Channel cable and the 1866 permanent transatlantic cable, London securities traders also teamed up with the Post Office, telegraph companies, and news agencies to rapidly expand international financial trade. In the 1850s London financiers, bankers, and merchants petitioned the House of Lords for a British global telegraph network. Once constructed, stockbrokers became a lead user group. Firms such as the Anglo-American Telegraph Company and the Commercial Cable Company opened stations in the London exchange and operated connections to the New York Stock Exchange, an increasingly important trade partner.

As for news agencies, Paul Julius Reuter operated a Paris–Berlin carrier pigeon link that beat financial news exchanges by mail train. However, his pigeons were no match for the new Paris–Berlin telegraph line, and in 1851 Reuter moved to London to deal in financial news on the Channel telegraph cable. A large number of client subscriptions to this service allowed him to negotiate cheaper cable tariffs and develop a thriving business. In the 1860s the Reuter's Telegram Company Ltd circulated premium financial information to London stockbrokers, co-sponsored a French transatlantic cable, and built its own private cable from Britain to the German coast to access Asian financial information via the Germany–Turkey–India telegraph connection.

By the mid 1870s London stockbrokers could access a global telegraph network for financial news and deal with traders as far away as Australia, South Africa, and Latin America. Traffic between the London and New York exchanges dominated international financial contacts with some 4,000 telegrams per day by 1909. Another 3,000 messages served continental Europe, 90 percent of which covered the Berlin, Frankfurt, Paris, Amsterdam, and Brussels exchanges.

By then, brokers also used telephone lines to gain information advantages and to match buyers and sellers. In 1888 stockbrokers had collectively threatened to leave the London exchange unless it invested in premium telephone facilities; soon the exchange owners established public telephone connections to provincial stock exchanges as well as private leased lines, which London brokers kept open throughout the working day for instant and continuous communication. International telephone connections to Paris in 1891 and Brussels in 1903 expanded this practice to the Continent, where the Amsterdam, Rotterdam, Antwerp, Brussels, Bremen, Hamburg, and Berlin bourses had already been telephonically hooked up. Since only larger London firms could afford private leased lines, about ten brokerages increasingly dominated London's intermarket trading.[36]

Other stock exchanges followed the London example and became local, national, or international telecommunication hubs. In complex processes of competition and collaboration, these financial system-builders welded the world's exchanges into an impressive telecommunications-based capital market. By 1910, when our American observer Solomon Huebner noted that stocks and bonds represented the pulse of economic life, telecommunication links connected about 120 stock exchanges worldwide into an impressive transnational financial system. This eurocentric prewar operation counted over fifty exchanges in Europe and just under seventy in current and former colonies, divided about equally over North America, Latin America, Africa, Asia, and Australasia. Only a few existed outside the European diaspora, such as Japan's Tokyo and Osaka exchanges. Thus, concluded Huebner, "The modern systems of long distance telephony, telegraphy, and cabling...have made it possible for investors to trade on any of the above mentioned stock markets at will."[37]

The capital market was not a homogeneous space, however. First, its transnational geography was characterized by a particular mix of international, national, and local circulations. Huebner and his peers agreed that London was the undisputed global center. Financial traders around the world accessed the London Stock Exchange to buy or sell any asset of sufficient size or quality. Tellingly, the share of British government bonds in the London exchange trade had decreased from 70 percent in 1853 to merely 10 percent by 1913. Sales in colonial and foreign government debts had increased to 21

Fig. 4.5 Telegraphy at the Stock Exchange: *The entanglement of the capital market and the telegraph system is best illustrated by the so-called stock ticker—a telegraphic printer producing strips of paper containing alphabetic symbols for a particular company, followed by the price data for a recent transaction. It was used at stock exchanges and in investors' meeting places roughly between the late 1860s and 1960s. In this 1918 photo, young women operate stock exchange tickers and boards in the Waldorf-Astoria Hotel in New York City.*

percent, and (foreign and domestic) private equity accounted for no less than two-thirds. About half of the London trade was in foreign assets. Foreign securities also made up half of the trade at the Paris Bourse, which specialized in government bonds from continental Europe and the Mediterranean.

By contrast, foreign assets accounted for only 6 percent at the Berlin Bourse and 1 percent in Vienna. These were national components of the transnational system, as were the New York Stock

Exchange and a wide array of national exchanges from Madrid to St. Petersburg. Often their governments required them to focus on domestic assets in order to prevent unchecked capital outflow. This practice in turn drove investors to London and Paris for trading in foreign securities. Overall, around 1910 some 20 million investors worldwide held a nominal value in securities of over 32 billion pounds sterling; about 9 billion was international investment, indicating that in the ICT-based transnational financial system, most capital still circulated within national borders.

Within these boundaries, moreover, local exchanges continued to thrive. Even in Britain, London traders saw no need for centralization of the entire market, since they had telecom access to all provincial exchanges. Instead they set up a division of labor, in which local exchanges expanded their trade in local assets and specialties. Sheffield focused on engineering shares, Glasgow on iron and coal, Cardiff on shipping, and Liverpool on insurance. Austria-Hungary, France, Germany, Italy, and Russia each counted a handful of such local exchanges. In Spain the Barcelona and Bilbao exchanges served their local industries. In the Netherlands the Rotterdam Bourse did not manage to follow the success of its harbor. It existed as a local junction, but yielded the harbor's big business to the Amsterdam Bourse.[38]

Second, we may observe that Europe's financial space of flows reproduced local, continental, and global inequalities that also characterized Europe's telecommunications geography.[39] Even within leading telecommunications and financial hubs such as London, some quarters had premium access to financial services, while others were bypassed. On continental and global scales, the financial system echoed the Western European telecommunications bias. In all international financial trade, Western European investors owned a staggering 90 percent of the assets. British investors alone accounted for 40 percent. Their major targets were assets in the United States (16 percent), Russia and Canada (both 8 percent), and Argentina, Austro-Hungary, Spain, and Brazil (all between 8 and 5 percent). Capital moved structurally from Western Europe outward. For instance, British investors overwhelmingly financed the debts of the Canadian government, and owned virtually all the Canadian and Argentinean railroads so important to Europe's intercontinental food economy. French investors financed the Spanish and Russian infrastructure boom.

Capital & Crisis

Between roughly 1914 and 1970, this impressive transnational system splintered along national lines, as did Europe's food economy and, to a lesser (but substantial) extent, its chemical economy.

This change is remarkable because the prewar system seemed quite stable. The incidental "international contagion" of financial crises that telecommunications connections also carried, affected the overall system at most temporarily. The 1878 collapse of the large City of Glasgow Bank triggered the failure of a few smaller banks in Wales and England, but did not cause further disruption. Underscoring the tight infrastructure coupling of distant places, bank-runs in Argentina triggered the 1890 insolvency of Britain's oldest merchant bank, Baring Brothers, which again reverberated into the Argentina, Brazil, and Uruguay markets. Still, the Bank of England prevented further infection of the overall system as a lender of last resort. Barings survived another century until the days of Nick Leeson.

The New York panic of 1907 was the system's greatest challenge. A number of bankruptcies had already hit the New York Stock Exchange when United Copper Company directors attempted to drive up the price of their stock by aggressive buying. However, they did not control sufficient shares and stock prices dropped again. The speculators could not sell their expensive stock as planned and went bankrupt. Panicking creditors then withdrew their deposits from the many American trusts and banks that the bankrupted speculators controlled. These also collapsed. Exchange indices dropped by almost half, and commentators expected a major national economic depression.

However, the global capital market absorbed much of the shock: international telegraph connections delivered the liquidity that the American market lacked, buying American stakeholders time to organize a domestic rescue mission and restore investor confidence. While politicians and media, then as now, accused stock market speculators of immoral greed and endangering the real economy, financial system-builders explained that the transnational system had prevented, rather than caused, the crisis. Financial markets cushion shocks, they contended. Indeed, each and every day banks and firms in acute financial stress avert bankruptcy by instantly drawing funds from the telecommunications-based capital market: "What may seem so apparent in the case of important crises, it should be remembered, occurs almost daily in a less sensational way," noted Huebner in 1910.[40] To financial system-builders, populist politicians were the real danger to financial stability. If the government would curtail the London-centered capital market, warned London stock-jobbers Medwin & Lowy in 1909, "in time of financial stress those who are compelled to release securities would have no means of disposing of their holdings, and what might have been a temporary stringency could easily develop into an alarming crisis...the international character of the London market forms the safety-valve of financial disturbance."[41] Politicians and financial experts would continue to blame each other for financial crises, and continue to do so today.

Either way, the panic of 1907 did not crash the prewar transnational financial system. In the following decade, government initiatives did.[42] When Austria-Hungary declared war on Serbia on July 28, 1914, a shock wave hit the stock markets. Anticipating massive bond selling and ruin for investors, the Paris Bourse had partially suspended trade already on July 25. On July 28 panic sales triggered closure of the Madrid, Montreal, and Toronto exchanges. On July 29 Amsterdam, Antwerp, Berlin, Brussels, Budapest, Rome, Vienna and others followed. Among the last exchanges to stop trading were London, St. Petersburg, the South American markets, and Johannesburg.

A few years later Europe's governments reopened national stock exchanges under strict political control, particularly to raise funds for warfare. The capital market fragmented when government bonds flooded all domestic markets: the German national debt rose twenty-fold, the British ten-fold, the French and Italian debts five-fold. Large investors sold international securities to buy these domestic war bonds for financial or patriotic reasons, or because their governments obliged them to. This happened not only in belligerent Germany, France, Britain, and Greece, but also in neutral Spain, Sweden, and Norway. Many national exchanges banned non-national traders and securities. Government campaigns also lured small savers into war bonds. Financial border-builders and national system-builders ruled the day.

The infamous 1929 crash of the New York Stock Exchange illustrated several aspects of this new situation. After the war, the exchange had profited from national protectionism in Europe. The U.S. federal government had promoted national and international investment at the New York Stock Exchange, and American brokerages in London successfully exploited new transatlantic radio-telephony to offer British investors and brokers direct access to the New York exchange (as they would with transatlantic telephone cables in the 1950s). New York surpassed London as the global capital center.

In this context of tighter European national capital borders and the radiotelephonic flight of international trade across the Atlantic, the 1929 Wall Street crash hit hard. Politicians as usual blamed financial traders, while financial analysts saw the crash as a market correction of an American speculative bubble that was bound to occur. From a financial systems perspective, the difference with 1907 was the lack of a large global market to cushion financial shocks. Locally the crash therefore hit exceptionally hard: only in 1954 would the leading American stock market index Dow Jones Industrial Average regain its pre-1929 level. On the other hand, the prevalence of national borders in financial trade also implied limited contagion to Europe's stock markets. These experienced mild decline rather than steep collapse; 1929 did not represent a significant breaking point in the London Stock Exchange's performance.[43]

During the 1930s governments continued to cut international capital links and strengthen national financial circulation. In the 1910s and 1920s governments had paid for warfare, recovery, and war reparations by printing stacks of money, causing hyperinflation, and borrowing heavily from domestic banks, leaving banks low on reserves and vulnerable to payment failures by major customers. In response, governments increasingly protected domestic banks and currencies. In the summer of 1931 the Austrian and German governments reacted to major bank collapses by installing controls on capital and currency outflows. The British government also installed exchange controls: "this country is not in my judgment at present in a position to invest large sums at long-term in foreign countries," noted British Minister of Finance (and soon Prime Minister) Neville Chamberlain.[44] As other countries followed and the remaining international capital market collapsed, alliances between governments and domestic banks became the key elements of nationally-fragmented financial systems in Europe.

After the Second World War, the wave of infrastructure nationalizations on both sides of the Iron Curtain in effect moved railroad, telecommunication, and power company financing from capital markets to government budgets; this further shrank the capital market relative to state and bank financing. State-run programs such as the Marshall Aid program dominated international value flows. In tandem with these developments, central banks, domestic banking sectors, and post offices replaced stock exchanges in leading financial ICT innovation. By the mid-1960s they introduced automated cashless payment systems to serve financial traffic among domestic banking institutions. In the mass payments sector, banks also offered cashless wage and salary payment in the form of checks and electronic transfers.[45]

Finally, it is important to note that the remaining securities trade responded to the demise of the free capital market by strengthening national exchanges at the expense of local ones. The French and Belgian governments formed national broker companies to reduce domestic competition, and by the late 1970s the Paris Bourse handled 98 percent of all French trading. In Britain 22 local stock exchanges first consolidated into three regionals, before all British exchanges merged into the National Stock Exchange in 1973. The national exchange provided access for all brokers to all trading floors. In stark contrast to the pre-1914 system, provincial brokers now used telecommunications to centralize the remaining capital trade in London. As in France, British regional trading floors closed. In the Netherlands this happened after 1972. In Germany, Frankfurt came to dominate the more fragmented market.[46]

Capital in Cyberspace

On Monday, October 27, 1986, the so-called "Big Bang" at the London Stock Exchange catapulted Europe's leading capital market into yet another era. Following North America and preceding continental Europe, the London Stock Exchange liberalized, internationalized, and innovated. The change had been long in the making, and ICT infrastructure once more stood at center stage.

At the height of the national capital market fragmentation, banks and other institutional investors had sought ways to bypass national barriers. They for instance established multinational companies to access stock markets in different countries. New York's Merrill Lynch employed transatlantic communications to operate forty-eight overseas offices by 1972. Conversely, European banks such as *Crédit Suisse, Algemene Bank Nederland, Commerzbank,* and *Crédit Lyonnais* became members of the New York Stock Exchange via American subsidiaries. In addition, institutional investors pushed the integration of communications and computing into electronic trading systems to bypass physical stock exchanges altogether. In the U.S. Jerome Pustilnik and Herbert Behrens envisioned automatic, computer-mediated trading. They established Institutional Networks (Instinet) in 1969 as an electronic securities market directly connecting banks and insurance companies. In 1971 the U.S. National Association of Securities Dealers inaugurated its Automated Quotations system NASDAQ: by 1975 dedicated telephone links supplied the latest rates on computer screens to almost three thousand members, dispersed over nearly six thousand offices. They still did their actual trading, however, by telephone conversation. In response to the new competition, the New York Stock Exchange abolished minimum commissions, accepted foreign brokers as members, and installed its own electronic information system.[47]

In Britain, the London Stock Exchange preserved its information monopoly until the 1979 Thatcher government, in an attempt to revive the London financial sector and fuel economic growth, abolished exchange controls and demanded deregulation of the British capital market. Those negotiations resulted in the Big Bang: overnight the exchange ended minimum commissions, accepted foreign members, and inaugurated the Stock Exchange Automatic Quotation system SEAQ, which like NASDAQ combined on-screen prices with oral telephone trading. "Within five minutes of [the] Big Bang, on Monday morning, it was clear to me that the floor was dead. I'm not bragging. I was the last person in the City to figure it out!" confessed Anthony Abrahams, managing director of the leading jobber firm Smiths Brothers. An era of floor trading closed: "I was horrified. Horrified. Absolutely shattered. It had been a great club," noted James Capel's head of equities, John Wilson.[48] In Paris the *Commission des Operations de Bourse* followed London, engineered *le petit bang*, and introduced screen trading. The Amsterdam Exchange followed in 1988. German banks

Fig. 4.6 a+b Stocks in Cyberspace: *Electronic trading radically changed the spatial dynamics in stock exchange buildings. The image to the left shows the Amsterdam exchange's trading floor in 1938. The floor did not change much until the 1980s. The photo to the right shows the same trading floor after the introduction of computer-based trading in 1988.*

Fig. 4.6b

established their electronic trading system IBIS in 1989 outside the traditional stock exchanges. By then financial news information firms had activated satellite and FM radio transmissions to relay financial news to customers. A few U.S. markets offered computerized trading services; the New York Stock Exchange allowed investors to connect computers running automatic trading programs to the exchange computer system. In London, observers still found "program trading virtually non-existent."[49]

The dawning age of financial liberalization and electronic trading almost immediately revealed its own capacity for crisis. The October 1987 crash suggested that international capital market contagion had returned. In the usual crisis blame game, policy makers now pointed at stockbroker immorality combined with novel technology: "Program trading was the principal cause," remembers Edward J. Markey, chairman of the U.S. House of Representatives' subcommittee on telecommunications and finance.[50] At the New York Stock Exchange, investor computers were pre-programmed to massively dispatch automatic selling orders to the exchange computer system in case of price drops. Declines in foreign markets triggered massive computerized selling when the floor opened on Monday October 19. Printers in trade floor workstations jammed, leaving sellers and buyers unclear about current prices and the status of their transactions. Investors panicked, sold out, and stock values dived. The panic then bounced back and forth through electronic media between Asia, Europe, and the United States epicenter; it heavily affected such peripheral markets as New Zealand, where the market dropped by a record 60 percent.

Financial experts, for their part, again saw the crisis as a foreseeable market correction and as a signal of underlying instabilities in the real economy. Some freed program trading from blame, demonstrating that the crash actually began in Hong Kong and spread with the morning opening of exchange floors via Europe to the United States, the only place where program trading was important. In a joint statement, thirty-three of the world's leading economists blamed the crisis on the monetary and trade policies of governments across the world and predicted a new Great Depression.

Either way, from a financial systems perspective, it seems that resilience had returned with international contagion. Soon the world's stock markets absorbed much of the shock, and global

Fig. 4.7 **Capital in Crisis:** *The crash of 1987 shows the role of ICT in financial trade in two ways. First, ICT was one of the crisis' triggers. On Black Monday (October 19, 1987), drops in foreign markets sparked massive computerized selling of securities. Printers in workstations jammed; investors lost access to current ratings, panicked, sold out, and stock values dived even more. Second, the panic bounced back and forth through electronic media between Asia, Europe, and the United States epicenter, illustrating the cross-border connectivity of the financial system. The photo shows a desperate broker in London.*

Factory & Finance | 173

capital markets inclined upward. The October 1987 crash turned out to be a temporary dip. While the U.S. and other governments set new rules for program trading, stock exchanges responded with more and better electronic trading systems. The New York Stock Exchange upgraded its system to perform reliably under stress. NASDAQ, whose traders had not answered their telephones during the crisis, replaced telephone trading by full electronic trading systems such as its Small Order Execution System. It also announced that investors worldwide soon could dial-in on NASDAQ computers via its new PORTAL system. The London Stock Exchange, proud that SEAQ had remained functional during the crisis, also announced further investment in electronic trading platforms to keep up with its competitors.

In the 1990s, financial liberalization and electronic trading swept through the European continent. Governments released their controls over the financial system and capital trading, and boosted the securities business in several other ways. First, in East-Central Europe, post-communist governments promoted or founded stock exchanges. For example the Hungarian government authorized reopening the Budapest stock exchange in a 1989 Securities Act; the Polish State Treasury opened the Warsaw exchange in 1991; Russia's central bank established the Moscow Interbank Currency Exchange in 1992; and Albania's central bank established the *Bursa e Tiranës* in 1996. Second, in both East and West, governments massively privatized infrastructure and other state companies, feeding some $336 billion of private equity into Europe's capital markets (including the Soviet Union). Third, governments eschewed unpopular taxation for raising revenue and increasingly borrowed on the international capital market. In the 1990s lavish government borrowing made the Italian bond market a world leader—and its electronic bond trading platform (*Mercato telematico delle obbligazioni e dei titoli di stato*) became the future Eurozone's bond trade standard. By 2003 Portugese, German, and French government borrowing had exceeded the norms set in the EU stability pact that prepared the introduction of the Euro currency in 1999. By 2010 the national public debts of 14 of the 27 EU Member States exceeded the maximum norm of 60 percent of GDP. Greece topped the list with 142 percent. By contrast, Estonia had a public debt of merely 7 percent of its GDP.[51]

To profit from these rapidly rising stock and bond markets, financial system-builders engaged in yet another round of electronic infrastructure competition. The most promising arena was the market for high-tech company stocks in the image of the American NASDAQ. The European Association of Securities Dealers Automatic Quotation system (EASDAQ) was "designed expressly for a united Europe," and offered EU-wide electronic quotation and trading. Its story echoes that of the Trans European Network program.

By the early 1980s the European Commission had identified technological innovation as a means to lead the Community out of economic recession, spur competitiveness, and increase employment. Yet financing opportunities for high-tech startups were poor. European venture capitalists, for their part, complained that they could invest only in existing companies at national stock exchanges, while their American colleagues profited tremendously from Silicon Valley startups listed at NASDAQ. The Commission then teamed up with venture capitalists, jointly founding the European Venture Capitalist Association in 1985, to study the financing of small high-tech enterprises and the possibility of a Community-wide electronic trading system. The European Commission worked on its Investment Services Directive to break down national capital barriers; when it came into force in 1996, stock markets based in one country could in theory operate in others via electronic screens, networks, and computer terminals. Meanwhile venture capitalists, in close contact with the Commission, developed a trading system that could profit from the new directive and produce "a single Pan-European market ... rather than a multicenter approach."[52] Jos Peeters of Capricorn Venture Partners in Leuven chaired the working group that ultimately founded the non-profit European Association of Securities Dealers in 1994 and its for-profit EASDAQ company under Belgian law. It listed small high-tech companies and offered European Union-wide access to its electronic trading platform.

In response to the new competitor, Europe's national stock markets innovated and boosted the multi-center version of the European capital market that EASDAQ wanted to transcend. First, national exchanges quickly established their own NASDAQ-clones for small high-tech companies. Anticipating EASDAQ, the London Stock Exchange rapidly implemented its Alternative

Investment Market (later TechMARK). The French Treasury and the Paris Bourse agreed to pull out of EASDAQ and in 1996 founded the *Nouveau Marché* for high-tech startups. In 1997 the *deutsche Börse* established its *Neuer Markt* in Frankfurt and its *Xetra* (eXchange Electronic TRAding) system. Next followed Euro.NM Belgium, Amsterdam's *Nieuwe Markt* (both in 1997), Sweden's *Nya Marknaden* (1998), Italy's *Nuevo Mercato*, Swiss *SWX New Market*, Austria's *Growth Market* (all in 1999), Spain's *Nuevo Mercado*, Denmark's *KVX Growth market* (both in 2000), and others. The Paris Bourse claimed to have initiated a "European" dimension under the label *Euro.NM*, in which the new markets of Paris, Amsterdam, Brussels, and Frankfurt combined nationally organized trade with mutual access for all member traders. New Danish, Swedish, Swiss, Finnish and Norwegian markets were ready to join. Outside high-tech, the national exchanges of Amsterdam, Brussels, Paris, and soon Lisbon similarly joined forces in Euronext to combine national exchanges with mutual access by all traders in the pool.[53] The nation-based, "multicenter" approach to European financial collaboration rapidly outgrew the "panEuropean," "single market" approach.

At the turn of the millennium, the world's electronically mediated high-tech capital markets experienced their own crash. As usual, critics blamed the dot.com crash on greedy speculators and technology-out-of-control. Online brokers and their TV ads supposedly had led small and 'unqualified' investors and their home computers to turn the capital market into a global electronic casino.[54] Equally predictably, many sector analysts regarded the crash as a classic mania–panic cycle and a necessary market correction.

On a systemic level, the competition for high-tech start-ups had overcrowded the market, and individual exchanges lacked critical mass to absorb shocks. The "single market" initiative EASDAQ never obtained its envisioned 500 high-tech listings. It counted only 62 companies by 2001. Its chairman Stanislas Yassukovich regretted that "Investment banks that bring companies to the market for listing never bought into the idea ... Easdaq...was new, experimental, and had no home market...thus they opted for the [national] exchange."[55] As for the "multicenter" system, even the German *Neuer Markt* attracted only some three hundred companies at its height.

The dot.com crash hit all hard. EASDAQ was on the verge of bankruptcy when NASDAQ bought it, transformed it into NASDAQ Europe, but then closed it down in 2003. The Deutsche Börse shuttered the *Neuer Markt* and set up a smaller-scale high-tech listing called *TecDAX*. The "single market" as well as the nation-based "multicenter" versions of electronic European capital markets faced a deep crisis. The latter, however, were often rescued by their national parent exchanges; national exchanges continued to dominate Europe's capital market.

Flash Crash

Information and communication infrastructure remained a vital arena for Europe's capital markets and their crises in the new millennium. National exchanges continued to combine national listings with on-line access across national borders in the so-called multicenter system. Following the Euronext model, the Swedish electronic trading platform developer OM purchased the Stockholm exchange in 1998, merged it with the Helsinki exchange, creating the OMX in 2003, and subsequently added the Danish, Icelandic, Estonian, Latvian, Lithuanian, Armenian, and Norwegian national exchanges to its trading platform. The internationalization of Northern Europe's financial infrastructure now symbolized East–West integration after the Cold War. Fiber-optic cables on the bottom of the Baltic Sea enabled massive financial flows across the former East–West divide, where it had previously been impossible to make even a simple telephone call. The blackout of the Estonian exchange, due to a breakdown of the entire Nordic electronic trading platform on June 3, 2008, underscored the new East–West interdependency. Similarly, the Central Eastern Europe Stock Exchange group bought majority shares in the Vienna, Budapest, Prague, and Ljubljana exchanges and connected them into a single electronic trading platform. "We give companies the opportunity to be internationally connected and nationally located," said CEO Heinrich Schaller about his multicenter approach.[56] Indeed most listing and trading on national exchanges remained national. Euronext partners listed mostly domestic companies. Between 2001 and 2008 only seven foreign firms registered at *deutsche Börse*. In 2005 the Warsaw Stock Exchange listed 248 domestic and seven foreign companies.

On the other hand, the European Commission kept pushing for its so-called single financial market as an alternative to the nation-based multicentered system. Its Markets in Financial Instruments Directive (2004) forbade governments to route the securities trade through regulated national stock markets, and made way for so-called "unregulated players." Among these, Multilateral Trading Facilities such as Chi-X Europe, Turquoise, and BATS Europe became the new price fighters of the securities trade. They could offer low trading costs because they hosted no listings on their own, and instead brought together buyers and sellers electronically to trade in securities listed on other exchanges. National exchanges reacted with a new round of competition through electronic trading innovation, acquisitions, and mergers.

While this struggle for Europe's future capital market geography continued, another group of new, unregulated players stirred up emotions. In the words of New York Stock Exchange vice-president Joseph Mecane, a handful of large investors called High Frequency Traders now lead the "technological arms race."[57] Mecane observed that "what separates winners and losers is how fast they can move." High frequency traders specialize in short-time movement of high volumes of securities to profit from minimal deviations in supply and demand. Their powerful computer servers communicate by fiber-optic cables, microwave beams, or laser beams to nearby stock exchange computers so as to outrun other investors; their computer algorithms automatically exploit trading opportunities lasting just a few milliseconds. Between 2005 and 2010 the share of high frequency trading in the U.S. trade volume increased from under one fifth to over 70 percent, though it was executed by only 2 percent of the American trading firms. In Asia and Europe, and London in particular, high frequency trading grew rapidly.

In this context the European Commission and Europe's national regulators were particularly shocked by the events of May 6, 2010 in the United States. According to U.S. investigation reports, the so-called "Flash Crash" started on the futures derivatives market.[58] At 2.32 p.m. the trading house Wadell and Reed initiated an automatic selling program for 75,000 E-mini S&P future contracts worth $4 billion (U.S.). This was not unusual. By 2.41 p.m. high frequency trading programs picked up the sale. Programmed for short selling, they quickly purchased and sold on. Between 2.41 and 2.44 these programs traded over 140,000 E-Mini contracts with each other. In 14 seconds between 2:45:13 and 2:45:27 they traded over 27,000 contracts, while net purchases amounted to only two hundred. Intriguingly, the original seller program algorithm based its sales speed on the overall trade volume; when sales spiked, it offered more contracts and thereby reinforced the spiral. Then the E-mini trade stabilized; the high frequency traders seemed to have absorbed the price shock.

However, the turmoil now spilled over to the regular stock market. Equity investors' computer program safeguards reacted to the futures market instability with a time-out. Unable to monitor what was going on, panicky stock traders executed their own automatic selling programs or started selling manually. In the few minutes of the computer time-out, buyers were absent from the market, and stock values plunged sharply. When automatic trading programs came back on-line, liquidity flooded the market and the collapse was largely undone. For instance, Accenture stock traded for USD 39.98 at 2.46 p.m., collapsed to one cent by 2.47:53, and returned to 39.51 by 2.50 p.m. The market had fully recovered by 3.07 p.m. Observers found the Flash Crash's sudden recovery as astonishing as its sudden collapse.

The Flash Crash did not affect Europe through direct market contagion, but through fear, and European regulators and politicians demanded measures. Spokespersons of Europe's national financial authorities and the European Commission eagerly cited American authorities such as Nobel Prize winner, World Bank vice-president, and Flash Crash investigator Joseph Stiglitz, for believing that "high-frequency trading has negative social value." Jean-Pierre Jouyet, chair of the French *Autorité des Marches Financiers*, warned that "the excessive development of high-frequency trading has imperiled the functioning of markets." Andrew G. Haldane, Executive Director Financial Stability of the Bank of England, called the Flash Crash "a near miss" and pleaded for legislation to avoid a major crisis in the future.[59]

As in the earlier financial crises of 1907, 1929, 1987, and 2001, financial sector spokespersons had a radically different interpretation of the Flash Crash. In the U.S. the Chicago Mercantile Exchange, which specializes in derivatives, emphasized the stabilizing effect of high frequency trading: Its computerized reaction to very small price differences evens out fluctuations even before conventional traders step in. In the Flash Crash, too, high frequency trading "was a moderating factor ..., providing liquidity when it was needed the most." Prominent high frequency trader Jim Simons of Renaissance Technologies agreed that "the system worked beautifully compared to...October of 1987," when there had not been fast buyers to step in and reverse the crash. Their European colleagues picked up this line of argument and argued that "winding back the clock is a mistake."[60] The London Stock Exchange Group supported the new trading mechanism and established its own high frequency trading service.

Despite these counter arguments, political responses gathered momentum. The European Commission established a new European Securities and Markets Authority and defined entry requirements for high frequency traders and their electronic trading platforms. The British government's Office for Science advised the British cabinet to build its own large-scale, national or multi-national integrated computer system to track capital markets just like meteorologists track the weather. Campaigning during the French presidential election of 2012, the socialists' winning candidate François Hollande pledged to reassert political control over the transnational capital market. This was particularly ironic since Europe's main financial crisis during that time, the Eurozone souvereign debt crisis, was predominantly politician-made. Still, socialist candidates elsewhere in Europe took the same line of argument. Sitting French president Nikolas Sarkozy did not lag behind and promised to be tough on financial players. He promised to curtail high frequency trading: "What we want to do is create a shockwave and set an example that there is absolutely no reason why unregulated finance, those people who helped bring about the crisis, shouldn't pay to restore our accounts."[61] The fact that high frequency trading had little to do with either the credit crisis of 2007, or the government debt crisis of 2010, seems to matter little when politicians compete for votes.

Europe's capital markets and their occasional crises and blame games were in motion as ever. Meanwhile, information and communication infrastructure remains at the heart of financial system-building—just like messengers, carrier pigeons, and optic telegraphy had been tools of the trade in the time of the Blanc brothers.

5
Logistics of War

August 1914

"I saw immediately that something terrible had happened here. He was purple in the face, his pulse hardly countable. I had a desperate man in front of me."[1]

So wrote Eliza von Moltke, describing her husband Helmuth von Moltke in the evening of August 1, 1914. Von Moltke was at the time Chief of the German General Staff and responsible for the German armed forces. He had experienced a day full of sudden reversals. At 5 p.m. he had been present when Kaiser Wilhelm II, after much hesitation, had finally signed a mobilization order. The order implied that the main part of the German army in the coming two weeks would be called up and transferred to the country's western border, where it would prepare to attack France and Belgium. A smaller part of the army would be transferred to the eastern border to confront the Russians, who had already begun their own general mobilization on July 30.

Von Moltke, judging that a delay would have been dangerous, was relieved that the decision was taken. A few hours later, however, he was called back to the Kaiser, who explained that he had changed his mind. According to a telegram from the German ambassador in London, the British Foreign Minister had informed the Germans that both England and France would remain neutral in a forthcoming war—if Germany refrained from attacking France. The Kaiser interpreted this as a way to avoid the dreaded two-front war. In a happy mood, he said: "So we simply deploy the whole army in the East!" Von Moltke strongly objected. "If His Majesty insisted on leading the whole army to the East," he explained, "then he would not have an army that was ready to strike but a messy heap of disorderly, armed men without supplies." The Kaiser, unwilling to give in, replied that "it must be possible if I order it." Extremely upset, as his wife's account above testifies, von Moltke left.[2]

The General Staff had been planning to conduct a major war for several decades. Speed of mobilization was seen as a crucial factor, and the Kaiser's sudden departure from the plan revealed, in von Moltke's eyes, a lack of understanding of modern warfare's realities. There would, however, be one more surprise before the day ended. Later that evening von Moltke returned to the Kaiser, seeking to convince him. In the meantime a new telegram from London had made clear that Germany's conditions for British neutrality were unacceptable. The Kaiser, already in bed, told von Moltke that he could go ahead with the original mobilization plan: "Now do as you please; I don't care either way."[3]

The Kaiser's approval of the general mobilization set in motion an enormous machine. Millions of soldiers and officers received call ups by post and telegraph. All available railroad tracks and 11,000 trains brought them and their horses and equipment to predetermined destinations at the fronts. The entire operation took 13 days. The traffic was extremely intense, and at crucial points like the Hohenzollern Bridge in Cologne, a 54-car train passed every ten minutes, day and night.[4] The Russian and German mobilizations forced France and Austria to respond. Thus, in the first weeks of August more than ten million soldiers and two million horses were rolling to the various fronts in Europe at a pace of about 20 km per hour. Never before had railroads carried such a large volume of passengers and cargo.[5]

Unlike the Kaiser, Europe's military leaders knew well that modern warfare hinged on transport and communications, on moving armed forces and keeping them supplied. The importance of such military logistics forced von Moltke and his counterparts in other countries deeply to engage with a variety of infrastructure-related issues, ranging from the efficient use of civilian infrastructure for wartime purposes to the—often improvised—creation of dedicated military transport, communications, and energy systems at home and on foreign battlefields. Ultimately the centrality of infrastructure in the planning and making of war turned von Moltke and other leading strategists and commanders into military system-builders.

The previous two chapters detailed how economic system-builders used infrastructure to connect Europe in economic collaboration and development. This chapter will introduce military system-builders using infrastructure to make war with or against each other—on the ground, at sea, and in the air. These three theaters posed very different challenges from an infrastructure point of view. The chapter emphasizes the first half of the twentieth century, an era that witnessed the most devastating wars ever fought in Europe.

Railroads & Telegraphs in Military Planning

Logistics had been a crucial component of warfare long before Europe's infrastructure transition.[6] Unsurprisingly, then, military planners early on took an interest in the new logistical possibilities that railroads and telegraphs seemed to offer. Shortly after the first public railroad between Liverpool and Manchester opened in 1830, British military commanders used it for carrying a regiment sent to crush an upheaval in Ireland. In 1846 Prussian commanders transferred an Army Corps of 12,000 men on a newly-built railroad to Cracow to help quell a Polish uprising. And when Tsar Nicholas in 1849 intervened to help Austrian Emperor Franz Josef deal with a major Hungarian revolt, he used the new Warsaw–Vienna railroad to send 30,000 men with all their equipment to the Habsburg Empire. The advantage of rail transport was not only higher speed, but also that the troops arrived in good physical shape. The military potential of telegraph lines was also exploited. Telegrams enabled news about internal uprisings quickly to reach distant military headquarters, allowing commanders to take early action to assemble troops.[7]

From the 1850s railroads increasingly played a role in international conflicts as well. In the Crimean War, Great Britain and France sent 60,000 troops with heavy field guns to capture Sevastopol. The British troops established a front line 13 km from the port of Balaklava, which they controlled. Bringing in supplies by ship to Balaklava was easy, but the tiny road from there to the front was totally inadequate. Huge amounts of supplies piled up on the quays. When Samuel Peto, a leading British railroad contractor and Member of Parliament, heard about this, he proposed to solve the problem by constructing a railroad from the port to the front. Governmental approval allowed Peto quickly to assemble the necessary materials and a workforce of 250 experienced navvies, send them to Crimea, and build, in seven weeks, a crude railroad, pompously named the Grand Crimean Central Railway. On this rudimentary line, the British army could transport up to 700 tons of equipment a day to bombard Sevastopol on an unprecedented scale, ultimately forcing the Russians to surrender.[8]

At about the same time, Prussian military planners, and in particular Helmut von Moltke the elder—an uncle of the aforementioned general—started integrating railroads and telegraphs into war planning in a much more ambitious and systematic way. In 1857, the Danish-born von Moltke had become Chief of Prussia's General Staff. Having taken an interest in railroads for a long time, he was well aware of their potential for warfare. When preparing for combat with Austria in 1866, his Staff drew up a war plan based on a fast, large-scale railroad-based mobilization. As Prussia had five different railroads to the border, whereas the Austrians only had one, von Moltke was able to deploy his troops much faster on the Bohemian battle ground. With the help of telegraphy, he further managed to concentrate Prussian forces for a decisive battle at Königgrätz, where they defeated the Austrians.[9]

A problem for military planners, however, was that practically all existing railroads had been built for civilian purposes. After the Austro-Prussian War, von Moltke set out to adapt the existing railroad system to military needs, both physically and organizationally. In particular, he persuaded the government to invest in double-tracked railroads to border stations and to establish a military railroad corps specially trained for quick repairs of destroyed bridges, tunnels, and tracks. Moreover, he prepared a joint civilian–military management plan for railroads in times of war.[10]

Fig. 5.1 Mechanized Mobilization:
Railroads and telegraphs revolutionized warfare by making possible huge troop movements at the outbreak of war. In the 1866 Austro-Prussian war, the Prussians were able to bring 200,000 men and 55,000 horses to confront the Austrian troops on the Bohemian battle ground in just twenty-one days. The troops were not exhausted by long marches and thus proved ready for combat when arriving at their destination. The picture shows the embarking of cavalry in Düsseldorf at the beginning of the war.

The reforms were put to test shortly, in the Franco-Prussian War. Nearly 400,000 men reached their positions at the border within eighteen days after the declaration of war on July 15, 1870. The French mobilization was much slower, and the disorganized French lost all the battles in the first weeks. Near the end of August, half the French army surrendered, with Napoleon III being captured. Revolutionaries in Paris proclaimed a Republic and Prussian and German troops marched further west, some of them to besiege Paris. In this phase of the war, however, the railroads were unable to deliver supplies to the German troops, as the French railroad lines were frequently sabotaged and the railroad corps could not repair them fast enough.[11]

Prussia's staggering victories in 1866 and 1870 forced the other major European states to rethink their military planning. Austria, France, and Russia all launched reforms modeled after Prussia. Every country developed its own plan, but the growing role of alliances in war preparations from the late nineteenth century made logistical cooperation necessary. France and Russia in particular closely coordinated their war plans regarding the use of infrastructure and preparing for a two-front war with Germany. In the early 1910s their General Staffs met annually for this purpose. They also established reliable radiotelegraphy contact via two separate wireless telegraph routes, to be used in case of war.[12]

Infrastructure & Colonial Control

Outside Europe, Europeans made use of new infrastructure as an important tool in establishing and maintaining control over their colonies. In the nineteenth century Europe's imperial powers established networks of naval bases to support colonial expansion. Naval vessels of many nationalities protected the trade routes between distant colonies and Europe that were so important to the economic system-builders encountered earlier. The naval bases linked up with new inland transportation routes, particularly as steamships made many large rivers in colonial regions navigable. In the late 1830s, the British East India Company put into operation a dozen armed, iron-clad vessels on the Euphrates, the Tigris, and the Indus. In the Opium War with China a few years later, the British used similar gunboats, which sailed up the Yangtze River and defeated a Chinese fleet. Other colonial powers followed this example. King Leopold of Belgium, in particular, created a fleet of steamships on the Congo River to uphold his cruel dominion there.[13]

It took longer for military steamships to be introduced at sea. The main advantage with steam propulsion, compared to sail, was high and reliable speed irrespective of wind, but a downside was that much of the cargo space had to be reserved for coal and, more important, that steamships needed frequent refueling. Many new bases and coaling stations were necessary in the second half of the nineteenth century as navies introduced steam-propelled ships; in 1889 Britain had no less than 157 coaling stations at its disposal worldwide. It turned out that Wales rested on the world's best steamer coal, and a whole fleet of sailing-ship colliers soon transported this coal from Welsh harbors to fuel stations around the world. This was the first energy supply system with global coverage.[14]

Colonial officials rapidly recognized the potential of railroads to ensure colonial control. A few days after the inauguration of India's first railroad line in 1853, the British Governor-General, Lord Dalhousie, argued that further railroad-building "would enable the Government to bring the main bulk of its military strength to bear upon any given point, in as many days as it now requires months, and to an extent which is at present physically impossible."[15] Four years later a major revolt by Indian soldiers in the British Indian Army posed a severe threat to British rule. In the absence of railroads it took more than a year for the British to gather forces, crush the revolt, and regain control. Following this debacle, railroad building became a high priority task; and by 1872 Britain had built more than 8,000 km of railroads in India. This enabled the colonial power to exert military control over a vast territory using a fairly limited army. Other imperial states followed the British example, though no other colony came close to India in terms of the extent and density of its railroad networks.[16]

The rise of submarine telegraphy in the 1850s was another phenomenon that quickly interested the commanders of Europe's colonial powers. By 1900 underwater cables owned and operated by private companies connected all British naval bases. The French government enviously noted that "England owes her influence in the world perhaps more to her cable communications than to her navy." Indeed, these cables made it much easier to ensure that all the bases had sufficient supplies, while also enabling rapid redeployment of naval ships in case of crisis or war.[17]

The First World War

By the early 1910s, military system-builders in the major European countries had created impressive logistical systems and complex war plans that relied heavily on infrastructure use. On land, the First World War had three logistical phases. The first was mobilization, which, as noted earlier, had been minutely prepared. Staff officers in all countries shared a common "cult of the offensive"—a belief in the importance of fast mobilization and a conviction that a coming war would be short and the outcome decided during first few weeks of fighting. This explains why von Moltke the first was so eager to launch the German mobilization and why he was so upset when the Kaiser ordered the plan changed.[18]

In the second, offensive phase, things did not go as expected. The central idea of German war strategy—the famous Schlieffen Plan—was to encircle France through Belgium and then move southwards toward Paris, finally attacking French troops at the German border from behind. The Germans had expected Belgium to surrender immediately, but the Belgians fought back fiercely and systematically blew up railroad tunnels, bridges, and rolling stock to prevent the invaders from using them. As a result, German field commanders faced enormous supply difficulties as their troops entered France. At the September 1914 Battle of Marne, the German cavalry incurred heavy losses, partly because its horses, suffering from lack of fodder, were too weak to gallop. They were also too weak to pull the artillery's cannons. In contrast, the French Army and the British Expeditionary Force could use undamaged railroads quickly to transfer large number of troops and supplies to the battlefield.[19]

In the end the offensive phase blended into a third phase, for which no planning had been made. During this segment, dominated by trench warfare, commanders on both sides confronted the gigantic challenge of supplying millions of men and their horses living for four years in trenches along a haphazard front through northern France and Belgium with food, fodder, clothing, and ammunition. To enable this, they initiated a frantic repair of damaged railroads. When train traffic resumed, railheads close to the front became huge bottlenecks where immense volumes of materiel piled up. To improve transport from the railheads to the front, both sides set about building dense networks of new, light railroads, typically with a 60 cm gauge. Traffic on these railroads was dangerous and undertaken only at night. Small locomotives pulled the freight wagons the first kilometers from the regular railhead, but mules or men hauled them through the last part to the front, so as to minimize the noise. The light rails proved very flexible and could quickly be repaired if hit by bombardment.[20] They could also be used for carrying the wounded from the trenches to get medical care. In fact, improved transport and medical care enabled by infrastructure changed the death pattern in warfare. Before 1870 only one-fifth of all deaths occurred on the battlefields; the rest resulted from sickness. By 1918 this ratio had been reversed.[21]

Creating transport facilities was not enough; the enormous quantities of goods needed at the front had to be manufactured too. The entire economy in each belligerent country became "militarized," focusing on supplying its forces. States hastily constructed large industrial plants to mass produce arms and ammunition. In the first weeks of the war, France had lost a major part of its coal and steel industry to Germany and became dependent on large-scale imports from England and the United States. A British-led blockade gradually cut Germany off from overseas imports, and it had to develop an autarkic economy. In particular, shortages of nitrate for gunpowder and copper and other strategic metals posed severe problems. Military industrial complexes developed in the major belligerent countries and produced vast quantities of weapons and ammunition. In consequence, the volume of ammunition used at the fronts exceeded all previous wars by far.[22]

The massive firepower on both sides made it extremely difficult to advance through enemy lines. Moreover, if a breakthrough did occur, the defending side could quickly redirect troops on existing rail lines behind the front to halt the advance, while the attacking side had great difficulties in supplying its advancing troops. The battles of Verdun and the Somme in 1916 demonstrated in a terrifying way both the firepower that could be mustered and the difficulties in achieving a major breakthrough. The number of casualties, close to two million, was higher than in any other battle ever fought. And the deadlock continued. Not even during the final months of the war, when two million American troops with ample supplies strengthened the Allies, could commanders force a major breakthrough. Only the exhaustion of the German war economy eventually forced the Germans to seek an armistice.[23]

The sea was another major battle scene during the First World War. Europe's navies, like its armies, heavily relied on general transport and communications infrastructures for their operations. The navies made intense use not only of harbors, dredged channels, and well-charted sea lanes, but also of telegraph networks, radio stations, lighthouses, and energy supply systems. In addition, they drew upon dedicated military infrastructure in the form of specially-designed communications facilities, powerful naval bases, and a variety of seagoing vessels with very limited civilian utility.

The British Royal Navy and the German High Sea Fleet were the two most powerful seagoing forces the world had ever seen, with bases on opposite shores of the North Sea. They were the result of a frantic naval armament race during the preceding decade. A crucial British move in this competition was Admiral John Fisher's decision to substitute oil for coal as the main fuel for the Royal Navy. Apart from gains in speed, oil was more dense, easier to handle, and less dirty than coal. More space and more manpower could thus be devoted to the cannons aboard. Since oil-propelled vessels had longer range, they also needed fewer supply bases. However, Fisher realized that the transition to oil was linked to new risks in terms of fuel supply. While Britain had excellent steaming coal in abundant supply domestically, oil would have to be imported from far away. To secure supplies, the British government bought the majority of shares in the hitherto privately owned Anglo-Persian oil company, which controlled large oil fields and refineries in the Middle East, and purchased the necessary oil tankers for transporting critical fuels.[24]

Somewhat unexpectedly, the two fleets did not confront each other as war broke out. Neither side dared launch a large-scale attack in fear of losing their precious "dreadnoughts," their most powerful battleships. The German navy spent most of the war in its home base Wilhelmshaven, while the Royal Navy patrolled the waters between Scotland and Norway and the English Channel. This stalemate was only broken at the end of May 1916, when the German fleet left its home base and encountered patrolling British ships off the coast of Jutland. After a fierce battle the German fleet returned to its base and stayed there for the rest of the war. Instead, the war at sea mainly took the form of attempts to disturb and destroy enemy transport and communications. While Britain managed to disrupt most of Germany's overseas trade and, quite literally, cut its underwater telegraph cables, German U-boats obstructed the massive flows of goods that crossed the oceans en route to the British and French war economies. German U-boats armed with torpedoes could sneak past Britain's patrolling ships and chase Allied merchant ships. They also hauled up and cut some of Britain's subsurface telegraph cables.[25] The U-boats could operate for about 60 days without refueling, thus compensating for Germany's lack of bases on Atlantic shores. In February 1917 the Germans launched unrestricted submarine warfare, starting to sink merchant ships of all nationalities without prior warning. In particular, targeting tankers carrying oil for the Royal Navy was a crucial tactic. The U-boat attacks on U.S. merchant ships became an important factor in Washington's decision to enter the war, a move that fundamentally changed the balance of power and contributed to Germany's defeat.[26]

Blitzkrieg in Snow & Mud

After the First World War Europe's military system-builders judged that railroads had proven inflexible. In particular, they had been unable to support forward attacks. Tanks and trucks, which could use the much denser road networks, seemed to offer a higher degree of flexibility. Engineers thus set out to develop a variety of armored vehicles, with Germany taking particular interest in this new technology. The Versailles Treaty prohibited Germany from developing armored vehicles; but it secretly cooperated both with the Soviet Union and with Sweden. Hitler, once in power, openly rejected Versailles and initiated a fast build-up and modernization of the German army, with special "Panzer" divisions expected to play a crucial role in its next war.[27]

Another issue that was much discussed concerned the role of aircraft. As with the navy, military system-builders here developed a largely dedicated infrastructure, linked to already existing civilian systems only on the margin. Specially-designed airplanes and air bases, along with fuel supply arrangements and systems for communication and control formed the heart of the preparations made for warfare in the air. As it turned out, civilian aviation would profit more from the development of a military airways infrastructure than the other way round. Aircrafts' most important role in the First World War had been for reconnaissance of enemy positions and movements, but bombings of enemy cities, industrial plants, and military targets (to support troops on the ground) had also occurred. In 1921, Giulio Douhet, commander of wartime Italian air services, published an influential book, *Dominio dell'Aria*, in which he argued that large-scale bombing was bound to become decisive in the future. Bombers would first attack major enemy air bases, followed by cities, industries, and infrastructure. This would break the morale of the people and force governments to surrender.[28]

Nazi military planners envisaged a more versatile role for aircraft. The Spanish Civil War became an important test ground, wherein dive bombing to support attacking ground forces turned out to be particularly effective.[29] When Germany invaded Poland on September 1, 1939, its armored divisions received strong support from dive bombers. Hitler's forces broke through Polish lines and quickly penetrated deep into Poland's territory. Journalists and other observers of the war were astounded by the speed of the German attack, and used the term *Blitzkrieg* to describe it. Two weeks later the Soviet Union, in accordance with the Molotov–Ribbentrop Pact, attacked Poland from the East. Like the Nazis, the Red Army made massive use of tanks and aircraft. German and Soviet commanders alike became convinced of the insuperability of fast and flexible armored divisions supported by airplanes. Yet as it turned out, the blitzkrieg strategy had shortcomings and pitfalls.[30]

Three months after the German assault on Poland, on the morning of November 30, 1939, the soldiers at a Finnish border post 40 km east of the little village of Suomussalmi heard a strange rumbling sound from the Soviet side of the border. Soon hundreds of tanks came rolling out of the forest, followed by an immense number of trucks, cannons, horses, and soldiers. The attack came as a total surprise. A simultaneous move launched by the Soviets on the Karelian Isthmus had been expected, but not an attack in the sparsely populated and largely roadless areas further north. The Finns were unaware that the Soviets, in the preceding two months, had secretly built two roads of more than 200 km length from the Leningrad–Murmansk railroad to the Finnish border. The aim of the surprise attack, led by Major General Andrei Zelentsov, was to seize Suomussalmi and then continue toward the town of Oulu on the Gulf of Bothnia, cutting Finland into two isolated halves. Together with other divisions, Zelentsov would then advance south and attack the bulk of the Finnish army from the rear.[31]

The battle of Suomussalmi that ensued in the following weeks has become a classic in military history. Set in a landscape of endless forests, peat moors, and lakes, it was fought under extraordinary weather conditions, featuring deeply-drifted snow and

Logistics of War | 195

Fig. 5.2 **Winter Warriors:** *Finnish troops were able to withstand a massive Soviet attack during the harsh winter of 1939–40, not least due to their familiarity with winter conditions. While the heavily-mechanized Soviet troops were tied to the few available roads, the Finnish soldiers could move swiftly and quietly on skis and launch sudden attacks. The effective Finnish resistance was much admired abroad, as this cartoon from the British Daily Express on February 8, 1940 illustrates.*

temperatures below –40° C. It involved two very different military powers. The numerous, heavily armed, and motorized Soviet troops could rely on hundreds of tanks and cannons and thousands of trucks, horses, and wagons filled with ample supplies of food, fodder, and munitions, as well as air support. The Finnish troops, which were hastily sent to the area by train, were much fewer in number and had to fight mainly with guns and hand grenades.

The Finnish commander at Suomussalmi, Colonel Hjalmar Siilasvuo, identified a major weakness of the Soviet forces: they could only operate along the roads. Moreover, they were not well equipped for the harsh weather conditions. In contrast, his own troops were highly mobile. All his soldiers were experienced skiers who were used to the Finnish winter. Siilasvuo ordered the building of a temporary winter road from the nearest railroad station across a string of ice-covered lakes and moors. On this road trucks and horse-drawn carriages transported supplies of ammunition and food to the troops, while bringing back wounded and dead soldiers.[32] Well-hidden temporary camps with heated tents, kitchens, and even saunas, erected along the winter road, provided places where Finnish soldiers could eat, drink, and rest between their exhausting missions. The Finns dressed in all-white uniforms could advance close to the Soviet positions without being detected. This enabled them to launch quick, unexpected assaults and to retreat before the Soviets could make use of their cannons and tanks. The Russian soldiers had to be on the alert at all times and were soon exhausted from lack of sleep.[33]

Siilasvuo also had an information advantage over his enemy. Finnish radio intelligence was highly developed, allowing mobile vans west of Suomussalmi to eavesdrop on Russian radio traffic, send the signals to a center for crypto-analysis and translation, and return translated messages to Siilasvuo with only slight delay. In this way the Finns dealt effectively with the arrival of an additional Soviet Elite Division, sent to assist Zelentsov. Within three weeks the Finns had almost extinguished the two Soviet Divisions. War journalists reported horrifying scenes with thousands of corpses of men and horses frozen stiff, and hundreds of burnt out tanks and trucks. The Soviet commanders gave up seizing northern Finland, concentrating their forces, instead, on the Karelian Isthmus. There, they were more successful, eventually forcing the Finns to surrender.[34]

In June 1941 it was the Red Army's turn to face an unexpected attack. Abandoning the 1939 Molotov–Ribbentrop Pact, Nazi Germany launched "Operation Barbarossa." It was the largest military operation that has ever been conducted, involving nearly 3.5 million soldiers and more than half a million horses. The campaign was divided into three main army groups, one heading toward Leningrad, the second toward Moscow, and the third toward Ukraine and the Caucasus. Key components in the German war plan were the armored and motorized spearheads that had proven so efficient during campaigns in Poland, Belgium, and France. They were equally efficient in the early phase of the war against the Soviet Union, and time and again they were able to encircle and destroy or capture parts of the Red Army, which suffered huge losses.[35]

Yet the vast geographical scope of the operation made it uniquely challenging from a logistical point of view. The German planners had overlooked the poor quality of the Soviet Union's roads and railroads. In the case of rail, the German railroad corps set out to quickly convert the larger Soviet gauge (1.52 m) to the West European standard (1.45 m) so that German wagons and locomotives could be used. Until the conversion was complete, however, the Germans had to use captured Soviet rolling stock. This led to huge bottlenecks in the supply chains as all cargo had to be reloaded onto the enemy's wagons. Moreover, once the gauge had been changed, it turned out that the Soviet rails could not carry Germany's modern, heavier locomotives. The Nazis had to bring in older ones. As if this were not enough, Soviet coal could not be used in German locomotives, water supply stations were located too far apart, and Soviet signal and communications equipment proved inadequate. All in all, the carrying capacity of the railroads was much lower than expected.[36]

The severity of Soviet weather conditions was another factor that German planners had underestimated. During the first weeks of July, heavy rainfall turned many roads into quagmires, and within three weeks a quarter of the army's trucks had been damaged. The weather improved in the following months, but following additional rainfalls in October, the whole Soviet countryside turned into a morass. For about three weeks German troops were unable to move and could not receive any supplies from their home bases. In early November the winter frost set in, saving the troops from the wet and easing the transport situation. But the frost itself soon caused new problems. It became complicated to operate machinery, weapons, and motors in the cold. Worst of all, since the German locomotives' water supply pipes were not located inside their boilers, their steam engines could not operate under Soviet winter conditions. Hardly any German trains, loaded with badly needed winter equipment, made it to the front.[37]

Such logistical problems had an immense influence on the war. The failure of the blitzkrieg strategy gave the Soviets time to conduct a huge transport operation in which railroads were mobilized to evacuate whole industries to safe locations beyond the Urals. There, equipment and machinery installed in new factories geared up for war production. The slow German advance also gave the Red Army time to regroup and to muster new troops. In the ensuing Battle of Moscow, the German troops performed poorly, largely because railroads failed to supply them. The Red Army, by contrast, received arms and supplies along functioning railroads from the new factories in the East.

In the same week that the Soviet counter offensive commenced, the Japanese attacked Pearl Harbor, and the United States with its huge industrial capacity became an ally of the Soviet Union. As a result the Soviets started receiving U.S. weapons and supplies, shipped through Arctic convoys to the northern ports of Murmansk and Archangelsk. A year later the Soviet forces had become strong enough to defeat the Germans at Stalingrad. Precisely three years after the German attack on the Soviet Union, Soviet supreme commander Marshal Zhukov launched Operation Bagration, a massive assault on all German forces occupying Soviet territory. At that point, the Red Army had twice as many men, and between five and ten times as many tanks, aircraft, and artillery pieces. As the Germans retreated they carefully blew up every bridge they passed, but Zhukov, having foreseen this, had set up 68 special pontoon-bridge battalions. These battalions could build a one-mile bridge with a carrying capacity of 80 tons in only five hours. The careful preparations, the brute force, and the skills of the Red Army were decisive for the success of Operation Bagration, paving the way for Nazi Germany's final defeat.[38]

Bombing the Enemy

In Western Europe the air war was critical. In August 1940 Germany started massive air attacks on the British Isles. This "Battle of Britain" had been foreseen and feared by the British ever since the German bombings of London in June 1917, in which 162 people died. In a famous 1932 Parliamentary speech, the British conservative politician Stanley Baldwin had warned that "the bomber will always get through." He drew the conclusion that "the only defence is in offence, which means that you have to kill more women and children more quickly than the enemy if you want to save yourselves."[39] The Air Force would thus have to be given an offensive capacity in the form of bombers. At the same time, both Baldwin and the Air Staff argued that the aircraft themselves were merely one of several important components in a wider military aviation system. Other crucial components included air defense installations on the ground, efficient radio communications equipment, and fuel supply.

After the 1917 London bombings, Britons had constructed an early version of an air defense system, consisting of a chain of observation posts around London. The posts, linked by telephone lines to a control room, immediately informed commanding officers who communicated with anti-air gun batteries and airbases about enemy airplanes approaching their areas of responsibility. This system worked fairly well in May 1918 when thirty-eight German bombers attacked Britain in the war's largest raid. Seven of the bombers were successfully shot down or forced to land.[40]

During the interwar years, the speed of bomber aircraft increased, generating totally new demands on air defense systems. As Hitler came to power, leading British politicians and militaries increased their efforts to find a solution to the problem of early warning, setting up a Committee for the Scientific Survey of Air Defence, chaired by Sir Henry Tizard. In close cooperation with leading Air Force officers, the committee managed to build a working system, "Chain Home," based on a new technology, radar, which, using short pulses of radio energy, could determine the locations of aircraft in flight. A chain of radar stations was built along Britain's east and south coasts, tasked to detect all approaching bombers within their specified sectors. Operators analyzed radar signals and translated them into information about the position and altitude of approaching airplanes. This data proceeded through telephone lines—buried deep into the ground—to a "filter centre" at Fighter Command Headquarters, where specially trained operators evaluated all observations, trying to determine, in particular, whether an incoming plane was friendly or hostile. Their results flowed onward to three Fighter Command Groups responsible for different sectors of the air space. Here operators moved special markers representing enemy and friendly planes on a great map-table, like croupiers in a casino. Finally, the sector controllers, who were fliers themselves, watched the table from above and sent orders to the fighter pilots by radio-telephone, keeping contact with the pilots as they approached their targets.[41]

It was not until August 8, 1940, when the Luftwaffe launched its first large attack, that the system was put to test. Nazi Air Marshal Hermann Göring and his commanders sought to seize control of British airspace by bombing the country's air bases and radar stations. Although the Luftwaffe had more planes and more experienced pilots, the Chain Home system gave the British pilots early warning and efficient guidance to their targets, and Germany lost substantially more airplanes than did Britain. After four weeks the Germans gave up trying to control British airspace. Instead, they turned to night-time bombings of London and other cities.[42]

Fig. 5.3 **Locating the Luftwaffe:** *In the late 1930s Britain built a chain of radar stations along its eastern and southern coasts for detecting approaching enemy aircraft. Operators at radar stations telephoned their observations to colleagues at Fighter Command Headquarters, who marked the positions of incoming planes on a table almost like croupiers in a casino. Finally controllers watching the table from above sent orders by radio-telephone to the pilots to help them find and attack the intruders. The picture shows the Headquarters at Wiltshire in December 1942.*

Night attacks presented both Germany and Britain with new technical challenges. For the Luftwaffe the main difficulty was to navigate in the dark and identify the locations where bombs were to be dropped. In the late 1930s German scientists had developed a system for radio navigation called X-Gerät. A pilot flying along a special radio beam received a pure audio-frequency tone as long as he followed the beam, but as soon as he drifted away from it he would hear different sounds. The bomber pilot would follow the beam toward his goal until he intersected a beam from another radio station. As soon as he heard the second beam he would drop his bomb load.[43]

For the British the challenge was both to disturb the German radio stations and to target incoming aircraft. Engineers and technicians created a new radar system, based on small sets that could be installed in fighters. These had a range of only a few miles, so special ground-based radar stations were built for the purpose of helping fighter pilots fly sufficiently close to the bombers. In May 1941 more than a hundred German bombers were shot down as fighter planes used the new system. The next month the Luftwaffe ceased its attacks and regrouped toward the east to support Operation Barbarossa.[44]

By this time, British bombers were regularly attacking German cities and industries. A year later American bombers joined the air war, moving it decisively onto the Continent. The goal was primarily to destroy German war industries and the infrastructure necessary for supplying Hitler's troops in the Soviet Union and elsewhere. Radar and navigation systems became increasingly sophisticated; and British and German scientists and engineers struggled to understand each other's systems.[45] On one occasion the British even carried out a commando operation with 120 paratroopers, seizing vital parts of a radar station close to Le Havre and bringing them to Britain so scientists could develop countermeasures, notably jamming signals which interfered with the enemy's radio communications. The largest jamming operation during the war assisted the British bombings of Hamburg in July 1943. British aircraft dropped thousands of lightweight bundles of thin metal fibers. Appearing on German radar screens, they totally confused the radar operators. A few months later the Germans used the same technique when bombing British cities.[46]

A challenge for both warring parties was to organize fuel supply for their aircraft. While Germany's chemical industry had developed large plants for producing synthetic aviation fuel from coal, in the early 1940s, British research efforts in this field had not progressed beyond the laboratory stage. Moreover, Britain's refinery capacity was very limited, forcing the Royal Air Force to rely almost entirely on aviation fuel imported from the United States. This in turn posed a major transportation challenge, as the fuel had to be shipped across the Atlantic and then moved safely from ports to air bases. A special Oil Board was responsible for Britain's oil supply during the war. At the outbreak of the war it decided to divert most of the country's oil imports to west-coast ports, since these were less vulnerable to

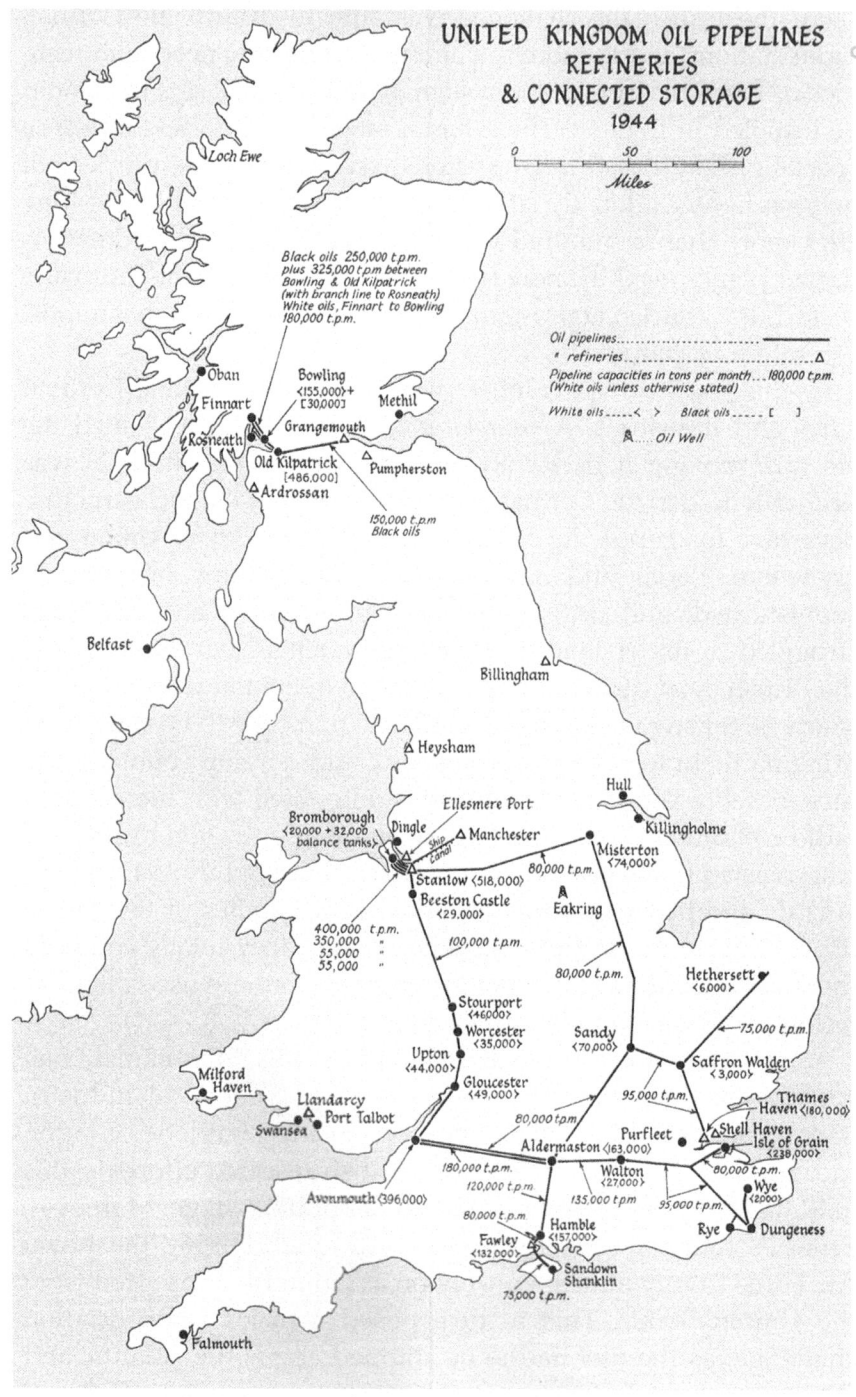

Fig. 5.4 **Fueling the Air Force:** *Between 1941 and 1943 the British government's Oil Board built an extensive pipeline system to supply air bases in eastern England with American aviation gasoline unloaded in British west coast ports. Trucks and trains lacked the necessary capacity and were more vulnerable to bombing. The pipelines were decisive in making possible the massive Allied bombings of Nazi Germany during the last two years of the war. The map depicts the pipelines, ports, and fuel storage facilities built by the Oil Board.*

bombing while also being logistically better placed for handling the U.S. supplies.[47]

To further improve the supply system, the Oil Board decided to build a network of pipelines from the western ports to the air bases. In summer 1941 it constructed a 170 km pipeline from Avonmouth eastward to Walton, not far from where most of Britain's air bases were situated. Half a year later, a 230 km pipeline from Avonmouth northward to Stanlow followed, interconnecting the two principal oil ports so that these could support each other if needed. The network worked very well and was intensely used, pumping nearly 100,000 tons of aviation fuel per month to the bases. When the U.S. entered the war, setting up its own air bases in the East Midlands, the Oil Board decided to extend the pipeline system by creating a full circuit, doubling the capacity and increasing redundancy. Following the circuit's completion in July 1943, the pipelines supplied the air bases with two-thirds of the fuel needed for the intensive bombardments of Germany during the last two years of the war.[48]

The Allies complemented the fuel supply infrastructure with the development of more energy-efficient aircraft engines and external drop-tanks, which could be dropped from the plane when the fuel had been used.[49] This made it possible to fly from England to Berlin and back, not only for bombers but also for protecting fighter planes. These Allied fighter planes shot down more than 2,000 of the most experienced German fighter pilots in the spring of 1944. Moreover, Allied bombers were able to destroy many German air fuel plants, causing a dramatic drop in production from 185,000 tons in March 1944 to 17,000 tons six months later. Thereby Allied air forces took control over most of the Continent's airspace, with devastating effects not only for the German war industry but also for the civilian population of the many cities that were terror-bombed. These bombings resulted in several hundred thousand civilians killed, three to six times as many as the victims of all German bombings of British cities.[50]

The Tonnage War

The third crucial theater of war in Europe was the Atlantic Ocean, which was of crucial importance for Allied military logistics.

Fig. 5.5 **Supplying Submarines:** *German submarines were a deadly threat to Allied convoys crossing the oceans. To increase the operating times of their submarines, Nazi Germany made use of a special category of submarines nicknamed "milk-cows." Their task was to bring fuel, torpedoes, and other supplies to attack submarines in the North Atlantic, so that these could operate longer before returning to their home base in Brittany. The picture shows the transfer of supplies from U 459 to U 571 in April 1942.*

Germany's occupation of most of the European continent in spring 1940 increased Britain's already very large dependence on imports—both military and civilian—from non-European sources. The United States emerged as Britain's most important supplier of tanks, trucks, aircraft, ships, weapons, ammunition, and oil products. Most of this cargo moved across the Atlantic in large convoys. Their vital importance for Britain's military strength, however, made them primary targets for German submarines.[51]

Having occupied large parts of France, the Germans were able to establish naval bases on its Atlantic coast. The most important was the U-boat base in Lorient in Brittany. Rear Admiral Klaus von Dönitz here created the operational center for a dreadful Atlantic "tonnage war." Von Dönitz developed advanced tactics for coordinated assaults on convoys by several U-boats. He commanded these "wolf packs" from Lorient by radio messages, encrypted by Enigma cipher machines. When news came in about convoys leaving U.S. harbors, U-boat commanders were immediately informed. A major weakness was that Germany lacked naval bases in the Atlantic, a circumstance that forced the U-boats to return as soon as their supplies of fuel, food, or torpedoes ran out. This could take several weeks if they were operating in the western part of the Atlantic. To increase operating times, von Dönitz complemented his fleet with larger U-boats that could cover longer distances and with special supply U-boats, nicknamed "milk-cows." These were designed to carry fuel, torpedoes, and other supplies, and with special equipment for transfer at sea.[52]

By the end of 1942 von Dönitz had 212 operational U-boats at his disposal, manned by some 10,000 sailors. This fairly limited force had become a severe threat to the entire Allied war effort. Allied merchant tonnage sunk increased from a monthly average of 180,000 tons in 1941 to 500,000 tons in the spring of 1942, and in the autumn surpassed 700,000 tons. As a result Britain's 1942 imports fell below 34 million tons—a third less than in 1939. In contrast, only 87 U-boats were destroyed by the Allied navies in 1942, making the ratio between sunk U-boats and merchant ships one in thirteen. The prospects for the Atlantic tonnage war looked extremely alarming for Allied commanders.[53]

For the many seamen who manned the merchant ships, the U-boats aroused deadly fear. Jacobus Tazelaar, a young Dutch telegrapher, was one of them. During most of the war he served on Dutch merchant ships participating in Allied convoys, where he repeatedly experienced how ships were sunk by the Germans:

> They just disappeared. When a ship was torpedoed, there was not a soul that cared about it. Keep on going. Get away, there is a U-boat. ... I lost many comrades this way. Fine guys. Never seen or heard again. Totally disappeared.[54]... The tankers were always in the middle. Because what said Adolf: "you must first get the tankers, because each sunk tanker means one air attack less."...But they were always situated in the heart of a convoy. Thus the U-boats dived under the outer boats, leaving them for later, heading for the tankers in the middle. They picked one or two, and then had to get away because they were hunted.[55]

Tazelaar was lucky and survived, but tens of thousands of seamen never returned home. In fact, the British merchant navy lost a higher proportion of personnel than any other armed service.[56]

In late 1942 Admiral Max Horton was appointed new commander responsible for anti-submarine warfare. He introduced new tactics and technologies based on careful analyses of previous attacks on convoys that had been pursued by analysts at the Admiralty. The deployment of convoys was done more skillfully, increasing their size and separating ships into slow and fast convoys. Protection was improved, not least through new long-range and heavily equipped Liberator bombers that could stay with the convoys all the way, and by supplying them with many more destroyers as escorts. Detection of U-boats increased due to better radar equipment and introduction of searchlights. Combating became more efficient by way of a new kind of anti-submarine mortars, "Hedgehogs," and more efficient depth charges. Moreover, after the Allies broke the Enigma code, they could intercept the German radio conservations between Lorient and the U-boats, making it easier to detect the latter. All these measures gradually changed the balance. In March 1943 the number of sunken Allied ships reached an all-time high, but after this the tide turned, and the number of sunken merchant ships decreased dramatically while the number of destroyed U-boats increased. During the rest of the year the ratio between sunken U-boats and merchant ships was one to one. In the first three months of 1944 no less than thirty-six U-boats were destroyed on the North Atlantic while only three merchant ships were sunk, making the ratio twelve to one. Von Dönitz now called back his U-boats and cancelled further operations against convoys.[57]

The Allied victory in the tonnage war made it possible to transfer across the Atlantic all the people and equipment necessary for the planned invasion of France. When the invasion was launched on June 6, 1944, 12,000 aircraft and over 1,000 naval ships supported the Allied troops. Since the Allies controlled both the seaways and the airspace, the German navy and air force could do nothing to intercept them. The invasion was the war's largest single logistic operation. Within a week more than 300,000 men, 50,000 vehicles, and 100,000 tons of supplies landed on five fairly small sand beaches. The Allies had hoped to quickly seize Cherbourg and its harbor to facilitate a further massive transfer of men and equipment. In reality, it took three weeks before they gained control, by which time the Germans had comprehensively demolished the harbor. Unable to use the regular maritime infrastructure, the Allies had to land most of their men and supplies on the invasion beaches, using temporary harbor equipment.[58]

When the Allied forces broke through the German ring around Normandy in late July 1944 and their armored divisions started advancing westward, a new logistic challenge emerged: fuel supply. There was sufficient gasoline onshore in Normandy by this time, but there were no appropriate railroad lines for transporting it eastward. Fuel truck convoys could not keep up with the needs of the quickly advancing Allied armies. By the end of August, the U.S. Third Army under General George Patton had reached the Meuse. From there, the Rhine, whose bridges were still intact, was within reach. Running out of gasoline, however, the tanks stopped. "My men can eat their belts, but my tanks have gotta have gas," Patton furiously erupted to Supreme Commander Dwight Eisenhower a few days later. According to war historian Lidell Hart, "the best chance of a quick finish [of the war] was probably lost when the 'gas' was turned off from Patton's tanks in the last week of August."[59]

Racial War

There was one other kind of warfare, of course. Ethnic cleansing had been practiced many times in Europe, but the large-scale racial war organized by the powerful Nazi organization *Schutz-Staffel* (SS) surpassed all previous pogroms. In line with Hitler's view that "Europe is not a geographic entity, it is a racial entity," the SS created a complex logistical system designed to kill millions of Jews and other unwanted Europeans. Prior to 1941, Nazi attempts to Germanize the *Reich* and its conquered lands centered on deportation. Adolf Eichmann, head of the Office of Jewish Evacuation, drew up concrete plans for relocating one million Jews per year to Madagascar and Palestine. The Franco–German peace treaty transferred Madagascar from France to Germany, and the SS planned to govern the island. Yet the Nazi failure to defeat Britain at sea thwarted this and similar schemes. Instead, the Nazi leadership worked out an industrial approach to physically annihilate—rather than deport—the Jews.[60]

Central to this "final resolution" of the Jewish Question were the infamous death camps constructed at sites such as Chełmno and Auschwitz in annexed Poland; Belzec, Majdanek, Sobibor, and Treblinka in occupied Poland; and Maly Trostinez near Minsk in Belarus. Auschwitz and Treblinka were by far the most important.

The death camps were supplemented by transit camps and ghettos in larger cities. The camps themselves, however, were only one component of the Holocaust system. They would have been meaningless without Europe's well-developed, integrated railroad system. When, in summer 1941, Eichmann and SS General Reinhard Heydrich started making detailed plans for moving Western and Southern Europe's Jews eastward, they took into account the fact that virtually all the involved countries were superbly connected with the *Reich* and occupied Poland through standard-gauge railroad tracks. Thus, locating the extermination camps at sites with excellent railroad connectivity was logical. Auschwitz, for example, was situated near Oderberg, a major railroad hub offering excellent connections both with Germany and with southern Europe. The centerpiece of the southern connection was the classical Warsaw–Vienna railroad, built a century before.

The availability of this infrastructure meant that once on board, the victims could be shipped across Europe using well-established technical and operational procedures, developed by railroad administrations for civilian purposes. In most cases the SS simply ordered the necessary transports from the German *Reichsbahn* or the railroad companies in the occupied territories, as if they were normal freight shipments. The per-person ticket price was set in accordance with an already established principle, according to which groups comprising more than 400 people could claim a 50 percent price reduction. The SS trusted the *Reichsbahn* and the other companies to carry out the ordered transports in a professional way. Since military and coal trains had priority, however, the deportee trains often made long stops in yards or side tracks. Speed was not important. Neither was food and water supply, which is why witnesses remember crying mothers holding up parched children during stops and why many victims—sometimes all—died before arrival.[61]

In 1942 the first death camps went operational. Before that, the railroads mainly moved Jews to the ghettos. In some cases it turned out upon arrival that the ghettos were too crowded. This was so especially at Lodz in occupied Poland. Several trains bound for Lodz were therefore diverted to destinations further east, notably Riga and Minsk, where the passengers were taken into nearby forests and shot. Most Jews in German-occupied territories in the Soviet Union were also shot, although in this case the killings took place without any preceding long-distance transport. All railroad

Fig. 5.6 **Departure for Death:** *Railroads played a crucial role in the Holocaust system. Auschwitz, Treblinka, Chełmno and the other death camps were all built close to major railroad hubs, thus enabling a smooth flow of victims. The German Reichsbahn and the railroad companies in occupied territories were duly paid by the SS for their services. Since military and coal trains had priority, the deportee trains often made long stops. The picture shows Polish Jews in an open cattle carriage at a railroad station in Warsaw in 1944.*

capacity on occupied Soviet territory was needed for supplying the German troops.[62]

The Holocaust system covered the entire Nazi sphere of influence, from Norway to the Greek Islands and from Western France to the occupied Soviet Union. In this zone the SS killed about six million Jews, half of whom died in the railroad-fed death camp system. Germans and their allies murdered the other half in the immediate vicinity of where they had lived, mainly in the Soviet Union. In addition to Jews, the Nazi state fed into the system astounding numbers of Soviet prisoners of war, ethnic Poles, Romani people, mental patients, homosexuals, Jehovah's Witnesses, and communists. In this morbid geography some national borders did matter while others did not. In the German *Reich*, occupied Poland, and the Soviet Union the Nazis erased close to 90 percent of the Jewish population, in the Netherlands 75 percent, and in Belgium 60 percent. In the Nordic countries, Nazi decision makers anticipated fierce resistance and pushed less hard. Thus Danish Jews could flee en masse by boat to Sweden and over 99 percent of Denmark's eight thousand Jews survived the Holocaust. Italy and Hungary likewise resisted massive deportations until Nazi Germany installed puppet governments in these countries. In Hungary, the new authorities managed to deport nearly half a million Jews to Auschwitz in only 70 days, from May to July 1944.[63]

Military System-Building in the Cold War

When Nazi Germany was finally defeated, the Red Army had occupied large parts of East-Central Europe, whereas American, British, and French armies controlled Germany west of the Elbe, and most of Austria and Italy. Relations between the Soviet Union and its former Western allies gradually became more hostile. In June 1948 a first major crisis erupted as the Soviet Union blocked all roads, railroads, and canals to Berlin from the British and American occupation zones in western Germany.

The Western allies responded with an airlift to supply the more than two million inhabitants of West Berlin. The task was daunting. There was only one airport in West Berlin, Tempelhof, with a single runway, and the available cargo planes available for the mission in western Germany were few. However, the Western allies quickly called in aircraft from bases as far away as Guam, Alaska, and Hawaii. William Tunner, a U.S. Air Force general with experience from wartime logistical operations in Asia, commanded the airlift. "In a successful airlift," he declared at the outset, "you don't see planes parked all over the place. They're either in the air, on loading or unloading ramps, or being worked on."[64] To achieve this he imposed rigid routines, so that planes were dispatched according to type, speed, and load, to avoid bunching up en route or on the ground. Furthermore, he ordered the building of an additional airport in West Berlin, Tegel, which became operational in November 1948. The air traffic control system was upgraded to allow take-offs and landings in fog and at night. At the peak in spring 1949, 225 cargo planes flew in 5,000–6,000 tons of supplies per day (equivalent to 2½–3 kg per inhabitant), mainly food and coal. Planes landed every ninety seconds and took off again within six minutes. The Western Powers also started a counter-blockade, prohibiting sales of hard coal, electrical motors, ball bearings, and other crucial items to eastern Germany. After eleven months the Soviet Union finally lifted its blockade and the trains, trucks, and barges started moving again across the interzonal border.[65]

The Berlin crisis had three significant consequences: it influenced the decision to create two German states; it made the U.S. commit to a significant military presence in Europe; and it contributed to the establishment of the North Atlantic Treaty Organization (NATO). When the Federal Republic of Germany became a NATO member in May 1955, the Soviet Union and the other communist countries in East-Central Europe responded by establishing the Warsaw Pact as an opposing military alliance.[66]

The two alliances each had a dominant power, the United States and the Soviet Union, the leading countries in developing ever more powerful nuclear weapons. The U.S. tested its first hydrogen bomb in 1952 and the Soviet Union in 1953. Nuclear weapons' growing threat strengthened the trend toward international cooperation. The offensive part of nuclear warfare depended crucially on the ability to guide bombers or missiles toward their intended goals. This could only be done through advanced infrastructure for communications and control.[67] To be effective, such infrastructure had to have a vast geographical coverage, and alliances covering a large surface thus became an essential part of military strategy. The defensive part of nuclear warfare involved difficult communications challenges, too, the most important being a capacity to detect enemy attacks early on. In the absence of such offensive and defensive communications infrastructure, nuclear arsenals would be useless.

Cooperation evolved very differently in East and West. In NATO, nuclear system-building became a highly controversial process fraught with internal commercial and political rivalry. The defensive infrastructure process started in earnest in 1953, when British and French officers at NATO's headquarters started discussing the need for an Early Warning System. It would involve infrastructural components in most of the member states. The warning system's enormous commercial importance, however, delayed the process significantly. By August 1961, the alliance's headquarters finally issued official requirements for what was called the NATO Air Defence Ground Environment (NADGE). British and French industries formed a joint consortium making a bid.[68] However, when American industries realized that NADGE was the largest common infrastructure effort since the founding of NATO, the U.S. demanded the design process be reopened. In the mid-1960s several international consortia were established for making bids. Each consortium included American, British, French, and German contractors, in proportion to their countries' contributions to NATO. The system that eventually resulted from this procurement process was completed only in 1973, in an environment of growing nuclear detente.[69]

In the Warsaw Pact a unified air defense system was discussed for the first time in January 1957, at a Moscow summit of Party leaders and government representatives.[70] Four months later, the Warsaw Pact's Soviet Chief of Staff sent a draft of an Anti-Aircraft Defense (AAD) system to all member countries. A key point was that "the Commander-in-Chief of the Soviet AAD Forces performs the coordination of all the issues related to AAD."[71] A year later another Moscow summit addressed the production and delivery of armament and equipment. The Soviet representatives suggested that conventional weapons be produced in all member countries, but "more modern complicated technical devices, air-missiles, rocketry, etc. shall be produced only in the USSR." All the representatives accepted this proposal except the Polish, who suggested that some models of air missiles and combat jets could be produced in their country. However, the Poles failed to mobilize support from other member countries and had to accept the Soviet proposal.[72]

Thus in the Warsaw Pact, the Soviet Union had a three-fold control of the Anti-Aircraft Defense system: Soviet system experts developed it, Soviet industries supplied the components, and its design enabled the Commander-in-Chief of the Soviet AAD Forces to coordinate the AAD in all member countries. The system commenced operation in May 1963—a decade earlier than its Western counterpart. It was further developed in later years; but the basic principles persisted—the Soviet Union stayed in control. Clearly, the Soviet Union had a much more dominant role in the Warsaw Pact than the U.S. in NATO, making the construction of "joint" infrastructure much easier. For the U.S., by contrast, the establishment of a military nuclear infrastructure was a matter of very delicate political and diplomatic negotiation.[73]

Importantly, military infrastructural cooperation was not always organized through the alliances. In some cases member states cooperated more intensely with formally neutral countries than with other member states in their respective alliance. Britain, for example, embarked on a close collaborative project with Sweden. Sweden had decided not to join NATO, but needed to strengthen

Fig. 5.7 Cold War Air Defense: *During the Cold War much effort was devoted to developing effective air defense systems able to detect approaching airplanes. However, both within NATO and the Warsaw Pact these developments spurred commercial rivalries among its members. Neutral Sweden built its own air defense system called STRIL-60 with radar and computer technology from the United Kingdom. When it went operational in 1964, it had few counterparts in the world. The picture shows a plan for the STRIL-60 system made by the British Decca firm in 1957.*

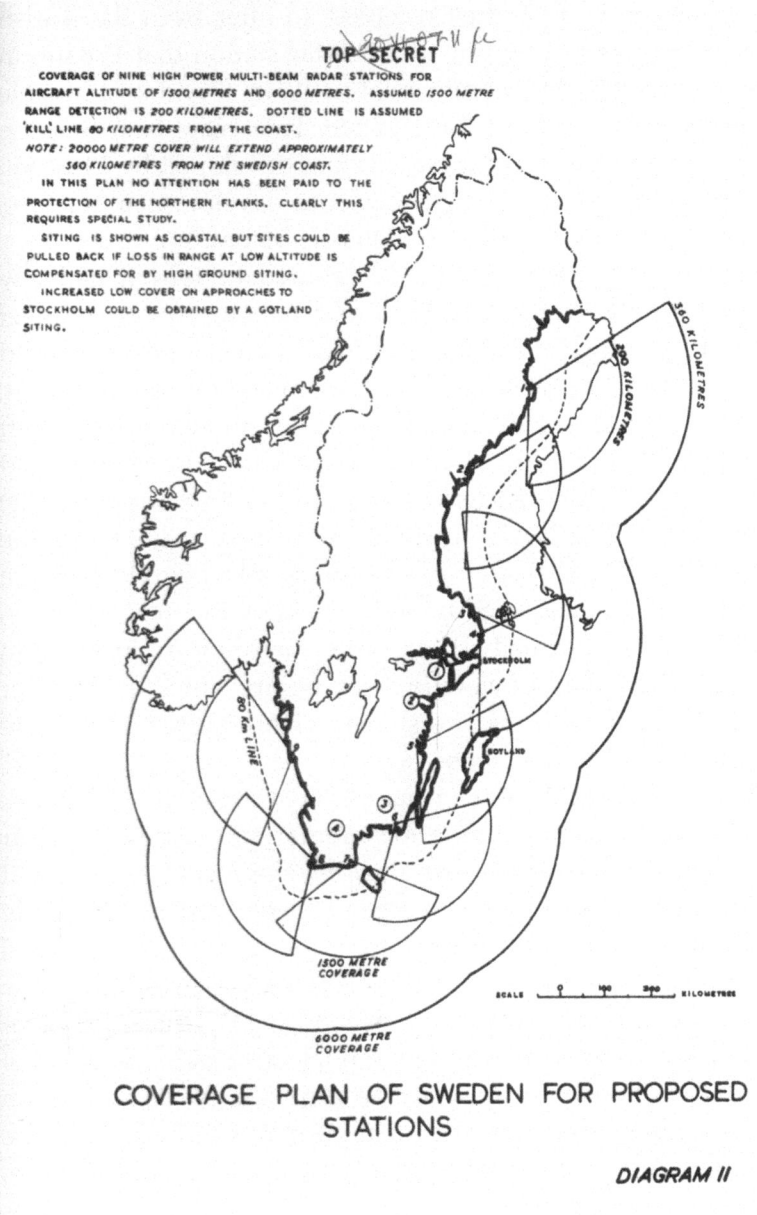

its Air Force to make its neutrality credible.[74] In 1952 the Air Force's leading commanders realized that their air bases were extremely vulnerable to attacks from low-flying enemy aircraft. They managed to establish close and trustful relations with colleagues in Great

Britain, however. In 1955 they received an offer from the British Ministry of Supply to buy a modern radar station that Britain, in the face of internal NATO commercial rivalries, found itself unable to sell to other members of the alliance. Two years later Sweden also procured a modern computer system developed by Marconi. The British company secured a contract to develop, manufacture, and install a complete Swedish air defense system.[75]

When the new system, STRIL-60, debuted in 1964 it had few counterparts in the world. Designed to detect approaching Soviet bombers at a distance of 360 km from the Swedish border, it could guide Swedish fighter planes to attack them 80 km from the coast. Moreover, the system enabled early warnings about Soviet aircraft en route to the British Isles. This was possible because Sweden and Norway operated cross-border communication links for air rescue purposes. Norway, a NATO member, was in turn linked to the British, and thus Swedish warnings could be relayed to Britain in a crisis situation. This was silently understood by the military actors involved, but never formally discussed or decided. All in all, from an infrastructural point of view, Sweden became integrated earlier and more strongly with the British air defense system than were Britain's fellow NATO members.[76]

As for offensive nuclear infrastructure, a particularly difficult task was to develop navigation aids for submarines carrying nuclear missiles. The United States led this development. Although it took place beyond NATO, the emergent system depended heavily on close cooperation with European allies. U.S. Chief of Naval Operations Admiral Arleigh Burke celebrated the virtues of a new weapon system, Polaris, organized around nuclear-fueled submarines armed with intermediate-range nuclear missiles. In spite of massive opposition both from his peers in the Navy, for whom more conventional ships was the main priority, and from Air Force commanders, who wanted to be the sole service for atomic warfare, Burke managed to push Polaris through.[77]

Burke and his colleagues developed a whole new strategy for nuclear warfare based on these submarines. In the mid-1950s the U.S. Air Force was preparing for a single massive nuclear attack on cities and counterforce targets such as air bases and missile silos in the Soviet Union. Such an attack would be conducted pre-emptively before the Soviets could do the same thing. Burke developed the alternative doctrine of "finite deterrence," whose core idea was to have Polaris submarines armed with nuclear missiles moving around in the oceans, invulnerable to Soviet nuclear attacks. If the Soviet Union launched a massive attack trying to destroy all U.S. air bases and missile ramps, the Polaris submarines would still be able to launch a devastating counterattack. If "the enemy knows we have and will use this capability, the deterrent is effective and the chances of a general war become less and less likely," Burke argued.[78]

One of the prerequisites for the Polaris system, however, was that submarine commanders could determine their underwater positions with great accuracy; otherwise the missiles launched from the vessels might miss their targets. Burke chose a navigation system that had been developed at MIT during the Second World War, LORAN-C. It allowed commanders to determine their position by measuring the time difference between the arrivals of radio signals from a number of widely spaced radio transmitters. However, the range of the first generation of Polaris missiles was only about 2,200 km, which meant that to reach major targets in the Soviet Union they would need to be launched from locations in the eastern part of the North Atlantic or in the Mediterranean. This in turn made it imperative to build LORAN-C radio stations on the European coast.[79]

Obtaining permission to construct European stations was far from straightforward. Norway, for example, had declared that "the Norwegian government will not accede to any agreement with other states which commits Norway to receive bases for the armed forces of foreign countries on Norwegian territory as long as Norway has not been attacked or subjected to threats of attack."[80] When Burke in May 1958 asked the U.S. Ambassador in Oslo, Frances Willis, to raise the topic with Norwegian Foreign Minister Halvard Lange, he thus instructed her not to tell the full story. The Norwegians learned only that the United States wished to erect a radio station in Lofoten in northern Norway, the purpose of which would be to guide civilian survey vessels carrying out a precise mapping of the seafloor. This mapping, in turn would make possible accurate navigation by the Polaris submarines. When formal decisions about the station were taken by the Cabinet and Parliament, the submarines were not mentioned at all. The general public was told that the Lofoten station would serve a range of civilian navigational purposes. However, the Norwegian technicians who took charge of its operation once it went on air in November 1959 came from the military.[81]

Similar stations appeared in Iceland and on the Faroe Islands. From the outset, Burke also planned for a transmitter in Wales. Since Britain was Washington's closest ally, this was assumed to be an easy project. However, commercial interests came in the way. The British Decca Navigation Company promoted its own Radio Navigation System and regarded the supposedly civilian LORAN-C system as a competitor. It thus did everything to block building such a station in Britain. The British government supported Decca and, after long negotiations, the United States gave up. Instead, Burke and his staff identified the Norwegian island Jan Mayen, 500 km northeast of Iceland, as a suitable location. The Norwegian government approved the U.S. request rapidly, and the station on Jan Mayen was built in great haste. It went on air on December 1, 1960, two weeks after the first Polaris submarine had gone out into the Atlantic on a patrol mission.[82]

The Soviet Union was probably well aware of the Loran-C stations and their purpose. For example, when an American survey team visited the Faroes in August 1958 to decide on the precise location of the LORAN-C station, its members discovered that the Soviet Assistant Naval Attaché in Copenhagen was staying in the same hotel. Thus in case of an actual war, these stations would probably have been high priority targets of Soviet nuclear attacks. This makes the Norwegian government's accommodating response to the U.S. requests an astounding decision.[83]

Luckily, the Cold War remained cold and no infrastructure built to guide or warn about nuclear attacks was used for its intended purpose. At times the tension between the two alliances was high and a few times full-scale war seemed near, particularly during the Cuban Missile Crisis in October 1962. This crisis highlighted the need for more mundane military communications infrastructure. At critical moments of the Cuban crisis, it took several hours to exchange messages through diplomatic channels, due to the need for coding, decoding, and translation. Hence, one of its outcomes was a decision to install a "hot line" between the White House and the Kremlin to allow secure, reliable, and swift communication in future crisis situations. In June 1963 the United States and the Soviet

Fig. 5.8 Crisis Communications: *The "hotline" between the Kremlin and the White House was constructed in 1963, after the Cuban Missile Crisis had demonstrated the tardiness in the communication between the leaders of the two superpowers. In the film Dr. Strangelove (1964) the "hotline" was depicted as a telephone connection; in reality it was a teletype link. This choice of technology was intended to reduce the risk for misinterpretations in a potential crisis situation. The British government was denied access to the hotline, which thus confirmed the role of the two new superpowers by excluding an earlier one.*

Union signed an agreement establishing a direct emergency communication link, and two months later the hotline became active.[84]

Stanley Kubrick's film *Dr. Strangelove* has created the popular misconception that the hot line was a telephone line. In reality it was a teletype link. A telephone line was seriously considered, but both sides agreed that a major disadvantage of a telephone line was that it could lead to misunderstandings. A hot line conversation would have to be translated instantly at both ends with a risk of misinterpretations. Furthermore, spontaneous and ill-considered remarks could be dangerous in a crisis situation. The teletype communication would minimize these risks. At first a single landline link routed through Helsinki, Stockholm, and London sufficed. After a Finnish farmer unknowingly cut the line while plowing his field a few years later, an added second link provided redundancy.[85]

European NATO member states opposed the bilateral nature of the hotline. When the British government discovered that the link would actually pass through London, it expressed a desire that a switchboard in London would make three-way communications possible. However, the leaders in Washington and Moscow refused. The hotline thus became a manifestation of the new Cold War realities in which major West European powers were reduced to second-rank players. Later on, the Soviet government used "hotline diplomacy" to sow dissension among NATO member states. When French President Charles de Gaulle visited Moscow in 1966, he signed an agreement authorizing a direct teleprinter line between the Elysée Palace and the Kremlin, but when the British government wanted a similar link, its request was rejected. Only in 1992 was a hotline finally established between the British and Russian governments.[86]

Losing Control of Colonies

On the European continent, the early Cold War was characterized by transboundary military system-building within NATO and the Warsaw Pact, and by diminishing influence of the traditional West European powers. On the global scene, Europe's colonial powers initially sought to maintain their overseas possessions and avoid their empires' disintegration. Increasingly, however, independence movements contested these aims.

A particularly fierce struggle took place in Indochina, a French colony since the 1880s following growing French penetration into the region earlier in the century. During the Second World War, Japan occupied Indochina, but as soon as the Japanese withdrew, France claimed sovereignty anew over the territory. The Viet Minh, a national liberation movement led by the communist Ho Chi Minh, refused to accept the return of French colonialism. After fruitless negotiations with the French government, the Viet Minh started a guerilla war in late 1946, with General Vo Nguyen Giap as its commander in chief. Three years later the communists in China came to power after a long civil war and began aiding Giap's troops with heavy weapons and other supplies. The Soviet Union followed suit, helping the Viet Minh to seize control of large parts of rural northern Vietnam, while the French controlled major cities and most of the south. In April 1953, Giap's troops entered Laos and attacked French outposts there as well, forcing the enemy to further disperse their resources.[87]

On the morning of November 20, 1953, 65 French Dakota air planes, filled with paratroopers, took off from the airport of Hanoi. An hour's flight later the planes reached their goal: the little village of Dien Bien Phu in Northern Vietnam, close to the Laotian border. As the 1500 paratroopers landed they met resistance from Viet Minh soldiers based in the village, but could soon seize control of the area. The French soldiers immediately repaired and upgraded an airstrip that had been constructed by the Japanese during the Second World War. During the following months the French flew in additional troops, weapons, and supplies and constructed strong fortifications around the air strip. The Dien Bien Phu base was intended to obstruct the Viet Minh's flow of men and supplies across the border, deemed necessary because the village was located strategically along one of the main roads to Laos.[88]

Hearing of the new French air base, General Giap decided to prepare a full-scale attack on it. The ensuing battle became a contest between two very different logistic systems. The French relied on their total command of the air for supplies. Giap organized a low-technology system to transport large quantities of weapons and supplies from the Chinese border to Dien Bien Phu, 800 km away. He mobilized 50,000 soldiers and more than 100,000 civilians to improve dirt tracks through dense jungles and across many mountains and rivers. Much work was devoted to camouflage; often the treetops were lashed together over roads to create tunnels, and bridges were

220 | Europe's Infrastructure Transition

Fig. 5.9 **Low-Tech Logistics:** *In the first months of 1954 the Viet Minh guerilla forces enrolled more than a hundred thousand peasants to complete a huge transport operation. They helped bring large amounts of arms and supplies from the Chinese border to the hills surrounding the heavily fortified French base at Dien Bien Phu, a distance of 800 km. With superiority of men, arms, and supplies, the Viet Minh defeated the French garrison after two months of fighting. The picture shows transport of food supplies in May 1954.*

built just below the surface of streams, making them invisible. This crude transport infrastructure sufficed for the Soviet trucks that Giap had at his disposal. Still, parts of the route were impassable for heavy vehicles, a problem that was solved by having local peasants, using bamboo rigs or bicycles, carry the loads. All this work had to be done under the constant danger of French air attacks.[89]

After four months, Giap was ready for the attack. Apart from the 50,000 soldiers under his command, he had placed more than 200 heavy field guns and well over 1,000 tons of ammunition in the forest-covered hills surrounding Dien Bien Phu. Moreover, he had reliable intelligence and knew that the French troops numbered 15,000 men armed with sixty guns. In contrast, the French commander, Colonel Christian de Castries, could not imagine that his opponent had mobilized such immense resources in this inaccessible part of the country. The battle lasted for eight weeks and the losses were huge on both sides. The final outcome was a complete victory for the Viet Minh. On May 7, 1954, Giap's men stormed the bunker housing de Castries and his staff officers, forcing them to surrender.[90]

This humiliating defeat shocked France and the Western world at large. For the first time an anti-colonial liberation movement had defeated a modern European power in full-scale battle. Dien Bien Phu did not only put an end to French rule in Indochina; it also meant the beginning of the end for France as a colonial power. By the mid-1960s the vast French empire in Africa and Asia had fragmented and disintegrated. Only French Guyana and a few islands in the Caribbean and the Pacific and Indian Oceans remained.[91]

Other West European nations saw their colonial empires fragmenting and dissolving in similar ways. In many colonies, independence movements commenced as guerilla warfare, and the colonial powers gradually realized that the high costs of maintaining and supplying troops far away prevented social reforms at home. This was so at least in Europe's democracies. In the case of authoritarian Portugal, the Salazar dictatorship clung to its African possessions much longer. It was only after a 1974 coup by war-weary leftist officers that its colonies achieved independence.[92]

The generally fast decolonization in Africa and Asia implied a concomitant European military withdrawal. In particular, almost all the naval bases that had once symbolized European global power—the "keys" that locked up the globe, as British Admiral Fisher had once put it—became property of the new independent nations.[93] However, the U.S. Navy, or in some cases the Soviet Navy, did subsequently take over some of them. The two superpowers thus assumed the global roles that a handful of Western European nations had played during the past 500 years.[94]

Yet concomitant technological developments partly reduced the negative effects of lost colonial bases. In particular, the greater range of modern ships—not least nuclear-powered ones—and advances in refueling at sea made navies more self-contained. Britain demonstrated this, for example, in the 1982 Falklands War. Shortly after the Argentinian invasion of the Falkland Islands (or, for Argentina, the Malvinas), the British government sent a Task Force to the archipelago, some 13,000 km from the British Isles. It comprised 127 ships, of which two-thirds were supply ships carrying 400,000 tons of fuel and 100,000 tons of freight. Many vessels had equipment for refueling at sea, thus making them independent of on-shore bases.

Britain also made effective use of the bases that it still controlled. Ascension Island, in particular, located in the middle of the South Atlantic, played an important role in the war. A British "Overseas Territory," it served as a staging post for the Task Force on its way to target. The airfield on the island had been rented out to the U.S. Air Force, but Prime Minister Thatcher managed to obtain U.S. President Reagan's permission to use it. Furthermore, British aircraft gained access to 40,000 tons of aviation fuel that the Americans had stockpiled on the island, which was subsequently used in destructive bombardments.[95]

The Infrastructure of a Dark Continent

"What was new in Europe's history was not the existence of conflict, but rather its scale," writes one historian, when contrasting the Franco-Prussian War's death toll, 184,000, with the 8 million killed in the First World War and the more than 40 million Europeans— half of them civilians—who died in the Second World War.[96] As this chapter has documented, this increase was closely linked to the incorporation of modern infrastructure into the planning and making of wars. As such it cannot be understood as a twentieth-century phenomenon only, but rather as part of a longer process begun in the mid-nineteenth century.

Military system-builders almost always understood the potential of new infrastructure as soon as it was introduced. From the 1860s, railroads and telegraphs became an integral part of military planning; and when war broke out large numbers of men were quickly mobilized and dispatched to the afflicted border regions by train, in massive logistical operations guided by modern communications. The huge number of soldiers on the battlefields and the efficiency with which they could be supplied with weapons and ammunition paved the way for a massive increase in deaths. Initially Europe's military planners and strategists believed that modern infrastructure would contribute to early decisive battles and thus to shorter wars. The First World War proved such expectations totally wrong. In fact, infrastructure contributed to the epic deadlock on the Western Front, where armies pounded one another month after month, year after year, with enormous loss of lives as a result.

In the interwar years the development of new transport technologies, notably armored vehicles and aviation, paved the way for a revival of the "cult of the offensive." When the Second World War broke out, Hitler's blitzkrieg strategy seemed to confirm this thesis. In the end, however, reliance on modern infrastructure had its limits; and, as in the First World War, it definitely did not succeed in putting an early end to the war. Instead, it enabled the

Fig. 5.10 **Death at a Distance:** *Nazi German Luftwaffe's 1937 bombing of Guernica in the Spanish Civil War caused massive destruction and many civilian casualties, as this picture shows. It demonstrated the capacity of bomber aircraft to bring about indiscriminate death at a distance; and through Picasso's famous painting, it has become a symbol of the cruelty of war. More generally, infrastructure contributed to the radical increase in the scale and scope of destruction in warfare from the mid-nineteenth to the mid-twentieth centuries.*

killing of millions of civilians. This was because, first, improved infrastructure allowed warfare to be conducted over much vaster areas, entailing that many more civilians were affected. Second, the fast build-up of a military aviation infrastructure enabled large-scale terror bombings far behind the fronts. Third, the Nazis launched a racial war to kill millions of Jews and other unwanted people, whereby Europe's integrated railroad infrastructure played a crucial role in transporting victims to Hitler's death camps.

During the Cold War, the potential scale of destruction in a war with nuclear weapons was almost unimaginable. The combination of warheads with extremely high destructive power and an infrastructure for launching them over long distances and with high precision created unprecedented threats. But this potential scale of a nuclear war had a restraining effect. Before 1950, "more than sixty million people died in wars or through state-sponsored violence; by contrast, the number of those who died in such a fashion after 1950 is well under one million, even taking the war in Yugoslavia into account."[97]

To a large extent, military system-builders appropriated infrastructure that had been built and designed primarily for civilian purposes. They did their best to modify the design of such systems for strategic or tactical purposes. For example, they built double track railroads to border stations that had little traffic in times of peace, and they designed bridges that could support heavy tanks—and be easily blown up if needed. In addition, potential combatants constructed dedicated military infrastructure. Naval and air bases formed logistical hubs for war. They were linked to each other and to remote sources of supply through increasingly sophisticated transport, communications, and energy systems. The infrastructure developed in this context often produced civilian spin-offs. For example, Britain's military pipeline system, designed during the Second World War, inspired commercial pipeline building in Europe during the postwar period. Similarly, the air traffic control systems developed in the context of terror bombing campaigns proved highly useful for civilian air traffic control purposes.

Finally, can we discern patterns specific to Europe through the perspective of military system-building? As armed forces have been tightly connected to nation states, Military Europe has basically conformed to the literally inter-national Europe that is so familiar from political history, with nation states struggling against each other and at times forming alliances to strengthen their positions. In the late nineteenth century, the major European countries developed elaborate war plans, coordinated with their allies and shaped to counter the plans that general staffs believed their adversaries had drafted. In this way Europe's military systems became increasingly interlocked, and when Russia started its mobilization in late July 1914, it more or less forced everybody else to do the same. In the course of the two World Wars, allies increasingly collaborated in military system-building and in crucial logistical efforts.

During the Cold War era the level of trans-boundary cooperation increased even further. Within the Warsaw pact, the Soviet Union had tight overall control, while NATO was less important in organizing such cooperation than one might have expected. The navigational infrastructure for the Polaris submarines, for example, was developed outside NATO; and in the end the system involved only the United States, Norway, Iceland, and Denmark. Britain refused to participate, while at the same time developing strong infrastructural links with a neutral, non-NATO member state such as Sweden in the field of air defense communications. Military Europe was thus divided not only by the Iron Curtain, but also by a number of boundaries that were invisible from a formal political point of view.

Importantly, the geographical structure of Europe in terms of already existing, civilian infrastructure had a marked impact on the course of wars. This was obvious already by the 1860s, when Prussia for the first time made large-scale use of railroads in its military campaigns. In the Second World War, Nazi Germany profited greatly from the fact that the railroads of both its allies and most occupied territories shared many technical characteristics, notably the European standard gauge. Among other things, this allowed for efficient transport of Jews from nearly all corners of Europe to the ghettos, killing fields, and death camps in the East. Conversely, Hitler's military commanders faced enormous difficulties supplying their dispersed troops in the Soviet Union due to the different technical characteristics of its railroads and roads.

All in all, from a military perspective Michel Chevalier's vision of the "circulation society" proved wholly in error. The rise of modern infrastructure and the intensification of economic cooperation did not prevent future wars. On the contrary, military system-builders skillfully exploited and extended Europe's infrastructure transition for murderous and destructive purposes, paving the way for wars to be fought on unprecedented scales and with greater loss of human life than anyone could have imagined two hundred years ago.

III
NETWORKING NATURE

6
Linking Land

Networked Mountain

Mount Brocken in the Harz chain is not extremely high with its 1,141 meter summit. Yet Northern Germany's tallest mountain, on the watershed of the Elbe and Weser rivers, always was a prominent landscape marker. Forests and bogs long made it inaccessible to human settlement. Tellingly, the mountain was a pagan refuge from Charlemagne's eighth-century Christianization campaigns to the late sixteenth century witch hunts. Contemporary myths identified Mount Brocken as the German center for the annual witch sabbath Walpurgis Night (*Walpurgisnacht*) and held that the mountain's inaccessibility necessitated that witches fly in on brooms. Equally telling, seventeenth-century botanists and physicians were among the first to climb to the summit on written record, to study the subalpine vegetation. Mount Brocken was a site of nature and social seclusion, but this was about to change.[1]

In the eighteenth century the local ruler, Count Christian Ernst zu Stolberg-Wernigerode, decided to exploit his property economically, and used infrastructure to open up Mount Brocken. A ring of peat works soon harnessed its subsoil energy for nearby towns and iron industries. Hiking trails to the summit and a summit inn attracted tourism to what the Count cleverly called "the mountain of all Germans."[2] By the 1820s some two thousand visitors annually signed the inn's guest book. Romantic poets now promoted the mountain as a symbol of the German nation itself: "Der Brocken ist ein Deutscher" wrote Heinrich Heine in 1824, praising the mountain for its "German thoroughness" and "German calmness, understanding, tolerance; because he can survey things so far and clear."[3] Romantic authors from August Wilhelm Schlegel to Hans Christian Andersen visited the Brocken to experience its sublime natural setting. Ironically, the region's last wolves and lynxes were now shot; bears had already disappeared. From the 1860s, nearby municipalities lobbied for a railroad to the summit to enable mass tourism, but botanists feared that the mountain's subalpine plant life would vanish too. Mount Brocken also entered environmental knowledge networks, with mixed success: in the 1820s the famous mathematician Carl Friedrich Gauss adopted the summit as a triangulation node for his geodetic survey of the Kingdom of Hanover, and meteorologists made the first temperature and air pressure measurements. In the 1860s, however, the Central Prussian Meteorological Institute closed the summit station, because regional weather predictions did not improve as expected.

By the 1890s botanists had installed a protected sub-Alpine summit garden, meteorologists staffed a new permanent weather station, postal services and a telegraph station served Brocken tourists, and the Nordhausen–Wernigerode Railway Company raised 5.5 million marks at the Berlin Bourse for a narrow-gauge track to the top. During the 1930s the railroad alone carried no less than 250,000 passengers uphill annually. Broadcasting infrastructure further enhanced the Brocken's role in German nation-building: A dirt road helped trucks to carry up an experimental TV station in 1935. The next year it broadcast the Berlin Olympic Games, through which the Nazi government attempted to advertise the Aryan race's physical superiority. Soon communication cables connected the Berlin television studios to a permanent summit TV tower, powered by a 15 kV line from the nearest electric power network. The Brocken had become a thoroughly-networked mountain by the time the German government declared the region a nature reserve in 1937.

The Cold War changed Mount Brocken from a node in national networks to a sensitive international border. As it was situated just east of the new demarcation line, East German *Volkspolizei* opened a summit station to obstruct illegal border traffic with West Germany. Mountain visits henceforward required a permit. Initially the new East German leader Walter Ulbricht still invited tourism for supporters of the new regime: "I can see the peaceful German lands from here," he told Eastern and Western youth at the summit in 1951; "but looking West I see the criminal preparation for a new war...I trust you are wise enough to walk for peace rather than lie on the front and be destroyed."[4] By 1960 the railroad annually carried up some 90,000, overwhelmingly Eastern, visitors. When Ulbricht and Khrushchev agreed to build the Berlin Wall in August 1961, however, "walks for peace" and railroad visits ended. The mountain summit turned into the Warsaw Pact's most western military bulwark, permanently staffed with East German and Soviet troops. NATO particularly worried about the Soviet espionage station *Jenissej* and its advanced East German counterpart *Urian*. *Urian* eavesdropped on civilian telephone conversations beamed in and out of West Berlin, captured police and military transmissions up to four hundred kilometers into Western territory, end relayed intercepted signals to analyst centers in Magdeburg and East Berlin by underground cable. To nature conservationists' regret, a 2,600 m long concrete wall sealed off the summit bulwark.

When the Berlin Wall fell in November 1989, local inhabitants climbed Mount Brocken's snow-clad slopes to challenge their own local wall. In early December thousands rallied for "free citizens, free Brocken." East German security forces were confused and left. Soviet soldiers provided hot tea—they would not abandon camp until 1994. Soon a new summit television tower relayed all-German programs, a new radar dome served all-German air traffic control, and the weather station tackled problems common to East and West such as acid rain measurements.

In the realm of nature, however, different visions of East–West reintegration clashed. Locals advertised Brocken's nature tourism as East–West reconciliation and pushed for reopening the summit railroad, which currently welcomes over a million people annually. Nature conservationists, by contrast, pushed for an integrated East–West nature plan. In December 1989 a conference of

Fig. 6.1 Reclaiming Mount Brocken: *Citizens reclaimed the military bulwark of Mount Brocken after the end of the Cold War in Germany on December 3, 1989. The mountain was at once an icon of nature and a key node in communication systems. The three summit installations from left to right are East Germany's old and new TV towers and its* Urian *espionage dome, known locally as the "Stasi mosque" (referring to East Germany's secret police—the Ministry for State Security or "Stasi").*

over three hundred conservationists from East and West agreed to turn the Iron Curtain barrier strip, where wildlife thrived in the absence of human settlement, into a protected corridor for plants and animals. Their scheme later evolved into one of Europe's most ambitious ecological system-building projects; the plan was that the so-called European Green Belt should interconnect nature reserves from the Barents Sea, along the Finnish–Russian border and Central Europe's former Iron Curtain, to the Mediterranean. In the Brocken region, situated within this belt, nature on either side of the former border should be integrated into a natural park; this park should serve as a priority node in Europe's hoped-for ecological infrastructure.[5] Because of these plans, ecologists loathed the Brocken railroad as "a dagger into the heart" of nature. In return, locals rallied against the new "green dictatorship" that threatened economic development.[6] By way of compromise, the new natural park would combine tourism with cultural heritage and nature conservation. The region's environmental flagship became the reintroduction of the Eurasian lynx, which in the age of infrastructure came with embedded GPS transmitters.

The networking of Mount Brocken illustrates several roles of infrastructure in the remaking of Europe's natural environment. Over the past two centuries transport, energy, communications, and hydraulic infrastructure firmly tied preindustrial landscapes and largely-untrodden nature into the modern human-built world. Even if marketed as celebrating nature, as in the case of the Brocken railroad and later Nazi motorway projects, these connections often interrupted ecological flows.[7] Conservationists responded to these interruptions with programs to reconnect Europe's "fragmented nature" into an ecological infrastructure. The connection and rupture of nature was part and parcel of Europe's infrastructure transition.

The chapters in Part III of this book inquire about the networking of Europe's natural environment—its landscapes, waters, and skies. They first address the virtual integration of Europe's environments into transnational scientific knowledge systems, such as geodetic associations developing coordinate grids overlaying European space, or meteorological societies modeling the European air. Such knowledge networks constituted an arena for European integration and fragmentation in their own right, but also reflected and informed the making of real environmental connections and ruptures: the incorporation of land, water, and air into Europe's infrastructure space, the associated fragmentation of European nature, and deliberate attempts to restore Europe's fragmented nature by means of green infrastructure.

Knowing Land

By the time Carl Friedrich Gauss climbed Mount Brocken for surveying the Kingdom of Hanover, the territorial state had already become a prominent organizational unit for generating land knowledge. Europe's medieval dynasties had had no maps and no concept of fixed and unified territory. Their realms had been patchworks of historically-acquired kingdoms, duchies, lordships, counties, boroughs, castles, towns, villages, and so on, held together by personal bonds rather than continuous territories, and routinely intersected by foreign enclaves. Administrators measured internal realm distances in travel time between centers. External borders usually remained undefined and unmarked. Historical atlases that retrospectively depict Europe's medieval dynasties as sharply-bounded territorial states are deeply anachronistic.

From the fifteenth century, however, geographers in Latin Christendom rediscovered Ptolemy's ancient concepts of longitude and latitude, abstract coordinate grids overlaid on the landscape, and cartographic projections (Islamic geographers had used these techniques all along). To assist military campaigns, road building, administration, and taxation, Europe's rulers increasingly hired geographers to map their realms.

The making of the famous Cassini map of France illustrates the difficulties of such knowledge system-building. By 1679 the French *Académie Royale des Sciences* and the famous military system-builder Vauban, who desired well-defined and fortified Kingdom borders, had convinced the Sun King to order a new map of France. Genoa-born Giovanni Domenico Cassini documented the Kingdom's contours within a few years, but surveying the inner Kingdom by triangulation—using the mathematical fact that if two points, the base line connecting them, and two angles of an imaginary triangle are known, the distance to a third point can be calculated—took much longer. When Cassini's eyesight faltered, his son Jacques took over and completed triangulating the length of France along the Paris meridian in 1718. Further triangulation, pushed by the *Corps des Ponts et Chaussées* for road building purposes, produced a virtual network of 800 adjoined triangles overlaying the landscape and an 18-sheet map of France (scale 1:878,000) by 1744. A third generation Cassini, César-François, led a more detailed triangulation for a 180-sheet topological map (1:86,400). His son Jean Dominique finally presented it to Parliament in 1789. By then French statesmen saw their country as a bounded territorial state represented by the Cassini map, which combined a national coordinate grid with depicting—in the words of French Revolution theorist Abbé Sieyès in 1789—"the smallest parishes and the finest details...to a great degree of exactitude."[8]

Equally time consuming, the first triangulation of Denmark ran from 1761 to 1820 and the Board of Ordnance's "principal triangulation of Britain" took from 1783 to 1853. The Napoleonic Wars gave a further boost to landscape knowledge production, and at the 1814–15 Vienna Peace Congress statesmen used maps and surveys to negotiate Europe's new state system in terms of territorially-sovereign states, separated by exact boundary lines. New states established by the Congress, such as the Kingdom of Hanover for which Gauss worked, lost no time to hook up their territories in the scientists' virtual knowledge networks.

Europe's land knowledge systems also expanded outward. The efforts of the British East India Company are illustrative. In the late eighteenth century, Bengal's Surveyor General, James Renell, used road length research to devise a large-scale Map of Hindoostan. This map innovatively depicted the Company's South Asian possessions as a coherent geographical region. In order to map this territory, Major William Lambton started his Great Trigonometric Survey of India in 1802; it would provide a common grid for the Company's local and regional cartography. Setting out from Madras in the south with a 10.8 km baseline, the triangulation reached the Himalayas in about forty years. The world's highest mountain was named after Lambton's assistant and successor, George Everest. The project reached completion in 1870. By then the British state (which had succeeded the East India Company as ruler of the subcontinent) and Indian nationalists alike understood India as a bounded territory.

In practice, however, local detail and large-scale grids did not always connect. Militaries, road and railroad builders, and local administrators rarely waited for large-scale reference grids to guide their local and regional surveys. Still, large-scale landscape knowledge increasingly fed global geopolitical imaginations: the far reaches of British land knowledge networks is perhaps best illustrated by the British Imperial Federation League's famous 1886 imperial map. Its designer, Walter Crane, visualized the Victorian imagination of empire in the form of a world map with clearly delineated and colored British possessions on all continents, connected by the main naval trade routes, surrounded by colonial imagery, and united under the banner of "freedom, fraternity, and federation."[9]

Meanwhile the emerging science of geodesy started linking isolated coordinate grids into international reference systems. The so-called Struve Geodetic Arc became an icon of

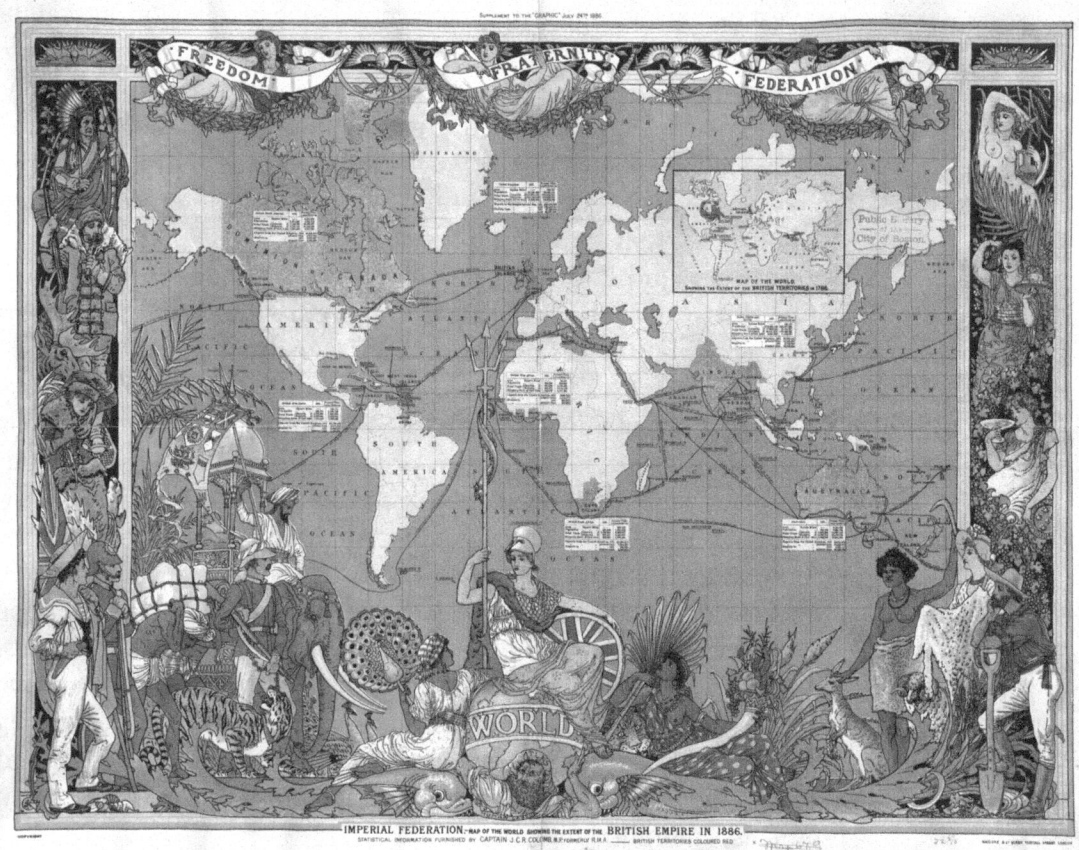

Fig. 6.2 **Mapping the Empire:** *Large-scale landscape knowledge infrastructure fed geopolitical imaginations. Artist and illustrator Walter Crane visualized the* Imperial Federation, map of the world showing the extent of the British Empire in 1886 *for the Imperial Federation League. The map, published in the London weekly,* The Graphic, *delineates British possessions on all continents, and connects them by naval trade routes centered on Britain.*

internationalist geodetic referencing. In the Russian Protectorate of Livonia, the Livonian Society for Public Utility and Economy and Tartu University hired astronomy professor Friedrich Georg Wilhelm von Struve in 1816 to map Livonia for three thousand silver roubles, a horse, and a wagon. Some 400 km further south, Imperial quartermaster-general Prince Piotr Mikhailovich Volkonsky assigned military topographer Carl Tenner to a similar project for the Vilnius Protectorate. While their regional triangulation assignments served road building and military logistics, Struve and Tenner envisioned a larger scientific by-product: the triangulation of the meridian, or at least a big part of it, would greatly contribute to the endeavor to measure the shape of the earth. Inspired by Lambton's and Everest's efforts in India, they worked together to measure the length of the arc from the northern coast of Norway to the Black Sea.

Fig. 6.3 Triangulating Territories: *Geographers measured land by means of triangulation—using the mathematical fact that if the position of two landscape points is known, the position of a third point can be calculated by measuring the angles of an imaginary triangle. Friedrich Georg Wilhelm von Struve, Carl Tenner, and their collaborators measured a large part of a meridian from Northern Norway to the Black Sea from 1816 to 1855, which became constituent of Europe's emergent coordinate grid. The 2,880 km arc required 258 triangles, and was connected to the known (astronomically determined) position of the Pulkovo Observatory near St. Petersburg.*

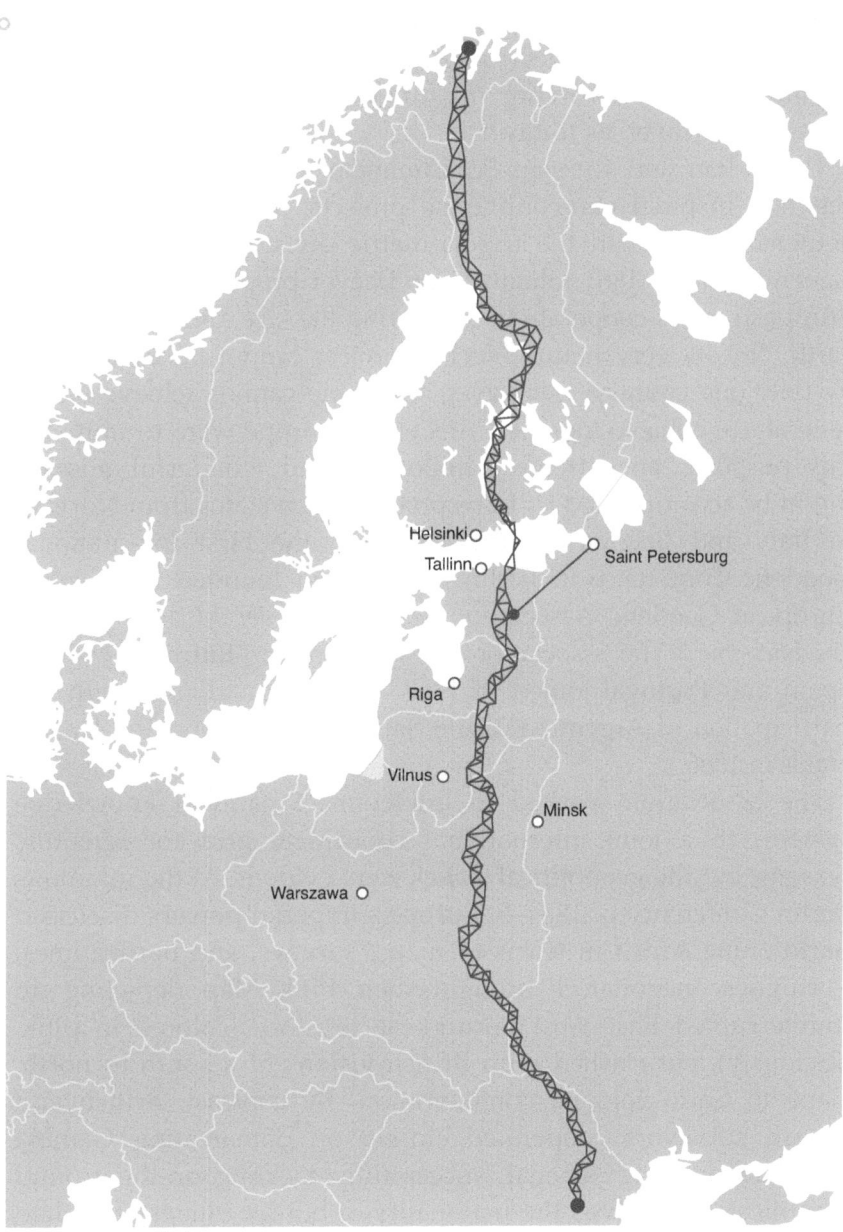

Colleague geodesists led the project work in Finland, Norway, and Sweden. Taking in hand iron bars to measure baselines and theodolites and other apparatus to determine angles, Struve, Tenner and their collaborators completed the 2,880 km arc with 258 main adjoined triangles in 1855. When UNESCO put the

Struve Geodetic Arc on its World Heritage List in 2005 it was still an integrative project, now in the form of a collaborative commemoration involving organizations in the ten countries that the arc traverses today.[10]

The Indian and Russian–Scandinavian arc measurement projects also inspired pan-continental projects. Recently retired as a lieutenant-general in the trigonometric division of the Prussian General Staff, in 1861 Johann Jacob Baeyer proposed that Central European states cooperate in measuring the size and shape of the earth: "by its very nature, such a project cannot be undertaken by only one country...However, what one cannot achieve alone, several can achieve together...if Central Europe were to unite for this purpose...an extremely important and wonderful mission might be accomplished."[11] In response, fifteen states from Norway to Italy and Belgium to Russia joined the First International Geodetic Conference in Berlin in 1864 and founded the Central European Geodetic Association (*Zentralbüro der Mitteleuropäische Gradmessung*). The association's name became "European" when Spain and Portugal joined in 1867 and "international" with the participation of Argentina, Chile, Japan, Mexico, and the United States in 1886.

The association worked to interconnect national knowledge systems in a joint international coordinate grid for scientific reasons, but the geopolitical stakes were evident. At the infamous Berlin Conference of 1884–5, Europe's imperial powers discussed partitioning Africa in terms of maps, surveys, and border lines. Portuguese negotiators brought their Pink Map depicting an uninterrupted East–West Portuguese territory (colored in pink, obviously), but clashed with British visions of a south to north, Cape to Cairo colonial confederation. By contrast, British and French surveyors cooperated closely on demarcating Gambia from surrounding Senegal, successfully tackling on-the-ground complications such as the nationality of border villages that had resulted from their diplomats' conference room negotiations. Newcomers in the imperial game quickly learned the rules. In 1890 Japan's foreign minister Aoki Shūzō recommended that "Korea should be made part of the Japanese map."[12] Upon annexation in 1910, Japan's Imperial Geodetic Committee moved in and tasked over eight hundred staff to triangulate Korea, reference it in the international coordinate system, and geodetically embed the new colony's legal status in international law. King Rama IV of Siam (Thailand) mapped his country as a territorial state to keep his British and French colonial neighbors at bay, and simultaneously gain control of his unruly border zones. For scientific or for political reasons, surveyors across the globe hooked up territories in huge transnational landscape grids. And so, they build a transnational knowledge system that organized Europe and the world in coordinates.

During the First World War, the association's neutral members kept going in the Reduced Geodetic Association Among Neutral Nations, which after the war transferred its activities to the International Union of Geodesy and Geophysics. By 1936 the Union had commissions for aligning the overall European network; better connecting the French, Belgian, and Italian triangulations; aligning French and Italian measurements in Morocco; and completing the African primary triangulation network and its connection to the European grid.

The virtual integration of Europe's land into one knowledge system had progressed impressively by 1946, when the Union's geodesy section became the International Association of Geodesy. However, noted U.S. Army Geodetic Division Chief Floyd W. Hough, in Europe "each country has established its own triangulation and computed the geographic position from its own selected astronomic initial."[13] These referencing differences induced errors into the European primary triangulation grid. So did differences in the equipment used. Hough pushed for an army-led, full-scale re-triangulation. When civilian geodesists protested against U.S. army leadership, he strategically placed the project under the international scientific association. Still its Cold War flavor was undeniable: In 1947 the U.S. Army General Staff had ordered a secret Geodesy for Guided Missiles program "to resolve to a common datum all existing worldwide geodetic surveys," starting with Hough's re-triangulation of Europe.[14] Thus Hough's new Land Survey Office in Occupied Germany reworked the geodetic archives captured from the German army (these in turn included military maps taken from the Russians). In addition it set up 714 first-order stations to re-triangulate the Central European network from Belgium to Latvia. This network in turn connected to a reanalysis of the Baltic Ring (Norway–Sweden–Finland–Estonia–Latvia–Denmark) that by the early 1950s included 820 points and some 1,000 triangles, including 3 flare triangulation nodes—flares dropped from airplanes by parachute to cover gaps of 100–300 km such as the Danish–Norwegian sea straits. Soon followed a southwestern bloc including North Africa and a southeastern bloc reaching into Ukraine. The new primary grid called European Datum 1950 became NATO's reference for European horizontal land knowledge. In 1955 followed the United European Leveling Network Western Europe to calibrate vertical landscape knowledge, so coordinates could be specified in three dimensions. Soviet geodesists used their System S42 standard centered on the Pulkovo observatory near Leningrad, founded by Struve a century earlier, for USSR state re-triangulation and, from 1957, as the standard for the Eastern European United Astronomic Geodetic Network. A year later the Eastern European Unified Precise Leveling Network commenced its research. Europe's landscapes were now framed in two coordinate grids on either side of the Iron Curtain.[15]

Land knowledge system-building received yet another boost from remote sensing technologies and Geographic Information Systems. First World War military airplane reconnaissance had promoted the so-called classical form of remote sensing, aerial photography surveys. In the 1920s the new discipline of aerial photogrammetry developed techniques to reference such photographs through geodetic grids, rectify perspective distortions, and account for gradients. The two-way interaction with transport system-building continued: young airline companies offered aerial photography services for topographic agencies. Infrastructure builders for their part referenced aerial photographs and cadastral maps in large-scale coordinate grids to project tunnels and bridges. By the late 1930s several European governments had ordered aerial photograph mapping; and by 1950 a prominent professor in geodesy, Willem Schermerhorn, had convinced the United Nations to establish an International Training Center for Aerial Survey at his Delft Polytechnic in the Netherlands. The new Center hosted European cooperation in aerial survey research and trained surveyors from developing countries to map the remaining 75 percent of the earth's land surface by aerial photogrammetry.[16]

Remote sensing from satellites, finally, promised to revolutionize large-scale landscape knowledge systems in two ways. First, satellite navigation radio signals further boosted work on geographic reference grids and positioning. Second, optical remote sensing enabled views of land cover and land use on a continental scale, providing a 'satellite view' of Europe's landscape connections and fragmentations.

After the famous launch of the Soviet *Sputnik* satellite in 1957, the Soviet military and the U.S. Department of Defense had worked vigorously on radio-based satellite positioning to guide bombers, missiles, and submarines. By the 1980s the Soviet programs had developed into the Global Navigation Satellite System (*Globalnaya Navigatsionnaya Sputnikovaya Sistema* or GLONASS), the U.S. programs into the Global Positioning System (GPS). In both systems, ground station or mobile computers calculated their location by triangulating radio signals from several satellites. The Soviet system remained a military-only technology until the 2000s, but the Global Positioning System produced a civilian spin-off. The Americans had already put a number of military GPS satellites in orbit when, on September 1, 1983, autopilot navigation problems led Korean Air Line Flight 007 from New York to Seoul into Soviet territory. Soviet military commanders on duty interpreted the flight as a spying mission and ordered an interceptor plane to shoot down the craft, killing all 269 people on board. A major Cold War blame game erupted, with U.S. President Ronald Reagan responding to what he called a "crime against humanity" by ordering part of the GPS signals open to civilian use, free of charge, to avoid similar navigational errors in the future.

After 1989 a new generation of GPS satellites provided high-precision signals to the U.S. military and less-precise signals for civilian use. Europe's geodesists immediately tapped into the new resource to serve vehicle navigation producers and EUROCONTROL's air traffic controllers, who found the European Datum 1950 standard outdated. In 1987 Europeans in the International Association for Geodesy teamed up with the European Committee for Official Cartography to build GPS stations at 300–500 km distance and triangulate the European Terrestrial Reference Frame (ETRF89), which the European Commission later adopted as its standard for European map making. In the 1990s followed a re-triangulation of many former communist states. The military significance of landscape knowledge surfaced occasionally, as in 1995, when the Ukrainian military halted geodetic association staff and confiscated measurements from fifteen Ukrainian GPS stations. Russia, Belorussia, and Moldavia did not join the new standard; as in much other infrastructure, the Iron Curtain had not dissolved but moved eastward. By the mid-1990s the European commission also asked for an upgrade of the vertical reference standard; the European Vertical Reference Network would henceforward calibrate coordinate systems in 3D with a precision in the centimeters range—years before the European Union and the European Space Agency started their own civilian navigation satellite program, GALILEO in the early 2000s.[17]

Using Land

The second way in which satellites transformed Europe's large-scale landscape knowledge was by photographing the uses of land on a Pan-European scale. These data were fed into Geographic Information Systems, which then projected what Europe looked like in terms of human-made and ecological infrastructure.

Satellite imagery initially seemed unable to even approach the resolution of aerial photography: "seeing more than the contours of the most general features of nature from satellite images...seems completely out of the question," noted a photogrammetrist in 1957.[18] However, optical satellite imagery increasingly proved useful for large-scale land use inquiries, thanks to multi-spectral scanning and computer manipulation of data in geographic information systems, which developed rapidly in the 1960s. By the late 1960s the UN International Training Center in Delft was involved in multi-spectral scanner imagery research for NASA's New Earth Resources Technology satellites (soon known as LANDSAT). When LANDSAT I became operational in 1972, Europe's land knowledge system-builders had access to its multi-wavelength optical images.

The European Communities' Joint Research Center in Ispra, Italy, henceforward used LANDSAT data to map Community land cover. During the 1970s its overriding aim was to estimate agricultural production better, which at that time consumed most

Fig. 6.4   Europe from Above: *From 1985 the European Communities' Joint Research Center in Ispra, Italy, used satellite photographs to map Community land cover. Satellite data was stored, combined, and checked in the geographic information system CORINE (Community-wide Coordination of Information on the Environment). Of the EU-25 area (the 25 countries of the European Union in 2006), CORINE classified 47% as Agricultural Class, 31% as Forest Class, 16% as Nature Class, and 4% as Artificial Class. Inland waters made up the remainder. This map is based on a slightly different CORINE dataset, and also includes some non-EU countries.*

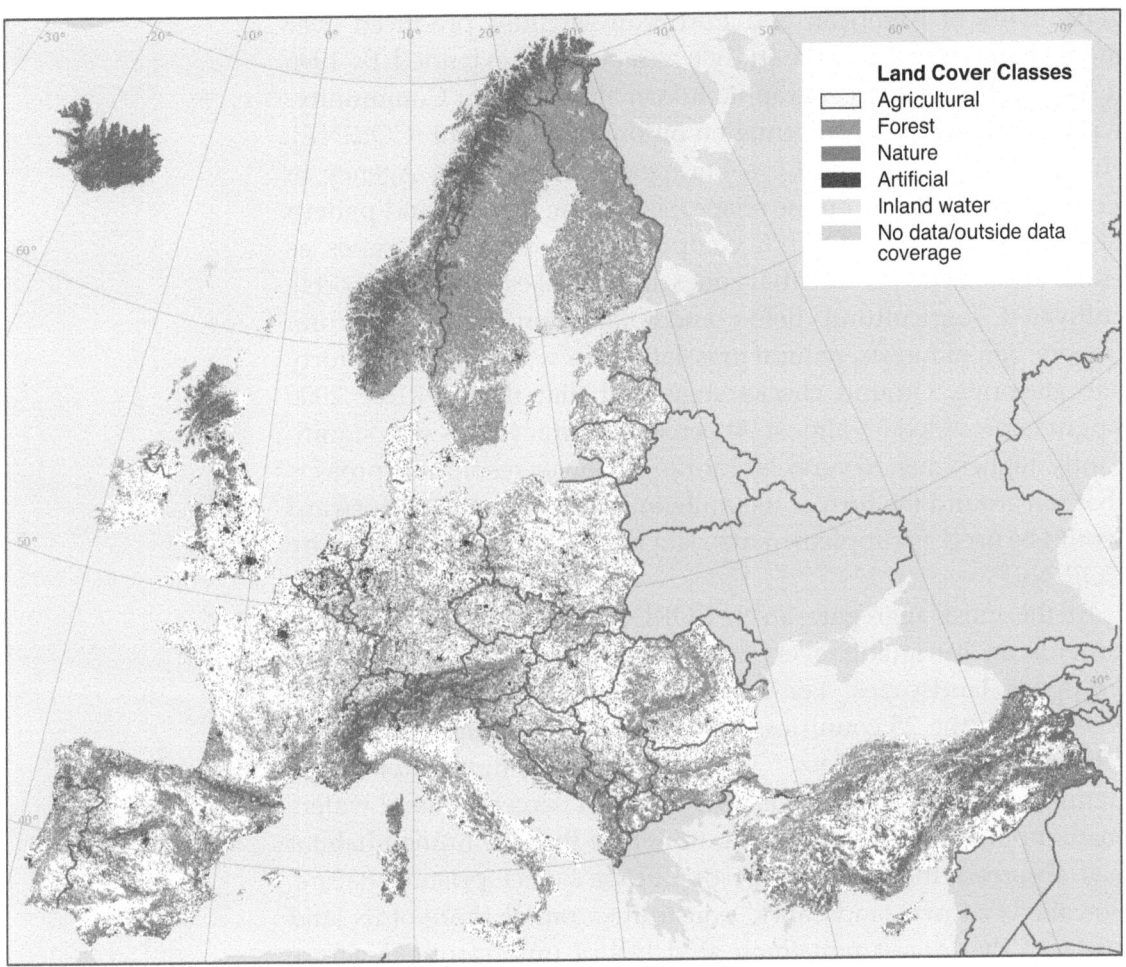

of the Community budget, and which hitherto had depended on member state statistical offices with their different standards and categories. The Center combined satellite imagery, having an initial accuracy of about eighty meters, with other digitalized data sources such as aerial scanning and classical agronomic surveys, into a geographic information system for agricultural land cover—the Advanced Agriculture Information System. In the 1980s the Center also mapped West African river and agricultural systems to assist Community responses to drought and starvation in the Sahel region.

In 1985, the Center started an influential study of European land cover to inform Community nature preservation policies. New generations of American and European satellites produced ever more accurate data, and the study was repeatedly extended. By 1996 it had produced the geographic information system Community-wide Coordination of Information on the Environment (CORINE), currently hosted by the EU's European Environment Agency in Copenhagen.[19] Based on the shape, size, color, texture, and pattern of satellite images, CORINE computers classified landscapes as either artificial (say residential zones, industrial estates, or airports), cultivated (agricultural fields and plantation forests), natural (moors, boreal forests, natural grasslands), or water, with over forty subcategories. Ground checks suggested that the CORINE 2000 upgrade provided an almost 90 percent accuracy. This was significantly higher than several larger-range, lower-resolution projects that ran around the turn of the millennium, and that henceforward would be used as supplementary data for territories not covered by CORINE.[20]

At the most aggregate level, CORINE-based land cover maps provide an intriguing overview of connections and ruptures in European landscapes. For example, roughly 47 percent in the EU-25 area (the 25 countries of the European Union in 2006) was labeled "agricultural class." The corresponding figures for forest, nature, and artificial class were 31, 16, and 4 percent. Inland waters made up the rest. The first thing to note is that the human habitat has absorbed the greater part of Europe's once-pristine nature. So-called "natural landscapes" constitute a minor share of its land surface. The largest remaining stretches of uninterrupted nature today follow mountain ranges along the Swedish–Norwegian border, the cross-border Alpine and Carpathian Mountain Ranges, the Balkan and Iberian mountain systems, the Italian Apennines, and the Scottish Highlands.

Equally remarkable, although the European Environment Agency today worries chiefly about natural landscape fragmentation by road infrastructure and urbanization, such "artificial surfaces" make up only a few percent of Europe's present-day landscape. If we exclude city parks and other urban greenery, the remaining "sealed soil" irreversibly lost to housing, infrastructure, and other construction work occupies less than 2 percent of the Agency's thirty-eight member and partner states' territories. This coverage ranges from over 13 percent in Malta and 7 percent in the Netherlands and Belgium to under 1 percent in Estonia,

Montenegro, and Albania and under 0.5 percent in Sweden, Norway, and Iceland.[21]

Agriculture and forestry appear to be much more invasive human activities. Agricultural belts make up almost half of the surface of today's European Union. Commercial human-made forests cover another third and dominate the landscape in Scandinavia. This brings the share of human-made landscapes up over 80 percent of Europe's land cover; nature zones and inland waters make up the rest. The remainder of this chapter discusses how these different land uses entwined with Europe's infrastructure transition, and what kind of landscape connections and ruptures they produced.

Urban Systems

Whereas artificial surfaces make up just a tiny part of Europe's modern landscapes, they form the core of its human habitat. And although this human-built world seems highly fragmented on large-scale satellite images, in practice it is firmly interconnected by the transnational infrastructure discussed throughout this book. Transport, communication, energy, and hydraulic infrastructure as well as food, industrial, and service networks usually gravitated into, and interconnected, human settlements. Indeed urban system-builders such as municipal governments, city engineers, and urban planners worked hard to align infrastructure and urban development projects into internally- and externally-connected artificial landscapes.

Urban system-builders undoubtedly devoted most of their effort to creating internally connected cityscapes. Europe's "walking cities" had typically evolved from the Middle Ages along a complex maze of lanes, alleys, and waterways full of dead ends. Most streets were extensions of private spaces beyond a front door, where shopkeepers displayed their goods, barbers provided their services, and locals held animal fights. With the late eighteenth-century and nineteenth-century population surges, breaking of city walls, and incipient infrastructure transition, city engineers and administrators increasingly reorganized cities into singular, accessible, manageable, and public spaces. In the words of Baron Georges-Eugène Haussmann, charged with the reform of Paris in the mid-nineteenth century, the task at hand was to "regularize the disordered city, to disclose its new order by means of a pure, schematic layout...to give unity to and transform the operative whole."[22] Haussmann proceeded radically by demolishing medieval quarters and building large boulevard-based street systems, flanked by multi-story buildings with underground sewerage.

Throughout Europe and beyond, urban governments were fascinated. Even thousands of kilometers from Paris, on Europe's natural geography border with Asia, Ottoman rulers reformed the Empire's Capital after the French model. Istanbul's urban engineers eschewed Haussmann's radical demolitions, but used the spaces left by devastating blazes for redevelopment. Here they broadened, straightened out, and extended streets, created thoroughfares, built squares, and eliminated dead ends. The new road structure would also provide easy access for police forces; creating an accessible city came with the policy aim of centralizing control over its residents. Next, the administration used its new public streets for infrastructure services such as horse-driven streetcars, waste disposal, piped water supply and sewage, and gas lines for street lighting. In 1875 the city inaugurated its *tünel*, the first metro on the Continent modeled after the London Underground. As in many other cities, however, the modernized networked city spaces served only the more wealthy districts in "European" Istanbul. The poorer "Asian" districts were reconfigured only from the 1910s and 1920s, when the modern infrastructure ideal of universal access increasingly held sway in urban planning.[23] By then Europe's urban system-builders had professionalized; they developed and spread the idea of urban infrastructure in exchange visits or conventions from the first international hygienic congress (1876) to the congresses of the influential French *Association Générale des Techniciens et Hygiénistes Municipaux* (founded 1905), the *Union Internationale des Villes* (1913), International Garden Cities and Town Planning Association (1913), or the *Congrès Internationaux d'Architecture Moderne* (1928).[24]

New generations of urban planners increasingly used local railroads and automobile roads to expand overcrowded cities into suburbs. Le Corbusier's famous 1930 concept of "the radiant city" for the "machine age" focused on express motorways connecting functional residential, industrial, and business zones. After the

Second World War, urban planners in the West built ring roads, feeder roads to suburbs, and multi-story car parks in larger and smaller towns. By now most new housing was constructed in suburbs. In Eastern Europe some 1,200 new socialist industrial towns followed a similar layout, emblematically represented by the schematic "national steel towns" such as prewar Magnitogorsk in the Soviet Union and postwar Nowa Huta in socialist Poland, Eisenhüttenstadt in the GDR, and Kunčice in Czechoslovakia. Urban infrastructure remains a key arena for reorganizing cityscapes today. In the era of Europeanization and climate change, urban planners tackle competitiveness by investing in accessibility, and address resource management challenges by supporting sustainable energy, mobility, and supposedly clean information infrastructure.[25]

Externally, Europe's urban system-builders worked hard to connect their cities to other commercial and population centers and thereby produced extended urban systems.[26] In the prototypical seventeenth-century urban clusters of the Low Countries, city governments had organized, financed, and built the new inland navigation networks on a bilateral basis. When during the nineteenth century centralized state governments took the lead in infrastructure matters, urban elites remained involved. As discussed earlier, the Rotterdam, Antwerp, and Amsterdam city councils, as well as their upstream Rhine valley colleagues from Cologne to Basel, perpetually boosted their connectivity, which in turn favored urban growth in this particular corridor.[27] When a cartographic team studied French territory in a European context in the late 1980s, they depicted the Rhine corridor—which bypassed most of France—and its maritime and alpine tunnel extensions to England and Northern Italy as Europe's "great population backbone that organizes European space and defines its city networks."[28] In this "line of power in European space," soon dubbed the Blue Banana by the media, urban densities coincided with seaport, airport, telecom, financial, knowledge, industrial, and commercial infrastructure concentrations. For the researchers, the Blue Banana was a planning concept that should inspire the French authorities to connect communities to Europe's economic artery, instead of focusing solely on Paris. In response, others developed planning concepts such as the Golden Banana from Valencia to Milan or the Yellow Banana from Paris via Cologne and Berlin to Warsaw.

However, the use of infrastructure for building city-anchored settlement systems was not a historical necessity. For example, Belgian public intellectuals and politicians revolted against the "French" city-centered model of spatial organization. In the mid-1860s liberal Minister of Public Works Jules Vander Stichelen proposed that Parliament develop cities and the countryside "following the principle of equality."[29] In stark contrast with earlier Belgian railroad planning, secondary railroads and tramways should now provide rural communities direct access to the national railroad grid rather than only to urban centers. Thus the state purchased secondary railroad lines, introduced extremely cheap worker fares and housing loans, and founded the National Company of Local Railways to build interlocal tramways connecting rural communities to their nearest railroad station.

By 1903 the prominent socialist politician Emile Vandervelde could observe that settlements of 2,000 to 5,000 flourished along dense tramway networks; he estimated that since 1886 merely 4 out of Belgium's 41 administrative regions suffered rural exodus into cities. In France this was the case for 61 out of its 87 *départments*. Great Britain too suffered from a depopulated countryside. Critics such as the modernist architect Renaat Braem would later condemn Belgium as "the ugliest country of the world," because it resembled neither a city nor a rural landscape. Vandervelde, by contrast, proudly spoke of the "Belgian garden," a giant garden city on a national scale. The British sociologist Benjamin Seebohm Rowntree agreed and praised Belgian infrastructure and housing policies for furnishing the countryside working class with houses and gardens.[30]

Connection & Rupture in Agriculture

Europe's artificial landscapes were much better connected than the isolated red dots on satellite land use imagery suggests, and their spatial architecture of integration and fragmentation is a recurring theme throughout this book. Conversely, Europe's seemingly uninterrupted belts of agriculture and forestry, which came to make up about three-quarters of its land cover, turn out to be much more fragmented than the imagery suggests. While urban system-builders used infrastructure to link settlements, agricultural system-builders only integrated fields locally. They built and used roads to tie local field systems to the nearest settlements, from which agricultural produce might reach distant users via the transnational food infrastructure described earlier. Likewise, local field drainage and irrigation infrastructure tied fields into the nearest waterways and thereby to Europe's waterway system, more fully discussed below. Europe's fields did not make up a transcontinental system of their own.

Accordingly, the construction of agrarian and plantation landscapes usually took the form of local and regional projects, even if they arose on state initiatives or were dressed up in nationalist rhetorics. From Estonia to Italy, such projects transformed the most fertile preindustrial and extensive farming terrains into intensive agriculture and forestry grounds, while abandoning less fertile areas. Today extensive agriculture, characterized by spatial diversity, crop rotation, and grazing, remains prominent only on the Iberian Peninsula. The 3 million – 6 million remaining hectares of Portuguese *montados* and Spanish *dehesas* consist of Savanna-like grasslands hosting cereal crops and livestock pastures and are scattered with oak trees providing cork, and acorns for fodder. Conservationists regard them as models for sustainable agriculture in view of their high levels of biodiversity.[31]

Even on the Iberian Peninsula, however, local, regional, and national agricultural system-builders made intensive agriculture the dominant form of farming. As elsewhere in Europe, the Spanish state privatized the commons in the period of *Desamortización* (1821–1924). The leading development area, the Ebro River basin in North-Eastern Spain covering some 17 percent of Spanish territory, illustrates local and regional infrastructure's pivotal role. On the lower Ebro, private investors had already improved some land by irrigation when the Urgel canal, a regional circular canal from the Segre River, delivered water to some 15,000 additional hectares between 1860 and 1880. Soon after so-called *regeneracionistas*, such as Lucas Mallada y Pueyo and his colleagues, mobilized agricultural societies to cure the "diseases of the fatherland" by correcting its "defective" geographical and hydrological conditions. Many local communities built country roads and local irrigation systems to produce geometric, intensively-farmed field structures; others did

Fig. 6.5 Making Agricultural Land: *The Danish Heath Society (det danske hedelskab) turned the vast heathlands of Jutland into fertile agricultural fields, and inspired similar projects elsewhere in Europe. In the economic crisis of the 1930s, state subsidies enabled the massive use of unemployed workers for planting windbreaking bushes.*

not, underscoring the prevalence of local initiative in agricultural system-building.

After the turn of the century, agricultural lobbies secured central government support via the Ebro hydrological confederation (*Confederación Hidrográfica del Ebro*, 1926). This institution built regional canals to which farmers connected new ditches on their leveled lands. The Franco government's "internal colonization" policies pushed further hydrological works, and its national colonization institute (*Instituto Nacional de Colonización*) moved settlers to the new agricultural zones. During this process of agricultural intensification, the region moved from traditional vines and olives to high yield cereals, vegetables and fruits that thrived in well irrigated and fertilized environments. However, by the 1950s the irrigation infrastructure only reached 15 percent of all arable land in the region. Significant differences among neighboring communities suggested the persistence of Ebro agriculture's local dynamics and fragmentation.[32]

Further North, in some of Europe's most intensively farmed countries, local and regional projects also paved the way. As in Spain, Danish military road engineer Enrico Mylius Dalgas and his collaborators used national rhetorics to support large regional projects. They used the 1864 loss of Schleswig-Holstein to Prussia to argue for domestic land cultivation on the Jutland peninsula;

their approach would soon condense into Danish nationalism's slogan "what is externally lost must be regained internally." Their Danish Heath Society (*det danske hedeselskab*, 1866) built local transport and hydraulic infrastructure to transform the brushlands covering half of the peninsula into arable fields and conifer plantations. By 1907 it had halved Jutland's heath area; by 1950 merely a fifth remained.[33]

Dalgas and the Danish Heath Society were quite influential. For instance, in the Netherlands, which like Denmark became one of the most intensively-farmed countries in the world, provincial agricultural associations followed Dalgas's example and founded their own heath societies. Notably, these agricultural system-builders produced more cultivated land on the country's higher elevation inland soils than the renowned Dutch coastal polder agriculture reclamations.

Equally noteworthy, in the long term this regional and local agricultural system-building displayed a tragic irony: to compensate for the lost water buffer capacity of the former heath lands, without which local rivers periodically flooded fields, agricultural system-builders re-engineered small rivers and built extensive local field and forest ditch systems, later supplemented by pipeline drainage networks. In the Netherlands alone, the length of local field drainage pipelines today exceeds the public road network (which is one of the world's densest) by almost a factor of three.[34] However, this effective local drainage infrastructure eventually introduced periodic droughts hitherto unknown. Europe's agriculture system-builders again solved the problem with more infrastructure. The dry summer of 1976 triggered an irrigation system boom in Denmark, the Netherlands, France, and Germany to compensate for their effective drainage systems. Inland agricultural irrigation ultimately contributed more to Dutch summer water shortages than industry and households combined.

Land reforms that repeatedly whirled through Europe further underscored the local fragmentation of agricultural landscapes. Policy makers and reformers merged small local plots into larger, but still local, ones for scale and productivity gains. New local access roads, drainage and irrigation infrastructure, and electric power supply schemes structured such land reallotment projects. In Cold War Western Europe, the European Community's agricultural policy proved an important driver of such projects. Long-time

Agricultural Commissioner Sicco Mansholt's 1968 memorandum encouraging systematic farm amalgamation, which would make half of the Community's farmers superfluous, did fail, triggering personal threats and leaving him with the nickname of "farmer killer." However, by the mid-1980s the Commission could observe that farms of less than twenty hectares declined while larger ones increased throughout the Community, except in the UK. In communist Europe forced scale increases had taken the form of much larger collective farms; but when these were privatized after 1989, "agricultural fragmentation" became a prominent policy problem in, for instance, Romania and Bulgaria.[35] Time and again, the local remained the chief level of agricultural system-building.

Europe's plantation forests, finally, continue to evoke discussions about whether they belong to "nature" or "agriculture." Either way, Europe's forests today are largely human-made. By the late nineteenth century, timber and firewood demand had depleted forests in Europe's more densely populated regions. The influential German school of economic forest management pushed hard for reforestation programs that aimed for monofunctional, even-aged conifer forests optimized for timber output. These reforestation programs, rather than spontaneous regeneration, bent Europe's trend of forest decline into one of forest creation by the early 1900s.

Once again most new plantation forests took the form of rather isolated local and regionally-connected patches. For instance in Denmark, Dalgas's Heath Society and similar initiatives would more than double Denmark's forest area. They typically did so by building arable fields separated by local forest belts, which could provide timber and simultaneously shelter the new fields from winds and droughts. In Russia such forest shelter belts could be very long indeed: already in the 1890s the Russian soil scientist Vasily Dokuchaev had argued that turning the southern steppes into agricultural grounds required forest shelterbelts, typically along rivers, to prevent water runoff and break the hot dry winds. By the early 1940s the Soviet Union counted over a million hectares of forest defense belts. As a response to the 1946 drought and the resulting 1947 famine, Stalin's Great Plan for the Transformation of Nature (1948) aimed to create another 23 million hectares of forest shelter belts, consisting of oak, ash, elm, and poplar, to protect fields from temperature fluctuations, excess humidity and droughts, and devastating winds. Soviet foresters built green belts up to hundreds (and occasionally over a thousand) kilometers in length. Still we cannot speak of integrated forests, for these belts typically consisted of 30–100 m wide parallel strips that stood some hundreds of meters apart. About 20 percent of the envisioned scheme was constructed before the central government reallocated the funds in the mid-1960s.[36] Meanwhile international organizations such as the UNECE and the European Communities worked on forestry policies; but by 1986 the European Commission could observe that despite its efforts, forestry integration had worked poorly.[37]

In other cases, foresters connected new timber plantations to existing natural forests. In Switzerland, Germany, and France, for instance, they added plantations to natural mountain forests. In Switzerland fuel and timber needs had reduced the forest share to some 18 percent of the landscape by the mid-nineteenth century. The Swiss Forestry Society then convinced the federal government that deforestation caused flooding and avalanches; and the Forest Police Law of 1876 initiated replanting programs that would increase the area to some 29 percent.[38]

Their colleagues in Scandinavia created some of Europe's largest forest zones by transforming natural forest into plantations. In the second half of the nineteenth century, flourishing Swedish and Finnish sawmill industries had cut much of the large pine boreal forests. These were replaced by plantation forests. The peak transformation came in the 1940–1960s, when foresters drained wet areas with ditch systems and brought in fertilizer and pesticides. Government and especially private roads made the plantations accessible. Dense, even-aged fast-growing pine forests swept through Norway, Sweden and Finland; the Swedish Forestry Agency now reckons that these make up 85 percent of the nation's forests. Today ecologists in this area speak of a different kind of "fragmentation": old-growth, varied forest is systematically interrupted by even-age monotonous conifer plantations. Despite vigorous foresting in Russia's vast natural domains, the Cold War cleavage remains clearly visible on the Russian–Finnish border in the contrast between dominating old growths on the Russian side and monotonous plantations on the Finnish side.[39]

Preserving Land

Like many of his contemporaries, Canon Hardwicke Rawnsley felt increasingly alarmed by the perpetual expansion of human-built networks into natural landscapes. Just starting his career as an Anglican vicar in England's Lake District in 1878, he joined the ad hoc Thirlmere Defence Association to campaign against the Manchester water supply system's intrusion into the Lakelands. The association could do no more than stall construction of the Thirlmere dams and their 154 km aqueduct to Manchester. A few years later Rawnsley organized a more successful campaign against a proposed slate railroad, and co-founded the permanent Lake District Defence Society "to offer a powerful and consolidated opposition to the introduction of unnecessary railways into the Lake District, and all other speculative schemes which may appear likely to impair its beauty."[40]

In the mid-1890s, however, Rawnsley changed strategy. With his fellow campaigners Octavia Hill and Sir Robert Hunter, he founded the non-profit National Trust for Places of Historic Interest or Natural Beauty. This organization would not campaign and lobby, but instead purchase and own sites worthy of protection. The National Trust acquired its first cultural heritage site in 1896 and its first nature site, Wicken Fen wetlands in Cambridgeshire, in 1899. By 1907 it owned ten nature reserves.

On the European continent too, nature conservationists now purchased and protected reserves on a local or micro-regional scale. Today ecologists consider such reserves "biodiversity nodes" in continent-wide ecological networks: to counter the intrusion of the infrastructure-based human habitat, they interconnect reserves by means of "green corridors," creating a so-called "ecological infrastructure" for the circulation of plants and animals. In retrospect, the establishment of local and regional nature reserves constituted the first steps in ecological system-building. Remarkably, the European Environment Agency currently works for the construction of human-built European "green infrastructure" in order to forge territorial cohesion of the EU—a phrasing that echoes the legitimation of the EU Trans European Network programs of the 1990s.[41]

Of course, a number of nature conservation projects predated the National Trust, witness de facto nature zones such as the hiking area of Mount Brocken and Tsar Alexander II's formal protection of the European Bison in Białowieża Forest on the current Polish–Belorussian border in 1860 (which preserved these animals for aristocratic hunting!).[42] The Trust and other conservation organizations, however, drew their inspiration chiefly from across the Atlantic. The U.S. Congress had reserved Yosemite Valley as a California State Park in 1864, and established Yellowstone in 1872 as a federal National Park "reserved and withdrawn from settlement" and "set apart as a public park or pleasuring ground for the benefit and enjoyment of the people."[43] Luxury hotels and tourism followed. As in the case of Mount Brocken, the U.S. railroad infrastructure showed its Janus face in nature issues. Railroads had earlier claimed large swaths of wilderness and facilitated the near extermination of the American bison by facilitating the mass fur trade. In 1871, however, the Northern Pacific Railroad joined the lobby for Yellowstone Park and subsequently promoted lucrative nature tourism: "BISON once roamed the country now traversed by Northern Pacific. The remnants of these Noble Beasts are now found in Yellowstone Park reached directly only by this line," noted a 1904 advertisement.[44] This double entwinement of transport infrastructure with nature conservation persists today.

Governments in Australia (1879), Canada (1885), and New Zealand (1894) picked up the American national park idea. In Britain, the National Trust's early purchases were part of a larger vision to manage natural landscapes as a "national park, after the manner of the Yellowstone region in America."[45] Also in the 1890s, the Hungarian biologist Károly Sajó published several widely-read calls to establish American-style state parks in continental Europe. In response the German Bird Protection Association created bird reserves from the late 1890s, and the French poets Henry Cazalis and Sully Prudhomme founded the *Société pour la protection des paysages* in 1901 to preserve natural and architectural beauty. Prominent Dutch citizens initiated the Netherlands Nature Monuments Association in 1905. Paul Sarasin founded the Swiss Nature Protection League to found nature parks, as did botanist Julius Römer and his *Kronstädter Naturfreunde* in Transylvania, Karl Reinhold Kupfer's Riga Society of Naturalists in the Russian Protectorate of Livonia, and the new German Nature Park Association. The Swedish Parliament authorized no less than nine national parks totaling 3,600 square kilometers in

1909. On Sarasin's suggestion, in 1913 seventeen states initiated an International Consultative Commission for the Protection of Nature to further promote the national park idea. Nature reserves proliferated spectacularly from England to communist Russia, where conservationists succeeded in convincing Lenin to step up earlier Tsarist initiatives for defining nature sanctuaries. Imperial powers extended nature reserve policies to their colonies, and conservationists on either side of the Polish–Czechoslovakian border even managed to found the transboundary Pieniny reserve in 1931–2, after a decade of agitation and lobbying, land purchases, and bilateral government negotiation.[46]

While nature reserves proliferated, urban planners greatly boosted the notion of "green belts," in retrospect another key element of green network building. Organizations such as Sir Ebenezer Howard's Garden City Association of 1899, the *Deutsche Gartenstadt-Gesellschaft* of 1902, and *l'Association des cités-jardins* of 1904 advocated green belts around cities and suburbs to halt urban sprawl and ribbon development and preserve rural space for recreation. The 1924 International City Planning Conference in Amsterdam even acknowledged green belts among its seven principles for sound city planning. London soon became the greenbelt flagship. In the late 1920s Raymond Unwin became chief planner for Greater London, and by the mid-1930s he and his collaborators had persuaded the region's city councils to adopt a plan "to establish a Green Belt or girdle of open space...to provide a reserve supply of public open spaces and of recreational areas" and to purchase 11,400 hectares of land, permanently preserved under the 1938 Green Belt Act.[47] In other cities greenbelt discussions led to similar undertakings or other forms of greenery. The 1935 General Plan of Moscow introduced a green belt around the Russian capital, while Berlin and Copenhagen expanded along radial railroad lines separated by green wedges. Leningrad's communist authorities used green belts to separate suburban zones. Green belts, strips, or wedges also entered Amsterdam, Budapest, Frankfurt, Lisbon, Prague, Stockholm, and many smaller towns.

The unprecedented postwar boom in infrastructure, industry, settlement, agriculture, and plantation forests apparently triggered an equally unprecedented surge of nature reserve and urban green belt projects. In 1948 eighteen nations, seven international nature conservation organizations, plus over a hundred local and national ones, founded the International Union for Nature Protection (soon renamed International Union for the Conservation of Nature, IUCN) that quickly drew still more countries into nature site protection. In 1965, Western governments in the Council of Europe started awarding so-called European Diplomas for "protection of certain landscapes, reserves and natural features of European interest," and instituted the European Nature Conservation Year in 1970 to call for more reserves. Later the Council's Bern Convention on the Conservation of European Wildlife and Natural Habitats (1979) obliged signatories "to conserve wild flora and fauna and their natural habitats, especially those species and habitats whose conservation requires the co-operation of several States."[48]

On a global scale, the United Nations 1972 Conference on the Human Environment in Stockholm declared that "man...bears a solemn responsibility to protect and improve the environment for present and future generations."[49] The Stockholm Declaration triggered the European Economic Community and the Comecon apparatus; the former's 1979 Birds Directive, obliging member states to work for "preservation, maintenance and re-establishment of biotopes and habitats" is still influential today. Worldwide, private and government nature reserves multiplied from under 5,000 in the mid-1940s to over 30,000 in the 1980s.[50]

Green belt builders, too, made headway. Influential town planners such as Patrick Abercrombie advertised London's green belt domestically and internationally. By 1956 Minister of Housing Duncan Sandys told the House of Commons that he had sent all local authorities in England and Wales "a circular ... expressly asking them to establish Green Belts wherever appropriate." In response "preliminary plans for green belts have already been submitted for Birmingham, Coventry, Manchester and the southeast Lancashire conurbation, Merseyside, Derby, Nottingham, Oxford, South Tyneside and the Hertfordshire towns; and other proposals will be reaching me very shortly."[51] Internationally, Abercrombie co-founded the International Union of Architects and toured Australia, New Zealand, and Hong Kong to promote the green belt model. In 1965 the Soviet government decided on green belts around all large cities, industrial centers, and larger worker settlements for recreation and buffering of factory zones. Many green belts, however, did not materialize as planned; land owners and social reformers often opposed them for limiting the growth of cramped cities, resulting in abandonment or compromise.

Europe's Ecological Networks

In the shadow of this vast proliferation of nature reserves and green belts, nature conservationists started to combine green nodes and links into emergent notions of ecological networks. Their successors today locate the genesis of ecological networks in the Soviet republics of Estonia and Lithuania in the 1970s. In Western Europe, biologists and planners conceptualized the Netherlands' National Ecological Network in the 1980s, which in turn inspired Pan-European nature planning in the 1990s.[52]

Baltic ecological network builders did not credit new biological subdisciplines, such as systems ecology and ecological engineering, as their sources of inspiration, unlike their Western colleagues. Instead they drew on human-centered nature considerations in geography and topological planning. They eagerly cited the Russian geographer Boris Rodoman, who translated planning concepts of "polarized landscapes" and "functional zoning" into a management tool for biosphere preservation. In Rodoman's view, central planners should divide a given territory into separate zones with different functions. Intensive land use in urban, industrial, and cultivated zones should be flanked by integrated nature zones to purify the air, clean groundwater, prevent erosion, and protect habitats, in short, to compensate for the environmental damage done by humans. Such landscape polarization in economic and ecological zones entered central planning in a number of Soviet and Comecon states in the late 1970s and 1980s. Estonian university researchers and planners spoke of a "network of compensative areas" from the mid-1970s. Their Lithuanian colleagues agitated for a "nature frame" from the early 1980s, and their Czechoslovak peers started to work on a "system of landscape territorial stability."[53]

Ülo Mander, who worked at the Estonian Agricultural Academy from the late 1970s and chaired the Estonian Association of Landscape Ecology two decades later, noted in retrospect that the Estonian national ecological network "might be called an

| Linking Land   259

Fig. 6.6 National Ecological Networks: *From the 1970s, ecological system-builders have developed the concept of ecological networks or "green infrastructure." In Eastern Europe, the concept was pioneered by Estonian geographers. In Western Europe, the national ecological network of the Netherlands—one of the most ecologically-fragmented countries in the world—became paradigmatic. The network became a national policy objective in 1990. It connects isolated "core areas" and "nature development areas" (low-lying peat and clay areas, river forelands, sandy soils, dunes, and marine mudland ecosystems) by means of "ecological corridors."*

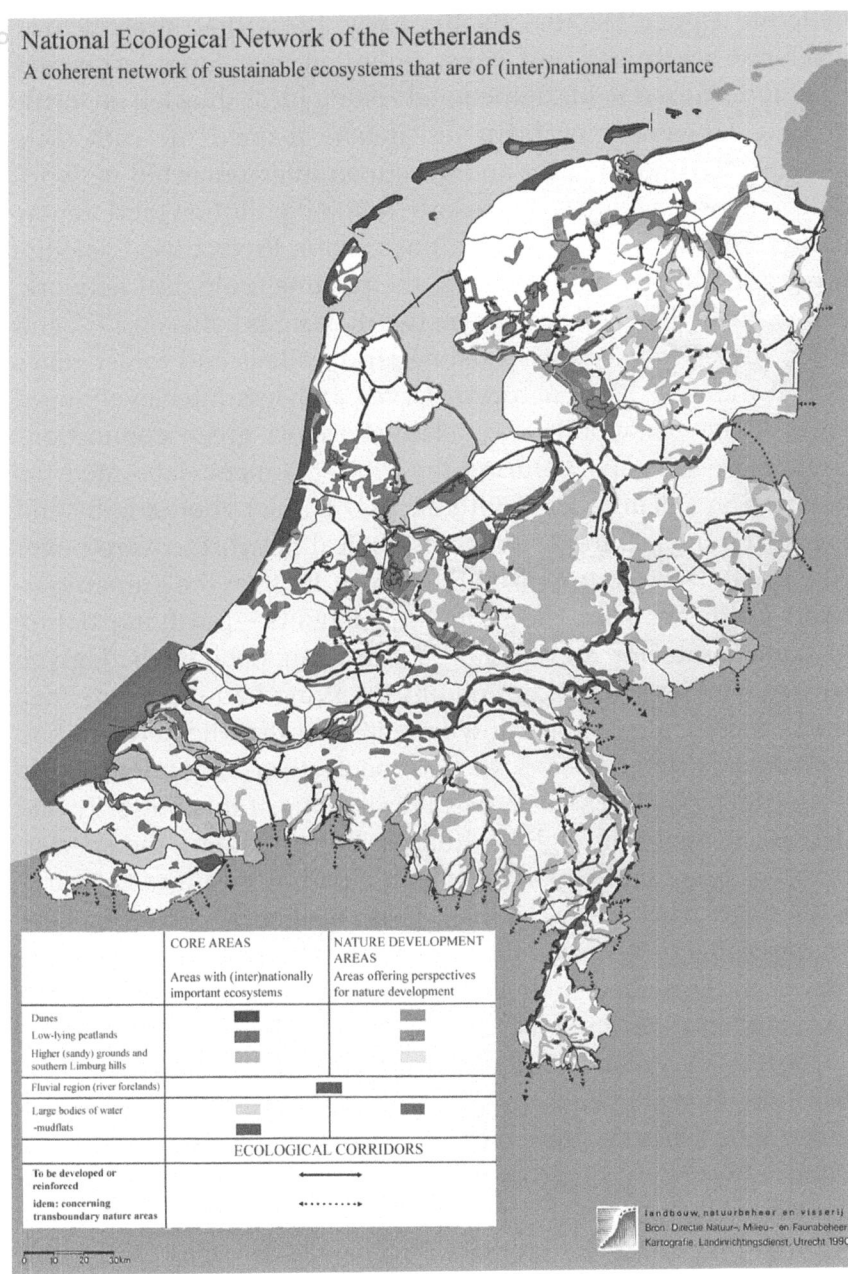

ecological infrastructure to compensate [for] intensive economic activities."[54] Mander and his colleagues remember how the stage had been set in Estonia. After the Soviet annexation, central planners had concentrated agriculture in collective or state farms in fertile Upper Estonia. By the early 1970s that strategy had produced severe soil and water pollution near large farms and heavily-fertilized fields. Functional zoning ideas thus fell on fertile ground. University of Tartu researchers teamed up with state planners to conceptualize and design an interconnected network of compensating areas to absorb human pollution and renew natural resources. Their Land Construction Project used satellite images to identify bottlenecks in the pristine ecological network, and published several national network designs between 1977 and 1983. These schemes used existing river valleys and forest zones as links among large nature reserves and less-intensively-used areas. A few new-built and relatively short green connections could close the gaps.[55] During the 1980s planners elaborated the network on a district scale with the aid of aerial photography and field data. In 2000 the Estonian ecological network covered over 50 percent of the country's land territory. By then the human-centered justification for the ecological network—purifying nature to compensate for and sustain the human habitat—had given way to the Western conception of preserving nature "for its own sake." Estonian ecologists now emphasized that the network had a positive effect on species such as the protected Clouded Apollo butterfly, *Parnassius Mnemosyne*. Populations of this butterfly had decreased vastly throughout Europe, but in Estonia the species' presence grew and expanded along riparian meadow corridors with alder strips on river banks. These ecological corridors, later studies suggested, hosted the larvae food plants and adult mating places and provided shelter for a butterfly population that seeks to avoid high speed winds.[56]

The human-centered Eastern European ecological network debate hardly resonated in Western Europe. Instead, Western advocates of green infrastructure drew on the nature-centered scientific disciplines of systems ecology and ecological engineering developed in the United States.

During the 1960s the brothers Eugene and Howard Odum had successfully promoted ecological systems as the appropriate study unit of biological organization. In a self-regulating ecosystem equilibrium, key inputs such as energy and carbon entered the system by photosynthesis in green plants and subsequently cycled through the system's natural food chains. The Odums and others called for human intervention and "ecological engineering" to create better initial conditions; after that ecosystems would be self-sustaining. Robert MacArthur and Edward O. Wilson's equilibrium theory of island biogeography further fueled the debate about how to engineer better nature reserves: larger and more diverse habitats allowed more species, because migration helped species evade local extinction by chance events. The International Union for the Conservation of Nature endorsed the theory in its World Conservation Strategy for "genetic diversity" of 1980.[57]

In the Netherlands, where intensive agricultural system-building had almost depleted nature, Fred Baerselman and Frans Vera studied these ideas as classmates in biology at Amsterdam Free University in the early 1970s. They joined biologist and activist critiques of the "unnaturalness of Dutch forest and nature zones," which dismissed traditional human-centered nature conservation as "large scale gardening." Instead they agitated for targeted interventions to create "real nature." As prominent policy entrepreneurs promoting ecological networks for the Ministry of Agriculture, Nature, and Food, they would later call the Netherlands an "ecological disaster area": land use statistics counted only 6 percent of the territory as "natural" (excluding some 8 percent of production forests).

Since omnipresent farm fields prevented the expansion of isolated nature reserves, they proposed "some unusual and unorthodox ideas to restore and develop nature... As always: necessity is the mother of invention."[58] To boost the possibilities for species to migrate, a 1981 nature policy proposal to Parliament aimed "to construct corridors or 'stepping stones' between nature reserves, so as to realize a kind of ecological infrastructure."[59] During the 1980s Baerselman, Vera, and a handful of others further developed the concept's key elements. "Ecological core areas" were nature reserves large enough for complete and self-regulating biotic communities, and "can also be used as reservoirs from which smaller wildlife areas can be supplied with plant and animal species."[60] Areas too small to be biodiversity generators could function as "stepping stones" for species migration. Finally, "ecological corridors" such as watercourses, wayside verges, or simply strips of greenery across agricultural lands should facilitate the migration of species between these ecological nodes.

The Dutch Parliament endorsed the proposal in its 1990 Nature Policy Plan, which projected a National Ecological Network for 2018. To the grave disappointment of Baerselman and Vera, their agency's director gave in to agriculture interests and abandoned a strict separation of nature from other land uses: "The concept of the ecological network has been endorsed ... but the ecological departure point has been partly put overboard, and the ecological network now comprises other activities such as production forests, military zones, and agriculture. The rhetorical power of the policy document ... legitimates the damaging of nature," complained Vera.[61] Nevertheless the construction of a national ecological network began. By 2011, when Government and Parliament quarreled about withdrawing corridor funds after the European sovereign debt crisis, provincial authorities had acquired some 50 percent of the targeted land and had built 30 percent of the network. In some 270 locations the national ecological network crossed motorways and railroads; here ecological system-builders built so-called green-grey junctions such as ecoducts (viaducts for plants and animals) and badger or toad tunnels.[62]

Baerselman and Vera's scheme had included cross-border corridors reaching Belgian and German nature areas and anticipated further upscaling: "The 'national ecological network' can be one of the starting points for a 'European Ecological Network', that should preferably be developed from several starting points simultaneously."[63] When the Dutch government held the rotating presidency of the European Communities in 1991 and hosted the ongoing negotiations on the Habitat Directive (an extension of the 1979 Birds Directive to other species), Dutch ecological network builders seized this opportunity.[64] Promoting their national solution as a European one, they used the CORINE land use database to draft an interconnected European Ecological Network and presented it to the Communities' Council of Environment Ministers. To the regret of the scheme's main author, Graham Bennett, the EU's Habitat Directive and *Natura 2000* vision (the combined nature reserve system of the bird and habitat directives) obliged governments to designate nature reserves, and put corridors second as a voluntary option.

Bennett and his collaborators then convinced the Dutch and Hungarian governments to host a major conference in Maastricht under the banner of the European Commission, the Council of Europe, and the International Union for the Conservation of Nature. The conference declaration announced a new European Center for Nature Conservation, which together with the Council of Europe

Linking Land | 263

Fig. 6.7 From Iron Curtain to European Green Belt: *One of the most ambitious attempts to reconnect Europe's nature is the European Green Belt project. Some 150 governmental and non-governmental organizations from 16 EU countries and 8 non-EU countries collaborate to turn the former Iron Curtain, where wildlife thrived in the absence of human settlement, into a green corridor. The belt measures 12,500 km, from the Russian–Norwegian border at the Barents Sea to the Mediterranean and the Black Sea. The photograph shows a part of the European Green Belt at the Austrian–Czech border near Linz, Austria.*

would propose an interconnected European ecological network at the upcoming "Environment for Europe" ministerial conference in Sofia. There forty-six governments promised to implement the so-called Pan-European Ecological Network, defined, following the Dutch model, as "a physical network of core areas ... linked by corridors and supported by buffer zones, thus facilitating the dispersal and migration of species."[65] After all, supporters proclaimed, "nature does not have any borders."[66]

Europe's ecological system-builders soon found out that the realization of such a pan-European network within ten years was overly optimistic, but nevertheless started a number of actions. Much effort went into developing indicative maps at a 1:3,000,000 scale for Central and Eastern Europe, South-eastern Europe, and Western Europe. To designate ecological core areas, they combined data on existing protection sites and threatened species with land cover data. The latter exercise required the complicated alignment of land use databases such as CORINE 2000 for the European Union, Swiss, and Norwegian land use data, and less detailed

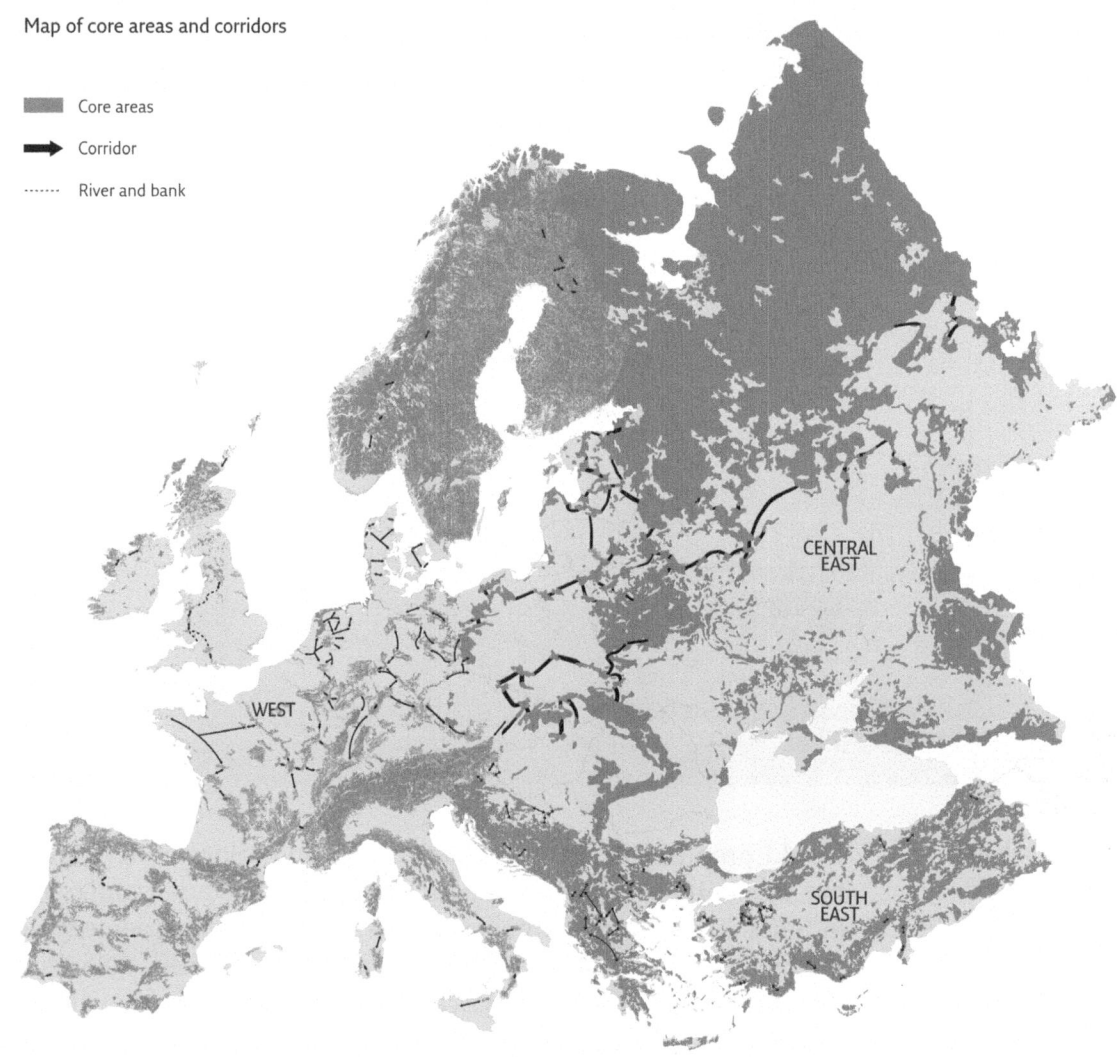

Map of core areas and corridors

Pan-European and global data sets. To determine the location of ecological corridors they drew on geographical data on river valleys and bird migration routes, as well as the opinions of national and (micro) regional experts, whose detailed knowledge on connection possibilities proved indispensable especially for densely-cultivated areas. Subsequent ministerial conferences endorsed the proposed maps, but did not enforce their implementation. Thus Europe's ecological network builders attempted to inspire and coordinate local, (micro) regional, national, cross-national governmental and non-governmental initiatives within the maps' framework. The European Green Belt traversing twenty-two countries along the former Iron Curtain is an example of international cooperation of non-governmental environmental associations coordinated by the International Union for the Conservation of Nature. Most programs, however, had a national focus such as the Baltic states', Dutch, German, Moldavian, Polish, Romanian, and Ukrainian government programs, or a regional approach such as the programs of Spain's Extremadura, Andalusia, and Catalonia Autonomous regions, the University of Aquila program in Italy's central Apennines, or Danish province-level corridor planning.[67] In the Baltic states, where ecological networks had been pioneered, the Pan-European initiative triggered a convergence with the Western network concept: "The existing network of protected areas as well as the ecological network should be re-evaluated at [the] European level," noted Estonian ecologists in 1999. They then proceeded to reshape their network in terms of core areas, corridors, buffer zones, and cross-border connectivity.[68]

Parnassius Mnemosyne *or* Lepus Europeus

Fig. 6.8 Mapping the Pan-European Ecological Network: *The most ambitious and challenging green infrastructure project proved to be the construction of a Pan-European Ecological Network (acronym: PEEN). The effort to connect nature zones by ecological corridors on a pan-European scale started in the late 1990s with the development of indicative maps, based on existing nature reserves, land cover databases, and geographical data on river valleys and bird migration routes. The thick lines on this overview map are green corridors.*

Estonian ecologists credited their networks for the revival of an endangered butterfly, the *Parnassius Mnemosyne* or Clouded Apollo. Their Dutch colleagues celebrated the successful spread of beavers, otters, badgers, and black storks alongside a wide array of other rare birds, reptiles, insects, and plants. Czech botanists found that one of their earliest local corridors—the merely 15 meter wide *Vracrov* link across agricultural land—and an early regional corridor showed successful sustenance of indigenous woody plants and willows, respectively.[69]

However, in a 2011 report the European Environment Agency suggested that the rapidly-declining Central European population of the European hare, the *Lepus europeus*, may be more representative of the current state of Europe's ecological system-building. Due to habitat fragmentation by agriculture and transport infrastructure, in several countries "its extinction seems impossible to prevent, as the 'point of no return' has probably been crossed several years ago."[70] On a higher level of aggregation the Agency observed that ongoing habitat fragmentation simply outran ecological network building: "In spite of the planning concept of preserving large unfragmented areas, fragmentation has continued to increase during the last 20 years, and many more new transportation infrastructure projects are planned, especially in Eastern Europe." On balance, "fragmentation of landscapes is rising and the remaining ecological network provides less and less connectivity."[71]

Unable to stop fragmentation, Europe's ecological system-builders had other problems as well. The binding legislation of the EU *Natura 2000* program drew available funds to nature reserves rather than ecological corridors. In addition, ecological network builders increasingly met opposition. French farmers protested fiercely against returning cultivated land to nature. The "Natura 2000 out of Bulgaria" movement protested all nature conservation efforts that hampered economic growth and employment. Norwegian locals lamented the increased circulation of lynx, wolverine, bear, and wolf that damaged livestock and scared people away from wandering through the woods; they loathed ecology as an urban elite project threatening rural lifestyles. Even in the pioneering Netherlands, farmers' organizations and their political allies clashed with nature managers, paying game hunters to position themselves at ecoducts to shoot red deer or lobbying for fences on top of expensive new ecoducts to prevent Belgian wild boar from eating Dutch crops. In addition, ecological networks may also carry so-called "invasive species"; some of these animals, plants, and microorganisms threaten indigenous species and reduce rather than sustain biodiversity (though most invasive species travel via transport infrastructure rather than ecological networks). Finally, ecological system-builders regretted their incapability to coordinate their own efforts: "ecological networks are being developed at the country or regional level, but at the European and global level there are mainly visions."[72]

Europe today hosts a number of ambitious cross-border ecological connection programs. The Green Lungs of Poland program, for instance, includes border crossings to Estonian, Belarusian, Latvian, Lithuanian, Russian, and Ukrainian nature zones. Nevertheless, for the reasons listed above, on aggregate Europe's transnational nature conservation constellation continues to gravitate around local and regional protected areas, with comparatively weak national and international linkages. Nature conservation's Europe, in other words, remains chiefly the Europe of local and regional initiative.

As for biodiversity, a number of species managed to cope with ongoing habitat fragmentation. They simply defied existing classifications, and settled inside the human habitat. The European Environment Agency recognizes that about half of Europe's biotopes and species now live in agricultural terrain. This makes upgrading agricultural fields with hedges, ditches, and other "semi-natural elements" an important conservation strategy. From this perspective, the human habitat–nature dichotomy and its exclusive focus on creating new wilderness might harm rather than boost European biodiversity. The Agency further notes that surprisingly many species even inhabit towns and cities; the so-called "urban forest" is made up of "urban wetlands, abandoned industrial sites, roadside verges, vacant lots and derelict lands, ruins, allotment gardens and cemeteries ... together with arboreta, residential gardens and villas, botanic gardens and individual balconies."[73] Europe's species, it seems, developed through complex interactions with ecological networks, as well as with the networked human habitat described throughout this book, and continue to do so today.

7

Troubled Waters

The "Molotov–Ribbentrop Pipeline"

Lubmin is a tiny, unremarkable seaside resort in the northeasternmost corner of Germany. At first glance, it would seem an odd place for presidents, prime ministers, and EU top officials to come together. Situated on the Baltic Sea, far away from Europe's political and economic centers, and struggling to survive as a resort, Lubmin enjoys none of the fame attached to the nearby holiday islands of Rügen and Usedom. Nor can it compete with the grandiose, prestigious flair of Heiligendamm an hour's drive to the west, which in 2007 hosted a much-publicized G8 summit.

Yet on Thursday, November 8, 2011, German Chancellor Angela Merkel, Russian President Dmitry Medvedev, Dutch Premier Mark Rutte, French Premier François Fillon, and EU Commissioner Günther Oettinger all arrived in Lubmin for a meeting considered to be of crucial importance, given that the political leaders were accompanied by 200 journalists and 500 other guests. The purpose was to inaugurate the new Nord Stream natural gas pipeline, designed for natural gas exports from Russia to Western Europe.

Similar ceremonies had taken place every few years or so ever since Austria's first gas imports from the Soviet Union in September 1968. It had become a well-established habit for political leaders to use the occasion of inauguration ceremonies to hail transnational infrastructure projects as symbols and fundaments of peace and friendly cooperation across the Continent. Nord Stream was no exception. Medvedev argued that the pipeline "opens a new page in our country's cooperation with the European Union," whereas Merkel emphasized that "Nord Stream is the biggest energy infrastructure project of our time." Rutte noted that the new infrastructure "came on stream at exactly the right time," and Oettinger spoke about an "important step in the development of a pan-European transport grid."[1]

But there was one major difference between Nord Stream and the other Russian export pipelines: instead of being routed through one or more Central European transit countries, it was laid on the bottom of the Baltic Sea. Lubmin was the place where the pipeline, diving into the Baltic at Vyborg in northwestern Russia, reached land again. President Medvedev emphasized that this circumstance implied that "for the first time, Russian gas will reach countries of the EU directly."[2] Given the many problems in preceding years with securing transit through Ukraine and Belarus, expanding the East–West gas system into the Baltic Sea offered major advantages for both exporter and importers. Buried in gravel and sand on the Baltic Sea floor, outside the territorial waters of any third parties, the pipeline would remain beyond the reach of troublesome transit countries, which thus far had been able to influence the gas flow. Turning Neptune's domain into an infrastructural space was seen to enhance both the security and efficiency of Europe's gas supply.

Yet following its launch in 2005, the project had been highly controversial. Interpreting it as an aggressive Russian and German foreign policy tool, Poland's foreign minister Radosław Sikorski dubbed it the "Molotov–Ribbentrop Pipeline," and former Polish President Aleksander Kwaśniewski named it "a mine at the fundament of EU solidarity."[3] Some thought that the pipeline was in reality one of Russia's hidden defense objects, a tool and an excuse for strengthening its military presence on the Baltic. The most controversial point in this context was the initial insistence from Nord Stream's side that a "service platform" would need to be erected off the Swedish island of Gotland. This component of the system was in the end abandoned following public protest.

The pipeline was also questioned on environmental grounds. Although pipelines had already been laid in both the North Sea and the Mediterranean, no one knew what impact Nord Stream would have on the Baltic Sea's particularly sensitive ecosystem and its unique brackish life-world. In the Nordic countries, with their long and populated Baltic shorelines, it was this issue rather than military and national security issues that had dominated the debate. The Baltic ecology was already in deep trouble, due to high concentrations of heavy metals, radioactive nuclides, chemicals, nitrogen, and phosphorus being dumped into it by numerous rivers. Increasing sea-bound transports, meanwhile, implied higher risk of oil spills. Just a few years before the gas pipeline's inauguration, a Polish container vessel had run into a Chinese bulk carrier, loaded with fertilizers, chemicals, and oil, causing the latter to sink off the Danish island of Bornholm and spoiling some of Sweden's best beaches. Small wonder, then, that coastal populations watched maritime energy projects such as Nord Stream with suspicion.

When it came to its actual construction, the Nord Stream pipeline ran into trouble due to the prevalence of dangerous wartime mines, which needed to be cleared from a zone surrounding its course. The crossings between the gas pipeline and already-existing telegraph, telephone, fiber-optic, and electricity cables that traversed the Baltic also needed to be carefully considered. Shipping companies, for their part, were disturbed by the fact that shipping lanes and the entry channel to the important Polish harbor of Świnoujście had to be changed to protect the pipeline. Historians and archeologists, in contrast, eagerly followed—and cooperated—with the pipeline company and the pipe layers. This was because several unique shipwrecks from the Middle Ages and later periods had been discovered on the sea floor in connection with preparing the route.

The Nord Stream story has been analyzed in earlier research from a variety of perspectives.[4] This chapter takes it as point of departure for a broader historical analysis of how Europe's infrastructure has interacted with Europe's wet environment. At focus are not only Europe's seas, but also its inland waters, examined in three segments. The first deals with the ways in which system-building has interacted with and influenced the aquatic sciences or, more generally, Europeans' knowledge about their rivers, lakes, and seas.

Fig. 7.1 **Contested Connection:** *Russian natural gas exports to Germany and other West European countries traditionally depended on onshore pipelines traversing much of East-Central Europe. The offshore Nord Stream Pipeline through the Baltic Sea offered a first direct connection between Russia and Germany. Poland's foreign minister Radosław Sikorski dubbed it the "Molotov–Ribbentrop Pipeline," and other actors criticized the project on environmental grounds. Here the pipeline is being lowered by the Italian vessel* Castoro Dieci *in summer 2011.*

The second turns to the issue of how system-builders have claimed Europe's waterscapes for infrastructural purposes and thereby also materially adapted them—often in destructive ways—to the demands of the network age. The third part, finally, addresses how system-builders and their creations have been held responsible for pollution—and how they have envisioned ever more infrastructure as a solution to wet environmental problems.

Charting Inland Waters

One of the most notable aspects of the Nord Stream pipeline project was its crucial dependence on accurate knowledge about the Baltic Sea, in terms of its winds, currents, salinity, its biological life-world, the characteristics of its seabed, and traces from earlier human activity. This forced the pipeline company to cooperate closely with oceanographers, hydrologists, biologists, geologists, archaeologists, fishery and military researchers, and other experts. Many scientists welcomed this, for the simple reason that it opened up new research and funding opportunities. Such interdependence between scientific activities and system-building has been a recurring theme in Europe's aquatic history.

In the case of inland waters, river manipulation and canal construction projects early on generated a demand for knowledge about the natural dynamics of rivers and lakes. The circulation of water traditionally was perceived as something highly mysterious. Renaissance scholars debated, in particular, whether rainfalls really sufficed to account for all the water that flowed in Europe's rivers. Star scientists like Johannes Kepler, René Descartes, and Athanasius Kircher considered this implausible or even impossible. A persistent theory was that of an unseen ocean within the earth, from which the rivers sourced much of their water. Moreover, rivers, lakes, and seas that appeared to be isolated from each other if viewed from the earth's surface were believed to be interconnected through a system of underground waterways. The Caspian Sea, for example, was supposedly linked to the Persian Gulf and the Black Sea, whereas the Rhine connected with the Danube and Sweden's Lake Vänern with Lake Vättern.[5]

Actual measurements to prove that precipitation was the only source of Europe's flowing water were first carried out in 1674 by the French geographer Pierre Perrault, who set out to map the flow dynamics of the Upper Seine. Perrault's and others' studies forced hydrologists to conceptualize Europe's aquatic geography in terms of nature-given "drainage basins" (the terms "river basin" and "catchment area" are also commonly used), separated from each other by "drainage divides" (or watersheds). Such conceptualizations led to a breakthrough in the hydrological sciences, with important long-term consequences for river engineering projects.[6]

Under the influence of the Enlightenment and further hydraulic engineering efforts in the eighteenth century, the drainage basin concept also started to be appropriated for political purposes. In 1752 the French cartographer Philippe Buache, in the service of King Louis XV, published an essay suggesting that a continent's landscapes be analyzed as a set of contiguous drainage basins. In the 1770s the German historian Johann Christoph Gatterer expanded this idea into a theory of the world's division into lands and regions. In the early nineteenth century, then, colorful atlases began being published in which the traditional political maps were complemented by hydrological visualizations of Europe.[7]

Fig. 7.2 **Alternative Geographies:** *Under the influence of the Enlightenment and intense hydraulic engineering efforts in the eighteenth and nineteenth centuries, historians and geographers developed new cartographic visualizations of Europe. This map from 1839 is aesthetically very similar to contemporary political maps, but Europe's internal structure looks totally different. The borders, which are not political, but hydrological, mark major drainage divides.*

Buache's and Gatterer's work strongly influenced political debates about territoriality and public administration. Advanced proposals for administrative restructuring of countries into provinces based on drainage basins developed almost everywhere, the argument being that this was the most natural way to organize a country. In France the notion was appropriated by revolutionaries and opponents to political centralization, and in Spain by leading *regeneracionistas* such as Joaquin Costa in the struggle against the traditional landowning elite. In Britain similar proposals were brought forward. In most cases, however, the vision of a natural political geography failed to materialize. The exception was Spain, where the administrative restructuring proposed by Costa actually became reality in 1865, the king ordering the partition of the country into ten hydrologically-defined districts.[8]

Since most drainage basins extended into more than one country, the new atlases also created a sense of tension and contradiction between natural and political geography. Some geographers came to the conclusion that most existing borders between countries were unnatural. Yet radical political reorganization was in most cases not a realistic approach to resolving the perceived mismatches. Instead, two principal alternatives for action took shape. The first was to interlink a country's drainage basins through the construction of artificial waterways. This was what most canal-building was about. The other was to relinquish the primacy of the nation state and establish close cooperation with foreign stakeholders in a shared hydrological region. This was the idea that led the Congress of Vienna, in the early nineteenth century, to stipulate the formation of a number of international navigational commissions. Later on, the riparian states in many drainage basins broadened their relations with one another to include further issues of common interest, such as flood protection, irrigation, fisheries, hydropower, and pollution. In the end, the perceived need to deal with the discrepancies between Europe's natural and political geography stimulated infrastructural activity both within and between countries.

Mapping the Sea

At sea, a basic prerequisite for much system-building has been the availability of accurate and reliable charts indicating the location and characteristics of coasts, islands, shoals, and harbors, along with information on depths, currents, and water characteristics. The revolution in maritime transport that set in from the late eighteenth century greatly stimulated the production of such information.

A key challenge was to develop a better understanding of the Atlantic Ocean. Both the British and the American hydrographic offices undertook to compile comprehensive Atlantic surveys. A former U.S. Navy commander, Matthew Fontaine Maury, who after a leg injury had turned to science for a new career, became the key person in this quest. Having been appointed director of the U.S. Navy's Depot of Charts and Instruments, Maury started collecting logbooks and observations from naval officers and merchant shipping captains. On this basis he was able to compile a novel set of nautical charts featuring useful data on winds and currents. When published in 1852, the charts aroused great attention not only in the United States, but also in Europe. Maury then took the initiative to widen his ocean surveying endeavor to include data from European shipmasters as well. The project was thereby elevated to a high political level, the U.S. government inviting "all the maritime states of Christendom" to a conference upon the subject. It was held in Brussels in August 1853.[9]

The Brussels conference recommended "a plan of observations which should be followed on board the vessels of all friendly nations" and which should be carried on "in peace and war." A chart was to be constructed by putting down "the tracks of many vessels on the same voyage, but at different times, in different years, and during all seasons, and by projecting along each track the winds and currents daily encountered." The countries represented agreed to "unite and cooperate in carrying out one system of philosophical research with regard to the sea. Though they may be enemies in all else, here they are to be friends."[10] The cooperation was also a sign of recognition that if Europe and America were to reach out to the Atlantic and the other oceans in the new network era, they would have to do so in a concerted effort. The mapping of the seas thus became a new arena for both intra-European and trans-Atlantic cooperation. The success of the venture became evident when reports started arriving from captains who had used the new charts, informing their makers that sailing times from Europe to many overseas destinations had been significantly shortened.[11]

Maury further widened his scientific ambitions by setting out to map the Atlantic seabed, with a particular focus on its depths. Apart from navigation, another infrastructural domain here emerged as an important ally of the scientists: the emerging business of underwater telegraphy. When Cyrus Field, the American entrepreneur, started taking serious interest in the possibility of a trans-Atlantic telegraph cable, Maury was the obvious person to approach when it came to determining its physical-geographical feasibility. Initial results from Maury's deep-sea soundings, carried out in the Atlantic's middle latitudes, hardly encouraged telegraph system-builders, as they suggested that there the seabed was extremely rugged and abrupt in shape. Further north, however, the

Fig. 7.3 **Symbiotic Relationship:** *Maritime transport and submarine telegraphy system-builders were important users of improved nautical charts, and the needs of these actors stimulated scientific progress in the aquatic sciences. The close connections between infrastructure and hydrography are made explicit on this map, which was published in the 1866 edition of Matthew Fontaine Maury's* The Physical Geography of the Sea. *Later scientific studies showed that the Telegraphic Plateau (shown in the upper part of the map), which at the time was believed to be a characteristic feature of the North Atlantic seabed, actually did not exist.*

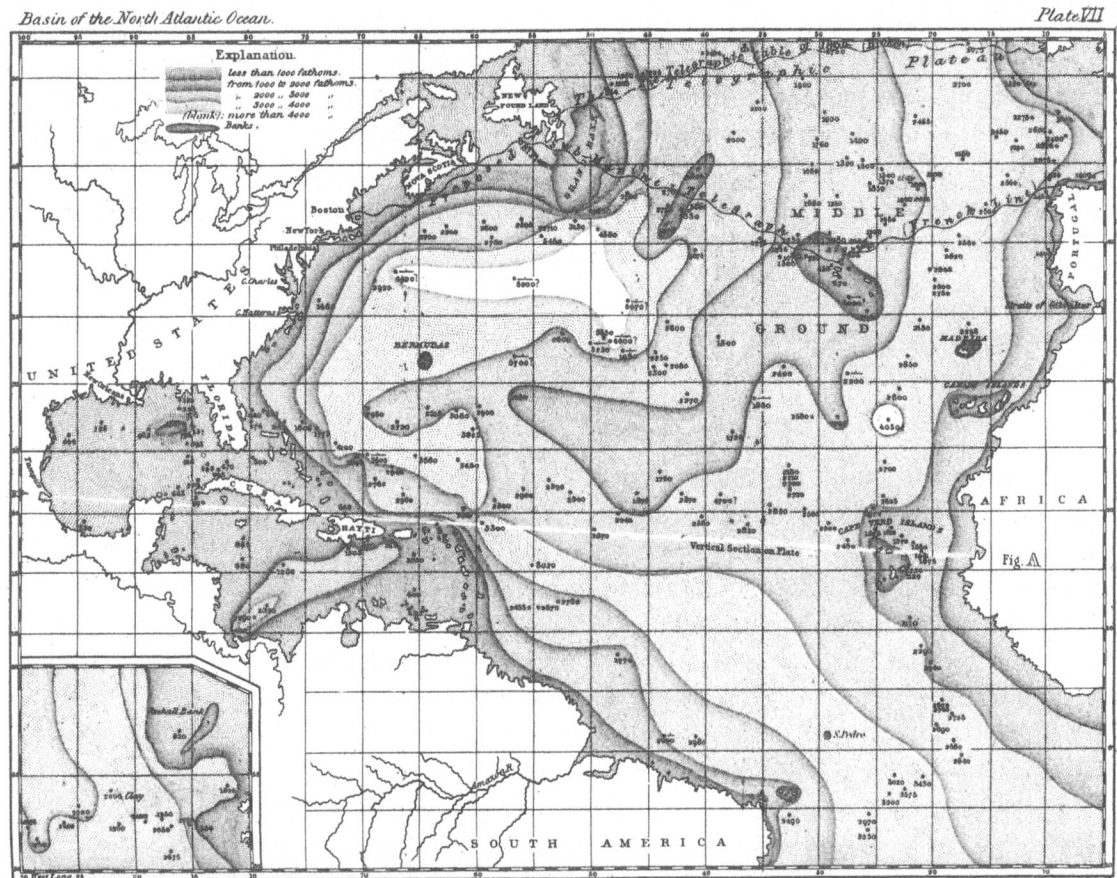
Basin of the North Atlantic Ocean. Plate VII

situation looked better. Corresponding with Field, Maury in 1854 confirmed that the northern Atlantic sea floor formed "a plateau, which seems to have been placed there especially for the purpose of holding the wires of the submarine telegraph, and keeping them out of harm's way."[12] He optimistically christened this underwater landscape the "Telegraphic Plateau."[13]

Like Maury, the scientists employed by the British Hydrographic Office were able to argue in favor of massive public support for their scientific projects by pointing to their infrastructural—and military—utility. Both the Crimean War and the American Civil War alerted the British to the importance for the world's leading imperial power of knowing the seas, whereby not only the Atlantic, but also the Mediterranean, the Black Sea, the Baltic, the Red Sea, and the Indian Ocean became important spaces for exploratory activities. By 1870, Britain had assumed world leadership in deep sea exploration. Ambitious charting projects were launched by other nations, too, including historically-important mapmakers such as France and the Netherlands, but also smaller, non-colonial powers such as Denmark and Sweden. For the latter, however, the practical part of the motivation had less to do with navigation or telegraphy and more with fishery interests.[14]

Improving Europe's Rivers

Hydraulic system-building contributed not only to new knowledge and new perceptions of European waterscapes. In the process Europe's seas and inland waters were also physically adapted to infrastructure's needs, often with profound—and destructive—impact on the natural environment. Major projects modified Europe's rivers, in particular, to such an extent that by the late twentieth century they were hardly distinguishable from human-built canals.

The most far-reaching river improvement efforts were undertaken on the Rhine. Already from the outset, they gave rise to controversy. Based on two agreements between the Grand Duchy of Baden and the Bavarian Palatinate, signed in 1817 and 1825, a skilled engineer in the service of Baden's government, Johann Gottfried Tulla, set out to rectify the Upper Rhine on its course from Basel to Worms, a distance of 340 km, by straightening it and quickening its current. This was a radical ambition because the stretch happened to include the Rhine's main floodplain. Downstream communities became worried about potentially adverse effects, particularly increased flooding. When in 1824 the Middle and Lower Rhine suffered a devastating flood, hydraulic engineers in the service of Hesse, Prussia, and the Netherlands rang the alarm bell, arguing that the flood was not natural, but a direct result of Tulla's upstream rectification project. Tulla dismissed this argument, claiming that his projects were much too insignificant for any radical effects to be possible on regions several hundred kilometers away.[15]

Downstream actors continued to oppose Tulla's Upper Rhine project, but they also took inspiration from it. While Prussian diplomats still argued the legal case against Baden and Bavaria,

Prussian hydraulic engineers began removing the famously dangerous Bingen reef, just downstream from Mainz, which for centuries had hindered navigation. Then, in 1851, a much larger effort, the Prussian Navigation Project, brought hydraulic engineers from the Prussian provinces of the Rhineland, Westphalia, and Nassau together to re-engineer the river on the whole stretch from Bingen to the Dutch border. In the Netherlands, meanwhile, the Department of Public Works and Water Management (*Rijkswaterstraat*) launched an integrated project to remake and rectify the various Rhine branches on Dutch territory. The German-dominated Rhine Commission, pointing to the growing importance of efficient transport connections between Germany and the North Sea, put pressure on the Dutch in this context.[16]

The Rhine projects, most of which took Tulla's engineering principles as point of departure, provided ample inspiration for the visions of system–builders active in other drainage basins. One of the most challenging was the Danube's. In its natural state, the Danube was much more complex than the Rhine; and it was seriously obstructed by rapids, shallows, sandbanks, and reefs. The greatest obstacle to efficient navigation was the 120 km gorge across the Carpathian Mountains known as the Iron Gates, where the river's course was constricted and the water flowed faster. Underwater reefs gave rise to rapids that were widely regarded as barriers to larger vessels and in particular to the enormous flat-bottomed barges that were traditionally sent down the Danube from Ulm in southern Germany. "If these difficulties were removed," one traveller speculated in 1833, "the whole of the East would communicate" with Germany.[17] A year later Austrian engineers arrived and, building on the recent experience of their Prussian peers, blasted away the rocks in the channel at the Iron Gates' upper end. Navigation was reportedly greatly improved.[18]

In parallel, efforts were launched to improve the lower Danube and the river's giant delta, where the watercourse split up into numerous and mostly unnavigable channels. Only three of them had traditionally been of any significance, though all were shallow and navigating proved hazardous due to shifting sands. The vessels that actually used them were mainly small grain transporters from Walachia and Bulgaria to Black Sea ports and Constantinople. In the 1830s this trade expanded, inspiring West European traders and shipping companies with financial muscles to seek greater access to the Black Sea region. Britain, in particular, eyed Danube grain as a contributor to meeting domestic food needs.

The Russians, however, who from 1829 controlled the river's delta, regarded the Danube grain trade as an unwelcome competitor to their own agricultural exports. Accordingly, they deliberately allowed at least one of the three delta channels, the Kilia Channel in the north, to silt up in such a way that it could no longer be used. With regard to the remaining two channels, nothing was done to improve them.[19]

Prospects for change increased after the Crimean War and the Ottoman reconquest of the delta. The Paris peace treaty of 1856 stated that the Lower Danube must be made accessible to all and ordered formation of the European Danube Commission. The commission included not only representatives of the Lower Danube states themselves (Russia and the Ottoman Empire), but also from Britain, France, Austria-Hungary, and Sardinia-Piedmont. Seated in Galati and with workshops at Sulina, the Commission secured the right to collect a toll on all ships passing through the delta and use this fund to finance physical improvement projects. This made the European Danube Commission a much stronger organization than its counterpart on the Rhine.[20]

In what followed, the course of the Sulina Channel, the middle of the Danube's three main deltaic arms, was narrowed with the help of dykes, forcing the water to flow more swiftly and using this more powerful current to increase the scour. In this way the channel was successfully deepened to 5 meters. The increased accessibility made it possible for the total tonnage of ships visiting the delta to increase six-fold in the half century from 1856 to 1907.[21]

During that period mechanization, progress in machine-building, naval architectural innovations, stronger materials, and the development of new explosives generated further opportunities for Europe's river engineers. In an initial and highly laborious effort to carve out a navigable channel along the scenic Middle Rhine, which was full of underwater rocks, workers blasted away 30,000 cubic meters of rock between 1851 and 1879. Upon the project's completion, however, the channel was already insufficient to accommodate the larger vessels that by then had started navigating the Rhine. In the 1890s, improved technology made it possible for the Prussians to remove nearly ten times as much rock from the river bed in one-third as much time. Similarly on the Danube, massive explosives, used in the period from 1883 to 1898, helped construct a canal within the river's course at the Iron Gates. Combined with the availability of more powerful steam engines, this bypass allowed first a tugboat and later a railroad locomotive to pull ships upstream against the current.[22]

Steam-powered dredging technology paved the way for another, even more far-reaching revolution. Small-scale dredging had taken place for centuries on many waterways, but the new mechanical dredging and pumping machinery facilitated projects on a grander scale. For the first time, the depths and widths of navigable channels could be standardized throughout a river's course. Hydraulic engineers, notably in Germany and Austria-Hungary, even started contemplating a Europe-wide standardization of rivers and canals, so that a 1,000 ton barge would be able to move across the Continent without transshipment. The Rhine, Europe's busiest inland waterway, was designed for a minimum depth of 2 meters on the section from Bingen to St. Goar, 2.5 meters on the section from St. Goar to Cologne and 3 meters from there to the Dutch border. In Holland, Dutch engineers, as part of a larger project, redesigned the Waal so that it, too, would maintain a minimum depth of 3 meters.[23]

The remaking of the Rhine, the Danube, and other European rivers continued throughout the late nineteenth and most of the twentieth centuries. From a navigational point of view, the improvement works were enormously successful. But the new designs also turned out to be flawed in several respects. The fears debated so hotly already in the 1820s concerning increased risks of flooding could not be unequivocally confirmed, but there was no lack of other unintended effects. One problem was that faster currents generated greater erosion. Another was the inherent instability of Europe's modernized rivers. Continuous follow-up work, mainly in the form of massive "maintenance dredging," was in most places necessary. This had adverse impacts on the riverine fauna and flora. The salmon, in particular, lost its spawning places in the rivers' gravel beds. By the mid-twentieth century, the salmon, once of immense importance for food supply and local economies in the Rhine's drainage basin, had all but disappeared. Contrary to common belief, it was not pollution that made this happen, but continuous dredging in combination with the erection of dams and other artificial obstacles.[24]

The Coming of Hydropower

The next phase in the re-engineering of Europe's rivers, starting in the late nineteenth century, focused on the construction of weirs and dams. Most dams spanned small rivers, where they fulfilled a variety of functions. Irrigation was a main purpose of dam-building in arid regions, notably in southern Europe and parts of Russia, whereas in key industrial areas such as the Ruhr, the dammed water was mainly intended for industrial use, along with consumption by rapidly-growing urban populations. In forest and mining regions, dams facilitated log driving and provided mechanical energy. In many places the purpose of dams was to even out seasonally changing flows in feeder streams and tributaries, so as to guarantee sufficiently deep navigation channels in the mainstream throughout the year.[25]

From the 1880s, hydroelectric power generation emerged as a new motive for dam construction. Scandinavia, the Soviet Union, and the Alpine region became the most important hydroelectric areas in Europe. In Scandinavia, the forest industry had traditionally been the main agent in weir construction. The arrival of power companies spurred controversy. The log-driving community felt threatened, fearing that its logs would be trapped in the new dams or destroyed in artificial waterfalls. Fishing interests also opposed the projects. Gateway technologies such as fish ladders and specially-designed logways, handled the conflicts; but the net effect, at least from a fishery point of view, was clearly negative. The contest between electricity and log-driving interests ultimately faded away as road transport reoriented logging in the 1960s. In the case of Sweden, concerns over fish and a growing environmental movement led the Parliament, in a 1970 decision, to protect four of the country's remaining northern rivers from further exploitation; but this was the exception that proved the rule.[26]

Russia's hydro-electrical potential was also very large. In this case dam-building for energy purposes closely intersected with navigational, water supply, and especially agricultural interests. In 1916 the Tsar's Ministry of Agriculture launched a first report on the empire's immense hydroelectricity potential. A few years later, Lenin's GOELRO engineers took over and vastly scaled up the plans. The key organization in the ambitious projects subsequently launched was *Gidroproekt*, an engineering institute. Under the strong leadership of Sergei Zhuk, it grew into an extraordinarily powerful organization.[27]

Actual construction, with ample use of forced labor from the Gulag, accelerated under Stalin. In 1933 the first major Soviet dam, on the middle Dnepr, began operations. With an installed capacity of 560 MW, it was one of the world's largest hydropower stations. In addition, by making the Dnepr navigable for large barges all the way from Central Ukraine to the Black Sea, it served transport interests. The Dnepr dam was a mighty symbol of Soviet technological capability, but it was also criticized internally by agricultural interests, who argued that Soviet hydraulic engineering efforts should be concentrated on the country's arid regions and serve irrigation purposes. Moreover, the project arguably diverted resources from the construction of booming Moscow's badly needed reservoir for municipal water supply, a project that hinged on completing a major canal linking Moscow with the Volga.[28]

The Volga became the main focus of *Gidroproekt*'s engineers from the early 1930s. Stalin himself early on argued for large-scale irrigation programs in the Volga basin, the main purpose being to end droughts in the arid regions around Samara, Saratov, and Astrakhan. Multiple interests were at stake, ranging from hydropower and transport to water supply and fishing. The internal Soviet debate ran high when it came to distribution of water among competing interests. Planners and engineers also debated the pros and cons of small versus large dams. Those arguing for small hydroelectric power stations, whose main advantage would be their limited inundation of farmland, ultimately lost out to a more radical plan. Cascades of huge hydropower stations took shape on Soviet drawing boards, with giant reservoirs able to regulate the water for year-round flow. Vast areas of farmland along the Volga would have to be sacrificed and whole populations moved, but this would be compensated for by newly-developed land and living space elsewhere.[29]

By the eve of the Second World War, Zhuk's hydraulic projects had already inundated 663 cities, villages, and towns. But the main thrust was still to come. The Nazis, on their retreat, had destroyed much of what had been built up before the war, including the great Dnepr dam—much as Allied air raids targeted and destroyed several large German dams. Stalin's response was to launch, as

Fig. 7.4 **Damming the Volga:** *The Volga, Europe's longest river, early on stimulated the imagination of Soviet engineers. As in many other European river basins, multiple interests were at stake when large hydraulic projects started to take shape along the river. The Volga Hydroelectric Station, pictured here while still under construction in 1958, today remains Europe's largest hydroelectric facility. The huge reservoir above it totally changed the region's geography.*

part of his Great Plan for the Transformation of Nature, a massive hydraulic system-building initiative. Twelve major hydroelectric power stations were eventually built along the Volga, complemented by several smaller ones. At the Kuibyshev station, the largest, the Volga was dammed in such a way that a 600 km long water reservoir gathered upstream. Several such ultra-large bodies of water, both on the Volga and other rivers, totally changed the Soviet Union's natural geography. Perhaps half a million people were displaced as their homes were inundated.[30]

In Western and Central Europe, the Alps hosted the most promising hydropower potential, but much effort also went into electrifying non-Alpine stretches of great European rivers such as the Rhine and the Danube. This fueled international political controversies. For example, after the First World War when France set about exploiting the Rhine's hydropower potential by constructing a lateral canal—essentially moving the Rhine into France—and building a series of dams along it, the Germans on the river's other side were perplexed. They regarded the project as disastrous, for with all normal discharges diverted into the canal, the old river course would only be used for peak discharges. Navigation on the original Rhine would become impossible. The "Grand Canal," as the French proudly called it, would likely have far-reaching negative consequences for Baden's agriculture, while also having a detrimental impact on the Rhine valley's landscape. Nazi propaganda warned that the French project would set in motion the "steppification" of Germany, and the Upper Rhine development became one of Hitler's arguments for war preparations.[31]

On the Danube, Europe's politically most complex river, Austria and Germany built the first dams in the early twentieth century. After the First World War, the League of Nations and other actors pointed to the need for multilateral cooperation, though in practice little happened. Following the Second World War, Gunnar Myrdal's UNECE created a Danube Study Group, which along with several individual visionaries increasingly argued that the American Tennessee Valley Authority (TVA) should be adopted as a model for managing the Danube basin. This reflected optimism that the conflicts between different potential uses of the river could be resolved and that environmental impacts could be minimized. The TVA also inspired—and was inspired by—analogous efforts elsewhere in Europe, for example, along the Rhône in France and in some smaller Balkan river basins.[32]

Actual projects started to take form in the 1950s, though not so much linked to UNECE's visions. Yugoslavia and Romania worked out bilateral projects for harnessing the Iron Gates' hydropower potential, while combining it with navigational improvements and irrigation projects. Hungary and Czechoslovakia agreed on two similar multipurpose projects along their border. In practice, however, dam construction and other concrete projects were slow in coming. Approved projects were subsequently scaled down. The first Iron Gates' dam was eventually completed in 1972. Five years later Czechoslovakia and Hungary signed a treaty on their projects. At the time of communism's collapse in 1989, however, none of them was operational. The Hungarian environmental movement, which was also a disguised anti-communist movement, made the project a main target. Other nascent environmental movements in communist Europe, notably in Latvia, likewise organized themselves to oppose hydropower projects.[33]

By the late twentieth century, only a very few rivers in Europe had avoided being dammed. The dams were preceded by careful measurements and analyses of water flows, sedimentation, and the river's ecology. But the real effects of the dams were always more far-reaching than indicated by the scientific reports on which decisions to launch the projects were based. Toward the late twentieth century, analysts started to recognize that virtually all dams had a destructive impact on Europe's environment and ecosystems.

The most obvious effects were local, that is, at and around the dam site. The nearby landscape was completely altered and the conditions of life changed radically as the reservoir basin was stripped of trees, plants, and humus. Filled with water, it looked like a lake, but biologically, it was not. It was much more difficult for flora and fauna to establish themselves both in the reservoir and along its shores. In 1911 the German limnologist August Thienemann showed that reservoirs were biotopes that favored a certain kind of species: those that were able to adapt to changing conditions. Over the longer term, even these species tended to disappear, being kept up only by fish-farming. Needless to say, dams also presented an obstacle to migratory fish, from the sturgeon to the salmon.[34]

On a larger geographical scale, dams had far-reaching impacts on the seas as well. Scandinavia's 240 dams significantly altered the seasonal flow of fresh water into the Baltic. The Mediterranean was affected not only by European hydraulic engineering, but also by megaprojects in Africa and the Middle East. Egypt's Aswan dam trapped the Nile's silt, causing this river's great delta to shrink and depriving the Mediterranean of nutrients. This in turn destroyed sardine and shrimp fisheries.[35] Such findings hinted at the need to view every river not only in the context of its own drainage basin, but as interconnected with the marine environment and with other river basins that emptied into the same sea. The full recognition of these interdependencies, however, would come only in the age of pollution.

Transferring Water

Most Renaissance scholars erroneously believed that different drainage basins were connected with each other through a system of invisible, subterranean waterways. Creating real connections between drainage basins became a task for Europe's engineers. In most cases, such links, taking the form of canals, sought to facilitate transport, but some had a totally different purpose: to redistribute water resources across drainage divides. Such projects challenged Europe's natural division into a set of clearly-defined catchment areas.

The Soviet Union and Spain launched Europe's most radical interbasin water transfer projects. In the Soviet case, Stalin's hydraulic engineers soon recognized that the massive irrigation projects in the Volga basin would strip out much of the river's water. Rather than cancel the projects, however, the Soviet Academy of Sciences proposed to add more infrastructure. More precisely, it proposed to make additional water volumes available through diverting several northern Russian rivers into the Volga.[36]

Planning started in earnest in the 1960s, as increased irrigation assumed a key role in countering the country's agricultural crisis. In 1971, then, engineers from *Gidroproekt*, which had now become the Ministry of Land Reclamation and Water Resources, arrived at the watershed separating the Kama River (one of the Volga's main tributaries) from the Pechora River (which emptied into the Barents Sea). There, several giant nuclear charges were detonated along a 70 km stretch, the goal being to assess the feasibility of completely levelling the ground and thus removing the drainage divide altogether.[37]

In light of environmental concerns and the Soviet Union's key role in ongoing international negotiations on nuclear disarmament, this radical strategy proved unsustainable. Yet in the late 1970s the diversion project gained momentum again. The new strategy was to pump huge amounts of water across the watershed, rather than physically eliminating it. A set of giant pumps would lift the water 97 meters. Soviet engineers considered the project crucial not only in its own right, but also as a model for larger undertakings that were planned further east, involving the great Siberian rivers.

However, the nascent Soviet environmental movement, and in particular a group within it known as Living Water, strongly opposed the Volga diversion project. The Kremlin did its best to censor the debate as it was unfolding in the Soviet media, but the project still failed to take off due to massive critique from within the scientific community. Then, in the turmoil following the Chernobyl nuclear disaster and the first effects of new Soviet leader Mikhail Gorbachev's *glasnost* policy, the Politburo opted to shelve the diversions. The Soviet environmental movement celebrated the decision as a defining event.[38]

Spain came further than the Soviet Union in actually implementing its river diversion visions. This was partly linked to the ambitious attempts to transform the country's agriculture, discussed in the previous chapter. Under Franco, the country's hydraulic engineers got unprecedented opportunities to realize their dreams. Alfonso Peña Boeuf, Franco's long-term Minister of Public Works, spotted river diversions as the logical way of correcting the country's "hydrological disequilibrium," which had led to unfair distribution of wealth. "We are prepared to make sure that not a single drop of water is lost and that not a single injustice remains," Franco himself assured his people in 1959, taking pride in his ambition to "change the geography of Spain."[39] A "grand geographical reorganization" of Spain's water resources ensued, with trans-basin diversions forming the backbone of an imagined national water grid.[40]

The skeleton of the system emerged during the last decade of Franco's rule, although it was not completed until after his death. Its main constituent was a 286 km canal, of which 69 km were in tunnels, which started transferring massive volumes of water from the upper Tagus, which flowed westward and emptied into the Atlantic at Lisbon, to the smaller Segura River, which emptied into the Mediterranean near Alicante, where water was needed partly for irrigation but increasingly to support a booming tourist industry. To enable this, Franco's engineers built facilities to pump the Tagus' water over a height of no less than 300 meters.[41]

Portugal and several autonomous regions in Spain were highly critical of the Tagus–Segura diversion project. Political tensions escalated following serious droughts in southern and central Spain and Portugal in the early 1990s. The regional government of Castilla-La Mancha, for example, noted that its farmers "see the water passing by while their fields are often dry."[42] Castilla-La Mancha managed to secure a Supreme Court declaration confirming that the transfer was unlawful. The EU, meanwhile, exploited the Iberian water crisis for its own purposes by arguing that controversies like this one could be resolved most efficiently if supranational agencies were allowed to play a greater role in European water management activities. By the early twenty-first century, the future of inter-basin water transfers in the Iberian Peninsula seemed highly uncertain.[43]

Improving Europe's Seas

While massive projects adapted and re-engineered the natural courses of rivers, engineers also transformed and manipulated Europe's seas. At focus were at first waters near land. Many river mouths and estuaries, ocean ports, and natural coastscapes proved inappropriate for transport and flood protection purposes.

Some significant improvements had taken place in the seventeenth and eighteenth centuries—notably in France and the Low Countries—but in the nineteenth century the situation grew increasingly acute as ports needed to deal with ever larger oceangoing vessels. A fierce competition ensued among Europe's ports to attract passengers and commerce, and successful adaptations of waterscapes near harbors became a prerequisite for survival.[44]

Rotterdam, for example, was still a fairly minor port in 1850. In fact, its prospects looked gloomy due to its problematic location between the Rhine–Meuse river delta and the North Sea's tides. Without human involvement, the site would quickly have become unreachable for the ever larger Rhine barges and new ocean steamers. The inland waterways tended to naturally change their course and the sand and silt that they deposited threatened accessibility. Moreover, siltification in the delta worsened further following the many hydraulic projects carried out on the Lower, Middle, and Upper Rhine.

Determined to prevent nature from having its way, Dutch system-builders made use of newly-available steam power to cut a new connection for Rotterdam to the sea—the New Waterway, completed in 1872—and then successively deepen and broaden it by further dredging to accommodate ever larger vessels. At the same time, the Dutch did everything to prevent a corresponding adaptation process with regard to the Scheldt, on which Belgium's Antwerp, Rotterdam's main rival, was located, but whose wide estuary was within Dutch borders.

Harbors located on rocky coasts were in a more troublesome position. Docks could rarely be excavated from the land, but were, instead, created at the expense of the sea through construction of artificial wave breakers and stone piers. Yet this strategy was feasible only in the immediate vicinity of the shoreline, and further growth could only take place through lateral expansion. The French, for example, expanded the great port of Marseilles laterally over 20 km until it eventually reached the sandy Rhône delta. Once there, the river's deposits of mud and silt permitted a north European port-construction strategy. The result was the new port of Fos-sur-Mer, destined to become France's strategic import point for oil and gas from North Africa and the Middle East.[45]

Rapid growth in the size of ships, notably oil tankers, further increased the pressure on harbors. As of 1966, the largest oil tankers in the world had already a draught of 17 m and a deadweight of 300,000 tons. No ports in Europe could handle such monstrous vessels, the deepest harbor basins being designed for 100,000-ton tankers. The extreme draught of the new supertankers—and the way in which they were expected to continue growing—generated completely new dredging challenges, as not only sand and mud had to be removed, but increasingly also layers of hard earth or rocks. This sometimes made the projects prohibitively expensive. Moreover, it was often necessary to increase the length of the channels. Rotterdam's port authority, for example, concluded that it would have to build an 8 km channel out into the sea to enable ships with a 20 meter draught to reach the harbor. The length of the channel would have to be further extended to 40 and 55 kilometers for ships with draughts of 25 and 30 meters, respectively.[46]

In the 1970s, however, this development unexpectedly stagnated. Oil price shocks and overall economic stagnation led many ports to cancel ambitious channel projects. Today, contrary to what the 1960s forecasts predicted, very few oil tankers have a draught of 25 meters or more. Rotterdam eventually did invest in 20 and 25 meter channels, but as of the early twenty-first century it looks improbable that the 30 meter variant will ever be realized.[47]

In the wake of the First and especially the Second World War, maritime transports faced new challenges in which not only harbors, but also the high seas were at stake. Europe's saltwaterways had, quite literally, become minefields, making voyages in coastal regions and strategic straits hazardous. In 1948 the British Admiralty reported that Britain, since the war's end, had lost 172 ships through war-created hazards. The navies of countries with mined territorial waters responded by coming together and ordering a clean-up of the seas along certain corridors. The result was the North European and Mediterranean Routing Instructions (NEMEDRI) scheme. In the Baltic, North, and Mediterranean Seas, a system of carefully-mine-swept routes was created. A few miles wide, these sea lanes were marked by buoys, lightships (lighthouses mounted on vessels), and even the remnants of major wrecks. Adherence to the system was not compulsory, but all navigators were aware of the statement accompanying the routing instructions: "Mariners leave the channels at their peril."[48]

With time, congestion rather than mines became the most pressing problem, particularly so in the English Channel and

Fig. 7.5 The Dredging Revolution: *Steam-powered dredging machinery opened up totally new prospects for improving rivers and building canals. This image from the 1860s shows the Suez Canal being dredged during an early phase of its construction. Such projects were impossible to finish once and for all; unless continuous maintenance dredging took place, the quality of waterways was bound to steadily deteriorate.*

THE SUEZ CANAL: DREDGES AT WORK.

the southern part of the North Sea. Nowhere in Europe—or elsewhere in the world—was maritime traffic as dense as here. On the Borkum–Terschelling route, for example, off the Netherlands and West Germany, 350 ships passed on a daily basis already in 1962. Half the world's collisions were reported to take place between Dover and the Elbe. Positive and negative experiences from the NEMEDRI era inspired transport ministries, hydrographic offices, and shipping companies to respond by creating internationally-approved "Traffic Separation Schemes" (TSS). These gave the most densely trafficked of Europe's waters a new structure, carefully defining zones of access for different types of vessels.[49]

This development took off in 1961, when the Federal German Ministry of Transport, in collaboration with the shipping

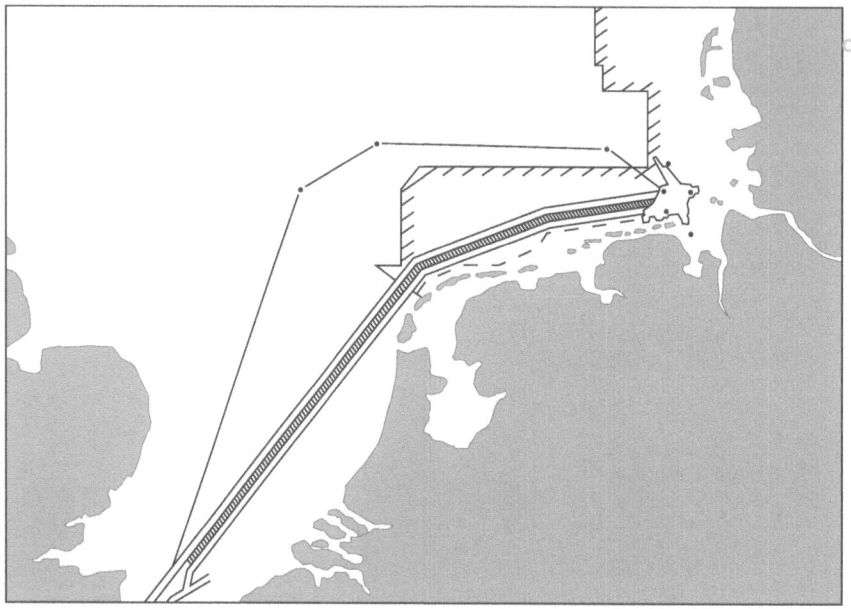

Fig. 7.6 **Maritime Highways:** *Europe's infrastructure transition turned the seas into clearly structured territories. The creation of sea lanes represented an important part of this process. Sea lane construction accelerated after the two World Wars as navigators sought to avoid mines. By the early 1960s congestion had become the main motivation for highway building at sea, stimulating further initiatives in which Traffic Separation Schemes (TSS) were at focus. This map shows one of the first proposed schemes for separation of eastbound and westbound traffic in the North Sea, including a special outer route for heavy-draught vessels.*

associations of the German North Sea ports, set up a North Sea Lanes Commission. The main objective was to enforce a northward dispersion of traffic off the German coast. The commission proposed that German and Dutch authorities cooperate in creating distinct eastbound and westbound lanes separated by a 2 mile safety zone, to be marked by buoys. For coastal shipping, an additional lane was proposed further south; whereas for vessels of heavy draught a new lane was to be created much further out in the North Sea.[50]

Similar anti-collision schemes developed in the Dover Strait. The British, French, and West German Institutes of Navigation—their Dutch and Belgian counterparts initially did not participate—created a joint Dover Strait Working Group, which emerged as the prime mover in establishing an early set of lanes. Following a period with several serious accidents in the years around 1970, the group's initiatives expanded, whereby the International Maritime Organization (IMO) of the United Nations became instrumental in extending and improving existing separation schemes. In 1972, the participants implemented a complex system of separation zones and created a special deep-draught route. The latter was reserved for vessels (notably supertankers) bound for Dutch, German, or Scandinavian ports, which needed water of such depth that only

Fig. 7.7 **Before GPS:** *The period from the mid-nineteenth to the mid-twentieth century became a golden era for Europe's lighthouse builders. Before the appearance of more modern communication technologies such as radar, RDF, and GPS, lighthouses formed the backbone of an immensely important communication system aimed at reducing navigational vulnerability. Many lighthouses, like this one on the Firth of Clyde, were architecturally impressive and picturesquely situated creations.*

a very narrow strip of the Dover Strait could guarantee them safe passage.[51]

In parallel with—and complementing—the introduction of these maritime motorways, state agencies worked hard to reduce navigational vulnerability by improving maritime communications. An impressive expansion of the lighthouse infrastructure had started in Europe already in the mid-nineteenth century. France, for example, which as late as 1800 had only 24 lighthouses in operation nationwide, possessed 360 in 1885, and 1,088 in 1987. The French Lighthouse Commission (*Commission des Phares*) led the way in Europe in creating nation-wide lighthouse systems, designed so that navigators would always have at least one lighthouse in sight while moving along or toward the coast. The nineteenth and twentieth centuries became a dynamic period of experimentation in lighthouse construction, both in terms of alternative energy sources and optical equipment. The strength of light signals increased dramatically. By the early 1990s, the lighthouse of Créac'h on the French coast had a reach of no less than 55 km. In the postwar period, ship radar, radio direction finding (RDF), the U.S.-based Global Positioning System (GPS), and other modern communication technologies began complementing lighthouses.[52]

Other engineering projects threatened rather than facilitated maritime transport. This concerned, in particular, the radical visions targeting some of Europe's key straits. The most far-reaching was the idea of eliminating the straits altogether. Hermann Sörgel's interwar Atlantropa project, for example, envisioned huge dams across the Strait of Gibraltar and even the Sicilian Straits. Sörgel observed that since there was a net inflow of water from the Atlantic into the Mediterranean, a dam would ultimately lower the Mediterranean's water level. This was seen advantageous both for electricity production and land reclamation. For navigational purposes, however, it was a nightmare. In northern Europe, a related proposal was brought forward in the early 1950s by the famous Swedish entrepreneur Ruben Rausing, who argued in favor of drying up the Swedish–Danish Sound. This project did not involve any hydropower potential or changes in the sea level. Instead, the focus was on land gains, urban expansion of Copenhagen and Malmö, and economic integration in the Swedish–Danish borderland. Luckily, neither Sörgel's nor Rausing's proposals ever materialized as projects.[53]

Energizing the Sea

The search for, production of, and transmission of energy was another infrastructural domain that strongly affected Europe's seas. The development took off in earnest when governments and oil companies, following the discovery of vast volumes of natural gas near the Dutch coast in 1959, identified the North Sea as a promising area for offshore oil and gas exploration. The Baltic Sea, the Bay of Biscay, the Mediterranean, the Black Sea, and the Caspian later on emerged as additional oil and gas targets. Yet the North Sea—and with time its northward extension into the Norwegian Sea and the Arctic Ocean—was by far the most important.

The maritime quest for fossil fuels was closely related to a renewed phase in the hydrographic surveying of Europe's seas, ultimately facilitating the determination of exact international borders in the blue. This border-building process, which was fraught with diplomatic controversy, relied on advanced scientific mappings of the seabed, especially Europe's continental shelves. Hydrographers and other scientists were just as happy as their predecessors in the nineteenth century to see Europe's infrastructure transition stimulate the development of their academic disciplines. In the neoliberal era that set in from the 1980s, UN-led invention of "exclusive economic zones" complemented the geographic partition of continental shelves, though in this case fishing rather than energy interests were at focus.[54]

The arrival of oil and gas drilling rigs totally changed the visual appearance and physical geography of Europe's seas. In the 1970s, large-scale oil and gas production commenced, carried out on giant platforms that stayed at sea on a quasi-permanent basis. In effect the platforms created an archipelago of artificial islands in a seascape that until recently had been dominated by stormy waters and empty horizons. Fishery interests and shipping companies were far from happy about these new obstacles. Below the surface, the seafloor also underwent dramatic change, as energy companies laid large-diameter pipelines for fuel transmission from offshore oil and gas fields to Britain, Scandinavia, and continental Western Europe. To protect these lines from trawlers, divers buried them in mud and sand. Pumping and compressor stations erected above the pipelines added to the North Sea's new look.[55]

Power companies also made use of the seafloor, laying transmission cables across the Baltic, the North Sea, and the Mediterranean. The first cable, bridging the Sound, began operating as early as 1915, but the breakthrough came in the 1960s when new HVDC technology allowed Swedish, Danish, and West German electricity companies to interconnect their grids. This was followed by additional cables from Sweden to Finland, Poland, and directly to Germany, from Finland to Estonia, from Norway to Denmark

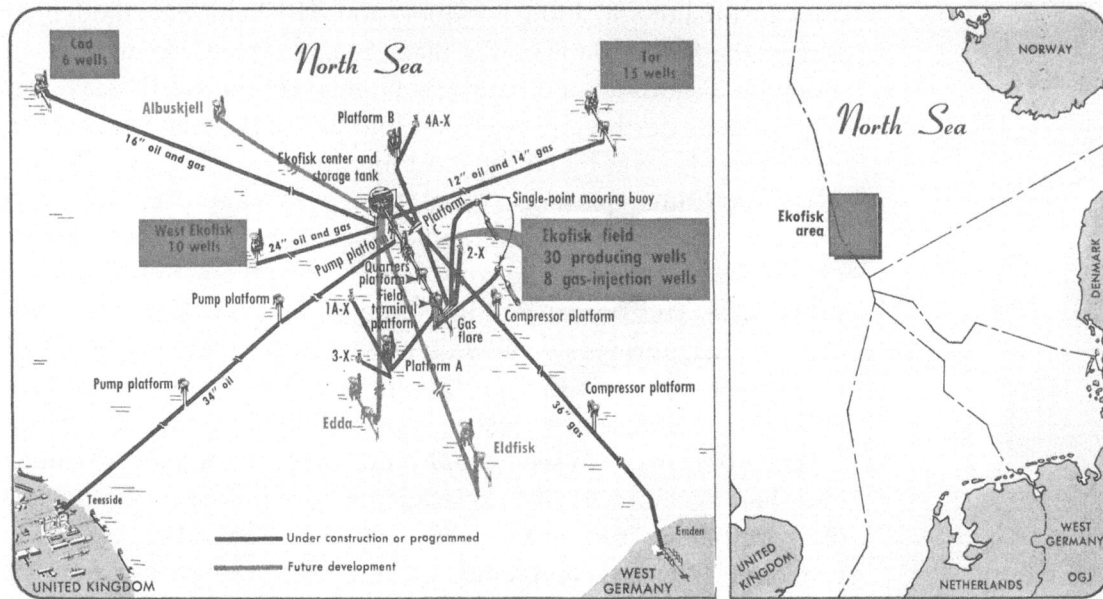

Fig. 7.8 **North Sea Networks:** *The discovery of oil and gas in the North Sea was one of the most spectacular aspects of Europe's twentieth-century energy history. The map to the left in this illustration from the Oil and Gas Journal shows the American oil company Phillips' system for producing and transmitting oil and gas from fields on the Norwegian continental shelf to Britain and Germany as of 1973. The map to the right shows the political shelf borders. These were settled through negotiations in the 1960s and early 1970s, the most contentious domain being the German one.*

and the Netherlands, from Britain to Ireland, France, and the Netherlands, from Italy to Greece, and from Spain to Morocco. Numerous domestic underwater connections further allowed many islands to link up with the grid. Environmental groups questioned this electrification of Europe's seas, pointing to possibly adverse effects on maritime flora and fauna. Yet the actual impact of the cables was clearly much less salient than that of offshore oil and gas installations.[56]

More radical in terms of its impact on coasts, seascapes, and ecosystems was the breakthrough of offshore wind power in the early twenty-first century. Again, the North Sea was a central site. Power companies set out to erect whole "farms" of wind turbines at sea, often close to newly-established shelf and zonal borders. Renewable electricity visionaries viewed such offshore wind farms as crucial components in the construction of "smart" and sustainable European electricity grids. It was in this context that nine European governments in 2009 agreed to build a joint power grid of high-voltage cables under the North Sea. Apart from wind power, high hopes were held for "tidal power" as a further contributor to maritime electricity production. Environmental organizations such as Greenpeace strongly favored such innovative projects.[57]

Fig. 7.9 Conquering the Caspian: *In the Soviet Union, the Caspian was the first sea to become subject to offshore oil exploration. Initially the focus was on areas in the immediate vicinity of land, whereby different oil fields were linked with each other and with onshore bases through roads built on semi-permanent bridges. The road shown on this image from 1978 interconnected numerous oil wells in the Serebrovsky offshore oil field.*

The Rise of Transnational Pollution

The remaking of Europe's waterscapes for the purpose of flood protection, navigation, water supply, and energy production certainly generated tensions and disputes. Increasingly, however, these controversies were overshadowed by another key concern: pollution. Pollution was largely the result of industrial and municipal actors' deliberate use of Europe's waters as natural sewage systems. The ability of rivers, in particular, to transport, dissipate, and destroy unwanted waste products had always been much appreciated. With the onset of the infrastructure transition, however, the volume of discharges increased dramatically on two fronts: on the one hand, municipalities started constructing centralized water supply and artificial sewage systems to increase urban sanitary standards and cope with rapidly-growing populations. On the other, an industrial economy of previously unimaginable dimensions took form.

Both trends generated a vastly growing demand for fresh water and a corresponding growth of wastewater. The previously local character of wet pollution was increasingly challenged by the suspicion that very large discharges of polluted wastewater from an upstream source might cause serious damage not only in the immediate vicinity of the discharge point, but several hundred kilometers downstream as well. Although water supply and wastewater disposal constituted local systems, insofar as their human-built constituents were concerned, they were increasingly perceived as interconnected with one another into larger, meso-regional systems.

The Rhine was a case in point. For example, dyestuff production, at the heart of chemical manufacturing throughout the second half of the nineteenth century, generated large amounts of toxic arsenic that needed to be disposed of. Several cases of arsenic poisoning in the 1850s made it politically impossible for upstream governments, in view of their relations with downstream communities, to allow dumping of arsenic directly into the Rhine. The Prussian government stipulated that all arsenic residues must be transported in sealed containers down to the sea and dumped there. The Dutch, however, regarded dumping into the sea as a potential threat to ocean fishery, and the transport itself on Rhine barges was also considered dangerous. In 1868 the governments of Prussia and the Netherlands signed a treaty to deal with the issue.[58]

Later on, the Ruhr's sprawling coal excavation and Alsace's potash mines emerged as additional threats. Dutch cities such as Rotterdam, which found itself totally dependent on the Rhine for its freshwater supply, processed the Rhine's water before it entered the urban distribution system, but this did not prevent the city's population from being plagued by waterborne typhus and other diseases. After 1911 several controversies concerning phenol-tasting drinking water and phenol-tasting salmon added to the worries. Chloride pollution was another problem. Humans and fish aside, large agricultural and horticultural interests were at stake.[59]

About 1927, a group of Dutch waterworks joined forces in a concerted effort to increase their knowledge about pollution in the Rhine and reduce emissions. Upstream German industrialists, however, thought it unnecessary to take any action. "Except to protect the fisheries, there is no rationale whatsoever to do anything about the pouring of wastewater in the Rhine because its water volume is so large that it can absorb and cleanse the waste itself," explained Karl Imhoff, the Managing Director of the Ruhr Cooperative, an organization formed to deal with wastewater discharges, as late as 1928.[60]

Seemingly powerless in the face of the upstream German interests, the Dutch efforts initially failed. Only in 1948 did they yield some tangible results, as the governments of France, Luxembourg, the Netherlands, Switzerland, and West Germany agreed to set up the International Commission for the Protection of the Rhine against Pollution (ICPR). Two decades later a major disaster, Hoechst's accidental dumping of the insecticide endosulfan into the Main, catalyzed attempts to come to grips with the problem. The incident caused massive fish kills and was front-page news for several days both in Germany and the Netherlands. For the first time the deteriorating quality of the Rhine's waters generated massive public unrest.[61]

A further climax surfaced in 1971, as the river's oxygen level reached an all-time low. Soon afterwards, ICPR received a charge to organize regular ministerial-level meetings, which became a new key arena for handling Rhine pollution and ecology issues internationally. In 1976, moreover, the European Communities joined ICPR as a contracting party. That year three important conventions went into force following approval at the Rhine Ministers' Conference. Designed to come to grip with chlorides, chemicals, and thermal pollution, respectively, they paved the way for "the most extensive revision of the Rhine river regime since the Congress of Vienna," as a leading Rhine historian put it.[62]

An intense period of municipal and industrial system-building for wastewater treatment followed. Dismantling the Rhine as a transnational sewage system and re-localizing wastewater treatment through investments in new local infrastructure became the new panacea. An alternative plan, intended to eliminate the main source of chloride pollution, ultimately failed. Project Eau Claire, as it was called, proposed by Alsace's vast potash industry, would have created a wastewater pipeline from Strasbourg to Rotterdam, where the chlorides would have been left for the North Sea to absorb. In the end this project proved too controversial, particularly as calculations showed that the system would only become economically feasible if other industrial pollutants also made use of it. Instead, the involved actors decided to store the chlorides locally in underground limestone formations near Mulhouse.[63]

The Sandoz disaster of November 1986, in which 30 tons of mercury and pesticides washed into the river, wiping out most of the Upper Rhine's fish stock, helped accelerate the trend toward international cooperation. A Rhine Action Plan for Ecological Rehabilitation, with a more aggressive agenda than the previous conventions, gained approval in 1987, specifying targets for water quality to be reached. Towards the end of the century, it was already clear that the impact of the new agreements and regulations signed in the 1970s and 1980s had been enormously positive. Concentrations of heavy metals, chlorides, chemicals, and most other pollutants—the most notable exception being nitrates—had all radically decreased. Oxygen levels had likewise increased to near normal levels.[64]

Other rivers faced similar challenges. In the cases of the Elbe and the Danube, which flowed across the Iron Curtain, pollution management was extremely challenging politically. The Elbe earned a reputation as "the most polluted river in Europe."[65] The Danube was to a certain extent cleaner, if only because the total discharge of the Danube was extraordinarily large (about three times that of the Rhine). In oil pollution, the Danube was much worse off than the Rhine, however. This chiefly resulted from navigation and the transport, in Eastern Europe, "of oil in old and poorly maintained pipelines and tanks." Yet recognizing that this was the case did not generate international cooperation.[66]

After several years of negotiations, the eight riparian countries adopted the Declaration of the Danube Countries to Cooperate on Questions Concerning the Water Management of the Danube, Especially to Protect the Danube from Pollution in 1985. Yet their efforts lagged far behind those on the Rhine. Cooperation gained momentum only after the fall of communism, and in particular after a major environmental disaster in 2000—"the worst since Chernobyl," as the BBC put it—when massive amounts of cyanide and heavy metals spilled from the Baia Mare goldmine in Romania. The main victims were in Serbia and in Hungary on the large Danube tributary Tisza, where nearly all wildlife was wiped out along a major stretch. Numerous municipal waterworks had to temporarily close down.[67]

The way accidents such as the 1969 endosulfan and the 2000 cyanide spills hit major tributaries to the Rhine and the Danube, from where the pollutants quickly spread to the mainstream, reminded environmental stakeholders of the necessity to view every river as part of a larger aquatic system. Only now, toward the late twentieth century, did the ultimate implications of the river basin concept, originally developed in the seventeenth and eighteenth centuries, become clear. Populations living on the banks of major rivers increasingly discovered their vulnerability to potential incidents in a multitude of tributaries and feeder streams. On the basis of this insight, effective environmental cooperation eventually developed along the Rhine, the Danube, and elsewhere.

Moreover, since most rivers emptied into one or another sea, stakeholders along Europe's coasts also became part of European pollution's political geography. Just like rivers, the seas could transport and spread waste across national borders; and a substantial part of this pollution arrived by way of Europe's large river mouths. In the North Sea, the south–north going current guided pollution from the Rhine, Meuse, Scheldt, and the British rivers to the German Bight. Toward the end of the 1970s, oxygen depletion and fish disease began being observed there. The enormous algae blooms and the widely publicized seal death in the German Bight in 1988 highlighted the intricate relations between inland waters and the maritime world. About half of heavy metal pollution came to the sea via rivers. Actors engaged in protecting the North Sea, notably the intergovernmental Oslo and Paris Commissions (established in 1972 and 1974, respectively), following pollutants to their sources, became very active in pushing ICPR and other Rhine actors to enforce a reduction in riverine pollution. The two North Sea commissions also played a main role in the campaign that eventually compelled the Alsatian potash industry to abandon its Strasbourg–Rotterdam wastewater pipeline plan.[68]

Industrial pollution from coastal sources added other problems. Areva, for example, the French operator of a nuclear reprocessing plant at La Hague, discharged vast volumes of liquid radioactive waste into the English Channel, from where it flowed to the North Sea, Skagerrak, and Kattegat. Britain's BNFL likewise used the Irish Sea as a nuclear sewer for its Sellafield reprocessing facility, constructing a special wastewater pipeline that extended 3 km beyond the high-water mark. In fact, it was precisely the possibility of getting rid of voluminous liquid pollutants that made seaside locations so attractive for nuclear reprocessors. For their part, hydrologists were happy for the opportunity that radioactive substances offered to enhance scientific knowledge about water movements. Coastal populations around the North Sea, including faraway Norway and Denmark, were less enthusiastic.

Their emerging awareness of inhabiting a maritime nuclear waste distribution system made them active in pushing Areva and BNFL to shut down their facilities or at least put an end to their waste discharges.[69]

In addition, Europe's seas had to cope with pollution from maritime transport and energy supply. Oil spills from tankers en route from Russia, the Middle East, and North Africa to European refineries and pipeline grids ignited major concerns in Europe, while also generating the first international attempts to come to grips with maritime pollution. The Mediterranean countries, greatly dependent as they were on their sprawling tourist industries, were particularly worried. The Suez Canal and Soviet oil exports through the Bosporus had turned the Mediterranean into a major transport artery for oil. By the 1960s there were "tactile tar balls on many Mediterranean beaches."[70]

The defining event in the history of European oil spills, however, was the 1967 grounding of the *Torrey Canyon* supertanker in the English Channel. En route from Kuwait to Milford Haven, the ship spilled 121,200 tons of crude oil into the sea. In 1978, the *Amoco Cádiz* spilled another 228,000 tons off Brittany. After the latter accident, new legislation demanding safer transports yielded a marked reduction in spills. Like the chemical disasters on the Rhine and other European rivers, the mediated drama of oil spills, with pictures of oil-smeared beaches, birds, and fish, were highly effective in mobilizing both the general public and governments to respond. Yet from a statistical point of view, the tanker accidents accounted for only a small share of maritime oil pollution. Much more pervasive were the smaller, but almost continuous—and often deliberate—discharges of oil from tankers and other large vessels trafficking Europe's major sea lanes.[71]

Toward Ecological System-Building

Fighting pollution was considered an urgent task because it directly jeopardized fresh water and food supply, tourism, and the use of sediment for land reclamation projects. Growing environmental consciousness in the early 1970s, however, increasingly addressed the intrinsic value of an unspoiled nature. Biodiversity, whose

Fig. 7.10 After the Storm I: *The rapid growth of maritime oil transports generated totally new kinds of environmental problems. This photo from March 1967 shows volunteers attempting to clear oil at Lands End in Cornwall, after the oil tanker* Torrey Canyon *had run aground on the Seven Stones rocks, spilling its cargo. The oil from the ship threatened an environmental disaster, only avoided when British jets bombed the ship and burnt off the oil.*

importance for humanity's survivability remained contested, was more and more considered important for its own sake.[72]

On the Rhine, the salmon became an iconic species. It had once been of immense importance for local economies and food supply throughout the basin. Starting in the mid-nineteenth century catches had begun decreasing, and a century later the salmon had all but disappeared. Pollution and overfishing were among the contributing factors, but by far the most destructive force was river improvement through dredging and the construction of artificial weirs and dams. Dredging destroyed the salmon's best spawning and smolting grounds, while dam construction made its migration nearly impossible. When the ICPR issued an "Ecological Plan for the Rhine" in 1989, it argued for restoring a sustainable salmon population in the river basin. Its centerpiece was an artificial infrastructure designed to enable the salmon's return.

Advertised as Salmon 2000, the project involved several components. Its first step identified tributaries and feeder streams that still possessed suitable gravel beds for spawning. Then, specially-designed fish passages enabled the salmon's migration from the sea to the gravel beds. In the Netherlands, hindrances were removed at the river's main mouths. System-builders set out to reconstruct coastal sluiceways on the IJsselmeer (especially at the Afsluitdijk) and to add fish passages to the weirs on the Nederrijn-Lek and Meuse rivers. A particularly important part of the project was redesigning the Haringvlietdam, aimed to allow salmon migrations up the common Meuse–Rhine delta. The engineers then continued their work farther upstream, first in North Rhine-Westphalia, then on the Middle and Upper Rhine. Other measures took the form of undoing earlier improvement projects by, for example, removing dikes, artificial embankments, and weirs that no longer served any important function. ICPR regarded the outcome as highly successful, although it acknowledges that "Rhine salmon is not yet independent of human help and stocking exercises."[73]

The salmon project aside, the ICPR initiated the Habitat Patch Connectivity Project, which focused on "re-establishing the alluvial corridor that once stretched uninterrupted from Lake Constance to Hoek van Holland." The ultimate goal was "to provide migration and colonization paths for animals and plants." "Envisaged is a riverscape in which the most ecologically valuable and near-natural core areas are linked together so that every organism can reach every biotope," the ICPR declared in 1998.[74]

The seas were similarly subject to ecological infrastructure visions. In the Baltic, for example, the main problem was de-oxygenation of deep bottoms, a phenomenon that scientists agreed was essentially caused by eutrophication. The problem was not perennial. Great storms pushing vast volumes of oxygen-rich North Sea salt water into the Baltic tended to solve it in a natural, but irregular way. Unfortunately, however, storms powerful enough for this outcome were exceptionally rare, occurring only a few times a century. Hence Swedish and Danish engineers elaborated radical geo-engineering solutions aiming to bring in salt water by artificial means. One proposal was to build 12 parallel tunnels, each 10 meters in diameter, through southern Sweden. Another was to lay pipelines on the bottom of the Sound, although this would require no less than 1,576 parallel lines if each had a diameter of 1.2 meters. Other, more advanced variants included the removal of the subsea thresholds in the Danish straits with dynamite, and a huge mechanical system to increase the "pulses" of salt water into the Baltic.[75]

Europe through the Lens of Wet Systems

This chapter has examined Europe's infrastructure transition through the lens of water. The focus has been on different levels of interaction between infrastructure system-building and Europe's waterscapes. Core issues included how infrastructure influenced—and was influenced by—changing perceptions and new knowledge about European waters; how system–builders increasingly claimed rivers, lakes, and seas for a variety of purposes; and how they in this process destroyed the natural environment. However, more infrastructure—ranging from sewage treatment plants to ecological networks—also became a panacea for coming to grips with many wet environmental problems.

In the case of inland waters, the Rhine played a unique role. Growing awareness of how the Rhine's drainage basin functioned as a single hydrological system formed the point of departure for anchoring an integrated European region. While actors could draw on pre-modern antecedents, interactions among geographically-dispersed actors were vastly scaled up and diversified in the nineteenth and twentieth centuries. This was obvious in scientific endeavors, in river rectification projects, in dam and hydropower plant construction, in the evolution of wastewater discharge practices, and in joint efforts to address environmental problems. By the early twenty-first century, even the most remote corners of the Rhine basin had become part of this regional system.

Another notable hydrological region was Danube Europe, although from an infrastructural point of view this geographical entity was much slower in forming than Rhine Europe. This was so despite a number of grand nineteenth- and twentieth-century visions in which the Danube basin represented a point of departure for various ambitious projects. During the Cold War, the Iron Curtain, with which Rhine Europe never had to cope, was clearly salient. In the post-Cold War decades, however, infrastructural cooperation in the basin gained momentum. Coincidentally, the immediate post-Cold War era also featured the completion of the Rhine–Main–Danube canal—the first large-scale navigational and hydrological connection across the Main European Watershed.

The perception of the Rhine's and the Danube's drainage basins as integrated geographical entities is intriguing in view of the large number of riparian countries involved in their making. This strongly-transboundary dimension was less obvious in other drainage basins, although rivers such as the Western Dvina, the Vistula, the Oder, the Elbe, the Po, and the Rhône did flow through more than one country. Nationalists regarded the Western Dvina as distinctly Latvian, the Vistula as Polish, the Po as Italian, and the Rhône as French. Even the Rhine was famously perceived as German. Transboundary flows were thus rhetorically transformed into national ones. However, rivers that were widely perceived as national were not necessarily subject to more intense hydraulic engineering activities than their international counterparts. Motivated by the enormous potential benefits of cooperation in fields such as navigation and the struggle against pollution, system-builders in international river basins came together in infrastructure endeavors that often outpaced developments in national basins.

As for Europe's seas, improved transport brought the two classical European navigational spheres—the Mediterranean and the Black Sea, on the one hand, and the North and Baltic Seas on the other—closer together. Most system-building activities, however, focused on cooperation within smaller maritime regions. Of these, the North Sea was by far the most interconnected, particularly in transport and energy. The extent of interaction among coastal states—friendly and otherwise—was so great that the North Sea, plus the Rhine's and the nearby Meuse's river basins, may be taken as an alternative definition of Western Europe, thus challenging other—political, economic, and cultural—delimitations of this region.

In a similar vein, the post-Cold War Baltic Sea region, previously divided by the Iron Curtain, emerged as a competitor to—or extension of—culturally-constructed areas such as Scandinavia and the Nordic region. Encouraged by a parallel development in southern Europe, where the Mediterranean countries early on came together in efforts to counter environmental destruction, the Baltic Sea countries identified cooperation in fields such as sewage treatment plants and regional electricity markets as tools for forging a new European geography. The controversies surrounding projects such as the "Molotov–Ribbentrop" pipeline, however, testified to the fragility of the Baltic as an infrastructural space.

8
Common Skies

"A Cupola of Polluted Air over Europe"

On October 24, 1967, the influential Swedish newspaper *Dagens Nyheter* published an article with a rather boring title, "The Acidification of Precipitation." The message, however, was new and radical. The author, Svante Odén, claimed that "there is a more or less permanent cupola of polluted air over Europe." Sulfur, he wrote, being emitted in large quantities by power plants and industries all over Europe, was being transported through the air over vast distances and transformed into sulfuric acid through chemical processes in the atmosphere. Odén, an associate professor of soil science, further argued that when rain or snow brought the airborne sulfuric acid down, usually in places far away from where the emissions had taken place, it lowered the pH values in streams and lakes. In Sweden and Norway, this in turn drastically diminished the fish populations in many lakes. Moreover, he predicted that increasing acidity would reduce the future biological productivity of forests and of cultivated land, particularly so in the Nordic countries, which had soils that were especially sensitive to acidification.[1]

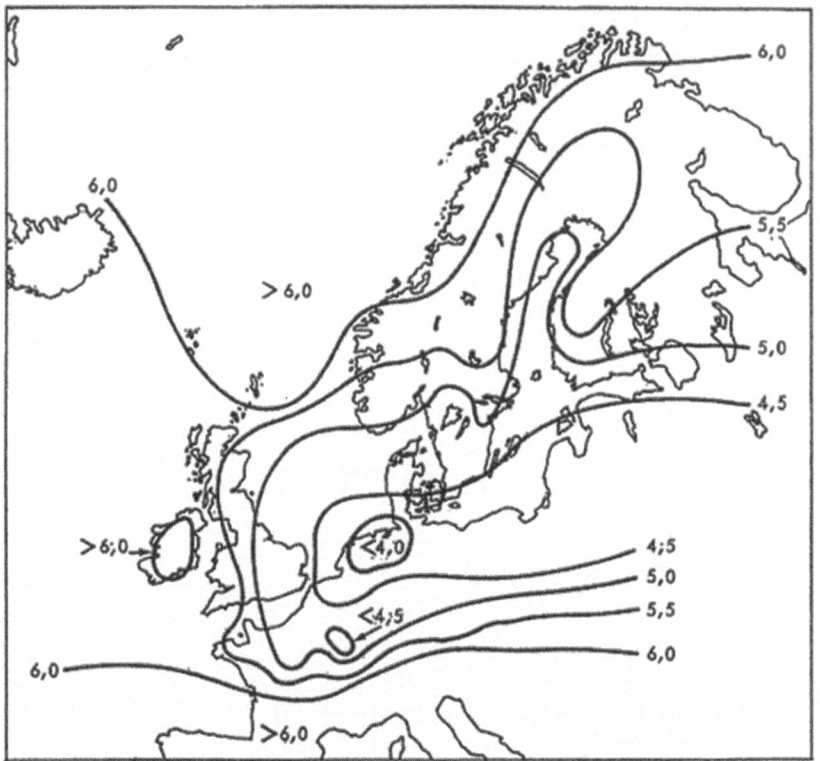

Fig. 8.1 **Continental Pollution:** *This map is one of the first depicting air pollution on a European scale; the lines represent the acidity of rainwater. The map was first published in the Swedish newspaper* Dagens Nyheter *on October 24, 1967, illustrating an article on "The acidification of Precipitation." The caption read: "A map of the pH of precipitation over Europe in 1962. Note the acidic finger that extends up over the Baltic."*

By publishing his findings in a leading daily paper, rather than a scientific journal, Odén was able to immediately attract attention to his alarming message far beyond the academic community. Officials at the newly-established Swedish Environmental Protection Agency (SEPA) became very concerned, while industry representatives questioned his findings, fearing that the government might respond by taxing sulfur emissions. SEPA, recognizing the international dimension of acidification, or "acid rain" as it was soon called, brought the issue to the OECD's Air Quality Committee. There, Odén's scientific findings encountered massive skepticism. One by one, the air quality experts present "stood up and explained that, outside an inner zone of only a few kilometers, sulfur emissions were no problem," as SEPA's representative Göran Persson later recalled.[2]

The dominant view at the time was that air pollution was primarily a local phenomenon. The atmosphere was seen as a giant diluting machine, offered by nature for free. Most experts viewed the building of tall smokestacks as the most effective measure to deal with air pollution, arguing that sufficiently tall stacks led to an effective dispersion of sulfur and other pollutants, rendering their concentrations harmless before they hit the ground.[3] Odén seriously questioned this prevailing consensus, arguing that the atmosphere must rather be seen as an efficient transport infrastructure capable of redistributing pollutants from industrial regions to many particular places elsewhere in Europe. Put differently, he claimed that Europe had a "common sky." The political implication was clear: the problem of air pollution would have to be addressed on an international level.[4]

Acid rain was the latest in a series of challenges that Europeans had come to face as a result of the commonality of Europe's sky. All were closely related to Europe's infrastructure transition, and the ways they were engaged contributed decisively to the making of Europe in the air. Resonating with the preceding two chapters, this chapter commences by unveiling the interdependence between infrastructure and scientific knowledge about Europe's air. The focus is on the interaction between the making of modern meteorology as a scientific field and new uses of transport and communications technologies, starting in the 1850s. The chapter then turns to two concrete cases of system-builders' struggles to appropriate—or claim—the air for infrastructure purposes: radio communication and aviation. Both saw their breakthroughs in the early twentieth century, and both generated fierce debates and controversies over Europe's skies. The final part of the chapter returns to the issue of air pollution, elaborating on this theme from an infrastructural point of view. It also discusses the role of Europe's common sky in the construction of ecological networks.

Mapping the Sky

In the midst of the Crimean War a terrible storm hit the Black Sea on November 14, 1854, largely destroying the French–British fleet off the coast of Crimea. Thirty ships sank, several hundred sailors drowned, and important supplies were lost. A storm had been observed the day before over the Mediterranean and France's Minister of War asked the director of the Paris Astronomic

Observatory, Urbain le Verrier, to investigate whether it was in fact the same storm and if the catastrophe could have been prevented by a telegraphic warning. Le Verrier contacted astronomers and meteorologists all over Europe requesting information concerning the weather they had observed between November 12 and 16. He received 250 answers; and by compiling all this information, he was able to trace the path of the storm, concluding that it would indeed have been possible to warn the fleet.[5]

This finding spurred Le Verrier to develop a plan for a "weather telegraphy network" that could alert mariners and others about approaching storms. He presented the plan to Napoleon III, who approved it, and in the spring of 1855, commissioned 13 weather observatories close to telegraph stations across France, their tasks being to send regular reports to the Paris Observatory. This French network worked well and Le Verrier set out to extend it through international cooperation. He convinced his colleagues at the observatories in St. Petersburg, Vienna, Geneva, and other European cities to organize similar national weather telegraphy networks and to start exchanging weather reports with each other. In the early 1860s observatories over a large part of the European continent (except the Ottoman Empire) and the British Isles were exchanging daily weather reports.[6]

The weather telegraphy network had a profound impact on meteorology. By combining synchronous data from many places, meteorologists were able to discover new patterns in the atmosphere. In particular they realized that low pressures were a key determinant of winds; that there is generally a counter-clockwise flow of air about a low pressure center; that the speed of the wind is proportional to the decline in air pressure; and that there is a tendency for atmospheric conditions to move from west to east due to the rotation of the Earth.[7] Moreover, the telegraphy network enabled more reliable weather forecasts. Here again Le Verrier made an important contribution. In 1863 the Paris Observatory started to publish daily European weather maps based on the international telegraphic exchange of weather data. The maps visualized the current weather situation with the help of isobar lines, and they also showed the movement of low pressure nodes during the past few days. This cartographic technique spread quickly and a decade later weather maps were being printed in daily newspapers in most European capital cities, providing a user-friendly tool, predicting winds, storms, and rain. The forecasts were of great utility—they

Capt. Frain saving the sole survivor from the *Wild Wave*.   *Pride of Ocean*. H.M.S. *Retribution*. *Medora*. *Lady Valiant*. H.M.S. *Vulcan*. *Mercia*.
STORM IN BALACLAVA BAY.

Fig. 8.2   After the Storm II: *A terrible storm off Crimea in November 1854 destroyed French and British naval ships bringing supplies to the troops besieging Sevastopol. The storm had been observed beforehand in the Mediterranean and gave rise to the idea that telegrams could warn of approaching storms. This idea resulted in the establishment of a European weather telegraphy network with weather stations close to telegraph stations. It was coordinated by the Paris Observatory. A main task of this network was to warn sailors about approaching storms.*

could warn sailors of approaching storms, help farmers plan their harvests, guide travelers, and so on. The exchange of weather data was seen as such a valuable public utility that telegraph companies all over the world—both public and commercial—agreed to transmit such data free of charge.[8]

Within twenty years after the Crimean catastrophe, Le Verrier and his European colleagues had created a whole meteorological knowledge system. Infrastructure, and in particular telegraphy, was a critical component. Telegraphy helped meteorologists assemble weather data from stations all over Europe. Together with newspapers it also enabled efficient dissemination of forecasts to the public.[9] By the end of the nineteenth century, the system encompassed thousands of weather stations spanning several continents, all linked through telegraph networks. This international collaboration made it possible for meteorologists to analyze characteristic and recurrent patterns of the European weather, such as the importance of low pressures coming in from the North Atlantic to Western Europe. In the Mediterranean, many seasonal winds had since long had traditional names like the Mistral, the Levante, the Bora, and the Ostro; and now they were

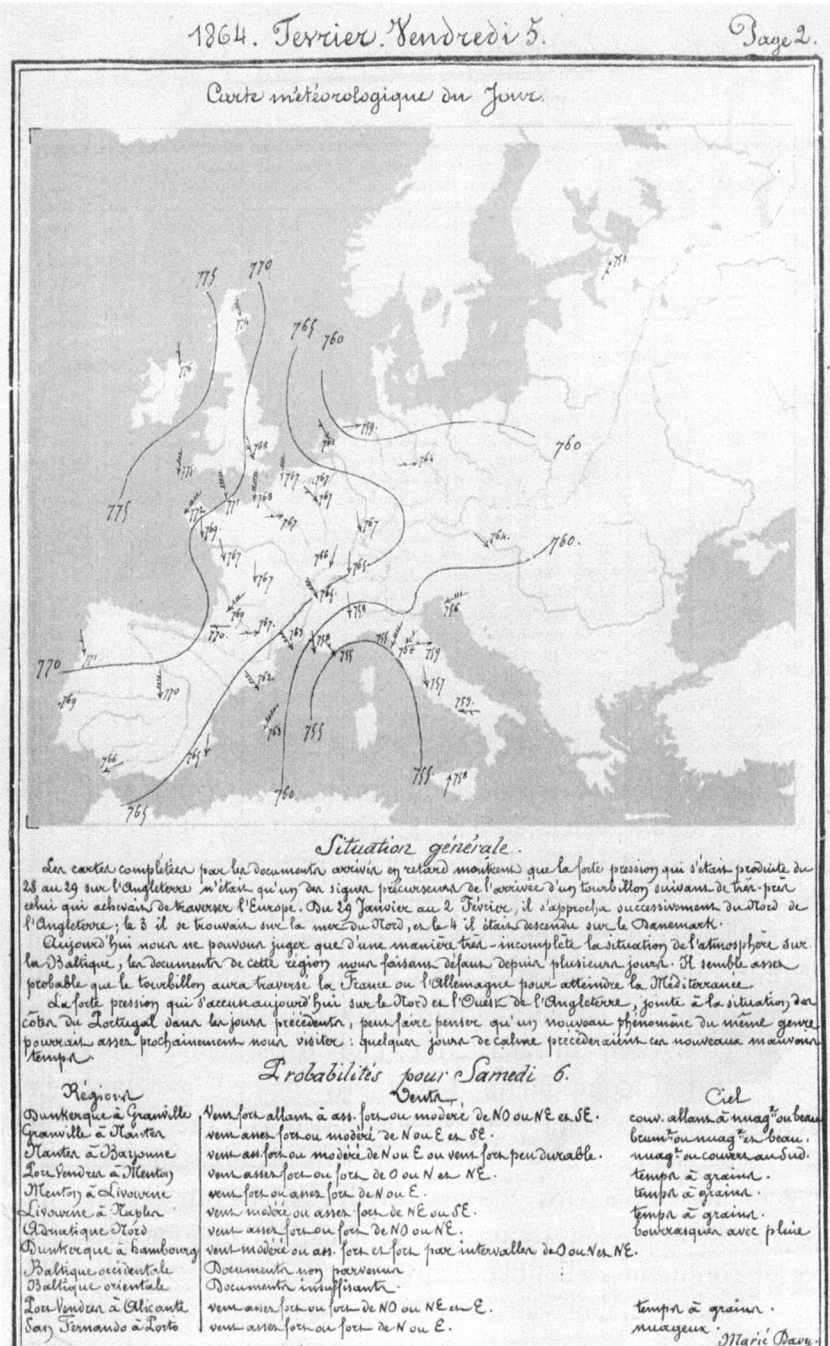

**Fig. 8.3
Meteorological Maps:** *Through the weather telegraphy network much data was assembled from many parts of Europe; and in the early 1860s French meteorologists developed a new kind of map to illustrate the weather situation by depicting isobar lines. These proved to be helpful for making weather forecasts. The picture shows a weather map from the Paris Observatory for February 5, 1864. The extent of the isobars (and in particular the dots with observations) reflects the coverage of the network of observatories that participated in the daily exchange of weather data by this time.*

scientifically analyzed. For example, the Austrian meteorologist Julius von Hann gave a theoretical explanation of the Bora and the Mistral as katabatic winds, caused by cold, heavy air created at high mountain plains moving fast through valleys down to the sea propelled by gravitation.[10]

The impressive knowledge system, coordinated by the International Meteorological Organization (IMO) established in 1873, had one important limitation: all observations were made on the ground while the dominant meteorological theories emphasized the importance of circulations in the atmosphere. On March 1, 1893 a balloon equipped with a number of instruments for making very precise measurements of physical properties of the sky made its first ascent with three men aboard. Richard Assman

Fig. 8.4 **Scientists in the Sky:** *On March 1, 1893 a research balloon called* Humboldt *made its first trip with three scientists aboard. Kaiser Wilhelm II supported the endeavor and was present at the ascent. This drawing, made by the crew member Hans Gross, depicts the balloon at 5,000 meters altitude above the city of Stettin. The balloon was well equipped with instruments for making precise measurements of a range of physical properties. Richard Assman from the Prussian Meteorological Institute in Berlin led the balloon crew. He broke his leg during the subsequent landing.*

from the Prussian Meteorological Institute in Berlin led the team opening up this new domain for meteorological research. He had been able to muster support from very influential scientists and industrialists for this endeavor—even Kaiser Wilhelm II had personally donated 50,000 Marks.[11] By naming the balloon after the prominent scientist Alexander von Humboldt—famous for his arduous expedition in Latin America—Assman and his colleagues strived to put themselves in the same heroic tradition of exploring unknown territories. Their expeditions proved to be arduous too. Assman broke his right leg during the landing after the maiden trip, and two months later the hydrogen-filled *Humboldt* caught fire after a landing and was destroyed. Luckily the balloonists were not injured.[12]

The German balloon ascents spurred meteorologists elsewhere. French scientist Léon Teisserenc de Bort designed unmanned balloons that could reach higher than manned ones. They carried packets of recording instruments, which automatically parachuted down to the ground after having completed their measurements. Measurements made in these manned and unmanned balloons paved the way for formulating the theory of a layered atmosphere, a fundamental discovery that would later turn out to be of crucial importance for other system-builders in the air.[13]

The close links between meteorology and infrastructure were further strengthened in the 1920s, when several countries attempted to use radio technology for transmitting weather data from unmanned balloons and kites at high altitudes. The name "radio-sonde" was coined for this kind of device. In the 1930s several radio-sonde designs were manufactured and more and more observations were assembled from high altitudes.[14] In parallel radio technology was also introduced for assembling weather observations from airplanes, ships, and from distant weather stations that could not be connected to the telegraph network. This increase of observations from high altitudes improved the quality of forecasts. Moreover, when radio broadcasting spread in the 1920s, weather reports became very popular programs among listeners all over Europe, and particularly among farmers, fishermen, and sailors for whom warnings of storms or rain were of vital importance. Fishermen and sailors could even listen to weather reports while at sea. Radio technology thus revolutionized both the assembly of observations and the dissemination of forecasts.

Weather & War

In peacetime there was a simple logic in the field of international meteorological cooperation coordinated by the IMO: it improved the forecasts for all participants involved. This logic came to an abrupt end with the outbreak of the First World War. Accurate observations of the prevailing winds were crucial for artillery's effectiveness and forecasts of rain and wind directions were essential for planning attacks, in particular when poison gas was to be used. Furthermore, airplane and Zeppelin pilots needed meteorological observations to plan their missions. Identifying high-quality weather forecasts as a crucial tool in warfare, all combatants sought to produce better forecasts than their enemies, and the international exchange of data ceased immediately. All combatant nations established military weather services and invested heavily in training meteorologists. Toward the end of the war, military commanders on the Western Front received detailed weather reports several times a day.[15]

Once the war was over there was no more need for secrecy, and the meteorologists quickly resumed their prewar international weather exchanges. However, when the Second World War broke

Fig. 8.5
Meteorologists at War: *During the First World War, regular weather observations became crucial both for the precision of artillery and for planning attack, in particular when poison gas was used. All belligerent nations set up military weather services, and the picture shows members of the German weather service preparing the release of a weather balloon.*

out the international exchange of weather data ceased again. All warring nations again sponsored weather services for assisting military commanders. The planning for D-Day shows more than anything else the crucial importance of meteorology as a military science. The invasion of Normandy was planned to take place on the morning of June 5, 1944 because the tide would be unusually low. Suitable weather was also crucial for the success of the operation; the air force stipulated that there be no fog or low clouds, and for the amphibious landings, on-shore winds must not exceed 12 mph. Meteorologists thus had a crucial role in preparing the invasion, and five forecasting centers around the British Isles continuously analyzed data gathered from numerous ground stations and weather airplanes.

On June 1 the Chief Meteorological Officer, Captain John Stagg, reported to General Dwight Eisenhower and his staff that a complex system of low-pressure areas was approaching from the west; and on the following day strong winds and heavy rain came in over England and France. In the early morning of June 4, when the final decision whether to launch the invasion or not had to be taken, Stagg presented disappointing forecasts and Eisenhower decided to postpone the launch for 24 hours. Early the next morning the staff met anew, and Eisenhower later described the setting of the meeting: "our little camp was shaking and shuddering under a wind of almost hurricane proportions and the accompanying rain seemed to be travelling in horizontal streaks."[16] To his surprise Stagg reported that the weather would likely improve the next day; and Eisenhower made the decision to go ahead with the invasion, well aware of the risk that the meteorologists could be mistaken. It turned out that the German meteorologists had made a different forecast and predicted an invasion as highly unlikely because of bad weather. The German troops were therefore not on alert, and were taken by surprise.[17]

Computers & Satellites

During the Second World War much effort was devoted to the development of computing machines, and the first electronic general purpose computer called ENIAC was completed in late

1945, after the war had ended. Mathematician John von Neumann looked for a showcase application for ENIAC and identified weather prediction as a promising candidate. He contacted a leading meteorologist, Carl-Gustav Rossby, who became enthusiastic. Securing funding was easy because military commanders now realized the importance of accurate weather predictions. The two developed a numerical model for weather prediction and were supplied with data from the weather services. However, it turned out that the ENIAC was too slow. To make a 24 hour weather forecast took a little more than 24 hours, so the forecasts produced were of no practical use. A few years later Rossby became a professor at the University of Stockholm and got the chance to resume the endeavor. In 1953 a fast electronic computer called BESK came onstream in Stockholm; and with BESK, computing a 24 hour forecast took only 40 minutes. Now, the assembly and feeding of data into the computer became the bottleneck instead, and Rossby convinced his sponsor, the Swedish Air Force's weather service, to send a car with fresh data once a day to BESK. Within 6 hours from the observation, the computer processed the data. The numerical forecasts produced proved to be fairly reliable and demonstrated the potential of computer-based weather forecasts.[18]

The Stockholm researchers inspired colleagues in many other countries, and meteorologists soon became very prominent computer users, second only to the designers of nuclear weapons. Computing was one of the key technologies of the Cold War era; and the U.S., which was the leader in this field, unsurprisingly tried to prevent the export of computing technologies to the Soviet Union. This meant that it also restricted exports to its allies; and thereby access to supercomputers became an obstacle for European meteorologists on both sides of the Iron Curtain. In Western Europe an international meteorological collaboration emerged in the late 1960s on the initiative of the Council of Ministers of the European Communities. This led to the 1974 establishment of the European Centre for Medium-Range Weather Forecasts (ECMWF), located at Shinfield Park in England and equipped with a very powerful computer. The high-quality telecommunications that the British could provide was important to the location decision, as huge quantities of data were drawn from a vast area. Participation in the ECMWF was restricted; no Comecon countries were accepted as members. The Cold War division thus became noticeable in European meteorological (non)cooperation.[19]

Numerical forecasts depended on quick and ample weather data, not only on the ground but also at higher altitudes. Satellites, another key Cold War technology, soon offered new possibilities for assembling such data. Satellites were a field in which the Soviet Union stood at the forefront, after the launching of *Sputnik* in 1957 and the first manned spacecraft in 1961. While satellites had major military importance for surveillance purposes, both superpowers tried to disguise this function by emphasizing civilian uses. Assembling meteorological data provided a suitable cover, and in 1959 the United States launched a satellite, *Explorer VII*, which carried both meteorological instruments and a very sensitive camera for military espionage. Two years later the United Nations General Assembly urged member states and the UN's World Meteorological Organization (WMO)—established in 1950 as a successor of the IMO—to cooperate in the use of satellites and other platforms for gathering weather data.[20]

Despite the Cold War tensions, the WMO was able to gradually develop such cooperation. Toward the end of the twentieth century this generated a very complex and sophisticated global knowledge system. Today the WMO-coordinated meteorological network encompasses surface weather stations, weather ships, aircraft, weather radar, ocean data buoys, automatic stations at remote locations, and not least a number of geostationary and polar orbiting satellites. Currently satellite data outnumber those generated by all other instruments combined tenfold. All data are delivered by wire-bound and wireless telecommunication networks in a number of global, regional, and national meteorological centers. There, huge computers perform analyses that produce numerical weather forecasts, which are in turn distributed to the public via the press, radio, TV, and the Internet.[21]

Sharing & Allocating Radio Waves

Meteorologists strove to *understand* the sky, while others set out to *use* the sky for various purposes. These ambitions triggered controversies early on. One of the first uses of the sky was for radio communications. In spring 1902 Kaiser Wilhelm II's brother Prince Heinrich was returning to Germany after a trip to the United States, travelling on the ocean-liner *Deutschland*. When he wanted to send a telegram to Berlin, he was informed that this was impossible. From a technical point of view, European engineers had already learned to use the air for communications purposes. Political obstacles, however, prevented the German prince from using the recently-developed technology. The British Marconi Company owned all coastal radio stations in the vicinity; and these refused to communicate with *Deutschland* because it operated wireless equipment manufactured in Germany. This made Prince Heinrich furious, and, once back in Berlin, he took action. The result was the German government's decision to organize a first international radiotelegraph conference.[22]

Representatives of Austria, France, Great Britain, Hungary, Italy, Russia, Spain, and the United States attended the August 1903 Berlin conference. The Marconi Company's "non-intercommunication" policy anchored the discussions. Germany proposed a resolution that "radio telegrams coming from and sent to ships shall be received and transmitted without regard to the system employed." It was accepted by all delegates except the British and Italian, which backed the Marconi Company. The resolution therefore had little effect, and Europe remained divided in the field of radio communication.[23]

In 1906 Germany convened a follow-up conference. By then international interest in wireless communications had grown markedly; and representatives from no fewer than 30 nations participated. Again, Marconi's policy of "non-intercommunication" was high on the agenda. Another important issue, however, concerned the allocation of frequencies. A growing number of public and private actors wanted to use radio waves, and actors had started to perceive the electromagnetic spectrum as a scarce resource. Germany proposed reserving the longer waves (600–1600 meters) for government and military purposes, leaving only the shorter (300–600 meters) to private companies like Marconi. This would prevent the latter from handling long-distance communications as short wave stations had a more limited range. Negotiations about these two issues led to a compromise. Britain gave up its support for non-intercommunication in exchange for reserving wave lengths above 1600 meters for commercial uses. The 1906 conference also led to the establishment of the International Radiotelegraph Union (IRU), which became a branch of the International Telegraph Union (ITU). An international institutional framework for using and sharing the newly-discovered natural resource of electromagnetic waves had thus been created.[24]

The limits to this new resource became obvious, particularly in Europe where an increasing number of actors sought to use wireless capabilities. This demand spurred inventors and entrepreneurs to improve radio technology. Marconi's system of spark transmitters produced many waves of varying frequency and intensity. It had two major disadvantages: Marconi sets could produce only Morse signals, which took up a large part of the available spectrum. In the decade before the First World War, inventors developed new kinds of transmitters, the most important being the high-speed alternator, which could produce continuous radio signals with so called amplitude modulation, AM. This made it possible to transmit speech and music. Another advantage was that these AM waves occupied only a small part of the spectrum. Furthermore, inventors developed transmitters able to generate higher frequencies, to expand the range of the spectrum available for radio transmissions. The combination of greater precision and broader range dramatically increased the available "channels" for communication.

Another strand of development involved expanding radio's geographical reach. This was of particular interest to the German and French governments, both of which sought ways to communicate with faraway colonies without having to use British-controlled undersea telegraph lines. Germany's Telefunken built the world's most powerful transmitting station in Nauen, near Berlin. In 1914, it was equipped with a 200 kW generator and an antenna covering two square kilometers. This enabled the station to reach the German protectorate Togo in West Africa, and from there messages could be relayed to stations in Germany's other African colonies. The station could also communicate with the United States. At the same time, the French governor in Indochina decided to erect a 300 kW station in Saigon to be able to communicate with Paris. However, the First World War broke out just as the generator was to be shipped from Marseille. It was set up in Lyon instead and served as a connection to Russia and the United States during the war.[25]

Radio communication became crucial in warfare; and Europe's radio infrastructure expanded enormously in the belligerent

Fig. 8.6 By-Passing the British: *In 1914 the Nauen radio station near Berlin was equipped with a 200 kW generator and an antenna covering two square kilometers, which made it the most powerful in the world. With this station the German government could communicate with its colonies in Africa without having to use British-controlled undersea telegraph lines. This picture from 1914 shows two maintenance workers on the antenna of the station.*

nations. This also spurred further technological development. Vacuum-tube technology, for example, developed by the Bell Company for long-distance telephony ten years earlier, was used for constructing high-frequency oscillators. These could generate much shorter wavelengths than before. The new technology could be used in directional beam antennas, which could transmit radio signals over long distances with fairly low power. At the same time most ships and many aircraft were furnished with radio equipment, and many young men and women were trained to serve as radio technicians.[26]

One of the most intriguing aspects of radio communication, from a scientific point of view, was the observation that radio waves bounced in the atmosphere. In the 1920s, the British physicist Edward Appleton, who had served as a radio technician during the war, decided to use radio signals as a tool for exploring the atmosphere. He was able to establish cooperation with the BBC and used its transmitter at Bournemouth and a receiver station that he built in Cambridge. By systematically analyzing the reflection of radio waves he demonstrated the existence of several "bouncing layers," consisting of concentrations of ionized particles. He discovered that the ionization densities of the layers varied diurnally and that the reflection of radio waves took place at different altitudes at different times of the day (and night). Appleton further revealed a long-term variation depending on sunspot activity, with a 50 per cent higher density in years of sunspot maxima. Appleton's main purpose was to unveil the physical properties of the atmosphere; he received the 1947 Nobel Prize in Physics for his scientific contributions.[27] However, his research also greatly interested inventors of new radio equipment and negotiators at international conferences charged with allocating radio frequencies. Such conferences became very important for Europe's radio infrastructure following the introduction of radio broadcasting.

The enthusiasm for broadcasting in the early 1920s led to a boom in new radio stations.[28] Most chose frequencies for their broadcasts in what was then called the medium wave band, comprising wavelengths between 200 and 600 meters. This soon led to broadcast interference, as a transmitter used for reaching listeners within, say, a 200 km radius, would at certain times of the day send waves much further away. After bouncing in the ionosphere they could disturb broadcasts from stations in a distant country using the same frequency. Stations first response to this phenomenon was to increase the power of their own transmitters, to drown out the disturbance from others. But when all parties acted the same way, the effect was like a cocktail party where the sound level gradually increases.[29]

The IRU did not address this dilemma. Instead the founder of the first Swiss radio station, Maurice Rambert, organized an international meeting in Geneva in April 1924 to do so. By inviting representatives from broadcasting companies, the radio industry, and governments, Rambert hoped to find a common solution. The conference helped create the non-governmental International Broadcasting Union (IBU).[30] The most urgent problem for Rambert and his colleagues was what they called "the congestion of the European ether." The IBU appointed a technical commission which prepared a "frequency plan" for Europe. The total number of available wavelengths was a little less than 100, if a separation of 10 kHz between each wavelength was applied; and the crucial question was how to distribute these frequencies in a "fair" way among Europe's nations. The engineers in the commission came up with an elaborate mathematical formula, according to which each country should receive frequencies in proportion to its area, population, and economic development. Furthermore, the commission tried to allocate neighboring frequencies to stations far apart to minimize interference.[31] The plan defined a Broadcasting Europe, consisting of 29 countries located between a meridian through Ireland and Portugal in the West, and another through the Soviet Union close to Odessa in the East. Having adopted the frequency plan at a meeting in July 1926, IBU set up a Technical Centre in Brussels, tasked to monitor member countries' actual adherence to the plan.[32]

Rambert and his colleagues worked to create order in the European ether. The key objective of this "IBU order" was to preserve the national character of broadcasting, and to avoid listeners being disturbed by foreign radio stations. But in addition, the IBU's work derived from its ideology of contributing to mutual understanding between the peoples of Europe. To achieve this, the IBU organized construction of a physical network consisting of high-quality telephone lines through which radio stations in member states interconnected. The network was used for exchanging radio programs. In 1931 a program called "European Concerts" debuted, so that a concert performed in one member country could be relayed through the network and transmitted at each participating station. These broadcasts became very popular and continued with great regularity until the outbreak of the Second World War.[33]

The "IBU order" met several challenges in the 1930s. Not all radio station owners were satisfied with the focus on domestic broadcasts. Some had in fact explicitly intended to reach international audiences. The Vatican, for example, founded Radio Vatican to reach Catholics worldwide. When inaugurated in January 1932, the Pope's voice was heard on five continents by the largest audience that had ever listened to a single man.[34] In the same vein, the Soviet government established Radio Moscow to spread a socialist message, primarily to listeners in East-Central Europe. The League of Nations, meanwhile, set up Radio Nations, principally for worldwide broadcasts in emergency situations. Finally, businessmen in Luxembourg created Radio Luxembourg, a station with light entertainment and regular advertisements primarily intended for a British audience. These stations thus rejected the national character of broadcasting that the IBU tried to maintain.[35]

Another difficulty was the rapid increase in Europe's radio stations, as well as in their average power. The number of stations doubled between 1926 and 1933, forcing the IBU to modify its frequency plan on several occasions. It did so mainly by squeezing stations more tightly together, with only 4.5 kHz separations. Greater power meant that stations could reach audiences in neighboring countries. Hitler and Mussolini increasingly used broadcasting for political propaganda, and this created political tensions. The IBU's policy was to prevent cross-border propaganda programs, but the organization had no means to actually do so.[36]

The Second World War collapsed the "IBU order" altogether. Propaganda programs became the rule rather than the exception, accompanied by strict censorship and "jamming" of enemy stations. After the war, the Soviet Union and its allies opted to leave IBU, establishing, instead, the *Organisation International de Radiodiffusion*. The capitalist countries in Western Europe responded by setting up the European Broadcasting Union. The International Telegraph Union convened a worldwide conference in Atlantic City in 1947 to restore some order after the war. The following year it also arranged a regional conference for Europe in Copenhagen. However, this attempt to implement a new pan-European frequency plan failed, one reason being that Germany was excluded. The occupying forces in Germany established radio stations, ignoring the plan. In particular, the United States started broadcasting to its own troops and to audiences behind the Iron Curtain on frequencies that it was not supposed to use. As a result, by the early 1950s radio interference proliferated across European borders, both intended and unintended.[37]

In what followed, however, radio stations in West Germany, which had been given no frequencies at all, started to experiment with broadcasting at Very High Frequencies (VHF). This part of the spectrum was not regulated by the ITU. The Germans found that frequency modulation or FM, a new technology developed by the Americans in the 1930s, worked very well in the VHF band. Such FM stations had very good sound quality, as well. Moreover, they had a short range, which meant minimal interference among stations. The West German success inspired other countries to introduce FM broadcasting in the 1950s, easing the pressure on lower frequencies. Moreover, due to FM transmitters' limited range, international interference occurred only in border regions. When TV broadcasting developed in the mid-1950s, stations were also often allocated to the VHF band, mainly for quality reasons but partly also to avoid cross-border interference. Thus, the problem of congestion in the European ether was solved by a transition to new parts of the spectrum, and the interwar broadcasting order could partly be re-established.[38]

Thirty years later a new technological transformation in transmission technology occurred, again disrupting the order. This time it was not expansion to new regions of the spectrum, but the launching of communication satellites owned by private companies, that brought about the change. Positioned in a geo-stationary orbit, such satellites could transmit TV and radio programs directly to individual households equipped with a parabolic antenna. In the suburbs of large European cities with many immigrants, houses totally changed their appearance as they were increasingly covered with parabolic antennas. The new technology made it possible for families to watch programs in their native languages, irrespective of their country of origin. However, they had to pay a fee to the companies providing the service. A new Broadcasting Europe emerged in which the re-established "IBU order" with undisturbed national broadcasting was combined with satellite-provided programs from faraway countries.[39]

Creating an Aviation Infrastructure

A few years after Marconi and others introduced radio communication, other system-builders exploited Europe's sky for aviation purposes, again generating tensions and controversies among countries. In July 1909 the French aviator and engineer Louis Blériot for the first time flew an airplane across the English Channel. Landing close to Dover after a 40-minute flight, he was met by soldiers and policemen tasked to salute and welcome him. Four years later, when another French aviator, Brindejonc de Moulinais, landed at an airport near London after crossing the Channel, the police were also present. This time, however, they arrested the pilot and put him on trial. The different receptions of these two aviation pioneers reflected a dramatic shift with respect to the legal status of the sky.[40]

This issue had started to be discussed as early as 1902 at Brussels' Institute of International Law. The prominent French lawyer Paul Fauchille presented a draft international air law based on the concept of the freedom of the air. He argued that the air was similar to the high seas and that the same principles should be applied. In the law of the sea, the notion of territorial waters defined the first three nautical miles off a country's coast as an integral part of its space. Fauchille suggested in analogy that the first 1500 meters above the ground be defined as "territorial air," while the air above this limit should be free to use for all. In 1906, however, the British law professor John Westlake presented an alternative view. He referred to land property right and particularly a classic formulation of it in medieval Roman law: "For whoever owns the soil, it is theirs all the way to Heaven and to Hell." This law had been adopted in many countries and implied that mineral resources below the ground belonged to the owner of the land above it. Westlake argued that this principle should also be applied to the air above the ground, and that the air should reflect the sovereignty of the nation below it. Two very different principles for the legal status of the air thus stood opposed: one primarily based on a horizontal, the other on a vertical structuring.[41]

These academic debates drew the demarcation line in the heated political discussions that followed. In May 1910, a year after Blériot's legendary cross-Channel flight, France organized a first political conference to consider the issue of the air's legal status. Delegates from nineteen European countries convened in Paris to discuss the principles for future international aviation in Europe. The German and French delegations, following Fauchille's line of thought, argued for an extensive freedom of flight, while the British delegation, following Westlake, emphasized the national sovereignty view. The majority of the delegates reached agreement on a draft convention based on the German–French position, but due to British resistance the convention could not be adopted.[42]

An important reason for British reluctance was their early recognition that aviation was bound to generate a military threat of a completely new type. In 1911 and 1913 the British Parliament passed Aerial Navigation Acts stipulating that a foreign aircraft wishing to visit Great Britain had to make a first landing within 5 miles of the coast to get clearance for further flying. This legislation was applied when Brindejonc de Moulinais was arrested after his landing in London in May 1913. In court Brindejonc explained that he had lately flown over Spain, Belgium, the Netherlands, and Germany, none of which had questioned his right to fly, and he found it impossible to be acquainted with the specific laws of each country. The judge understood this view, assured Brindejonc that he was "glad to welcome a clever and brave airman," and then freed him with the warning that the law would be strictly applied in the future.[43]

When the Great War broke out in August 1914, Fauchille's concept of the air as a borderless domain suddenly vanished in continental Europe as well. All European countries declared their air boundaries closed. Even if aviation had a limited impact on the war's outcome, military strategists realized that it had enormous potential for future wars. This insight influenced the Paris Peace Conference negotiations on international regulation of aviation (among the winners). The resulting Paris Convention became the cornerstone for international civil aviation in the twentieth century.[44] In the first paragraph the signatories of the Convention recognized that "every Power has complete and exclusive sovereignty over the air space above its territory."[45] National air space included "both that of the mother country and of the colonies, and the territorial waters adjacent thereto."[46]

The Paris Convention also sought "to encourage the peaceful intercourse of nations by means of aerial communication."[47] A new intergovernmental organization, called the International Commission for Air Navigation (ICAN) and tasked to implement the Convention, began work in 1922. A French lawyer and decorated flyer from the Great War, Albert Roper, became its first Secretary General, a post he held for no less than 30 years. ICAN operated under the League of Nations, and the defeated nations were not allowed membership. Several other international organizations concerned with international aviation appeared in the early 1920s, assuming responsibility for harmonizing practical matters like the marking of air routes, formalizing routines for weather forecasting, promoting the use of wireless for airport safety, as well as developing international legislation for aviation.[48] The new airline companies emerging after the war, for their part, established the International Air Transport Association (IATA). It had a much more welcoming attitude then the Paris Convention; in fact two representatives from *Deutsche Luft Reederei* were among its founders.[49]

All these new organizations cooperated closely—with Roper serving as an unflagging coordinator—in a joint effort to build an international infrastructure. A primary goal was to increase the safety of flying, which at the time was a very risky business. In the early 1920s there was about one fatal accident in every 3,000 flights. Hence air travel was estimated to be 160 times riskier than rail travel. In addition, more than one out of twenty flights ended in an unforeseen landing, on small airfields, farmlands, or roads. It was not uncommon that engines stopped or that propellers, rudders, and other crucial components broke in flight. Furthermore, cruising altitudes were low, typically between 500 and 1,000 meters; and at that height, the atmosphere was very turbulent. Unexpected storms or clouds were thus a common cause for crashes. Finally, airplanes could not carry much fuel and had to make frequent stops, and most accidents occurred at landings and take-offs.[50]

Early aviation was, nonetheless, a transnational business; and pilots from many countries used its infrastructure. This created a demand for standardization and common procedures, and the international organizations played a key role to achieve this. In fact, a very positive atmosphere prevailed within these organizations among the aviation experts, many of whom had been flyers during the war. ICAN's British representative, Sir Sefton

Brancker, spoke of "an extraordinary *camaraderie*" that did not exist in any other walk of life.[51] In the same vein the authors of an IATA Report in 1935 declared that "IATA has created between all its members a kind of solidarity and technical friendship...and the attempt to vanquish nature in a domain still full of unknown dangers."[52]

ICAN, IATA, and other organizations made great efforts to standardize and harmonize the aviation infrastructure, but nation states were responsible for building and managing it. Air Ministries or equivalent institutions built and operated regular airports as well as smaller emergency landing fields along major air routes. To help pilots navigate, they mandated large visual markings with numbers, letters, and colors on the ground (or the roofs of big buildings) that could be seen from above. These markings were correlated with special aeronautical maps. In the late 1920s Air Ministries also established lighting systems at larger airports to assist takeoffs and landings in poor weather conditions. Lighting expanded in the 1930s when night flying became common for delivering airmail between major cities. Another important part of the infrastructure concerned meteorology, as airports became nodes in meteorological networks supporting pilots with up-to-date forecasts. Visual signals at airports were used to communicate current weather conditions on the ground. ICAN developed obligatory rules and standards for all these signs and other aids.[53]

Landing and take-off were accident-prone moments in flights; and in the early 1920s airport managers created air traffic control systems to improve safety. The first attempt was at the Croydon Aerodrome in London in 1922. A specially-trained traffic officer, attended by a wireless operator, communicated with pilots in approaching aircraft, giving instructions about when to land, also advising pilots who were ready to take off. This system became a model for many other airports both in Britain and other parts of Europe.[54] In the 1930s many countries extended the air control around airports to a system for en route control between airports. This enabled traffic officers to guide pilots during entire trips. Before departing the pilot would submit a flight plan, including departure time, intended route, and landing time, and send it by radio to the control units along the flight corridor. Each control unit was given responsibility for a certain area or "sector," as it was called. When

Fig. 8.7 **Failed Flight:** *Aviation was a risky business and more than one out of twenty flights ended in unforeseen landings in the early 1920s, sometimes because pilots had lost their orientation. International organizations organized the creation of air routes with markings on the ground to help pilots navigate. This illustration from the French journal* Le Petit Parisien *in November 1910 illustrates both the danger of flying and early attempts to create visual aids on the ground.*

an aircraft left one sector and entered another, the pilot first tuned in on the wavelength of the new control unit and reported to the traffic officer who checked his position against the plan. The officer then kept contact with the pilot until he (it was almost always a man) entered the next sector. The traffic officers' primary duty was to make sure that safe distances existed between airplanes within his sector, but he could also help a pilot to navigate when visibility was poor or warn of weather disturbances. ICAN established international rules for air control, and English was agreed upon as the common language for aerial communication.[55]

In the interwar years aircraft were tightly bound to a terrestrial infrastructure in an almost literal sense; and the notion of airways and air routes had a very concrete meaning. As long as a pilot was flying within an airway, he had help from many visual markings or lighting aids and could use emergency landing fields if needed. But if he lost his way or deliberately departed from it, he was in trouble. The structure of the European aviation sky can thus be described as a network of invisible "tunnels" with a radius of about one kilometer, above a marked air route on the ground. But there were natural and political limitations to the scope of this infrastructure. High mountain ranges like the Alps and the Pyrenees could not be flown over, and large seas like the Mediterranean, not to speak of the oceans, were difficult to cross. Moreover, a number of governments, chiefly in Southern Europe, used the sovereignty over their airspace for political or commercial purposes, placing special demands on airlines seeking landing rights.[56]

Handling Congestion in the Air

In the 1930s, the aviation industry sought to develop aircraft that could fly at higher altitudes. Such planes would offer several advantages. Cruising speed would increase due to lower air pressure, longer distances could be covered, and much weather disturbance would be avoided. High-altitude sickness, however, posed an obstacle. To prevent passengers and crew from becoming ill or even fainting when an aircraft climbed above 3,000 meters, pressurized cabins were necessary. Several aircraft manufacturers worked hard to develop such cabins in the 1930s, but the breakthrough came during the Second World War, when cabin pressure was achieved in high-flying bombers.[57] Also the payloads of bombers increased enormously. When these technical advances reached civilian aviation after the war, aircraft were no longer tied to the ground-based airways, and they could fly much farther. Nature's barriers, high mountains and vast oceans, now receded in significance. Political barriers, however, remained important. In particular, crossing the Iron Curtain became a complicated affair.[58]

In the 1950s and 1960s, the rise of jet propulsion radically increased an aircraft's speed and range and enhanced aviation's attractiveness in relation to other modes of transport. Rapid growth of air transport, however, increased the stress on European air traffic control as the risk of collisions increased. Aviation ministries improved their interwar systems by introducing radar technology. They also established new air corridors, to allow commercial aircraft to fly at higher altitudes, and enlarged the air sectors to cope with higher speeds. Larger sectors meant that pilots did not have to contact as many controllers along their routes. An important limitation, however, was that these air systems were national. This meant that an air sector could not be larger than a single country. In the small Benelux countries, this constraint created increasingly stressful workloads for both air controllers and pilots.[59]

Another problem was coordination with military air traffic, which had a considerable volume during the Cold War. Commercial and military aviation had separate systems for air traffic control, and while civil operators expected pilots to fly along predetermined routes and demanded strict application of minimum distances between aircraft, military operators were trained to provide their pilots freedom of movement and tactical flexibility. In 1955 ICAN, now renamed ICAO, and NATO set up a Committee on European Airspace Coordination, with the aim to solve the coordination issue among six West European NATO member states—Belgium, France, the Federal Republic of Germany, Luxembourg, and the Netherlands.[60] Committee discussions led to a growing consensus about better control arrangements and improved coordination between military and civilian aircraft in upper airspace (above 6,000 meters). In 1960 the six agreed to create an international organization, Eurocontrol, to which member states would delegate responsibility for civilian traffic in the participating countries' upper airspace. This was a radical initiative in the sense that it challenged the central role of the nation state in European air transportation.[61]

As a first step Eurocontrol assumed management of the upper airspace for Belgium and Luxembourg by taking over existing facilities at Brussels airport in 1964. The next step was to develop a totally new system for air control, based on digital computers, and to establish a joint control center. An international team of engineers and scientists, headed by Germany's Dr. Hansjürgen von Villiez, worked many years to develop a reliable system, putting it in operation in 1972. The system was based on five radar installations transmitting data to the center, located in Maastricht at the Netherlands' southernmost tip. Every controller could handle up to 12–15 aircraft at the same time, whereas in the non-computerized systems a controller could guide only 6–7 aircraft. Eurocontrol's new system was widely acknowledged as the most advanced in the world.[62]

However, cooperation's political side did not develop as fully as the technological. Already in 1963, France and the United Kingdom declared that they were not willing to accept supranational control of their upper airspaces. The official reasons were national sovereignty and the need for coordination with military aviation, but requests from trade unions of air traffic control personnel fearing job losses were also significant. The four remaining countries continued to pursue the supranational agenda. By 1974 the Maastricht center controlled the airspaces of Belgium, Luxembourg, and the northern part of West Germany. In 1975, it was to assume control also over Dutch airspace. However, Amsterdam's air control personnel protested forcefully against the transfer of jobs to another part of the country, and the Dutch government sought to avoid a domestic conflict. As a result, Amsterdam airport retained control of Dutch airspace until 1986. The political turmoil led to a renegotiation of Eurocontrol's purpose. In 1981 a new convention was signed defining a more modest role for Eurocontrol as a facilitator of cooperation, and the computer-mediated air traffic system it had developed was transferred to national air control organizations.[63]

The primary purpose of air traffic control was to reduce the vulnerability of air traffic, and it had been quite successful in this endeavor, mainly by separating them aloft. However, the low vulnerability, critics argued, had been attained at the cost of an inefficient use of the air. Increasingly, the aviation industry began to regard European airspace congestion as a major challenge. In the 1980s Eurocontrol experts launched a new approach to reduce it. The basic idea was to coordinate the flight plans for aircraft flying through the joint airspace, trying to spread them out more evenly in space and time. This would require the assembly of all flight plans and a calculation of a suitable take-off time and route for each flight. Eurocontrol's engineers set about developing the necessary software and computer systems; and in 1988 twelve databases for flight plans, covering the airspace of all member states, commenced operation. The databases, initially located in five places, had by 1995 concentrated at only two Central Flow Management Units—one in Brussels responsible for northern Europe and one in Paris responsible for southern Europe. Eurocontrol's flow management project had proven a success, as it led to reduced delays. This gave the organization considerable prestige, and several new countries applied for membership. Following the end of the Cold War, neutral countries such as Sweden and Switzerland, as well as a range of former Comecon countries and even ex-Soviet republics such as Ukraine and Moldova, joined Eurocontrol.[64]

However, air traffic continued increasing rapidly in Europe and congestion problems reappeared. In this situation the European Union launched the Single European Sky initiative in 1999. The initiative followed up on Eurocontrol's work by aiming to reorganize European airspace into functional blocks, according to traffic flows rather than national borders. Within each functional block, air control and flow management would be integrated; and Eurocontrol would continue to be responsible for these services. To enable this project, in 2004 and 2008 the European Parliament adopted common rules and procedures at a European level. However, their implementation has been contested and delayed, partly due to opposition by trade unions representing 14,000 employees of the present national air control companies, which have considerable negotiating power through their ability to obstruct air traffic. It thus remains to be seen whether the Single European Sky will become a reality.[65]

Using the Sky as a Sink

Europe's air could be used not only for radio and aviation purposes, but also, as noted in the introduction to this chapter, for diluting pollutants. Smokestack technologies, designed to distribute

Fig. 8.8 Diluting Emissions: *Until the 1960s high smoke stacks were seen as the most effective way to handle emissions from power plants and industries. The atmosphere was seen as a diluting machine, and high smoke stacks were believed to disperse emissions to sufficiently low concentrations to be harmless when they again reached the ground. The picture shows a 145 meter high smoke stack at the smelting plant in Rönnskärsverken in Northern Sweden. At its inauguration in 1928 it was the tallest stack in Europe.*

pollutants over as large an area as possible, played an important role in this context. By the early twentieth century, some smokestacks had become immense architectural constructs. In 1928, for example, a 145 meter tall chimney was built to serve a new smelting plant on a small island close to Skellefteå, a coastal town in northern Sweden. With a diameter of 20 meters at the base and 4.5 meters at the top, it was the tallest smokestack Europe had yet seen. Four years earlier a Swedish mining engineer, Oscar Falkman, had discovered a rich deposit of copper, gold, and silver at Boliden, only 30 km to the west of Skellefteå. The metal ore also contained much arsenic and pyrite, which no smelters in Sweden could handle. Falkman established the Boliden Mining Company and made a study tour to the U.S. in the mid-1920s to explore how the ore could be processed. He visited the Anaconda Mining Company in Montana, which had a smelter processing very similar ores to the ones in Boliden and was amazed at its smokestack, which at 178 meters was then the world's tallest. It had been built to disperse the emissions from the plant, hoping to avoid conflicts with local farmers about damage caused by air pollution. Back in Sweden, Falkman decided to build a similar device to avoid conflicts. To reduce the degree of local pollution even further, he chose to build the smelter on an island rather than next to the mine itself. The idea was to make use of prevailing winds to distribute most of the emissions out over the sea. In addition, Falkman hoped that the sea currents would help dilute possible arsenic acid leaks.⁶⁶

The company magazine hailed the new smokestack with a joking little poem: "Skorsten kallar vi det rör, som till Ryssland röken för" (Smokestack we call the pipe, which leads the fumes to Russia).⁶⁷ Even if Falkman hardly believed that much of the smoke would actually reach Russia, Sweden's century-old enemy served nicely as a metaphor for getting rid of the emissions as far away as possible. The smokestack symbolized the company's environmental consciousness, even though it turned out that the local damage the smelter caused was quite substantial. There was little local complaint, however, as the company paid compensation to those affected. Moreover, the whole region seemed to profit from the company's mining and refining. It was not until the late 1960s that the smelter was recognized as Sweden's most polluting industrial plant by far. From then on, the smokestack became a symbol of large-scale pollution.⁶⁸

The Boliden smokestack exemplified air pollution management in most European countries. In the nineteenth century, emissions from the combustion of coal and industrial processes increased dramatically in industrial towns and regions all over Europe. The air became heavily polluted and severe local health effects soon appeared. However, the pollution met little resistance, for it was seen as a more or less inevitable consequence of industrial production, which gave work opportunities and prosperity to most of the people affected. In many cases, the only measure to combat air pollution that was deemed feasible was precisely to build higher smokestacks. When gases and particles were emitted into the atmosphere at high altitude, winds dispersed them across the surrounding landscape, reducing the concentrations of hazardous substances—or so it was believed—to levels that were no longer harmful.

But even if industries provided tall smokestacks, innumerable household furnaces still emitted pollutants. Occasionally this produced dangerous "smog." In December 1952 London faced a combination of cold weather, intensive use of furnaces, and an absence of wind, generating very high concentrations of smoke particles in the city. Some 4,000 people lost their lives. This tragedy contributed to a change in British perceptions of air pollution. In response to the "killer smog," Parliament passed a Clean Air Act, introducing severe restrictions for smoke emissions in heavily-polluted areas. In "smoke control areas" households and industries could only use "smokeless furnaces," being forced to switch from coal to electricity, gas, or low-sulfur oil.[69]

The Clean Air Act was a first step toward a new paradigm for reducing air pollution developed by newly-professionalized environmental experts. In this paradigm dedicated energy systems such as electricity, gas, and district heating played a key role. These systems converted "dirty" fuels into user-friendly and fairly clean energy carriers and then distributed them via a specially-designed physical network. Large plants, where the combustion process could be carefully controlled and the amount of pollutants reduced, accomplished this conversion. The remaining smoke was emitted through high chimneys. This new paradigm to reduce pollution was applied in many European countries from the 1950s onwards in somewhat different ways.

The skeptical reaction of the OECD Air Quality Committee to the Swedish assertions of large-scale air pollution in Europe, as referred to in this chapter's introduction, should be seen in the context of this new paradigm. The large, centralized smokestacks, regarded as key components for reducing local and regional pollution, now stood accused of causing large-scale trans-border pollution. Moreover, this alleged pollution was not the traditional smoke, consisting of visible—and smelly—particles of mainly carbon soot that had been in focus in previous decades, but instead, invisible and odorless chemicals like sulfur and nitrogen oxides, reaching the ground by way of "acid rain." Even if Committee members were skeptical at the outset, they agreed that the Swedish report gave "clear indication of a problem which required continuing study" and decided to set up a research project to do so.[70]

In 1972 the OECD launched a Co-operative Technical Programme to Measure the Long Range Transport of Air Pollutants, the purpose being to determine the relative importance of local and distant sources of sulfur compounds over different regions. Eleven West European countries joined.[71] After five years of intense collaborative work, the study's scientists and experts published a report with unequivocal findings, confirming that "sulphur compounds do travel long distances (several hundred kilometers or more) in the atmosphere" and that "the air quality in any one European country is measurably affected by emissions from other countries."[72] The report further demonstrated that air pollution in Europe had an asymmetric character with distinct net "donators" and net "receivers" of emissions. A set of maps showed the spatial patterns of this Acid Europe. The fact that leading scientists from eleven countries stood behind the report gave it high credibility.[73]

The asymmetrical character of the acidification problem posed special political challenges for reaching international agreements. While the net importing countries had a strong interest in introducing measures to diminish the emissions, the exporting countries did not want to impose extra costs on their polluting industries. What complicated the matter even more was that some of the exporters were big and powerful nations like West Germany and Great Britain, while the main importers were the small Nordic countries. Moreover, the Cold War made it difficult to achieve broad political cooperation between countries on opposite sides of the Iron Curtain. A political deadlock thus seemed inevitable.[74]

A political development that had little to do with environmental politics would break this deadlock. In 1975, attempts to achieve détente between the two superpowers led to the Helsinki Declaration, which set the stage for international cooperation in areas like disarmament, democratization, and economic exchange. In actual practice, however, it proved difficult to launch such cooperation. In this situation, the Soviet Union proposed cooperation in the environmental arena, perceived as a politically less sensitive field. The Western countries responded positively.[75] Looking for suitable environmental issues in which cooperation might prove fruitful, Soviet experts quickly identified acid rain as a possibility. They knew that this was a deep concern among the Scandinavian countries, while Russian scientists had also found that the Soviet Union was a major net importer of air pollution. In 1978 the Kremlin invited the Norwegian Minister of Environmental Protection, Gro Harlem Brundtland, to Moscow. Her hosts suggested cooperation within the UNECE framework, with the aim to achieve a convention on air pollution. The Soviets would push their East European allies, while the Norwegian government would exert "moral pressure" on Western European countries by referring to the OECD report.[76]

Intensive negotiations during the following year resulted in the Geneva Convention on Long-range Transboundary Air Pollution (LRTAP), signed by representatives from 33 countries in November

Fig. 8.9 Monitoring the Invisible: *The transnational air pollution from sulfur and nitrogen oxides discovered in the 1960s and 1970s differed from previous local forms of air pollution—it was invisible and odorless and could only be registered with the help of scientific instruments. In the realm of international research projects, a whole chain of measuring stations was set up for monitoring pollution of air and precipitation. The picture shows the station in Oulanka in Northern Finland.*

1979. The Convention was only a general framework and did not imply any binding obligations for the signatory countries. This reflected the fact that most European governments did still not regard acidification as a major problem. Yet the Convention did create a template for further negotiations. Its Secretariat became a coordinating body within a growing international community of air pollution experts, and it also meant the continuation of ongoing monitoring and modeling efforts.[77]

The expert community played a key role in the further struggle to reduce emissions. In the early 1980s scientists discovered large-scale damage to forests in Central Europe, and this strongly affected public opinion in several countries. *Waldsterben*, as the Germans dramatically called it, paved the way for the conclusion of a first "Sulphur Protocol" in 1984, in which the signatories agreed to reduce their sulfur dioxide emissions by 30 percent within a decade. Some 18 of the 30 members of the LRTAP Convention opted to sign the protocol. The forerunners could demonstrate that it was possible to reduce emissions without huge economic sacrifices. They did so mainly by purchasing coal and oil with low sulfur content, and by constructing desulfurization plants. Moreover, they exercised a moral pressure on the non-signing countries. The Sulphur Protocol spurred negotiations on additional Protocols for nitrogen oxides in 1988, volatile organic compounds in 1991, and heavy metals in 1998, as well as a second Sulphur Protocol in 1994.[78]

Signing the protocols remained voluntary, but gradually more and more countries decided to join the agreements. An important reason was that Europe's energy infrastructure was in a state of flux. In the 1970s and 1980s, the boom in natural gas pipeline construction facilitated radical growth in the use of this sulfur-free gas as a fuel in many countries. It is hardly a coincidence that the two key players behind the LRTAP Convention, Norway and the Soviet Union, were also major gas exporters. In Britain, another gas-rich country, Prime Minister Margaret Thatcher was eager to phase out much of the nation's inefficient, state-run coal industry, and managed to do so after a fierce struggle with the National Union of Mineworkers. This cleared the way for using more natural gas and for Great Britain to cut sulfur emissions and sign the protocols.

In a similar vein, the expansion of nuclear power and electricity supply in many countries made it easier to reduce overall emissions. Nuclear power, however, generated totally new long-range air pollution risks. This was dramatically demonstrated in April 1986 following the Chernobyl disaster. The Soviet government tried to keep the Ukrainian tragedy secret—both from its own population and from the outside world. Two days later, however, enhanced radioactivity levels were detected at Sweden's Forsmark nuclear power plant, a hundred kilometers to the north of Stockholm. Swedish nuclear and meteorological experts were able to document that the radioactivity came from a nuclear power accident somewhere in the Soviet Union. When the Swedish ambassador in Moscow informed Gorbachev's government of these findings, the Soviets admitted that an accident had indeed occurred in Chernobyl. In the week after the accident, radioactive fallout was detected in many parts of Europe, depending on how the winds blew and where it rained. Western media trumpeted reports about the radiation, causing much anxiety in the affected regions. Many people refused to let their children play outside, milk and food was discarded, and national agencies for radiation protection had a hard time trying to calm the general public. As a result, Chernobyl generated a dramatically enhanced public awareness of the transboundary nature of air pollution.[79]

Moreover, two new forms of air pollution came to the fore in the West European public debate at this time. The first concerned the thinning of the "ozone layer." This was linked to potentially-serious health effects, with the ozone loss seemingly caused primarily by chlorofluorocarbons (CFCs), a group of human-made chemicals. The second concerned an increase of carbon dioxide in the atmosphere with potential effects on the global climate, this caused largely by combustion of fossil fuels. The debates about these new threats soon generated international negotiations that led to conventions and protocols fairly similar to the ones negotiated in Europe for acid rain but on a global scale. Whereas the struggle to prevent the ozone layer's thinning was widely recognized as a success story, attempts to come to grips with climate change remained highly problematic. As of the 2010s, greenhouse gas emissions were measured as increasing faster than ever.

Although climate change was largely caused by energy and transport system-building, far-reaching visions of countering it relied on constructing even more infrastructure. One idea brought forward took the form of an inverted version of the tall smokestacks built in the nineteenth and twentieth centuries. This time the idea was not to create pipes into the sky but into the deep underground, with a long-term vision of connecting these new underground pipes with an infrastructure of pipelines through which carbon dioxide could be collected from many polluting plants and isolated.[80]

Norway emerged as a forerunner in the development of this "carbon capture and storage" (CCS) technology. This was not surprising, in light of the apparent contradiction between Norway's high ambitions in the field of "sustainable development"—a concept coined by an international commission led by Gro Harlem Brundtland—and its role as a major oil and gas producer. In his 2007 New Year's speech, Norwegian Prime Minister Jens Stoltenberg addressed climate change, linking it to a new national ambition:

> When President Kennedy said that the Americans would land on the moon within ten years, no American had been in space. They went to the moon in ten years. They set goals. And they reached the goals. Our vision is that we within seven years will have the technology in place that makes it possible to clean emissions from climate gases. It will be an important breakthrough for reducing emissions in Norway, and when we succeed I believe the world will follow us.[81]

The construction of the CCS plant that Stoltenberg referred to had already begun in Mongstad, a town on Norway's Atlantic Coast. As it turned out, however, Stoltenberg's ambitions could not be met. The plant was delayed, costs skyrocketed, and it was criticized in political debates. Finally, despite the symbolic significance and the national prestige linked to the CCS project, and with seven billion NOK spent on it, Stoltenberg's government terminated Mongstad as a full-scale carbon capture project. The energy minister stated that a "carbon test center" would be built at the site, and that the state's ambition was to build a full-scale plant in another location. However, it will be very difficult for the Norwegians to regain confidence in the idea of capturing carbon by way of pipes.[82]

Ecological Networks for Birds

More successful, as of the early twenty-first century, were attempts to protect Europe's common sky as an ecological infrastructure. As in the cases of meteorology, radio, aviation, and pollution, air-based system-building was here strongly linked to activities on the ground. Migratory birds were the focus, and bird protectors became proponents for establishing protected areas—often wetlands—along their routes.

Bird protection had a long history in Europe, going back to the late nineteenth century. At this time there was a fashion for women to wear exotic feathers in hats and literally millions of birds died annually in West India, Brazil, and East India to provide such feathers.[83] Protests led by women against this trade resulted in the establishment of the Royal Society for the Protection of Birds in Great Britain, the *Deutscher Bund für Vogelschutz* in Germany, and similar associations in other European countries. These early environmental organizations initiated national bird conservation legislation in many European countries early in the twentieth century.

Bird protection took a new turn in the 1970s. Recognizing that protection was typically a trans-frontier environment problem, new and more radical NGOs in several West European countries—notably the Dutch *Stichting Mondiaal Alternatief*, (SMA), the German *Komitee gegen den Vogelmord* (KV), and the Italian *Lega nazionale contro la destruzione degli ucelli* (LNDU)—jointly started lobbying the EC to take action. In 1974 they submitted the petition Save the Migratory Birds to the EC Commission, arguing that the extinction of insect-eating birds would lead to a dramatic increase of insects resulting in large-scale destruction of crops, posing a threat to human survival. These NGOs gained public support and, by the end of 1976, the Commission had received more than 50,000 letters supporting the petition. Moreover, a leading German member of the European Parliament, the Christian Democrat Hans Edgar Jahn, also advocated measures to protect bird species; this double pressure spurred the Commission to take action.[84]

The focus of the petition was on the need to prevent the killing of birds. This, however, gave rise to fierce reactions from the strong European hunting lobby; and responsible EC officials commissioned an eminent British ornithologist, Stanley Cramp, to provide a scientific report. Rather than proposing any general ban on hunting or the like, Cramp suggested a more infrastructural approach; he emphasized the need to "preserve, maintain or re-establish a sufficient diversity and area of habitats" for wild birds.[85] A patchwork of such habitats, isolated from each other on the ground but connected with each other through the air, by way of the birds' flying routes, was the answer.[86]

In 1979 the EC adopted a Directive on the Conservation of Wild Birds along these lines. It was binding legislation that went beyond the nation states. The environmental groups that were instrumental in the process behind the Directive also engaged in monitoring its implementation. Indeed on several occasions, the Commission even took governments to the European Court of Justice for having failed to properly implement it. The Directive's most direct result was that EU member states designated Special Protection Areas for birds, which presently cover more than 7 percent of the EU's territory (all new members have adopted it as well). These 3,600 scientifically-identified areas, oftentimes wetlands, provided a terrestrial infrastructure supporting the seasonal flows of migrating birds through the European sky. According to a scientific investigation, they have had a positive effect on bird populations. The previous declining trend was broken, with population recovery being particularly strong in member states that dedicated the most territory as Special Protection Areas.[87]

Intermeshed Appropriations of the Sky

Europe is a region of the world in which the concept of a common sky is particularly relevant, due to the large number of countries occupying a fairly small area. This chapter has documented how human-made infrastructure has been crucial for exploring and appropriating the sky in a number of ways. Most of this infrastructure was and still is terrestrial, including telegraph lines, antennas, airfields, smokestacks, and bird protection areas, but it also included flying objects ranging from balloons and kites to aircraft and satellites. This infrastructure brought about new kinds of transnational flows and services of crucial importance for Europeans' daily lives: reliable weather forecasts, broadcasting and wireless communication, and smooth international air travel. It also helped reduce air pollution and protect migratory birds. Furthermore, the different appropriations of the sky have become increasingly intermeshed. Aviation, for example, is critically dependent on radio communications, on reliable meteorological data, and even on low levels of pollution (as demonstrated in the spring of 2011 when an "ash cloud" from the Icelandic volcano Eyafjallsjökul caused a near-collapse of European air transportation).

These explorations and appropriations fostered new interpretations of the sky and not least of its structure: meteorologists and radio physicists discovered a number of layers in the atmosphere influencing the circulation of air and the propagation of radio waves. Meteorologists mapped dominant wind patterns that affect not only the weather in different parts of Europe, but also the asymmetrical dispersion of emissions. When new kinds of flows across national borders arose in the early twentieth century, questions of ownership and control of the sky were brought to the fore, a process which also produced different interpretations of the sky's structure. Some legal experts and politicians argued that the air should be regulated like the sea, free for all above a certain altitude, while others claimed that states should have ultimate control and responsibility for the air space above their territories. The experiences of the First World War supported the latter and the principle of national sovereignty over airspace was first codified for aviation. It was later transferred to radio waves and emissions as well. However, experiences of cross-border interference led to a qualification of this principle; at the 1972 United Nations Conference on the Human Environment in Stockholm, delegates agreed that while states "had the sovereign rights to exploit their own resources pursuant to their own environmental policies" they also had "the responsibility to ensure that activities within their jurisdiction or control do not cause damage to the environment of other States."[88]

For obvious reasons Chevalier's vision of a circulation society did not include circulations in the air, but remarkably, it is in the common sky above Europe that his vision has come closest to fulfilment. From the late nineteenth century onwards, specific professional groups of Europeans realized the mutual dependencies that followed from flows through the sky across national borders. In response they established new forms of international organization and cooperation in Europe: the IMO organized exchanges of weather observations; the IBU and ITU made frequency plans; the ICAN and IATA standardized a cross-border aviation infrastructure; the Eurocontrol coordinated flight plans; the Convention on LRTAP negotiated emission reductions; and the EC/EU adopted legislation to protect breeding grounds for birds. The leading actors behind these forms of infrastructure cooperation understood the mutual benefits it produced. They were enduring and persistent; even if they could not prevent the breakdown of cooperation in times of war, they quickly restored it again when peace returned. This does not mean of course that cooperation was without tensions and conflicts, but, nevertheless, actors from different countries realized that they had more to gain from cooperation than open conflict. In the European sky the metaphor of sitting in the same boat became completely convincing.

Conclusion

Michel Chevalier had a dream about the future of Europe: railroads, steam shipping lines and other infrastructure, in combination with the abolition of tariffs, would give rise to a "circulation society," in which Europeans cooperated closely and enjoyed huge economic benefits. Poverty would vanish and natural obstacles would cease to hinder trade and other activities. Moreover, war would become almost impossible among peoples and countries closely cooperating in all spheres of life. When Chevalier died in 1879, he had seen much of his dream come true: railroads crisscrossed the European continent, steam ships provided fast and regular transport across the oceans, and telegraph cables connected cities around the globe, enabling almost instant communications. Large volumes of goods were indeed traded across borders and over long distances, thanks to new infrastructure and free trade agreements.

However, in one crucial respect his dream had crashed: war still plagued Europe. If anything, humanity's destructive capabilities had increased rather than decreased, and Chevalier's cherished infrastructure networks were heavily involved. His own country, France, had experienced a humiliating defeat by Germany, mainly because the Prussian militaries had been much more skillful than the French in employing railroads and telegraphy for warfare.

Moreover, while grasping infrastructure's potential to overcome physical obstacles in Europe's natural geography, he did not anticipate its highly destructive impact on ecosystems and the natural environment.

Chevalier had an impressive understanding of the transformative potential of the new infrastructure being established in the early 1830s. It is the realization of this potential until today that we have analyzed in this book; and in doing so we have been much inspired by the works of another Frenchman, who lived almost precisely a hundred years after Chevalier: the historian Fernand Braudel (1902–85). He was one of the leading members of the "Annales School," scholars aiming to write a new kind of total history, encompassing economic, political, environmental, technical, social, and cultural aspects. Braudel wrote two impressive works of this comprehensive nature. The first was a more than 1,000-page volume about the Mediterranean world in the second half of the sixteenth century, and the second, a three-volume series about the emergence of mercantile capitalism in Europe between the fifteenth and eighteenth centuries.[1] In these works he time and again emphasized how fundamental geographical conditions provided by nature were stable elements for European societies: "For whole centuries, all movement was dominated by the primacy of water and ships, any inland location being an obstacle and a source of inferiority. The great European points of growth...were situated along the coastal fringes."[2] As we have shown, many of the obstacles and hindrances that these geographical conditions posed were overcome through creating new networks in the nineteenth and twentieth centuries. This meant a fundamental conversion from a nature-based to a network-based geography, which is at the heart of Europe's infrastructure transition.

Braudel used three time scales in his analysis: the short time span of "events," predominant in political history that foregrounds individual actors; the medium range of gentle rhythms often used by economic and social historians to describe varying aggregate phenomena such as price levels, trade volumes, or birth rates; and the long trajectory of exceedingly slow changes in the relations of societies and their environments, which he called the *long durée.* Braudel argued that historians need to take all these three time spans into account, so as to see how events are dependent both on cycles and the *long durée,* and how events and cycles contribute to the incremental change of the *long durée*. This is what we have done. Foremost, we used an event perspective when analyzing how various system-builders at different places and times developed visions and mobilized supporters and resources for their network-building endeavors. We have used a medium time perspective when discussing how the intensity of system-building and border-building activities changed over time, due to booms and busts in overall economies, periods of war and peace, etc. And in a *long durée* perspective we demonstrated how all these networks, taken together, gradually and cumulatively altered the material preconditions of European societies in fundamental ways.

Europe's Infrastructure Transition highlights a specific class of historical actors that we call system-builders.[3] The system-builders we presented built—or tried to build—systems of many different kinds: basic infrastructure, economic, and military systems, scientific knowledge systems, and ecological networks. Some built entirely novel operations, while others created combinations of existing networks focusing on overcoming technical or organizational obstacles for interconnections. Their visions, choices, and endeavors produced durable systems with long-lasting influence. However, network systems enabling large flows across borders oftentimes met opposition and spurred another class of actors—border-builders—to try to prevent, reduce, and control such flows. We argue that by focusing on system-builders and border-builders we add a new dimension to earlier research on the history of Europe.

In this concluding chapter we summarize and reflect upon our main findings by returning to the questions posed in the first chapter about how Europe's infrastructure emerged, how it altered economic relations and warfare, and how it interacted with Europe's natural environment.[4]

How Did Europe's Infrastructure Space Emerge?

In 1938, the Swedish author and journalist Ludvig Nordström set out on a tour to investigate living conditions in the Swedish countryside. His venture became almost literally a muckraking experience. He encountered an abundance of dirt and poverty, households without electricity, running water, or central heating often living in damp and filthy homes. He first presented his findings in a series of radio programs and later published a book with the title "Filth-Sweden."[5] A few years later he wrote another book in which he contrasted the dreadful countryside life with what he saw as the shining city life:

> Stockholm like every modern city is basically a wonderful creation by spirit, fantasy, calculation, inventiveness, passion, a feeling of duty to serve all the people of the city to a reasonably decent life. Lying down, I can see this wonderful creation of the human spirit in its entirety: first the whole invisible city beneath the ground with its galleries, drums, halls, machine rooms, in which pipes of different kinds, quiet and unknown to the general public, work and enable, that it can quench its thirst with clean, bacteria free water, can wash itself, shower, bath, keep a level of cleanliness, making it a little group in the large civilized world. I see the shining power stations, with turbines humming as smooth as purring cats, I see the coking in Värtan, where gas is manufactured, the telephone central's muddle of cables, so that within a second all these Stockholmers can come in contact with each other.[6]

What Nordström found so fascinating in Stockholm was the multitude of networks available to its inhabitants and the wide range of services they provided. Those networks indeed were a fundamental aspect of the expansion of Europe's infrastructure space. Moreover, many of these systems complemented each other, which increased the overall services even more. For example, in the mid-nineteenth century economic system-builders created intermodal transport chains combining everything from horses and carriages, canal barges, trains, sailing ships, and steamships. These chains extended tentacles deep into all continents of the world, like steamships on the Congo River or railroads across the vast Pampas of Argentina. The challenge when trying to create such chains was managing transshipment at interfaces like harbors and railroad stations. Here the economic system-builders had to erect storage facilities that could preserve their goods or install efficient equipment for lifting goods from one carriage to another. But when the Rotterdam harbor authorities and stevedoring companies introduced new machinery to increase the efficiency of transshipment, harbor workers resisted violently, afraid of losing their jobs. System-building was never a smooth affair.

Other system-builders created additional kinds of complementarity. Railroad companies early on realized that by building telegraph lines along railroad tracks, train traffic could be better managed, increasing both capacity and safety. For telegraph companies railroads delivered a welcome "right of way" and facilitated maintenance and repair. This kind of complementarity of transport and communication systems became increasingly important over time. In the 1880s when submarine telegraph cables had been sunk, connecting most major harbors around the world, shipping companies were able to communicate with their captains when they arrived at far away harbors, and could thereby control their fleets in a totally new way. Moreover, at the turn of the century, radio technology gave them additional opportunities to communicate with ships while at sea. In the interwar period, radio communication became effective for aviation, enabling flight controllers on the ground to assist pilots to find their way and to land safely. Such air control systems became indispensable for managing the rapidly increasing flows of airplanes in the European sky from the 1950s onwards.

In a similar way transport systems became entangled with energy systems. While renewable energy sources were available locally almost everywhere in Europe, fossil fuel resources had a very uneven distribution. To make coal accessible beyond the mining regions, new transport networks were needed; indeed some of the first canals and railroads in England were built for this purpose. The growing supply of cheap coal in turn spurred the further growth of railroad and steamship traffic, making it possible to transport coal over long distances and across borders; and a vast intra-European coal trade emerged with Great Britain and Germany as the main suppliers. Near the end of the nineteenth century oil was introduced, but oil resources had a very different geographic distribution to coal, the main suppliers being the United States, the Dutch Indies, the Middle East, Galicia, Romania, and Azerbaijan. Tankers, trains, and trucks carried the oil, and these transport systems again largely depended on the energy source they carried. However, new forms of infrastructure also developed for distributing energy independently of transport systems through dedicated networks. In the nineteenth century, system-builders constructed urban gasworks and electricity networks, and in the twentieth century their successors created transnational grids for electricity, oil, and natural gas which have grown dramatically and become the backbones for energy supply.

The multitude of networks did not expand according to an overall master plan. On the contrary, they were often first built one by one and by system-builders representing many kinds of interests. Later on other system-builders interconnected different networks either "horizontally," with similar networks in another region or country, or "vertically," with networks of different kinds. Consequently the overall growth of the ensemble of networks had a rather haphazard nature.

Chevalier had foreseen a leading role for France, England, and Germany in the future circulation society; and in these countries the growth of networks was indeed rapid early on, as they had financial resources for the huge investments involved. But their canals, railroads, and telegraph lines, which were primarily built to connect urban areas, bypassed their vast rural districts. This urban–rural divide was even more salient in Europe's poorer and less densely populated countries. However, even if rural areas were not directly integrated into the new networks, they could still be heavily influenced as corridors of modernization often evolved along major railroad lines.[7] The marked urban–rural divide in the provision of infrastructure decreased toward the mid-twentieth century with the advent of new systems in many parts of Europe. Radio broadcasts could be received equally well by rural and urban households, and the growing numbers of cars, buses, and trucks provided better transport facilities in the countryside. Also electricity and telephone networks eventually reached rural areas, and water and sewage followed. The grimy conditions of rural households that Ludvig Nordström had encountered did gradually improve.

The pace of infrastructure development was closely related to overall political and economic changes. After a rapid expansion from the mid-1850s to 1914, the two World Wars and the depression in the 1930s delayed network growth and spurred border-building activities. Many countries introduced new protectionist legislation; and harbors, airports, and border stations on rails and roads became crucial points for monitoring cross-border flows of goods and people. During the Cold War the pace of infrastructure

Fig. 9.1 Europe's New Border: *This picture from May 2014 shows African migrants sitting on the border fence around the Spanish enclave Melilla in North Africa. The Spanish Guardia Civil on the one side and the Moroccan Army on the other are waiting for the migrants to climb down. This fence is a little link in the increasingly complex border arrangements coordinated by Frontex, aiming to prevent migrants reaching Europe but encouraging ever more desperate and dangerous attempts. It has transformed the Mediterranean from a bridge to a wall.*

expansion became rapid anew, but only within East-Central and Western Europe, not in between. Border-building expanded too, and the Iron Curtain evolved from a metaphor in a political speech to a fortified corridor many hundred kilometers long through the heart of Europe. At times border-builders developed innovative technologies like the "derailing points" in East Germany, which automatically derailed unauthorized trains that tried to pass a border station. But we have also seen that some system-builders were able to penetrate the Iron Curtain nonetheless. In the 1970s and 1980s energy companies built an impressive natural gas grid interconnecting Siberian gas fields with the grids of Austria, Germany, France, and Italy. Leading politicians in both West and East approved these links, hoping that the new economic interdependency would reduce political tensions.

The end of the Cold War led to the dismantling of the Iron Curtain and an opening of the borders that had divided Europe for almost half a century. Instead, a new ambitious border-building endeavor began, this time strengthening the European Union's external borders particularly along the Mediterranean. The main purpose was to prevent illegal migrants from Africa and Asia reaching Europe. In 2004, the EU created a special agency called FRONTEX for managing its external borders, and this agency introduced sophisticated surveillance infrastructure to create "smart borders." This in turn spurred migrants and smugglers to devise ever more dangerous routes with thousands of drowned people as a result.

Ludvig Nordström was fascinated by the multitude of systems that a city like Stockholm could provide for its inhabitants in 1941. Since then many more systems have been introduced; many of them also reached rural households. In the postwar era, more and more Europeans became critically dependent on the services of the infrastructures around them, and this made their *reliability* a crucial issue. One strategy used by system-builders to address this challenge was to create "horizontal" connections in the form of international linkages. This was common for power companies, which by connecting their grids with grids in neighboring countries could import power when there was a local shortage. Likewise West European gas companies started to purchase gas from the Soviet Union to decrease their dependency on Dutch, North African, or domestic suppliers. However, these international connections also led to new kinds of vulnerabilities and dependencies. For example, a major power failure in Northern Germany on November 4, 2006 cascaded all the way to Croatia and North Africa. On January 1, 2006, the Russian gas company Gazprom interrupted its gas deliveries to Ukraine when negotiations for a new gas contract had failed following the "Orange Revolution." As Ukraine was the major transit country this led to gas shortages also in Hungary, Slovakia, and Austria. An even worse gas supply crisis followed in 2009. The 2014 Russian–Ukrainian conflict renewed concerns about the political implications of transnational energy supply relationships in Europe.

Another strategy that system-builders used for increasing reliability was to make "vertical" connections; for example information and communication systems were introduced for monitoring and controlling electricity, railroads, and aviation. However, this in turn led to growing complexity that created new kinds of vulnerabilities. In the mid-1990s the U.S. government began to talk of "critical infrastructure," in particular referring to the increasing role of information and communication technologies and set up a commission to investigate how to handle vulnerabilities. Following the terrorist attacks in the United States on "9/11" (September 9, 2001) and in Madrid and London, this concept has also become a core policy issue in the EU. Thus much attention has been devoted in the past years on how to reduce the vulnerability of critical infrastructure.[8]

How Did Infrastructure Alter Europe's Economic Relations & Warfare?

Friedrich Engelhorn, the founder of the *Badische Anilin- & Soda-Fabrik* (BASF) in Ludwigshafen in 1865 represents a telling example of an economic system-builder. Early on, he understood the opportunities provided by new infrastructure, specifically that the many by-products from newly-built gasworks were not just waste, but could be used to produce a range of chemical products. He established BASF to build factories to do so, and then recognized that the by-products from these plants could in turn yield additional products. Gradually one of the world's first comprehensive chemical complexes emerged in Ludwigshafen with many chemical plants interconnected by a very dense network of local railroads, conveyor belts, and other modes of transport. The output from these factories reached distant markets all over the world by way of river barges, railroads, and steamships. Engelhorn and his associates in BASF thus made use of new general-purpose infrastructure that had been built by others, linked with local transport infrastructure specific for their own needs, to create a worldwide production system.

We further encountered a number of other economic system-builders that in similar ways adapted new infrastructure to their own needs, often by complementing them with specific devices in production systems. Depending on the nature of their businesses these system-builders used different kinds or combinations of infrastructure: the chemical industry relied heavily on energy systems, the food industry on transport systems, and finance on communication systems. From the mid-nineteenth century, system-builders in these three spheres created vast transnational systems combining long-distance flows with local hubs or "complexes," thereby transcending the limitations that natural conditions had previously posed.

However, time and again these efforts of economic system-builders to create transnational systems were confronted by border-builders, who aimed to reduce or even disrupt flows across borders. The first instance was when cheap grain from North America and Argentina started "flooding" Europe in the 1870s. Millions of European farmers felt threatened and created influential lobby groups which brought about protectionist food policies in most countries. The experiences of the two World Wars, when food flows were dramatically interrupted, strengthened these policies even further: in 1960 no less than 90 percent of all food consumed in Western Europe was produced nationally, even though the potential capacity for long-distance food transports was immense. In the following decades, the Common Agricultural Policy encouraged cross-border food trade within the EEC/EU, but retained high barriers toward the rest of the world. Agricultural policies in East-Central Europe followed a similar pattern during the Cold War.

In the case of organic chemicals, the German global dominance in world production of dyestuffs and fertilizers came to an end during the First World War, when this industry was transformed to produce explosives instead. The other belligerent countries had quickly to set up their own facilities, and in the interwar period these companies and the German ones formed a powerful cartel. During the Cold War, oil gradually replaced coal as the preferred feedstock for chemicals and thus economic system-builders created huge chemical complexes along transnational oil and ethylene pipelines on both sides of the Iron Curtain.

Financial system-building also went through dramatic changes, following a similar rhythm. London's role as the globe's leading capital market broke down in August 1914, when all national stock exchanges closed down. After the war, the New York Stock Exchange took over London's role until the 1929 crash, when most European governments imposed harsh restrictions on transborder capital flows, lasting until the 1970s. In the 1980s economic system-builders could profit both from liberal ideologies and from enhanced information and communication technologies to create global electronic trading systems. The financial crashes in 1987, 2001, and 2008 demonstrated the resulting interdependencies.

In these three economic branches and in many others as well, various border-builders recurrently obstructed the growing transnational flows and the increasing international division of labor that new infrastructure provided. Nonetheless, these border-builders have not been able to prevent the realization of Chevalier's "circulation society," and today trans-border flows of goods and capital are immense, compared to 150 years ago. Also the flows of people have grown dramatically, even if great efforts are made to prevent "illegal" migrants from entering the EU.

Turning to military system-builders, they quickly realized the opportunities that new infrastructure offered. For example, they almost instantly started using railroads for transporting troops, at first for quelling local revolts. Transporting whole armies by railroad was a much bigger challenge. The Prussian General Staff developed great skills in managing such operations and created a specialized bureaucracy for making elaborate mobilization plans. These plans prepared for an extreme, intensified use of infrastructure, in stark contrast to the even and regular use that most economic system-builders strived to attain. Mobilization would employ the maximum carrying capacity of networks; and indeed, at the outbreak of the First World War, European railroads carried more passengers and goods than they had ever done.

The nature of military system-building changed dramatically during the course of a war. Plans could be made for the early phases, but further developments could not be foreseen, which forced military system-builders to improvise and adapt to changing conditions. For example, none of the First World War's military planners had foreseen that millions of their men would be living for four years in trenches along a haphazard front through northern France and Belgium. Supplying all these men and their horses with food, fodder, ammunition, and other supplies became a huge logistical challenge and both sides built flexible light rail networks for transporting goods from the railheads to the front. The Finnish Colonel Hjalmar Siilasvuo, who organized the defense against two invading Soviet Divisions at Suomussalmi in December 1939, provides another example. He was a splendid improviser and quickly established a temporary winter road across frozen lakes and moors to supply his troops. He also used the high mobility of his skiing soldiers to encircle the Soviet troops and cut off their supply lines.

Besides using existing civilian infrastructure, military system-builders also developed specific infrastructure for military purposes. Early on, European colonial powers established global networks of naval bases for replenishing their commercial and armed vessels. These bases became even more important when naval steam ships were introduced from the 1850s and onwards. In fact, the coaling stations built in the late nineteenth century constituted the world's first energy system with a global reach. In a similar way military system-builders in the new Air Forces constructed air bases, and England's first oil pipelines were completed in 1941 to ensure Britain's supply of aircraft fuel. They also developed electronic systems using radar and other radio technology for guiding their own aircraft and for detecting enemy formations. Similar infrastructure was also introduced in naval warfare, in particular for detecting and fighting submarines. During the Cold War, U.S. Admiral Arleigh Burke devoted much effort to establish a network of special radio stations in the northwest of Europe needed for accurate navigation of American nuclear submarines. Much of this infrastructure developed by military system-builders has been reworked for civilian purposes. Air control is the most prominent example.

The most pervasive change in warfare brought about by infrastructure was the increase of speed, scale, and scope. Not only could huge masses of soldiers be assembled on battlefields, they could also be supplied with powerful weapons and enormous quantities of ammunition for effectively killing each other, as demonstrated at the Western Front in the First World War. In the Second World War the increasing mobility and growing spatial scope of warfare, combined with indiscriminate air bombings of urban areas and the railroad-based Holocaust, led to huge civilian losses. During the Cold War military system-builders created infrastructure for nuclear war of unthinkable proportions. This has so far had a restraining effect: the number of war casualties in the second half of the twentieth century was only a fraction of the total in the first half.

Warfare is sometimes compared to a chess game. Using this metaphor, the game has changed totally in character, due to Europe's infrastructure transition: the board has grown in size; a number of new long ranging pieces have been introduced replacing the pawns and the knights; the most valuable new pieces can move both below and above the board; and the spectators of the game have become its most likely victims.

How Did Infrastructure Interact with Europe's Natural Environments?

When the government of the Grand Duchy of Baden wanted to improve conditions for transport on the Upper Rhine in the early 1820s it hired the hydraulic engineer Johann Gottfried Tulla to straighten the river's course. This project was looked upon with suspicion by officials in downstream countries, and, when a devastating flood occurred in the lower Rhine in 1824, they blamed it on Tulla's project, although Tulla himself rejected these accusations. This controversy raised questions about what factors determined the variations of the water flow in major rivers and to what extent human intervention can have an effect. The "improvement" of the Rhine and other similar projects to appropriate or adapt nature for infrastructure purposes created a need for better knowledge of the grounds, waters, and skies of Europe. Hence, in the mid-nineteenth century scientists and surveyors made a number of large-scale mapping and measuring efforts.

Much of this mapping was done on a national level, but in some cases scientists and surveyors organized transnational collaborations. For example, the German-Russian astronomer Friedrich Georg Wilhelm von Struve, in the Tsar's service, arranged the construction of a triangulation chain all the way from the Barents Sea to the Black Sea in order to produce maps of high accuracy. The Director of the U.S. Navy's Depot of Charts and Instruments, Matthew Fontaine Maury, came up with the ingenious idea of assembling logbooks with their meteorological observations for documenting the annual rhythms of currents and winds and producing nautical charts of the oceans with suggestions for fast and safe routes. French meteorologist Urbain le Verrier had another brilliant idea—to utilize the new telegraph network for gathering weather observations, in order to warn about storms and to produce weather maps suited for forecasts. These three men were knowledge system-builders who created transnational projects for assembling and processing observations. Their efforts have been continued and expanded by organizations like the World Meteorological Organization, which has developed an extremely complex system for global weather analysis including balloons, radiosondes, airplanes, and satellites for assembling data, large-scale computers for processing it, and multiple communication technologies for distributing it. Knowledge system-builders were critically dependent on infrastructure of many kinds, and at the same time they provided services that were essential for the safe operation of aviation, shipping, power systems, and the like.

Tulla's endeavors to enhance conditions for transport on the Rhine came in conflict with other interests, downstream and upstream, groups that used the river for other purposes like fishing, water consumption, sewage, and mechanical power and had different visions of how to "improve" the river. These conflicts also highlighted the issue of ownership and control over rivers like the Rhine and the Danube, which flowed through several countries. The affected governments at times agreed to establish special international commissions or study groups for negotiating "improvements," but in most cases with little success. It was often easier to resolve conflicts concerning rivers that did not cross national borders, either through compromises like multi-purpose dams or when the strongest interest group could impose its will. Today almost all European rivers have been radically transformed by hydraulic system-builders. This has not only destroyed the flora and fauna, but also altered the annual variations of the currents. The multitude of improvement works notwithstanding, devastating floods continue to occur.

The seas were affected by hydraulic system-builders. In the Netherlands, for example, they transformed a large bay, the Zuiderzee, into a lake, the IJselmeer, by building a long embankment. They also altered the "interface" between the North Sea and Rotterdam harbor by carving new, deep canals out into the sea, allowing entry of oil tankers with a 25 meter draught. When oil companies discovered oil and gas in the North Sea in the 1960s, the question arose about "ownership": which nation had the right to exploit such resources beyond territorial waters? After long negotiations, the riparian states agreed on a partitioning of the North Sea's continental shelf. This paved the way for oil and gas companies to build production platforms far out at sea, plus a whole network of pipelines on the North Sea floor. Submarine networks were not new, for sure—subsurface telegraph cables had existed for over a century—but the oil and gas pipelines posed much greater risks of ecological damage.

In the beginning of the twentieth century the European sky became another important arena for system-builders: the Marconi Company and its competitors wanted to build radio stations for long-distance communication, and aviation enthusiasts wanted to create airfields and other facilities for long-distance flights. This raised questions about the legal status of the sky and of how to create international rules for using it. At a 1906 international radiotelegraphy conference in Berlin, the delegates agreed to reserve different parts of the electromagnetic spectrum for different purposes and to establish the International Radiotelegraph Union, IRU, for allocating frequencies among states. At a similar 1910 conference on civil aviation in Paris, opinions differed profoundly among the delegates. The French and Germans supported a proposal to divide the sky in a similar way as the sea, with a lower level above the ground as "territorial air" and the air above it free to use for all, while the British argued for national sovereignty of all the air above a country. The conference could not reach a consensus, but at the Paris Peace Conference nine years later, a Convention based on the British principle was unanimously agreed upon. The war had demonstrated the danger of unwanted aircraft above national territories.

The international cooperation within aviation and radio had different aims, particularly in the interwar years. Aviation had its competitive advantage over long distances and this made international coordination crucial to facilitate cross-border travel. Aviation was also a very risky business and aviation authorities in neighboring countries jointly strived to "tame the air"; they developed weather services, established air routes with clear markings on the ground, and built radio communication facilities for assisting pilots, not least in bad weather. However, some countries also used their air sovereignty as a political weapon, rejecting passage by airplanes from certain countries. Within the radio system, international coordination was also crucial but for almost the opposite reason, to avoid unwanted radio signals across nation borders that could disturb domestic broadcasting. Many broadcasting companies, worried about a growing "congestion of the European ether" in the mid-1920s, formed the International Broadcasting Union, which developed a frequency plan for Europe. The basic idea of the plan was that each country should have its own frequency(ies), and that frequencies near one another on the spectrum should be allocated to countries far apart. The plan worked fairly well even though some radio stations—like Radio Vatican, Radio Moscow, and Radio Luxemburg—were established deliberately for reaching far away listeners. Hardly surprisingly, all these forms of international cooperation in the sky broke down during the Second World War and were difficult to restore afterwards.

The ground has, of course, also been an important arena for infrastructure builders and the location and routing of networks was often contested, not least because of feared effects on the environment. Today, roads, rails, canals, power lines, and the like, cover substantial areas particularly in urban regions, but, perhaps surprisingly, "artificial surfaces" cover only a few percent of Europe's land surface. The most important impact of infrastructure building on the ground has been indirect by stimulating more intensive use of land. Today agricultural areas and commercial forests cover about 80 percent of Europe's land mass, which leaves less than 20 percent for nature zones and inland waters. Infrastructure entanglements with the ground have not been negotiated internationally in the same way as for rivers, seas, and the sky, as the cross-border effects are not as obvious. But the increase of farming monocultures and the decrease and partitioning of nature zones have had effects on fauna and flora that affect large parts of Europe. In the 1970s nature conservationists in Estonia (then a Soviet republic) and the Netherlands developed similar ideas about "ecological networks," featuring corridors between nature zones to enable animals and plants to spread and thereby avoid losses of biological diversity. In the early 1990s the EU adopted the notion of a European ecological network. An intriguing example of cross-national collaboration in this field is the establishment of an ecological corridor along the former Iron Curtain. What used to be the main symbol for separation of people in Europe has thus become a symbol for interconnection of its fauna and flora!

In the 1950s an environmental movement gradually emerged in Europe, which focused in particular on environmental impacts of infrastructure building. The environmentalists protested against polluting or dangerous power plants, against urban motor ways causing pollution and noise, against airports close to cities, against dams altering rivers, and so on. Most of these struggles concerned what activists regarded as local or regional problems, but in the late 1960s the transnational character of pollution became unmistakable:

In 1967 a supertanker, *Torrey Canyon*, was shipwrecked off the coast of Cornwall and caused a huge spill of crude oil that affected beaches far away; two years later a large accidental dumping of an insecticide into a tributary of the Rhine caused massive fish starvation downstream; and at the same time environmental researchers in Scandinavia started arguing that the large-scale emissions from industries and power plants in continental Europe and the British Isles caused acidification in Scandinavian streams and lakes, leading to severe environmental damage.

Environmentalists, experts, and policymakers argued that international cooperation was necessary to handle these threats. An International Commission for the Protection of the Rhine against Pollution had in fact been established in 1948, but had been fairly idle. It was reinvigorated in the early 1970s and got the riparian governments to agree on making huge investments in sewage treatment plants and the like along the river and a remarkable improvement of water qualities was achieved. Other large rivers like the Elbe and the Danube had even worse pollution problems; but in the context of the Cold War, it was difficult to achieve joint action. In the case of the Danube, cooperation gained momentum only after a major disaster in 2000, when huge amounts of cyanide and heavy metals spilled from a gold mine in Romania and wiped out much of the wildlife downstream. As for trans-border air pollution, representatives from countries with large-scale power plants and industries initially denied that their emissions could cause pollution at long distances; but a large international research project substantiated the Scandinavian claims in the mid-1970s. Still there was much reluctance from the emitting countries to impose restrictions on their own industries and power stations. When the Soviet Union joined forces with the Scandinavian countries, this paved the way to the signing of a Convention on Long-range Transboundary Air Pollution in 1979, providing a platform for further negotiations and agreements that have contributed to substantial reductions of emissions.

The negative environmental impacts of infrastructure building have thus been increasingly highlighted in the past half century, and large efforts have been made to come to grips at least with some of them. In a number of cases, international collaboration has produced rather impressive improvements. There have also been some attempts to restore landscapes and waterscapes to their pre-industrial shape. However, many of the ecological transformations made by system-builders in the past two centuries are so huge and vast that they seem irreversible. Leading scientists have even suggested that a new geological epoch, the "anthropocene," has emerged characterized by the far-reaching impacts on the earth's ecosystems from human activities.[9] This leads back to Fernand Braudel. In his writings about European societies in the sixteenth to eighteenth centuries, he emphasized the fundamental geographical obstacles to human activities provided by nature. While Europe's infrastructure transition overcame many of these natural obstacles to human activities, there now seems to be a need to install new kinds of self-imposed obstacles or boundaries for human activities in Europe and beyond to avoid an escalating degradation of the natural environment. A major challenge for future system-builders will be to help keep societies within such boundaries.[10]

Endnotes

Introduction: Chevalier's Dream

1. Chevalier, *Système de la Méditerranée*, 6. See also: Chevalier, *Politique Européenne*; Chevalier, *Economie politique*. Translations are ours unless otherwise noted.
2. Chevalier, *Système de la Méditerranée*, 6. Compare Saint-Simon and Thierry, *Reorganisation de la société européenne*.
3. Chevalier, *Politique Européenne*, 7.
4. In Dutch: Chevalier, *De ijzerbanen*.
5. Chevalier, "Chemins de fer."
6. Jennings, "Democracy before Tocqueville"; Drolet, "Industry, Class and Society"; Kaiser and Schot, *Writing the Rules*.
7. Reagan, "Facebook's Mission Statement." On Chevalier and the history of networking thinking: Williams, "Cultural Origins"; Mattelart, *Invention of Communication*, 85–110; Mattelart, *Networking the World*; Giessmann, *Netze und Netzwerke*, 81–96. On today's network society: Castells, *Rise of the Network Society*.
8. Hobsbawm, *Age of Extremes*; Mazower, *Dark Continent*; Snyder, *Bloodlands*.
9. Chevalier, *Système de la Méditerranée*, 48.
10. Grin et al., *Transitions*. Our focus on infrastructure entanglements with economy, war, and nature sets this book apart from existing European infrastructure history books such as, in order of appearance: Merger et al., *Les réseaux européens transnationaux*; Van der Vleuten and Kaijser, *Networking Europe*; Badenoch and Fickers, *Materializing Europe*; Ambrosius and Henrich-Franke, *Integration von Infrastrukturen* (which has a good literature review); Högselius et al., *Making of Europe's Critical Infrastructure*; Schiefelbusch and Dienel, *Linking Networks*. For explorations of these entanglements: Van der Vleuten, "In Search of the Networked Nation" and "Networking Technology, Society, Nature"; Roth and Schlögel, *Neue Wege in ein neues Europa*; Disco and Kranakis, *Cosmopolitan Commons*.
11. De Vries and Van de Woude, *First Modern Economy*; Van Lottum, "Labour Migration."
12. These are orders of magnitude, not precise figures. Livi Bacci, *Population of Europe*, 116–22; Lucassen and Lucassen, "Mobility Transition in Europe"; Lucassen and Lucassen, "From Mobility Transition." For an example of local fragmentation even in urbanized regions see: Van der Woud, "Town and Country," 188.
13. Radkau, "Zum ewigen Wachstum."
14. As quoted in Anastasiadou, *Constructing Iron Europe*, 11. Compare Anastasiadou and Tympas, "Iron Silk Roads."
15. We here follow Woolf, "Europe and its Historians"; Cole and Ther, "Introduction"; Scranton, "Writing a New History." Compare, in the history of technology, Hecht, "Colonial Networks of Power."
16. Graham and Mavin, *Splintering Urbanism*; Badenoch, "Myths of the European Network." Channel Tunnel: Van der Vleuten and Kaijser, "Networking Europe."

17. On system-builders: Hughes, "Electrification of America"; Kaijser, "System Building from Below"; Disco and Van der Vleuten, "Politics of Wet System Building"; Van der Vleuten et al., "Europe's System Builders."
18. Myrdal, "Twenty Years," 626. See further this volume, chapter 3.
19. For a 2005 evaluation of the EU's influence on infrastructure: Merger, "Great European Infrastructure Projects," 421. Historically: Schipper and Van der Vleuten, "Trans-European Network Development."
20. This is the New Transnational History proposed in Tyrell, "American Exceptionalism." Compare Van der Vleuten, "Toward a Transnational History"; Saunier, *Transnational History*.
21. Janáč, *European Coasts of Bohemia*.
22. "Papoutsis, Besson, Malmström and Laitinen visit RABIT operational area," *Frontex News Release*, November 5, 2010; Leonard, "Creation of FRONTEX"; Human Rights Watch, *EU's Dirty Hands*; Hayes and Vermeulen, *Borderline*.
23. Chevalier, *Système de la Méditerranée*, 9.
24. We here follow Van der Vleuten, "Networking Technology, Society, Nature." Inspired by Braun, "Geflügelte Saurier," who, for a different purpose, writes of "first order system builders" (our infrastructure system-builders) and "second order system builders" (our economic, military, and knowledge system-builders).
25. Edwards, "Meteorology as Infrastructural Globalism"; Edwards, *Vast Machine*; Disco and Kranakis, *Cosmopolitan Commons*.
26. European Environment Agency, *Landscape Fragmentation in Europe*, 6.
27. European Environment Agency, *Green Infrastructure*. Compare Van den Belt, "Networking Nature."
28. Bowker, *Science on the Run*, calls this historiographical move of foregrounding society's background infrastructure "infrastructural inversion."
29. Davies, *Europe*, preface.

1 Manipulating Space & Time

1. *From the Finland Station* was Theodore Hamerow's response in the form of a book on the fates of Europe's revolutionary movements after the October Revolution. See: Wilson, *To the Finland Station*; Hamerow, *From the Finland Station*.
2. On Lenin's journey: Pearson, *The Sealed Train*; Krupskaya, "Departure for Russia"; Wesson, *Lenin's Legacy*, 60.
3. The most common route in this context is by road through southern Sweden to Stockholm, followed by ferry transshipment across the Baltic Sea and from there through Finland to the Russian border near St. Petersburg. There is hardly any cargo going through Haparanda and Tornio, though.
4. Svedberg, "Saint-Simon's Vision of a United Europe," 154–58; Van der Vleuten and Kaijser, *Networking Europe*, 9.
5. *Final Act of the Congress of Vienna/General Treaty*, Articles CVIII–CIX. Available online at http://en.wikisource.org/wiki/Final_Act_of_the_Congress_of_Vienna (accessed May 15, 2014). Article CXIII further stipulated that "each state bordering on the rivers is to be at the expense of keeping in good repair the towing paths, which pass through its territory, and of maintaining the

necessary works through the same extent in the channels of the river, in order that no obstacle may be experienced to the navigation."

6 For an overview of road-building in nineteenth-century Europe, see: Pounds, *Historical Geography of Europe 1800–1914*, 430–32. For some national case studies, see: Guldi, *Roads to Power* (Britain); Kaijser, *I fädrens spår*, 130 (Sweden); and Johansen, "Danish Coastal Shipping," 36 (which despite the title also deals with road transport); and Mentzel, *Transportation Technology and Imperialism* (for the Ottoman Empire). For an overview of waterway-building in different European countries, see the case studies in Kunz and Armstrong, *Inland Navigation*.

7 This was the case, for example, along the Rhine. See: Cioc, *Rhine*. The notable exception was the remaking of the Danube's treacherous delta, where the European Danube Commission took charge of improvement works following the Crimean War. Chamberlain, *Regime of International Rivers*; Pounds, *Historical Geography of Europe 1800–1914*, 446–49. See further: chapter 7, this volume.

8 Pounds, *Historical Geography of Europe 1800–1914*, 353; Armstrong, "British Coastal Shipping," 20.

9 Armstrong, "British Coastal Shipping," 20; Scholl, "Bremerhaven," 205.

10 See: Miller, "Steamships," 977.

11 Schivelbusch, *Railway Journey*, 29.

12 As quoted in De Block, "Designing the Nation," 705.

13 Ibid., 703–32.

14 Pounds, *Historical Geography of Europe 1800–1914*, 454–56.

15 Janáč, *European Coasts of Bohemia*, 31–32.

16 For the case of Belgium, see: De Block, "Designing the Nation"; for the Netherlands, see: Buiter, "Internationality of Dutch Railways"; for Switzerland, see: Schueler, *Materialising Identity*; for Italy, see: Schram, *Railways and the Formation of the Italian State*; for Greece, see: Anastasiadou, *Constructing Iron Europe* and Tympas and Anastasiadou, "Constructing Balkan Europe."

17 Kaiser and Schot, *Writing the Rules*; Anastasiadou, *Constructing Iron Europe*, 79–81 and 134; Henrich-Franke, "Changing Patterns of Infrastructure Governance," 17.

18 Schueler, *Materialising Identity*.

19 For the Danish case, see: Johansen, "Danish Coastal Shipping," 36; for the Scandinavian–German connections, see: Roth, "Implikationen."

20 Tympas and Anastasiadou, "Constructing Balkan Europe," 30.

21 Ibid.

22 Ibid.

23 For the history of the building of the Trans-Siberian Railway, see in particular: Marks, *Road to Power*.

24 For railroads in Central Asia and in the Russo-British "Great Game," see: Hopkirk, *Great Game*, 430–46, and Sergeev, *Great Game*, in particular 154 and 290.

25 Anastasiadou, *Constructing Iron Europe*; McMeekin, *Berlin-Baghdad Express*.

26 Schueler, *Materializing Identity*, 69.

27 Hugill, *Global Communications*, 25–27; Headrick and Griset, "Submarine Telegraph Cables," 545.

28 Standage, *Victorian Internet*, 69; Harvard, "Modernitetens depescher?," 30; Fickers and Griset, *Communicating Europe*, chapter 1.
29 Standage, *Victorian Internet*, 68–73; Headrick and Griset, "Submarine Telegraph Cables," 546; Kaijser, *I fädrens spår*, 109; Harvard, "Modernitetens depescher?," 30.
30 Headrick, *Invisible Weapon*, 17–22; Standage, *Victorian Internet*, 73–84.
31 Headrick, *Invisible Weapon*, 20–24. For the early visions of a trans-Siberian connection between Europe and North America and on-land connections to India, see: Hugill, *Global Communications*, 36–39.
32 Headrick, *Invisible Weapon*, 28–115. The historical origins of trans-Atlantic telegraphy is further discussed in chapter 7, this volume. An intriguing account of the Portuguese role in the global telegraph network from the late nineteenth century is offered by Silva and Diogo, "From Host to Hostage."
33 Kaijser, "From Invention to Global System," 127–29.
34 Europe's radio communications are further discussed in chapter 8, this volume. See also: Fickers and Griset, *Communicating Europe*.
35 Kunz, "Economic Performance," 58–60 and 68; Giuntini, "Inland Navigation in Italy," 151; Ojala, "Finnish Coastal Shipping," 69; Gómez-Mendoza, "Light and Shade"; Pounds, *Historical Geography of Europe 1800–1914*, 353–54. For a good overview of the complexity of tolls in medieval Europe, see: Newman, *Travel and Trade*.
36 Torpey, *Invention of the Passport*, 111–17.
37 Howkins, "Railway Geography," 290–91; Kunz, "Economic Performance," 60–66.
38 Kolb, "Reichsbahn," 137; Howkins, "The Adjustment of International Rail Passenger Services," 151.
39 "International Communications," *Railway Gazette* 53 (1930): 767, as quoted in Anastasiadou, *Constructing Iron Europe*, 109.
40 *Zeitschrift für Paneuropa* 1 (1924): 31–32, as quoted in Schipper, *Driving Europe*, 86.
41 Hantos, "Une Nouvelle Organisation des Transports en Europe Central," 271–72, as quoted in Anastasiadou, *Constructing Iron Europe*, 116–17.
42 Davies, *History of the World's Airlines*, 11–17; see also: Kranakis, "European Civil Aviation," 290–326.
43 Cohen, *IATA*, chapters 1 and 3.
44 Cooper, *Right to Fly*, 145; Lissitzyn, "Diplomacy of Air Transport."
45 Van der Vleuten et al., "Europe's System-Builders," 328.
46 Schipper, *Driving Europe*, 92–95; Anastasiadou, *Constructing Iron Europe*, 69–70.
47 Schipper, *Driving Europe*, 106–7; Kaiser and Schot, *Writing the Rules*, Introduction.
48 As quoted in Anastasiadou, *Constructing Iron Europe*, 68.
49 Anastasiadou, *Constructing Iron Europe*, 67–68, 82–83, 102–3, and 109; Janáč, *European Coasts of Bohemia*, 32; Schipper, *Driving Europe*, 77; see also: Schipper et al., "New Connections for an Old Continent."
50 Schipper, *Driving Europe*, 98–99; Janáč, *European Coasts of Bohemia*, 35–37; Anastasiadou, *Constructing Iron Europe*, 115–16.
51 As quoted in Anastasiadou, *Constructing Iron Europe*, 116.
52 Schipper, *Driving Europe*, 98–99; Janáč, *European Coasts of Bohemia*, 35–37; Anastasiadou, *Constructing Iron Europe*, 115–16.

53 Janáč, *European Coasts of Bohemia*, 27–84.
54 Anastasiadou, *Constructing Iron Europe*, 42–48.
55 Ibid., 52.
56 Ibid., 49–52.
57 Ibid., 36–50.
58 Davies, *History of the World's Airlines*, 11–17. See also: Kranakis, "European Civil Aviation," 290–326; Jones, "Rise and Fall of Aeroflot."
59 Davies, *History of the World's Airlines*, chapter 11.
60 Laborie, "A Missing Link?"; Kaijser, "From Invention to Global System," 127–29. On radio broadcasting during the interwar years, see chapter 9, this volume, and Fickers and Griset, *Communicating Europe*.
61 Zeller, *Driving Germany*.
62 Schmitt, *Path to European Union*, 12, as quoted in Schipper, *Driving Europe*, 162.
63 Janáč, *European Coasts of Bohemia*, 70; Blackbourn, *Conquest of Nature*, chapter 4; Joachimsthaler, *Breitspurbahn*; Zeller, *Driving Germany*.
64 Schipper, *Driving Europe*, 164–70.
65 Van der Vleuten et al., "Europe's System-Builders," 341.
66 Ibid., 340–45; Henrich-Franke, "Mobility and European Integration," 64–82; Janáč, *European Coasts of Bohemia*, 166–67.
67 This was the formulation used by Ronald Reagan in a famous speech delivered in Berlin on June 12, 1987. "Raze Berlin Wall, Reagan Urges Soviet," *New York Times*, June 13, 1987.
68 Bock, *Interzonenzüge*, 9–16; Nicholls, "Zusammenbruch und Wiederaufbau"; Gonser, *Geteilte Eisenbahn*.
69 Bock, *Interzonenzüge*, 26–27.
70 Water and road transport faced an analogous situation. In the case of water, only the Elbe remained open to traffic, and in the case of roads six border-crossing points were retained. Bock, *Interzonenzüge*, 26–27; Scheffer, *Burned Bridge*, 97–99. A similar concentration of traffic to only a few limited frontier stations took place at about the same time elsewhere on the Iron Curtain. Along the 500 km long Greek–Bulgarian border, for example, all cross-border traffic was concentrated to a single frontier station. Karas, "Infrastructuring Europe," 5.
71 Bock, *Interzonenzüge*, 47 and 54.
72 Ibid., 98.
73 Ibid., 98–100.
74 Gonser, *Geteilte Eisenbahn*.
75 Schipper, *Driving Europe*, 187–218.
76 Ibid.; Schipper, "Changing the Face of Europe," 211–28; Mom, "Roads without Rails"; Schot, "Infrastructures and European Integration," 86–88; Blomqvist, "Roads for Flow – Road for Peace"; Lundin, *Bilsamhället*. For the complex links between ECE, ECMT, OEEC, and other organizations in the road field, see: Schot and Schipper, "Experts and European Transport Integration," which also discusses the failure of the EEC to develop a common transport policy.
77 Janáč, *European Coasts of Bohemia*, 131–244.
78 Ibid., 202.
79 Ibid., 131–244.
80 Laborie, "A Missing Link?," 196–97; Högselius, *Dynamics of Innovation in Eastern Europe*; Campbell, *Soviet and Post-Soviet Telecommunications*, 15–23.

81 Tsaglioti, "Infrastructuring Europe: Report No. 3," 7 and 22; "Inszenierte Sicherheit: Die Datenschnüffler vom BND," *taz*, June 23, 2013.
82 Laborie, "A Missing Link?"
83 Abbate, *Inventing the Internet*, 154; for the background of EURONET, see: Fickers and Griset, *Communicating Europe*, chapter 3.
84 Abbate, *Inventing the Internet*. See further: Fickers and Griset, *Communicating Europe*, chapter 3. Data networks were envisioned also in Eastern Europe, see, for example, Gerovitch, "Internyet."
85 Westwood, *Soviet Railways to Russian Railways*, 18–21.
86 As quoted in ibid., 21–22.
87 Ibid., 21–22.
88 Ibid., 22.
89 See: Kaiser and Schot, *Writing the Rules*, chapters 3 and 5, where an account of analogous problems in the post-First World War era is found.
90 Westwood, *Soviet Railways to Russian Railways*, 22–26; Buchhofer, "Transport Infrastructure in the Baltic States."
91 Buchhofer, "Transport Infrastructure in the Baltic States," 70–72; Butkevicius, "Development of Passenger Transportation."
92 For a good study of post-Soviet air traffic in the Baltic Sea region, see: Nilsson, "Östersjöområdet."
93 Högselius, *Dynamics of Innovation in Eastern Europe*, 92–95.
94 Ibid.
95 For a comprehensive discussion of these issues, see, in particular, Johnson and Turner, *Strategy and Policy for Trans-European Networks*, 27–47.
96 Ibid., 34.
97 Ibid.
98 Ibid., 43.
99 Ibid.
100 Ibid., 112.
101 Ibid., 112–13.
102 Barrett, "Sustainability of the Ryanair Model."
103 Kaijser, *I fädrens spår*.
104 De Block, "Designing the Nation," 715.
105 Schueler, *Materialising Identity*, 83.
106 Schivelbusch, *Railway Journey*, 36.
107 Ibid., 38–39.
108 Schueler, *Materialising Identity*, 66–67.
109 Schivelbusch, *Railway Journey*, 10.
110 Standage, *Victorian Internet*, 83.
111 Harvard, "Modernitetens depescher?," 45; Kaijser, "From Invention to Global System."
112 Howkins, "Adjustment of International Rail Passenger Services," 154.
113 Anastasiadou and Tympas, "Iron Silk Roads."

2 Fueling Europe

1 The 2006 gas crisis: Fredholm, *Gazprom in Crisis*. The Nord Stream Pipeline is further discussed in Chapter 7, this volume.
2 This event is well documented in UCTE, *Final Report*. For further analysis see: Van der Vleuten and Lagendijk, "Transnational Infrastructure Vulnerability."

3   Van der Vleuten and Lagendijk, "Interpreting Transnational Infrastructure Vulnerability."
4   Dutch peat transports: De Vries, *The European Economy in an Age of Crisis*, 165–6. For the role of canals in European coal transports, see the national case studies in: Kunz and Armstrong, *Inland Navigation*.
5   Russian coal imports: Izmestieva, "Integration of the European Coal Market." Swedish coal imports: Avango, *Sveagruvan*. For a discussion of the prohibitive costs of overseas coal supplies, see: Barbier, *Scarcity and Frontiers*, 378–79.
6   For the pre-First World War development of the Galician oil industry, see: Rambousek, "Die ÖMV-Aktiengesellschaft." The Romanian oil industry: Murgescu, "Anything but Simple." Russia and its relation to developments elsewhere: Yergin, *The Prize*, 56–77.
7   Yergin, *The Prize*, 58–63.
8   Tomory, "Building the First Gas Network." Paquier and Williot, *L'industrie du gaz en Europe*, contains a good collection of case studies of early gas histories from various parts of Europe.
9   Hughes, *Networks of Power*.
10 Cordovil, "De-electrifying the History of Street Lighting"; Del Curto and Landi, "Gas-Light in Italy"; Kaijser, "Stadens ljus"; Izmestieva, "Integration of the European Coal Market"; Gorshkov, "Gazosnabzhenie Leningrada," 27.
11 Cordovil, "De-Electrifying the History of Street Lighting"; Del Curto and Landi, "Gas-Light in Italy."
12 Schönholzer, "Ein elektrowirtschaftliches Programm für Europa," 385 (emphasis in original).
13 Gall, "Atlantropa."
14 Lagendijk and Van der Vleuten, "Inventing Electrical Europe."
15 Lagendijk, *Electrifying Europe*, 117.
16 As quoted in ibid., 165–7.
17 Ibid.
18 Ibid.
19 As quoted in Lagendijk and Van der Vleuten, "Inventing Electrical Europe."
20 Ibid.
21 For a detailed discussion see: Lagendijk, *Electrifying Europe*, 144–45; Lagendijk and Van der Vleuten, "Inventing Electrical Europe."
22 Kaijser, "Trans-border Integration of Electricity and Gas," 7–10.
23 Lagendijk, *Electrifying Europe*, 151–52.
24 Högselius, "Connecting East and West?," 249–50; Holmberg, "Survival of the Unfit."
25 Sistemnyi operator edinoi energeticheskoi sistemy, "Istoriya."
26 Tchalakov et al., "Bulgarian Power Relations"; Hegmann, "Die Entwicklung der Zusammenarbeit im RGW," 21.
27 Lagendijk, *Electrifying Europe*, 157–212.
28 Ibid., 192–94; Tympas et al., "Border-Crossing Electrons"; Tsaglioti, "Infrastructuring Europe: Report No. 2"; Tchalakov et al., "Bulgarian Power Relations," 150.
29 Bayernwerk, "Company History"; Lagendijk, *Electrifying Europe*, 169–72.
30 Myllyntaus, *Electrifying Finland*; Michelsen, "Uneasy Alliance."
31 Sens, "Energieversorgung Mecklenburg-Vorpommerns," 201–52; Högselius, *Deutsch-deutsche Geschichte des Kernkraftwerkes Greifswald*, 13–28.
32 Yergin, *The Prize*.

33 Ibid., 62 and 137. Britain's military pipelines are discussed further in chapter 6, this volume.
34 On the Western part of the system, see: "Trans-Europe Crude Line Considered," *Oil and Gas Journal*, July 16, 1956. On the Balkan pipeline visions, which were formulated later than the West European ones, see: "Final Agreement Reached on TAL Spur," *Oil and Gas Journal*, July 3, 1967.
35 See, for example, *gwf*, June 10, 1966, 653; Tsaglioti, "Infrastructuring Europe: Report No. 2," 4–5.
36 Yergin, *The Prize*, 479–98.
37 "Soviet Line Will Supply Satellites Crude," *Oil and Gas Journal*, June 8, 1959.
38 "How Europe View Threat of Red Exports," *Oil and Gas Journal*, April 13, 1959.
39 See: *gwf*, December 10, 1965.
40 Derzhavnyy komitet, *Nafta i gaz Ukrayiny*, 143–45; Elshtein, "Gazovaya promyshlennost v Polshe," 49; Högselius, *Red Gas*, 14.
41 See: "French Push Gas Project," *Oil and Gas Journal*, July 28, 1958.
42 As of 1961, Hassi R'Mel was believed to contain up to a trillion cubic meters of recoverable gas, making it the second-largest gas field in the world (after the Panhandle-Hugoton field in the United States). See: "Major Gas Areas of the World," *Oil and Gas Journal*, April 24, 1961, 106. For the UNECE's involvement, see: Högselius, *Red Gas*, 26–28, and Högselius et al., "Natural Gas in Cold War Europe," 32.
43 Högselius, *Red Gas*, 28; Högselius et al., "Natural Gas in Cold War Europe," 32.
44 Kaijser, "Striking Bonanza."
45 Ibid.
46 Bokserman, *Razvitie gazovoi promyshlennosti*, 80.
47 Högselius et al., "Natural Gas in Cold War Europe," 33.
48 Högselius, *Red Gas*, 67–88; Högselius et al., "Natural Gas in Cold War Europe," 33–34.
49 Högselius, *Red Gas*, 91–93.
50 Ibid., 105–34. Esso, which regarded the Soviet gas as a competitor to its own German activities, lobbied Washington seeking to prevent the deal, though in vain. The German government inquired of the US embassy whether it would object, but was given the green light from the Nixon administration.
51 Högselius et al., "Natural Gas in Cold War Europe," 35–36.
52 Britain: Arapostathis et al., "Governing Transitions."
53 Victor and Victor, "Bypassing Ukraine."
54 Hayes, "Transmed and Maghreb"; Evans, "Changing Policy Perspectives."
55 Hecht, "The Power of Nuclear Things," 10–20.
56 As quoted in ibid.," 15.
57 Ibid., 10–20.
58 Magnus von Bonsdorff (former CEO of TVO), author interview, November 10, 2006.
59 Högselius, "Connecting East and West?"
60 Voloshin, "Electric Power in the Comecon European Countries," 741; Karapetian et al., "Energy Conservation in the Transmission and Distribution of Electricity," 1107–10; see also: Tchalakov et al., "Bulgarian Power Relations."

61 Högselius, "Decay of Communism"; Högselius, "Challenging Chernobyl's Legacy."
62 Lagendijk and Van der Vleuten, "Inventing Electrical Europe," 86; Thue, "Connections, Criticality, and Complexity"; Högselius and Kaijser, "Art of Acting on Mulitple Arenas"; Högselius and Kaijser, *När folkhemselen blev internationell*.
63 For an extensive discussion of Trans-European Networks in energy, see: Johnson and Turner, *Strategy and Policy for Trans-European Networks*, 134–77.
64 Cf. Lagendijk and Van der Vleuten, "Inventing Electrical Europe."
65 Maltby, "European Union Energy Policy Integration," 438.
66 Thue, "Connections, Criticality, and Complexity."
67 Högselius, *Red Gas*, 197–216.
68 Ibid.
69 Henningsen et al., "Berlin Creates 380-kV Connection with Europe."
70 Lagendijk and Van der Vleuten, "Inventing Electrical Europe"; Högselius, "Connecting East and West?" The new link across the Gulf of Finland was a High-Voltage Direct Current (HVDC) line.
71 Hayes, "Transmed and Maghreb," 189; Lagendijk and Van der Vleuten, "Inventing Electrical Europe."
72 Rutledge and Wright, "World Coal and UK Energy Policy"; Ekawan and Duchene, "Evolution of Hard Coal Trade"; Smith, "World Coal Trade."
73 Ericsson and Nilsson, "International Biofuel Trade."
74 Zakaria and Wakker, *Failing Governance*.

3 Networked Food Economy

1 Mol, *Memories van een havenarbeider*; *Algemeen Handelsblad*, July 8, 1907; Van Lente, "Machines and the Order"; Van Driel and Schot, "Radical Innovation."
2 Van Driel and De Goey, *Rotterdam Cargo Handling Technology*.
3 Betz and Thorbecke as quoted in Bosch and Van der Ham, *Twee eeuwen Rijkswaterstaat*, 86.
4 *Staatsspoorwegen* Director-General Vrolik as quoted in Van de Woud, *Een nieuwe wereld*, 316. Telecommunications: De Wit, *Telefonie in Nederland*, 83. Electricity: Van den Noort, *Licht op het GEB*. Oil: Boon, "Energy Transition."
5 As quoted in Blom, *One Hundred Years*, 46.
6 As quoted in http://tentea.ec.europa.eu/en/ten-t_projects/30_priority_projects/priority_project_5/priority_project_5.htm (accessed November 27, 2013).
7 Van der Vleuten, "Networked Nation," 86–87. The authoritative source is the Parliamentary Inquiry report Tijdelijke Commissie Infrastructuur, *Reconstructie Betuweroute*.
8 Castells, *Network Society*; Ribeill, "Les 'Services agricoles' des grands réseaux"; Vahrenkamp, *Logistic Revolution*; Van der Vleuten, "Networking Technology, Society, Nature."
9 Disco, "Taming the Rhine"; Klemann and Wielenga, *Deutschland und die Niederlande*; Davids, "Fabric of Production."
10 Brunet, *Villes Européennes*; Brunet, "Lignes de force"; Hospers, "Beyond the Blue Banana?"

11 As quoted in Heywood, *Modernising Lenin's Russia*, 56.
12 Hughes, *Networks of Power*, 289–91, 319–23, 350–62; Millward and Singleton, *Political Economy of Nationalization*; Millward, *Private and Public Enterprise*.
13 Economic Commision for Europe, *Fifteen Years of Activity*, 2.
14 Rostow, "Economic Commission for Europe"; Wightman, *Economic Co-operation in Europe*, 11–51; Berthelot, "Unity and Diversity"; Berthelot and Rayment, "ECE: Bridge between East and West."
15 Michael Hoffman in *New York Times Magazine*, September 12, 1948, as quoted in Blomkvist, "Roads for Flow," 173.
16 Myrdal, "Twenty Years," 625. Economic Commision for Europe, *Fifteen Years of Activity*, 50–51; Wightman, *Economic Co-operation*, 155–56.
17 On the League: Schipper et al., "New Connections for an Old Continent." On *Grossraumrechnik*: Maier, "Systems Connected"; Janac, *European Coasts of Bohemia*; Wagner, *Grossraumtechnik*.
18 OEEC, *Europe's Growing Needs*, 15.
19 Kapitonov, "Important Instrument of the CMEA," 113; Kapitonov, "CMEA: A New Sphere," 41; Grant-Friedman, "Standing in the Mirror." For the tensions between nationalism and internationalism in energy compare Hristov, *Communist Nuclear Era*.
20 Emphasis added. Myrdal, "Twenty Years," 626. Schot and Schipper, "Experts and European Transport Integration"; Laborie, "A Missing Link?"; Van der Vleuten and Lagendijk, "Interpreting Transnational Infrastructure Vulnerability"; Padgett, "Single European Energy Market," 56.
21 On food transitions: Grigg, "Nutritional Transition"; Grigg, "Changing Geography of World Food Consumption"; Oddy and Petráňová, "Diffusion of Food Culture." Health: Livi Bacci, *Population of Europe*; Kim, "Nutrition and the Decline of Mortality"; Muraskin, "Nutrition and Mortality Decline"; Fogel, *Escape from Hunger*.
22 Oldenziel and Hård, *Consumers, Tinkerers, Rebels*.
23 Mansholt, *Over de internationale arbeidsverdeling*, as quoted in Westerveld, *Graanrepubliek*, 61. Overseas transport: Headrick, *Tentacles of Progress*; Hugill, *World Trade since 1431*. Britain: Magee and Thompson, *Empire and Globalisation*; Daunton, "Britain and Globalisation I"; Edgerton, *Britain's War Machine*, 15 and 19 (flows are measured in tonkilometer = metric tons of freight transported over 1 km); "Commonwealth Contributions to the British Diet."
24 Magee and Thompson, *Empire and Globalisation*, 17.
25 This international contract is reproduced in Friis, "International Handel med Korn." Also Eskildsen, "Danske Former for Handel."
26 Critchell and Raymond, *History of the Frozen Meat Trade*, 191.
27 Ibid., 27.
28 *The Argus*, October 30, 1879, 10.
29 De Kerbrech, *Harland & Wolff's Empire Food Ships*, 3; Edgerton, *Britain's War Machine*, 20–21.
30 Edgerton, *Britain's War Machine*, 24.
31 Thévenot, *History of Refrigeration*, 83, note 1, and 84.
32 Finstad, "Varme visjoner og frosne fremskritt," especially 51–57.
33 As quoted in Maybury-Lewis, "Genocide against Indigenous Peoples," 45. Pulley, "Railroad and Argentine National Development"; Pyenson, "Athena's Retinue."

34 Bird Rose, *Hidden Histories*, 150; Anthony, "Labour Relations on Northern Cattle Stations."
35 Thévenot, *History of Refrigeration*, 114–15 and 137–38.
36 Van der Laan, "Modern Inland Transport"; Brooks, "Peanuts and Colonialism"; Bowman, "'Legitimate Commerce'."
37 Cooper, "'Our Strike'."
38 Hogendorn and Scott, "East African Groundnut Scheme."
39 McCalla, "Protectionism in International Agricultural Trade"; Morilla Critz et al., "'Horn of Plenty'," 337.
40 As quoted in Aldenhoff-Hübinger, "Agrarhandel zwischen Integration," 199.
41 Daunton, "Britain and Globalisation since 1850 II"; Westerman, *Graanrepubliek*, 91–92; Berend, "Failure of Economic Nationalism."
42 Conservative estimates speak of at least 20 million deaths from starvation, malnutrition, and associated diseases, and a similar number of military deaths (including soldiers starving while fighting). Collingham, *Taste of War*, 28–29 and 514, note 5.
43 Economic Commission for Europe, *Ten Years of Agricultural Trade*, 4–5. Johnson, "Some International Angles."
44 The 1945 MALM report as quoted in Homberg, "Public Health, National Security," 207. Also: Jörgensen, "Neutrality and National Preparedness."
45 Robbins, *Famine in Russia*; Robbins, "Russia's System of Food"; Smith, "Bread for the Russians."
46 Cited in Heywood, *Modernizing Lenin's Russia*, 49.
47 On famines: Davies et al., "Stalin, Grain Stocks, and the Famine"; Kuromiya, "Soviet Famine"; Fisher, *Famine in Soviet Russia*. For documents on the 1932-3 famine see: http://www.rusarchives.ru/publication/famine/famine-ussr.pdf (accessed 25 August 2011). On food system-building: Thévenot, *History of Refrigeration*; Chossudowsky, "Rationing in the USSR"; Goldman, "Marketing Structure in the Soviet Union"; Taylor, "Problems of Food Supply Logistics."
48 Domestic food system-building: De la Bruhèze and Van Otterloo, "Milky Way"; Van der Vleuten, "Networked Nation," 97–101. Retail: Van Reenen, *Afzetorganisatie van de Nederlandse tuinbouw*; Vermeulen and Van Helvoort-Segerink, *75 jaar Spar* (with English summary); Van de Plassche, "Betekenis van het wegennet"; Priester, "Melkveehouderijbedrijf." National diet: Jobse-van Putten, *Eenvoudig maar voedzaam*.
49 Orland, "Milky Ways"; Thévenot, *History of Refrigeration*; Stoilova, "Bulgarian Yogurt."
50 Collingham, *Taste of War*, 37–38 and 180–81.
51 In reality Churchill refused food aid to all but the Greeks until his American colleagues convinced him otherwise. Quotation: Collingham, *Taste of War*, 152. Also: Mukerjee, *Churchill's Secret War*.
52 Thévenot, *History of Refrigeration*; Finstad, "Varme visioner og frosne fremskritt," 137–57; Wos, "Economie et organisation"; Fleck, "Evolution de l'économie agricole"; Komlo, "Révolution agraire et industrialisation"; O'Hagan, "National Self-Sufficiency in Food"; Emilya Karaboeva, personal communication.
53 Economic Commision for Europe, *Ten Years of Agricultural Trade*. Calculated as the ratio of accumulated domestic production and accumulated national

food availability (production + net imports) in weight% or value%. The UN ECE used membership of the OEEC as a proxy for the category "Western Europe."

54 Secretariat of the Economic Commission for Europe, "Survey on Transport of Perishable Foodstuffs," UNECE Archives, G.IX 13/5/1/7, Box 1338, Index 6567. Also: Van der Vleuten, "Feeding the Peoples of Europe."
55 Ibid., Annex 2, p. 2.
56 Inland Transport Committee, "Transport of Perishable Foodstuffs. Resolution No. 18." UNECE Archives, G.IX 13/5/1/1, Box 1337, Index 3323.
57 ECE Secretariat, "Review of the Working Party's Programme," UNECE Archives, G.IX 13/5/2/2 Box 1342, Index 6688.
58 Economic Commision for Europe, *Fifteen Years of Activity*, 44; *Agreement on International Carriage*; *Agreement on the International Carriage (2003 Amendment)*, 73, 81.
59 "Transfrigoroute Europe," UNECE Archives, G.IX 13/5/2/11, Box 1345, Index 13106; Rohen, *50 Years of Transfrigoroute*.
60 Economic Commision for Europe, *Agricultural Trade in Europe*, 54; Grigg, "Food Consumption." For changes in national food balance sheets see the FAO historical database (http://faostat.fao.org/site/368/default.aspx#ancor).
61 Economic Commision for Europe, *Ten Years of Agricultural Trade*, 13. Greece: Tsaglioti, "Infrastructuring Europe: Report No. 1," 3 and 24.
62 Economic Commision for Europe, *Ten Years of Agricultural Trade*, 6–8. Compare Deutsch, *The Food Revolution*.
63 Emilya Karaboeva, personal communication.
64 In value%. For East-Central Europe precise numbers lacked. Economic Commision for Europe, *Ten Years of Agricultural Trade*, 12–15; Economic Commision for Europe, *Agricultural Trade. Volume II*, 40–43.
65 Westerveld, *Graanrepubliek*, 161; Van Merriënboer, *Mansholt*. On the CAP: Thiemeyer, "Failure of the Green Pool"; Patel, "Paradefall der Integration?"; Patel and Schot, "Twisted Paths to European Integration."
66 For example:, Directives 88/128/EEC; 89/108/EEC, 92/1/EEC, and 92/2/EEC; *Control of the Cold Chain*; Van der Vleuten, "Feeding the Peoples of Europe"; "Frigoscandia Leads the Way in European Frozen Food Logistics," *Quick Frozen Foods International*, January 2000; *Guide to Refrigerated Transport*.
67 Mansholt cited in Westerveld, *Graanrepubliek*, 31; Economic Commision for Europe, *Agricultural Trade. Volume II*, 16 and 51.
68 Despite its image as the most integrated economy of the world, Nitsch found in 2000 that an average EU country exports seven to ten times more to itself than to a partner country (the so-called "home bias"). Nitsch, "National Borders"; Head and Mayer, "Non-Europe."
69 As quoted in Westerveld, *Graanrepubliek*, 228.
70 Rempe, "Airy Promises"; Rempe, "Fit für den Weltmarkt."

4 Factory & Finance

1 Schröter, *Friedrich Engelhorn*.
2 The company's founding document as quoted in Abelshauser et al., *German Industry and Global Enterprise*, 12. Perkin: Robinson, "Sir William Henry Perkin"; Travis, "Perkin's Mauve."

3   As quoted in Abelshauser, *German Industry and Global Enterprise*, 5. A detailed survey of Europe's chemical activity in 1900 is Witt, *Chemische Industrie*.
4   Count Corti, *Magician of Homburg and Monte Carlo*.
5   MP Fulchiron as quoted in Flichy, "Birth of Long Distance Communication," 98.
6   As quoted in Count Corti, *Magician of Homburg and Monte Carlo*, 24. Also: Smith, *Monaco and Monte Carlo*, 285–86.
7   For studying industry not as factories, but as geographically-extended Large Technical Systems see: Hughes, *American Genesis*, 184–249; Davids, "Fabric of Production."
8   Data from Abelshauser et al., *German Industry and Global Enterprise*. Ludwigshafen: Roggersdorf, *Im Reiche der Chemie*; *BASF 1865–1965*.
9   Ibid.; Harris, "Ruhr Coal-Mining District," 215–18; Banken, *Industrialisierung der Saarregion*, 141–6; Aftalion, *History of the International Chemical Industry*, 47; Richardson, "Development of the British Dyestuffs Industry," 112; Scherzer, "Fortschritt der Erdgasversorgung."
10 Roggersdorf, *Im Reiche der Chemie*; Abelshauser et al., *German Industry and Global Enterprise*; Chandler, *Shaping the Industrial Century*, 116; Morris and Travis, "History of the International Dyestuff Industry"; Aftalion, *History of the International Chemical Industry*; Richardson, "Development of the British Dyestuffs Industry."
11 Richardson, "Development of the British Dyestuffs Industry"; Hopkins, "Chemical Industry and Trade of England"; Reed, "British Chemical Industry."
12 Richardson, "Development of the British Dyestuffs Industry," 120. Other national system-building: Morris and Travis, "History of the International Dyestuffs Industry"; Hopkins, "Chemical Industry and Trade of France"; Langlinay, "Kuhlmann at War 1914–1921"; Conti, "Development of the Chemical Industry in Italy"; Dobb, "Soviet Agriculture and Chemical Industry"; Kragh and Styhr Petersen, *En nyttig videnskab*; Homburg, "Eerste Wereldoorlog"; Hopkins, "Chemical Industry and Trade of Switzerland"; Simon, "Rise of the Swiss Chemical Industry."
13 As quoted in Richardson, "Development of the British Dyestuffs Industry," 119.
14 Royal Dutch/Shell director Colijn as quoted (in English) in Homburg, "Operating on Several Fronts," 136. Also: Homburg, "Explosives from Oil."
15 For the BASF negotiations and the full quote see: Jonker et al., *History of Royal Dutch Shell, Vol. 1*, chapter 6. Shell in America: Beaton, *Enterprise in Oil*, 502–53.
16 Schröter, "Cartels as a Form of Concentration," 124. Also: Schröter, "International Dyestuffs Cartel 1927–39"; Woolcock, "International Dyestuffs Situation"; Haynes, "Cartels and Consolidations"; Schröter, "German Question"; Schröter, "Risk and Control in Multinational Enterprise."
17 Welsch, *Geschichte der chemischen Industrie*; Sagers and Shabad, *Chemical Industry in the USSR*.
18 Czechoslovakian analyst Peter Kolar (Radio Free Europe Evaluation and Analysis Department), as quoted in "Background Research: The Comecon Pipeline," September 6, 1960, Open Society Archives, Radio Free Europe/Radio Liberty, fond HU-OSA-300-8-3, file 122-1-92. Available at http://www.

osaarchivum.org (accessed October 6, 2011). On USSR gas and petrochemical policy: Sladkov, "Chemistry and the Building of Communism"; Dienes, "Natural Gas Industry of the USSR."

19 *Pravda*, December 19, 1963, as quoted in Mayevsky, "Chemistry and Politics," 34. See also: Khimii, "Chemistry and the Building of Communism."

20 Belarus: "Hard-Pressed Soviet Pipeliners Head for Ever Tougher Tasks," *Oil and Gas Journal*, June 21, 1965, 120–23; "First Unit in Soviet Plant Open," *Oil and Gas Journal*, March 25, 1963, 86; "Russia's Pipeline Plans Limping Behind Schedule," *Oil and Gas Journal*, October 26, 1964, 82. Poland: "Soviet Line to Feed Satellite Refineries," *Oil and Gas Journal*, June 27, 1960, 94–95. GDR and Czechoslovakia: Welsch, *Geschichte der chemischen Industrie*, 187–93. Hungary: "New Pipeline Gives Russian Crude Easier Access to Europe," *Oil and Gas Journal*, October 29, 1962, 124, and "Hard-Pressed Soviet Pipeliners Head for Ever Tougher Tasks," *Oil and Gas Journal*, June 21, 1965, 120–23; "Hungary Approves Refinery, Pipelines," *Oil and Gas Journal*, November 27, 1972, 52.

21 *Oil and Gas Journal*, August 11, 1958, 126, and March 30, 1959, 111. Also, western Ukrainian gas was piped to a nitrogenous fertilizer production complex at Pulawy, Poland. *Oil and Gas Journal*, 18 October 1965, 67. "Hungary Opens Purse to Hike Industry," *Oil and Gas Journal*, September 14, 1970, 48–49; Sagers and Shabad, *Chemical Industry in the USSR*.

22 As quoted in Harry Trend, "RFE/RL Background Reports: Projected Comecon Ethylene Pipeline Network," November 8, 1971, Open Society Archives, Radio Free Europe/Radio Liberty, fond HU-OSA-300-8-3, file 125-5-51, 6–7. Available at http://www.osaarchivum.org/greenfield/repository/osa: 98133 4e2-104b-454e-b389-768b1316342e (accessed October 6, 2011). Also: "Czechs Start Work on 280-Mile Extension to Comecon System," *Oil and Gas Journal*, April 8, 1963, 65.

23 "Western Europe Expands on All Fronts," *Oil and Gas Journal*, October 31, 1960, 78–79; Wever, "Olieraffinaderij en petrochemische industrie."

24 Blom, *One Hundred Years of Shell Pernis*; Van Zanden et al., *History of Royal Dutch Shell, Vol. 2*, chapter 4; Homburg et al., "Industrialisatie en industriecomplexen."

25 Timm as quoted in Abelshauser et al., *German Industry and Global Enterprise*, 485.

26 *Oil and Gas Journal*, December 29, 1958, 109; "Rhine Valley Gets More Crude," *Oil and Gas Journal*, July 18, 1960, 84; "Trans-Europe Crude Line Considered," *Oil and Gas Journal*, July 16, 1956, 76; "Big Inch Crude Line Approved," *Oil and Gas Journal*, March 23, 1959, 71; "Big Inch Line to Serve Expanding Markets in Europe," *Oil and Gas Journal*, February 12, 1962, 94–95; Boon, "Energy Transition"; "Groningen Gas Beating on Swiss Door," *Oil and Gas Journal*, October 28, 1968, 58–59; *Oil and Gas Journal*, October 5, 1959, 120; "German Oil, Chemical Firms to Merge," *Oil and Gas Journal*, November 11, 1968, 114; "W. Germany Due to Shift to Gas," *Oil and Gas Journal*, November 25, 1968, 48; "Product Line to Serve Big German Plant," *Oil and Gas Journal*, December 21, 1964, 64; "European Ethylene Network Shaping Up," *Oil and Gas Journal*, August 26, 1968, 76.

27 Molle and Wever, "Oil Refineries and Petrochemical Industries."

28 Finland: "Finland Builds Its Petrochem Industry," *Oil and Gas Journal*, December 4, 1972, 53–55. Yugoslavia: Zdenko Antic, "Green Light for

Yugoslav-Hungarian Pipeline," RFE/RL Background Reports, July 9, 1973, Open Society Archives, Radio Free Europe/Radio Liberty, fond HU-OSA-300-8-3, box 35-4-273. Pappas: Tsaglioti, "Infrastructuring Europe: Report No. 2." Soviet exports: "Export Commitments Are the Key to Twin Soviet Petrochem Complexes," *Oil and Gas Journal*, October 10, 1977, 86–87.

29 Economic Commission for Europe, *East–West Trade in Chemical Products*, 4.
30 Association of Petrochemicals Producers in Europe, "Trans European Olefins Pipeline Network"; European Parliament, "Amendments 19-49," April 1, 2005, PE 355.761v01-00; "Olefins Pipeline under Scrutiny," ICIS.com, April 4, 2005; European Commission, *Energy Infrastructure Priorities*, 8.
31 Huebner, "Scope and Functions," 483.
32 Plotnikov, "Certain Problems of the Development of Finance," 36. Western companies: Da Rin, "Finance and the Chemical Industry."
33 Michie, *Global Securities Market*; Michie, *London Stock Exchange*, 89; Killick and Thomas, "Provincial Stock Exchanges."
34 Interviews of German financial experts as quoted in Meier, "Working in the Skyline," 123; Wenzlhuemer, "Metropolitan Telecommunication."
35 For the following: Michie, *London Stock Exchange*; Michie, "Friend or Foe?"; Michie, "London Stock Exchange"; Michie, "London and New York Stock Exchanges"; Nalbach, "'Poisoned at the Source'?"; Beauchamp, *History of Telegraphy*, 80.
36 Michie, *London Stock Exchange*.
37 Huebner, "Scope and Functions," 489. Michie, *Global Securities Market*, 136 identifies 53 exchanges in Europe (excluding Constantinople), 16 in North America, 10 in Latin America, 11 in Africa, 14 in Asia, and 15 in Australasia.
38 Figure in the previous paragraphs: Michie, *London Stock Exchange*, 4 and *Global Securities Market*, 132–3. See also: Michie, *Global Securities Market*, chapters 4 and 5; Cassis, *Capitals of Capital*; Hermans and De Wit, "Bourses and Brokers."
39 Michie, *London Stock Exchange*, 4 and *Global Securities Market*, 132–3.. For communication infrastructure inequalities: Wenzlhuemer, "Dematerialization of Telecommunication"; Wenzlhuemer, "Metropolitan Telecommunication."
40 Huebner, "Scope and Functions," 500.
41 As quoted in Michie, *London Stock Exchange*, 135. The contagion classic is Kindleberger and Aliber, *Manias, Panics, and Crashes*. For the stability argument: Michie, *London Stock Exchange*, 52; Michie, *Global Securities Market*, 3; Marate, "Contagion Effects"; Eichengreen and Bordo, "Crises Now and Then," 40, table 5; Ferguson, "Political Risk and International Bond Market." 1907 Panic: Richie, *Global Securities Market*, 154.
42 Michie, *Global Securities Market*, chapter 6; Ferguson, "Political Risk and International Bond Market."
43 White, "Stock Market Boom and Crash," 80, figure 6. Depression: Clavin, *Great Depression in Europe*.
44 Chamberlain as quoted in Michie, *London Stock Exchange*, 183. Monetary policy and crises: Eichengreen, *Globalizing Capital*; Eichengreen, *Capital Flows and Crises*.
45 Eichengreen and Bordo, "Crises Now and Then," 40–41 (Tables 5–6). Banking innovation: Bonhage, "Eurocheque." Compare lagging banking innovation

in the nineteenth century as discussed in Mooij, "History of International Financial Communications"; Michie, "One World or Many Worlds?"
46 Michie, *Global Securities Trade*, chapters 6 and 7.
47 Ibid. On financial news and trading communications: Office of Technology Assessment, *Trading Around the Clock*.
48 Cited in Clemons and Weber, "London's Big Bang," 237–38. On Paris: ibid., 237, note 9.
49 HM Treasury, "Note on LSE Paper," February 9, 1988. Disclosed on www.hm-treasury.gov.uk/foi_stock1987_290605.htm (accessed January 25, 2012).
50 As quoted in Bozzo, "Players Replay the Crash." Also: Rochlin, *Trapped in the Net*, 75; Arshanapalli and Doukas, "International Stock Market Linkages"; Shiller et al., "Investor Behavior"; Yang and Bessler, "Contagion"; *Resolving the Global Economic Crisis*; Michie, *Global Securities Trade*, 294; Office of Technology Assessment, *Trading Around the Clock*.
51 Michie, *Global Securities Trade*; Lesova, "In Russia." Government monetary policy: Eichengreen, *Globalizing Capital*.
52 Cited from Tirez, "Easdaq Benefits from European Framework." On EASDAQ and other NASDAQ copycats: Weber and Posner, "Creating a Pan-European Equity Market"; Abbanat, *Feasibility Study*; Posner, *Origins of Europe's New Stock Markets*. Investment Services Directive: Warren, "European Union's Investment Services Directive."
53 Posner, *Origins of Europe's New Stock Markets*.
54 Stäheli, "Inklusionsmedier der Börsenkommunikation."
55 Cited in Abbanat, *Feasibility Study*, 22.
56 Schaller as quoted in Launder, "No Urge to Merge." See also: Dunkley, "Pan-Europe vs. the Nationals"; Kaszuba, "East and Central Europe Stock Exchange Markets"; Engelen and Grote, "Stock Exchange Virtualisation"; Belgrade: Vuksanović, "Information System of Stock Exchange Market"; Reszat, *European Financial Systems*, 83–92; Wójcik, "Geography and the Future of Stock Exchanges."
57 Joseph M. Mecane as quoted in Duhigg, "Stock Traders Find Speed Pays."
58 *Findings Regarding the Market Events*.
59 Stiglitz as quoted in Spicer, "Special Report"; Jouyet as quoted in Brunsden, "EU Should Toughen High-Frequency Trade Proposals"; Haldane, "The Race to Zero."
60 Quotes from: CME Group, "What Happened"; Corkery, "Jim Simons on Flash Crash."
61 Sarkozy as quoted in "Sarkozy's Shock Tax on Share Trading"; Cliff and Northrop, *Global Financial Markets*.

5 Logistics of War

1 Mombauer, *Helmuth von Moltke*, 222.
2 Ibid., 219–22; see also: Tuchman, *Guns of August*, 87–99.
3 Mombauer, *Helmuth von Moltke*, 224.
4 Bucholz, *Moltke, Schlieffen and Prussian War Planning*, 278.
5 Westwood, *Railways at War*, chapter 5.
6 See, for example, Van Creveld, *Supplying War*; Lynn, *Feeding Mars*; McNeill, *Pursuit of Power*; Howard, *War in European History*.

7   Westwood, *Railways at War*, 6; Pratt, *Rise of Rail-Power in War and Conquest*, 8; Showalter, "Soldiers into Postmasters?"
8   Wolmar, *Engines of War*, 22–29.
9   Showalter, *Railroads and Rifles*; Bucholz, *Moltke and the German Wars*; Westwood, *Railways at War*, 57–58.
10 Showalter, *Railroads and Rifles*, 38–39; Van Creveld, *Supplying War*, 67; Mitchell, *Great Train Race*, 65.
11 Van Creveld, *Supplying War*, 89–96.
12 Doughty, "French Strategy in 1914."
13 Harkavy, *Strategic Basing and the Great Powers*, 44–51; Headrick, *Tools of Empire*, 43–54, and 196–99.
14 Harkavy, *Strategic Basing and the Great Powers*, 55; Tetsuro Sumida, "British Naval Operational Logistics," 460–61.
15 Headrick, *Tenctacles of Progress*, 63.
16 Ibid., 65–66.
17 Kennedy, "Imperial Cable Communications and Strategy"; Kennedy, *Rise and Fall of British Naval Mastery*, 206.
18 Bucholz, *Moltke, Schlieffen and Prussian War Planning*; Evera, "Cult of the Offensive."
19 Van Creveld, *Supplying War*, 125. An often-told story about the battle of Marne is how a fleet of 600 Parisian taxicabs were used for transporting 6,000 men to the front at a crucial point of the battle. This story exaggerates the role of the motor car for the French victory; the overwhelming majority of French soldiers traveled by train.
20 Wolmar, *Engines of War*, 186.
21 Ibid.; Howard, *War in European History*, 116.
22 McNeill, *Pursuit of Power*, 317–28.
23 Ibid., 339–40.
24 Yergin, *The Prize*, 150–64; Sumida, "British Naval Operational Logistics," 464.
25 Headrick, *Invisible Weapon*, 140–45.
26 Kennedy, *Rise and Fall of British Naval Mastery*, chapter 9.
27 Wulff, "Sweden and Clandestine German Rearmament Technology." The German officer Heinz Guderian was the most elaborate proponent of fast "mechanized" warfare, presenting his ideas in his 1938 book *Achtung—Panzer!*.
28 Douhet, *Command of the Air*, 22.
29 Budiansky, *Air Power*, 200–214.
30 Lidell Hart, *History of the Second World War*, chapter 3.
31 This section is based on the following literature: Appel, *Finland i krig*; Meinander, *Finlands historia, del 4*; Trotter, *Frozen Hell*; Siilasvuo, *Striderna i Suomussalmi*; Järvinen, *Finsk och rysk taktik under vinterkriget*; Van Dyke, *Soviet Invasion of Finland 1939–40*.
32 The Finnish soldiers killed in the war were, whenever possible, brought home to be buried in their local cemetery. This was a considerable logistic effort but contributed significantly to morale.
33 Siilasvuo's book, *Striderna i Suomussalmi*, gives accounts of his assessments and considerations. This book is, of course, literally the winner's history. See also: Järvinen, *Finsk och rysk taktik*, 240–41.
34 Trotter, *Frozen Hell*, 152.

35 Bellamy, *Absolute War*; Lidell Hart, *History of the Second World War*; Van Creveld, *Supplying War*; Kennedy, *Engineers of Victory*; Stahel, *Operation Barbarossa*.
36 Stahel, *Operation Barbarossa*, 136, 248, and 332–33; Van Creveld, *Supplying War*, 157.
37 Van Creveld, *Supplying War*, 155–74.
38 Kennedy, *Engineers of Victory*, 197.
39 Ibid., 85.
40 Rose, "Radar and Air Defense," 224.
41 Brown, *Radar History*, 63; Kirby, *Operational Research*, 80; Gough, *Watching the Skies*, chapter 1.
42 Kennedy, *Engineers of Victory*, 88–99.
43 Brown, *Radar History*, 114–15.
44 Ibid., 116–19; Gough, *Watching the Skies*, 10–13.
45 Brown, *Radar History*, 116. R.V. Jones was a key British actor in this electronic war and has written a fascinating book about it, *Most Secret War*.
46 Jones, *Most Secret War*, chapter 27; Gough, *Watching the Skies*, 19–20.
47 Payton-Smith, *Oil*, 65–69.
48 Ibid., 332–35.
49 Of particular importance was the combination of U.S. Mustang fighters with British Rolls-Royce engines, resulting in an energy efficient and fast aircraft, see Kennedy, *Engineers of Victory*, 120–30.
50 Ibid., 137; Edgerton, *Britain's War Machine*, 285 and 379.
51 Edgerton, *Britain's War Machine*, chapters 2 and 3.
52 Padfield, *War Beneath the Sea*, chapter 4; Kennedy, *Engineers of Victory*, chapter 1.
53 Kennedy, *Engineers of Victory*, chapter 1; Lidell Hart, *History of the Second World War*, chapter 24.
54 Tazelaar points at a particularly cruel aspect of the convoy warfare; when one ship was hit the other ships in the convoy were not allowed to assist it as this would make them easy targets for the U-boats. This was in sharp contradiction with traditional seamen ethics. Danish author Casper Jensen writes about this conflict in his novel *We, the Drowned*.
55 The interview with Tazelaar was done within a Dutch oral history project "Getuigenverhalen," see www.getuigenverhalen.nl (accessed November 15, 2010).
56 Edgerton, *Britain's War Machine*, 163.
57 Kennedy, *Engineers of Victory*, chapter 1; Lidell Hart, *History of the Second World War*, chapter 24.
58 Kennedy, *Engineers of Victory*, chapter 4; Lidell Hart, *History of the Second World War*, chapter 31.
59 Yergin, *The Prize*, 384–88; Lidell Hart, *History of the Second World War*, 562 and 567.
60 Mazower, *Dark Continent*, 167–84; *Hitlers Table Talk 1941–1944*, 24.
61 Hilberg, "German Railroads/Jewish Souls"; Mierzejewski, *Most Valuable Asset of the Reich*, 115–26; Mierzejewski, "A Public Enterprise in the Service of Mass Murder"; Gottwald, "'Logistik des Holocaust'."
62 Mierzejewski, *Most Valuable Asset of the Reich*, 115–26.
63 Mazower, *Dark Continent*, 170–84; "The Minutes from the Wannsee Conference, January 20, 1942," as translated for the Nuremberg trials and adapted for

publication at http://www.holocaustresearchproject.org/holoprelude/Wannsee/wanseeminutes.html (accessed January 9, 2014).
64 Clay Large, "Great Rescue."
65 Ibid.
66 Judt, *Post War*, 146–49.
67 Wilkes and Gleditsch, *Loran-C and Omega*, 5–8.
68 Gough, *Watching the Skies*, 230–7.
69 Ibid.
70 Mastny and Byrne, *Cardboard Castle?*, xxvi.
71 Baev, "Organizational and Doctrinal Evolution," 5.
72 Ibid., 6.
73 Germuska, "Logistics and Infrastructures in the Warsaw Pact."
74 This air force became the fourth largest in the world by the end of the 1950s, largely consisting of aircraft produced domestically by SAAB.
75 Gribbe, *Stril 60*.
76 Ibid.
77 MacKenzie, *Inventing Accuracy*, 136; Bruzelius, *Polaris and Scandinavia*, 45–54.
78 As quoted in Bruzelius, *Polaris and Scandinavia*, 51; MacKenzie, *Inventing Accuracy*, 149–50.
79 MacKenzie, *Inventing Accuracy*, 143–44.
80 Wilkes and Gleditsch, *Loran-C and Omega*, chapter 12.
81 Ibid.
82 Bruzelius, *Polaris and Scandinavia*, 104–5; Wilkes and Gleditsch, *Loran-C and Omega*, chapter 12.
83 Bruzelius, *Polaris and Scandinavia*, 98 and 108.
84 Egilsson, "Origins, Use and Development of Hot Line Diplomacy."
85 Ibid.
86 Ibid.
87 Fall, *Hell in a Very Small Place*.
88 Ibid., chapter 1; Windrow, *Last Valley*, chapter 7.
89 Fall, *Hell in a Very Small Place*, 125–33. This art of building and maintaining roads and trails resilient to air attacks became of crucial importance also in the Second Indochina War when the so-called Ho Chi Minh trail became a lifeline for supplies from North to South Vietnam, see: Kane, *Military Logistics and Strategic Performance*, chapter 4.
90 Fall, *Hell in a Very Small Place*, chapters 5–11.
91 Abernethy, *Dynamics of Global Dominance*, 153–57.
92 Ibid., 148.
93 As quoted in Kennedy, *Rise and Fall of British Naval Mastery*, 206.
94 Harkavy, *Bases Abroad*, chapter 10.
95 Webb, "Continued Importance of Geographic Distance."
96 Mazower, *Dark Continent*, 396–97.
97 Ibid., 399.

6 Linking Land

1 Richter, *Brocken*; Schmidt and Korsch, *Brocken*.
2 As quoted in "Ein Dolchstoss ins Herz," *Der Spiegel* 34/1991, 80. On nature and nature management in the Harz region: Genath, *"Es geht fast täglich,"* 89–130.

3   As quoted in Schmidt and Korsch, *Brocken*, 66 (our translation). On Romantic experiences of Brocken nature: Köhler-Zülch, "Hans Christian Andersen und die Harzer Sagentopographie."
4   As quoted in Richter, *Brocken*, 152. On television: Dittmar, "GDR Television in Competition."
5   Ibid. and Acker et al., "MT. Brocken, a Site for a Cloud Chemistry Measurement Programme"; Terry et al., *Green Belt of Europe*.
6   As quoted in "Ein Dolchstoss ins Herz," *Der Spiegel* 34/1991, 84.
7   Zeller, *Driving Germany*; Ciocl et al., *How Green Were the Nazis?*.
8   As quoted in in Biggs, "Putting the State on the Map," 385. Branch, "Mapping the Sovereign State"; Brown, *Story of Maps*.
9   Stone, "Imperialism, Colonialism and Cartography"; Kalpagam, "Cartography in Colonial India"; Edney, *Mapping an Empire*; Collier, "Colonial Survey Committee"; Biltcliffe, "Walter Crane and the Imperial Federation Map"; Driver, "In Search of the Imperial Map."
10 Batten, *Resolute and Undertaking Characters*; Smith, "Struve Geodetic Arc"; Viik and Randjärv, "How Struve and Tenner Started the Work of Their Life."
11 As quoted (in English) in Levallois, "History of the International Association of Geodesy," 249. See also: Baeyer, "Entwurf zu einer mitteleuropäischen Gradmessung"; Baeyer, *Über die Grösse und Figur der Erde*; Torge, *Geschichte der Geodäsie in Deutschland*; Angus-Leppan, "Note on the History of the International Association of Geodesy"; Ádám, "Update of the History of the International Association of Geodesy."
12 As quoted in Fedman, "Triangulating Chōsen"; Collier, "International Boundary Surveys"; Branch, "Mapping the Sovereign State."
13 Hough, "Adjustment of the Central European Triangulation Network," 64.
14 Cited in Warner, "Political Geodesy," 368. Doel, "Constituting the Postwar Earth Sciences."
15 Whitten, "Adjustment of European Triangulation"; Simonsen, "Remarks on the Calculation"; Weber, "European Triangulation Net South East"; Ihde, "Some Remarks on Geodetic Reference Systems."
16 Disco, *60 Years of ITC*; Berkers, *De aarde verdeeld*, 154–57; Cousins and Ihse, "Methodological Study."
17 Adam et al., "European Reference System"; Greaves and Cruddace, "Adoption of ETRS89"; Pace et al., *Global Positioning System*.
18 Cited in Disco, *60 Years of ITC*, 37.
19 Contzen, "Benefit of Remote Sensing Activities"; Briggs, "Integrating Land Resource Data"; Commission of the European Communities, *Results of the CORINE program*; Feranec et al., "Corine Land Cover Change Detection."
20 In the *Pan-European Land Cover Monitoring* (PELCOM) project, Alterra coordinated a land cover information system explicitly on a pan-European scale; Meteo-France hosted the International Geosphere and Biosphere Programme's *Data and Information System* (in 2001 transferred to the International Water Management Institute's Global Irrigated Area Map). European Environment Agency, *Thematic Accuracy of Corine*; Mücher, "Geo-Spatial Modelling and Monitoring."
21 European Environment Agency, *European Environment*; European Environment Agency, *Landscape Fragmentation*.
22 As quoted in Graham and Marvin, *Splintering Urbanism*, 55. Tarr and Dupuy, *Technology and the Rise of the Networked City*; Hård and Misa, *Urban Machinery*.

23 Demirakın, "Study of Ottoman Modernisation"; Dinçal, "Arenas of Experimentation." Buiter, "Constructing Dutch Streets"; Graham and Marvin, *Splintering Urbanism*; Coutard, "Placing Splintering Urbanism."
24 Saunier, "Sketches from the Urban Internationale."
25 Germuska, "Between Theory and Practice"; Jajeśnak-Quast, "In the Shadow of the Factory"; Lundin, "Mediators of Modernity"; Kasanko et al., "Are European Cities Becoming Dispersed?"; Turok and Mykhnenko, "Trajectories of European Cities"; Næs, "Urban Planning and Sustainable Development."
26 Pumain, "An Implicit Large Territorial-Technical System."
27 De Vries and Van der Woude, *First Modern Economy*; Van der Vleuten, "Networked Nation," 87; Disco, "Taming the Rhine"; Bruinsma and Rietveld, "Urban Agglomerations in European Infrastructure"; Dupuy and Stransky, "Cities and Highway Networks in Europe."
28 Brunet, *Villes Européennes*, 6. See also: Brunet, "Lignes de force de léspace Europeén"; Hospers, "Beyond the Blue Banana?"
29 De Block, "Engineering the Territory," 169; De Block and Polasky, "Light Railways and the Rural-Urban Continuum."
30 De Block, "Engineering the Territory," 157.
31 Mander and Palang, "Changes of Landscape Structure in Estonia"; Agnoletti, "Degradation of Traditional Landscape"; Meeus et al., "Agricultural Landscapes in Europe"; Stoate et al., "Ecological Impacts of Arable Intensification"; Plieninger et al., "Traditional Land-Use and Nature Conservation."
32 Gómes Mendoza and Ortega Cantero, "Hydraulics and Forestry in Spain"; Pinilla, "Development of Irrigated Agriculture"; Clar and Vicente, "Path Dependence and the Modernisation of Agriculture."
33 Lüttichau, "Opdyrkning af heden og moser."
34 There were 375,000 km of drainage pipes compared with 135,000 km of public roads. Driessen, *Waardebepaling kleine ondergrondse infrastructuur*. See also: Van de Ven, *Man-Made Lowlands*, 211–26; Commission of the European Communities, *State of the Environment*, 111.
35 Westerman, *De graanrepubliek*, 173; Commission of the European Communities, *State of the Environment*, 100; Van Dijk, "Scenarios of Central European Land Fragmentation."
36 Komarov, "Destruction of Nature"; Josephson, *Industrialized Nature*, 109 and 122–24.
37 Commission of the European Communities, *State of the Environment*, 96.
38 Mather and Fairbairn, "From Floods to Reforestation."
39 Kouki et al., "Forest Fragmentation in Fennoscandia"; Ericsson et al., "Forest of Grazing and Logging"; Swedish Forest Agency, *Swedish Statistical Yearbook of Forestry*.
40 As quoted from a 1885 brochure in Ritvo, *Dawn of Green*, 121. Judy, "'Unbroken towards the Sea'."
41 Jongman, "Nature Conservation Planning in Europe"; European Environment Agency, *Green Infrastructure and Territorial Cohesion*.
42 Genath, "*Es geht fast täglich*," 63–88; Evans, *History of Nature Conservation in Britain*; Baigent, "'God's earth will be sacred'."
43 United States Congress, "Act Creating Yellowstone National Park."
44 As quoted in Isenberg, *Destruction of the Bison*, 181.
45 An 1898 National Trust report cited in Judy, "'Unbroken towards the Sea'."

46. Vig, "On Whose Shoulders We Stand"; Genath, *"Es geht fast täglich,"* 63–88; Lefeuvre, "De la protection de la nature"; Van den Belt, "Networking Nature"; Oszlányi et al., "Nature Conservation in Central and Eastern Europe"; Shtilmark, *History of the Russian Zapovedniks*; Jepson and Whittaker, "Histories of Protected Areas."
47. The plan is cited in Reeder, "Social Construction of Green Space," 65. See also: Amati and Yokohari, "Establishment of the London Green Belt"; Clark, *European City and Green Space*; Amati, *Urban Green Belts*.
48. Quotations from: Council of Europe, *European Diploma for Certain Protected Landscapes*; Council of Europe, *Convention on the Conservation of European Wildlife*. See also: IUCN, *Tenth Anniversary 1948–1958*; Jepson and Whittaker, "Histories of Protected Areas"; Rink, "Environmental Policy and the Environmental Movement"; Meyer, "L'européanisation de la politique environnementale."
49. United Nations, *Declaration of the United Nations Conference*.
50. Figures from IUCN, *2003 United Nations List of Protected Areas*, 25–26, which for the first time included areas smaller than 10 km^2 and unclassified areas.
51. House of Commons Debates, Volume 556 (July 9, 1956), p. 52, available at http://hansard.millbanksystems.com (accessed March 14, 2012). See also: Clark, *European City and Green Space*; Amati, *Urban Green Belts*.
52. Jongman, "Nature Conservation Planning in Europe"; Jongman et al., "European Ecological Networks and Greenways."
53. Sepp and Kaasik, *Development of National Ecological Networks*; Miklós, "Most Successful Landscape Ecological Concepts."
54. Mander and Palang, "Changes of Landscape Structure in Estonia," 53. See also: Sepp et al., "Prospects for Nature and Landscape Protection in Estonia"; Meier et al., "Riparian Buffer Zones"; Külvik, *Ecological Networks in Estonia*.
55. Jagomägi, "Ökoloogiliselt tasakaalustatud maa"; Aaviksoo, "Changes of Plant Cover."
56. Meier et al., "Riparian Buffer Zones."
57. Odum, "Man and Ecosystem"; Odum, "Strategy of Ecosystem Development"; Mitsch and Jørgensen, "Ecological Engineering"; IUCN, *World Conservation Strategy*.
58. Baerselman and Vera, *Nature Development*, 57. Statistics Netherlands, *Vijfenegentig jaren statistiek*, 12. Verduijn et al., "Discursive Framing and Network Strategies"; Van der Windt et al., "Valuing Nature in the Context of Planning."
59. Tweede Kamer der Staten Generaal, *Structuurschema Natuur en Landschapsbehoud*, 34.
60. Baerselman and Vera, *Nature Development*, 42.
61. As quoted in Schmit, "Landbouw dicteert meer dan ooit." See also: Verduijn et al., "Discursive Framing and Network Strategies."
62. Bennett and Mulongoy, *Review of Experience with Ecological Networks*; Jongman and Bogers, "Current Status of the Practical Implementation of Ecological Networks."
63. Baerselman and Vera, *Nature Development*, 43.
64. Wurzel, "European Union Environmental Policy."
65. As quoted in Benett and Wolters, "European Ecological Network," 16.

66 Bouwma, "Progress in the Development," 17.
67 Jongman et al., "Pan-European Ecological Network"; Remm et al. "Design of the Pan-European Ecological Network." Project overviews: Jongman, "Nature Conservation Planning in Europe"; Jongman et al., "European Ecological Networks"; Bennett, "Interaction between Policy Concerning Spatial Planning and Ecological Networks in Europe."
68 Sepp et al., "Prospects for Nature," 162; Sepp and Kaasik, *Development of National Ecological Networks*.
69 Bouwman et al., *Public Secret*; Calle et al., "De libellen"; Buček et al., "Ecological Network Creation in the Czech Republic."
70 European Environment Agency, *Landscape Fragmentation in Europe*, 13.
71 Ibid., 7 and 9.
72 Keulartz, "European Nature Conservation"; Andersen et al., *Large Predators and Human Communities*; Marijnissen, "Voorlopig liever niet te veel herten"; Van Lierop, "Zwijnen zwermen uit"; Jongman et al., "Pan-European Ecological Network," 322; Bennett, "Green Infrastructure in Europe," 14–15.
73 European Environment Agency, *10 Messages for 2010. Message 6*, 6. Biodiversity in Agriculture: Bignal and McCracken, "Low-Intensity Farming Systems"; High-Level Conference on Mapping and Assessment of Ecosystems and Their Services (MAES) in Europe, "Cropland and Grassland."

7 Troubled Waters

1 Nord Stream, "Flows through Nord Stream Line 1," November 8, 2011 (press release).
2 Ibid.
3 "Europe Is Awakening for Russia…with a Heavy Hangover," *euinside*, December 12, 2011.
4 On the Nord Stream debate: Larsson, *Nord Stream, Sweden and Baltic Sea Security*; Whist, *Nord Stream: Not Just a Pipeline*; Karm, "Environment and Energy."
5 Biswas, *History of Hydrology*, 165–202 (especially 198); Corbin, *Lure of the Sea*, 12; Magris, *Danube*; Jakobsson, "Understanding Lake Vänern."
6 Biswas, *History of Hydrology*, 208–13; Molle, "River-Basin Planning and Management," 485.
7 Gatterer, *Abriss der Geographie*; Molle, "River-Basin Planning and Management," 485. Buache defined a river basin as "the set of all slopes on which fall the waters that converge to a same river or creek."
8 Pritchard, *Confluence*, 31; Molle, "River-Basin Planning and Management," 486; Swyngedouw, "Technonatural Revolutions."
9 Maury, *Physical Geography of the Sea*, ix; Houvenaghel, "International Maritime Conference 1853," 563; Houvenaghel, "First International Conference on Oceanography," 330–36.
10 Maury, *Physical Geography of the Sea*, xi.
11 Ibid.
12 As quoted in Headrick and Griset, "Submarine Telegraph Cables," 548, and Rozwadowski, *Fathoming the Ocean*, 82–84.
13 Ibid.

14 Rozwadowski, *Fathoming the Ocean*, 92–95; Ritchie, *Admiralty Chart*, 197; Headrick and Griset, "Submarine Telegraph Cables," 547. On Sweden: Eriksson, "Kartläggarna," 115–19. On Germany: Matthäus, *Germany and the Investigation of the Baltic Sea Hydrography*.
15 Radkau, *Nature and Power*, 199; Cioc, *Rhine*, 70–71.
16 Cioc, *Rhine*, 56–60. For a comprehensive overview of modern Dutch hydraulic engineering, see: Van de Ven, *Man-Made Lowlands*.
17 As quoted in Pounds, *Historical Geography of Europe 1800–1914*, 447;
18 Ibid.
19 Chamberlain, *Regime of International Rivers*.
20 Lagendijk, "Divided Development."
21 Pounds, *Historical Geography of Europe 1800–1914*, 446–49; Cattell, "Politics of the Danube Commission," 383; Castner, "Regulierung der Donau am Eisernen Thor," 785–89; Chamberlain, *Regime of International Rivers*.
22 Cioc, *Rhine*, 58; Pounds, *Historical Geography of Europe 1800–1914*, 448.
23 Janáč, *European Coasts of Bohemia*; Cioc, *Rhine*, 56 and 60–61.
24 Cioc, *Rhine*, 68.
25 Blackbourn, *Conquest of Nature*.
26 Jakobsson, "Industrialisering av älvar"; Törnlund and Östlund, "Mobility without Wheels."
27 Weiner, *Little Corner of Freedom*, 415.
28 Josephson, *Industrialized Nature*, 19–25.
29 Ibid.; Weiner, *Little Corner of Freedom*, 415.
30 Josephson, *Industrialized Nature*, 26 and 31–34.
31 Huisman et al., "Transboundary Cooperation in Shared River Basins," 87; Cioc, *Rhine*, 67. See also: Disco, "From Sea to Shining Sea."
32 Lagendijk, "Divided Development"; Pritchard, *Confluence*; Tsaglioti, "Infrastructuring Europe: Report No. 3," 7–8.
33 Lagendijk, "Divided Development"; Fitzmaurice, *Damming the Danube*; Högselius, "Connecting East and West?"
34 Blackbourn, *Conquest of Nature*, 231–32.
35 Ibid.
36 Josephson, *Industrialized Nature*.
37 Podvig, *Russian Strategic Nuclear Forces*, 477; "Saving the Caspian," *Time*, March 17, 1975.
38 Weiner, *Little Corner of Freedom*, 414–29; Kelly et al., "Large-Scale Water Transfers in the USSR."
39 As quoted in Swyngedouw, "Technonatural Revolutions," 12.
40 Ibid.
41 Ibid.; WWF, *Tagus-Segura Water Transfer*, 1.
42 As quoted in Llamas, "Transboundary Water Resources in the Iberian Peninsula," 340.
43 Ibid., 340–42; Correia and Silva, "International Framework," 93.
44 On pre-nineteenth-century activities: Shallat, *Structures in the Stream*, 14–17.
45 Oudet, "Crisis in the Increase of Tonnage," 309.
46 Ibid., 310–12.
47 Ibid., 312; Molenaar, "End of the Sea," 186.
48 Kemp, "Coastal Navigation in the Mid-20th Century," 534; Plant, "International Traffic Separation Schemes," 136.

49 Sibthorp, *North Sea*, 47; Sohnke, "Routing in the North Sea," 386.
50 Sohnke, "Routing in the North Sea," 386–90.
51 Ibid., 385; Sibthorp, *North Sea*, 47–48.
52 Mollat du Jourdin, *Europe and the Sea*, 182–83; Levitt, *Short Bright Flash*; Kemp, "Coastal Navigation in the Mid-20th Century," 533.
53 Gall, "Atlantropa"; "Entreprenörer i politiken," *Svensk Tidskrift*, April 5, 2000.
54 Franckx, "EC Maritime Zones," 243–44; Papanicolopulu, "Note on Maritime Delimitation," 383.
55 Nowadays, "underwater production units (on the seafloor) have taken over for the surface platforms. Gone are the days when production rigs filled the North Sea." Andersen, "Changing Technology, Changing Commons," 91.
56 See, for example, Alm, "Nationell kraft och lokal motkraft."
57 "Europe Plans a North Sea Grid," *IEEE Spectrum*, March 2010, 12.
58 Andersen, "Pollution and the Chemical Industry," 186–88; Cioc, *Rhine*, 122.
59 Disco, "Accepting Father Rhine?," 389.
60 As quoted in Cioc, *Rhine*, 96; Disco, "Accepting Father Rhine?," 393.
61 Disco, "Accepting Father Rhine?," 401.
62 Huisman et al., "Transboundary Cooperation," 89; Cioc, *Rhine*, 177–79.
63 Cioc, *Rhine*, 179–80.
64 "The Rhine Struggles to Survive," *New York Times*, February 15, 1987; Huisman et al., "Transboundary Cooperation," 92; Cioc, *Rhine*, 109 and 182–83. In 1993 it was concluded that the target values had been reached for 38 substances.
65 Vink et al., "Development of the Heavy Metal Pollution Trends," 215. This negative reputation for the Elbe was a simplification, as it concerned some but not all forms of wet pollution.
66 Nachtnebel, "Danube River Basin Environmental Programme," 5.
67 Salewicz, "Management of Large International Rivers," 58; Linneroth, "Danube River Basin," 637; "Death of a River," BBC News, February 15, 2000; European Environmental Agency, *Mapping the Impacts of Natural Hazards and Technological Accidents in Europe*, 121.
68 Huisman et al., "Transboundary Cooperation," 93; MacGarvin, *North Sea*, 60; Cioc, *Rhine*, 178.
69 Teclaff, "International Law and the Protection of the Oceans from Pollution," 535; Hermann et al., "Distribution of Artificial Radionuclides," 427 and 453.
70 Quoted in Haas, *Saving the Mediterranean*, 66–67.
71 Ibid., 2. As of 1990, only 12 percent of all oil spills were the result of tanker accidents.
72 Disco, "Remaking 'Nature'," 208.
73 Cioc, *Rhine*, 186–88, 194; ICPR, *Salmon 2020*.
74 As quoted in Cioc, *Rhine*, 196.
75 Aydin et al., *Restaurering av Östersjön*.

8 Common Skies

1 Lundgren, *Acid Rain on the Agenda*.
2 Persson, "…och än faller regnet," 9–10 (our translation).
3 Persson, "Acid Rain Story."
4 The Swedish government put the issue on the agenda of the first United Nations Conference on the Human Environment that it hosted in Stockholm in 1972 by presenting a report authored by a group of Swedish experts,

chaired by Bert Bolin, *Air Pollution across National Boundaries: The Impact on the Environment of Sulfur in Air and Precipitation*.
5 Khrgian, *Meteorology*, chapter 4.
6 Ibid.
7 Nebeker, *Calculating the Weather*, 28.
8 Ibid., 37.
9 In harbour and fishing towns the telegraph stations had special optical devices to communicate storm warnings.
10 Barry, *Mountain Weather and Climate*, 140.
11 Höhler, *Luftfarhrtforschung and Luftfarthmythos*; Greene, "High Achiever."
12 Höhler, *Luftfarhrtforschung and Luftfarthmythos*, 164–65.
13 Ibid.; Greene, "High Achiever."
14 DuBois et al., *Invention and Development of the Radiosonde*.
15 Friedman, *Appropriating the Weather*, 103–5; Nebeker, *Calculating the Weather*, chapter 7.
16 As quoted in Nebeker, *Calculating the Weather*, 112.
17 Ibid., 111–13. A Swedish meteorologist, Anders Persson, argues that the forecast that Stagg and his colleagues made "was right for the wrong reason." The actual weather situation on D-day differed significantly from the forecasted but still meant higher visibility and somewhat weaker winds than on previous days. See: Persson, "Rätt av fel orsak?"
18 Staff Members, Institute of Meteorology, University of Stockholm, "Results of Forecasting," *Tellus* 6 (1954): 139–49.
19 Edwards, *Vast Machine*, 137; Edwards, "Predicting the Weather"; Woods, *Medium-Range Weather Prediction*, 19–21. The Council of Ministers wanted to strengthen scientific and technical research in the EC through international cooperation, and chose meteorology as a key area of cooperation, as meteorologists had complained about insufficient computer capacities.
20 Edwards, *Vast Machine*, 215–27.
21 Ibid.
22 Headrick, *Invisible Weapon*, 119–20.
23 Ibid.
24 Ibid.; Tomlinson, *International Control of Radiocommunications*, chapter 1; Hills, *Struggle for Control of Global Communications*, chapter 3.
25 Headricks, *Invisible Weapon*, 129–30.
26 Hugill, *Global Communications since 1844*, chapter 5.
27 Appleton, "Ionosphere."
28 See also: Fickers and Griset, *Communicating Europe*.
29 Wormbs, "Technology-Dependent Commons."
30 Lommers, *Europe—On Air*, 57–71.
31 An interesting aspect of the plan is that it allotted frequencies also to countries that were not yet members of the Union, and many of these indeed became members in the following years.
32 Wormbs, "Technology-Dependent Commons."
33 Fickers and Lommers, "Eventing Europe."
34 The inventor Guglielmo Marconi, who actively assisted the Vatican in the construction of the station, was present at the first broadcast.
35 Lommers, *Europe—On Air*, chapter 4. Radio Moscow's station was formally owned by Comintern, a private global organization of national communist parties.

36 Ibid., chapter 5; Spohrer, "Threat or Beacon?"
37 Wormbs, "An Expanding Resource"; Spohrer, "Threat or Beacon?"
38 Ibid.
39 Wormbs, *Vem älskade Tele-X?*
40 "Bleriot Tells of His Flight," *New York Times*, July 26, 1909; Wohl, *Passion for Wings*, 55–57; Simonsen, "Transnationale rum." The question was not entirely new, as balloons had been crossing borders for years but only on rare occasions. The fast development of aviation made it more urgent.
41 Jönsson, *International Aviation and the Politics of Regime Change*, 77–78.
42 Ibid., 80–81; Cooper, *Right to Fly*, 18–20.
43 Simonsen, "Transnationale rum," 64–67.
44 Cooper, *Right to Fly*, 22 and 27–32; Jönsson, *International Aviation and the Politics of Regime Change*, 83–87.
45 As quoted in Cooper, *Right to Fly*, appendix.
46 Ibid.
47 Ibid.
48 The former was called the International Aeronautical Conference (CAI) and the latter the International Technical Committee of Aerial Legal Experts (CITEJA). For an overview of all international aviation organizations see: Kranakis, "'Good Miracle'."
49 Cohen, *IATA*, 15–17.
50 Staniland, *Government Birds*, 15; Kranakis, "'Good Miracle'."
51 As quoted in Macmillan, *Sir Sefton Brancker*, 332. Cohen, *IATA*, has also many examples of this close collaboration.
52 As quoted in Cohen, *IATA*, 58.
53 Kranakis, "'Good Miracle'"; Cohen, *IATA*.
54 Gough, *Watching the Skies*, 78.
55 Ibid.; Heide, "EUROCONTROL"; Cohen, *IATA*.
56 Cooper, *Right to Fly*, 145; Lissitzyn, "Diplomacy of Air Transport"; Davies, *History of the World's Airlines*, 156–70.
57 Chapin, "Patent Interferences."
58 Nicklin, "Formal and Informal Governance of Civil Aviation across the Iron Curtain."
59 Heide, "EUROCONTROl."
60 Sochor, *Politics of International Aviation*, chapter 6. Originally Italy participated in the discussions but it did not join Eurocontrol, while Britain and Ireland joined Eurocrit in the late 1960s.
61 Ibid.; McInally, *Eurocontrol History Book*, 40–43.
62 Heide, "EUROCONTROL."
63 Ibid.
64 Ibid.; McInally, *Eurocontrol History Book*, 69.
65 McInally, *Eurocontrol History Book*; Turner, "Unions Mobilise."
66 Grönberg, "'Skorsten kallar vi det rör som mot Ryssland röken för'."
67 As quoted in ibid.
68 Ibid.
69 Brimblecombe, *Big Smoke*, 161–78.
70 Persson, "Acid Rain Story."
71 Austria, Belgium, Denmark, Finland, France, FRG, the Netherlands, Norway, Sweden, Switzerland, and the U.K. were full participants. Moreover, Iceland and Italy were adjunct participants.

72. As quoted in OECD, *OECD Programme on Long Range Transport of Air Pollutants*, chapter 11.
73. Ibid. The research project was chaired by Mr Reed from the British Ministry of the Environment.
74. Kaijser, "Under a Common Acid Sky."
75. Gehring, *Dynamic International Regimes*, chapter 2.
76. Sokolovsky, "Fruits of Cold War."
77. The full text of the Convention and its subsequent Protocols can be downloaded from the homepage of UNECE.
78. Gehring, *Dynamic International Regimes*, 155–56; Levy, "European Acid Rain"; Bäckstrand, *What Can Nature Withstand?*.
79. Swedish government, *Efter Tjernobyl*; Birgitta Dahl (former Swedish Energy Minister), author interview, January 18, 2010. See also: Josephson, *Red Atom*, which discusses the much more severe local effects around Chernobyl.
80. Hansson, *Kolets återkomst*.
81. Stoltenberg, "Statsministerens nyttårstale 2007" (our translation from the Norwegian).
82. Doyle, "Norway Drops Carbon Capture Plan."
83. Adams, *Against Extinction*.
84. Meyer, "Saving Migrants."
85. As quoted in ibid.
86. Ibid.
87. Meyer, "Greening Europe?"; Meyer, "Saving Migrants"; Donald et al., "International Conservation Policy."
88. As quoted in paragraph 21 of the Declaration of Principles, which can be downloaded from the website of the United Nations Environment Program.

Conclusion

1. Braudel, *Mediterranean*; Braudel, *Civilization and Capitalism*.
2. Braudel, *On History*, 32–33.
3. Following Hughes, *Networks of Power*, but using it in a slightly wider sense.
4. In the following we mention people, projects, and places that have been introduced in earlier chapters without explicitly referring to these chapters. The index makes it easy to find them.
5. Nordström, *Lort-Sverige*. See also: Oldenziel and Hård, *Consumers, Tinkerers, Rebels*, 76–80.
6. Nordström, *En dag i mitt liv*, 23 (our translation from the Swedish).
7. For example, the little Swedish village of Malexander, located 25 km from a major railroad line built in 1873, went from a local economy dominantly of self-subsistence character to an economy entangled with global markets in just a few decades, see: Kaijser, "Nature's Periphery."
8. Högselius et al., *Making of Europe's Critical Infrastructure*.
9. Crutzen and Stoermer, "'Anthropocene'"; Robin et al., *Future of Nature*, part 10.
10. The concept of "planetary boundaries" has been introduced by the Swedish ecologist Johan Rockström, see: Rockström et al., "A Safe Operating Space for Humanity."

Bibliography

Aaviksoo, Kiira. "Changes of Plant Cover and Land Use Types (1950s to 1980s) in Three Mire Reserves and their Neighborhoods in Estonia." *Landscape Ecology* 8 (1993): 287–301.

Abbanat, Robert. *Feasibility Study: A Pan-European Market for Technology Growth Companies.* EASDAQ, 2004.

Abbate, Janet. *Inventing the Internet.* Cambridge, MA: MIT Press, 1999.

Abelshauser, Werner, Wolfgang von Hippel, Jeffrey Allan Johnson, and Raymond G. Stokes. *German Industry and Global Enterprise: BASF: The History of a Company.* Cambridge: Cambridge University Press, 2004.

Abernethy, David. *The Dynamics of Global Dominance: European Overseas Empires, 1415–1980.* New Haven, Yale University Press, 2000.

Acker, K., D. Möller, W. Wieprecht, and St. Naumann. "Mt. Brocken, a Site for a Cloud Chemistry Measurement Programme in Central Europe." *Water, Air and Soil Pollution* 85 (1995): 1979–84.

Ádám, József. "Update of the History of the International Association of Geodesy." *Journal of Geodesy* 82 (2008): 662–74.

——— et al. "The European Reference System Coming of Age." In *International Association of Geodesy Symposia, Volume 121*, edited by K.P. Schwarz, 47–54. Heidelberg: Springer, 2000.

Adams, William M., *Against Extinction: The Story of Conservation.* London: Earthscan, 2004.

Aftalion, Fred. *A History of the International Chemical Industry.* Philadelphia: Chemical Heritage Foundation, 2001.

Agnoletti, Mauro. "The Degradation of Traditional Landscape in a Mountain Area of Tuscany during the 19th and 20th Centuries." *Forest Ecology and Management* 249 (2007): 5–17.

Agreement on the International Carriage of Perishable Foodstuffs and on the Special Equipment to be Used for Such Carriage (ATP). New York and Geneva: United Nations, 1976.

Agreement on the International Carriage of Perishable Foodstuffs and on the Special Equipment to be Used for Such Carriage (ATP) as amended on 7 November 2003. ECE/TRANS/165. New York and Geneva: United Nations, 2003.

Aldenhoff-Hübinger, Rita. "Agrarhandel zwischen Integration, Desintegration und transnationaler Kooperation, 1850–1914." In *Integration und Europäische Integration im Vergleich*, edited by Christian Henrich-Franke, C. Neutsch, and G. Thiemeyer, 193–202. Baden-Baden: Nomos, 2007.

Alm, Maria. "Nationell kraft och local motkraft: en diskursanalys av konflikten kring SwePol Link." PhD thesis, Linköping University, 2006.

Amati, Marco, ed. *Urban Green Belts in the 21st Century.* London: Ashgate, 2008.

———, and M. Yokohari. "The Establishment of the London Green Belt: Reaching Consensus over Purchasing Land." *Journal of Planning History* 6 (2007): 311–37.

Ambrosius, Gerold, and Christian Henrich-Franke. *Integration von Infrastrukturen in Europa im historischen Vergleich. Band 1: Synopse.* Baden-Baden: Nomos, 2013.

Anastasiadou, Irene. *Constructing Iron Europe: Transnationalism and Railways in the Interbellum.* Amsterdam: Amsterdam University Press, 2012.

———, and Aristotle Tympas. "Iron Silk Roads: Comparing Interwar and Postwar Transnational Railway Projects." In *Linking Networks: The Formation of Common Standards and Visions for Infrastructure Development*, edited by Martin Schiefelbusch and Hans-Liudger Dienel. Farnham: Ashgate, forthcoming.

Andersen, Arne. "Pollution and the Chemical Industry: The Case of the German Dye Industry." In *The Chemical Industry in Europe 1850–1914: Industrial Growth, Pollution, and Professionalization*, edited by Ernst Homburg, Anthony S. Travis, and Harm G. Schröter, 183–202. Dordrecht: Kluwer, 1998.

Andersen, Håkan With. "Changing Technology, Changing Commons." In *Cosmopolitan Commons: Sharing Resources and Risks across Borders*, edited by Nil Disco and Eda Kranakis. Cambridge, MA: MIT Press, 2013.

Andersen, Reidar et al., eds. *Large Predators and Human Communities in Norway*. Trondheim: NINA, 2003.

Angus-Leppan, P.V. "A Note on the History of the International Association of Geodesy." *Journal of Geodesy* 58 (1984): 224–29.

Anthony, Thalia. "Labour Relations on Northern Cattle Stations: Feudal Exploitation and Accommodation." *The Drawing Board: An Australian Review of Public Affairs* 4 (2004): 117–36.

Appel, Erik et al., *Finland i krig, 1939–1940. Första delen*. Esbo: Schildts förlag, 2001.

Appleton, Edward V. "The Ionosphere." Nobel Lecture, December 12, 1947. http://www.nobelprize.org/nobel_prizes/physics/laureates/1947/appleton-lecture.html (accessed May 15, 2014).

Arapostathis, Stathis, Anna Carlsson-Hyslop, Peter J. G. Pearson, Judith Thornton, Maria Gradillas, Scott Laczay, and Suzanne Wallis. "Governing Transitions: Cases and Insights from Two Periods in the History of the UK Gas Industry." *Energy Policy* 52 (2013): 25–44.

Armstrong, John. "British Coastal Shipping: A Research Agenda for the European Perspective." In *Coastal Shipping and the European Economy 1750–1980*, edited by John Armstrong and Andreas Kunz, 11–24. Mainz: Verlag Philipp von Zabern, 2002.

Arshanapalli, Bala, and John Doukas. "International Stock Market Linkages: Evidence from the Pre- and Post-October 1987 Period." *Journal of Banking and Finance* 17 (1993): 193–208.

Association of Petrochemicals Producers in Europe and European Chemical Industry Council. "Trans European Olefins Pipeline Network (8 April 2004)." http://www.petrochemistry.net (accessed November 4, 2011).

Avango, Dag. *Sveagruvan: svensk gruvhantering mellan industri, diplomati och geovetenskap 1910–1934*. Stockholm: Jernkontoret, 2005.

Aydin, Helen, Silvana Bajlovic, Johanna Cedergren, Tina Jacobsson, Ronja Krische, and Jenny Molén. *Restaurering av Östersjön*. Stockholm: Kungliga Tekniska Högskolan, 2006.

Bäckstrand, Karin, *What can Nature Withstand? Science, Politcs and Discourse in Transboundary Air Pollution Diplomacy*. Lund: Lund Political Studies 116, Lund University, 2001.

Baerselman, Fred, and Frans Vera. *Nature Development: An Exploratory Study for the Construction of Ecological Networks*. The Hague: Ministry of Agriculture, Nature Management and Fisheries, 1995 (Dutch original 1988).

Badenoch, Alec. "Myths of the European Network: Constructions of Cohesion in Infrastructure Maps." In *Materializing Europe: Transnational Infrastructures and the Project of Europe*, edited by Alec Badenoch and Andreas Fickers, 47–77. Basingstoke: Palgrave Macmillan, 2010.

———, and Andreas Fickers, eds. *Materializing Europe: Transnational Infrastructures and the Project of Europe*. Basingstoke: Palgrave Macmillan, 2010.

Baerselman, Fred, and Frans Vera. *Nature Development: An Exploratory Study for the Construction of Ecological Networks*. The Hague: Ministry of Agriculture, Nature Management and Fisheries, 1995 (Dutch original 1988).

Baev, Jordan. "The Organizational and Doctrinal Evolution of the Warsaw Pact (1955–1969)." Accessed May 15, 2014. http://www.coldwar.hu/html/en/publications/organizational.html.

Baeyer, J.J. "Entwurf zu einer mitteleuropäischen Gradmessung." Handwritten document, April 1861. Print version 1862.

———. *Über die Größe und Figur der Erde. Eine Denkschrift zur Begründung einer mittel-europäischen Gradmessung*. Berlin: Georg Reimer, 1861.

Baigent, Elizabeth. "'God's earth will be sacred': Religion, Theology, and the Open Space Movement in Victorian England." *Rural History* 22 (2011): 31–58.

Banken, Ralf. *Die Industrialisierung der Saarregion 1815–1914*. Volume 2. Stuttgart: Franz Steiner Verlag, 2003.

Barbier, Edward B. *Scarcity and Frontiers: How Economies Have Developed through Natural Resource Exploitation*. New York: Cambridge University Press, 2011.

Barrett, Sean D. "The Sustainability of the Ryanair Model." *International Journal of Transport Management* 2 (2004): 89–98.

Barry, Roger G. *Mountain Weather and Climate*. London: Routledge, 1992.

BASF 1865–1965. Ein Jahrhundert Badische Anilin & Soda Fabrik AG. Annex to *Mannheimer Morgen* (no date).

Batten, Alan Henry. *Resolute and Undertaking Characters: The Lives of Wilhelm and Otto Struve*. Boston, MA: Reidel, 1988.

Bayernwerk. "Company History." http://www.fundinguniverse.com/company-histories/bayernwerk-ag-history (accessed May 15, 2014).

Beaton, Kendal. *Enterprise in Oil: A History of Shell in the United States*. New York: Appleton-Century-Crofts, 1957.

Beauchamp, Ken. *History of Telegraphy: Its Technology and Application*. IEE History of Technology Series 26. London: Institution of Electrical Engineers, 2001.

Bellamy, Chris. *Absolute War: Soviet Russia in the Second World War*. London: Pan Books, 2009.

Bennett, Graham. "Interaction between Policy Concerning Spatial Planning and Ecological Networks in Europe: Overview Report." Tilburg: ECNC, 2008.

———. "Green Infrastructure in Europe—Past Lessons/Future Challenges." In *Towards a Green Infrastructure for Europe*, 14–15. Brussels, 2009.

———, and Kalemani Jo Mulongoy. *Review of Experience with Ecological Networks, Corridors and Buffer Zones*. CBD Technical Series No. 23. Montreal: Secretariat of the Convention in Biological Biodiversity, 2006.

———, and Rob Wolters. "A European Ecological Network." In *Perspectives on Ecological Networks*, edited by Peter Nowicki et al., 11–18. Tilburg: ECNC, 1996.

Berend, Ivan T. "The Failure of Economic Nationalism: Central and Eastern Europe before World War II." *Revue économique* 51 (2000): 315–22.

Berkers, Eric. *De aarde verdeeld, verbeeld, en getekend*. Zutphen: Walburg Pers, 2004.

Berthelot, Yves. "Unity and Diversity of Development: The Regional Commissions' Experience." In *Unity and Diversity in Development Ideas. Perspectives from the*

UN Regional Commissions, edited by Yves Berthelot, 1–50. Bloomington: Indiana University Press, 2004.

———, and Paul Rayment. "The ECE: A Bridge between East and West." In *Unity and Diversity in Development Ideas. Perspectives from the UN Regional Commissions*, edited by Yves Berthelot, 51–131. Bloomington: Indiana University Press, 2004.

Biggs, Michael. "Putting the State on the Map: Cartography, Territory, and European State Formation." *Comparative Studies in Society and History* 41 (1999): 374–405.

Bignal, Eric M., and David I. McCracken. "Low-Intensity Farming Systems in the Conservation of the Countryside." *Journal of Applied Ecology* 33 (1996): 413–24.

Biltcliffe, Pippa. "Walter Crane and the Imperial Federation Map Showing the Extent of the British Empire (1886)." *Imago Mundi* 57 (2005): 63–69.

Bird Rose, Deborah. *Hidden Histories: Black Stories from Victoria River Downs, Humbert River and Wave Hill Stations*. Canberra: Aboriginal Studies Press, 1991.

Biswas, Asit K. *History of Hydrology*. Amsterdam: North-Holland Company, 1970.

Blackbourn, David. *The Conquest of Nature: Water, Landscape and the Making of Modern Germany*. New York: Norton, 2006.

Blom, Wim. *One Hundred Years of Shell Pernis: A Century of Refining and Petrochemicals in the Port of Rotterdam*. The Hague: Shell Nederland, 2002.

Blomqvist, Pär. "Roads for Flow—Road for Peace: Lobbying for a European Highway System." In *Networking Europe: Transnational Infrastructures and the Shaping of Europe, 1850–2000*, edited by Erik van der Vleuten and Arne Kaijser, 161–86. Sagamore Beach, MA: Science History Publications, 2006.

Bock, Peter. *Intezonenzüge: Eisenbahnverkehr im geteilten Deutschland 1945–1990*. Munich: GeraNova Zeitschriftenverlag, 2000.

Bokserman, Yuli I. *Razvitie gazovoi promyshlennosti SSSR*. Moscow: Gosudarstvennoe nauchno-tekhnicheskoe izdatelstvo neftyanoi i gorno-toplivnoi literatury, 1958.

Bolin, Bert et al., *Air Pollution across National Boundaries. The Impact on the Environment of Sulphur in Air and Precipitation*. Stockholm: Royal Ministry for Foreign Affairs, 1971.

Bonhage, Barbara. "Eurocheque: Creating a 'Common Currency' European Infrastructure for the Cashless Mass Payments System." In *Materializing Europe: Transnational Infrastructures and the Project of Europe*, edited by Alec Badenoch and Andreas Fickers, 182–97. Basingstoke: Palgrave Macmillan, 2010.

Boon, Marten. "Energy Transition, Suez Crisis and Transnational Transport: The Case of the Rotterdam-Rhine Pipeline 1955–1960." Paper presented at the 15th EBHA Conference, Athens, August 24–26, 2011.

Bosch, A., and W. van der Ham. *Twee eeuwen Rijkswaterstaat 1798–1998*. Zaltbommel: Europese Bibliotheek, 1998.

Bouwma, Irene. "Progress in the Development of the Pan European Ecological Network." In 1st International Symposium on the Pan European Ecological Network "Nature Does not Have Any Borders: Towards Transfrontier Ecological Networks." Proceedings. *Environmental Encounters No. 44*, 17–22. Paris: Council of Europe, 2000.

Bouwman, Dorrit et al. *A Public Secret: The Success of the National Ecological Framework*. Hoevelaken: Nationaal Groenfonds, 2010.

Bowker, Geoffrey C. *Science on the Run: Information Management and Industrial Geophysics at Schlumberger, 1920–1940*. Cambridge, MA: MIT Press, 1994.

Bowman, Joye L. "'Legitimate Commerce' and Peanut Production in Portuguese Guinea, 1840s–1880s." *Journal of African History* 28 (1987): 87–106.

Bozzo, Albert. "Players Replay the Crash." http://www.cnbc.com/id/21136884 (10–12–2007) (accessed January 31, 2012).

Branch, Jordan. "Mapping the Sovereign State: Technology, Authority, and Systemic Change." *International Organization* 65 (2011): 1–36.

Braudel, Fernand. *The Mediterranean and the Mediterranean World in the Age of Philip II.* Berkeley: University of California Press, 1995 (French original 1949).

———. *On History.* Chicago: University of Chicago Press, 1982 (French Original 1969).

———. *Civilization & Capitalism 15th–18th Century.* Berkeley: University of California Press, 1992 (French original 1979).

Braun, Ingo. "Geflügelte Saurier. Zur intersystemischen Vernetzung grosser technischer Netze." In *Technik ohne Grenzen*, edited by Ingo Braun and Bernward Joerges, 446–500. Frankfurt a.Main: Suhrkamp, 1994.

Briggs, David. "Integrating Land Resource Data into a European Geographical Information System: Practicalities and Problems." *Applied Geography* 9 (1989): 5–20.

Brimblecombe, Peter *The Big Smoke: A History of Air Pollution in London since Medieval Times.* London: Methuen, 1987.

Brooks, George E. "Peanuts and Colonialism: Consequences of the Commercialization of Peanuts in West Africa, 1830–70." *Journal of African History* 16 (1975): 29–54.

Brown, Lloyd A. *The Story of Maps.* Boston: Little, Brown and Company, 1949.

Brown, Louis, *A Radar History of World War II. Technical and Military Imperatives.* Bristol: IOP Publishing, 1999.

Bruhèze, Adri A. Albert de la, and Anneke H. van Otterloo. "The Milky Way: Infrastructures and the Shaping of Cold Chains." *History and Technology* 20 (2004): 249–69.

Bruinsma, Frank, and Piet Rietveld. "Urban Agglomerations in European Infrastructure Networks." *Urban Studies* 30 (1993): 919–34.

Brunet, Roger, ed. *Les villes Européennes. Rapport pour la DATAR.* Montpellier: RECLUS, 1989.

———. "Lignes de force de l'éspace Européen." *Mappemonde* 66 (2002): 14–19.

Brunsden, Jim. "EU Should Toughen High-Frequency Trade Proposals, Jouyet Says." http://www.bloomberg.com/news/2011-11-24/eu-should-toughen-high-frequency-trade-proposals-jouyet-says.html (accessed December 14, 2011).

Bruzelius, Nils, *Polaris and Scandinavia: The Deployment of the Fleet Ballistic Missile U-boats and the U.S. Policy towards the Scandinavian Countries.* Saarbrücken: VDM Verlag, 2011.

Buček, Antonin, Petr Maděra, and Luboč Úradníček. "Ecological Network Creation in the Czech Republic." *Ekologie krajiny* 2008: 12–24.

Buchhofer, Ekkehard. "Transport Infrastructure in the Baltic States during the Transformation to Market Economies." *Journal of Transport Geography* 3 (1995): 69–75.

Bucholz, Arden, *Moltke, Schlieffen and Prussian War Planning.* Oxford: Berg Publishers, 1991.

———. *Moltke and the German Wars, 1864–1871.* Basingstoke: Palgrave Macmillan, 2001.

Budiansky, Stephen, *Air Power: The Men, Machines and Ideas That Revolutionized War from Kitty Hawk to Gulf War II*. London: Viking, 2004.

Buiter, Hans. "Constructing Dutch Streets: A Melting Pot of European Technologies." In *Urban Machinery: Inside Modern European Cities*, edited by Mikael Hård and Thomas J. Misa, 141–62. Cambridge, MA: MIT Press, 2008.

———. "The Development of the Internationality of Dutch Railways, 1832–2000." Paper presented at the 4th Tensions of Europe Plenary Conference, Sofia, June 17–20, 2010.

Butkevicius, Jonas "Development of Passenger Transportation by Railroad from Lithuania to European States." *Transport Geography* 22 (2007): 73–79.

Calle, P., G. Kurstjens, and B. Peters. "De libellen van de Gelderse Poort: natuurlijk rivierenlandschap soortenrijker dan verwacht." *Brachytron* 9 (2006): 49–57.

Campbell, Robert. *Soviet and Post-Soviet Telecommunications: An Industry under Reform*. Boulder, CO: Westview Press, 1995.

Cassis, Youssef. *Capitals of Capital: A History of International Financial Centres 1780–2005*. Cambridge: Cambridge University Press, 2006.

Castells, Manuel. *The Rise of the Network Society*. Oxford: Blackwell, 1996.

Castner. "Die Regulierung der Donau am Eisernen Thor." *Prometheus* 3 (1892).

Cattell, David T. "The Politics of the Danube Commission under Soviet Control." *American Slavic and East European Review* 19 (1960): 380–94.

Chamberlain, J.P. *The Regime of International Rivers: Danube and Rhine*. New York: Columbia University, 1923.

Chandler, Alfred D. Jr., *Shaping the Industrial Century: The Remarkable Story of the Evolution of the Modern Chemical and Pharmaceutical Industries*. Cambridge, MA: Harvard University Press, 2005.

Chapin, Seymour L. "Patent Interferences and the History of Technology: A High-flying Example." *Technology & Culture* 12 (1971): 414–46.

Chevalier, Michel. *Economie politique et politique. Articles extraits du Globe*. Paris, Bureau du Globe, 1832.

———. *Politique Européenne. Articles extraits du Globe*. Paris: Bureau du Globe, 1832.

———. *Système de la Méditerranée. Articles extraits du Globe*. Paris: Bureau du Globe, 1832.

———. *De ijzerbanen beschouwd als de voornaamste materiele middelen, ter bevestiging van den vrede in Europa, en ter bestendiging van het geluk des menschdoms*. Rotterdam: J.A. van Belle, 1838.

———. "Chemins de fer." In *Dictionnaire de l'économie politique*. Vol. I, 337–62. Paris: Librairie de Guillaumin et cie, 1852.

Chossudowsky, E. M. "Rationing in the USSR." *The Review of Economic Studies* 8 (1941): 143–65.

Cioc, Mark. *The Rhine: An Eco-Biography, 1815–2000*. Seattle: University of Washington Press, 2002.

———, Franz-Josef Brueggemeier, and Thomas Zeller, eds. *How Green Were the Nazis? Nature, Environment, and Nation in the Third Reich*. Athens: Ohio University Press, 2005.

Clar, Ernesto, and Pinilla Vicente. "Path Dependence and the Modernisation of Agriculture: A Case Study of Aragon." *Rural History* 22 (2011): 251–69.

Clavin, Patricia. *The Great Depression in Europe, 1929–1939*. Basingstoke: Palgrave Macmillan, 2000.

Clay Large, David, "The Great Rescue." in *The Cold War: A Military History*, edited by Robert Cowley, 20–34. New York, Random House, 2005.

Clemons, Eric, and Bruce Weber. "London's Big Bang: A Case Study of Information Technology, Competitive Impact, and Organizational Change." In *System Sciences, 1989. Vol. IV: Emerging Technologies and Applications Track. Proceedings of the Twenty-Second Annual Hawaii International Conference*, 233–42. Kona, Hawaii: IEEE, 1989.

Cliff, Dave and Linda Northrop. *The Global Financial Markets: An Ultra-Large-Scale Systems Perspective*. London: UK Government Office for Science, 2011.

CME Group, "What Happened on May 6th." www.cmegroup.com (May 10, 2010). (accessed December 14, 2011).

Cohen, Ralph, *IATA:. The First Three Decades*. Montreal: IATA, 1949.

Cole, Laurence, and Philip Ther. "Introduction: Current Challenges of Writing European history." *European History Quarterly* 40 (2010): 581–92.

Collier, Peter. "The Colonial Survey Committee and the Mapping of Africa." Paper Presented at the International Symposium on the History of Colonial Cartography 1750–1950, Utrecht, August 21–23, 2006.

———. "International Boundary Surveys and Demarcation in the Late 19th and Early 20th Centuries." *Survey Review* 41 (2009): 2–13.

Collingham, Lizzie. *The Taste of War: World War Two and the Battle for Food*. London: Allen Lane/Penguin, 2011.

Commission of the European Communities. *The State of the Environment in the European Community 1986*. Luxembourg: EC Official Publications, 1987.

———. *Results of the CORINE Program. SEC(91) 958 Final*. Brussels, 1991.

Conti, Prince Piero Ginori. "The Development of the Chemical Industry in Italy." *Industrial and Engineering Chemistry* (October 1926): 999–1002.

Control of the Cold Chain for Quick-Frozen Foods Handbook. Paris: International Institute of Refrigeration, 1999.

Contzen, J.P. "The Benefit of Remote Sensing Activities of the Joint Research Centre (JRC) in Europe and Africa." *Photogrammetria* 43 (1989): 311–22.

Cooper, Frederick. "'Our Strike': Equality, Anticolonial Politics and the 1947–48 Railway Strike in French West Africa." *Journal of African History* 37 (1996): 81–118.

Cooper, John. *The Right to Fly*. New York: Henry Holt & Co., 1947.

Corbin, Alain. *The Lure of the Sea: The Discovery of the Seaside in the Western World, 1750–1840*. London: Penguin, 1995 (French original 1988).

Cordovil, Bruno. "De-Electrifying the History of Street Lighting: Energies in Use in Town and Country (Portugal, 1780s-1930s)." In *The Culture of Energy*, edited by Mogens Rüdiger, 30–81. Cambridge: Cambridge Scholars Publishing, 2008.

Corkery, Michael. "Jim Simons on Flash Crash: High Frequency Traders Saved the Day." *Wall Street Journal*, September 13, 2010.

Correia, Francisco Nunes, and Joaquim Evaristo da Silva. "International Framework for the Management of Transboundary Water Resources." *Water International* 24 (2009): 86–94.

Council of Europe. *European Diploma for Certain Protected Landscapes, Reserves and Natural Features (Adopted by the Ministers' Deputies on 6th March 1965). Resolution (65)6*. Council of Europe, 1965.

———. *Convention on the Conservation of European Wildlife and Natural Habitats. CETS No. 104*. Council of Europe, 1979.

Count Corti. *The Magician of Homburg and Monte Carlo*. London: Thornton Butterworth, 1934.

Cousins, Sara, and Margareta Ihse. "A Methodological Study for Biotope and Landscape Mapping Based on CIR Aerial Photographs." *Landscape and Urban Planning* 41 (1998): 183–92.

Coutard, Olivier. "Placing Splintering Urbanism: Introduction." *Geoforum* 39 (2008): 1815–20.

Critchell James, and Joseph Raymond. *A History of the Frozen Meat Trade*. London: Constable, 1912.

Crutzen, Paul and Stoermer, Eugene, "The 'Anthropocene'." *Global Change Newsletter* 41 (2000): 17–18.

Da Rin, Marco. "Finance and the Chemical Industry." In *Chemicals and Long Term Growth*, edited by Ashish Arora, Ralph Landau, and Nathan Rosenberg, 301–19. New York: Wiley, 1998.

Daunton, Martin. "Britain and Globalisation since 1850. I: Creating a Global Order 1850–1914." *Transactions of the Royal Historical Society* 16 (2006): 1–38.

———. "Britain and Globalisation since 1850. II: The Rise of Insular Capitalism 1914–1939." *Transactions of the Royal Historical Society* 17 (2007): 1–33.

Davids, Mila. "The Fabric of Production: The Philips Industrial Network." *History and Technology* 20 (2004): 271–90.

Davies, Norman. *Europe: A History*, second edition. London: Pimlico, 1997.

Davies, R.E.G. *A History of the World's Airlines*. London: Oxford University Press, 1964.

Davies, R.W., M.B. Tauger, and S.G. Wheatcroft. "Stalin, Grain Stocks, and the Famine of 1932–1933." *Slavic Review* 54 (1995): 642–57.

De Block, Greet. "Designing the Nation: The Belgian Railway Project, 1830–1837." *Technology and Culture* 52 (2011): 703–32.

———. "Engineering the Territory: Technology, Space, and Society in 19th and 20th Century Belgium." PhD thesis, Katholieke Universiteit Leuven, 2012.

———, and Janet Polasky. "Light Railways and the Rural-Urban Continuum." *Journal of Historical Geography* 37 (2011): 312–28.

De Kerbrech, Richard P. *Harland & Wolff's Empire Food Ships 1934–1948. A Link with the Southern Dominions*. Freshwater, Isle of Wight: Coach House Publications, 1998.

De Vries, Jan. *The European Economy in an Age of Crisis, 1600–1750*. Cambridge: Cambridge University Press, 1976.

———, and Ad van de Woude. *The First Modern Economy: Success, Failure, and Perseverance of the Dutch Economy 1500–1815*. Oxford: Oxford University Press, 1996.

De Wit, Onno. *Telefonie in Nederland 1877–1940*. Amsterdam: Otto Cramwinckel, 1998.

Del Curto, Davide, and Angelo Landi. "Gas-Light in Italy between 1700s & 1800s: A History of Lighting." In *The Culture of Energy*, edited by Mogens Rüdiger, 2–29. Cambridge: Cambridge Scholars Publishing, 2008.

Demirakın, Isık N.A. "Study of Ottoman Modernisation of the City: The Sixth Municipal District of Istanbul (1856–1877)." MA thesis, Bilkent University, 2006.

Derzhavnyi komitet naftovoi, gazovoi ta naftopererobnoi promyslovosti Ukrainy. *Nafta i gaz Ukrainy*. Kiev: Naukova Dumka, 1997.

Deutsch, Robert. *The Food Revolution in the Soviet Union and Eastern Europe*. Boulder, CO: Westview Press, 1985.

Dienes, Leslie. "The Natural Gas Industry of the USSR." MA thesis, University of British Colombia, 1965.

Dinçal, Noyan. "Arenas of Experimentation: Modernizing Istanbul in the Late Ottoman Empire." In *Urban Machinery: Inside Modern European Cities*, edited by Mikael Hård and Thomas J. Misa, 49–69. Cambridge, MA: MIT Press, 2008.

Disco, Cornelis. "Remaking 'Nature': The Ecological Turn in Dutch Water Management." *Science, Technology and Human Values* 27 (2002): 206–35.

———. "Accepting Father Rhine? Technological Fixes, Vigilance, and Transnational Lobbies as 'European' Strategies of Dutch Municipal Water Supplies 1900–1975." *Environment and History* 13 (2007): 381–411.

———. "Taming the Rhine: Economic Connection and Urban Competition." In *Urban Machinery: Inside Modern European Cities*, edited by Mikael Hård and Thomas J. Misa, 23–47. Cambridge, MA: MIT Press, 2008.

———, and Erik van der Vleuten. "The Politics of Wet System Building." *Knowledge, Technology & Policy* 14 (2002): 21–40.

Disco, Nil. *60 Years of ITC: The International Institute for Geo-Information Science and Earth Observation*. Eindhoven: Stichting Historie der Techniek, 2010.

———. "From Sea to Shining Sea: Making Ends Meet on the Rhine and the Rhone." In *Materializing Europe: Transnational Infrastructures and the Project of Europe*, edited by Alec Badenoch and Andreas Fickers, 255–85. Basingstoke and New York: Palgrave Macmillan, 2010.

———, and Eda Kranakis, eds. *Cosmopolitan Commons: Sharing Resources and Risks across Borders*. Cambridge, MA: MIT Press, 2013.

Dittmar, Claudia. "GDR Television in Competition with West German Programming." *Historical Journal of Film, Radio and Television* 24 (2004): 327–43.

Dobb, Maurice. "Soviet Agriculture and the Chemical Industry." *Slavonic and East European Review* 24 (1946): 127–32.

Doel, Ronald E. "Constituting the Postwar Earth Sciences: The Military's Influence on the Environmental Sciences in the USA after 1945." *Social Studies of Science* 33 (2003): 635–66.

Donald, Paul F. et al. "International Conservation Policy Delivers Benefits for Birds in Europe." *Science*, August 10, 2007: 810–13.

Doughty, Robert, "French Strategy in 1914: Joffre's Own." *Journal of Military History* 67 (2003): 433–35.

Douhet, Guilio. *The Command of the Air*. London: Faber and Faber, 1943.

Doyle, Alister. "Norway Drops Carbon Capture Plan it Had Likened to 'Moon Landing'." *Reuters*, September 20, 2013.

Driessen, J. *Waardebepaling kleine ondergrondse infrastructuur Vervangingswaarde van kabels en leidingen in Nederland. Rapport 13/99059363/JOD, revisie D3*. Houten: Grontmij, 2005.

Driver, Felix. "In Search of The Imperial Map: Walter Crane and the Image of Empire." *Historical Workshop Journal* 69 (2010): 146–57.

Drolet, Michael. "Industry, Class and Society: A Historiographic Reinterpretation of Michel Chevalier." *English Historical Review* 123 (2008): 1229–71.

DuBois, John, Robert Multhauf, and Charles Ziegler. *The Invention and Development of the Radiosonde*. Smithsonian Studies in History and Technology 53. Washington, DC: Smithsonian Institute Press, 2002.

Duhigg, Charles. "Stock Traders Find Speed Pays, in Milliseconds." *New York Times*, July 23, 2009.

Dunkley, Emma. "Pan-Europe vs. the Nationals." *Wall Street Journal*, October 10, 2011.

Dupuy, Gabriel, and Vaclav Stransky. "Cities and Highway Networks in Europe." *Journal of Transport Geography* 4 (1996): 107–21.

Economic Commission for Europe. *Ten Years of Agricultural Trade in Europe 1951–1960*. Geneva: United Nations, 1962.

———. *Fifteen Years of Activity of the Economic Commission for Europe 1947–1962*. New York: United Nations, 1964.

———. *Agricultural Trade in Europe*. New York: United Nations, 1972.

———. *East-West Trade in Chemical Products among ECE Member States*. ECE/CHEM/39. Geneva: UNECE, 1982.

———. *Agricultural Trade. Volume II of Agricultural Review for Europe No. 27, 1983 and 1984*. New York: United Nations, 1985.

Edgerton, David, *Britain's War Machine: Weapons, Resources and Experts in the Second World War*. London: Allen Lane, 2011.

Edney, Matthew. *Mapping an Empire: The Geographical Construction of British India*. Chicago: University of Chicago Press, 1997.

Edwards, Paul, "Predicting the Weather. An Information Commons for Europe and the World," in *Cosmopolitan Commons. Sharing Resources and Risks across Borders*, edited by Nil Disco and Eda Kranakis, 153–84. Cambridge, MA: MIT Press, 2013.

———. "Meteorology as Infrastructural Globalism." *Orisis* 21 (2006): 229–50.

———. *A Vast Machine: Computer Models, Climate Data, and the Politics of Global Warming*. Cambridge, MA: MIT Press, 2010.

Egilsson, Haraldur Tor. *The Origins, Use and Development of Hot Line Diplomacy*. Discussion Papers in Diplomacy. The Hague: Netherlands Institute of International Relations "Clingendael." 2003.

Eichengreen, Barry. *Capital Flows and Crises*. Cambridge, MA: MIT Press, 2004.

———. *Globalizing Capital: A History of the International Monetary System*, second edition. Princeton: Princeton University Press, 2008.

———, and Michael D. Bordo. *Crises Now and Then: What Lessons from the Last Era of Financial Globalization*. NBER Working Paper Series 8716 (2002).

Ekawan, Rudianto, and Michel Duchêne. "The Evolution of Hard Coal Trade in the Atlantic Market." *Energy Policy* 34 (2006): 1487–98.

Elshtein, A. "Gazovaya promyshlennost v Polshe." *Gazovaya promyshlennost*, February 1958: 49–53.

Engelen, Ewald, and Michael H. Grote. "Stock Exchange Virtualisation and the Decline of Second-Tier Financial Centers—The Cases of Amsterdam and Frankfurt." *Journal of Economic Geography* 9 (2009): 679–96.

Ericsson, Karin, and Lars J. Nilsson, "International Biofuel Trade: A Study of the Swedish Import." *Biomass and Bioenergy* 26 (2004): 205–20.

Ericsson, Staffan, Lars Östlund, and Anna-Lena Axelsson. "A Forest of Grazing and Logging: Deforestation and Reforestation History of a Boreal Landscape in Central Sweden." *New Forests* 19 (2000): 227–40.

Eriksson, Gunnar. "Kartläggarna: Naturvetenskapens tillväxt och tillämpningar i det industriella genombrottets Sverige 1870–1914." PhD thesis, Umeå University, 1978.

Eskildsen, F.S. "Danske Former for Handel med Korn." In *Korn II*, edited by A. Ranløv, 5–45. Copenhagen: Alfred Jørgensens Forlag, 1943.

European Commission. *Energy Infrastructure Priorities for 2020 and Beyond—A Blueprint for an Integrated European Energy Network.* COM(2010) 677/4. Brussels: European Communities, 2010.

European Environment Agency. *The Thematic Accuracy of Corine Land Cover 2000. Technical report No 7/2006.* Copenhagen: EEA, 2006.

———. *10 Messages for 2010. Message 6: Urban Ecosystems.* Copenhagen: EEA, 2010.

———. *The European Environment: State and Outlook 2010. Land Use.* Copenhagen: EEA, 2010.

———. *Mapping the Impacts of Natural Hazards and Technological Accidents in Europe: An Overview of the Last Decade.* EEA Technical Report No. 13. Copenhagen: EEA, 2010.

———. *Green Infrastructure and Territorial Cohesion.* EEA Technical Report No. 18. Copenhagen: EEA, 2011.

———. *Landscape Fragmentation in Europe.* EEA Report No. 2. Copenhagen: EEA, 2011.

Evans, David. *A History of Nature Conservation in Britain*, second edition. London: Routledge, 1996.

Evans, I.M. "Changing Policy Perspectives for Natural Gas in the Netherlands." *Energy Policy* 9 (1981): 232–36.

Evera, Stephen, "The Cult of the Offensive and the Origins of the First World War." In *Military Strategy and the Origins of the First World War*, edited by Steven Miller, Sean Lynn-Jones, and Stephen van Evera, 59–108. Princeton: Princeton University Press, 1991.

Fall, Bernard B. *Hell in a Very Small Place: The Siege of Dien Bien Phu.* Oxford: Alden Press, 1966.

Fedman, David. "Triangulating Chōsen: Maps, Mapmaking, and the Land Survey in Colonial Korea." *Cross-Currents: East Asian History and Culture Review* 1 (2012): 205–34.

Feranec, Jan, Gerard Hazeu, Susan Christensen, and Gabriel Jaffrain. "Corine Land Cover Change Detection in Europe." *Land Use Policy* 24 (2007): 234–47.

Ferguson, Niall. "Political Risk and the International Bond Market between the 1848 Revolution and the Outbreak of the First World War." *Economic History Review* 59 (2006): 70–112.

Fickers, Andreas, and Pascal Griset. *Communicating Europe: Technologies, Information, Events.* Basingstoke and New York: Palgrave Macmillan, forthcoming.

———, and Suzanne Lommers. "Eventing Europe: Broadcasting and the Mediated Performances of Europe." In *Materializing Europe: Transnational Infrastructures and the Project of Europe*, edited by Alexander Badenoch and Andreas Fickers, 225–51. Basingstoke and New York: Palgrave Macmillan, 2010.

Findings Regarding the Market Events of May 6, 2010. Washington DC: US Commodity Futures Trading Commission and the US Securities and Exchange Commission, 2010.

Finstad, Terje. "Varme visjoner og frosne fremskritt. Om fryseteknologi i Norge, ca. 1920–1965." PhD thesis, NTNU Trondheim, 2011.

Fisher, H.H. *The Famine in Soviet Russia 1919–1923: The Operations of the American Relief Administration.* New York: Macmillan, 1927.

Fitzmaurice, John. *Damming the Danube: Gabcikovo/Nagymaros and Post-Communist Politics in Europe.* Boulder, CO: Westview Press, 1995.

Fleck, Joseph. "Evolution de l'économie agricole en Tchecoslovaquie." *Économie rurale* 83 (1970): 39–44.

Flichy, Patrice. "The Birth of Long Distance Communication: Semaphore Telegraphs in Europe (1790–1840)." *Réseaux* 1 (1993): 81–101.

Fogel, Robert William. *The Escape from Hunger and Premature Death 1700–2100. Europe, America, and the Third World.* Cambridge: Cambridge University Press, 2004.

Franckx, Erik. "EC Maritime Zones: The Delimitation Aspect." *Ocean Development & International Law* 23 (1992): 239–58.

Fredholm, Michael. *Gazprom in Crisis.* Russian Series 06/48, Conflict Studies London: Research Centre, Defence Academy of the United Kingdom, 2006.

Friedman, Robert Marc. *Appropriating the Weather: Vilhelm Bjerknes and the Construction of Modern Meteorology.* Ithaca, NY: Cornell University Press, 1989.

Friis, E. "International Handel med Korn." In: *Korn I*, edited by A. Ranløv, 385–462. Copenhagen: Alfred Jørgensens Forlag, 1942.

Gall, Alexander. "Atlantropa: A Technological Vision of a United Europe." In *Networking Europe: Transnational Infrastructures and the Shaping of Europe, 1850–2000*, edited by Erik van der Vleuten and Arne Kaijser, 99–128. Sagamore Beach: Science History Publications, 2006.

Gatterer, J.C. *Abriss der Geographie.* Göttingen: Joh. Christian Dietrich, 1775.

Gehring, Thomas, *Dynamic International Regimes: Institutions for International Environmental Governance.* Berlin: Peter Lang, 1994.

Genath, Peter. "*Es geht fast täglich auf den Brocken ...!" Der Arbeitsalltag der Ranger im Nationalpark Hochharz aus volkskundlicher Perspektive.* Münster: Waxmann, 2005.

Germuska, Pál. "Between Theory and Practice: Planning Socialist Cities in Hungary." In *Urban Machinery: Inside Modern European Cities*, edited by Mikael Hård and Thomas J. Misa, 233–55. Cambridge, MA: MIT Press, 2008.

———. "Logistics and Infrastructures in the Warsaw Pact." Unpublished report, 2012.

Gerovitch, Slava. "InterNyet: Why the Soviet Did Not Build a Nationwide Computer Network." *History and Technology* 24 (2008): 335–50.

Giessmann, Sebastian. *Netze und Netzwerke. Archäologie einer Kulturtechnik 1740–1840.* Bielefeld: Transcript Verlag, 2006.

Giuntini, Andrea. "Inland Navigation in Italy in the Nineteenth Century." In *Inland Navigation and Economic Development in Nineteenth-Century Europe*, edited by Andreas Kunz and John Armstrong, 147–54. Mainz: Verlag Philipp von Zabern, 1995.

Goldman, Marshall I. "The Marketing Structure in the Soviet Union." *Journal of Marketing* 25 (1961): 7–14.

Gómez-Mendoza, Antonio. "Light and Shade in Spanish Coastal Shipping in the Second Half of the Nineteenth Century." In *Coastal Shipping and the European Economy 1750–1980*, edited by John Armstrong and Andreas Kunz, 101–16. Mainz: Verlag Philipp von Zabern, 2002.

———, Josefina, and Nicolás Ortega Cantero. "Hydraulics and Forestry in Spain (1855–1936)." *Geojournal* 26 (1992): 173–79.

Gonser, Simon. *Die geteilte Eisenbahn: Schienenverkehrsströme von 1945 bis 1989 in BRD und DDR.* Munich: GRIN Verlag, 2004.

Gorshkov, V.A. "Gazosnabzhenie Leningrada." *Gazovaya promyshlennost* (November 1957): 27–30.
Gottwald, Alfred. "Die Logistik des Holocaust als mörderische Aufgabe der Deutschen Reichsbahn im europäischen Raum." In *Neue Wege in ein neues Europa: Geschichte und Verkehr im 20. Jahrhundert*, edited by Ralf Roth and Karl Schlögel, 261–80. Frankfurt a.Main: Campus Verlag, 2009.
Gough, Jack, *Watching the Skies*, London: HMSO, 1993.
Graham, Steve, and Simon Marvin. *Splintering Urbanism: Networked Infrastructures, Technological Mobilities, and the Urban Condition*. London: Routledge, 2001.
Gränberg, Per-Olof, "'Skorsten kallar vi det rör som mot Ryssland röken för'. Om konstruktionen av Europas högsta skorsten vid Rönnskärsverken." *Polhem* 2 (2005): 25–42.
Grant-Friedman, Andrea. "Standing in the Mirror of World Capitalism: Economic Globalization, the Soviet Union, and the COMECON." Department of Sociology, UCLA, 2004. http://escholarship.org/uc/item/1gj5351j (accessed December 1, 2013).
Greaves, Mark, and Paul Cruddace. "The Adoption of ETRS89 as the National Mapping System for GB." Paper presented at the EUREF Symposion, 2001. http://www.euref-iag.net (accessed 15 June 2012).
Greene, Mott T. "High Achiever: The Discovery of the Stratosphere Laid the Foundations of Geophysics." *Nature* 407 (2000): 947.
Gribbe, Johan, *Stril 60: Teknik, vetenskap och svensk säkerhetspolitik under det kalla kriget*. Möklinta: Gidlunds förlag, 2011.
Grigg, David. "The Nutritional Transition in Western Europe." *Journal of Historical Geography* 22 (1995): 247–61.
———. "Food Consumption in the Mediterranean Region." *Tijdschrift voor Economische en Sociale Geografie* 90 (1999): 391–409.
———. "The Changing Geography of World Food Consumption in the Second Half of the Twentieth Century." *Geographical Journal* 165 (1999): 1–11.
Grin, John, Jan Rotmans, and Johan Schot, eds. *Transitions to Sustainable Development: New Directions in the Study of Long Term Transformative Change*. New York: Routledge, 2010.
Guide to Refrigerated Transport. Paris: International Institute of Refrigeration, 1995.
Guldi, Jo. *Roads to Power: Britain Invents the Infrastructure State*. Cambridge, MA: Harvard University Press, 2012.
Haas, Peter M. *Saving the Mediterranean: The Politics of International Environmental Protection* New York: Columbia University Press, 1990.
Haldane, Andrew G. "The Race to Zero." Speech at the International Economic Association Sixteenth World Congress, Beijing, July 8, 2011.
Hamerow, Theodore S. *From the Finland Station: The Graying of Revolution in the Twentieth Century*. New York: Basic Books, 1990.
Hansson, Anders. *Kolets återkomst : Koldioxidavskiljning och lagring i vetenskap och politik*. Linköping : Institutionen för Tema, Linköping unversity, 2008.
Hård, Mikael, and Thomas J. Misa, eds. *Urban Machinery: Inside Modern European Cities*. Cambridge, MA: MIT Press, 2008.
Harkavy, Robert. *Strategic Basing and the Great Powers, 1200–2000*. London: Routledge, 2007.
Harkavy, Robert E. *Bases Abroad: The Global Foreign Military Presence*. Oxford: Oxford University Press, 1989.

Harris, Chauncy D. "The Ruhr Coal-Mining District." *Geographical Review* 36 (1946): 194–221.

Harvard, Jonas. "Modernitetens depescher? Telegrafen och den norrländska pressens tidshorisonter, 1850–1870." *Presshistorisk årsbok* 24 (2007): 27–47.

Hayes, Ben, and Mathias Vermeulen. *Borderline: The EU's New Border Surveillance Initiatives*. Berlin: Heinrich Böll Foundation, 2012.

Hayes, Mark. H. "The Transmed and Maghreb Projects: Gas to Europe from North Africa." In *Natural Gas and Geopolitics: From 1970 to 2040*, edited by David G. Victor, Amy M. Jaffe, and Mark H. Hayes, 49–90. Cambridge: Cambridge University Press, 2006.

Haynes, Williams. "Cartels and Consolidations." *Industrial and Engineering Chemistry* 23 (1931): 588–93.

Head, Keith, and Thierry Mayer. "Non-Europe: The Magnitude and Causes of Market Fragmentation in the EU." *Review of World Economics* 136 (2000): 284–314.

Headrick, Daniel. R. *The Tools of Empire: Technology and European Imperialism in the Nineteenth Century*. Oxford: Oxford University Press, 1981.

———. *The Tentacles of Progress: Technology Transfer in the Age of Imperialism, 1850–1940*. Oxford: Oxford University Press, 1988.

———. *The Invisible Weapon: Telecommunications and International Politics 1851–1945*. New York: Oxford University Press, 1991.

———, and Pascal Griset. "Submarine Telegraph Cables: Business and Politics, 1838–1939." *Business History Review* 75 (2001): 543–78.

Hecht, Gabrielle. "Colonial Networks of Power: The Far Reaches of Systems." *Annales historiques de l'électricité* 2 (2004): 147–58.

———. "The Power of Nuclear Things." *Technology & Culture* 51 (2010): 1–30.

Hegmann, Margot. "Die Entwicklung der Zusammenarbeit im RGW." *Zeitschrift für Geschichtswissenschaft* 19 (1971): 15–53.

Heide, Lars, "EUROCONTROL: Negotiating Transnational Air Transport in Europe." In *The Making of Europe's Critical Infrastructure*, edited by Per Högselius, Anique Hommels, Arne Kaijser, and Erik van der Vleuten, 191–212. Basingstoke and New York: Palgrave Macmillan, 2013.

Henningsen, Claus G., Klaus Polster, and Dietmar Obst. "Berlin Creates 380-kV Connection with Europe." *Transmission & Distribution World* 50 (1998): 33–43.

Henrich-Franke, Christian. "Mobility and European Integration: Politicians, Professionals, and the Foundation of the ECMT." *Journal of Transport History* 29 (2008): 64–82.

———. "Changing Patterns of Infrastructure Governance in the Transport and Communication Sectors in Europe." In *Internationalization of Infrastructures: Proceedings of the 12th Annual International Conference on the Economics of Infrastructures*, edited by Jean-Francois Auger, Jan Jaap Bouma, and Rolf Künneke, 13–36. Delft: Technical University of Delft, 2009.

Hermann, J., P.J. Kershaw, P. Bailly du Bois, and P. Guegueniat. "The Distribution of Artificial Radionuclides in the English Channel, Southern North Sea, Skagerrak and Kattegat, 1990–1993." *Journal of Marine Systems* 6 (1995): 427–56.

Hermans, Janneke, and Onno de Wit. "Bourses and Brokers: Stock Exchanges as ICT Junctions." *History and Technology* 20 (2004): 227–47.

Heywood, Anthony. *Modernising Lenin's Russia: Economic Reconstruction, Foreign Trade and the Railways*. Cambridge: Cambridge University Press, 1999.

High-Level Conference on Mapping and Assessment of Ecosystems and Their Services (MAES) in Europe. "Cropland and Grassland." http://biodiversity.europa.eu/topics/ecosystems-and-habitats/agro-ecosystems-and-grasslands (accessed August 6, 2012).

Hilberg, Raul, "German Railroads/ Jewish Souls." *Society* 35 (1998): 162–74.

Hills, Jill, *The Struggle for Control of Global Communication. The Formative Century*. Urbana-Champaign: Illinois University Press, 2002.

Hitler's Table Talk 1941–1944: His Private Conversations. New York: Enigma Books, 2000.

Hobsbawm, Eric. *The Age of Extremes 1914–1991*. London: Abacus, 1994.

Hogendorn, J.S., and K.M. Scott. "The East African Groundnut Scheme: Lessons of a Large Scale Agricultural Failure." *African Economic History* 10 (1981): 81–115.

Högselius, Per. *Die deutsch-deutsche Geschichte des Kernkraftwerkes Greifswald: Atomenergie zwischen Ost und West*. Berlin: Berliner Wissenschaftsverlag, 2005.

———. *The Dynamics of Innovation in Eastern Europe: Lessons from Estonia*. Cheltenham and Northampton, MA: Edward Elgar, 2005.

———. "Connecting East and West? Electricity Systems in the Baltic Region." In *Networking Europe: Transnational Infrastructures and the Shaping of Europe, 1850–2000*, edited by Erik van der Vleuten and Arne Kaijser, 245–77. Sagamore Beach, MA: Science History Publications, 2006.

———. "Challenging Chernobyl's Legacy: Nuclear Power Policies in Europe, Russia and North America in the Early 21st Century." In *Nuclear Energy Development in Asia: Problems and Prospects*, edited by Xu Yi-Chong, 190–210. Basingstoke and New York: Palgrave Macmillan, 2010.

———. "The Decay of Communism: Managing Spent Nuclear Fuel in the Soviet Union, 1937–1991." *Risk, Hazards, and Crisis in Public Policy* 1 (2010): 83–109.

———. *Red Gas: Russia and the Origins of European Energy Dependence*. New York: Palgrave Macmillan, 2013.

———, Anna Åberg, and Arne Kaijser. "Natural Gas in Cold War Europe." In *The Making of Europe's Critical Infrastructure: Common Connections and Shared Vulnerabilities*, edited by Per Högselius, Anique Hommels, Arne Kaijser, and Erik van der Vleuten, 27–61. Basingstoke and New York: Palgrave Macmillan, 2013.

———, Anique Hommels, Arne Kaijser, and Erik van der Vleuten, eds. *The Making of Europe's Critical Infrastructure.:Common Connections and Shared Vulnerabilities*. Basingstoke and New York: Palgrave Macmillan, 2013.

———, and Arne Kaijser. *När folkhemselen blev internationell: elavregleringen i historiskt perspektiv*. Stockholm: SNS Förlag, 2007.

———, and Arne Kaijser. "The Politics of Electricity Deregulation in Sweden: The Art of Acting on Multiple Arenas." *Energy Policy* 38 (2010): 2245–54.

Höhler, Sabine, *Luftfahrtforschung und Luftfahrtmythos. Wissenchaftliche Ballonfahrt in Deutschland, 1880–1910*. Frankfurt: Campus, 2001.

Holmberg, Gustav. "Public Health, National Security and Food Technology in the Cold War." In *Science for Welfare and Warfare. Technology and State Initiative in Cold War Sweden*, edited by Per Lundin, Niklas Stenlås, Johan Gribbe, 195–212. Sagamore Beach, MA: Science History Publications, 2010.

Holmberg, Rurik. "Survival of the Unfit: Path-Dependence and the Estonian Oil Shale Industry." PhD thesis, Linköping University, 2008.

Homburg, Ernst. "De Eerste Wereldoorlog: Samenwerking en concentratie binnen de Nederlandse chemische industrie." In *Techniek in Nederland in de twintigste eeuw. Volume II: Delfstoffen, Energie, Chemie*, edited by Johan Schot, Harry Lintsen, Arie Rip, and Adri A. Albert de la Bruhèze, 316–31. Zutphen: Walburg Pers, 2000.

———. "Explosives from Oil: The Transformation of Royal Dutch/Shell during World War I from Oil to Petrochemical Company." In *Gunpowder, Explosives and the State: A Technological History*, edited by Brenda J. Buchanan, 385–407. Ashgate: Aldershot 2006.

———. "Operating on Several Fronts: The Trans-National Activities of Royal Dutch/Shell, 1914–1918." *Frontline and Factory: Comparative Perspectives on the Chemical Industry at War, 1914–1924*, edited by Roy MacLeod and Jeffrey Allan Johnson, 123–44. Dordrecht: Springer, 2006.

———, Aat van Selm, and Piet Vincken. "Industrialisatie en industriecomplexen." In *Techniek in Nederland in de twintigste eeuw. Volume II: Delfstoffen, Energie, Chemie*, edited by Johan Schot, Harry Lintsen, Arie Rip, and Adri A. Albert de la Bruhèze, 376–401. Zutphen: Walburg Pers, 2000.

Hopkins, O.P. "The Chemical Industry and Trade of England." *Journal of Industrial and Engineering Chemistry* 13 (1921): 189–97.

———. "The Chemical Industry and Trade of France." *Journal of Industrial and Engineering Chemistry* 13 (1921): 6–13.

———. "The Chemical Industry and Trade of Switzerland." *Journal of Industrial and Engineering Chemistry* 13 (1921): 285–92.

Hopkirk, Peter. *The Great Game: The Struggle for Empire in Central Asia*. New York: Kodansha, 1990.

Hospers, G.J. "Beyond the Blue Banana? Structural Change in Europe's Geo-Economy." *Intereconomics: Review of European Economic Policy* 3 (2002): 76–85.

Hough, Floyd W. "The Adjustment of the Central European Triangulation Network." *Bulletin Géodésique* 22 (1948): 64–93.

Houvenaghel, Guy. "The First International Conference on Oceanography (Brussels, 1853)." *German Journal of Hydrography* 22 (1990): 330–36.

———. "International Maritime Conference 1853." In *The Palgrave Dictionary of Transnational History*, edited by Akira Iriye and Pierre-Yves Saunier, 563–64. Basingstoke and New York: Palgrave Macmillan, 2009.

Howard, Michael. *War in European History*. Oxford: Oxford University Press, 2009.

Howkins, Trevor J. "Railway Geography and the Demarcation of Poland's Borders 1918–1930." *Journal of Transport Geography* 4 (1996): 287–99.

———. "The Adjustment of International Rail Passenger Services to New State Boundaries—The Eastern Marchlands of Europe 1918–39." *Journal of Transport Geography* 7 (1999): 147–58.

Hristov, Ivaylo. *The Communist Nuclear Era: Bulgarian Atomic Community during the Cold War, 1944–1986*. Amsterdam: Amsterdam University Press, 2014.

Huebner, S.S. "Scope and Functions of the Stock Market." *Annals of the American Academy of Political and Social Science* 35 (1910): 483–505.

Hughes, Thomas P. "The Electrification of America: The System Builders." *Technology & Culture* 20 (1979): 124–61.

———. *Networks of Power: Electrification in the Western World 1880–1930*. Baltimore: Johns Hopkins University Press, 1983.

———. *American Genesis: A Century of Invention and Technological Enthusiasm*. New York: Penguin Books, 1989.
Hugill, Peter J. *World Trade since 1431: Geography, Technology, and Capitalism*. Baltimore: Johns Hopkins University Press, 1993.
———. *Global Communications since 1844: Geopolitics and Technology*. Baltimore: Johns Hopkins University Press, 1999.
Huisman, Pieter, Joost de Jong, and Koos Wieriks. "Transboundary Cooperation in Shared River Basins: Experiences from the Rhine, Meuse and North Sea." *Water Policy* 2 (2000): 83–97.
Human Rights Watch, *The EU's Dirty Hands: Frontex Involvement in Ill-Treatment of Migrant Detainees in Greece*. New York: Human Rights Watch, 2011.
ICPR. *Salmon 2020*. International Commission for Protection of the Rhine. http://www.iksr.org (accessed May 15, 2014).
Ihde, Johannes. "Some Remarks on Geodetic Reference Systems in Eastern Europe in Preparation of a Uniform European Geoid." *Bulletin Géodésique* 67 (1993): 81–85.
Isenberg, Andrew C. *The Destruction of the Bison: An Environmental History, 1750–1920*. New York: Cambridge University Press, 2000.
IUCN. *Tenth Anniversary 1948–1958: From Fontainebleau to Delphi*. Brussels: IUCN, 1958.
———. *World Conservation Strategy: Living Resource Conservation for Sustainable Development*. Gland: IUCN, 1980.
———. *2003 United Nations List of Protected Areas*. Gland: IUCN, 2003.
Izmestieva, Tamara. "Integration of the European Coal Market and Russian Coal Imports in the Late 19th and Early 20th Century." In *Integration of Commodity Markets in History*, edited by Clara Eugenia Núñez, 79–90. Proceedings of the Twelfth International Economic History Congress, Madrid, August 1998.
Jagomägi, Jüri. "Ökoloogiliselt tasakaalustatud maa." *Eesti Loodus* 26 (1983): 219–24.
Jajeśnak-Quast, Dagmara. "In the Shadow of the Factory: Steel Towns in Postwar Eastern Europe." In *Urban Machinery: Inside Modern European Cities*, edited by Mikael Hård and Thomas J. Misa, 187–210. Cambridge, MA: MIT Press, 2008.
Jakobsson, Eva. "Industrialisering av älvar: studier kring svensk vattenkraftutbyggnad, 1900–1918." PhD thesis, Gothenburg University, 1996.
———. "Understanding Lake Vänern: Science History Perspectives on Sweden's Largest Lake, 1600–1900." In *Transference: Interdisciplinary Communications 2008/2009*, edited by W. Østreng [unpaged]. Oslo: CAS, 2010. http://www.cas.uio.no/publications_/transference.php (accessed May 15, 2014).
Janáč, Jiří. *European Coasts of Bohemia. Negotiating the Danube-Oder-Elbe Canal in a Troubled Twentieth Century*. Amsterdam: Amsterdam University Press, 2012.
Järvinen, Yrjö. *Finsk och rysk taktik under vinterkriget*. Stockholm: Söderströms, 1949.
Jennings, Jeremy. "Democracy before Tocqueville: Michel Chevalier's America." *The Review of Politics* 68 (2006): 398–427.
Jepson, Paul, and Robert J. Whittaker. "Histories of Protected Areas: Internationalisation of Conservationist Values and their Adoption in the Netherlands Indies." *Environment and History* 8 (2002): 129–72.
Joachimsthaler, Anton. *Die Breitspurbahn: Das Projekt zur Erschliessung des grosseuropäischen Raumes, 1942–1945*. Munich: Herbig, 1985.

Jobse-Van Putten, Jozien. *Eenvoudig maar voedzaam. Cultuurgeschiedenis van de dagelijkse maaltijd in Nederland.* Nijmegen: SUN, 1995.

Johansen, Hans Christian. "Danish Coastal Shipping c. 1750–1914." In *Coastal Shipping and the European Economy 1750–1980*, edited by John Armstrong and Andreas Kunz, 25–44. Mainz: Verlag Philipp von Zabern, 2002.

Johnson, Debra, and Colin Turner. *Strategy and Policy for Trans-European Networks.* Basingstoke: Palgrave Macmillan, 2007.

Johnson, Rex. "Some International Angles on Postwar Agricultural Trade." *Journal of Marketing* 11 (1946): 174–78.

Jones, David R. "The Rise and Fall of Aeroflot: Civil Aviation in the Soviet Union, 1920–91." In *Russian Aviation and Air Power in the Twentieth Century*, edited by Robin .Higham, John T. Greenwood, and Von Hardesty, 236–68. London: Frank Cass, 1998.

Jones, R.V. *Most Secret War.* Worcester: Trinity Press, 1978.

Jongman, Rob. "Nature Conservation Planning in Europe: Developing Ecological Networks." *Landscape and Urban Planning* 32 (1995): 169–83.

———, and Marion Bogers. "Current Status of the Practical Implementation of Ecological Networks in the Netherlands." Alterra/European Centre for Nature Conservation, 2008.

———, Irene Bouma, Arjan Griffioen, Lawrence Jones-Walters, and Anne van Doorn. "The Pan-European Ecological Network: PEEN." *Landscape Ecology* 26 (2011): 311–26.

Jongman, Rob H.G., Mart Külvik, and Ib Kristiansen. "European Ecological Networks and Greenways." *Landscape and Urban Planning* 68 (2004): 305–19.

Jonker, Joost, Jan-Luiten van Zanden, Stephen Howarth, and Keetie Sluyterman. *A History of Royal Dutch Shell. Volume 1: From Challenger to Joint Industry Leader 1890–1939.* New York: Oxford University Press, 2007.

Jönsson, Christer, *International Aviation and the Politics of Regime Change.* London: Frances Pinter, 1987.

Jörgensen, Hans. "Neutrality and National Preparedness: State-led Agricultural Rationalization in Cold War Sweden." In *Science for Welfare and Warfare. Technology and State Initiative in Cold War Sweden*, edited by Per Lundin, Niklas Stenlås, and Johan Gribbe, 173–93. Sagamore Beach, MA: Science History Publications, 2010.

Josephson, Paul R. *Industrialized Nature: Brute Force Technology and the Transformation of the Natural World.* Washington, DC: Island Press, 2002.

———. *Red Atom: Russia's Nuclear Power Program from Stalin to Today.* Pittsburgh, PA: University of Pittsburgh Press, 2005.

Judt, Tony, *Post War: A History of Europe since 1945.* London: Penguin, 2005.

Judy, Chelsea. "'Unbroken Towards the Sea': The National Trust and the Rise of Coastal Preservation in Late 19th and 20th Century Britain." *Voces Novae* 2 (2011): 81–96.

Kaijser, Arne. "Stadens ljus: etableringen av de första svenska gasverken." PhD thesis, Linköping University, 1987.

———. *I fädrens spår: den svenska infrastrukturens historiska utveckling och framtida utmaningar.* Stockholm: Carlssons, 1994.

———. "From Invention to Global System." In *The World's Largest Machine: Global Telecommunications and the Human Condition*, edited by Magnus Karlsson and Lennart Sturesson, 106–38. Stockholm: Carlsson, 1995.

———. "Trans-Border Integration of Electricity and Gas in the Nordic Countries, 1915–1992." *Polhem: Tidskrift för teknikhistoria* 15 (1997): 4–43.

———. "Striking Bonanza: The Establishment of a Natural Gas Regime in the Netherlands." In The *Governance of Large Technical Systems*, edited by Olivier Coutard, 38–57. London: Routledge, 1999.

———. "System Building from Below." *Technology & Culture* 43 (2002): 521–48.

———. "Nature's Periphery: Rural Tansformation by the Advent of Infrasystems." In *Taking Place: The Spatial Contexts of Science, Technology and Business*, edited by Enrico Baraldi, Hjalmar Fors and Anders Houltz, 151–86. Sagamore Beach, MA: Science History Publications, 2005.

———. "Under a Common Acid Sky. Negotiating Transboundary Air Pollution in Europe." In *Cosmopolitan Commons: Sharing Resources and Risks across Borders*, edited by Nil Disco and Eda Kranakis, 213–42. Cambridge, MA: MIT Press, 2013.

Kaiser, Wolfram, and Johan Schot. *Writing the Rules for Europe: Experts, Cartels, International Organizations*. Basingstoke and New York: Palgrave Macmillan, 2014.

Kalpagam, U. "Cartography in Colonial India." *Economic and Political Weekly* 30 (1995): 87–98.

Kane, Thomas, *Military Logistics and Strategic Performance*. London: Frank Cass, 2001.

Kapitonov, V. "Important Instrument of the CMEA Countries' Economic Integration." *International Affairs* 22 (1976): 105–13.

———. "CMEA: A New Sphere of Cooperation." *International Affairs* 24, (1978): 39–47.

Karapetian, I.G., A.L. Kudoyarov, U.S. Zhelezko, and V.E. Vorotnitski. "Energy Conservation in the Transmission and Distribution of Electricity in the Soviet Union." *Energy* 12 (1987): 1107–10.

Karm, Ellen. "Environment and Energy: The Baltic Sea Gas Pipeline." *Journal of Baltic Studies* 39 (2008): 99–121.

Kasanko, Marjo et al. "Are European Cities Becoming Dispersed?" *Landscape and Urban Planning* 77 (2006): 111–30.

Kaszuba, Stanislaw. "East and Central Europe Stock Exchange Markets in the Ages of Globalization." *International Journal of Trade, Economics and Finance* 1 (2010): 89–92.

Kelly, P.M., D.A. Campbell, P.P. Micklin, and J.R. Tarrant. "Large-Scale Water Transfers in the USSR." *GeoJournal* 9 (1983): 201–14.

Kemp, John. "Coastal Navigation in the Mid-20th Century." *Journal of Navigation* 64 (2011): 533–50.

Kennedy, Paul. "Imperial Cable Communictions and Strategy." *English Historical Review* 86 (1971): 728–52.

———. *The Rise and Fall of British Naval Mastery*. London: Allen Lane, 1976.

———. *Engineers of Victory: The Problem Solvers Who Turned The Tide in the Second World War*. New York: Random House, 2012.

Keulartz, Jozef. "European Nature Conservation and Restauration Policy—Problems and Perspectives." *Restauration Ecology* 17 (2009): 446–50.

Khimii, Uspekhi. "Chemistry and the Building of Communism." *Russian Chemical Reviews* 30 (1961): 623–24.

Khrgian, Aleksandr, *Meteorology: A Historical Survey*. Jerusalem: Israel Program for Scientific Translations, 1970.

Killick J.R., and W.A. Thomas. "The Provincial Stock Exchanges 1830–1870." *Economic History Review*, New Series 23 (1970): 96–111.

Kim, John. "Nutrition and the Decline of Mortality." In *The Cambridge World History of Food*, Volume II, edited by Kenneth Kiple and Kriemchild Conée Ornelas, 1381–9. Cambridge: Cambridge University Press, 2000.

Kindleberger, Charles P., and Robert Aliber. *Manias, Panics, and Crashes. A History of Financial Crises*, fifth edition. Hoboken, NJ: Wiley, 2005.

Kirby, Maurice. *Operational Research in War and Peace. The British Experience from the 1930s to 1970s*. London: Imperial College Press.

Klemann, Hein A.M., and Friso Wielenga eds. *Deutschland und die Niederlande. Wirtschaftsbeziehungen im 19. und 20. Jahrhundert*. Niederlande Studien 46. Münster: Waxman, 2009.

Karas, Serkan. "Infrastructuring Europe: Report No. 2, Part 1." Unpublished, Athens, 2011.

Köhler-Zülch, Ines. "Hans Christian Andersen und die Harzer Sagentopographie." In *Erzählkultur: Beiträge zur kulturwissenschaftlichen Erzählforschung*, edited by Rolf Wilhelm Brednich, 173–90. Berlin and New York, 2009.

Kolb, Eberhard. "Die Reichsbahn vom Dawes-Plan bis zum Ende der Weimarer Republik." In *Die Eisenbahn in Deutschland: Von den Anfängen bis zur Gegenwart*, edited by Lothar Gall and Manfred Pohl, 109–64. Munich: C.H. Beck, 1999.

Komarov, Boris. "Destruction of Nature in the Soviet Union." *Society* (July/August 1981): 39–49.

Komlo, Laszlo. "Révolution agraire et industrialisation du complexe alimentaire hongrois." *Économie rurale* 83 (1970): 113–23.

Kouki, Jari et al. "Forest Fragmentation in Fennoscandia." *Scandinavian Journal of Forest Research* 16, Supplement 3 (2001): 27–37.

Kragh, Helge, and Hans Jørgen Styhr Petersen. *En nyttig videnskab. Episoder fra den tekniske kemis historie i Danmark*. Copenhagen: Gyldendal, 1995.

Kranakis, Eda. "European Civil Aviation in an Era of Hegemonic Nationalism: Infrastructure, Air Mobility, and European Identity Formation, 1919–1933." In *Materializing Europe: Transnational Infrastructures and the Project of Europe*, edited by Alec Badenoch and Andreas Fickers, 290–326. Basingstoke and New York: Palgrave Macmillan, 2010.

———. "The 'Good Miracle': Building a European Airspace Commons, 1919–1939." In *Cosmopolitan Commons: Sharing Resources and Risks across Borders*, edited by Nil Disco and Eda Kranakis, 57–96. Cambridge, MA: MIT Press, 2013.

Krupskaya, Nadezhda. "Departure for Russia." In *Reminiscences of Lenin*. Moscow: Foreign Languages Publishing House, 1959.

Külvik, Mart. *Ecological Networks in Estonia—Concepts and Applications*. Tartu: Tartu University Press, 2002.

Kunz, Andreas. "The Economic Performance of Inland Navigation in Germany." In *Inland Navigation and Economic Development in Nineteenth-Century Europe*, edited by Andreas Kunz and John Armstrong, 47–76. Mainz: Verlag Philipp von Zabern, 1995.

———, and John Armstrong, eds. *Inland Navigation and Economic Development in Nineteenth-Century Europe*. Mainz: Verlag Philipp von Zabern, 1995.

Kuromiya Hiroaki. "The Soviet Famine of 1932–1933 Reconsidered." *Europe-Asia Studies* 60 (2008): 663–75.

Laborie, Léonard. "A Missing Link? Telecommunications Networks and European Integration, 1945–1970." In *Networking Europe: Transnational Infrastructures and the Shaping of Europe, 1850–2000*, edited by Erik van der Vleuten and Arne Kaijser, 187–215. Sagamore Beach, MA: Science History Publications, 2006.

Lagendijk, Vincent. *Electrifying Europe: The Power of Europe in the Construction of Electricity Networks*. Amsterdam: Aksant, 2008.

———. "Divided Development: Postwar Ideas on River Utilisation and their Influence on the Development of the Danube." *The International History Review* 36 (2014).

———, and Erik van der Vleuten. "Inventing Electrical Europe: Interdependencies, Borders, Vulnerabilities." In *The Making of Europe's Critical Infrastructures: Common Connections and Shared Vulnerabilities*, edited by Per Högselius, Anique Hommels, Arne Kaijser, and Erik van der Vleuten, 62–104. Basingstoke and New York: Palgrave Macmillan, 2013.

Langlinay, Erik. "Kuhlmann at War 1914–1921."In *Frontline and Factory: Comparative Perspectives on the Chemical Industry at War, 1914–1924*, edited by R.M. MacLeod and J.A. Johnson, 145–66. Dordrecht: Springer 2006.

Larsson, Robert. *Nord Stream, Sweden and Baltic Sea Security*. FOI Base data report. Stockholm: FOI, 2007.

Launder, William. "No Urge to Merge." *Wall Street Journal*, October 10, 2011.

Lefeuvre, Jean-Claude. "De la protection de la nature á la gestion du patrimoine naturel." In *Patrimoines en Folie*, edited by Henri Pierre Jeudy, 29–76. Paris: Éditions de la Maison des sciences de l'homme, 1990.

Leonard, Sarah. "The Creation of FRONTEX and the Politics of Institutionalisation in the EU External Borders Policy." *Journal of Contemporary European Research* 5 (2009): 371–88.

Lesova, Polya. "In Russia, It's a Start." *Wall Street Journal*. October 10, 2011.

Levallois, J.J. "The History of the International Association of Geodesy." *Bulletin Géodésique* 54 (1980): 249–313.

Levitt, Theresa. *A Short Bright Flash: Augustin Fresnel and the Birth of the Modern Lighthouse*. New York and London: Norton, 2013.

Levy, Marc. "European Acid Rain: The Power of Tote-Board Diplomacy." In *Institutions for the Earth: Sources of Effective International Environmental Protection*, edited by Peter Haas, Robert Keohane, and Marc Levy, 75–132. Cambridge, MA: MIT Press, 1993.

Lidell Hart, Basil. *History of the Second World War*. New York: Putnam, 1971.

Linneroth, Joanne. "The Danube River Basin: Negotiating Settlements to Transboundary Environmental Issues." *Natural Resources Journal* 30 (1990): 629–60.

Lissitzyn, Oliver. "The Diplomacy of Air Transport," *Foreign Affairs*, Vol 19, No 1 (Oct. 1940): 156–70.

Livi Bacci, Massimo. *The Population of Europe: A History*. Oxford: Blackwell, 2000.

Llamas, M. Ramón. "Transboundary Water Resources in the Iberian Peninsula." In *Conflict and the Environment*, edited by Nils Petter Gleditsch, 335–53. Boston: Kluwer, 1997.

Lommers, Suzanne, *Europe—On Air: Interwar Projects for Radio Broadcasting*. Amsterdam: Amsterdam University Press, 2012.

Lucassen, Jan, and Leo Lucassen, *The Mobility Transition in Europe Revisited, 1500–1900: Sources and Methods*. International Institute of Social History Research Paper 46. Amsterdam: IISG, 2010.

———. "From Mobility Transition to Comparative Global Migration History." *Journal of Global History* 6 (2011): 299–307.

Lundgren, Lars. *Acid Rain on the Agenda: A Picture of a Chain of Events in Sweden, 1966–1968*. Lund: Lund University Press, 1998.

Lundin, Per. *Bilsamhället: ideologi, expertis och regelskapande i efterkrigstidens Sverige*. Stockholm: Stockholmia, 2008.

———. "Mediators of Modernity: Planning Experts and the Making of the 'Car-Friendly' City in Europe." In *Urban Machinery: Inside Modern European Cities*, edited by Mikael Hård and Thomas J. Misa, 257–79. Cambridge, MA: MIT Press, 2008.

Lüttichau, Christian. "Opdyrkning af heden og moser." In *Danmarks kultur ved Aar 1940. Volume 5*, edited by Svend Dahl, 74–103. Copenhagen: Det danske forlag, 1942.

Lynn, John. *Feeding Mars: Logistics in Western Warfare from the Middle Ages to the Present*. Boulder, CO: Westview Press, 1993.

MacGarvin, Malcom. *The North Sea*. London: Collins and Brown/Greenpeace, 1990.

MacKenzie, Donald. *Inventing Accuracy: A Historical Sociology of Nuclear Missile Guidance*. Cambridge, MA: MIT Press, 1990.

Macmillan, Norman. *Sir Sefton Brancker*. London: Heinemann, 1935.

Magee, Gary B., and Andrew S. Thompson. *Empire and Globalisation: Networks of People, Goods and Capital in the British World, c. 1850–1914*. Cambridge: Cambridge University Press, 2010.

Magris, Claudio. *The Danube*. London: Harvill Press, 2001 (Italian original 1986).

Maier, Helmut. "Systems Connected: IG Auschwitz, Kaprun, and the Building of European Power Grids up to 1945." In *Networking Europe: Transnational Infrastructures and the Shaping of Europe, 1850–2000*, edited by Erik van der Vleuten and Arne Kaijser, 129–58. Sagamore Beach, MA: Science History Publications, 2006.

Maltby, Tomas. "European Union Energy Policy Integration: A Case of European Commission Policy Entrepreneurship and Increasing Supranationalism." *Energy Policy* 55 (2013): 435–44.

Mander, Ülo, and Hannes Palang. "Changes of Landscape Structure in Estonia during the Soviet Period." *Geojournal* 33 (1994): 45–54.

Mansholt, Derk. *Over de internationale arbeidsverdeling en de prijsvorming van het broodkoren*. St. Anna Parochy, 1896.

Marate, Ashraf A. "Contagion Effects of Three Late Nineteenth Century British Bank Failures." *Business and Economic History* 23 (1994): 102–15.

Marijnissen, Hans. "Voorlopig liever niet te veel herten over het ecoduct." *Trouw* 13, November 2012.

Marks, Stephen G. *Road to Power: The Trans-Siberian Railroad and the Colonization of Asian Russia, 1850–1917*. Ithaca, NY: Cornell University Press, 1991.

Mastny, Vojtech, and Malcolm Byrne, eds. *A Cardboard Castle? An Inside History of the Warsaw Pact, 1955–1991*. Budapest: Central European University Press, 2005.

Mather, A.S., and J. Fairbairn. "From Floods to Reforestation: The Forest Transition in Switzerland." *Environment and History* 6 (2000): 399–421.

Mattelart, Armand. *The Invention of Communication*. Minneapolis: University of Minnesota Press, 1996.

———. *Networking the World 1794–2000*. Minneapolis: University of Minnesota Press, 2000.

Matthäus, Wolfgang. *Germany and the Investigation of the Baltic Sea Hydrography during the 19th and Early 20th Century*. Warnemünde: Leibniz-Institut für Ostseeforschung, 2010.

Maury, Matthew Fontaine. *The Physical Geography of the Sea*. New York: Harper & Brothers, 1855.

Maybury-Lewis, David. "Genocide against Indigenous Peoples." In *Annihilating Difference: The Anthropology of Genocide*, edited by Alexander Laban Hinton, 43–53. Berkely: University of California Press, 2002.

Mayevsky, Viktor. "Chemistry and Politics." *The Current Digest of the Soviet Press* 15 (1964): 34.

Mazower, Mark. *Dark Continent: Europe's Twentieth Century*. London: Penguin, 1999.

McCalla, Alex F. "Protectionism in International Agricultural Trade 1850–1968." *Agricultural History* 43 (1969): 329–43.

McInally, John. *Eurocontrol History Book*. Brussels: Eurocontrol, 2010.

McMeekin, Sean. *The Berlin-Baghdad Express: The Ottoman Empire and Germany's Bid for World Power*. Cambridge, MA: The Belknap Press of Harvard University Press, 2010.

McNeill, William. *The Pursuit of Power: Technology, Armed Force, and Society since AD 1000*. Chicago: University of Chicago Press, 1982.

Meeus, J.H.A., M.P. Wijermans, and M.J. Vroom. "Agricultural Landscapes in Europe and their Transformation." *Landscape and Urban Planning* 18 (1990): 289–352.

Meier, Kadri, Valso Kuusemets, Jaan Luig, and Ülo Mander. "Riparian Buffer Zones as Elements of Ecological Networks: Case Study on Parnassius Mnemosyne Distribution in Estonia." *Ecological Engineering* 24 (2005): 531–37.

Meier, Lars. "Working in the Skyline: Images and Everyday Action." *Encountering Urban Places: Visual And Material Performances in the City*, edited by Lars Frers and Lars Meier, 119–34. Aldershot: Ashgate, 2007.

Meinander, Henrik, *Finlands historia, del 4*. Esbo: Schildts Förlag, 1999.

Mentzel, Peter. *Transportation Technology and Imperialism in the Ottoman Empire, 1800–1923*. Washington, DC: American Historical Association, 2006.

Merger, Michèle. "The Great European Infrastructure Projects and their Outcome." In *Neue Wege in ein neues Europa: Geschichte und Verkehr im 20. Jahrhundert*, edited by Ralf Roth and Karl Schlögel. Frankfurt a.Main: Campus Verlag, 2009: 417–30.

———, Albert Carreras, and Andrea Giuntini, eds. *Les réseaux européens transnationaux: XIXe et XXe siècles: Quels enjeux?* Nantes: Ouest Éditions, 1995.

Meyer, Jan-Henrik. "Greening Europe? Environmental Interest Groups and the Europeanization of a New Policy Field." *Comparativ* 3 (2010): 83–104.

———. "Saving Migrants: A Transnational Network Supporting Supranational Bird Protection Policy in the 1970s." In *Transnational Networks in Regional Integration: Governing Europe 1945–1983*, edited by Wolfram Kaiser, Brigitte Leucht, and Michael Gehler, 176–98. Basingstoke: Palgrave Macmillan, 2010.

———. "L'européanisation de la politique environnementale dans les années 1970." *Revue d'histoire* 20 (2012): 117–26.

Michelsen, Karl-Erik. "An Uneasy Alliance: Negotiating Infrastructure at the Finnish-Soviet Border." In *The Making of Europe's Critical Infrastructures: Common Connections and Shared Vulnerabilities*, edited by Per Högselius, Anique

Hommels, Arne Kaijser, and Erik van der Vleuten, 108–30. Basingstoke and New York: Palgrave Macmillan, 2013.

Michie, Ranald C. "The London Stock Exchange and the British Securities Market, 1850–1914." *Economic History Review*, New Series 38, No. 1 (1985): 61–82.

———. "The London and New York Stock Exchanges, 1850–1914." *Journal of Economic History* 46 (1986): 171–87.

———. "Friend or Foe? Information Technology and the London Stock Exchange since 1700." *Journal of Historical Geography* 23 (1997): 304–26.

———. *The London Stock Exchange: A History*. Oxford: Oxford University Press, 1999.

———. "One World or Many Worlds? Markets, Banks, and Communications 1850s–1990s." In *European Banking Overseas, 19th–20th Century*, edited by Ton de Graaf, Joost Jonker, and Jaap-Jan Mobron, 227–48. Amsterdam: ABN AMRO Historical Archives, 2002.

———. *The Global Securities Market: A History*. Oxford: Oxford University Press, 2006.

Mierzejewski, Alfred C. *The Most Valuable Asset of the Reich: A History of the German National Railway. Volume 2, 1933–1945*. Chapel Hill, NC: University of North Carolina Press, 2000.

———. "A Public Enterprise in the Service of Mass Murder: The Deutsche Reichsbahn and the Holocaust." *Holocaust Genocide Studies* 15 (2001): 33–46.

Miklós, László. "The Most Successful Landscape Ecological Concepts in the Practice." *Problems of Landscape Ecology* 28 (2010): 15–22.

Miller, Michael B. "Steamships." In *The Palgrave Dictionary of Transnational History*, edited by Akira Iriye and Pierre-Yves Saunier, 976–79. Basingstoke and New York: Palgrave Macmillan, 2009.

Millward, Robert. *Private and Public Enterprise in Europe: Energy, Telecommunications and Transport 1830–1990*. Cambridge: Cambridge University Press, 2005.

———, and John Singleton. *The Political Economy of Nationalization in Britain 1920–1950*. Cambridge: Cambridge University Press, 1995.

Mitchell, Allan. *The Great Train Race: Railways and the Franco-German Rivalry, 1815–1914*. New York: Berghahn Books, 2000.

Mitsch William J., and Sven E. Jørgensen. "Ecological Engineering: A Field Whose Time Has Come." *Ecological Engineering* 20 (2003) 363–77.

Mol, Hein. *Memories van een havenarbeider*. Nijmegen: SUN, 1980 (orig. 1932).

Molenaar, Henk. "The End of the Sea." In *Struggling for Leadership: Antwerp-Rotterdam Port Competition 1870–2000*, edited by Reginald Loyen, Erik Buyst, and Greta Davos, 179–93. Heidelberg: Physica-Verlag, 2003.

Mollat du Jourdin, Michel. *Europe and the Sea*. Oxford: Blackwell, 1993.

Molle, Francois. "River-Basin Planning and Management: The Social Life of a Concept." *Geoforum* 40 (2009): 484–94.

Molle, Willem and Egbert Wever. "Oil Refineries and Petrochemical Industries in Europe." *GeoJournal* 9 (1984): 421–30.

Mom, Gijs. "Roads without Rails: European Highway Network Building and the Desire for Long-Range Motorized Mobility." *Technology and Culture* 46 (2005): 745–72.

Mombauer, Annika. *Helmuth von Moltke and the Origins of the First World War*. Cambridge: Cambridge University Press, 2001.

Mooij, Joke. "A History of International Financial Communications: the Netherlands since the 1850s." In *European Banking Overseas, 19th-20th Century*, edited by Ton de Graaf, Joost Jonker, and Jaap-Jan Mobron, 249–70. Amsterdam: ABN AMRO Historical Archives, 2002.

Morilla Critz, José, Alan L. Olmstead, Paul W. Rhode. "'Horn of Plenty': The Globalization of Mediterranean Horticulture and the Economic Development of Southern Europe 1880–1930." *Journal of Economic History* 59 (1999): 316–52.

Morris Peter T.J., and Anthony S. Travis. "A History of the International Dyestuff Industry." *American Dyestuff Reporter* 81 (1992): 59–100 and 192–95.

Mücher, Sander. "Geo-Spatial Modelling and Monitoring of European Landscapes and Habitats Using Remote Sensing and Field Surveys." PhD thesis, Wageningen University, 2009.

Mukerjee, Madhusree. *Churchill's Secret War: The British Empire and the Ravaging of India during World War II*. New York: Basic Books, 2010.

Muraskin, William. "Nutrition and Mortality Decline: Another Vie." In *The Cambridge World History of Food, Volume II*, edited by Kenneth Kiple and Kriemchild Conée Ornelas, 1389–97. Cambridge: Cambridge University Press, 2000.

Murgescu, Bogdan. "Anything but Simple: The Case of the Romanian Oil Industry." in *History and Culture of Economic Nationalism in East Central Europe*, edited by Helga Schultz and Eduard Kubu, 231–50. Berlin: Berliner Wissenschafts-Verlag, 2006.

Myllyntaus, Timo. *Electrifying Finland: The Transfer of a New Technology into a Late Industrialising Economy*. London: Macmillan, 1991.

Myrdal, Gunnar. "Twenty Years of the United Nations Economic Committee for Europe." *International Organization* 22 (1968): 617–28.

Nachtnebel, H.P. "The Danube River Basin Environmental Programme: Plans and Actions for a Basin Wide Approach." Paper presented at the EU-SADC Conference on Shared River Basins, Maseru, Lesotho, May 1997.

Næs, Petter. "Urban Planning and Sustainable Development." *European Planning Studies* 9 (2001): 503–24.

Nalbach, Alex. "'Poisoned at the Source'? Telegraphic News Services and Big Business in the Nineteenth Century." *Business History Review* 77 (2003): 577–610.

Nebeker, Frederik. *Calculating the Weather: Meteorology in the 20th Century*. San Diego: Academic Press, 1995.

Newman, Paul B. *Travel and Trade in the Middle Ages*. Jefferson, NC: McFarland, 2011.

Nicholls, Anthony James. "Zusammenbruch und Wiederaufbau: Die Reichsbahn während der Besatzungszeit." In *Die Eisenbahn in Deutschland: von den Anfängen bis zur Gegenwart*, edited by Lothar Gall and Manfred Pohl, 245–80. Munich: C.H. Beck, 1999.

Nicklin, Sean. *Formal and Informal Governance of Civil Aviation across the Iron Curtain: The Case of Czechoslovakian Airlines (CSA) 1945–1970*. Tensions of Europe and Inventing Europe Working Paper series, working paper No. 2010/ 16, http://tensionsofeurope.eu/www/en/publications/working-papers (accessed 5 January 2015).

Nilsson, Jan Henrik. "Östersjöområdet: studier av interaktion och barriärer." PhD thesis, Lund University, 2003.

Nitsch, Volker. "National Borders and International Trade: Evidence from the European Union." *The Canadian Journal of Economics* 33 (2000): 1091–1105.

Nordström, Ludvig. *Lort-Sverige*. Stockholm: Kooperativa förbundets bokförlag, 1938.

———. *En dag i mitt liv: lite vardagsdemokrati*. Stockholm: Kooperativa förbundets bokförlag, 1942.

Oddy, Derek, and Lydia Petráňová. "The Diffusion of Food Culture." In *The Diffusion of Food Culture in Europe from the Late 18th Century to the Present Day*, edited by Derek Oddy and Lydia Petráňová, 18–28. Prague: Academia, 2005.

Odum, Eugene P. "The Strategy of Ecosystem Development." *Science*, New Series 164 (1969): 262–70.

Odum, H.T. "Man and Ecosystem." *Bulletin Connecticut Agric. Station* 1962.

OECD. *OECD Programme on Long Range Transport of Air Pollutants: Measurements and Findings*. Paris: OECD, 1977.

OEEC. *Europe's Growing Needs of Energy: How Can They Be Met?* Paris: OEEC, 1956.

Office of Technology Assessment. *Trading Around the Clock: Global Securities Markets and Information Technology*. Background Paper, OTA-BP-W-66. Washington, DC: U.S. Congress Office, 1990.

O'Hagan, J. P. "National Self-Sufficiency in Food." *Food Policy*, Vol. 1, No. 5 (1976): 355–66.

Ojala, Jari. "Finnish Coastal Shipping 1750–1850." In *Coastal Shipping and the European Economy 1750–1980*, edited by John Armstrong and Andreas Kunz, 63–74. Mainz: Verlag Philipp von Zabern, 2002.

Oldenziel, Ruth, and Mikael Hård. *Consumers, Tinkerers, Rebels: The People Who Shaped Europe*. Basingstoke and New York: Palgrave Macmillan, 2013.

Orland, Barbara. "Milky Ways: Dairy, Landscape, and Nation Building until 1930." In *Land, Shops, and Kitchens: Technology and the Food Chain in Twentieth Century Europe*, edited by Carmen Sarasúa, Peter Scholliers, and Leen Van Molle, 212–54. Turnhout: Brepols, 2005.

Oszlányi, Július, Krystyna Grodzínska, Ovidiu Badea, and Yuriy Shparyk. "Nature Conservation in Central and Eastern Europe." *Environmental Pollution* 130 (2004): 127–34.

Oudet, L. "The Crisis in the Increase of Tonnage." *Journal of Navigation* 21 (1968): 305–19.

Pace, Scott et al. *The Global Positioning System: Assessing National Policies*. Santa Monica, CA: Rand Corporation, 1995.

Padfield, Peter. *War Beneath the Sea: U-Boat Conflict during World War II*. New York: Wiley, 1995.

Padgett, Steven. "The Single European Energy Market: The Politics of Realization." *Journal of Common Market Studies* 30 (1992): 53–75.

Papanicolopulu, Irini. "A Note on Maritime Delimitation in a Multizonal Context: The Case of the Mediterranean." *Ocean Development & International Law* 38 (2007): 381–98.

Paquier, Serge, and Jean-Pierre Williot, eds. *L'industrie du gaz en Europe aux XIXe et XXe siècle. L'innovation entre marchés et collectivités publiques*. Brussels: Lang, 2005.

Patel, Kiran Klaus. "Paradefall der Integration? Die Gemeinsame Agrarpolitik der EWG und die Agrarintegration nach dem Zweiten Weltkrieg." In *Integration und*

Europäische Integration im Vergleich, edited by C. Heinrich Franke, C. Neutsch, and G. Thiemeyer, 203–19. Baden-Baden: Nomos, 2007.

———, and Johan Schot. "Twisted Paths to European Integration: Comparing Agriculture and Transport Policies in a Transnational Perspective." *Contemporary European History* 20 (2011): 383–403.

Payton-Smith, Derek J., *Oil: A Study of War-Time Policy and Administration*. London: HMSO, 1971.

Pearson, Michael. *The Sealed Train*. London: Macmillan, 1975.

Persson, Anders. "Rätt av fel orsak? Väderprognosen för D-dagen 1944." *Svenskt militärhistoriskt bibliotek presenterar*, March 2013.

Persson, Göran. "...och än faller regnet." In Naturvårdsverket, *Miljö för Miljoner. Svensk miljövård 1985*, 7–22. Stockholm: Naturvårdsverket, 1985.

———. "The Acid Rain Story." In *International Environmental Negotiations: Process, Issues and Contexts*. edited by G. Sjöstedt, U. Svedin, and B. Hägerhäll Aniansson, 105–16. Stockholm: Utrikespolitiska Institutet and Forskningsrådsnämnden, 1993.

Pinilla, Vicente. "The Development of Irrigated Agriculture in Twentieth-Century Spain: A Case Study of the Ebro Basin." *Agricultural History Review* 54 (2006): 122–41.

Plant, G. "International Traffic Separation Schemes in the New Law of the Sea." *Marine Policy*, April 1985: 134–47.

Plieninger, Tobias, Franz Höchtl, and Theo Speck. "Traditional Land-Use and Nature Conservation in European Rural Landscapes." *Environmental Science and Policy* 9 (2006): 317–21.

Plotnikov, K. "Certain Problems of the Development of Finance and Credit in the Process of Building Communism." *Problems of Economics* 7 (1965): 31–40.

Podvig, Pavel. *Russian Strategic Nuclear Forces*. Cambridge, MA: MIT Press, 2001.

Posner, Elliot. *The Origins of Europe's New Stock Markets*. Cambridge, MA: Harvard University Press, 2009.

Pounds, N.J.G. *An Historical Geography of Europe, 1800–1914*. Cambridge: Cambridge University Press, 1985.

Pratt, Edwin, *The Rise of Rail-Power in War and Conquest, 1833–1914*. London: P.S. King and Son, 1915.

Priester, P.R. "Het melkveehouderijbedrijf." In *Techniek in Nederland in de twintigste eeuw. Vol. 3: Landbouw en voeding*, edited by Johan Schot, Harry Lintsen, Arie Rip, and Adri A. Albert de la Bruhèze, 99–125. Zutphen: Walburg Pers, 2000.

Pritchard, Sara B. *Confluence: The Nature of Technology and the Remaking of the Rhône*. Cambridge, MA: Harvard University Press, 2011.

Pulley, Raymond H. "The Railroad and Argentine National Development, 1852–1914." *The Americas* 23 (1966): 63–75.

Pumain, Denise. "An Implicit Large Territorial-Technical System: Settlement Systems." *Flux* 21 (1994): 11–20.

Pyenson, Lewis. "Athena's Retinue: Nineteenth-Century Scientists Embedded in the Army." *The British Journal for the History of Science* 45 (2012): 377–400.

Radkau, Joachim. "Zum ewigem Wachstum verdammt? Jugend und Alter grosstechnischer Systeme." In *Technik ohne Grenzen*, edited by Ingo Braun and Bernward Joerges, 50–106. Frankfurt a.Main: Suhrkamp, 1994.

———. *Nature and Power: A Global History of the Environment*. New York: Cambridge University Press, 2008.

Rambousek, H. "Die ÖMV-Aktiengesellschaft: Entstehung und Entwicklung eines nationalen Unternehmens der Mineralölindustrie." PhD thesis, Wirtschaftsuniversität Wien, 1977.

Reagan, Gillian. "The Evolution of Facebook's Mission Statement." *New York Observer*, July 13, 2009.

Reed, Peter. "The British Chemical Industry and the Indigo Trade." *British Journal for the History of Science* 25 (1992): 113–25.

Reeder, David A. "The Social Construction of Green Space in London before the Second World War." In *The European City and Green Space 1850–2000: London, Helsinki, Stockholm, and St. Petersburg 1850–2000*, edited by Peter Clark, 41–67. London: Ashgate, 2006.

Remm, K., M. Külvik, Ü. Mander, and K. Sepp. "Design of the Pan-European Ecological Network: A National Level Attempt." In *Ecological Networks and Greenways*, edited by R. Jongman and G. Pungetti, 151–70. Cambridge: Cambridge University Press, 2004.

Rempe, Martin. "Airy Promises: Senegal and the EEC's Common Agricultural Policy in the Nineteen-Sixties." In *Fertile Ground for Europe? The History of European Integration and the Common Agricultural Policy since 1945*, edited by Kiran Klaus Patel, 221–40. Baden-Baden: Nomos, 2009.

———. "Fit für den Weltmarkt in fünf Jahren? Die Modernisierung der senegalesischen Erdnusswirtschaft in den 1960er Jahren." In *Entwicklungswelten. Zur Globalgeschichte der Entwicklungszusammenarbeit*, edited by Hubertus Büschel and Daniel Speich, 241–74. Frankfurt a.M.: Campus Verlag, 2009.

Resolving the Global Economic Crisis: After Wall Street. A Statement by Thirty-Three Economists from Thirteen Countries. Washington: Institute for International Economics, 1987.

Reszat, Beate. *European Financial Systems in the Global Economy*. Chichester: Wiley, 2005.

Ribeill, Georges. "Les 'Services agricole' des grands réseaux: de grands moyens pour quelle efficacité?" *Revue d'histoire des chemins de fer* 41 (2009): 61–87.

Richardson, H.W. "Development of the British Dyestuffs Industry before 1939." *Scottish Journal of Political Economy* 11 (1964): 110–29.

Richter, Wolfram. *Der Brocken—ein deutscher Berg. Bilder, Texte, Dokumente*, ninth edition. Claustal-Zellerfeld: Pieper, 2004.

Rink, Dieter. "Environmental Policy and the Environmental Movement in East Germany." *Capitalism Nature Socialism* 13 (2002): 73–91.

Ritchie, George Stephen. *The Admiralty Chart: British Naval Hydrography in the Nineteenth Century*. London: Hollis & Carter, 1967.

Ritvo, Harriet. *The Dawn of Green: Manchester, Thirlmere, and Modern Environmentalism*. Chicago: University of Chicago Press, 2009.

Robbins, Richard G. Jr. "Russia's System of Food Supply Relief on the Eve of the Famine of 1891–92." *Agricultural History* 45 (1971): 259–69.

———. *Famine in Russia 1891–1892: The Imperial Government Responds to a Crisis*. New York/London: Columbia University Press, 1975.

Robin, Libby, Sverker Sörlin, and Paul Warde, eds. *The Future of Nature: Documents of Global Change*. New Haven: Yale University Press, 2013.

Robinson, Robert. "Sir William Henry Perkin: Pioneer of Chemical Industry." *Journal of Chemical Education* 34 (1957): 54–58.

Rochlin, Gene I. *Trapped in the Net: The Unanticipated Consequences of Computerization.* Princeton: Princeton University Press, 1997.

Rockström, Johan et al. "A Safe Operating Space for Humanity." *Nature* 461 (2009): 472–75.

Roggersdorf, Wilhelm. *Im Reiche der Chemie. 100 Jahre BASF.* Düsseldorf/Wien: Econ-Verlag, 1965.

Rohen, Beatrice. *50 years of Transfrigoroute International: A Retrospective of the Early Years and the Most Important Developments.* Bern, 2005.

Rose, Alexander. "Radar and Air Defense in the 1930s." *Twentieth Century British History* 9 (1998): 219–45.

Rostow, W.W. "The Economic Commission for Europe." *International Organization* 3 (1949): 254–68.

Roth, Ralf. "Wirtschaftliche, politische und kulturelle Implikationen der Eisenbahn im deutsch-skandinavischen Raum—1870 bis 1914." In *Die Internationalität der Eisenbahn 1850–1970*, edited by Monika Burri, Kilian T. Elsasser, and David Gugerli, 131–48. Zürich: Chronos Verlag, 2003.

———, and Karl Schlögel, eds. *Neue Wege in ein neues Europa. Geschichte und Verkehr im 20. Jahrhundert.* Frankfurt a.Main: Campus Verlag, 2009.

Rozwadowski, Helen. *Fathoming the Ocean: The Discovery and Exploration of the Deep Sea.* Cambridge, MA: Belknap Press of Harvard University Press.

Rutledge, Ian, and Philip Wright. "World Coal and UK Energy Policy: A Company Level Perspective." *Energy Policy* 21 (1993): 788–97.

Sagers Matthew J., and Theodore Shabad. *The Chemical Industry in the USSR: An Economic Geography.* Boulder, CO: Westview Press, 1990.

Saint Simon, Comte de and A. Thierry. *De la reorganisation de la société Européenne.* Paris: Adrien Égron, 1814.

Salewicz, K.A. "Management of Large International Rivers: Practical Experiences from a Research Perspective." In *Hydrology for the Water Management of Large River Basins*, Proceedings of the Vienna Symposium, August 1991, IAHS Publ. No. 201, 1991, 57–69.

"Sarkozy's Shock Tax on Share Trading 'a Political Gesture'," *Irish Independent Newspaper* on *Independent.ie* (January 31, 2012). (accessed January 31, 2012).

Saunier, Pierre-Yves. "Sketches from the Urban Internationale." *International Journal of Urban and Regional Research* 25 (2001): 380–403.

———. *Transnational History.* Basingstoke: Palgrave Macmillan, 2013.

Scheffer, Edith. *Burned Bridge: How East and West Germans Made the Iron Curtain.* New York: Oxford University Press, 2011.

Scherzer, Günther. "Der Fortschritt der Erdgasversorgung in der Bundesrepublik und seine Auswirkungen auf die Gaswirtschaft in Bayern." *gwf* 108 (1967): 230–39.

Schiefelbusch, Martin, and Hans-Liudger Dienel. *Linking Networks: The Formation of Common Standards and Visions for Infrastructure Development.* Farnham: Ashgate, forthcoming.

Schipper, Frank. "Changing the Face of Europe: European Road Mobility during the Marshall Plan Years." *Journal of Transport History* 28 (2007): 211–28.

———. *Driving Europe: Building Europe on Roads in the Twentieth Century.* Amsterdam: Aksant, 2008.

———, Vincent Lagendijk, and Irene Anastasiadou. "New Connections for an Old Continent: Rail, Road and Electricity in the League of Nations Organisation for Communications and Transit." In *Materializing Europe: Transnational*

Infrastructures and the Project of Europe, edited by Alec Badenoch and Andreas Fickers, 113–43. Basingstoke and New York: Palgrave Macmillan, 2010.

———, and Erik van der Vleuten, "'Trans-European Network Development and Governance in Historical Perspective." *Network Industries Quarterly* 10 (2008): 5–7.

Schivelbusch, Wolfgang. *The Railway Journey: The Industrialization of Time and Space in the Nineteenth Century*. Berkeley, CA: University of California Press, 1986 (German original 1977).

Schmidt, Thorsten, and Jürgen Korsch. *Der Brocken: Berg zwischen Natur und Technik*, sixth edition. Wernigerode: Schmidt, 2009.

Schmit, Hans. "Landbouw dicteert meer dan ooit natuurplannen van de overheid." *Trouw*, February 22, 1993.

———. *The Path to European Union: From the Marshall Plan to the Common Market*. Baton Rouge: Louisiana State University Press, 1962.

Scholl, Lars U. "New York's German Suburb: The Creation of the Port of Bremerhaven." In *Harbours and Havens: Essays in Port History in Honour of Gordon Jackson*, edited by Lewis R. Fischer and Adrian Jarvis, 191–211 St. John's, Newfoundland: International Maritime Economic History Association, 1999.

Schönholzer, Ernst. "Ein elektrowirtschaftliches Programm für Europa." *Schweizerische Technische Zeitschrift* 23 (1930): 385–97.

Schot, Johan. "Transnational Infrastructures and the Origins of European Integration." In *Materializing Europe: Transnational Infrastructures and the Project of Europe*, edited by Alec Badenoch and Andreas Fickers, 82–109. Basingstoke and New York: Palgrave Macmillan, 2010.

———, and Frank Schipper. "Experts and European Transport Integration, 1945–1958." *Journal of European Public Policy* 18 (2011): 274–93.

Schram, Albert. *Railways and the Formation of the Italian State in the Nineteenth Century*. Cambridge: Cambridge University Press, 1997.

Schröter, Harm G. "Risk and Control in Multinational Enterprise: German Business in Scandinavia 1918–1939." *Business History Review* 62 (1988): 420–43.

———. "Cartels as a Form of Concentration in Industry: The Example of the International Dyestuffs Cartel from 1927 to 1939." *German Yearbook on Business History 1988*, 113–44. Dordrecht: Springer, 1990.

———. *Friedrich Engelhorn: Ein Unternehmer-Porträt des 19. Jahrhunderts*. Landau: Pfälzische Verlag, 1991.

———. "The International Dyestuffs Cartel 1927–39, with Special Reference to the Developing Areas of Europe and Japan." In *International Cartels in Business History*, edited by Akira Kudo and Terushi Hara, 33–56. Tokyo: University of Tokyo Press, 1992.

———. "The German Question, the Unification of Europe, and the European Market Strategies of Germany's Chemical and Electrical Industries 1900–1992." *Business History Review* 67 (1993): 369–405.

Schueler, Judith. *Materialising Identity: The Co-Construction of the Gotthard Railway and Swiss National Identity*. Amsterdam: Aksant, 2008.

Scranton, Phil. "Writing a New History of Europe: Six Considerations for Discussion. Making Europe Book Series Discussion Note." Unpublished paper, December 2010.

Sens, Ingo. *Die Geschichte der Energieversorgung in Mecklenburg und Vorpommern von ihren Anfängen bis zum Jahr 1990*. Rostock: Hanseatische Energieversorgung AG, 1996.

Sepp, Kalev, and Are Kaasik, eds. *Development of National Ecological Networks in the Baltic Countries in the Framework of the Pan-European Ecological Network.* Warsaw: IUCN, 2002.

———, Hannes Palang, Ülo Mander, and Are Kaasik. "Prospects for Nature and Landscape Protection in Estonia." *Landscape and Urban Planning* 46 (1999): 161–67.

Sergeev, Evgeny. *The Great Game 1856–1907: Russo-British Relations in Central and East Asia.* Baltimore: Johns Hopkins University Press, 2013.

Shallat, Todd. *Structures in the Stream: Water, Science, and the Rise of the US Army Corps of Engineers.* Austin: University of Texas Press, 1994.

Shiller, R.J., K. Fumiko, and T. Yoshiro. "Investor Behavior in the October 1987 Stock Market Crash: The Case of Japan." *Journal of the Japanese and International Economies* 5 (1991): 1–13.

Showalter, Dennis. "Soldiers into Postmasters? The Electric Telegraph as an Instrument of Command in the Prussian Army." *Military Affairs* 37 (1973): 48–52.

———. *Railroads and Rifles: Soldiers, Technology, and the Unification of Germany.* Hamden: Archon Books, 1975.

Shtilmark, Feliks. *History of the Russian Zapovedniks 1895–1995.* Edinburgh: Russian Nature Press, 2003.

Sibthorp, M.M., ed. *The North Sea: Challenge and Opportunity. Report of a Study Group of the David Davies Memorial Institute of International Studies.* London: Europa Publications, 1975.

Siilasvuo, Hjalmar. *Striderna i Suomussalmi.* Stockholm: Medéns förlag, 1940.

Silva, Ana Paula, and Maria Paula Diogo. "From Host to Hostage: Portugal, Britain and the Atlantic Telegraph Networks." In *Networking Europe: Transnational Infrastructures and the Shaping of Europe, 1850–2000*, edited by Erik van der Vleuten and Arne Kaijser, 151–86. Sagamore Beach, MA: Science History Publications, 2006.

Simon, Christian. "The Rise of the Swiss Chemical Industry Reconsidered." In *The Chemical Industry in Europe 1850–1914*, edited by Ernst Homburg, Anthony S. Travis, and Harm G. Schöter, 9–28. Dordrecht: Kluwer, 1998.

Simonsen, Dorthe. "Transnationale rum. Om luft, territorialitet og mobilitet." In *Transnationale historier*, edited by Anne Magnussen, Sissel Bjerrum Fossat, Klaus Petersen, and Niels Arne Sorensen, 61–77. Odense: Odense Universitetsforlag, 2009.

Simonsen, O. "Remarks on the Calculation of the Denmark-Norway Connexion by Flare Triangulation." *Bulletin Géodésique* 27 (1953): 39–60.

Sistemnyi operator edinoi energeticheskoi sistemy. "Istoriya." http://www.so-ups.ru/index.php?id=925 (accessed May 15, 2014).

Sladkov, A. M. "Chemistry and the Building of Communism." *Russian Chemical Reviews* 30 (1961): 623–24.

Smith, Adolphe. *Monaco and Monte Carlo.* London: Grant Richards, 1912.

Smith, Greg. "The World Coal Trade: A Commentary." *Energy Policy* 22 (1994): 443–46.

Smith, Harold F. "Bread for the Russians: William C. Edgar and the Relief Campaign of 1892." *Minnesota History* 42 (1970): 54–62.

Smith, J.R. "The Struve Geodetic Arc." 2005. http://www.fig.net/hsm/struve/struve_arc_smith_2005.pdf (accessed 17 December, 2014).

Snyder, Timothy. *Bloodlands: Europe between Hitler and Stalin*. New York: Basic Books, 2010.

Sochor, Eugene. *The Politics of International Aviation*. Iowa City: University of Iowa Press, 1991.

Sohnke, F. "Routing in the North Sea." *Journal of Navigation* 17 (1964): 385–90.

Sokolovsky, Valentin. "Fruits of Cold War." In *Clearing the Air: 25 Years of the Convention on Long-Range Transboundary Pollution*, edited by Johan Sliggers and Willem Kakebeeke, 7–17. New York: United Nations, 2004.

Spicer, Jonathan. "Special Report: Globally, the Flash Crash is No Flesh in the Pan." *Reuters*, October 15, 2010.

Spohrer, Jennifer. "Threat or Beacon? Recasting International Broadcasting in Europe after World War II." In *Airy Curtains in the European Ether: Broadcasting and the Cold War*, edited by Alexander Badenoch, Andreas Fickers, and Christian Henrich-Franke, 29–50. Baden-Baden: Nomos, 2013.

Stahel, David, *Operation Barbarossa and Germany's Defeat in the East*. Cambridge: Cambridge University Press, 2009.

Stäheli, Urs. "Inklusionsmedier der Börsenkommunikation: Medienutopien und Inklusionsvorstellungen." In *Vernetzte Steuerung: Soziale Prozesse im Zeitalter technischer Netzwerke*, edited by Stefan Kaufmann, 83–94. Zürich: Chronos, 2007.

Standage, Tom. *The Victorian Internet: The Remarkable Story of the Telegraph and the Nineteenth Century's On-line Pioneers*. New York: Walker, 1998.

Staniland, Martin. *Government Birds: Air Transport and the State in Western Europe*. Lanham: Rowan and Littlefield, 2003.

Statistics Netherlands. *Vijfenegentig jaren statistiek in tijdreeksen 1899–1994*. The Hague: CBS, 1994.

Stoate, C. et al. "Ecological Impacts of Arable Intensification in Europe." *Journal of Environmental Management* 63 (2001): 337–65.

Stoilova, Elitsa. "Bulgarian Yogurt: Manufacturing and Exporting of Authenticity." PhD thesis, Plovdiv University/Eindhoven University of Technology, forthcoming.

Stoltenberg, Jens. "Statsministerens nyttårstale 2007." http://www.regjeringen.no/nb/dokumentarkiv/stoltenberg-ii/smk/taler-og-artikler/2007/statsministerens-nyttarstale-2007.html?id=440349 (accessed January 3, 2014).

Stone, Jeffrey C. "Imperialism, Colonialism and Cartography." *Transactions of the Institute of British Geographers*, New Series 13 (1988): 57–64.

Svedberg, The. "Saint-Simon's Vision of a United Europe." *European Journal of Sociology* 35 (1994): 145–69.

Swedish Forest Agency. *Swedish Statistical Yearbook of Forestry 2010*. Jönköping: Swedish Forest Agency, 2009.

Swedish Government, *Efter Tjernobyl*, Stockholm: DsI 1986:11, 1986.

Swyngedouw, Erik. "Technonatural Revolutions: The Scalar Politics of Franco's Hydro-Social Dream for Spain, 1939–1975." *Transactions of the Institute of British Engineers* 32 (2007): 9–28.

Tarr, Joel, and Gabriel Dupuy, eds. *Technology and the Rise of the Networked City in Europe and America*. Philadelphia: Temple University Press, 1988.

Taylor, David H. "Problems of Food Supply Logistics in Russia and the CIS." *International Journal of Physical Distribution & Logistics Management* 24 (1994): 15–22.

Tchalakov, Ivan, Tihomir Mitev, and Ivaylo Hristov. "Bulgarian Power Relations: The Making of a Balkan Power Hub." In *The Making of Europe's Critical*

Infrastructures: Common Connections and Shared Vulnerabilities, edited by Per Högselius, Anique Hommels, Arne Kaijser, and Erik van der Vleuten, 131–56. Basingstoke and New York: Palgrave Macmillan, 2013.

Teclaff, Ludwik A. "International Law and the Protection of the Oceans from Pollution." *Fordham Law Review* 40 (1972): 529–64.

Terry, Andrew, Karin Ullrich, and Uwe Rieken, eds. *The Green Belt of Europe: From Vision to Reality*. Gland: IUCN, 2006.

Tetsuro Sumida, Jon. "British Naval Operational Logistics, 1914–1918." *Journal of Military History* 57 (1993): 447–80.

Thévenot, Roger. *A History of Refrigeration throughout the World*. Paris: International Institute of Refrigeration, 1979.

Thiemeyer, Guido. "The Failure of the Green Pool and the success of the CAP: Long Term Structures in European Agricultural Integration." In *Fertile Ground for Europe? The History of European Integration and the Common Agricultural Policy since 1945*, edited by Kiran Klaus Patel, 47–60. Baden-Baden: Nomos, 2009.

Thue, Lars. "Connections, Criticality, and Complexity: Norwegian Electricity in its European Context." In *The Making of Europe's Critical Infrastructure: Common Connections and Shared Vulnerabilities*, edited by Per Högselius, Anique Hommels, Arne Kaijser, and Erik van der Vleuten, 213–38. Basingstoke and New York: Palgrave Macmillan, 2013.

Tijdelijke Commissie Infrastructuur. *Reconstructie Betuweroute: De besluitvorming uitvergroot*. The Hague: Sdu Publishers, 2004.

Tirez, Dirk. "Easdaq Benefits from European Framework." *International Financial Law Review*, November 1997.

Tomlinson, John. *International Control of Radiocommunications*. New York: Arno Press, 1979.

Tomory, Leslie. "Building the First Gas Network, 1812–1820." *Technology & Culture* 52 (2011): 75–102.

Torge, Wolfgang. *Geschichte der Geodäsie in Deutschland*, second edition. Berlin: De Gruyter, 2009.

Törnlund, Erik, and Lars Östlund. "Mobility without Wheels: The Economy and Ecology of Timber Floating in Sweden, 1850–1980." *Journal of Transport History* 27 (2006): 48–70.

Torpey, John. *The Invention of the Passport: Surveillance, Citizenship and the State*. Cambridge: Cambridge University Press, 2000.

Travis, Anthony S. "Perkin's Mauve: Ancestor of the Organic Chemical Industry." *Technology and Culture* 31 (1990): 51–82.

Trotter, William. *A Frozen Hell: The Russo-Finnish Winter War of 1939–1940*. Chapel Hill, NC: Algonquin Books, 1991.

Tsaglioti, Fotini. "Infrastructuring Europe: Report No. 1." Unpublished, Athens, 2011.

———. "Infrastructuring Europe: Report No. 2." Unpublished, Athens, 2011.

———. "Infrastructuring Europe: Report No. 3." Unpublished, Athens, 2011.

Tuchman, Barbara. *The Guns of August*. New York: Ballantine Books, 2004 (original 1962).

Turner, Aimee. "Unions Mobilise to Halt Further European Reform." *Air Traffic Management Net*, June 9, 2013. http://www.airtrafficmanagement.net/2013/06/unions-mobilise-to-halt-further-european-reform (accessed January 3, 2014).

Turok, Ivan, and Vlad Mykhnenko. "The Trajectories of European Cities 1960–2005." *Cities* 24 (2007): 165–82.

Tweede Kamer der Staten Generaal. *Structuurschema Natuur en Landschapsbehoud. DEEL A: Beleidsvoornemen*. Zitting 1980–81, 16820, no. 2.

Tympas, Aristotle, and Irene Anastasiadou. "Constructing Balkan Europe." In *Networking Europe: Transnational Infrastructures and the Shaping of Europe, 1850–2000*, edited by Erik van der Vleuten and Arne Kaijser, 25–50. Sagamore Beach, MA: Science History Publications, 2006.

———, Stathis Arapostathis, Katearina Vlantoni, and Yiannis Garyfallos. "Border-Crossing Electrons: Critical Energy Flows to and from Greece." In *The Making of Europe's Critical Infrastructures: Common Connections and Shared Vulnerabilities*, edited by Per Högselius, Anique Hommels, Arne Kaijser, and Erik van der Vleuten, 157–86. Basingstoke and New York: Palgrave Macmillan, 2013.

Tyrell, Ian. "American Exceptionalism in an Age of International History." *American Historical Review* 96 (1991): 1031–55.

UCTE. *Final Report System Disturbance on 4 November 2006*. Brussels: UCTE, 2007.

United Nations. *Declaration of the United Nations Conference on the Human Environment*. United Nations, 1972.

United States Congress. "Act creating Yellowstone National Park, March 1, 1872." http://www.ourdocuments.gov/doc.php?doc=45 (accessed March 4, 2012).

Vahrenkamp, Richard. *The Logistic Revolution: The Rise of Logistics in the Mass Consumption Society*. Lohmar/Köln: Josef Eul Verlag, 2012.

Van Creveld, Martin, *Supplying War: Logistics from Wallenstein to Patton*. Cambridge: Cambridge University Press, 1977.

Van de Plassche, A.W. "De betekenis van het wegennet voor de tuinbouw." *De Ingenieur* 62 (1950): A.26–27.

Van de Ven, G.P., ed. *Man-Made Lowlands: History of Water Management and Land Reclamation in the Netherlands*. Utrecht: Uitgeverij Matrijs, 2004.

Van de Woud, Auke. "Town and Country: Work in Progress." In *Accounting for the Past 1650–2000: Dutch Culture in a European Perspective, Volume 5*, edited by Douwe Fokkema and Frans Grijzenhout, 175–96. Basingstoke: Palgrave Macmillan, 2004.

———. *Een nieuwe wereld. Het ontstaan van het moderne Nederland*. Amsterdam: Bert Bakker, 2006.

Van den Belt, Henk. "Networking Nature, or, Serengeti behind the Dikes." *History and Technology* 20 (2004): 311–33.

Van den Noort, Jan. *Licht op het GEB. Geschiedenis van het Gemeente- Energiebedrijf Rotterdam*. Rotterdam: GEB, 1993.

Van der Laan, H. Laurens. "Modern Inland Transport and the European Trading Firms in Colonial West Africa." *Cahiers d'Études africaines* 84 (1981): 547–75.

Van der Vleuten, Erik. "In Search of the Networked Nation: Transforming Technology, Society, and Nature in the Netherlands during the Twentieth Century." *European Review of History* 10 (2003): 59–78.

———. "Networking Technology, Networking Society, Networking Nature." *History and Technology* 20 (2004): 195–203.

———. "Toward a Transnational History of Technology: Meanings, Promises, Pitfalls." *Technology and Culture* 49 (2008): 974–94.

———. "Feeding the Peoples of Europe." In *Materializing Europe: Transnational Infrastructures and the Project of Europe*, edited by Alec Badenoch and Andreas Fickers, 148–77. Baskingstoke: Palgrave Macmillan, 2010.

———. "Networked Nation: Infrastructure Integration of the Netherlands." In *Technology and the Making of the Netherlands. The Age of Contested Modernization 1890–1970*, edited by Johan Schot, Arie Rip, and Harry Lintsen, 46–123. Zutphen: Walburg & MIT Press, 2010.

———, Irene Anastasiadou, Vincent Lagendijk, and Frank Schipper. "Europe's System Builders: The Contested Shaping of Transnational Road, Electricity, and Rail Networks." *Contemporary European History* 16 (2007): 321–47.

———, and Arne Kaijser. "Networking Europe." *History and Technology* 21 (2005): 21–48.

———, and Arne Kaijser, eds. *Networking Europe: Transnational Infrastructures and the Shaping of Europe, 1850–2000*. Sagamore Beach, MA: Science History Publications, 2006.

———, and Vincent Lagendijk. "Transnational Infrastructure Vulnerability: The Historical Shaping of the 2006 European 'Blackout'." *Energy Policy* 38 (2010): 2042–52.

———, and Vincent Lagendijk. "Interpreting Transnational Infrastructure Vulnerability: 4/11 and the Historical Dynamics of Transnational Electricity Governance." *Energy Policy* 38 (2010): 2053–262.

Van der Windt, Henny, Jaques Swart, and Josef Keulartz. "Valuing Nature in the Context of Planning: An Exploration." In *Visions of Nature: A Scientific Exploration of People's Explicit Philosophies Regarding Nature in Germany, the Netherlands and the United Kingdom*, edited by Riyan van den Born, Rob Lenders, and Wouter de Groot, 211–35. Berlin: LIT-Verlag, 2006.

Van Dijk, Terry. "Scenarios of Central European Land Fragmentation." *Land Use Policy* 20 (2003): 149–58.

Van Driel, Hugo, and Ferry de Goey. *Rotterdam Cargo Handling Technology 1870–2000*. Zutphen: Walburg Pers, 2000.

———, and Johan Schot, "Radical Innovation as a Multilevel Process: Introducing Floating Grain Elevators in the Port of Rotterdam." *Technology & Culture* 46 (2005): 51–76.

Van Dyke, Carl. *The Soviet Invasion of Finland 1939–40*. London: Frank Cass, 1997.

Van Lente, Dick. "Machines and the Order of the Harbour: The Debate about the Introduction of Grain Unloaders in Rotterdam 1905–1907." *International Review of Social History* 43 (1998): 79–110.

Van Lierop, Olga. "Zwijnen zwermen uit over de regio." *Eindhovens Dagblad*, July 25, 2013.

Van Lottum, Jelle. "Labour Migration and Economic Performance: London and the Randstad, c. 1600–1800." *Economic History Review* 64 (2011): 531–70.

Van Merriënboer, Johan. *Mansholt: A Biography*. Brussels: Peter Lang, 2011.

Van Otterloo, A.H. "Prelude op de consumptiemaatschappij in voor- en tegenspoed 1920–1960." In *Techniek in Nederland in de twintigste eeuw. Vol. 3: Landbouw en voeding*, edited by Johan Schot, Harry Lintsen, Arie Rip, and Adri A. Albert de la Bruhèze, 262–79. Zutphen: Walburg Pers, 2000.

Van Reenen, R.M. *De afzetorganisatie van de Nederlandse tuinbouw*. The Hague: Centraal Bureau voor Tuinbouwveilingen, 1950.

Van Zanden, Jan Luiten, Joost Jonker, Stephen Howarth, and Keetie Sluyterman, eds. *A History of Royal Dutch Shell. Vol. 2: Powering the Hydrocarbon Revolution, 1939–1973*. New York: Oxford University Press, 2007.

Verduijn, Simon, Huub Ploegmakers, and Sander Meijerink. "Discursive Framing and Network Strategies: How a Small Group of Policy Entrepreneurs Pushed the Idea of 'Nature Development' in the Netherlands." Paper presented at the 6th Annual European Consortium for Political Research Conference, Reykjavik, August 25–27, 2011.

Vermeulen, Ton, and Marieke van Helvoort-Segerink. *75 jaar Spar*. Rotterdam: Van Well, 2007.

Victor, Nadezha, and David Victor. "Bypassing Ukraine: Exporting Russian Gas to Poland and Germany." In *Natural Gas and Geopolitics: From 1970 to 2040*, edited by David G. Victor, Amy M. Jaffe, and Mark H. Hayes. Cambridge: Cambridge University Press, 2006.

Vig, Károly. "On Whose Shoulders We Stand: The Pioneering Entomological Discoveries of Károly Sajó." *ZooKeys* 157 (2011): 159–79.

Viik, Tõnu, and Jüri Randjärv. "How Struve and Tenner Started the Work of Their Life." *Baltic Astronomy* 20 (2011): 169–78.

Vink, Rona, Horst Behrendt, and Wim Salomons. "Development of the Heavy Metal Pollution Trends in Several European Rivers: An Analysis of Point and Diffuse Sources." *Water Science and Technology* 39 (1999): 215–23.

Voloshin, Vladimir I. "Electric Power in the Comecon European Countries." *Energy Policy* 18 (1990): 740–46.

Vuksanović, Emilija. "Information System of Stock Exchange Market in Serbia." *Management Information Systems* 5 (2010): 7–12.

Wagner, Kurt. *Grossraumtechnik: Die Technik im neuen Europa*. Berlin: Otto Elsner Verlag, 1944.

Warren, Manning Gilbert. "The European Union's Investment Services Directive." *University of Pennsylvania Journal of International Business Law* 15 (1994): 181–220.

Warner, Deborah Jean. "Political Geodesy: The Army, the Air Force, and the World Geodetic System of 1960." *Annals of Science* 59 (2002): 363–89.

Webb, K. "The Continued Importance of Geographic Distance and Boulding's Loss of Strength Gradient." *Comparative Strategy* 26 (2007): 295–310.

Weber, G. "The European Triangulation Net South East." http://www.euref-iag.net (accessed June 15, 2012).

Weber, Steven, and Elliot Posner. "Creating a Pan-European Equity Market: The Origins of EASDAQ." *Review of International Political Economy* 7 (2000): 529–73.

Weiner, Douglas R. *A Little Corner of Freedom: Russian Nature Protection from Stalin to Gorbachev*. Berkeley: University of California Press, 1999.

Welsch, Fritz. *Geschichte der chemischen Industrie: Abriss der Entwicklung ausgewählter Zweige der chemischen Industrie von 1800 bis zur Gegenwart*. Berlin: Deutscher Verlag der Wissenschaften, 1981.

Wenzlhuemer, Roland. "The Dematerialization of Telecommunication: Communication Centres and Peripheries in Europe and the World, 1850–1920." *Journal of Global History* 2 (2007): 345–72.

———. "Metropolitan Telecommunication: Uneven Telegraphic Connectivity in 19th-Century London." *Social Science Computer Review* 27 (2009): 437–51.

Wesson, Robert G. *Lenin's Legacy: The Story of the CPSU*. Stanford: Hoover Institution Press, 1978.

Westerman, Frank. *De graanrepubliek*. Amsterdam: Olympus, 2010 (first edition 1999).

Westwood, John N. *Railways at War*. Colchester: Osprey Publishing, 1980.

———. *Soviet Railways to Russian Railways*. Basingstoke and New York: Palgrave Macmillan, 2002.

Wever, Egbert. "Olieraffinaderij en petrochemische industrie: Ontstaan, samenstelling, voorkomen van petrochemische complexen." PhD thesis, Groningen University, 1974.

Whist, B.S. *Nord Stream: Not Just a Pipeline*. FNI Report 15/2008. Oslo: Fridtjof Nansen Institute, 2008.

White, Eugene N. "The Stock Market Boom and Crash of 1929 Revisited." *Journal of Economic Perspectives* 4 (1990): 67–83.

Whitten, C.A. "Adjustment of European Triangulation." *Bulletin Géodésique* 26 (1952): 187–206.

Wightman, David. *Economic Co-operation in Europe: A Study of the United Nations Economic Commission for Europe*. London: Stevens & Sons, 1956.

Wilkes, Owen, and Nils Petter Gleditsch, *Loran-C and Omega: A Study of the Military Importance of Radio Navigation Aids*. Oslo: Norwegian University Press, 1987.

Williams, Rosalind. "Cultural Origins and Environmental Implications of Large Technological Systems." *Science in Context* 6 (1997): 377–403.

Wilson, Edmund. *To the Finland Station: A Study of the Writing and Acting of History*. London: Fontana/Collins, 1960.

Windrow, Martin, *The Last Valley: Dien Bien Phu and the French Defeat in Vietnam*. Cambridge: Perseus Books, 2004.

Witt, Onno N. *Die chemische Industrie auf der internationalen Weltausstellung zu Paris 1900*. Berlin: Hermann Heyfelder, 1902.

Wohl, Robert, *A Passion for Wings: Aviation and the Western Imagination 1908–1918*. New Haven: Yale University Press, 1994.

Wójcik, Dariusz. "Geography and the Future of Stock Exchanges: Between Real and Virtual Space." *Growth and Change* 38 (2007): 200–223.

Wolmar, Christian. *Engines of War: How Wars Were Won & Lost on the Railways*. London: Atlantic Books, 2010.

Woods, Austin, *Medium-Range Weather Prediction: The European Approach*. Berlin: Springer, 2005.

Woolcock, W.J.U. "The International Dyestuffs Situation." *Journal of the Society of Dyers and Colourists* 43 (1927): 5–9.

Woolf, Stuart. "Europe and its Historians." *Contemporary European History* 12 (2003): 323–37.

Wormbs, Nina, *Vem älskade Tele-X? Konflikter om satelliter i Norden 1974–1989*. Stockholm, 2003.

———. "Technology-Dependent Commons: The Example of Frequency Spectrum for Broadcasting in Europe in the 1920s." *International Journal of the Commons* 5 (2011): 92–109.

———. "An Expanding Resource: Radio Spectrum for Broadcasting in Europe Before and After WWII." In *Cosmopolitan Commons: Sharing Resources and Risks across Borders*, edited by Nil Disco and Eda Kranakis, 97–122. Cambridge, MA: MIT Press, 2013.

Wos, Augustyn. "Economie et organisation de l'agriculture en Pologne." *Économie rurale* 83 (1970): 13–20.

Wulff, Petter. "Sweden and Clandestine German Rearmament Technology." *Icon* 11 (2005): 33–50.

Wurzel, Rüdiger. "European Union Environmental Policy and Natura 2000: From Adoption to Revision." In *Legitimacy in European Nature Conservation Policy: Case Studies in Multilevel Governance*, edited by J. Keulartz and G. Leistra, 259–82. Dordrecht: Springer, 2008.

WWF. *The Tagus-Segura Water Transfer: Lessons from the Past*. World Wildlife Foundation. www.panda.org/dams (accessed May 15, 2014).

Yang, Jian, and David A. Bessler. "Contagion around the October 1987 Stock Market Crash." *European Journal of Operational Research* 184 (2008): 291–310.

Yergin, Daniel. *The Prize: The Epic Quest for Oil, Money and Power*. London: Simon & Schuster, 1991.

Zakaria, Adriani, and Eric Wakker. *Failing Governance—Avoiding Responsibilities: European Biofuel Policies and Oil Palm Plantation Expansion in Ketapang District, West Kalimantan (Indonesia)*. Amsterdam: Milieudefensie/WALHI, 2009.

Zeller, Thomas. *Driving Germany: The Landscape of the German Autobahn*. Oxford and New York: Berghahn Books, 2007.

Illustration Credits

Permissions to reproduce the illustrations and photographs in this book have generously been granted by the institutions and collections named here, and are gratefully acknowledged by the editors, the authors, the Foundation for the History of Technology, and Palgrave Macmillan.

The Foundation for the History of Technology has carefully tried to locate all rights holders. Parties who despite this feel that they are entitled to certain rights are requested to contact the Foundation for the History of Technology (www.histech.nl).

Cover: Armoured train Smialy, Poland. From the collection of Adam Jonca. Permission by Adam Jonca.

0.1 Workers and locals here celebrate the meeting of the two bores of the Gotthard Tunnel in 1880. The full train service started in 1882 when the approach lines had been completed. Plate from the *Illustrated London News* 80/1, 257. Permission by Science Museum / Science & Society Picture Library. Ref. no. 10413079. 7

0.2 Armoured train, Smialy, Poland. From the collection of Adam Jonca. Permission by Adam Jonca. 13

0.3 Original caption: "Natuurbrug Best - 2012." Aerial photo A2 highway Eindhoven – 's-Hertogenbosch (the Netherlands), 2012 by Joop van Houdt. Permission by https://beeldbank.rws.nl, Rijkswaterstaat / Joop van Houdt. 15

1.1 The arrival of Communist leader Vladimir Ilich Lenin at the Finland Station in Petrograd, Russia, April 1917. Joseph Stalin, who was not actually present at the event, is fictitiously depicted standing behind Lenin. Soviet painting, ca. 1930s. Courtesy of Library of Congress, Prints and Photographic Division. Reproduction number LC-UXZ62–102123. 22

1.2 Original caption: "Dover Pier. Arrival of the Continental Mails. London, Chatham and South-Eastern Railway." Illustration from *The Book of Trains, a children's railway book*, ca. 1890–1891. Permission by National Railway Museum / Science & Society Picture Library. © National Railway Museum / Science & Society Picture Library. All rights reserved. Ref. no. 10302990 – inventory no. NRM/85/49/28. 28

1.3 Trans-Siberian Railway station, Khilok, 1900. Photo by DeAgostini/Getty Images. Permission by DEA Picture Library / Getty Images. Ref. no. 142086779. 31

1.4 HMS *Agamemnon* laying the Atlantic Telegraph cable in 1858. A whale crosses the line. Drawing by Robert Charles Dudley (1826–1900). Watercolor over graphite 1865–66. In collection of The Metropolitan Museum of Art, gift of Cyrus W. Field. Courtesy of The Metropolitan Museum of Art (www.metmuseum.org). Accession number 92,10,68. 35

Illustration Credits

1.5	Map drawn by Camiel Lintsen (Kade 05) for the Foundation for the History of Technology. Map based on: Trevor J. Howkins, "Railway Geography and the Demarcation of Poland's Borders 1918–1930," *Journal of Transport Geography* 4 (1996), 291, figure 2.6. Courtesy Foundation for the History of Technology, Eindhoven.	38
1.6	Map by Piero Puricelli (1883–1951), 1931. Published in: Frank Schipper, D*riving Europe: Building Europe on Roads in the 20th Century* (Amsterdam: Amsterdam University Press 2008), 108. Courtesy Frank Schipper.	41
1.7	Original caption: "Belgique-Congo par avion Sabena." Poster Sabena airlines 1930s. Permission by AKG Images. Ref. no. AKG115268.	44
1.8	Original caption: "Planung der transkontinentalen Breitspur-Fernbahnen, 1943." Photo by Ralf Roletschek for Wikimedia. Collection Deutsch Bahn AG, Verkerhsmuseum Nürnberg. Reference http://commons.wikimedia.org/wiki/File:2011–03–05-eisenbahnmuseum-nuernberg-by-RalfR-30.jpg.	46
1.9	Original caption: "Entgleisungsweiche 51, Grenzbahnhof Staaken." Photo by Peter Bock. Published in Peter Bock, *Interzonenzüge: Eisenbahnverkehr im geteilten Deutschland 1945–1990* (Munich: GeraNova Zeitschriftenverlag, 2000). Permission by Peter Bock.	49
1.10	Interoute network map by Interoute / Speed Communications. Courtesy Interoute / Speed Communications.	59
2.1	A horse-drawn coal barge crossing the Barton Swing Aqueduct, carrying the Bridgewater Canal across the wider span of the Manchester Ship Canal. Postcard ca. 1905 by M. Banks. Permission by Mary Evans / Grenville Collins Postcard Collection. Ref. no. 10290674.	68
2.2	Josef Stalin addresses a meeting of oil workers in Baku, Azerbaijan, 1908. Postcard. Permission by Mary Evans / John Massey Stewart Collection. Ref. no. 10284495.	69
2.3	A coalman carries in a large sack of coal for a terraced house in Salford, Manchester. Photograph by Shirley Baker, 1964. Permission by Mary Evans Picture Library / Shirley Baker. Ref. no. 10239504.	71
2.4	Map drawn by Camiel Lintsen (Kade 05) for the Foundation for the History of Technology. Map based on various sources. Courtesy Foundation for the History of Technology, Eindhoven.	73
2.5	Original captions: "Abb. 40, Das Raubtier 'Mensch'. Europa is ein grosser Käfig mit Einzelstellen" and "Abb.41. Statt trennender Mauern: bindende Leitungen!" Illustrations by Herman Sörgel (1885–1952). Originally published in: Herman Sörgel, *Die drei grossen. "A" Grossdeutschand und italienisches Imperium, die Pfeiler Atlantropas* (Munich, 1931), 91. Also published in: Alexander Gall, "Atlantropa. A Technological Vision of a United Europe," in: Erik van der Vleuten and Arne Kaijser (eds), *Networking Europe: Transnational Infrastructures and the Shaping of Europe, 1859–2000* (Sagamore Beach, MA: Science History Publications, 2006), 114.	75
2.6	Map drawn by Camiel Lintsen (Kade 05) for the Foundation for the History of Technology. Map based on: Per Högselius, "Connecting East and West? Electricity Systems in the Baltic Region", in: Erik van der Vleuten and Arne Kaijser (eds), N*etworking Europe: Transnational Infrastructures and the Shaping of Europe, 1859–2000*	

	(Sagamore Beach, MA: Science History Publications, 2006), 249. Courtesy Foundation for the History of Technology, Eindhoven.	78
2.7	Map produced by the United Nations Economic Committee for Europe (UNECE). Published in: Vincent Lagendijk, *Electrifying Europe: The Power of Europe in the Construction of Electricity Networks* (Amsterdam: Amsterdam University Press 2008), 182; Scan available in author's collection. Courtesy Vincent Lagendijk.	81
2.8	Original caption: "Das Europäische Ferngasnetz." Bayerisches Hauptstaatsarchiv, "Nachlass Schedl, Box. 200." Permission by Bayerisches Hauptstaatsarchiv.	88
2.9	LNG *Adamawa* tanker passing through the Strait of Gibraltar, carrying gas from the Saharan dessert – 2007. Photo by Nigel Lawrence, editor of *Shipping Today and Yesterday*. Permission by Nigel Lawrence – *Shipping Today and Yesterday*.	90
2.10	Protests against the transport of containers carrying highly radioactive nuclear waste in 1997 near Gorleben in Lower Saxony, Germany. Photo by Dietmar Scherf. Permission by Ullstein Bild – Dietmar Scherf. Ref. no. 1003759355.	92
2.11	Desertec plan. Courtesy Desertec Founcation. Reference: http://www.desertec.org.	97
2.12	Gazprom control room, 2006. Photo by Alexey Panov. Permission by Ria Novosti – Alexey Panov. Ref. no. #133384.	99
3.1	Original caption: "Overslag Rotterdam 1961." Photo by Frits J. Rotgans (1912–1978). Permission by Nederlands Fotomuseum – Frits J. Rotgans. Ref. no. bae84f3–3d9a-9116–15ea-7c858821217d.	109
3.2	Original caption: "The *Waipawa* as Yard Number 932, being prepared for launching, June 1934." Permission by National Museums Northern Ireland. © National Museums Northern Ireland – Collection Harland & Wolff, Ulster Folk & Transport Museum.	119
3.3	Original caption: "Afrique Occidentale Chargement des Arachides sur un Vapeur en Rivière." Original postcard in collection Foundation for the History of Technology. Courtesy Foundation for the History of Technology, Eindhoven.	123
3.4	Famine Russia 1920–1922, transport of bodies. Permission by Ullstein Bild. Ref. no. 00103536.	127
3.5	Loading fish into a refrigerated goods wagon of Interfrigo, September 12, 1959. Photo by D.C. Gerdessen (Nederlandse Spoorwegen). Permission by Het Utrechts Archief – D.C. Gerdessen (Nederlandse Spoorwegen). Ref. no. 168412.	133
3.6	Packages of butter in a freezer storehouse in Gross-Gerau, January 19, 1979. Photo by Heinz Wieseler. Permission by dpa-International – Heinz Wieseler. © dpa – International – Heinz Wieseler.	136
4.1	The BASF factory complex at Ludwigshafen, Germany, in 1881. Painting by Robert Friedrich Stieler (1847–1908). Courtesy BASF Company Archives (BASF Unternehmensarchiv).	145
4.2	Control panel of the Druzhba pipeline near the city of Almetyevs, Russia. Photo taken in 1971. Permission by Rianovosti / Science Photo Library. Ref. no. C021/4403.	153
4.3	The petrochemical zone Rotterdam-Moerdijk-Vlissingen-Terneuzen-Antwerp. Original map made for Foundation for the	

	History of Technology (2000), new translated English version 2015. Originally published in J.W. Schot et. al. (eds) *Techniek in Nederland in de 20e eeuw, II Delfstoffen, Energie, Chemie* (Zutphen: Walburg Pers 2000), 399. Courtesy Foundation for the History of Technology, Eindhoven.	155
4.4	The BASF Ludwigshafen complex. Permission by Press Photo BASF.	157
4.5	Girls operate stock boards at the Waldorf-Astoria Hotel. Provided to Wikimedia Commons by the National Archives and Records Administration as part of a cooperation project. Ref. no. NARA - 533759.	163
4.6a+b	Amsterdam Exchange in 1938 and in 1988. Courtesy Stichting Capital Amsterdam.	170–71
4.7	Original caption: "A businessman covers his face as the market crashes, October 1987." Photo by *The Independent* / Rex Features. Permission by *The Independent* / Rex Features. Ref. no. 152179b.	173
5.1	Original caption: "Auszug des 11. Westfälischen Husaren-Regiments aus Düsseldorf." Woodcut 1866. Permission by BPK Images. Ref. no. 30011226.	187
5.2	Original caption: "Finlands secret weapon." Cartoon from the British *Daily Express*, February 8, 1940. Permission by Express Newspapers.	195
5.3	Royal Air Force Fighter Command, 1939–1945, general view of the Operations Room at No. 10 Group Headquarters, Rudloe Manor, Wiltshire, showing WAAF plotters and duty officers at work. Photo December 1942. Permission by Getty Images – IWM. Ref. no. 154422364.	200
5.4	Map originally published in: D.J. Payton-Smith, *Oil: A Study of War-Time Policy and Administration* (London: HMSO 1971). Map may be used according to UK Open Government License for public sector information.	202
5.5	German U-Boats U-571 and U-459 transfer supplies. Permission by Bundesarchiv. Bild 101II-MW-4835–18.	204
5.6	Deportation of Polish Jews in open cattle carriages in Warsaw, Poland. Photo ca. 1944. Permission by Ullstein Bild. Ref. no. 00805824.	209
5.7	Original caption: "Coverage plan of Sweden for proposed stations. Diagram II." Permission by Krigsarkivet Stockholm.	213
5.8	Poster of film *Dr. Strangelove*, 1964. Permission by Rue des Archives.	217
5.9	Food supplies transport through the forest during Dien Bien Phu Battle, Vietnam. Permission by Getty Images – Collection Jean-Caude Labbe. Ref. no. GAR 113977014.	220
5.10	Guernica ruins, 1937. Permission by Bundesarchiv. Bild 183-H25224.	223
6.1	March to reclaim Mount Brocken from the military. Photo by Hansjörg Hörseljau, December 3, 1989. Permission by Hansjörg Hörseljau Fotograf.	232
6.2	Map of the world showing the extent of the British Empire in 1886. Drawn by Walter Crane (1845–1915), published as a	

supplement to *The Graphic*, July 1886, as the "Imperial Federation." Statistical information furnished by Captain J.C.R. Colomb, MP formerly RMA. Wikimedia Commons. Reference http://commons.wikimedia.org/wiki/File:Imperial_Federation,_Map_of_the_World_Showing_the_Extent_of_the_British_Empire_in_1886.jpg. 236

6.3 Reconstruction of the triangulation of the Von Struve Geodetic Arc project. Map drawn by Camiel Lintsen (Kade 05) for the Foundation for the History of Technology. Map based on J.R. Smith, *The Struve Geodetic Arc* (International Institution for History of Surveying & Measurement 2005), 2. Courtesy Foundation for the History of Technology, Eindhoven. 237

6.4 Figure based on Corine Land Cover 2006, the map shows the distribution of aggregated land cover classes. Created March 8, 2013, last modified July 10, 2013. Published by the European Environment Agency. Permission by the European Environment Agency (EEA). Reference: http://www.eea.europa.eu/data-and-maps/figures/corine-land-cover-types-2006. 243

6.5 Workers digging drainage ditches, 1930s, near Aarle Rixtel, the Netherlands. Original source Directoraat Generaal Rijkswaterstaat, Directie Noord-Brabant. In collection Foundation for the History of Technology. Courtesy Foundation for the History of Technology. 250

6.6 The Netherlands National Ecological Network. Published in *Natuurbeleidsplan* (The Hague 1990). 259

6.7 European Green Belt near Linz. Photo by Klaus Leidorf. Permission by Klaus Leidorf. 263

6.8 Pan-European Ecological Network map. Permission by Alterra, Wageningen UR and ECNC. 264

7.1 Castoro Dieci lowering a pipeline, 2011. Permission by Nord Stream AG. 272

7.2 Map of Europe's river basins and drainage divides. Made by Adolf Stieler (1755–1836). Published in Adolf Stieler and Christian Gottlieb Reichard, *Hand-Atlas über alle Theile der Erde und über das Weltgebäude* (first edn 1839, revised 1843). 274

7.3 Original caption: "Basin of the North Atlantic Ocean." Map included in: M.F. Maury (1806–1873), *The Physical Geography of the Sea*. (New York: Harper & Brothers Publishers, 1866 edition). 277

7.4 A view over The Volga Hydroelectric Station under construction. Photo taken May 3, 1958. Permission by Photo ITAR-TASS / Makletsov. 284

7.5 Original caption: "The Suez canal: dredgers at work." Drawing 1860s. Permission by Mary Evans Picture Library. Ref.no. 10119545. 291

7.6 Map drawn by Camiel Lintsen (Kade 05) for the Foundation for the History of Technology. Map based on F. Sohnke, "Routing in the North Sea," *Journal of Navigation* 17 (1964), 389. Courtesy Foundation for the History of Technology, Eindhoven. 292

7.7 "The Firth of Clyde," British Railways poster ca. 1960. Permission by NRM Pictorial Collection / Science and Society Picture Library. © NRM Pictorial Collection / Science and Society Picture Library. Ref. no. 10171589. 293

7.8 Overview of Phillips' North Sea system for producing and transmitting oil and natural gas from the Ekofisk and surrounding fields in

	Norway to England and Germany as of 1973. Published in *Oil and Gas Journal*, May 7, 1973, 35. Permission by *Oil and Gas Journal*.	296
7.9	Road bridge connecting oil wells in the Serebrovsky offshore oil field, in the Caspian Sea, near Baku, Azerbaijan. Photo by Valeriy Shustov, June 1978. Permission by Ria Novosti – Valeriy Shustov. Ref. no. #97437.	297
7.10	Volunteers attempt to clear oil at Lands End, Cornwall, after the oil tanker *Torrey Canyon* had run aground on the Seven Stones rocks spilling its cargo of oil. Photo taken March 27, 1967. Permission by Getty Images – Popperfoto. Ref. no. 79028592.	303
8.1	Original caption: "A map of the pH of precipitation over Europe in 1967." Originally published in *Dagens Nyheter*. Also published in: Arne Kaijser, "Under a Common Acid Sky. Negotiating Transboundary Air Polution in Europe," in: Nil Disco and Eda Kranakis (eds), *Cosmopolitan Commons: Sharing Resources and Risks across Borders* (Cambridge, MA: MIT Press 2013), 213–44. Courtesy Arne Kaijser.	310
8.2	Original caption: "Storm in Balaclava Bay." Drawing published in *Illustrated London News* 1854. Vintage print in collection Foundation for the History of Technology. Courtesy Foundation for the History of Technology, Eindhoven.	313
8.3	Original caption: "Carte météorologique du jour 1864 février vendredi 5." Permission by Lóbsevatoire de Paris.	314
8.4	Balloon Humboldt, 1893. Drawing by Hans Groß (1860–1924), published in Richard Aßmann und Arthur Berson (eds), *Wissenschaftliche Luftfahrten, Band 1* (Vieweg, Braunschweig 1899). Permission by BPK Bildagentur. Ref. no. 10024666.	315
8.5	Meteorological Station German Army World War I, ascending weather balloon. Permission by AKG Images. Ref. no. 1062206.	317
8.6	Original caption: "Zweihundert Meter über der Erde. In Königswusterhausen bei Berlin wird augenblicklich der größte Funkturm Deutschlands im Auftrage der Reichspost durch die Honeffwerke-Baden erbaut." Photo ca. 1914. Permission by Bundesarchiv. Bild 102–11475.	323
8.7	Landing of an airplane on a roof, in Issy-Les-Moulineaux (top); Testing of new flight routes by the Eiffel Tower (below). Frontpage of French newspaper *Le Petit Parisien*, November 6, 1910. Photo by Leemage. Permission by Getty Images. Ref. no. 14484707.	332
8.8	Picture of the smokestack at Rönnskär. Permission by Boliden Rönnskär.	337
8.9	Oulanka Station. Published in: Arne Kaijser, 'Under a Common Acid Sky. Negotiating Transboundary Air Polution in Europe', in: Nil Disco and Eda Kranakis (eds), *Cosmopolitan Common:s Sharing Resources and Risks across Borders* (Cambridge, MA: MIT Press 2013), 213–44. Courtesy Arne Kaiser.	341
9.1	African migrants sitting on the border fence around the Spanish enclave Melilla in North Africa. Photo by Jose Colon (AFP), May 2014. Permission by Getty Images. Ref. no. 453593934.	355

Making Europe: Series Acknowledgements

Making Europe is the result/product of an unusual collaboration among a host of individuals and organizations. The *Making Europe* authors and series editors feel extremely fortunate to be working with them. We list here individuals and organizations who contributed to the entire series. Each volume in the series also has its own separate acknowledgements.

Making Europe was initiated by:

- Foundation for the History of Technology (www.histech.nl)

Making Europe is sponsored by:

- Eindhoven University of Technology (www.tue.nl)
- Fonds 21 (www.fonds21.nl) – formerly known as SNS REAAL Fonds
- Next Generations Infrastructures (www.nextgenerationsinfrastructures.eu)
- Foundation for the History of Technology Corporate Program (www.histech.nl) that includes:
  - DSM (www.dsm.com)
  - EBN (www.ebn.nl)
  - FrieslandCampina(www.frieslandcampina.com)
  - Philips (www.philips.nl)
  - SIDN (www.sidn.nl)
  - TNO (www.tno.nl)

Making Europe has been made possible thanks to:

- Tensions of Europe Network (www.tensionsofeurope.eu)
- European Science Foundation EUROCORES Programme Inventing Europe – Technology and the Making of Europe, 1850 to the Present (www.esf.org)
- Research Theme Group Grant of the Netherlands Institute of Advanced Studies (NIAS) in 2010–11 (www.nias.nl)
- European University Institute in Florence, Italy for providing the support in developing the series and for the founding workshop (3–6 July 2008) (www.eui.eu)

Making Europe benefited from the feedback of a community of scholars who have been involved in the series from the start:

Håkon With Andersen, Alec Badenoch, Robert Bud, David Burigana, Cornelis Disco, Paul Edwards, Valentina Fava, Karen Johnson Freeze, Andrea Guintini, Gabrielle Hecht, Rüdiger Klein, Eda Kranakis, John Krige, Leonard Laborie, Vincent Lagendijk, Suzanne Lommers, Slawomir Lotysz, Dagmara Jaješniak-Quast, Karl-Erik Michelsen, Matthias Middell, Thomas J. Misa, Dobrinka Parusheva, Kiran Patel, Pierre-Yves Saunier, Emanuela Scarpellini, Frank Schipper, Michael Strang, Ivan Tchalakov, Frank Trentmann, Aristotle Tympas, Hans Weinberger

Making Europe: Series Acknowledgements

Making Europe relied on the unflagging support of:

Picture editors

- Katherine Kay-Mouat
- Giel van Hooff
- Jan Korsten (Management)
- Camiel Lintsen – Kade 05 Eindhoven (graphs and maps)

Text editors

- Lisa Friedman
- James Morrison

PalgraveMacmillan

- Jenny McCall (Publisher)
- Holly Tyler (Editorial Assistant)
- Philip Hillyer (Copy-Editor and Editorial Services Consultant)
- Susan Boobis (Indexer)

Office Foundation for the History of Technology:

- Sonja Beekers (Secretarial Support)
- Jan Korsten (Business Director)
- Loek Stoks (Bookkeeping)
- Henk Treur (Volunteer)

Board Foundation for the History of Technology:

- Hans de Wit (chair)
- Jacques Joosten (treasurer)
- Saskia Blom
- Dirk van Delft
- Herman de Boon
- Eric Fischer
- Frans Greidanus
- Emmo Meijer
- Michiel Westermann
- Harry Lintsen (advisor)
- Martin Schuurmans (advisor)

Index

Abercrombie, Patrick 257
Abrahams, Anthony 169
acid rain 309, 310 Fig. 8.1, 311, 339
Adria Pipeline 158
Advanced Agriculture Information System 243
aerial warfare 193–94, 198, 199 Fig. 5.3, 200–201, 202 Fig. 5.4, 203
   air defence systems 211–12, 213 Fig. 5.7, 214
   Blitzkrieg 194
   Chain Home radar system 199–200
   fuel supplies 201, 202 Fig. 5.4, 203
Africa 11, 31, 45, 50, 74, 91, 93, 100, 102–4, 121–22, 123 Fig. 3.3, 161, 162, 221, 238–40, 286, 289, 302
   Desertec 97 Fig. 2.11, 98
   migration from 355 Fig. 9.1
   oil and gas 83, 84, 88 Fig. 2.8, 90, 95
   radio communication 323 Fig. 8.6
   railroads 32, 34, 43, 44 Fig. 1.7, 63
agriculture 245, 248–53, 259–60, 265, 364
   Advanced Agriculture Information System 243
   see also Common Agricultural Policy; food chains
air defence systems 211–12, 213 Fig. 5.7
   STRIL-60 213 Fig. 5.7, 214
air pollution 309, 310 Fig. 8.1, 311, 336–44
   acid rain 309, 310 Fig. 8.1, 311, 339
   chlorofluorocarbons (CFCs) 343
   Clean Air Act 338–39
   monitoring 341 Fig. 8.9
   smog 338–39
   smoke stacks 336, 337 Fig. 8.8, 338
   Sulphur Protocol 341–42
air traffic control 334–36
Albania 80, 174, 244
Algeria
   natural gas 86, 90, 100
   SONATRACH 91
Amoco Cádiz disaster 302
Amsterdam Stock Exchange 170–71 Fig. 4.6
Andersen, Hans Christian 230

Anglo-American Telegraph Company 35, 161
aniline dyes 142, 145
Appleton, Edward 324
Argentina 120–21, 222
arsenic pollution 298, 337–38
Ascension Island 222
Assman, Richard 315–16
Association of European Petrochemicals Producers 158
Association of German Railway Administrations 29, 42
Atlantic Ocean
   convoys 203, 204 Fig. 5.5, 205–07
   surveys 275–76, 277 Fig. 7.3, 278
Atlantropa project 74, 75 Fig. 2.5, 97 Fig. 2.11, 98, 294
Austria 284, 321
   gas imports 270
   gas shortages 65, 356
   ÖMV 88
   Verbund 80
Austria-Hungary 13 Fig. 0.2, 42, 164, 166, 280, 281
Austro-German Telegraph Union 33
Austro-Prussian War 14, 187 Fig. 5.1
aviation 39–40, 43, 44 Fig. 1.7, 58–59, 363
   air traffic control 334–36
   Eurocontrol 334–36
   infrastructure 328–33
   military air traffic 334–35
   radar 199–201, 334
   Single European Sky initiative 336
   see also aerial warfare

Backe, Herbert 129
Baden Gas Company (*Badische Gesellschaft für Gasbeleuchtung*) 141
Badische Anilin- & Soda-Fabrik (BASF) 142, 144, 145 Fig. 4.1, 146, 150, 156, 357
   Leuna complex 151
   Ludwigshafen complex 146, 147, 154, 157 Fig. 4.4
Baerselman, Fred 261–62

Baeyer, Johann Jacob 238
Bahr, Egon 90
Baia Mare goldmine pollution incident 300
Baku oil production site 69 Fig. 2.2
Baltic Ring 239–40
Baltic Sea 272–73
Baltic States 8, 23, 54–55
  see also individual states
bananas 120
Baring Brothers 165
BATS Europe 178
Bayer 144
Bayernwerk 80
Behrens, Herbert 169
Belarus 54, 78, 87, 99, 100, 152, 207, 266, 270, 380
Belgium 115
  Distrigaz 87
  railroads 26–27
  REFRIBEL 129
  Sabena 44 Fig. 1.7, 45
  urban systems 237–38
Bell Company 36
Bennett, Graham 262–63
benzene 142, 155 Fig. 4.3
Berlin airlift 210
Berlin Conference (1884–5) 238–39
Berlin Wall 49, 231
  fall of 53
Berlin–Baghdad railroad 32
BESK computer 319
Betz, Gerardus Henry 108
Biilmann, Einar 148
biodiversity 4, 15 Fig. 0.3, 249, 254, 261, 266–67, 303
birds, protection of 344–45
Blanc, François and Louis 142–43, 160
Blitzkrieg 193, 194, 197, 223 Fig. 5.10
Blue Banana 112, 247
Blue Star Line 12, 120
Boeuf, Alfonso Peña 287
Boldingh, Gerrit Hondius 148
Bora 313, 315
border-building 36–40, 355 Fig. 9.1, 356
  smart borders 11, 356
Bosch, Carl 150
Braem, Renaat 248
Brandt, Willy 49, 90, 104
Braudel, Fernand 350–51, 366

Brenner railroad 29
Brett, John 34
Brezhnev, Leonid 79
Briand, Aristide 40
Bridgewater Canal 67, 68 Fig. 2.1
Britain see UK
British Dyes Ltd 147
British Dyestuffs Corporation 147, 149
British East India Company 188, 235
British Imperial Federation League 235, 236 Fig. 6.2
British United African Company 122
Brundtland, Gro Harlem 340
Brustling, Maria Magdalena 141
Buache, Philippe 273
Bulgaria 8, 50–51, 79–80, 90, 93, 104, 131, 134–35, 153, 252, 266, 279
  food chains 129
Buna Werke chemical complex 151
Bundesnachrichtendienst 52
Burke, Arleigh 214, 215, 360

canals
  Bridgewater Canal 67, 68 Fig. 2.1
  Danube–Oder–Elbe canal 11, 51
  Panama Canal 3
  Rhine–Main–Danube Canal 51, 63, 306
  Suez Canal 3, 30–31, 84, 291 Fig. 7.5
capital markets *see* financial sector
carbon capture and storage 343–44
Cassini, Giovanni Domenico 234
Cassini map 234
Castries, Christian de 221
Cazalis, Henry 255
Central Eastern Europe Stock Exchange group 177
Central European Economic Conference (*Mitteleuropäische Wirtschaftstagung*) 42
Central European Geodetic Association 238
Central European Pipeline 156–57
Centrale des Matières Colorantes (CMC) 147
Chain Home radar system 199–200
Chamberlain, Neville 167
Channel telegraph cable 161
Channel Tunnel 8, 57
Chappe, Claude 32–33

chemical industry 141–81, 357, 358
   aniline dyes 142, 145
   Cold War 151–59
   Four Party Cartel 150
   pollution by 298–300
   see also individual companies
Chernobyl nuclear power plant 93–94, 287, 300, 342
Chevalier, Michel 1–2, 12–13, 24, 60, 63, 225, 349–50, 354, 359
Chi-X Europe 178
chloride pollution 298
chlorine gas 156
chlorofluorocarbons (CFCs) 343
circulation society 2, 225, 349, 359
Cisler, Walker 76
City of Glasgow Bank, failure of 165
Claudel, Paul 43
climate change 4, 96, 247, 343
coal 67–70, 100, 144, 145 Fig. 4.1, 146
Cobden–Chevalier Treaty 3, 37, 117
"cold chain" *see* refrigeration
Cold War 11, 47–53, 62, 82, 99, 103, 210–18, 225, 231, 306, 354–55
   air defence systems 211–12, 213 Fig. 5.7
   chemical industry 151–59
   computing 319
colonial control 188–89
   loss of 218–22
Comecon 47, 51, 62, 79, 80, 84, 99, 104, 114, 134–35, 151, 153–54 Fig. 4.2, 158, 257–58, 319, 336
Commercial Cable Company 161
Commission of the European Communities 56, 94
Common Agricultural Policy 136 Fig. 3.6, 137, 251–52, 358
   food dumping 137, 138
Communism, collapse of 53–56
Community-wide Coordination of Information on the Environment *see* CORINE
competing visions 40–46
computers 318–20
Congress of Vienna 2, 24–25, 36, 275, 279
conservation 232–33, 265–67
   nature reserves 254–56
Consultative Committee for International Telephony (CCIF) 45

CORINE land use database 242 Fig. 6.4, 244, 265, 386
Costa, Joaquin 274
Coudenhove-Kalergi, Richard 40
Council of Mutual Economic Assistance *see* Comecon
Cramp, Stanley 345
Crampton, Thomas 34
Crane, Walter 235, 236 Fig. 6.2
Crimean War 37, 186, 277, 280, 311
Cuban Missile Crisis 216, 217 Fig. 5.8
Cunard, Samuel 26
Czechoslovakia 42, 84, 88, 104
   Aussiger Verein 148, 149, 150, 151
   Communist invasion 89
   split 53

Dalgas, Enrico Mylius 250–51, 252
Dalhousie, Lord 189
dams 282–83, 284 Fig. 7.4, 285–86
Danube River 279–81, 362
   hydropower 284–85
   Iron Gates 280, 281, 285
   Kilia Channel 280
   pollution 300
   Sulina Channel 280
Danube–Oder–Elbe canal 11, 51
Darré, Richard Walther 125, 129
Davies, Norman 17
DE SPAR cooperative 128, 137
Declaration on the Construction of Main International Traffic Arteries 50
Delors, Jacques 56, 95
Denmark
   agriculture 250 Fig. 6.5, 251
   chemical industry 148
   railroads 30
Descartes, René 273
Desertec Foundation 97, 97 Fig. 2.11
Deterding, Henry 149
Deterling, Harry 49
Distrigaz 87
Dokuchaev, Vasily 252
dot.com crash 177
Douhet, Giulio 193
Dow Chemical 156, 158
Dr Strangelove 217 Fig. 5.8, 218
drainage basins 273–75, 286, 306
   water transfer 286–88
dredging 281, 291 Fig. 7.5

Druzhba oil pipeline 84–85, 152, 153 Fig. 4.2
DuPont 156
Dutch Golden Age 67
Dutch Oil Company 87

E-road plan 10, 50, 62, 114
EASDAQ 175, 177
East African Groundnut Scheme 122–23
East Germany *see* German Democratic Republic
Eastern Telegraph Company 35
Eastman, T.C. 118
École des Mines 1
École Polytechnique 1
ecological networks 254, 258, 259 Fig. 6.6, 260–65, 302–05, 364
   bird protection 344–45
   see also environment
economic recession 57
economic system-building 111–15, 142–43, 357–60
Egerton, Francis 67
Eichmann, Adolf 207
Eisenhower, Dwight 207, 318
electricity 66, 70–71, 72–82, 99–100, 114
   alternating current 72
   East–West divide 81 Fig. 2.7
   high-voltage direct current 77
   hydropower 74, 282–86
   integration and fragmentation 73 Fig. 2.4
   North Western Ring 77, 78 Fig. 2.6
   pan-Europeanism 74, 75 Fig. 2.5
Empire food ships 119 Fig. 3.2
endosulfan pollution incident 299
energy 65–103, 353–54
   entrepreneurship 141–44
   infrastructure 70–72, 71 Fig. 2.3, 101–04
   international linkages 356
   renewable 101
   supply security 96
   tidal 296
   see also specific sources
energy entrepreneurs 141–44
Enfantin, Barthélemy 1, 2
Engelhorn, Friedrich 141–42, 159, 357
ENI 88, 89, 91
ENIAC computer 318–19

Entgleisungsweichen 49 Fig. 1.9
environment 14, 15 Fig. 0.3, 57, 361–66
   biodiversity 4, 15 Fig. 0.3, 249, 254, 261, 266–67, 303
   bird protection 344–45
   conservation 232–33, 265–67
   ecological networks 254, 258, 259 Fig. 6.6, 260–65, 302–05
   land preservation 254–58
   nature reserves 254–56
   pollution
      skies 309, 310 Fig. 8.1, 311
      waterways 297–302
E.ON Netz 66
ESSO Chemical 156
Estonia 55–56, 78–79, 100, 174, 177, 244, 249, 265
   ecological network 258, 259 Fig. 6.6, 260, 364
Estonia ferry disaster 55
ethnic cleansing 207–09
ethylene 153–54, 156, 158
Euratom 94
Eurocontrol 334–35
EURONET 52
European Association of Securities Dealers Automatic Quotation system *see* EASDAQ
European Bank for Reconstruction and Development 55
European Central Inland Transport Organization 47
European Centre for Medium-Range Weather Forecasts (ECMWF) 319
European Coal and Steel Community 94
European Commission 66–67, 97, 104, 109
   Directive on the Conservation of Wild Birds 345
   single market 167–77
European Conference of Ministers of Transport 47
European Conference of Post and Telecommunication Administrations 9–10
European Danube Commission 37, 280
European Datum 1950 240, 241
European Economic Community 10, 89, 135, 136 Fig. 3.6

European Environment Agency 244, 254
European External Border Surveillance System *see* EUROSUR
European Geodetic Association 14–15, 238–39
European Green Belt 232, 263 Fig. 6.7
European Infrastructure Agency 57
European Network of Transmission System Operators for Electricity (ENTSO-E) 96
European Network of Transmission System Operators for Gas (ENTSOG) 96
European Recovery Program 76
European Round Table of Industrialists 56
European Securities and Markets Authority 180
European Terrestrial Reference Frame (ETRF89) 241
European Union 4, 7, 11, 23, 137, 245
  border control 355–56
  Common Agricultural Policy *see* Common Agricultural Policy
  Trans-European Networks 10, 57, 95, 97, 109
European Union of Coachbuilders 132
European Venture Capitalist Association 175
EUROSUR 11
Everest, George 235
explosives industry 147, 149, 280, 358

Falklands War 222
Field, Cyrus 34, 35 Fig. 1.4, 276
Fillon, François 269
financial crisis 165–68
  "Big Bang" 168, 169, 172, 173 Fig. 4.7
  Flash Crash 177–81
  1914 stock market crash 166
  Wall Street Crash 166–67
financial sector 159–64
  electronic trading systems 168–77
  high frequency trading 178–80
  liberalization 174
Finland 81
  Neste Oil 101, 158
  TVO 93
Finland Station 21, 22 Fig. 1.1
First World War 37, 61, 72, 74, 146, 183–85, 189–93, 223, 239, 290
  aircraft 193
  Battle of Jutland 192
  Battle of Marne 190
  Battle of the Somme 191
  Battle of Verdun 191
  logistics 189–90, 359
  manufacturing 190–91
  munitions 191
  naval warfare 191–92
  Schlieffen Plan 190
  stock market crash 166
  trench warfare 190
  U-boats 192–93
fish ladders 16, 282
Flash Crash 177–80
food chains 115–39, 358
  bananas 120
  contracts 117–18
  failures 122, 123 Fig. 3.3, 124
  long-distance transport 118
  meat 118, 119 Fig. 3.2, 120
  national food systems 124–31
  protectionism 124–25, 135
  refrigeration *see* refrigeration
  regional integration 131–39
  self-sufficiency 125
  tariffs 124, 125
forestry 245, 248–49, 253
fossil fuels 67–70, 144, 295
France 115
  Cassini map 234
  chemical industry 147
  Commissariat for Atomic Energy 92
  loss of Indochina 218–21
  natural gas 86–87
  Paris Bourse 142, 143, 163, 166, 168, 176
  railroads 27
  Second French Revolution 1
  stock exchange *see* Paris Bourse
  urban systems 245–46
  X.25 Transpac network 52–53
Franco-Prussian War 13, 187, 222
French Equatorial Africa shipping company 122
Friendship Bridge 8
Friis, E. 117
FRONTEX 11, 355 Fig. 9.1

Galician gas line 86, 87
garden cities 256

gas *see* natural gas
Gas Light and Coke Company 70
Gatterer, Johann Christoph 273
Gauss, Carl Friedrich 230, 233
Gaz de France 87
Gaz Maghreb Europe pipeline 100
Gazprom 65, 98, 99 Fig. 2.12, 356
Geneva Convention on Long-range Transboundary Air Pollution (LRTAP) 340–41
geodesy 235–41
geographic information systems 240
German Bird Protection Association 255
German Democratic Republic 49, 84
Germany 115
  Bayernwerk 80
  chemical industry 141–46
  electricity 66, 80, 82
  food chains 129
  Lufthansa 43
  Mount Brocken 229–31, 232 Fig. 6.1, 233, 255
  Nazi regime *see* Nazi Germany
  railmilk system 129
  railroads 27–28
  rivers *see* Danube River; Rhine River
  Ruhrgas 86, 87, 89
  Thyssengas 87
  Verein deutscher Handelsmüller 107
  see also First World War; Second World War
Giap, Vo Nguyan 219–20
Global Positioning System (GPS) 241–42, 294
globalization 9, 10, 63, 100, 117
Golden Banana 247
Göring, Hermann 200
Gotthard Tunnel 7 Fig. 0.1, 29, 32, 60
grain, pneumatic pumping of 107–08, 109 Fig. 3.1
Grand Crimean Central Railway 186
Gray, Thomas 26
gray-green junctions 15 Fig. 0.3
Great Depression 74, 124, 172
Great War *see* First World War
Greece
  Hellenic Oil 158
  PPC 80
green belts 256, 257–58
green corridors 254

greenhouse gases 343
groundnuts 122, 123 Fig. 3.3, 124
Gulf Oil 156
gutta percha 34

Haldane, Andrew G. 179
Hantos, Elemer 39
harbors 107–10, 289–90
  Rotterdam 101, 107–08, 109–10, 109 Fig. 3.1, 289–90
Hassi R'Mel gas field 86
Haussman, Georges-Eugène 245–46
Heine, Heinrich 60, 230
Hellenic Oil 158
Helsinki Declaration 340
Hercules Corporation 156
Heydrich, Reinhard 208
Hill, Octavia 254
Hindenburgdamm 38–39
Hitler, Adolf 45, 46 Fig. 1.8, 194, 223
  see also Nazi Germany
Hollande, François 180
Holocaust 207–08, 209 Fig. 5.6, 360
horizontal connections 356
Horton, Max 205
Hough, Floyd W. 239
Howard, Ebenezer 256
Huebner, Solomon S. 159, 162, 166
Humboldt, Alexander von 316
Humboldt research balloon 315 Fig. 8.4
Hungary 50
  Danube River 8
  electricity 79, 81 Fig. 2.7, 285
  gas shortages 65, 356
  Holocaust 209
  oil supply 84
  pollution 300
  see also Austria-Hungary
Hunter, Robert 254
hydropower 74, 282–86

IG Farben group 148, 150, 151
Ignalina nuclear power plant 93
Imhoff, Karl 298
Imperial Chemical Industries (ICI) 147, 156
Indochina 218–21
Industria Nazionale Colori di Anilinia 148
information and communication technology (ICT) 144

Infrastructure transition 5–8
Inland Transport Committee 113–14
inland waters 272–73, 274 Fig. 7.2, 275
　see also canals; rivers
Inman Line 26
Institutional Networks (Instinet) 169
intangible networks 2
INTERFRIGO 133 Fig. 3.5, 134, 137
intermodality 56
International Association of
　Geodesy 239
International Bank for Reconstruction
　and Development 50
International Broadcasting Union
　(IBU) 9, 325–26, 363–64
International Commission for the
　Protection of the Rhine against
　Pollution (ICPR) 299, 304
International Consultative
　Commission for the Protection
　of Nature 256
International Energy Agency 104
International Freight Train Time Table
　Conference 132
International Labour Organisation
　(ILO) 40
International Maritime
　Organization 292
International Meteorological
　Organization (IMO) 14–15, 315
International Radiotelegraph Union
　(IRU) 322, 363
International Railway Company for
　Refrigerated Transport *see*
　INTERFRIGO
International Railway Congress
　(1910) 7
International Railway Union 9, 132
International Road Federation 50
International Road Transport
　Union 132, 134
International Sleeping Car
　Company 29
International Telegraph Union
　(ITU) 33, 322, 326
International Union for the
　Conservation of Nature
　(IUCN) 257
internet exchange points (IXPs) 58
internet geographies 59 Fig. 1.10
Internet Protocol (TCP/IP) 52, 58

Iron Curtain 8, 48, 49 Fig. 1.9, 62, 80,
　82, 99, 113, 355
　deconstruction of 85–91
Italy 115
　chemical industry 148
　ENI 88, 89, 91
　food chains 129
　railroads 29–30

Jacobsen, Johannes 120
Jahn, Hans Edgar 345
James Capel 169
joint stock companies 160
Jouyet, Pierre 179
Junkers, Hugo 9

Kaiser Wilhelm II 183–84
Kepler, Johannes 273
Kircher, Athanasius 273
knowledge system building 15, 230,
　233–35, 236 Fig. 6.2, 238–42, 247,
　264, 313, 315, 320, 351, 361–62
Kosovo 53
Kroes, Nelie 110
Kubec, Jaroslev 11
Kubrick, Stanley 217 Fig. 5.8, 218
Kupfer, Karl Reinhold 255
Kwaśniewski, Aleksander 270

Lambton, William 235
land knowledge 229–67, 364
　agriculture 248–53
　geodesy 235–40
　geographic information
　　systems 240
　land use 242, 243 Fig. 6.4, 244–45
　maps *see* mapping
　Mount Brocken, Germany 229–31,
　　232 Fig. 6.1, 233, 255
　plantation forests 252–53
　satellite imaging 240–41, 242, 243
　　Fig. 6.4
　state boundaries 234–35
　triangulation 236, 237 Fig. 6.3
　urban systems 245–48
land preservation 254–58
LANDSAT 242
Lange, Halvard 215
Latvia 87
Le Globe 1–2
le Verrier, Urbain 312, 361

League of Nations 41, 74, 114
Lecocq, Francisco 118
Leeson, Nick 165
Lenin, Vladimir Ilyich 21, 22 Fig. 1.1, 61, 126
Lepus europeus (European hare) 265
Lesseps, Ferdinand de 30–31
liberalization 57, 95
life expectancy 6
lighthouses 293–94, 293 Fig. 7.7
Line of 45th Parallel 43
liquefied natural gas (LNG) 86, 90 Fig. 2.9, 98
List, Friedrich 27
Lithuania 87, 100
London Corn Trade Association 117
London Stock Exchange 161, 162, 169
   Alternative Investment Market 175–76
      "Big Bang" 168, 169, 172, 173 Fig. 4.7
      SEAQ 169, 174
LORAN-C navigation system 215–16
Luxembourg 115

Maastricht Treaty 57
MacArthur, Robert 261
McGlade, Jacqueline 15
Main European Watershed 62–63
Mallada y Pueyo, Lucas 249
malnutrition 132
Mander, Ülo 258–59
Mansholt, Derk 117
Mansholt, Sicco 117, 135, 137–38, 252
mapping 361
   drainage basins 273, 274 Fig. 7.2, 275
   land 234–35, 236 Fig. 6.2, 237 Fig. 6.3, 238–39
   seas and oceans 275–76, 277 Fig. 7.3, 278
   skies 311–12, 313 Fig. 8.2, 314 Fig. 8.3, 315 Fig. 8.4, 316
Marconi Company 36, 321–22
maritime transport *see* shipping
Markey, Edward J. 172
Markmann, Fritz 46
Marshall Plan 47, 76, 77, 114, 168
Maury, Matthew Fontaine 275–76, 277 Fig. 7.3, 278, 361
meat trade 118, 119 Fig. 3.2, 120

Mecane, Joseph 178
mechanical cargo handling 107–08, 109 Fig. 3.1
Medvedev, Dmitry 269
mega-cities 5
Merkel, Angela 269
meteorology
   computers and satellites 318–20
   Humboldt research balloon 315 Fig. 8.4
   maps 314 Fig. 8.3
   wartime 317 Fig. 8.5, 318
   weather forecasting 312, 313 Fig. 8.2
military
   aerial warfare 193–94
   logistics 195–98, 359–60
   naval warfare 191–92
   tank warfare 193, 194–95
   see also warfare
Mistral 313, 315
mobile telecommunications 55–56, 57–58
Mol, Hein 108, 116
Moldova 87, 336
Molotov–Ribbentrop Pipeline *see* Nord Stream pipeline
Monte Carlo 143
motorways 40, 41 Fig. 1.6
Mount Brocken, Germany 229–33, 255
   Urian espionage dome 231, 232 Fig. 6.1
munitions 191, 194
Myrdal, Gunnar 10, 74, 113, 114, 115, 132, 285

Nackelmackers, Georges 29
naphtha 156
Napoleon III 3, 13, 187
NASDAQ 169, 173, 174, 175
national debt 160
national food systems 124–31
National Trust 254, 255
nationalization 112
NATO 77, 99, 104, 211, 214, 225, 231
NATO Air Defence Ground Environment (NADGE) 211
natural gas 65–66, 70, 85–86, 114, 153, 356
   "European long-distance gas grid" 88 Fig. 2.8
   Galician line 86, 87

natural gas – *continued*
  Gaz Maghreb Europe pipeline 100
  Hassi R'Mel field 86
  Lacq deposit 86
  liquefied (LNG) 87
  liquified (LNG) 90 Fig. 2.9, 98
  Nord Stream pipeline 66, 269–71, 272 Fig. 7.1
  Slochteren field 87, 90, 156
  Trans-European Pipeline 88
  Trans-Mediterranean Pipeline 91
nature reserves 254–56
naval warfare 191–92
Nazi Germany 45–46, 46 Fig. 1.8, 114, 125, 225
  Blitzkrieg 194, 223 Fig. 5.10
  death camps 207–08
  ethnic cleansing 207–09
  food diversion policy 129
  High Sea Fleet 191–92
  Holocaust 207–08, 209 Fig. 5.6, 360
  Luftwaffe 200
  Operation Barbarossa 16–17, 196–97
  Schutz-Staffel (SS) 207
  U-boats 192–93, 204–06
  see also Second World War
Neporozhny, Piotr 79
Neste Oil 101, 158
Netherlands 115
  agriculture 251
  Amsterdam Stock Exchange 170–71 Fig. 4.6
  Betuwe route project 110
  chemical industry 148
  Dutch Golden Age 67
  ecological network 261–63
  Europoort harbour complex 109
  food chains 128
  KLM 45
  Nature Monuments Association 255
  New Waterway 108, 289
  Rotterdam 101, 107–08, 109–10, 109 Fig. 3.1, 289–90
  Slochteren gas field 87, 90, 156
network age 2, 3
networks *see* system-building
Neumann, John von 319
New York Stock Exchange 161, 162, 166, 172
  Wall Street Crash 166–67

Nord Stream pipeline 66, 269–71, 272 Fig. 7.1
Norddeutscher Lloyd 26
Nordic Mobile Telephony 55
Nordström, Ludvig 351–52, 354, 356
North Atlantic Treaty Organization *see* NATO
North European and Mediterranean Routing Instructions (NEMEDRI) scheme 290
North Sea Countries Offshore Grid Initiative 97
North Sea oil fields 296 Fig. 7.8
North Western Ring 78, 78 Fig. 2.6, 99
North–West oil pipeline 156
Norwegian Fish Fillet Company 120
nuclear power 91, 92 Fig. 2.10, 93, 342
nuclear weapons 211, 224
  air defence systems 211–12, 213 Fig. 5.7
  Polaris submarines 214–16

Oberle, Bruno 15
Odén, Svante 309
Odum, Eugene and Howard 260–61
Oettinger, Günter 269
offshore oil industry 295, 296 Fig. 7.8, 297 Fig. 7.9
oil 82–85
  East-Central Europe 84
  North Sea fields 296 Fig. 7.8
  offshore 295, 296 Fig. 7.8, 297 Fig. 7.9
  switch from coal 153 Fig. 4.2, 154–56
  vulnerability of supply 84–85
oil pipelines
  Adria 158
  Central European 156–57
  Druzhba 84–85, 152, 153 Fig. 4.2
  North–West 156
  Rotterdam–Rhine 109
  Southern European 156
  Trans-Alpine 83, 85, 157
oil tankers 289–90
  Amoco Cádiz disaster 302
  Torrey Canyon disaster 302, 303 Fig. 7.10, 365
Oliven, Oskar 9, 74
ÖMV 88, 89
Operation Barbarossa 16–17, 196–97, 201

Orange Revolution 65–66, 356
Organization for Economic
    Co-operation and Development
    (OECD) 339
Orient Express 31–32
Overseas Food Corporation 123
ozone layer 343

pacifism 1–2
palm oil 101
Pan-European Ecological
    Network 263, 264 Fig. 6.8
Pan-Europeanism 11
Panama Canal 3
Pantoflicek, Jan 154
Pappas, Tom 83, 158
Paris Bourse 142, 143, 163, 166, 168, 176
Parnassius mnemosyne (Clouded
    Apollo) butterfly 260, 265
Patton, George 207
Pecqueur, Constantin 60
Peeters, Jos 175
Pender, John 35
Perkin, William Henry 142, 147
Perrault, Pierre 273
Persson, Göran 310–11
Peto, Samuel 186
petrochemicals 145, 152, 153–54,
    157–58
  see also chemical industry
petroleum 69, 69 Fig. 2.2
Pflimin, Pierre 135
Poland 23, 84
  Green Lungs program 266
  invasion of 194
Polaris submarines 214–16
Polish–German Border 37, 38 Fig. 1.5
pollution 365
  chemical industry 298–300
  incidents 299–301
    Amoco Cádiz disaster 302
    Baia Mare goldmine 300
    Chernobyl 342
    Sandoz disaster 299–300
    Torrey Canyon disaster 302, 303
      Fig. 7.10, 365
  skies see air pollution
  waterways 297–302
Pompidou, Georges 92
post trains 28 Fig. 1.2
Posthuma, Frans 155

precipitation 273
Prudhomme, Sully 255
PTTs 45, 51, 52–53, 55, 58
public telegraph and telephone
    administrations see PTTs
public works 24, 40
Puricelli, Piero 9, 41 Fig. 1.6
Pustilnik, Jerome 169

Raaschou, Peter Esch 148
radar 199–201, 334
  Chain Home radar system 199–200
radio communication 320–27, 354, 363
  amplitude modulation 322
  broadcast interference 324–25
  frequency allocation 325
  medium wave 324–27
  Nauen radio station, Germany 323
      Fig. 8.6
  non-intercommunication policy 321
  reflection of radio waves 324
  satellites 327
  vacuum-tube technology 323–24
  VHF 327
  warfare 322–23
radioactive waste 92 Fig. 2.10, 301–02
radiosondes 316, 362
railroads 2–3, 4, 7 Fig. 0.1, 26–32,
    42–43, 63, 117, 349, 353
  coal transport 67–68
  colonial control 188–89
  military planning 185–88, 190
  post trains 28 Fig. 1.2
  role in Holocaust 208, 209 Fig. 5.6
  South America 120–21
  strikes 122
  trans-Alpine 29–30, 60
  war trains 13 Fig. 0.2
  see also specific routes
Railway Transport Council 53–54
Rambert, Maurice 325
Rausing, Ruben 294
Rawnsley, Hardwicke 254
Reagan, Ronald 241
refrigeration 118, 119 Fig. 3.2, 120,
    126–27, 130, 133 Fig. 3.5, 134, 137
  European standards 133–34
Renell, James 235
reservoirs 261, 283, 284 Fig. 7.4, 286
Reuter, Paul Julius 161
Reyes, Federico Nin 118

Rhine Action Plan for Ecological
    Rehabilitation 300
Rhine River 111, 278–79, 305, 362
    hydropower 284
    pollution 298–300
    Prussian Navigation Project 279
    salmon 304
Rhine–Main–Danube Canal 51, 63, 306
Rhodes, Cecil 32
Ridder, Gustave de 27
River Gambia Trading Company 122
rivers 278–81, 362
    dams 282–83, 284 Fig. 7.4, 285–86
    Danube 279–81, 284–85, 362
    dredging 281, 291 Fig. 7.5
    pollution 297–302
    Rhine 111, 278–79, 305, 362
road transport 55, 62
Roca, Julio A. 121
Rodoman, Boris 258
Rogier, Charles 27
Romania 8, 38, 50, 66, 69, 79, 90, 93,
    131, 153, 158, 252, 265, 285
    Baia Mare goldmine pollution
        incident 300
Rossby, Carl-Gustav 319
Rotterdam 101, 107–08, 109–10, 109
    Fig. 3.1, 289–90
Rotterdam-Antwerp chemical
    complex 154, 155 Fig. 4.3, 156
Rotterdam–Rhine oil pipeline 109
Rowntree, Benjamin Seebohm 248
Royal Dutch/Shell 109, 111, 148, 150,
    154–55
Royal Navy 191–92
Ruhrgas 86, 87, 89
Russia *see* Soviet Union
Rutte, Mark 269
Ryanair 58–59

St. Petersburg 21, 54
    gasworks 72
Saint Simon, Claude Henri de 2, 24
Saint Simonians 1, 60
Sajó, Károly 255
Sandoz disaster 299–300
Sandys, Duncan 257
Sarasin, Paul 255
Sarkozy, Nikolas 180
satellite imaging 240–41, 242, 243 Fig. 6.4
    meteorology 318–20

satellite radio communication 327
Scandinavia
    plantation forests 253
    see also individual countries
Schaller, Heinrich 177
Schedl, Otto 83, 88
Schermerhorn, Willem 240
Schlieffen Plan 190
Schönholzer, Ernst 74
seas and oceans 269–81, 362
    energy from 295–96
    improvements to 288–94
    inland waters 272–75
    lighthouses 293–94, 293 Fig. 7.7
    mapping 275–76, 277 Fig. 7.3, 278
    underwater telegraphy 34, 35
        Fig. 1.4, 276
Second French Revolution 1
Second World War 45–46, 61, 74, 112,
    125, 151, 223, 290, 326, 360
    aerial warfare 198, 199 Fig. 5.3,
        200–201, 202 Fig. 5.4, 203
    Atlantic convoys 203, 204
        Fig. 205–07
    Battle of Britain 198
    Battle of Moscow 197
    Battle of Suomussalmi 194, 195
        Fig. 5.2
    Blitzkrieg 194, 223 Fig. 5.10
    D-day landings 318
    ethnic cleansing 207–09
    Holocaust 207–08, 209 Fig. 5.6, 360
    Operation Bagration 198
    Operation Barbarossa 16–17, 196–97,
        201
    Pearl Harbor 197
    tank warfare 193, 194–95
    see also Nazi Germany
Semmering railroad 29
Senegal merchant shipping
    company 122
Shantung Railway 68
shipping
    Empire food ships 119 Fig. 3.2
    oil tankers *see* oil tankers
    pollution by 302
    sea lanes 291, 292 Fig. 7.6
    steamships 3, 4, 25–26, 59, 117, 188–89
    see also waterways
Shuzo, Aoki 238
Siberian Unified Power System 93–94

Siilasvuo, Hjalmar 195–96, 359
Sikorski, Radoslaw 270
Simons, Jim 180
Simons, Pierre 27
Simplon Tunnel 3
Single European Act 95
Single European Sky initiative 336
skies 309–48, 363
   air defence systems 211–12, 213 Fig. 5.7
   aviation 39–40, 43, 44 Fig. 1.7, 58–59, 328–33
   bird protection 344–45
   mapping 311–12, 313 Fig. 8.2, 314 Fig. 8.3, 315 Fig. 8.4, 316
   pollution *see* air pollution
   radio communication 320–27
Slochteren gas field 87, 90, 156
Slovakia 88
   gas shortages 56, 356
   see also Czechoslovakia
smart borders 11, 356
Smetana, Jan 51
Smits, Pierre 76
Smrček, Antonin 11, 42
Smyers, Guillaume 141
Sömera, Toomas 55
SONATRACH 91
Sörgel, Hermann 74, 75 Fig. 2.5, 97 Fig. 2.11, 98, 294
Southern European Pipeline 156
Soviet Railway Ministry 53
Soviet Union 8
   Aeroflot 43
   Bureau for Aniline Manufacture 148
   chemical industry 152
   dissolution of 53–54
   electricity network 77–78, 78 Fig. 2.6
   five-year plans 112, 126
   food shortages 121, 125–26, 127 Fig. 3.4, 128
   gas exports 65–66, 88
   Gazprom 65, 98, 99 Fig. 2.12, 356
   Great Plan for the Transformation of Nature 252–53
   hydropower 282–84
   New Economic Policy 126
   nuclear power 93
   oil 69 Fig. 2.2, 84–85, 151–52
   railroads 21–24, 30–31
   Trans-Siberian Railway 17, 30, 31 Fig. 1.3
   water transfer projects 286–87
   see also Cold War
Spain
   agriculture 249–50
   inland waters 274–75
   water transfer projects 287–88
Spanish Civil War 223 Fig. 5.10
Stagg, John 318
Stalin, Joseph 69 Fig. 2.2, 126, 252–53
Stanczyk, Jan 113
Standing Commission on Electric Power 79
Stasi 49, 52
steam propulsion 25–26
steamships 3, 4, 25–26, 59, 117
   military 188–89
Stiglitz, Joseph 179
Stock Exchange Automatic Quotation system (SEAQ) 169, 174
stock exchanges 159–62
stock ticker 163 Fig. 163
Stockton–Darlington line 68
Stolberg-Wernigerode, Christian Ernst zu 229–30
Stoltenberg, Jens 343
Struve, Friedrich Georg Wilhelm von 236, 237 Fig. 6.3, 361
Struve Geodetic Arc 235, 237 Fig. 6.3, 238
Submarine Telegraph Company 34
submarine telegraphy 34, 189
subscriber trunk dialing 52
Suez Canal 3, 30–31, 84, 291 Fig. 7.5
Sulphur Protocol 341–42
Swedish Environmental Protection Agency (SEPA) 310
Swiss Nature Protection League 255
Sympher, Leo 42
system builders/system-building 9–16, 351
   Cold War 47–53
   ecological 254, 258, 259 Fig. 6.6, 260–65, 302–05, 344–45, 364
   economic 111–15, 142–43, 357–60
   energy 65–103
   food supply 115–39
   infrastructure 5–8
   knowledge 15, 230, 233–35, 236 Fig. 6.2, 238–42, 247, 264, 313, 315, 320, 351, 361–62
   land-based 229–67
   military *see* military; warfare

system builders/system-
    building – *continued*
  railroads 25–32
  seas and oceans 269–81
  skies 309–48
  telegraphy *see* telegraphy

tangible networks *see* infrastructure
tank warfare 193, 194–95
Tazelaar, Jacobus 205
TechMARK 176
Teisserenc de Bort, Léon 316
telecommunications 36, 45
  Cold War 51–52
  EURONET 52
  financial sector 161–62
  international 62
  internet exchange points (IXPs) 58
  internet protocol (TCP/IP) 52, 58
  mobile *see* mobile
    telecommunications
  PTTs *see* PTTs
  subscriber trunk dialing 52
  X.25 Transpac network 52–53
  see also telegraphy
telegraphy 8, 32–36, 45, 117, 353
  costs of 61
  financial sector 161, 163 Fig. 163
  hacking of 142–43
  military planning 185–88
  submarine 189
  underwater cables 34, 35 Fig. 1.4, 276
Tellier, Charles 118
Tenner, Carl 236, 237 Fig. 6.3
Thatcher, Margaret 95, 342
thermal power 76
Thienemann, August 286
Thomas, Albert 40, 41 Fig. 1.6
Thorbecke, Johan Rudolph 108
Thyssengas 87
tidal energy 296
Timm, Bernhard 156
TIR carnet 114
Tizard, Henry 199
tolls 36–37
Tolstoy, Leo 126
Torrey Canyon disaster 302, 303
    Fig. 7.10, 365
Trans-Alpine Pipeline 83, 85, 157
Trans-European Networks (TENs) 10, 57, 95, 97, 98, 109
Trans-European Pipeline 88

Trans-Mediterranean Pipeline 91
Trans-Mediterranean Renewable
    Energy Cooperation 98
Trans-Siberian Railway 17, 30, 31
    Fig. 1.3, 121
transition
  communications 58–63
  economic 12
  energy 70–72, 102, 192
  food 12, 116, 132, 137
  infrastructure 5–8, 9, 15 Fig. 0.3
  land use 245
  maritime 292 Fig. 7.6, 295
  military 225
  transportation *see specific modes of*
    transportation
  see also system builders/system
    building
transnational Rhine economy 111
transportation 5, 7 Fig. 0.1
  revolution in 24–32
  see also specific modes of transportation
travel 6
trench warfare 190
triangulation 236, 237 Fig. 6.3, 238
trinitrotoluene (TNT) 147
Tulla, Johann Gottfried 278–79, 361, 362
Tunner, William 210
Turquoise 178
TVO 93

U-boats 192–93, 204–06
Ukraine 88, 129, 356
  food shortages 127 Fig. 3.4, 128
Ulbricht, Walter 231
Union for the Coordination of
    Production and Transmission of
    Electricity (UCPTE) 77, 96, 104
United Africa Company 122
United Kingdom
  Clean Air Act 338–39
  Dyestuffs Act (1920) 147
  food chains 124–25, 130
  garden cities 256
  Gas Light and Coke Company 70
  Imperial Airways 45
  National Trust 254, 255
  Royal Navy 191–92
  stock exchange *see* London Stock
    Exchange
  telegraph system 8

United Nations 9
  Economic Commission for Europe (UNECE) 47, 50, 62, 75–76, 80, 81 Fig. 2.7, 113–14, 132, 136, 137, 253, 285
  Food and Agriculture Organization (FAO) 132
  International Maritime Organization 292
  Relief and Rehabilitation Administration (UNRRA) 130
  World Meteorological Organization (WMO) 320
United States
  European Infrastructure Agency 57
  Flash Crash 177–81
  national parks 255
  stock exchange *see* New York Stock Exchange
  Tennessee Valley Authority 285
  Wall Street Crash 166–67
universal association 3
Unwin, Raymond 256
urban systems 245–48

Valensi, Georges 9
van Well, Adriaan 128
Vander Stichelen, Jules 248
Vandervelde, Emile 248
Vera, Frans 261–62
Versailles Treaty 193
vertical connections 356–57
Vestey, Edmund 12, 120
Vestey, William 12, 120
Viet Minh 219, 220 Fig. 5.9
Villiez, Hansjürgen von 335
vinyl chloride 155
Vitali, Philippe 30
Volga River 283, 284 Fig. 7.4
Volkonsky, Piotre Mikhailovich 236
von Dönitz, Klaus 204–05, 206
von Moltke, Eliza 183
von Moltke, Helmut (the elder) 186
von Moltke, Helmut (the younger) 14, 183–84, 189

Walesa, Lech 98
Wall Street Crash 166–67

warfare 183–225, 349–50, 357–60
  aerial *see* aerial warfare
  explosives 147, 149, 276
  munitions 191, 194
  naval 191–92
  nuclear weapons *see* nuclear weapons
  radio communication 322–23
  weather forecasting 317 Fig. 8.5, 318
  see also military; and individual wars
Warsaw Pact 211–12, 231
  Anti-Aircraft Defence system 212
Warsaw–St. Petersburg railroad 21–24
Warsaw–Vienna railroad 208
wastewater 297–99, 301, 305
water transfer 286–88
waterways 24, 25, 42, 62–63
  canals *see* canals
  coal transport 67–68, 68 Fig. 2.1
  Cold War 51
  drainage basins 273–75, 286, 306
  rivers 278–81, 306
  seas and oceans 269–81
weather forecasting *see* meteorology
West European Telegraph Union 33
White Star Line 26
wildlife crossings 15 Fig. 0.3
Willis, Frances 215
Wilson, Edmund 21
Wilson, Edward O. 261
Wilson, John 169
wind power 296
winds 313, 315
wireless telegraphy 36
World Bank 55
World Meteorological Organization (WMO) 320, 361

X-Gerät system 200
Xchlegel, August Wilhelm 230
Yellow Banana 247

Yeltsin, Boris 98
Yugoslavia 53, 80, 158

Zelentsov, Andrei 194, 196

The manufacturer's authorised representative in the EU is Springer Nature Customer Service Centre GmbH, Europaplatz 3, 69115 Heidelberg, Germany. If you have any concerns regarding our products, please contact ProductSafety@springernature.com

Printed and bound by CPI Group (UK) Ltd, Croydon, CR0 4YY

23/03/2026

02076458-0020